Washington State University Centennial Histories

The Crimson and the Gray

100 YEARS WITH THE WSU COUGARS

RICHARD B. FRY

Washington State University Press
Pullman, Washington
1989

Washington State University Press, Pullman, Washington 99164-5910
Copyright 1989 by the Board of Regents of Washington State University
All Rights Reserved
First Published 1989
Printed and bound in the United States of America

99 98 97 96 95 94 93 92 91 90 1 2 3 4 5 6 7 8 9 10

Library of Congress Cataloging in Publication Data

Fry, Richard B. 1923-
The crimson and the gray: 100 years with the WSU Cougars/
Richard B. Fry
p. cm.
Bibliography: p.
ISBN 0-87422-057-2 : $24.95

ISBN 0-87422-057-2 (hardbound)

This book is printed on pH-neutral, acid-free paper.

DUST JACKET PHOTO: *Shawn Landrum blocks a Husky punt in the fourth
quarter of WSU's Apple Cup victory over UW in 1988.* (Chris Anderson,
Spokesman Review)

Table of Contents

Foreword

It is important to understand that sports have made a major contribution to the history and traditions of Washington State University. Since the beginning, athletics has been a part of our legacy. Within days of the school's opening on January 13, 1892, the young men and women who made up the first student body organized the Washington Agricultural College Athletic Association. Two months later, a WAC baseball team engaged in the school's first athletic contest, a 26-0 victory over Pullman Military College.

Richard B. Fry's *The Crimson and the Gray: 100 Years with the WSU Cougars* is the stirring saga of the winning tradition begun on that March day nearly a century ago. It is also the second volume in a trilogy titled the *Washington State University Centennial Histories* that is being published by Washington State University Press during WSU's 100th anniversary. *The Crimson and the Gray* will be followed in the spring of 1990 by George Frykman's comprehensive study, *Creating the People's University: Washington State University, 1890-1990*. These books, along with William L. Stimson's *Going to Washington State: A Century of Student Life*, published earlier this year, will present us with the most complete investigation of WSU's past ever undertaken. We take pride in the history these three volumes are making available to Washington State University and to its extended family of alumni, friends, and supporters. I know you will agree with me that *The Crimson and the Gray*, the story of athletics at WSU, gives us another reason to be proud of our great university.

Samuel H. Smith, President
Washington State University
October 1989

Dedication

Athletics have always been a part of campus life at America's great colleges and universities, and Washington State University is no exception. All sports in which Cougars have participated over the years have contributed much to the lives of players, fans, students, alums, and friends—as well as to the University.

I am delighted to be able to take part in the celebration of WSU's first hundred years that is taking place in 1989 and 1990. I am also honored to have been invited to dedicate Richard B. Fry's salute to Cougar athletes, *The Crimson and the Gray*, a book that commemorates their century of excellence, perseverance, integrity, and achievement at an outstanding institution of higher learning.

Dr. Weldon B. "Hoot" Gibson
Class of 1938

Preface and Acknowledgments

TWO QUESTIONS, YOU SAY?

Why hasn't someone written a history of athletics at Washington State University long before this, and why isn't a Cougar writing this one?

Good questions. I can't answer the first, but, hey, I'm a Cougar! And like old Pullman junk dealer Scrappy Richardson used to say about his sanity, "I've got a certificate to prove it." The WSU Board of Regents made me an Honorary Cougar in 1985.

No school in the American West has had a more colorful sports history than Washington State University. True, the Cougars haven't won everything in sight, but they've had their share of championship teams and individuals, and who can match the likes of "Doc" Bohler, "Lone Star" Dietz, "Babe" Hollingbery, "Buck" Bailey, "Ike" Deeter, and the old "Fox of the Palouse" Jack Friel? Great characters and greater coaches, and all here in the "Golden Age."

Like diamonds, Washington State Cougars are forever!

From the time it began, as the Agricultural College, Experiment Station and School of Science of the State of Washington the school has been something special to all who have attended. Starting with "Farmers! Hayseeds! Pumpkins! Squash! W.A.C.! By Gosh!"—one of the first school yells—students have left no doubt as to how they felt about their college. No ag-school inferiority complex here! Students at WAC relished the remoteness of their campus, recognized from the beginning that it was "one for all and all for one!" out there midst the wheat fields, and always have enjoyed the times when the *farmers* skinned the *city slickers*.

Athletic competition began at WAC less than two months after the school opened its doors. One of the players who participated in the first athletic contest involving a WAC team said he thought that game "turned the tide toward the agricultural institution." It seems appropriate, as WSU observes its Centennial (1890-1990), that some of the people and some of the memorable moments in the school's colorful athletic history since that auspicious beginning be recorded for posterity.

The Crimson and the Gray: 100 Years with the Washington State Cougars is the first attempt at a full-scale history of the intercollegiate athletic program at WSU. Former President E. A. Bryan, ably assisted by Isobel Keeney, '28 (now Mrs. Arnold Leber and living in South Bend, Washington), gave some of the early athletic history of the institution in his epic *Historical Sketch of the State College of Washington, 1890-1925.*

This was followed in 1958 by *E. O. Holland and the State College of Washington*, in which Professor Emeritus of History William M. Landeen noted a few highlights of the athletic program at WSC between 1926 and 1942 and listed some of the school's outstanding athletes and their achievements.

I have drawn from both of these books, and I'm grateful to the three authors for their efforts. But it has been nearly fifty years since any WSU athletic history has been recorded in book form. A master's thesis, written in 1948 by an old Cougar fullback, Harold Gus Smith, '38, provided some good information on both men's and women's athletics at the college from 1892 to 1905, and William E. Heath's biography of J. Fred "Doc" Bohler, written as a master's thesis in 1951, gave me excellent background on one of the most unforgettable characters in Cougar Athletics.

Practically all of the football, basketball, and baseball statistics used in this book, up to the mid-seventies, were compiled by Robert J. (Bob) Guptill, '74, of Colfax, now Sports Information Director at Central Washington University in Ellensburg. "Gups" researched all the Cougar stats, from the beginning in 1892, while working as a student assistant in the Sports Information Office at WSU. It was a monumental task, and he accomplished most of it nights and weekends as a "labor of love" while carrying a full academic load.

In most cases, I have credited my sources as part of the narrative in this book, or in footnotes. But I would like to acknowledge some of them again, for only they know how often I have returned to these "wells" of information over the past three years: Robert W. Bucklin, '25, of Bellevue. Bob's knowledge of Cougar sports starts in 1896, when his father, Robert Eben Bucklin, was playing football and pole vaulting for WAC, and continues right down to today. Ivan R. Shirrod, '41, Pullman, has been collecting WSU and Whitman County historical materials and photographs for many years, and he shared them most generously. Jim Price, sports information director at Eastern Washington University in Cheney, is writing his own book on baseball teams and players in this region, but that didn't stop him from giving me information on old Cougar players, and other stories as well.

WSU Sports Information Director Rod Commons has been at my beck and call for information, stats, and photos since this project began and has never failed to deliver. Robert Burks, '54, Bellingham, made his collection of Cougar football scrapbooks, which date to the early 1900s, available to me on many occasions, saving untold hours of researching newspaper files. Jack and Catherine Mathews Friel, and Ike and Claire Rose Deeter, Washington State graduates all, regularly reached into their wonderful memories to come up with a name, an event, or a fact that I might never have been able to locate. Since they have lived in Pullman nearly three-quarters of the century I'm dealing with, you can imagine how much help they've been. Jerry Jones, editor of the Colfax *Gazette* and grandson of WAC's first Graduate Manager, John Hugh Jones, '03, came up with a number of items for me on early WAC/WSC history from the old *Gazette* files.

The chapter on "The Blair Case," WSU's landmark lawsuit involving sex discrimination in athletics, was written for me by June Bierbower, a long-time colleague, writer and editor in the WSU News Service. She's a Cornhusker by birth and graduation, but June knows more about Cougar athletics than most of us will ever learn—and she can write it, too! I also borrowed some of June's material on Babe Hollingbery's early life.

It was thrilling to be able to locate Mrs. L. Colleen Conroy, of Hardin, Montana, a granddaughter of the first Indian football coach at the College. I am indebted to Dianna Scheidt, acting director of the Big Horn County Historical Museum in Hardin, who steered me to Mrs. Conroy.

I am grateful to John Guido's staff in Manuscripts and Archives in WSU's Holland Library, particularly Lawrence R. Stark and Carol Lichtenberg, for helping me locate photos and materials; to the Reference staff at Holland for their knowledge and patience in directing me to sources; to David H. Stratton, Professor of History, and William Willard, Professor of Comparative American Cultures, for information and research guidance; to Sally Meyer, Director of Faculty Personnel Records, and her staff, particularly Maxine Rauch, for information on early-day faculty; to Gen DeVleming, executive assistant to WSU Presidents, for giving me access to the Regents' files; to Alumni Director Keith Lincoln and his staff; and to Registrar C. James Quann, who allowed me to prowl the records for names, hometowns, and graduation years of thousands of Cougar athletes, with assistance from Dean Pearson, Diane Wilson, and, sometimes, Karen Bloomfield. (She locked me in the vault one night!)

Sports Information and Alumni Records offices at the Universities of Oregon, Idaho, Washington, Wisconsin, Michigan, Minnesota, Illinois, Tennessee, and Houston, and at North Carolina State, Oregon State, Auburn, Cornell, Princeton, and Stanford were generous with their time, and Dr. Owen V. Johnson, '68, assistant professor of Journalism History at Indiana University, in Bloomington, guided me to several sources in Big Ten country and provided tips on other Cougar sports stories from his years in Pullman and at WSU.

Archivists Keith Richard, University of Oregon; Rick Ryan, Princeton University; G. A. Rudolph, University of Nebraska; Tim Bernardis, Little Big Horn College, Crow Agency, Montana; Penelope Krosch, University of Minnesota; Cassandra Volpe, University of Colorado, and Larry Dodd, Whitman College, were particularly helpful, along with D. W. Wuerthele, registrar at Springfield College, Springfield, Massachusetts.

Also at WSU, Don Ferrell, Director of Student Publications, opened up the photo files there to me, as did Pat Caraher, editor of *Hilltopics.*. Charm Arneson, of the Sports Information Office, patiently guided me through their photo and records files, and Glen Ames of the Alumni Office staff was always ready with his computer to find a name or date for me.

Pullman residents Don Downen, '36, long-time Chairman of the WSU Athletic Hall of Fame Committee; Barbara Jean Clark Collins, '40; Earl and Marge Rounds Muir, both '54; Dale Ruark, Mildred Hunt Vatnsdal,

'24; Merrill R. Ebner, '27; Raymon Smeltz, '32; Mary Ellen Gorham, '46; and Leonard Young gave me background information on the town and campus and geography of the area, along with some "color" stories, and, in the case of Mrs. Collins, provided history and photos, some of which belonged to her father, old Rose Bowl Captain Asa V. "Ace" Clark, '16.

Dr. Carol E. Gordon, former Chairman of the Department of Physical Education for Women, and Dr. Mary Lou Enberg, '50, Professor Emeritus of Physical Education, were of much help in backgrounding me on women's athletics from the 1950s through the 1970s, and Associate Athletic Director Marcia Saneholtz and Sally Savage, Senior Assistant Attorney General at WSU, helped June Bierbower gather material for her chapter on "The Blair Case."

I'm saddened that several people who provided me with material for this book did not live to see their contributions in print. Erich S. Klossner, '18; Esther Pond Smith, '47; Jack Koppel; and George Poler, all of Pullman; Ron Broom, '31, Spokane, and his brother, Larry, '39, Waitsburg; and John D. McCallum, '47, Tacoma, the noted sports historian and author, all passed away while the book was in progress. I am deeply indebted to all of them for their help.

Jeff Jordan, sports editor of the *Spokesman-Review*; Harland Beery, of the Bremerton *Sun*; Dick Rockne, of the Seattle *Times*, and Bob Payne, of the Tacoma *News-Tribune* helped me with photos and information.

In 1987, I had a delightful visit at his Menlo Park, California, home with John F. Bohler, '34. The love and admiration he had for both his parents in no way distorted the picture John gave me of life with "Doc" Bohler from the time of the first Rose Bowl game in 1916 all the way up to his father's death in 1960. I hope the warmth of John's stories comes through.

Orin E. Hollingbery, Jr. (Buster), allowed me to read the hundreds of letters that were written to his father in 1962 when friends staged "A Day for the Babe" in Yakima. The letters emphasized again what respect and adoration the man inspired from teammates, players, fellow coaches, opponents, parents, friends and business associates during the course of his long and successful life. Maybelle Hollingbery Ferrier, '37, graciously related stories and incidents in her father's life during an interview in her Lacey, Washington, home in 1987. Old Rose Bowler Clem Senn, '33, of Sunnyside, visited with me on several occasions about Babe and his teams in 1930-1932 when Clem lettered here.

We have used approximately 150 photographs in this book. Where the photographer is known, he or she has been credited, but in many cases pictures have had to be labeled simply *Daily Evergreen*, Manuscripts, Archives, and Special Collections, Washington State University Libraries, *Hilltopics*, or WSU Photo Service because there was no identification on the photos. Bob Bullis and Norm Nelson of the WSU Photo Service took many of the sports action pictures in the 1950s-1970s, and Rod Commons shot a number of those since. If a picture is not credited to a specific photographer, we just were unable to come up with a name. If there are errors, we apologize. They are the result of misinformation or no information at all. Millie Swales Liebel, '45, Pullman, made her father's photo albums from the 1907-1908 era available and we have used several. Millie said her dad, Osbourne "Oz" Swales, '10, of Everett, used to take pictures early in the first half of WSC football games, rush back to his dorm and turn out prints, then go and sell the photo-postcards in the stands. Janet Miller, of Spokane, gave me several pictures of the great WSC team of '06, on which her father, William "Bad Bill" Miller, '08, was a 167-pound tackle. Myrna Morrison, of Zillah, graciously made a collection of historic WSC sports photo-postcards from the 1900-1913 era available to me and asked that they be credited to the late Charles and Anne (Dornquist) Morrison, '22, from whose scrapbooks they came.

Stan Schmid, WSU Vice President for University Relations, had the vision to set up the Centennial Histories Series, and I thank him for giving me the opportunity of writing this sports history. And also Tom Sanders, Director of the Office of University Publications, Printing, and the WSU Press, and his staff, for their assistance. I am particularly grateful to Glen Lindeman, Jane Fredrickson and Dave Hoyt for their contributions.

WSU Press Editor in Chief Fred Bohm has been most patient during what must have seemed a very long gestation period as this history was coming together and I am most grateful to him.

I want to acknowledge the support of Dr. Weldon B. Gibson in this project. As always, where WSU is concerned, "Hoot" has been there, behind the scenes, working, in this case to ensure the success of the Centennial Books.

So many people have had a hand in putting this book together, it concerns me that I might have overlooked some of those who helped me along the way. As painful as this may be, I hope those who feel left out will understand that such oversights are even more painful to me.

I would like to dedicate this book to all those who have worn the colors so proudly—from the Pink and Blue to the Crimson and Gray—and to my family, and especially my wife, Marilyn, who have provided so much encouragement and support over the past three years.

Go, Cougars!

Richard B. Fry
Pullman, Washington
October 1989

The First Decade, 1892-1900

Play Ball!

IT WAS ONE OF THOSE FALSE SPRING DAYS IN THE PALOUSE COUNTRY; THE TEMPERA-
ture was only fifty-five but it felt like seventy-five. A steady string of
wagons and buggies headed out the old River Road toward Guy
(Albion), some folks rode horses, others walked. Just about every
winter-weary resident in Pullman and the surrounding countryside
came out that day to see the baseball game between the Pullman Military
College and the team representing the new college up on the other hill.

The date was Saturday, March 12, 1892, just one day shy of two
months after the Washington Agricultural College, Experiment Station
and School of Science—soon shortened to "WAC"—opened its doors.
The game was the first athletic contest played by students of the new
college.

Ira G. Allen, later to become Pullman's postmaster, played third base
for the cadets that day. In 1923, in an article in the *Powwow*, WSC's
alumni magazine, Allen recalled the event:

> The Military College came to Pullman first [in 1891], and had a
> very imposing college building on Military hill [at the corner of
> True and State streets], besides a couple of dormitories, or
> barracks, as they called them. This college at that time naturally
> had the largest number of students, and was very popular with
> the Pullman people, and when the ball game was announced it
> was considered a cinch that the soldiers would win. We had
> several students who claimed to be pretty good at the national
> sport, especially Lieutenant Brooks and Sergeant Spores, who
> were to constitute the battery. Elbridge Hammond, the son of a
> local merchant, had enrolled at the Military College, but for
> some reason had changed his mind and entered WAC. Reports
> began to reach the soldiers that Hammond could throw a ball so
> fast you could not see it, and that no one had been found who
> could hit it, but we knew that he could not throw a curve, and
> believed the Military team contained about nine men who could
> slam his offerings to all corners of the lot.
>
> The game was played on the flat down the creek, below the
> [J.K.] Smawley place [about where the Pullman sewage treatment
> plant is now], and every man, woman and child in Pullman was
> out to witness it, and most of them rooting for the Military boys.
>
> The game had not progressed far before we began to realize
> that the reports of Hammond's speed had not been exaggerated,
> for he sent us to the bench in amazing regularity, and the game
> ended 26 to 0 in favor of WAC.

OPPOSITE: *Arthur L. Hooper, captain
and tackle on the 1901 football
team, was the first of the Hoopers, a
famous athletic family in Washington State University annals.* (Manuscripts, Archives, and Special
Collections, Washington State
University Libraries)

The *College Record*, the original WAC student newspaper, confirmed the score and added some colorful details in an article in the edition for April 1892:

> The game was progressing finely, with the exception of a few broken fingers, when John Jacobs, in making first, collided with [Hale] Daggett, first baseman, and unfortunately broke a bone in Daggett's arm.
> The "hay seeds" were too much for the "soldier boys," and at the end of the sixth inning the latter conceded the game to the agricultural boys, who were proud of the score—26 to 0.

The importance of the victory in this first athletic outing by a college team was underscored by Allen, who wrote:

> I believe this game was what turned the tide of local popularity toward the agricultural institution, as new students seemed to favor it, and the military school shortly after [in 1893] burned down and was never rebuilt.

Imagine that. A "turning point" in the very first game!

The lineup for WAC in that historic contest deserves to go into the record books along with the score. Frank McReynolds, of Guy, was the catcher and Captain; Elbridge R. Hammond pitched; Bert Laney played first base; Lew Harris, second; Harold West, third, and Arthur Moody was the shortstop. Floyd Moore was in left field, E. Quimby Merriman in center, and John Jacobs in right. All the WAC players except McReynolds were from Pullman or off farms in the immediate area.

In these early years, students in the Preparatory Department often participated in college sports and activities. In that first baseball game, Hammond, the winning pitcher for WAC, had been enrolled at the Military College and then "transferred" to WAC. The fact that the eighteen-year-old fireballer is not recorded as having registered at the college until April 6 was no big deal. There were no eligibility rules. Hammond, by the way, was good enough to pitch and play outfield for Helena in the old professional Montana State and Northwestern leagues after leaving college.

When the student newspaper referred to the winning WAC team as "hay seeds," no one took offense. For nearly thirty years the college athletic teams had no official nickname. Sometimes they were "Hayseeds," generally the label was "Farmers," occasionally "Aggies." Far from resenting these descriptions, the athletes—and the student body in general—appeared to delight in them. According to the 1899 *Chinook*, the first college yearbook, one of the most popular yells of the day was:

> Farmers! Hayseeds! Pumpkins! Squash!
> W.A.C.! By Gosh!

Students adopted a variety of "mascots" in these early years, one of the first being a black terrier some wit dubbed "Squirt." He had four white feet, a spot atop his nose, and a white blaze on his chest. "A neat and bright looking little dog," the *Evergreen* commented. Squirt appears in several team pictures in the early yearbooks, and even made an occasional trip with the teams. In 1903, when the WAC team made a

Intramural and inter-class competition began at the college as soon as there were enough students to make up teams. Departments also had teams. (The Vet-Pharmic football game was one of the earliest of these rivalries. That one lasted until 1957 when the attrition rate became so high they "officially" cancelled the football competition. Students and faculty of the two colleges still go after each other in basketball.)

swing into the Willamette Valley for football games with Oregon Agricultural College and the University of Oregon, Squirt was "dog-napped" by some OAC students, "but escaped and rejoined the team in time for the game," the student newspaper reported. On this same trip the players picked up a black bear named "Toodles" and brought it back to campus where it enjoyed a brief place in the sun as another mascot.

The Athletic Association

That was no pick-up team representing WAC in the win over the Military College. It was the WAC Baseball Club, and it was sponsored by the Washington Agricultural College Athletic Association.

Washington Agricultural College opened its doors January 13, 1892. The college was housed in one building, the "Crib," situated atop a bleak, snow-covered hill on the northeast side of Pullman, a village of some 900 people in Washington's rich, rolling wheat country known as the Palouse. Eighty-four students enrolled at the college in the first year; most signed up in the "Preparatory Department." Pullman had no high school at the time. The "Prep" division filled this void.

A little more than a month after the opening of the school, a group of students got together and organized the Washington Agricultural College Athletic Association. On February 26, 1892, they elected Orin Stratton, a civil engineering student from Pullman, president. That was just four days after the first meeting, with Professor of Horticulture E. R. Lake serving as advisor, to discuss what sort of athletic club the college should have. Stratton and his fifteen-year-old sister, "Frankie" (Frances), and Elbridge Hammond, comprised a committee which recommended formation of the WACAA.

Serving with President Stratton as officers of that first athletic association, the predecessor to the Department of Intercollegiate Athletics, were Alice "Allie" Lyle, vice president; John Klemgard, secretary, and Floyd Moore, treasurer. Hammond was chosen business manager. All were from Pullman, but then most of the students at the college were locals.

The Athletic Association's first purchase was an outfit of bats, balls, and gloves. An investment which paid off quickly—and handsomely—in that 26-0 win!

An Arbor Day to Remember

On April 15, 1892, Arbor Day was observed for the first time on the campus of Washington Agricultural College. One of the featured speakers was Orin Stratton, president of the new WAC Athletic Association. The *College Record* for April 28 reported his Arbor Day message:

> Ladies and gentlemen, we have gathered here for the purpose of planting a tree to represent the college Athletic Association. An American White Ash has been selected.
> The ash is used in making boats, oars, carriages, furniture, bows, baseball bats, etc., by reason of its great strength, elasticity and endurance, and so we think it will be a fair representative of an athletic association.

> This tree that we are going to plant, like the Association, is small now, but we hope as time advances that the tree and the Association will grow.
>
> And he planted the tree.

It's there today, on the lawn in front of Bryan Hall in the same grove with the Lowell Elm. Orin Stratton's hope was fulfilled; both the tree and intercollegiate athletics have grown—and thrived!

The Victory Bell

"The construction of a small lake on the college farm near the athletic grounds will begin next week," the Pullman Herald reported on July 7, 1900. "This lake will be a great addition to the landscape, also serving as an ice pond and skating rink during the winter months." (It was given the unlikely name "Silver Lake." WAC students soon renamed it, more appropriately, "Lake de Puddle.")

Longest standing of all Washington State University traditions is that of the "Victory Bell." Acquired originally to serve as a signal for the beginning and ending of class periods, and as a fire alarm, the bell first "proclaimed its melodious sound" on Thanksgiving Day 1892. At that time it occupied a small tower atop old College Hall, the second building on campus. Erected in the summer of 1892, it stood about where Murrow Communications Center is today. (A story in *Powwow* in 1919 described College Hall as a square, three-story, wooden structure, "painted a flaming red on the outside and a dusty color on the inside.")

The bell soon began serving two additional purposes, announcing a victory by WAC athletic teams, and getting the frosh out to guard against an "invasion" by Idaho. One of the popular sports of those early years was a sort of "snipe hunt" for uninitiated freshmen. The bell would start ringing in the middle of the night and someone would holler "Idaho's here! Idaho's here!" and the chase was on.

Tommy Woods of Colfax, '03, was the best ever at this they said, standing out in front of Ferry and in "that great, deep, roaring voice howling 'Idaho! Idaho!'"

"Fellows piled out of doors and windows armed with socks full of sand, clubs, ropes, and so on," wrote Dr. Sophus B. Nelson, the first veterinary chairman, in *Powwow* (1920), recounting escapades of the days when the college was young.

> Woods went roaring over the hills, shouting for everybody to follow him. He was on the heels of the Idaho gang. They followed him and followed him far out into the country, the entire male part of the student body; till, finally circling his path, Woods joined the pursuers, and helped hunt the enemy whose presence he had proclaimed. Along toward morning the weary, bedraggled pursuers filtered back, disgusted because once more Idaho had raided the camp and gotten away.

When College Hall was razed in 1908 to make room for Bryan Hall, the bell was taken down and for eight or nine years sat rather forlornly on the ground near the new building. Old College Hall had become so rickety, it was said, that it swayed when Custodian George Grimes climbed to the roof to ring the bell.

The bell wasn't down from its tower long until some enterprising students removed the clapper one morning and no class bell sounded. Rumor had it that Idaho had stolen the clapper, but "Dad" Waller (O. L. Waller, Professor of Civil Engineering and Vice President) knew better. He sent a notice down to the civil engineering students informing them

The Victory Bell in transit. First installed on old College Hall, the bell was moved out near what is now Murrow Center when Bryan Hall was built on the College Hall site. Then, when new College Hall was completed, the bell was moved to its roof, where it still resides. (Ivan Shirrod)

that the college had need of the clapper. Covered with mud, it appeared in the Ad building the next morning. The surveyors confessed they had buried the clapper, hoping to have an excuse for being late to class.

Someone at Idaho obviously read in the *Evergreen* about the prank for it was not long after—following a loss to WSC in football—that the clapper disappeared again, this time for good.

The death-like silence which hung over the campus was relieved only after the mechanical engineers came forward with a new clapper they made in the shops down the hill.

Unfortunately, the *Powwow* reported, their calculations must have gone awry. "The gong moaned drearily every time the clapper came into contact with it." Finally, a new clapper was ordered and installed, but the problems with the bell continued. On another occasion it was filled with cement, which had set so hard when the prank was discovered the following morning that workmen had a devil of a time removing the stuff.

A few years later, some men stationed themselves around the gong to guard it during a football contest with Idaho. After the game it was discovered that the clapper was missing again. Further inquiries revealed the strange fact that the "guards" were Idaho students!

After this incident authorities decided the bell should be removed to a safer location and its campus travels came full circle. Relocated to the roof of the new College Hall, it continued to ring until a campus bell system was installed in 1919. Since that time it has been rung by members of the Cougar Guard Chapter of Intercollegiate Knights to signal victories by athletic teams.

The old "Victory Bell" also rang out gloriously at the conclusion of World Wars I and II, honoring all Washington State students, faculty, and alumni who had served their country.

An Interstate Rivalry Begins

The WAC Baseball Club of 1892 chalked up many "firsts" in its initial season of sports competition: first game played by a school athletic team; first win; first shutout. Unfortunately, the individual achievements, first hit, first run, etc., were not deemed important enough at the time to be recorded. That 1892 club did get some good coverage on its first "road" game, however, and that's of historical interest. It's also fascinating to read the story of the event. The front page account in the *College Record* for April 28, 1892, gives a good picture of the transportation of the day and also the friendly and rather formal atmosphere surrounding some of the sports contests of those early years. The sports reporting was a little different also:

> On a challenge by the Moscow U.S. baseball nine, the following named athletes boarded the U.P. train on April 16 at 8 a.m. for Moscow, viz: L. P. Farr, Frank McReynolds, H. L. West, J. F. Shanks, H. E. True, E. R. Hammond, W. R. Hull, Mr. [Thomas J.] Hardwick, Otis Baird, Eugene Chilberg and W. D. Barkhuff, while Dr. [Charles E.] Munn [veterinary faculty], Ira Allen, Arthur Moody, Orin Stratton, Lew Harris, Arthur Hill and J. W. Hampton proceeded on horseback. Those on the train arrived at 8:45 and were met at the depot by a representative of the U.S. nine, who escorted them to the Commercial hotel. At 11:30 the W.A.C.'s were invited into the dining-room, where a fine repast was spread, of which all heartily partook, and at 12:25 a buss [*sic*] was in waiting to convey them to the fair grounds, where the ball teams arrived at 12:40, and Mr. Farr was chosen umpire. The game began at 1:25 with the U.S. at bat. [At this time, the visiting team was given its choice of batting first or taking the field.]

WAC pounded eight runs across in the first two frames and took a 10-4 win in the seven-inning game.

> The crowd arrived [back] at the hotel at 3:45 p.m., where all waited until 5:10 when the out-of-town boys departed for home, feeling jubilant over the pleasant trip and the royal way they had been received and welcomed by the boys of the prosperous city of Moscow.

The Moscow U.S. nine was the number two baseball team in that city in 1892 and was sponsored by the U.S. Store, a sort of surplus store of its day, selling everything from general merchandise to furniture, farm equipment, and vehicles. Most of the Moscow U.S. players were of college age and matched up very well with the WAC squad.

Several of the Moscow players, including Gainford "Gub" Mix, a pitcher, later joined the WAC team for some of the games played during the summer schedule.

Four games were played between WAC and the Moscow U.S. nine that spring, with WAC winning three.

The WAC baseball team of 1892 finished with a season record of 11-1, including two more games with the U.S. team in Moscow that fall. The *College Record* took note of the season-ender played at Moscow on November 5 and won by WAC, 7-5:

●

The WAC Athletic Association was reorganized April 18, 1894, with Peter Brown, Pullman, president. Some consider this, rather than the 1892 organization, to be the first Athletic Association.

●

Saturday's game was very much retarded by the wind and
dust, also by the cold weather. Some of the boys had to play
with their overcoats on, but they got there just the same.

Who said "Bobo" Brayton invented "fall ball?" Captain Frank McReynolds and his "hay seeds" were playing "winter ball" way back in 1892!

WAC BASEBALL SEASON SUMMARY 1892

WAC 26 Pullman Military 0	WAC 18 Guy 7
WAC 10 Moscow U.S. 4	WAC 18 Pullman Pros 11
WAC 11 Moscow U.S. 15	WAC 23 Johnson 17
WAC 23 Guy (Albion) 2	WAC 9 Pullman Married Men 0
WAC 11 Moscow U.S. 9	WAC 12 Moscow U.S. 6
WAC 15 Moscow U.S. 14	WAC 7 Moscow U.S. 5

The "Spoils of Victory"

Track was the second sport started at WAC. The first meet was held
in June 1892, also with Pullman Military Academy. Races were run on
a course mowed through an oat field about where Martin stadium is
today.

"The stubble had previously been uprooted by dragging the ground
with a railroad rail," a story in *Powwow* related. "We won the meet by
a good margin, and in consequence claimed as a reward the sixteen-
pound iron shot of the academy. We had practiced with a large rock."

The first "Field Day" was held June 14, 1892, and became a spring
tradition at WAC. It was sort of a play-day, with track and field
competition, usually an intramural or student-faculty baseball game
and, on this first occasion, a "sparring exhibition." A track meet with the
University of Idaho, a natural regional rival because of its location just
eight miles to the east in Moscow, soon became the centerpiece of the
Field Day and eventually replaced it entirely.

*Robert Eben Bucklin clearing eight
feet, seven inches in the pole vault
on Rogers Field, in May 1897.*
(Robert W. Bucklin)

The importance attached to the Field Day is evident from the formal four-page "Programme" printed on quality paper that was sent out announcing the event.* Gold medals were awarded winners of individual track and field events. It is interesting to compare some of the marks established at that first Field Day:

100-yard dash (under 15)—Eddie Webb, Pullman, 14 seconds
100-yard dash—Frank McReynolds, Guy, 11 1/2 seconds
16-pound shot—Levi P. Farr, Pullman, 19 ft. 4 in.
Running broad jump—Henry Van de Walker, Moscow, 16 ft. 6 in.
Running high jump—William Hull, Olympia, and Henry Miller,
    Colfax, tie, 4 ft. 5 in.

•
D.A. Brodie, *crack halfback on the football team of 1895, was named Superintendent of the Western Washington Experiment Station at Puyallup in 1899 at an annual salary of $1,000.00.*
•

WAC students participated in a Field Day at the University of Idaho on June 9, 1893, the first mention found of track and field competition between athletes of the two schools. No score was reported, but among WAC entries Edgar Thompson, of Waterville, won the fifty-yard dash in five-and-a-half seconds; George Wagner, Blaine, took the standing high kick at seven feet, four inches, and the twelve-pound shot, thirty-six feet, four inches, and Frank McReynolds, quite an all-around athlete, won the 220 in twenty-eight seconds. Ira Kennedy, Spokane, was second in the ten-pound hammer throw. (No distance reported.)

Sports in the Doldrums

After such an auspicious start, 11-1, it might seem surprising that baseball went into the doldrums at WAC after the 1892 season and did not really get going again until 1898. Finances and weather were two very big problems.

"In the disturbed condition of the college in the spring of 1893 [politicians and some regents were still trying to move the institution to Yakima or Tacoma] and the meager attendance in the following autumn athletics reached the low water mark in its history," President Bryan wrote.

"Meager attendance" is right! Only twenty-three students enrolled at WAC in the fall of 1893 when Bryan's presidency began. The nation also was in the throes of the financial Panic of 1893.

The 1899 *Chinook* said a baseball team was organized at WAC in the spring of 1893 but that no games were played. The *Pullman Herald*, however, mentions that Guy (Albion) lost to "the college team" 16 to 8 that spring.

The ball field at the college had not yet been developed to the point where it was really playable. Occasional races and some jumping events and weight tosses were held down on the flat near "Tanglewood," but the baseball fields in use at this time were down on the old Albion road where that first game was played and on the flat by the river at the other end of town, just east of where the city softball complex is now. Both of these fields were right down on the "creek" (Palouse River) and were extremely vulnerable in any kind of high water.

*Ivan R. Shirrod, '41, of Pullman, has a prized copy.

Baseball in the loess! Notice the topsoil on WAC's baseball diamond in this photograph of Frank "Cack" Barnard fielding a throw at first base. The first baseball field was located where Martin Stadium is today. The batters hit toward Lake de Puddle, over the rise in right field, in the direction of today's Mooberry Track. (Manuscripts, Archives, and Special Collections, Washington State University Libraries)

The rains that destroyed crops in the Palouse in the fall and early winter of 1893, bringing added financial distress to the farmers and businessmen of the area, continued into the spring of 1894. An article in the Pullman *Herald* for April 6 of that year noted:

> . . .the baseball ground, on which so much work was put last summer, is now in bad shape, the floods of the spring having cut it up in deep trenches and carried tons of earth down the creek. It would take an immense amount of labor to get it in shape again. [Presumably, this field was at the east end of town, down on the river near where the Franz Koppel dairy was later.]

WAC records show that a single baseball game was played in 1896. This is important only because it was a 6-4 win over the University of Idaho, at Moscow. Although the schools had played two football games by this time, the baseball game in 1896 appears to have marked the start of the diamond rivalry between the neighboring institutions.

In 1898 WAC renewed baseball with an eight-game schedule, of which five were won. "Intercollegiate" baseball really began at the college that year. Three games were played with Idaho and three with Whitman College, WAC winning two from each school.

Baseball continued to struggle, however, with only six games played in 1899 (4-2) and but three in 1900, the first time the college team failed to win a game.

The 11-1 record of that first WAC team in 1892 remained the best by any of the college teams (except for the 6-0 record in the war-shortened season of 1917) until Doc Bohler's 1918 outfit chalked up a 13-1 mark in winning the Eastern division of the old Northwest Conference.

The "Iron Men"

"Of all the interests dear to the heart of the average alumnus, athletics usually takes precedence, and the acme of athletics in the minds of most alumni is football." Historian William M. Landeen wrote those words in 1958 in an introduction to a brief discussion of intercollegiate athletics at WSC in his book, *E. O. Holland and the State College of Washington, 1916-1944*. Professor Landeen knew his sports fans!

Football came to Washington Agricultural College in the fall of 1894, almost three years after competition in baseball and track began at WAC. After just one game, a 10 to 0 win over the team from the University of Idaho, the favorite autumn sport had infected the entire student body—and a large section of the local citizenry—with an incurable case of football madness.

Although WAC's victory in the 1894 game is not argued, the Idahos claim to this day that the first football game between the two schools actually took place a year earlier, in 1893 on the WAC campus, and that they won, strangely enough by an identical 10-0 score! (At that time a touchdown counted four points and the conversion two.)

President Bryan, who began his tenure at WAC in that fall of 1893, pooh-poohed the Idees' claim and wrote:

> An amusing story has been told of an attempted football game in the fall of 1893, in which there were not even goal posts and in which the Pullman boys lent to the Moscovites [sic] enough players to fill out, but nobody knew even the first elements of the game.

There are other versions, one related by long-time WAC Registrar Harry M. Chambers in 1924 when he was Alumni Director and Editor of the *Alumnus* magazine:

> Although not recorded in the official books of the State college, the first clash between the Cougars and Vandals came about in 1893. What a battle it must have been. Rival schools had been practicing a little and they finally arranged for a game. But neither team realized that it was practicing a different type of football from the other until the day of the game.
>
> Idaho's warriors arrived Friday, a day early, but that didn't halt proceedings. After considerable discussion they agreed to play that day but when they came to line up for battle they discovered that Washington State had been rehearsing rugby football while Idaho had been practicing the American type of play.
>
> On a sloping hill of bunchgrass back of where College hall now stands rooters of the rival institutions journeyed to see their respective teams play. After further conference, Idaho agreed to teach WAC some of the more important phases of the American game. After a hurried course in the new game, the two outfits went to bat [sic]. Both sides were smarting a little under the skin over the several difficulties and they tore at each other ferociously.
>
> The game finally ended in a row with each team claiming victory, according to the old-timers.

And they've been arguing ever since!

• Robert E. Bucklin, *of Port Blakely, writing to his parents in the winter of 1897-1898 to allay their fears of football injuries: "Padding on legs and shoulders is often over two inches thick. A rubber contrivance protects the mouth and nose, and shin guards protect the shins. So a man can tumble around a great deal and be protected by his padding." Now that should have been reassuring. Unfortunately, young Robert added: "The Spokane grounds were just covered with stones, and of course falling on them isn't going to improve a man's health."* •

There is yet another version of this first game, and it virtually proves that the game was no "game" at all, but merely a bunch of students from the two schools bumping heads.

The Pullman *Herald* for June 16, 1893, reported: "The football team from the university of Idaho came to Pullman last Saturday [June 9] and won a game from the agricultural college team, by a score of 12 to 0. The college team can't seem to play foot ball."

June 9, 1893, also was the date of a "Field Day" at the University of Idaho, and Frank McReynolds, among others from WAC, participated and won the 220. There is no way two major events such as a football game and a Field Day would have been scheduled on the same day.

What were they doing playing football in June anyway!

No, the first football game played by a team representing Washington Agricultural College, was on November 18, 1894, against a team from the University of Idaho on the old fairgrounds baseball field at Moscow. The first touchdown in WAC football history was scored by the old catcher, Frank McReynolds, this time playing at left halfback.

"McReynolds went through the line for the first touchdown after 13 1/2 minutes of play," the Pullman *Herald* reported in its November 23 issue. "Excitement reigned supreme; and the Moscow girls forgot to smile, and the cheers of the Washington Agricultural College aggregation were deafening."

Fred Long, of Chehalis, WAC Captain and right halfback, kicked the goal and the half ended with the score 6 to 0 in favor of the "Farmers." Long broke loose for a thirty-yard touchdown run six minutes into the second half. He missed his goal kick, "on account of the heavy wind that was blowing," making the final score 10-0.

"While the team of '93 had to play in overalls and old clothes, the team of '94 was outfitted in fine tight-fitting jackets and heavy trousers," the alumni magazine said, adding, "Nose guards and mustaches were common equipment for all back field men. . . ."*

The WAC Athletic Association bought that first set of football uniforms. (The mustaches must have come with them.) Frank Lowden, the varsity center and President of the WACAA in 1894, placed the order for the new uniforms with Hall Brothers, a store in Moscow. The total bill came to sixteen dollars.

Washington had been admitted to the Union as a state only five years before this game was played, and the college was less than three years old. It's interesting to note where these first football players came from. Only two, Long and Lowden, were "native sons." Kimmel was born in Iowa; Clemens and McCroskey in Tennessee; Chittenden in New York

At a meeting of the Athletic Association, October 22, 1899, Leo Totten, of Steptoe, presented a head-harness and guards to Captain (Boyd) Hamilton and Charles Goodsell of the football team. "These gifts were made by Mr. Totten on behalf of a number of students who are debarred from active participation in the athletic work, but who desire to show their interest," the College Record reported.

---

*Lining up for WAC in that first football game were: Milton P. McCroskey, Colfax, left end; Henry M. Chittenden, Spokane, left tackle; Edward Kimmel, Waitsburg, left guard; Francis M. Lowden, Jr., Walla Walla, center; John E. Clemens, Hay, right guard; Walter M. Savage, Pullman, right tackle, and William A. Hardwick, Pullman, right end. In the backfield with McReynolds and Long were Floyd L. Moore, Pullman, quarterback, and Joseph B. Winston, Spokane, fullback. (One reference has Edgar Thompson, of Waterville, listed as the starter at right end in place of Hardwick. Thompson is not listed in any WSU record book as a football letterman, however, and the 1899 *Chinook* has Hardwick as the starter in 1894.)

The first football team at Washington Agricultural College in 1894 poses with its new sixteen-dollar suits. That's the total price! Today, a football helmet costs more than $100.00. Front (left to right): Joe Winston, Captain Fred Long, and Frank Lowden. Middle: Edgar Thompson, John Clemens, Coach F. W. Waite, Milton McCroskey, and Tom Hardwick. Back: Walter Savage, Henry Chittenden, Floyd Moore, and Edward Kimmel. Frank McReynolds, who scored WAC's first touchdown (against Idaho), apparently missed the photo session. (Manuscripts, Archives, and Special Collections, Washington State University Libraries)

state; Savage in California; Hardwick in Kansas; Moore in Michigan; McReynolds in Montana; and Winston in North Carolina. Quite an all-America group!

The euphoria that resulted from that first football victory was short-lived. Spokane High School invited WAC to come to the north for a game on Thanksgiving Day, November 29, and Captain Long and his teammates readily accepted.

William Goodyear, the founder and publisher of The *Palouse City News*, "a weekly Democratic paper" in nearby Palouse, Washington, was an unpaid coach of that first team. Later, in 1934 when he was publisher of the Pullman *Herald*, Goodyear recalled the events surrounding the game with Spokane High School:

> The arrangement was that the boys were to go to Spokane the day before the game with their transportation and hotel expenses guaranteed. I went back to Palouse [after the win over Idaho] expecting to take the train from there. Wednesday afternoon the boys phoned that the Spokane management had given notice that it could not afford to meet their hotel bill and that they would have to come up on the freight train Thursday, which left Pullman anytime between 2 a.m. to 8 a.m. Knowing that they would be in no condition to play after such a trip I urged them to cancel the game, but they were rarin' to go and could not be stopped. Some of them camped in the depot all night so as to be sure to be on hand when the train arrived.
>
> The train reached Spokane about noon with the game scheduled for 2 o'clock. Most of the boys were so car sick they could not eat and those who tried promptly began vomiting. The quarterback was so dizzy that the first time the ball was passed back to him he did not even see it and the fullback recovered it for a loss of several yards.

> The boys put up a game fight but were too dead on their feet
> to do much against their opponents, who were reinforced by
> several older players from the Spokane Athletic Club.
>
> They all forgot their troubles and regained their appetites,
> however, at a big turkey dinner served at the hospitable home of
> Col. and Mrs. P. H. Winston, parents of Joe Winston, one of our
> players. [Winston played at fullback in this game but later
> switched to quarterback.]

The 18-0 loss in Spokane ended the first football season for WAC. It would be five years before the college team lost another game.

"Iron Men," who played both offense and defense and played the entire game, were the rule rather than the exception in this era. WAC did not make a substitution until the second football game of the 1897 season!

The *Chinook* for 1899, reviewing the school's gridiron achievements and recording its heroes, noted:

> The first game [of the 1897 season] was at Spokane with the
> Athletic Club. Our boys made two touchdowns in the first
> twelve minutes. It was just before the second touchdown that
> [Boyd] Hamilton [right end, from Colfax] had his knee cap
> broken and McCroskey [left end] had his neck seriously injured,
> but they both played through the game. The final score was 16
> to 8 in favor of the WAC team.
>
> The second game was played with Whitman College of Walla
> Walla. Larkin was substituted for Clemens, who had left college,
> and Bucklin and Troupe for Hamilton and McCroskey, who
> were injured in the Spokane game.

Charles Larkin, of Garfield; R. E. Bucklin, of Port Blakely, and Roy Troup (his name was misspelled in the *Chinook*), Nelson, British Columbia, thus became the first substitutes used by a WAC football team. The trio also became part of WAC football lore for another reason as well. The game against Whitman was remembered, as they say, in story and song by students and alumni for years to come.

Early on the morning of November 23, 1897, Ferry Hall at WAC burned to the ground, leaving ninety-six students—including most members of the football team—out in the cold with only the few items they were able to save as they fled the fire. Most of the students in the five-story men's dormitory lost everything they owned, clothing, trunks and suitcases, personal items, all their books. It was a miracle no lives were lost.

Fifteen football uniforms were destroyed. There was no gymnasium at WAC in 1897; a "shops" building erected in 1893 also served as a combination gymnasium/armory, but players kept their uniforms in their rooms in Ferry Hall.

The entire community of Pullman rallied to help the students. Churches gave a free Thanksgiving dinner and the people of Pullman and the surrounding area contributed money and clothing. "The relationship between the citizens of the town and the college became closer than ever before. . . ." President Bryan recalled.

The Ferry Hall fire occurred on Tuesday and Washington Agricultural College was scheduled to play Whitman College at Walla Walla on

Thursday. Captain Joe Winston took charge and demonstrated why his teammates had elected him their leader. The feisty little quarterback (145 pounds) telegraphed Frank Lowden, the 1895 Captain, who had returned to his hometown and was playing for the National Guard in Walla Walla. Lowden quickly rounded up uniforms for the WAC players who had lost their gear in the fire.

The WAC team boarded the train as scheduled, picked up the borrowed uniforms and other equipment in Walla Walla and went out and beat Whitman 16-4 on Thanksgiving Day to complete a third straight unbeaten season.

That's why all the old-timers remembered that team of 1897.

Frank Field, of Snohomish, lettered in football at WAC in 1897 and at the UW in 1899 and 1900 as "center rush."

Soldiers Field

The first athletic field at WAC was carved out of a sloping hillside where Martin stadium is now. Originally, it was called "Soldiers Field." The name was changed to "Rogers Field" in honor of Washington's third governor, John R. Rogers (1897-1901), who awarded diplomas to the first Washington Agricultural College graduating class in June 1897. It became Martin Stadium in 1972 when former Governor Clarence D. Martin's son and daughter-in-law, Dan and Charlotte Martin, of Los Angeles, California, capped off a new stadium drive with a gift of $250,000 to the university in the name of the man who served as Washington's chief executive from 1932 to 1940.

In the first years of the college, before excavating began to create the present athletic fields, the hillside behind Van Doren Hall, Holland Library, and the Compton Union Building sloped gently down to the area now occupied by three gymnasiums and the field house.

A photograph dated 1899, in Bryan's history, shows row crops planted on the slopes below where Van Doren and the Compton Union Building are now located, and the *College Record* for 1893 mentions "ball playing on Fulmer's beet patch." Chemistry professor Elton Fulmer grew sugar beets on the campus at the time as part of a research project. One of his "patches" must have been in this vicinity.

Thousands of yards of dirt were removed by primitive scrapers pulled by horses, and there was a lot of just plain digging, too, to create the flat which now appears so natural. President Bryan described the transition process:

> Just north of where the old grand stand is [south stands of present-day Martin stadium], a valley ran to the northward joining the valley in which Silver Lake was made. There were no willows there then and "Tanglewood" was a series of small nursery rows with 10,000 little forest plants a foot or two high. Professor [J.A.] Balmer [horticulture] had strewed apple pumice from the cider mill in a furrow and the seeds soon grew into the apple hedge [where the horseshoe end of the stadium is now].
>
> Farm teams and scrapers manipulated by willing student or faculty hands plowed and dragged the earth into the valley from east and west and south, and shovels, in other willing hands, leveled a field barely large enough for a football field. Around this a quarter-mile track [originally it was only a fifth of a mile] was later made and covered with cinders from the college heat

and power plant. Just west of this track there stood a hill about thirty feet high in the very middle of the present [practice/intramural] field. . . ."

John Bohler, son of WSU's long-time athletic director J. Fred "Doc" Bohler, remembers his father telling about races in 1909-1910 on this oval involving Jack Nelson, the college's great sprinter.

> Dad said you could not see the start of the 440 from the finish line because of that hill in the middle of the field. He said they'd hear the gun and then a few seconds later someone would holler "Here HE comes!" Nelson usually was so far out in front that he'd appear well ahead of any of the other runners.

When that original football field was scraped out it created a sort of one-sided amphitheater. Spectators at first sat on the grassy south hillside to watch games. Later, notches were cut into the hillside for seating. The first football stands, wooden bleachers, were erected on the north side of the playing field. They would be removed when baseball season started because they were then in "center field."

The first baseball field at WAC was laid out more or less across the football field. Home plate was down in the right-hand corner of the east end zone, as you look at the field today, and a wooden grandstand was built there for spectators. The short right field ended in "Tanglewood." Center field was on a line toward Silver Lake, or "Lake de Puddle" as the students called the pond created by damming the flow from several springs which arose where the Coliseum parking lot is now and trickled down and formed a swampy area where Hollingbery Field House later was built. Left field went almost to the sunset, after the hill Bohler spoke of was leveled.

The first real tennis courts on campus also were located in this area, at the base of the hill below where Van Doren Hall now stands. Four clay courts were scraped out on a flat at the west end of the present intramural field, perhaps eight feet above the level of the track. Later, the courts were moved to their present location east of Stadium Way, while the old court site was taken down to the level of the rest of the intramural/practice field and a track was constructed around the entire area, from the horseshoe end of Rogers Field to the base of the hill behind Van Doren. It was nearly a half-mile in length, one of the few in the country of that distance.

The First "Home" Game

Over the years, Washington State has played a number of "home" football games away from home, in Spokane, Tacoma, Seattle, and Portland, Oregon. The first of these was played on Thanksgiving Day, November 26, 1896 at nearby Colfax when the WAC team met and defeated a team from Walla Walla representing Company C of the Washington National Guard 22-0. (The score has been incorrectly listed as 24-0 in WSU records for years.)

Francis C. Lowden, Jr., of Walla Walla, the center on the first WAC team in 1894 and Captain of the 1895 team, was one of those instrumental in arranging the Colfax game. Lowden was Captain of the Company

The first athletic league in which WAC participated was formed in 1899, with Idaho and Whitman College as the other members.

This photo of the 1899 football team shows a variety of uniforms and equipment worn by early-day gridders. Note the shin guards and the helmets. The leather pendants hanging around some of the players' necks are nose and mouth guards. Front (left to right): Charles Goodsell, Boyd Hamilton, Chester Offner, Benjamin Mashburn, and Charles Proff. Middle: Peter Brown, Jim Elton, Robert Spencer, Fred Stone, Dennis Woods, and Fred Whittaker. Back: John Evans, James Rice, Steven Jayne, Fred Schnebley, Fred Poole, William Boone, Harry Jackson, Ernest Cobleigh, and L. H. Palmerton. (Manuscripts, Archives, and Special Collections, Washington State University Libraries)

C team and played right tackle in this game. WAC Captain Milton P. McCroskey lived near Steptoe and was a great favorite of the Colfax fans. These undoubtedly were factors that led to playing the game in Colfax, along with the fact that it was a "neutral" site, rail transportation was available, and it was closer for both teams.

In 1898, the *Evergreen* reported that "the first and second football teams gave an exhibition of ball on the fair grounds at Colfax Thursday," so there obviously was interest over there.

Bill Wilmot, long-time Publisher of the Colfax *Gazette*, uncovered these notes on that game in 1896, and other doings, from the pages of the *Gazette* for November 27:

> Foot ball is coming to be just as essentially a part of a regulation Thanksgiving as turkey dinner or special church services. Yesterday Colfax celebrated in the strictly regulation style, including the football game [between WAC and Co. C., W.N.G]. . . . The college students and their friends and supporters made the day hideous from the time they struck town until their train pulled out last night with
> "Ru, Rah, Ru Rah, Ru Rah, Ree!
> Washington, Washington, W.A.C.!"
> The officers [officials] were J. T. Bedell, umpire; D. A. Brodie, referee, and Ortis Hamilton, linesman. Two thirty minute halves were played. In the first the Pullman team made three 'touch downs' and kicked one 'goal' and in the second they made two touchdowns and missed both goals.
> [Joe] Winston, [Lester] Gammon and [William] Doty of the college team and [Charles] Crosby and [E. R.] Collins of the Walla Walla team were soon picked as favorites by the audience on their runs and tackles. [Winston was the WAC quarterback; Doty

played left half, and Gammon was at right half. For Walla Walla, Crosby played at right halfback and Collins was the quarterback.]

The day's biggest excitement came after the game:

> . . . the evening train to Pullman contained the college foot ball team, and when the train was forced to stop by finding three horses fast in a trestle, Captain McCroskey came out just as the train men were preparing to hitch chains to the horses to pull them out, expecting of course, in clearing the track to kill the horses. But the football hero called for a stay of proceeding and called out his chrysanthemum-locked eleven ["garlands of victory," no doubt], showed them the horses, said 4-11-44, or some thing like that, four men took hold of a horse, seven other men took hold of the four, there was a straining of muscles, and one horse was set on his legs by the side of the track and trotted off uninjured. The other two animals were rescued, and the train went on its way—passengers and train men rejoicing.
>
> Conductor Stevens of the Moscow run has an even better opinion of football players now than he had before.

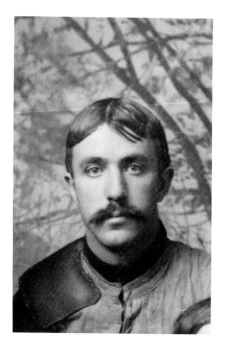

Robert R. Gailey played center-rush for the championship Princeton team of 1896. He "coached" the 1897 WAC team. (Princeton University Library)

Those Early-Day "Coaches"

There is considerable mystery surrounding the identity of some of the "coaches" of these early football teams at WAC. Bryan's history says the college teams—in any sport—did not have paid coaches until "Wild Bill" Allen came to coach the football team of 1900, and even he was not a regular college employee.

It is acknowledged that Goodyear, the newspaperman, and Professor W. J. Spillman, head of the Agriculture Department, "helped teach elements of the game" to the teams of 1894 and 1895.

The college yearbook of 1904, however, identifies a very young man in a dark, three-piece suit, wing collar and tie, as "Waite, Coach," under a picture of Washington Agricultural College's first football team. There was indeed a Fred Waite around WAC that fall; he was a nineteen-year-old freshman from Colfax.

As strange as it may seem today, there are reasons to believe this young fellow actually was the first football coach at WAC. For one, "F. Waite" is listed in the newspaper report as "umpire" of that first game with Idaho. For another, Waite's enrollment record at WAC says he had attended the University of Michigan before coming west with his father, who was in the hardware business in Colfax. In those days, anyone who had been around a big football school such as Michigan almost automatically qualified as an authority on the game. It is likely that young Waite knew something about football, and that would put him considerably ahead of most of the players on that first team.

Waite left school after one semester, but he stayed on the sports pages. The *College Record* for May 1895, reported: "Mr. Fred Waite, of Colfax, an ex-student of the W.A.C., lowered the state bicycle record for a mile on the Colfax track recently."

If another reason is needed for accepting young Waite as the coach of that team of 1894, the case of Robert R. Gailey might well be offered.

Gailey, from Princeton, has been listed for years in Washington State University football press books as coach of the 1897 team. Mr. Gailey's encounter with the college was even more brief than Mr. Waite's.*

The *Evergreen* for November 1897, noted:

> A visit from such men as Traveling Secretaries R. R. Gailey of Princeton, New Jersey, and J. A. Dummett of Portland, [for the Student Volunteer Movement, a predecessor to the YMCA] cannot be other than an encouragement and help to the institution. These men came to us on the noon train Saturday, Nov. 6. . . . At three o'clock all adjourned to the athletic grounds, where Mr. Gailey gave the foot ball team valuable instruction in the favorite autumn game.

The following day, Gailey went back to Portland and four months later was off to China, where he spent the next forty-three years. He was one of the founders of the World Service program of the YMCA. There is no record that he ever returned to Pullman, even for a visit, let alone pick up a check for "coaching."

Gailey must have been pleased, however, when he saw the sports page of the Sunday *Oregonian* on November 26, 1897, and read that WAC had defeated Whitman to complete its third straight unbeaten season (marred only by a 6-6 tie with the Lewiston Athletic Club in 1896). And Coach Gailey would have been downright proud had he known what obstacles those players overcame just to get out on that field.

Robert W. Bucklin, '25, has been chuckling for three-quarters of a century over a story his father told him about "Coach" Gailey. Bob's father, Robert Eben Bucklin, mentioned earlier as one of the first three substitutes in WAC football history, was out on the practice field that November day in 1897 when Gailey passed through Pullman.

> Dad said Gailey showed them a new "signal system" they used at Princeton. "Instead of barking out numbers and having the opposition steal your signals," Gailey said, crouching behind the center in that old T-formation, "you just tweak the center's fanny when you want him to snap the ball."

Frank Field, of Snohomish, was the center on that 1897 team. Do you suppose Frank was "bruised" after that win over Whitman?

Jokes aside, Gailey probably was very well qualified to offer some advice on "the favorite autumn game," as the *Evergreen* put it, and certainly on that "Hike!" signal. He was a graduate student at Princeton Theological Seminary in 1895 and 1896 and played center for Princeton University in those years. An obituary in 1950 noted that Gailey "was an All-American center on the championship [Princeton] team of 1896."

William Goodyear, one of the "technical advisors" of those first two WAC teams in 1894 and 1895, played some football at Williams College in Massachusetts before coming west in 1891. He said later his "coach-

Idaho won the Field Day at Moscow in 1896 by a score of 26-17, "and so elated did the representatives of the orange and white become over their victory that some of them forgot their positions as gentlemen, one man being carried so far as to use strong language in loud and boisterous terms." (Evergreen, May 1896)

---

*Fred Waite died in Ann Arbor, Michigan, in 1905 at age thirty and is buried in the cemetery at Colfax, Washington, along with his father and mother and three generations of the Waite family.

ing" was pretty much limited to "teaching some of the elements of the game." That undoubtedly was true, but it was a valuable contribution because the players knew so little about football at the time.

Professor W. J. Spillman, the brilliant young geneticist of the WAC faculty, had no background in athletics at all as an undergraduate at the University of Missouri, but Bryan describes Spillman, who came to WAC after teaching at the Oregon Normal School at Monmouth, as "bubbling over with enthusiasm." Some of it must have spilled over to football.

In a biography of his father, Dr. Ramsay Spillman explained the football coaching reference:

> It was when I asked Mr. [David A.] Brodie on what foundation my father coached football at Pullman, that I learned that he came to Pullman with a reputation as a coach at Monmouth.
> "When we decided at Monmouth in 1893 that we were going to play football, and wondered what we would do for a coach, your father stepped forward and said that he would coach". . . he brought out a group picture showing the team, and Professor Spillman as coach.

Brodie said Professor Spillman had a copy of Walter Camp's Football Rules, and he "studied them and coached."

In 1894, when Spillman came to Pullman, Brodie followed his mentor, and eventually became WAC's first graduate in Agriculture. He also was a crackerjack halfback on the 1895 team, and scored both touchdowns in WAC's 10-4 win over Idaho in the first football game played on Soldiers Field. In the second game of the season, Brodie scored an almost unheard of three touchdowns, one on a forty-five-yard run, in a 26-4 rout of the Spokane Amateur Athletic Club, to give WAC its first unbeaten season.

A professional coach he might not have been, but Spillman deserves to go into the WAC athletic record books somewhere. Maybe as the first "Recruiter?"

The first professional coach at WAC was William L. Allen, described in colorful fashion by President Bryan:

> In 1900, with the aid of voluntary contributions of faculty members and others, the athletic association was able to employ as coach "Wild Bill" Allen, a Michigan football star, inspired by the philosophy of "Hurry Up" Yost. He [Allen] gave the team some excellent training. Notwithstanding his notorious use of a two-inch cart rope as an incentive to speed in getting into the game and his profuse use of expletives more emphatic than ornamental, he contributed much to the development of a good team.

Allen, it turns out, was another of those "mystery" coaches.

President Bryan would be surprised to know that "Wild Bill," far from being a "star" at Michigan, might not have played there at all. Certainly he did not play for Fielding H. "Hurry Up" Yost, for Yost did not come to Michigan until 1901. Wolverine football records show an "Allen" (no first name given) as a "reserve" on the squads of 1897 and 1898 coached by Gustave H. Ferbert, and a "William Lindsay Allen" did receive an L.L.B. from Michigan in 1900, the first year "Wild Bill" was at WAC. Of course he could have graduated "in absentia" as they like to say around academe, but WAC's Allen coached at Seattle High School in 1899.

If indeed this is "Wild Bill" Allen, the story has a sad ending. He had an unbeaten (once tied, by the University of Washington) record at WAC in 1900, then left for undetermined reasons prior to the 1901 season. Allen returned in 1902 but his team posted a disappointing 2-3 record, defeating Idaho, 17-0, and Whitman, 6-5, but losing to the Lewiston Athletic Club, 12-0; Pacific University (of Forest Grove, Oregon), 6-5; and Washington, 16-0.

Allen left WAC after the 1902 season. University of Michigan Alumni Office records show that "William Lindsay Allen" died May 13, 1907, in Las Vegas, New Mexico, "of tuberculosis of the lungs," three months short of his thirty-first birthday.

First of the Indian Coaches

Between 1915 and 1925 Washington State had three consecutive football coaches who had been outstanding players at the Carlisle Indian School in Pennsylvania, William H. "Lone Star" Dietz, Gustavus A. "Gus" Welch, and Albert A. Exendine. But the first Indian coach, and very possibly the first *professional* coach the college had, was Frank S. Shively.

Many football fans can tell you about "Lone Star" Dietz and how he took WSC to the Rose Bowl in 1916, and quite a few people know about Welch and Exendine, who coached here after Dietz. Except for a note in President Bryan's history, little has been written or said about Shively, a prominent man in his own right. Bryan knew that Shively coached the WAC teams in 1898 and 1899, but that's about all he knew—or perhaps pretended to know. It could be that Bryan didn't want to know all the "arrangements."

WAC's first Indian football coach, Frank Shively (1898-1899) is shown in this 1905 photograph with the Crow chiefs Plenty Coups (left) and Big Shoulder Blade (right). (Smithsonian Institution, Office of Anthropology, Bureau of American Ethnology Collection)

It was with the beginning of the second period of the development of the college [1899] that the first provision for a football
coach was made, by the engagement of Frank Shively, a Nez
Perce Indian, trained at the famous Carlisle School for Indians.
Mr. Shively was not regularly employed, for at that time the
employment of an athletic coach from public funds would have
been a scandal, but his service was largely gratuitous and
inspired by his love for the great college game.

A short article in the Christmas edition of the *Evergreen* of 1909
provides a little better look at Shively and his place in WSU football
history:

The first coach at W.S.C. [*sic*] was Frank Shively, a full blooded
Crow Indian, graduate of Carlisle and clerk of the Indian Agency
at Lapwai [Idaho], who came up twice a week to instruct the
team, his salary being paid by collections taken from the players.

The "ubiquitous" Charles Goodsell, of Spokane, who quarterbacked
Shively's WAC teams in 1898 and 1899, wrote that postscript on his old
coach.

It turns out that Shively, whose Crow name was Braided Scalplock,
was half Crow. His father, Samuel Shively, was a prospector and later a
dispatch rider for the so-called "Pease Expedition." His mother, Girl
That Sees the Flower, was a Crow.

A small group of men led by Major (his title was honorary) Fellows
D. Pease built a couple of flatboats at Livingston, Montana Territory, and
floated down the Yellowstone to the Bighorn River where, in 1875, they
built a fort, planning to trade (primarily for furs) with the Crow.

Shively's mother died in childbirth and his father was killed in a
Blackfoot ambush near Big Timber in 1875, the year Frank Shively was
born. The orphaned infant was reared by his maternal grandmother at
Crow Agency, near Hardin, Montana.

In 1890, at the age of fifteen or sixteen, Shively was one of the so-
called "boarding school children," which the U.S. government ordered
sent from their reservations to the Carlisle Industrial School, and other
Indian schools in the East and Midwest, to fill up their rolls. Shively was
at Carlisle when football was introduced there in 1894, but a granddaughter, Mrs. Colleen Conroy, of Hardin, Montana, says her grandfather used to talk about competing in track, not football.* And the famous
Glenn S. "Pop" Warner, inventor of the Single- and Double-Wing
offenses, for whom Dietz, Welch, and Exendine all played at Carlisle,
did not arrive at the school until 1899. Warner didn't really get the
Indians on the warpath—beating all the big teams in the East—until
1907, well after Shively finished his coaching stint at WAC.

Shively's teams at Washington Agricultural College played a total of
three games in the seasons of 1898 and 1899 and his record was 1-1-1.
WAC and Whitman College tied 0-0 at Pullman on November 5, 1898,
the only game played in that war-shortened season. The Spanish-

---

* This background information on Shively came from Mrs. Conroy and her son, Harlan,
in Hardin; from Fred Hoxie, historian at the Newberry Library, Chicago; and David
Walter, of the Montana State Historical Society in Helena.

The WAC football team of 1897.
(Manuscripts, Archives, and Special
Collections, Washington State
University Libraries)

American War began on April 21, and prior to the football season of 1898 quite a few players left college to join the armed forces.

The most memorable game in Coach Shively's short tenure was played on Rogers field October 28, 1899. The Pullman *Herald* said it was an "ideal Indian summer day" and reported that a "large crowd of ladies and gentlemen (500) filled the grassy grandstand over looking the field."

Bryan's history took note of the game for another reason: "In 1899 Boyd Hamilton was Captain of the team and the ubiquitous Charles Goodsell quarter back. The great game of the season was that with Idaho which occurred on the home grounds . . . resulting in a glorious victory 11-0 for the college. . . ."

In recounting the feats of the day the college paper records: "At a very critical moment, when one of the Moscowites [it was George W. Kays, the Idaho Captain, on an end-around] got around the left end and was flying toward the goal, Goodsell sailed into the giant and rolled him over in his tracks. The Moscow man might as well have tried to run over the Ad. Building." (Goodsell was five feet four inches tall, Bryan added.)

Shively must have enjoyed the win; it was the first time WAC had played Idaho since 1895, due to bickering between the schools and bouts with the plague. (Diphtheria was rampant in Moscow a couple of these years and President Bryan would not allow the WAC boys to play.)

The final game of Shively's coaching career certainly was one no WAC fan ever forgot. The contest, between WAC and Whitman College at Walla Walla on November 10, 1899, ended in great turmoil. The umpire, Botany Professor R. Kent Beattie of WAC, declared it a 10-6 win for the Pullman team and Referee Walter Bratton, a professor on the Whitman faculty, ruled an 11-10 win for the home team.

"Just at the end of the game, in fact the linesman had called time," the *Evergreen* writer claimed, "Whitman attempted a place kick from the field which missed goal. All of her linemen were thus placed off side, but one of them run [sic] after the ball and fell on it, across the WAC goal line. Prof. Beattie as umpire declared it an off side play and ordered the ball back but game was called before it could be returned. Brattain [sic], the referee, said the ball had touched one of our men and, therefore, it was a touch-down."

The result remained in limbo for weeks. The *Evergreen* reported that the dispute had been referred to the Amateur Athletic Association of the Northwest "for settlement."

On December 6, nearly a month after the game was played, the *Evergreen* carried this sad message:

> The arbitrator ruled that the WAC earned the game and that the umpire's point of an off-side play was well taken but that he had been too slow in making his decision. He [the arbitrator], therefore, awarded the game to Whitman on the technicality.

An interesting sidelight to the whole affair is that professors Beattie and Bratton took turns being referee in the game. Beattie was the ref in the first half and Bratton the umpire. They switched jobs at halftime.

Although his coaching record certainly wasn't bad (by later standards, at least), it should be said for Shively that the Spanish-American War cost him several good players. Center and 1898 Captain-elect John Hugh Jones, of Wilbur, and Bucklin, a letterman end and one of the aforementioned first "subs" for WAC in that 1897 season, both left school to enlist, riding a farm wagon to Waitsburg to sign up. Bucklin suffered a severe thigh wound in the fighting near Manila, ending his athletic career.

Colonel Speed Sapp (that is his full name, not his rank; he was a noncommissioned officer), of Olympia, a two-year letterman at guard, played out the 1898 season but then went off to war and missed the 1899 schedule*.

Shively returned to the Crow reservation at Hardin, Montana, and was a clerk there in 1905. He later became prominent in tribal affairs and, since he spoke the Crow, Cheyenne, and Sioux dialects, on several occasions served as an interpreter at conferences and meetings between tribal elders and government officials in Montana and in the nation's capital. In 1913, Shively was a delegate from the Crow Nation at the laying of the cornerstone of the Memorial to the American Indians in Washington, D.C.**

The old coach spent his last years swapping stories with his good friend and drinkin' buddy Will James, the noted cowboy artist and author, whose ranch adjoined the Shively property at Hardin. He died of cancer in 1940 at age sixty-five.***

---

*Lieutenant Ford Fisher, of Seattle, a letterman on the 1895 football team, was killed in the Philippines, thus becoming the first Gray W man to lose his life for his country.

**See Charles Crane Bradley, Jr., "After the Buffalo Days," master's thesis, Montana State University, 1970.

***Conversation with Harlan Conroy, 1989.

Those Pesky "Idees"

The predictable rivalry between Washington State and Idaho, whose campuses are just eight miles apart in Pullman and Moscow, became so intense in the early years of athletic competition that presidential intervention was required to preserve the series.

An article by Idaho campus correspondent Allen Derr in the *Spokesman-Review* in 1950 recalled one of the opening salvos in this athletic "war," fired way back in 1896:

> . . . the Idaho team, entire student body, faculty and a large number of [Moscow] townspeople boarded a specially chartered train consisting of one steam engine and coach and chugged into Pullman. When they arrived not a sign of life could be found. Up on the hill school was going on as usual and no one seemed to know about the game. . . .
>
> So the Idaho team lined up in front of the college building, ran through a few signals and declared the game forfeited to Idaho. The Idaho delegation gave the college yell and went home.

A game was scheduled between the two schools in 1897, but President Bryan called it off because he'd been told there was an outbreak of diphtheria in Moscow.

In 1898, the game again was scheduled for Moscow, but when WAC showed up Idaho was found to have two players in uniform who were not on the roster WAC had received and approved, "big Ed Snow, who weighed 210 pounds stripped, and from the Nez Perce Indian reservation they recruited Chief [David] McFarland, halfback of all-American caliber," Derr wrote.

McFarland, from Lapwai, Idaho, apparently had played at Carlisle and was an excellent back. He earlier had applied for the football coaching job at WAC. As for Snow, Derr undershot big Ed's weight by at least forty pounds. His sons, Orval and Gerald, still living in the Moscow area, say their father, then nineteen, was 6-6 and 250, which was absolutely huge in that era, when "big" players were those over 185.

WAC arrived in Moscow fully intending to play. The Idaho team was out on the fairgrounds field and McFarland was limbering up with a few punts, Derr said. "He kicked the ball from one end of the field to the other. No one had even seen such punting. WSC [*sic*] immediately declared both Snow and McFarland ineligible. . . ."

The best part of the whole story, however, was told later by Gainford "Gub" Mix, who'd played for the Moscow U.S. Store in that game against the Washington Agricultural College baseball team. Mix was by this time sort of an athletic business manager for Idaho. He was at the gate that day in 1898 selling tickets. When it became evident there was disagreement over the eligibility of Snow and McFarland and that WAC might refuse to play, Mix "skipped to the bank with the entire $500 in gate receipts," Derr wrote.

President Bryan acknowledged in his history that the relationship between WAC and Idaho at this time as far as football was concerned was "characterized by more or less jangling. . . ." but it was agreed that the two schools had to get along and keep their natural athletic rivalry intact.

". . . to that end we established a system of equal division of gate receipts, and an understanding that rivalries must not go to the breaking point," Bryan wrote, taking note of the fact that WAC's next nearest neighbor was Whitman College in Walla Walla. "Beyond that, it was 400 miles to our next neighbor and athletic relations were hardly to be dreamed of."

Derr, an attorney in Boise for some years now, not only wrote about the Idaho-Washington State rivalry, he was part of it. In 1948, Derr and Dale Benjamin, a pledge at the Sigma Alpha Epsilon fraternity (now living in Pisgah Forest, North Carolina), were working on KUOI, the Idaho campus radio station. As a pledge prank, they made a record, "generally favorable to Idaho," is the way Derr puts it now, and very early one morning the week of the Idaho-WSC football game, drove over to Pullman, sneaked into the KWSC studios and, when the control room was vacant for a few minutes, put their "Idaho special" on the air over the WSC radio station.

"We tuned in KWSC and laughed almost all the way back to Moscow that morning," Derr recalled.

Unfortunately, WSC authorities did not join in the revelry. They reported the matter to the Federal Communications Commission and Derr, whose voice was on the record, was in deep stuff.

"Dr. [Jesse] Buchanan [the University of Idaho president] got a call and he decided I should be put under 'house arrest'," Derr said. "I missed the football game that weekend. Had to listen to it on the radio in the TKE house," Derr remembered, still laughing, forty years later.

Women's Athletics

Although Frankie Stratton served on the organizing committee for the first athletic association at WAC in 1892, and Allie Lyle was the association's first vice-president, there is little question that it was a men's organization right from the start.

The *College Record* for November 1892, reporting that the association had secured the assembly room in the "Crib" for an athletic room, noted, incongruously, "Just at present boxing seems to be the favorite *exercise* and several sets of gloves are in almost constant demand. Lady students may become honorary members of the Association by signing the constitution and by-laws."

Tennis was a popular sport on campus with both sexes in the early years. In May 1897, the Evergreen said "Considerable interest is being manifested in tennis among the young ladies as well as the gentlemen. Two courts on the campus are rapidly approaching completion." At one point the WAC Athletic Association was accused of discriminating against basketball (in favor of tennis). Association officers quickly rebutted the charge, pointing out that the lack of a gymnasium was the reason basketball was slow to become popular.

In November of 1897 women students in Stevens Hall formed their own athletic association. Luta Coffin, of Tekoa, was elected president,

The Board of Regents appropriated $175 for athletics at their meeting in April 1895. Part of the money was used in fitting up the armory with gymnastic apparatus and some to finance construction of the athletic grounds (first called "Soldiers Field," then "Rogers Field," now "Martin Stadium"). Four teams of horses, at three dollars per day, and one man at two dollars per day, were hired for four days. A farm team then was used for a day in harrowing and rolling the grounds. A ball field and one-fifth mile track were completed in time for the Field Day, June 8.

The faded printing on the basketball identifies this group as the "W.A.C. Basket Ball Team—1899." Unfortunately, the names of the players are not recorded. The first WAC women's basketball team to play an outside opponent was the team of 1901-1902, so this group must have competed with other class or club teams. (Manuscripts, Archives, and Special Collections, Washington State University Libraries)

with Ollie (Olivia) Laird, Garfield, vice president; Mary Allen, Spokane, secretary; Jessie Bratton, Oakesdale, treasurer; and Lucy (Lucyle) McCroskey, Elberton, field manager. The association voted to sponsor four sports, basketball, croquet, handball, and tennis. McCroskey replaced Coffin as president shortly thereafter and served until the association reorganized December 7, 1898, approved a constitution and by-laws and elected Josephine Hoeppner, of Colfax, president.* The association had seventeen members at this time.

The Reverend A. W. McLeod, pastor of the Baptist church in Pullman, was secured as a "trainer" for the Stevens Hall association and two basketball teams began practicing in the mechanical shops building three times a week "as the low ceiling and columns of the Stevens Hall gymnasium obstructed their playing," the *Evergreen* stated. (The "gymnasium" in Stevens Hall actually might have been the dining room. It had columns and a ten-foot ceiling. The floor in the shops building, also used by the men as both gymnasium and armory, measured twenty-five by sixty feet. By comparison, the main floor of the gymnasium opened in 1901 was sixty by one hundred feet. (Jack Friel said the gym looked "huge" when he came to WSC from Waterville in 1919.)

Women's basketball teams representing Stevens Hall and the College Athletic Association are pictured (but unfortunately the participants are not identified) in the 1899 *Chinook*. Undoubtedly there was intramural play well prior to that time, for the early yearbooks usually ran two seasons behind in reporting sports.

---

* Josephine Hoeppner Woods, Class of 1902, later taught German at the college and at the University of Washington, then married a mining engineer and spent several years in Peru. She recorded their experiences in a fascinating book, *High Spots in the Andes* (New York: G. W. Putnam's Sons, 1935).

In November of 1899 the student newspaper reported: "The girl members of the [WAC] Athletic Association have organized a basket ball team and are practicing twice a week under the direction of Coach Pat Lynch."

The first class in "Physical Culture" for women students was offered at WAC in the fall of 1900. Myrtle Graham, a tutor in the business school, was the instructor. She received fifty dollars per semester for this secondary assignment. ". . . particular stress being laid on the matter of correct breathing, the attainment of an erect, graceful figure, and adding to the vital strength of the body without overstraining or development along any particular line to the neglect of others," the student newspaper pointed out in reporting on the new class.

Ernest E. Hastings coached the first WAC women's basketball team to play an outside opponent. The game was against Walla Walla High School on December 18, 1901, at the Walla Walla Armory and drew a crowd of 500 persons. WAC won 14-12.

"The floor was very smooth, which fact greatly handicapped the W.A.C. players, causing them to foul often by crossing the line," the game account in the *Evergreen* said. Another "handicap" the *Evergreen* claimed, was the length of the floor, which was much shorter than the one in the old gym where the girls had been practicing. Mrs. C. V. Piper, wife of the WAC botany professor, "chaperoned" the team on the trip.*

Playing for WAC in this first game were Inez Allard, Pomeroy, and Ada Whittaker, Palouse, centers; Virginia McIntosh, Starbuck, and Mabel Price, Wardner, Idaho, forwards; and Helen Thompson, of Dayton, and Laura Onstot, of Theon (near Anatone), guards. The subs were Blanche Baum and Stella Pickell, both of Pullman, and Mary White, St. John.

The two teams played a return game in Pullman on March 1. The *Evergreen's* story of that game is a good example of the journalism of the day:

> The game was fast and snappy from start to finish. Brilliant plays were so frequent that they passed by unnoticed. Accurate passing, close guarding and pretty basket-throwing marked this as the best game of basketball played in Pullman.
>
> The WAC girls were the first to enter the gymnasium and they presented a pretty and attractive appearance in their crimson and gray suits. The Walla Walla girls soon followed, and they were becomingly attired in blue suits. They were somewhat smaller than the college girls, but their air of cool self-possession soon convinced the spectators that they were there to play basketball.
>
> Walla Walla won the toss, and chose the west goal to defend, and a moment later the game began. The "farmers" soon had the ball down to their opponents' goal, but could not hit the basket. The girls from the Prairie City forced it back, and Miss Wiseman scored two points for her team. The ball was again put into play

---

*Harold Gus Smith, "The History of Athletics and Physical Education at the State College of Washington from 1892 to 1905," a master's thesis, 1948. A 1938 WSC graduate, Smith grew up in Wapato. He was a football player in 1936-1937, and served on the Physical Education faculty of Linfield College, McMinnville, Oregon, for many years.

and Misses Onstat and Thompson worked it down the field and Miss McIntosh completed the play. The visitors next scored one, but Mabel Price couldn't bear to see the visitors ahead in her own gymnasium, and quickly threw a field goal. At this point, Helen Thompson did some of the prettiest and hardest work of the game; she seemed to be everywhere, and interfered with every pass the Visitors attempted. She was ably assisted by Miss [Anna] Tjossem [Ellensburg]. The latter part of the first half was marked by numerous fouls. Miss Wiseman improved the opportunity to the fullest and threw three goals in as many tries. This half closed in the Visitor's [*sic*] favor.

The second half was opened by very fast work on the part of the Visitors, but in their eagerness, they made several fouls which meant points for WAC, when Mabel Price was throwing goals.

A very disagreeable feature of the second half was the envelopment of the gymnasium in darkness. This made it homelike, however. After the machinery had been oiled and the dynamo started, the game was resumed and Miss Wiseman scored for the Visitors and Miss Price for the home team.

The writer did not bother to put the final score in the story; that was carried with the lineups that followed the game story, "W.A.C. 10, Visitors 6."

Mabel Price scored an almost unheard of twenty-two points in a game with Waitsburg Academy at Pullman on December 5, 1902. The *Evergreen* didn't bother to report the final score, noting, "While the game was too one sided to be ever in doubt, it was an enjoyable one."

On February 5, 1903, WAC defeated the girls' basketball team from the UW and the *Evergreen* pulled out all the stops, headlining:

Rah, Rah, Ree!
W.A.C.!
Champions By 'Gosh'

Purple and Gold Trailed in the Resin by the Crimson and Gray to the tune of 2-4.

It was the most closely contested game ever played in the state and gives our girls an undisputed claim to the championship of the state of Washington. The game was bitterly fought from beginning to end, and from the time our handsome representatives trotted out for their warming up practice until our bruised and tired little heroines were carried off the floor, the interest never waned. Of all the players individually the same can be said—they played basket ball.

The WAC scoring was described in superlatives: "Mabel [Price] located the draped circle early in the first half and later Bessie [Vermilye] threw the most difficult goal ever thrown in a match game in the local Gym." There was no scoring in the second half. Washington's only points came on two free throws.

The lineup for WAC in this game had Debbie Donley, of Rice, at center; Price and Bessie Vermilye, Colfax, at forwards; and Alma Prather, Pullman, and Thompson at guards. This team was coached by John B. Evans, '02, of Lewiston, Idaho, a star track man at WAC.

Helen Huse, the first professionally trained instructor in Physical Culture, took over the women's program in physical education and athletics in 1907. Miss Huse was a graduate of the School of Physical Education at the University of Nebraska and also had participated in several summer sessions at the Chatauqua School in New York. A year later, J. Fred "Doc" Bohler arrived at WSC from Nebraska to take over as Physical Director. His professional training very closely paralleled that of Professor Huse.

Whether it was an emphasis on physical education, as opposed to athletics, or whether the cost of maintaining off-campus athletic competition became prohibitive, there was a change in the women's program at WSC about the time that Prof. Huse arrived.

The women's basketball team played only two games in the 1903-1904 season, winning both, and one in 1905, an 8-3 loss to Colfax High School. WAC defeated Spokane High School 15-2 on January 16, 1904, with Vermilye "throwing five goals," and beat Lewiston High School 20 to 1. In its coverage of the Lewiston game, the *Evergreen* reported: "The guarding of the visitors was loose with the exception of Miss Kerns, who stuck to Capt. Vermilye like a blanket mortgage." Usually a high scorer, Vermilye had but two goals in this game. Ida Peterson [Stevens Point, Wisconsin] and Ada Whittaker picked up the scoring slack. They had four goals apiece.

Intramural, inter-class and club games replaced intercollegiate competition in women's athletics at WSC about this time. "Field Days" were held in the spring and fall months, but no scores of games with off-campus teams are found in the *Evergreen* or Pullman *Herald*, the two newspapers which normally covered all WSC activities.

The emphasis on "Physical Education" was apparent. In his history of physical education and athletics at the college from 1892 to 1905, Smith wrote:

> The development of Physical Education for women at Washington Agricultural College received earlier emphasis than that provided for men. This may be attributed to the division of men's activities into military training and athletics. As early as 1900 an instructor was provided for women's Physical Education [Miss Graham] and organized basket-ball competition was soon developed. Other activities included exercises, rhythms, and corrective gymnastics, and by 1905 the department was providing the primary leadership in women's Physical Education in the State of Washington.

The Power of the Press

Coverage of athletic events at the college by the press in the early years was pretty much limited to college papers and the Pullman *Herald*. When the college teams played away from home, little or no information was available until days after the events, and then the accuracy of the report was often suspect. If the team won, a player or coach usually would provide the local papers with a glowing account of the triumph—sometimes very short on facts and always without statistics—but if old WAC lost, readers would be fortunate to find a score.

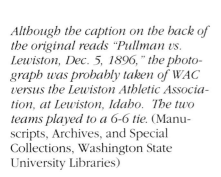

Although the caption on the back of the original reads "Pullman vs. Lewiston, Dec. 5, 1896," the photograph was probably taken of WAC versus the Lewiston Athletic Association, at Lewiston, Idaho. The two teams played to a 6-6 tie. (Manuscripts, Archives, and Special Collections, Washington State University Libraries)

In November of 1900, the Washington Agricultural College Athletic Association took note of the situation and voted to have a reporter from the *Evergreen* at every game to send back a write-up "at press rates, which were one-third of a cent per word. This was the first great step in getting athletics into the press, and the Athletic Association was responsible for this. . . ."*

It is likely that the first of these *Evergreen* reporters assigned to cover a college sports event off campus was W. D. Outman, of Waitsburg. President Bryan referred to Outman, although not by name, in telling of the first WAC-UW football game, which was played on November 29, 1900, shortly after that arrangement was made to have game reports telegraphed back to Pullman.

> This year for the first time the team traveled into distant parts—namely to Seattle—where on the University grounds the team fought that of the University to a 5 to 5 tie. The college reporter of this first game of football with our sister state institution, the University, evidently felt that an alibi was necessary for having failed to win and accordingly presented the following explanation: "The soil being of an entirely different kind from that on the east side, our team was hampered by having to wade through a different kind of mud from that which they had been accustomed to. . . ."**

Over the years, many students helped pay their way through school by reporting college events for one of the regional newspapers. Spokane,

---

* Harold Gus Smith, "The History of Athletics and Physical Education at the State College of Washington from 1892 to 1905," a master's thesis, 1948.

** Enoch Albert Bryan, *Historical Sketch of the State College of Washington, 1890-1925* (Pullman, Washington: Alumni and the Associated Students, 1928), p. 286.

Seattle, and Portland, Oregon, newspapers were among those main-taining "stringers" on campus in the early years. Some still do. One of these was Joseph L. Ashlock, '09, of Walla Walla, editor of the *Evergreen* in 1908 and later head of the Journalism program at WSC. Ashlock was the "Campus Correspondent" for several newspapers, and as such provided them with information on sports events as well as other campus news. (Joe must have had great "sources." From 1909 to 1916 he was Secretary to President Bryan, and from 1917 to 1922 was "Publicity Secretary" at the college.)

The first actual Sports Information Director at WSC (although that title was not used until the 1970s) was Howard B. Greer, '27, of Spokane. Greer was hired by Graduate Manager Earl V. Foster right after gradu-ation. One of his assignments as Publicity Editor for the Associated Students was to publicize the intercollegiate athletic program.

Greer was among the early college publicity men on the Pacific Coast (again demonstrating the foresight of the wily Foster), the late Don Liebendorfer, of Stanford, being the first in the nation in 1924. Greer was the WSC publicist for twenty-two years, with time out for Navy service during World War II.

Several men served as sports publicists at the college during the War years. News Bureau Manager Maynard Hicks handled the job (along with virtually every other "Information" chore at WSC), with help from Bill Chaplin, '44, of Alameda, California; Stan Mataya, '47, Cle Elum; John McCallum, '47, Tacoma; and others.

Greer returned in 1946 and held the job until 1948 when he left to join the *Daily Chronicle* staff in Spokane and Dave Stidolph, of Newtown, New York, a 1948 graduate of the University of Idaho became the sports publicist. Stidolph went to Cal in 1951 and was succeeded by Don Faris, sports editor of the Lewiston *Tribune*, who served six years. Faris resigned in 1957 to go into advertising in Spokane and Dick Fry moved over to Athletics from the WSC News Bureau. Fry lasted until 1970, when he returned to the News Bureau.

WSU again reached into the Lewiston *Tribune* staff, this time picking off Sports Editor Mike Wilson, a 1965 Cougar grad, to succeed Fry. Wilson stayed until 1976, when he became Sports Information Director at the University of Washington. Rod Commons, who had been an assistant to Johnny Eggers at Oregon State and then Sports Information Director at Brown University, Providence, Rhode Island, replaced Wilson. In 1988, recognizing the changing scene in intercollegiate athletics, WSU appointed Donna Murphy, from Chicago State Univer-sity, Co-Sports Information Director with Commons.

The Pink and Blue

People gasp, then they laugh, then they hoot, when first they learn that Washington State's school colors originally were pink and blue!

It makes for a good laugh, and a lot of good-natured ribbing from the fans of opposing schools occasionally, but there appears to be no argument, even though the first yearbook published by the students of

Washington Agricultural College, the *Chinook* for 1899, records on page six: "College Color: Blue."

Many people say the idea of pink and blue as the school colors stemmed from the name given the college's first building, the "Crib," a sobriquet derived from "The cradle of learning." Others contend that the pink and blue came from the beautiful sunsets in the Palouse country. Particularly in winter, the setting sun casts a warm pink glow over the rolling hills—and the campus buildings as well—while the sky above is a cool blue.

After that first football game with Idaho on November 18, 1894, the Pullman *Herald* headlined on its front page:

> FUN AT FOOTBALL
> The Pink and Blue Wave Victoriously
> Over the Orange and White
> The U of I Crack Football Team
> Defeated by the WAC Farmers

Relating the enthusiasm generated by the football game at Pullman the following year, when WAC defeated Idaho again (this time by the score of 10 to 4), President Bryan noted in his history ". . . H. K. Burch sold 200 yards of college colored ribbon on the grounds. The college colors at that time were pink and blue—think of it!"

Apparently, President Bryan followed his own advice, although it took him five years to make the move. Late in 1900 Bryan evidently decided it was time to get the matter of official school colors settled once and for all. The Pullman *Herald* for November 17, 1900, ran this article taken from the *Evergreen* of that week:

> The most enthusiastic of recent student meetings at WAC was that of last Tuesday, when the committee appointed by President Bryan to investigate the matter of changing the college colors made their report. There were three parties in the field. One championed the old pink and blue, another the blue and white and the third crimson and gray. After much discussion, motions and substitute motions, amendments and points of order the crimson and gray were adopted as the colors which shall represent the college in the future. May they never be trailed in the dust, but be followed by the same clean, honorable manhood that has carried their pink and blue predecessors to many a glorious victory. After the smoke of battle had cleared away the students, led by [Frank Fielding] "Jimmy" Nalder, gave three cheers and a tiger for the departing pink and blue. [Nalder, a New Zealand native whose family had emigrated to Waitsburg, was Yell King at the time, and a more ardent booster of the college there never was. He was WAC's third Registrar, 1903-1907, and later served many years as Director of General Extension programs.]

"The old banner," the article continued, "is to be inscribed with a record of all the victories won in athletics by the WAC and placed in the museum."

> Mr. Nalder was appointed a committee of one to communicate to the New York World such points of information concerning the WAC as are recorded of all other literary colleges of the

The football team of 1895. Note the variety of shirts and uniforms. Apparently, most of those sixteen-dollar suits from the 1894 season lasted only one year. Front (left to right): Ford Fisher, Fred Long, Captain Frank Lowden, Joe Winston, and Floyd Moore. Middle: C. S. Sapp, William Doty, and Milton McCroskey. Back: Charles Goodsell, David Brodie, John Clemens, Boyd Hamilton, and Edward Kimmel. (Manuscripts, Archives, and Special Collections, Washington State University Libraries)

country. A sample of the new colors adopted was placed on file with the secretary of the college to be used hereafter as a standard in determining the correct shade.

Unfortunately that "sample" of the new colors must have been lost somewhere along the way. For many years the Crimson has been found in a wide range of shades. During the period from 1968 to 1975 when two of the most forceful and, if you'll pardon the pun, "colorful" of Cougar coaches matched swatches, there came to be known in WSU uniforms the "Brayton Red" and the "Sweeney Red," and ne'er the twain did meet.

Baseball Coach Chuck "Bobo" Brayton held out for Webster's definition of Crimson: "any of several deep purplish reds," and picked the one he liked, perhaps hearkening back to a particular uniform color he remembered as a baseball, football and basketball letterman at Washington State in the 1940s.

Football Coach Jim Sweeney, the delightfully exuberant Irishman from Butte, Montana, preferred a little more life in his Crimson when he was picking colors for the Cougar uniforms in 1968-1975. Sure and begorrah, Sweeney's Crimson was red Crimson!

And maybe that's the way it should be, each Cougar putting a little personal touch to the old Crimson and the Gray.

Hey, it could have been Pink and Blue!

A "Foreign Field"

The first football game between Washington State and the University of Washington took place on November 29, 1900, in Seattle. It ended 5-5 and set the tone for the thrilling, often tumultuous, always hard-fought, games that would follow.

Winning first places for WAC in the three-way meet with the universities of Washington and Idaho at Pullman on May 7, 1900, were Lores L. Goodwin, *Kalama, discus, 95-2;* George Palmerton, *Pullman, 440, 54 4/5;* William Kruegel, *Pullman, mile, 4:55.1/5; and* John Jones, *Wilbur, pole vault, 9-7. Washington won with 74 points; WAC, 44, Idaho, 7. This was the first meeting between track teams representing Washington State and the UW.*

Right from the start weather and officiating headed the list of complaints. To this day, nothing has changed!

". . . the outcome of the game in Seattle was conceded by all who saw it to be largely the result of circumstances which militated very heavily against our team," wrote William D. Outman, of Waitsburg, a WAC student who covered that first game with the UW for the *Evergreen* and the Pullman *Herald.* Chief among these "circumstances," Outman wrote, was "the condition of the soil which, besides being of a different kind from that on the east side of the state, was rendered in such a terrible condition from the incessant rain preceding and during the game as to make thorough good playing absolutely impossible."

WAC came into that first meeting with its cross-state rival unbeaten and unscored on in four starts. Washington was struggling along at 1-1-1.

Opening with a 2-0 squeaker over the Lewiston Athletic Association in the Idaho city, WAC proceeded to shut out the Spokane Athletic Club 6-0 in Pullman, the Walla Walla Athletic Club 5-0 in Walla Walla, and the Spokane A.C. again, this time in Spokane, by a convincing 21-0.

In addition to a stingy defense, Coach "Wild Bill" Allen, the cart-rope wielder, had whipped up a pretty fair rushing game. The "ubiquitous" Charles Goodsell directed the WAC offense from the quarterback spot; Steven Jayne, of Davenport, was at left half; William Lasher, Cheney, played at right half; and Charles Proff, of Rosalia, was the fullback.

The WAC line was anchored by Fred Stone, Rosalia, at center; Robert Spencer, Pullman, and Albert Menig, Cheney, were the guards; Captain Jim Elton, The Dalles, Oregon, and Arthur Hooper, of Johnson, the tackles; and Frank "Cack" Barnard, Seattle, and Edward Cardwell, Wilbur, ends. (Barnard's nickname derived from his laugh, a high-pitched cackle that seemed to pop ventriloquist-like from barely parted lips.)

The game between the two major educational institutions in the state of Washington had an extra dimension in 1900. Considerable competition—bordering on ill feeling—had developed between WAC and Idaho. WAC had been scheduled to play Idaho on November 3 in Moscow, but in spite of President Bryan's warnings to "get along with Idaho!" another dispute had arisen. WAC claimed it had been notified the game would be played on the Moscow ball grounds where the two teams had met in 1894. At the last minute Idaho switched the site to "a sloping ground on the University campus not suitable for a real game," and WAC balked.

The "Farmers" countered with an offer to play the game in Pullman and give Idaho 150 dollars or all of the gate receipts, whichever was greater. Idaho refused. Several offers and counter-offers followed but there was no agreement.

The week before WAC played Washington, Idaho defeated the Sun Dodgers 12 to 6 in a game played in Spokane. WAC Coach Allen, seizing the opportunity to scout Washington, was in attendance. Charges later were hurled by Idaho that Allen, who had been a high school coach in Seattle the year before, had been "coaching" the Sun Dodgers from the sidelines, a contention which he denied, with acerbity no doubt.

This was the background against which WAC and the UW played.

Although it was a tie score, the game was strongly in our favor, reporter Outman wrote.

> It rained from start to finish, and every fumble was excusable. . . . By this time [early in the second half] the ball and suits were in a terrible condition from the mud.

Mr. Outman also suggested rather directly that there might have been some problem with the officials' eyesight on at least two occasions.

Goodsell had scored for WAC twenty minutes into the first half, but the goal kick was missed and the half ended 5-0. (In 1897, touchdowns became five points and conversions one.) Twenty-one minutes into the second half the UW scored, but also missed its goal kick. At this point Goodsell's ankle "gave out" and the little quarterback joined guard John Early, Northport, on the bench. Early had been sidelined before halftime by "a hard blow to the head" and was replaced by Roy McKenzie, Yelm.

With WAC on the Washington five, having driven the length of the field following the Sun Dodgers' score and subsequent kick-off, "We fumbled," wrote Outman, "and as I was standing within five yards of where the fumble was made, I am positive that our men fell on it, but it was ruled otherwise."

WAC forced a Sun Dodger kick and roared back to within three yards of goal, where "the referee ruled that necessary gains had not been made. This ruling also was rank. . . ." Outman wrote.

"The U. of W. did not have possession of the ball one-third of the time, and we shoved it twice as far as they did."

"We are the champions, in spite of rain, mud and bad luck. . . ," Outman concluded.

Thus ended the first visit to a "foreign" field by a team representing WAC. There would be many to follow, in which other "Outmans" would question the playing conditions and the officiating.

The First Decade, 1892-1900

"The Boys and Girls of Sweetwater Valley" would have been an appropriate title for a history of sports in the early days of Washington Agricultural College and School of Science. It was so innocent in those days.

The *College Record* for November 1892 recorded: "The sports indulged in during this month have been base ball, boxing, chiny, duck-on-the-rock, leap frog, foot ball, vaulting, and throwing weights."

It was difficult to tell the College students from those enrolled in the Preparatory department in 1892. Pullman had no high school then; some *College* students were admitted on a trial basis, and many were quite young. As far as sports were concerned, there were no organized leagues, no rules; age or enrollment status was unimportant. If you could run faster, throw harder, bat better, or were stronger than the next person, you were "eligible."

Right from the start, sports were the thing at WAC!

•

Orin Stratton "received a black eye by trying to catch a 'fly,'" the *College Record* reported on March 14, 1892. Stratton, the first president of the WAC Athletic Association, proved to be a better engineer than outfielder. A member of the first graduating class in 1897, with a B.S. in Civil Engineering, Stratton directed construction of many bridges in the Pacific Northwest, including the first iron bridge across the Gastineau Channel in 1935, connecting Juneau, Alaska, with Douglas Island.

•

On March 28, 1892, the Pullman Ladies' Golden Rule Society gave a social, the object of which was to discourage ball playing on Sunday. ". . . about one hundred young ladies and gentlemen, over ten and under twenty years of age, signed a pledge not to participate, or attend, games on the Sabbath. . . ."

•

"College Hill was covered with bunch-grass interspersed with the sunflower and lupine. There was not a tree in sight." (*W. J. Spillman's* recollection of his first view of the WAC campus in 1894, from a biography by his son, *Dr. Ramsay Spillman.*)

•

The *College Record* reported that Professor *O. L. Waller* (Math and Civil Engineering) "took great interest and helped the work along in many ways, raising money and superintending the necessary engineering work."

•

WAC defeated Idaho 81 to 18 in the first Field Day held on the new athletic grounds. Winners for WAC were *Frank McReynolds*, fifty-yard dash, 6 seconds; William Doty, Latah, high pole vault, 9-4; *Loring V. Corner*, Endicott, running high jump, 5-0; *Edgar D. Thompson*, Waterville, 100-yard dash, 11 1/5; *Carl Estby*, Snohomish, throwing 16-pound hammer, 80-6; *Frank Lowden*, putting 16-pound shot, 34-2; *McReynolds*, 440-yard run, 1 min.; *Lowden*, running high kick, 8-4; *Corner*, standing high jump, 4 feet; *Thompson*, 220-yard dash, 26-0; *Thompson*, standing hop, step and jump, 27-7; *Ed McMeekin*, Steptoe, running hop, step and jump, 38-8; *McMeekin*, running broad jump, 17-6.

•

John H. Jones, of Wilbur, and *Colonel Speed Sapp*, of Olympia, wrestled for the college title on December 19, 1896, as part of the athletic entertainment at the College Chapel. (Jones won.)

•

Arthur L. Hooper, of Johnson, was the first of four generations of Hoopers to attend Washington State. Arthur won his first letter in football in 1897 and was Captain of the baseball team that same year and the football team of 1901. *Frank, Albert (Pete)*, and *John Hooper*, also from Johnson, played basketball and baseball for the Cougars in the 1935-1942 era. "Pete" was elected to the WSU Athletic Hall of Fame in 1979. *Jeff Hooper*, of Bellevue, set all sorts of career records for Coach *"Bobo" Brayton's* Cougar baseball teams of 1984-1987 (including hits, 225; doubles, 47; home runs, 40; and RBI, 172.) *Grant Hooper*, of Mill Creek, Washington, continues the family's WSU tradition as the fourth generation Cougar and will graduate, appropriately, with the Centennial Class of 1990, rounding out a great first century for the Hooper Cougars!

•

Hans Mumm, WAC baseball and track letterman in the 1898-1901 era, was born in Schleswig, Germany. The family settled near Rosalia in 1880. Mumm was Captain of the 1901 baseball team and pitched. He was a sprinter in track.

•

"The Athletic Association wishes to extend its thanks to the Misses *Daisy Busby* [Pullman], *May Wilson* [Latah], *Cleo Holt* [Wawawai], *Elizabeth Mackay* [Pullman], and *Mary Grimes* [Pullman] for their courtesy and efforts in making the beautiful banner for the relay race. The U. of W. team said that out of the twelve banners that they have won, this one is by far the most beautiful." (May 1900 *Evergreen*)

The Second Decade, 1901-1910

The First "Gray W's"

THERE IS A DIFFERENCE OF OPINION AS TO WHEN THE FIRST "VARSITY" LETTERS WERE awarded at Washington Agricultural College. President Bryan said it was at the conclusion of the 1902 season and that twenty-three men "who had played in college games since its foundation were awarded the football W."

That's a pretty slim number, even in those days when substitutes were few and far between. WAC had been playing football for nine seasons by that time. Bryan's list includes sixteen members of the 1902 team, Dennis Woods, Jim Elton, John Early, Captain Arthur Hooper, John Hugh Jones, Bill Lasher, Al Menig, Roy McKenzie, Ed Cardwell, Clyde Gill, Charles Proff, Steve Jayne, William Lawrence, Frank Barnard, Alvin Coon, and Max Wells; Frank Lowden, Fred Long, Joe Winston, and Milton McCroskey from '94; Boyd Hamilton, '96; Charles Goodsell, '97; Ben Mashburn, '99; two managers, Browne, '01, and Adams, '02; and Coach "Wild Bill" Allen. McKenzie, Lawrence and Wells are not listed among the lettermen in the current WSU football press book and probably should be. Ford Fisher, '95; R. E. Bucklin, '97; and William Mashburn, '98, weren't on Bryan's list but they have been listed for some years, and should be.

The section on "Athletics" in the 1902 *Chinook* says regulations were adopted by the Athletic Association in the fall of 1900 regarding an athletic emblem to be won by members of the different college teams.

> A large Roman W was adopted for football; a somewhat smaller W inside a circle was adopted for the track men, and a similar W inside a diamond for the baseball men. All the W's, circles and diamonds are gray to be worn on a cardinal [here we go again!] sweater.

The matter is further confused by the 1902 *Chinook's* listing of fifteen men ". . . entitled to wear the College Emblem"—eleven of whom were members of the 1902 football team, plus Ben Mashburn, Goodsell, Coach Allen and Manager Browne, all from the 1900 team. (At the time, the yearbooks lagged a couple of years behind in their sports coverage.) It would not be fair—and certainly not accurate—at this late date to draw up a list of the "first" Gray W winners. Today there is no differentiation in sports; all Varsity letter winners receive the "Gray W."

OPPOSITE: *A man ahead of his time—and that was tough to do since Flyin' Jack Nelson equalled two world records in 1909-1910, running a 9 3/5 (9.6) 100 and a 21 1/5 (21.3) 220.* (Manuscripts, Archives, and Special Collections, Washington State University Libraries)

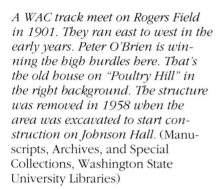

A WAC track meet on Rogers Field in 1901. They ran east to west in the early years. Peter O'Brien is winning the high hurdles here. That's the old house on "Poultry Hill" in the right background. The structure was removed in 1958 when the area was excavated to start construction on Johnson Hall. (Manuscripts, Archives, and Special Collections, Washington State University Libraries)

The 1902 *Chinook* had the right idea: "The regulations governing the winning of the W are so strict that it will be rather difficult for any large number of persons to have the emblem at any one time; thus making it a distinction worth working for, and one that should be jealously guarded by the [Athletic] Association."

The Sun Dodgers and the Webfoots

President Bryan called the WAC team of 1901 "undoubtedly the premier football team of early college history."

It was a good team, and one that was remembered for many a year. Arthur Hooper, of Johnson, was the captain and left tackle; Jim Elton, captain in 1900, was back at right tackle; John Hugh Jones, of Wilbur, who was to captain the 1902 team, played center; and Clyde Gill, of Pullman, captain of both the 1903 and 1904 teams, made the 1901 team at left end as a freshman. In addition, "lettermen" Bill Lasher, Charles Proff, John Early, Steven Jayne, Ed Cardwell and Frank Barnard were returning. Jones, Elton and Early all were veterans of the Spanish-American War. W. H. Namack, of Cornell, was the coach in 1901. He was assisted by the old quarterback, Charles Goodsell.

It is interesting to note the responsibilities students were given in the athletic program in these early years. Orville Adams, of Colfax, a senior in the fall of 1901, was the "Football Manager" appointed by the Athletic Association, and, according to the *Evergreen*, "obtained the services of a coach" (Namack). The Manager also set up schedules. How much faculty advising was involved in all this is not mentioned, but Adams' role in 1901 was important enough to earn him mention in Bryan's history, and he, along with Earl Browne, of Spokane, who was the first Football Manager, in 1900, received Varsity letters at the conclusion of the 1902 season, the first time "W's" were awarded.

The position of "Manager" evolved, with added responsibilities in the areas of student government and publications, into "Graduate Manager

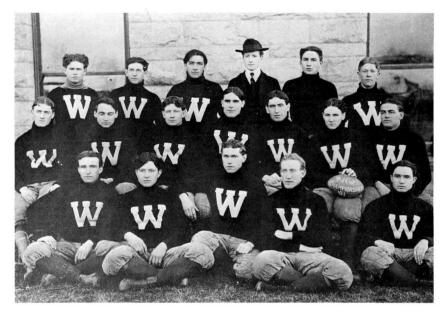

Pacific Northwest football champions in 1901. Front (left to right): Charles Proff, unknown, Steven Jayne, Ben Mashburn, and unknown. Middle: Frank Barnard, unknown, Dennis Woods, John Jones, John Early, Captain Arthur Hooper, and Clyde Gill. Back: Lawrence, Edward Cardwell, unknown, Manager O. L. Adams, unknown, and unknown. (Manuscripts, Archives, and Special Collections, Washington State University Libraries)

of Athletics," a position first occupied in 1909 by John Hugh Jones, of Wilbur, the highly regarded Captain of the 1902 football team and a graduate in mining engineering with the Class of 1903.

The football schedule in 1901 was the toughest yet attempted by a WAC team. It really was the first "intercollegiate" schedule in the school's history, opening on October 18 with Lewiston Normal (now Lewis-Clark State College), followed by Idaho, Washington, Oregon, and Whitman.

Highlights of the 1901 season were the appearances for the first time in Pullman of teams from the University of Washington, the "Sun Dodgers," and the University of Oregon, the "Webfoots." Washington Agricultural College opened with an easy 16-0 win over Lewiston Normal but must have been "looking ahead," as they say, when they went to Moscow on October 25 to play the pesky "Idees" and were upset 5-0. This was the real beginning of the WSU-Idaho football series, and it continued, unbroken except for the World War II years, until 1969.

WAC and Washington met on Friday, November 1. "The weather was bad, almost freezing," the *Evergreen* reported, "and on this account a poor crowd was present." Charles Proff, WAC's right halfback, scored a touchdown in each half, but William Lasher missed both extra points.

"High winds and rainy weather prevented accurate kicking," the Seattle *Post-Intelligencer* game account said. "The agricultural college boys were stronger, faster and displayed superior team work."

"Cack" Barnard, the WAC right end, described by the Seattle *Times* as "an old local high school boy who is playing on the Pullman team," analyzed the game in a letter to the newspaper: "The U's couldn't stand the tackle back. Old players that are not in training cannot play against men in good shape. That was the sequel to the whole thing," young Barnard wrote. (Barnard's father was a member of the WAC Board of Regents at the time. The Pullman *Herald* noted in its November 16 edition: "Regent F. J. Barnard came over from Seattle last week, saying

WAC's 1901 mile relay team, the best of its era, was composed of (left to right) Peter O'Brien, Van Williams, William Kruegel, and Arthur Annis. (Manuscripts, Archives, and Special Collections, Washington State University Libraries)

H. J. McIntire, Coach of the 1902 track squad. (Manuscripts, Archives, and Special Collections, Washington State University Libraries)

that he wanted to see that the boys were making the most of their superb educational advantages. He went away after the slaughter Saturday [16-0 win over Oregon] thoroughly satisfied with the progress of affairs.")

Another regent also appears to have been pleased with the state of affairs: "Regent and Mrs. J. W. Stearns [of Tekoa] entertained our football team at dinner to show their appreciation of the splendid work done by them on November first, when they defeated the University of Washington 10 to 0," the *Evergreen* reported on November 20.

> Everything was in keeping with the occasion—crimson and gray forming the color scheme for decoration in parlors and dining room, pen and ink sketches of football men were the place cards, and booklets in the shape of footballs, painted brown, and laced with crimson and gray ribbon were the souvenirs.
>
> The guests were W. H. Namack and C. H. Goodsell, coaches; O. L. Adams, manager; Captain Hooper, and Messrs, Early, Jones, Proff, Elton, [Ben] Mashburn, Jayne, [Dennis] Woods, Cardwell, Lasher, William Lawrence [Sequim], Barnard, Gill and Max Wells, Seattle. It was regretted that Mr. [Albert] Menig could not be there.

Washington Agricultural College did handle Oregon easily in their first meeting on Saturday, November 9, 1901, in Pullman. Proff again scored two touchdowns, one on a sixty-five-yard run, and Lasher got the third TD and kicked an extra point. It is only fair to point out, however, that Oregon had played a scoreless tie with Idaho in Moscow on Wednesday, November 6, before playing WAC on November 9. It was not uncommon in those years for teams to play two, even three, games on an extended football road trip. Oregon ended its three-game, eight-day grid safari by losing to Whitman on Tuesday, November 12, in Walla Walla.

The special correspondent of the Portland *Oregonian*, who accompanied the Oregon team on its "tour of defeat," (the Pullman *Herald* noted callously in its November 16 edition) says: "There is little difference between the play of Whitman and Agricultural. Both teams are stronger than Oregon. I should like to see them meet, as it will be a warm battle and fit for the gods."

The WAC-Whitman game in Walla Walla on November 28 (Thanksgiving) lived up to its billing. WAC prevailed 5-2 in a hard fought game and justly claimed its first Northwest Championship, since both Whitman and Washington had beaten Idaho, the only team to defeat WAC in that memorable 1901 season.

"It was a glorious day in the history of the Washington Agricultural College, when the football team defeated Whitman," the *Evergreen* cheered following the game.

> An excursion of one hundred and sixty persons from Pullman, Dayton and Waitsburg, together with people from in and around Walla Walla swelled the crowd at the game until there were twelve or fourteen hundred bystanders present. It was ideal football weather.
>
> The interference of both teams was excellent and as each well knew the other's tactics, no long gains were made.

"One noticeable feature of the game was the lack of wrangling over decisions and the good feeling that pervaded the players as well as the students of both institutions," the *Evergreen* writer observed, recalling no doubt the previous WAC-Whitman game in Walla Walla (November 10, 1899), when the final score was not settled for almost a month after the final gun!

An interesting thing about that Whitman game is that Captain Hooper scored the game's only touchdown, "on a one-yard run" the scoring summary says. Hooper was a tackle!

But the thing all the old Cougars remembered for so long about that season of 1901 was that the Sun Dodgers and the Webfoots made their first visits to Pullman and WAC beat 'em both!

A Gymnasium at Last!

"The Grand March of 143 couples began at 10:30 in the evening and was led by President and Mrs. Bryan. This was followed by twenty other dances which occupied the company until 2:30 in the morning," President Bryan wrote of the "Assembly Ball" held to dedicate WAC's new gymnasium in a two-day celebration February 7-8, 1902.

Great excitement prevailed on the WAC campus with the completion of the new gymnasium, located where the parking lot between Holland Library and the Compton Union Building is now. The 1900 legislature appropriated $10,000 for the building and the college had an ample supply of face brick on hand for the outside walls. Bricks sometimes were made on the campus in those early years. A clay bed behind Stevens Hall was dug out for much of the brick used in the Administration Building (now Thompson Hall). The old "Crib" was torn down and its brick used on the inside of the 1902 gymnasium.

The first indoor track meet at Washington Agricultural College was held February 23, 1901, in the Armory/Shops building. Winners were: 20-yard dash, J. W. Hungate, Pullman, 2 1/5; 25-yard hurdles, Lores L. Goodwin, Kalama, 4.0; standing high jump, Eugene Person, Spokane, 4-6; running high jump, Van E. Williams, Oakesdale, 5-3; standing broad jump, Williams, 10-6; pole vault, Hungate, 9-3; rope climb, William A. Clizer, Latah, (no time); shot put (twelve pound), Goodwin, 40-0.

A women's basketball game in the old gym (located between the present sites of Holland Library and the Compton Union Building). (Manuscripts, Archives, and Special Collections, Washington State University Libraries)

This photo, taken around 1906, shows a race finish on Rogers Field. The original gymnasium, built in 1901, is visible in the background. (Manuscripts, Archives, and Special Collections, Washington State University Libraries)

For almost ten years after the institution opened WAC had no indoor activity space even remotely resembling a regular "gymnasium." College catalogs as early as 1895 claimed there was one and that it was "well-equipped with apparatus for indoor exercise." That certainly was a bit of writer's license on the part of the editor. In the spring of 1892, shortly after it was organized, the WAC Athletic Association was granted permission to use the Assembly room in the "Crib" on a part-time basis as an "athletic room." Members could go there and work out with Indian clubs and other primitive exercise gear, and perhaps put on boxing gloves and spar a bit, but that was about it.

A building uphill from Carpenter Hall, near where Daggy Hall now stands, constructed in 1893 as a shops building and containing a power plant, began serving as a combination gymnasium and armory in 1895. The "gymnasium room" was twenty-eight by sixty feet and it had "bathrooms adjoining."

As early as 1899 the Administration Building was used as a women's gymnasium, and as late as the 1920s there were lockers and a dressing room there.

Catherine Mathews Friel, '23, and Mildred Hunt Vatnsdal, '24, have identical, frustrating memories of climbing the stairs to the fourth floor of the Administration Building, changing hurriedly into their gym clothes, running downstairs, then outside and over to Carpenter Hall, and up more stairs to the fourth floor where their physical education classes were held.

"All that and back again—and no shower of course—and get to class in ten minutes!" they recalled sixty years after, laughing.

When the young women used the fourth floor of the old Ad Building for basketball, workers on the floors below complained of the vibration. "The ink wells used to jump right out of the desk when those girls got to running upstairs," one clerk remembered.

Well, you can imagine the jubilation among the more athletic students at the college when the new gym opened. And in no time at all *Evergreen* sportswriters got downright snobbish about the new facility.

After Washington Agricultural College played its first basketball game, and lost 31 to 0 to the Spokane YMCA in Spokane (on December 7, 1901, a date that also will live in infamy), the *Evergreen* noted: ". . . our defeat was only to be expected, for the YMCA men had trained together for years, and their 'gym' is a great deal smaller than ours, which gave them a decided advantage."

The opening of the "Men's Gymnasium" marked the beginning of a new era in athletics and physical education at WAC. (It was "segregated" almost immediately; women's basketball teams did play there, but it was not known as the "Women's Gym" until the men moved into Bohler in 1928 and the old gym was turned over to the women.) For the first time the college had a building in which basketball could be played. There also was an indoor track—narrow and tight-cornered though it was—in the balcony above the basketball court ("17 laps to the mile," the college catalog for 1902 announced), showers, a handball court, lockers, and a swimming pool!

Women's physical education on the fourth floor of the Administration Building (now Thompson Hall) in the early years of the twentieth century. Note the basketball court markings on the floor. When the women got to jumping around, workers on the floors below claimed inkwells would fall from desks! (Manuscripts, Archives, and Special Collections, Washington State University Libraries)

A "plunge" they called it, eighteen by forty feet and six feet deep, but it was not completed for several years and never worked very well. It had to be drained at least once a week because there was no filter system. Even after it was finished they usually covered it during the winter with planking and used the space for additional lockers.

The building measured sixty-seven by one hundred and thirty-five feet, had main entrances on the south and west, and the gymnasium floor was sixty by one hundred feet and forty feet from floor to ceiling. The front (south) part of the building was two stories. Artificial lighting was helped by large, semi-circular windows above the balcony area and another large window in the east end.

The Men's Gym also served as the armory for the ROTC, which was another reason the appropriation from the legislature was forthcoming. As a Land Grant institution WAC was required to offer ROTC and all physically qualified male students had to take it for two years.

There were ten rooms, including office space for the first Physical Director, Ernest E. Hastings, from Springfield College in Massachusetts. He arrived in the fall of 1901 and lasted one semester, to be replaced by Herbert J. McIntire, also from Springfield. W. H. Namack, from Cornell, the football coach in 1901, had an office there, along with the Commandant of the ROTC.

With the completion of the first gymnasium and the "election" as President Bryan put it of a professionally trained Physical Director by the Board of Regents, the program in Physical Education and Athletics at WAC took on an entirely new look.

The first basketball game on campus (other than intra-squad affairs) was played on the morning of February 17, 1902, as WAC lost again to the Spokane YMCA, this time by a closer margin, 24-16. John Palmerton, of Pullman, had the honor of making the first basket in the new gymnasium. "The collegians soon had the ball in their opponents'

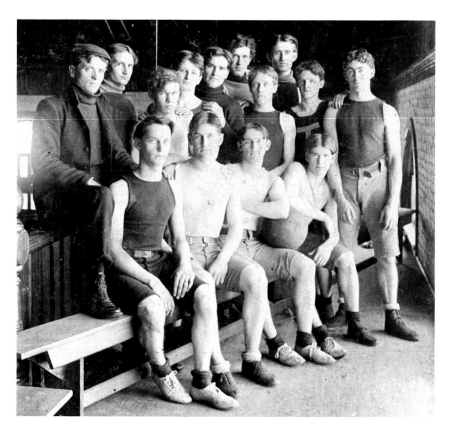

WAC's first men's basketball team, 1902. Coach John B. Evans is at the left, wearing a cap, but the identities of the others in the photograph are unknown. However, Fred Stone, Captain Fred Thiel, Forrest Grimes, Charles Shoemaker, and George Palmerton played on that first team. (Manuscripts, Archives, and Special Collections, Washington State University Libraries)

territory, and by brilliant team work approached their basket, when Palmerton threw a difficult goal," the *Evergreen* reported.*

The intercollegiate athletic program at WAC became fully rounded with the opening of the Men's Gym in 1902 and basketball joined baseball, track and football as "major" sports. It was not long before wrestling, tumbling (gymnastics), and boxing began.

The Saga of Johnny Bender

Washington Football War Song**

"Way out West in Washington
Where the football players come,
Hunting rivals whom they slaughter,
Rolling them in mud and water.
They are led by old Chief Bender,
He's a heap big war-fire tender,
When he leads them on the warpath,
Idaho's scalp they're sure to get."

---

*The lineup for Washington Agricultural College in that first home basketball game had Forrest Grimes, Pullman, and Glenn Stone, Clarkston, at forwards; Captain Fred Thiel, Ritzville, center; and Palmerton and Charles Shoemaker, Reardan, at the guards. John B. Evans, of Lewiston, Idaho, a member of the Class of 1902, coached the first two WAC teams. The 1902 team lost both games it played against the Spokane YMCA. In 1903, WAC split four games, winning at home and losing on the road to the Spokane YMCA and Spokane High School. The first win for a WAC basketball team came on December 13, 1903, at Pullman, when the "farmers" defeated the Spokane YMCA 18 to 13.

**Words and music by Emory D. Alvord, '15 (written in 1913).

John Rheinhold Bender came to Washington State College in 1906 as the school's first "Physical Director and Coach of Athletic Teams." From Sutton, Nebraska, Bender had won considerable acclaim as a running back and catcher for the Cornhuskers in 1901-1904. He coached at South Dakota State Normal in Spearfish the year before coming to WSC. It didn't take Bender long to become as legendary in Washington as he had been in Nebraska. His first football team at WSC in the fall of 1906 was unbeaten, untied, and unscored upon!

Bender kept things rolling in 1907. His second team, led by a slender wraith from Kent, Jerry "The Dane" Nissen, compiled a 7-1 record against tough opposition. The "Sons of Enoch" (a sportswriter's take-off on Whitman's "Sons of Marcus") beat the Sun Dodgers 11-5, in Seattle, and capped off the year with a win over St. Louis University, champions of the Missouri Valley Conference, in the first "intersectional" game played by a Washington State team.

Bender coached football, basketball and baseball at WAC, and he coached those teams very well indeed. His first basketball team in 1907 finished 5-4, but the sport was only six years old at the State College and none of the previous teams had a better record than Bender's first club. In 1908, Johnny's second hoop squad went 12-3.

The little speedster's great love probably was baseball. He played professionally in the Midwest with Omaha while coaching at WSC, and also put in some time with the Spokane Indians of the Northwest League. He quickly put WSC on the baseball map with a 16-3 record in 1907, his first season coaching the diamond sport at Pullman. WSC swept series with Oregon and Idaho and took two out of three against Whitman. The one loss to Whitman was the only defeat in the 1907 season at the hands of a college team. Merritt McCully, of Olympia, and Joe Halm, the great field goal kicker from Prosser, each won six games in 1907, with Nels Dolquest, of Everett, and James Garred, of Walla Walla, adding two wins apiece.

WSC went 14-4-1 in the 1908 baseball season, taking two of three games from Washington and Idaho and sweeping a three-game series with Whitman. Again, of the four losses two came against non-college opponents and the 2-2 tie was with the Spokane Indians, a professional team. That game went twelve innings.

"WSC had her half of the [twelfth] inning coming but could not play it because the 'Yanigans' had to make the evening train for Spokane," the Pullman *Herald* reported. That was the first "tie" in the college's baseball history; it came on April 11 at Pullman and Halm pitched all twelve innings for WSC. He allowed just four hits, struck out eight, and (Buck Bailey, where are you?) didn't walk a batter.

Johnny Bender's immortal football team of 1906 chalked up consecutive shutouts against Blair Business College of Spokane, 11-0 in Pullman, in what the *Evergreen* referred to as a "practice" game; Montana, 5-0 at Missoula; Spokane Amateur Athletic Club, 8-0 in Spokane; Idaho, 10-0 at Pullman; Spokane AAC again, 8-0 at Pullman; and Whitman College, 6-0 at Pullman. Harry E. Goldsworthy, of Oakesdale, later to become an outstanding regent (Goldsworthy Hall is named for him), was the Captain and right end of the 1906 team.

•

Colonel Speed Sapp, *an old football player (Yes, his first two names were "Colonel" and "Speed;" the WSU press book says he played six seasons between 1895 and 1905), returned from the Spanish-American war with a number of mementos, including a homemade cannon which he presented to the student body at an assembly on October 7. (Undoubtedly the same cannon that rocked the citizenry of Pullman on October 28, 1905, when 800 college students broke loose in a rally before the football game with Montana.)*

•

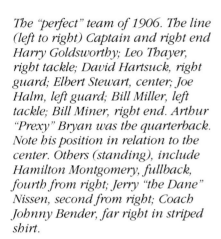

The "perfect" team of 1906. The line (left to right) Captain and right end Harry Goldsworthy; Leo Thayer, right tackle; David Hartsuck, right guard; Elbert Stewart, center; Joe Halm, left guard; Bill Miller, left tackle; Bill Miner, right end. Arthur "Prexy" Bryan was the quarterback. Note his position in relation to the center. Others (standing), include Hamilton Montgomery, fullback, fourth from right; Jerry "the Dane" Nissen, second from right; Coach Johnny Bender, far right in striped shirt.

In the big game against Idaho on November 9, the starting lineup for WSC had Goldsworthy and William Miner, Pullman, at ends; Allen "Big" Thayer, St. Paul, Minnesota, and "Bad Bill" Miller, Goldendale, tackles; Ben Hartsuck, Olympia, and "Bunch" Halm, Prosser, guards; and Elbert "Shorty" Stewart, of Walla Walla, at center. (He was the tallest man on the squad—and probably in school—at 6-4.)

The backfield was composed of Arthur "Prexy" Bryan (son of President and Mrs. Enoch A. Bryan), quarterback; Nissen and Cecil Cave, Pullman, halfbacks; and Hamilton Montgomery, Enumclaw, at fullback. Subs were Herb Wexler and Jim Fariss, both of Pullman; Lyle Buck, Mount Vernon; Robert Fancher, Espanola; Patrick Crane, Snohomish; and William McCarty, Spokane.

The win over Idaho in 1906 sent the campus into a frenzy of celebration. "Ten to zero! Oh! joy divine!" the *Evergreen* crowed, adding, "For four long weary years the faithful, ardent supporters of W.S.C. had waited for a victory." (Idaho put together a three-game win string in 1903-1905. This, and another in 1923-1925, were its longest of this venerable series.) WSC's margin of victory came on a twenty-six-yard field goal by "Bunch" Halm in the first half (four points then), and a seventy-yard punt return by Nissen, behind key blocks by Miner, Bryan and Stewart, with less than three minutes remaining in the game. Halm converted for the 11-0 final score.

". . . the gladdest, happiest roar that ever echoed across the Palouse hills or startled the polywogs [sic] in Lake d'Puddle" followed Halm's first half field goal, the paper said. "From the spectators' viewpoint the tackling by Goldsworthy and Miner and the gains by Nissen were spectacular," the *Evergreen* noted. "But remember it was the line that made this work possible. All honor to Stewart, Hartsuck, Halm, Miller and Thayer."

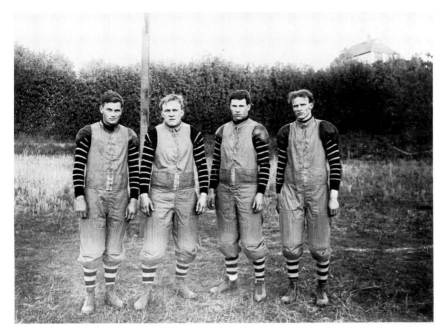

The starting backfield in 1906, the year that WSC's football team was unbeaten, untied, and unscored on (left to right): Arthur "Prexy" Bryan, Quarterback; George Hardy, right half; Lorne "Big" Thayer fullback; and Jerry "the Dane" Nissen, left half. (Manuscripts, Archives, and Special Collections, Washington State University Libraries)

To give you some idea of the feeling that existed between WSC and Idaho supporters at the time, 200 WSC students had taken a train to Moscow on October 25 and rooted for Oregon in the Webfoots' 12-0 win over the Idees. The *Evergreen* reported some Idaho fans were so incensed by these Crimson and Gray-clad "Oregon" rooters that an Idaho student knocked the WSC yell master down. A cartoon on the front page of the *Evergreen* for November 1 (following that Idaho-Oregon game) showed "Toodles," a small black bear, one of the college mascots of the day, draped with "WSC" and "Oregon" pennants and headed to Moscow (to root for Oregon).

One of the highlights of that unbeaten season occurred in the second half of the November 17 game against the Spokane AAC at Pullman. The Spokane *Spokesman-Review* game story headlined: "Bender Helps Farmers Win," and noted:

> There were many interesting features, but one which over-shadowed all others was the phenomenal playing of "Little Johnny Bender," the popular coach of the W.S.C. who made his first appearance as a player in the Pacific Northwest and won deafening rounds of applause by the most brilliant playing ever seen in this section of the country.
>
> Coming down the field, with hair streaming, dodging, twisting and throwing off tacklers right and left, he made three of the best runs ever seen here. Tonight the little coach is the hero of Pullman.

"A coach, playing?" you might well ask. The answer, of course, is that the game was not a "collegiate" contest. Spokane AAC had former college and high school players on its roster, among them Dr. T. E. Callahan, a Spokane physician who played right guard with great enthusiasm. (Callahan was "put off the field for roughness" by Umpire Hawkins in the first WSC-SAAC meeting that year in Spokane on November 3.)

Jerry "the Dane" Nissen breaks for a long one in WSC's 11-5 win over Washington at Denny Field in Seattle in 1907. (Janet Miller)

Bender very likely played in some of the college baseball games as well, at least in his first Pullman stay, 1906-1908.

It was not unusual for coaches, or faculty for that matter, to take part in some of the college games in those years. Professor (later Dean) H. V. Carpenter of the WSC Engineering Department, an old Illini hurler, regularly pitched for WAC in games against club and town teams. In fact, Carpenter pitched for WAC against the great Orval "Orvie" Overall of the University of California when the Bears made a barnstorming trip into the Pacific Northwest in 1902. Overall, who later pitched for Cincinnati and Chicago of the National League, struck out 16 and beat WSC 12-3 at Pullman on June 16. Governor Henry McBride was among the spectators that day. The WAC Coach in 1902 was Herbert E. "Bert" Lougheed, who had played four years at Stanford. Lougheed also played for the college team in that game against California. (He also played for the Spokane Indians during the summer and was so versatile he was used at practically every position at one time or another.)

Ah, those were the days!

Cougar fans who complain about coverage in today's sports pages would have noted a certain feeling of deja vu on Sunday, November 25, 1906, had they read the Spokane paper. On the front page, the *Spokesman-Review* headlined: "Yale Blue Waves Over Harvard," and the story ran a full column and a half. On page fifteen appeared the story of WSC's 6-0 win over Whitman the day before at Pullman, which completed a perfect season for "Johnny Bender's Farmers."

As great as that 1906 season was, two victories during 1907 probably did more for WSC's athletic program than anything that preceded them. An 11-5 win over the University of Washington November 21 on old Denny Field on the UW campus, and the 11-0 shutout of St. Louis University at Natatorium Park in Spokane on Christmas Day of 1907, were landmarks in WSC football history.

UW football records show the attendance was 3,000, and the Pullman *Herald* reported the game was played "On a sloppy field and in a drizzling rain. . . ." (Some things never change!) It was the first meeting of the two teams since Washington's 12-6 win, also in Seattle, in 1904.

St. Louis University warms up for the game with Washington State College on Christmas Day 1907 at Spokane's Recreation Park. (Janet Miller)

The schools had been "tiffing" over some player eligibility matters and did not play in 1905 and 1906. The game was scoreless through the first half, but Captain Nissen, WSC's speedy left half, returned the second half kickoff twenty-five yards and then passed to Goldsworthy who took the ball down to the Washington fourteen. It was the first pass attempt of the game for WSC. From there, fullback Ralph Rader, of Pullman, pounded down to the five and Nissen scored on a "crisscross." The extra point was missed.

Washington scored shortly thereafter, also missed the conversion, and the game was tied at 5-5 with seven minutes to play.

It was time for Nissen to shine again, and Pullman's star never was brighter!

WSC took Washington's kickoff and worked the ball down near midfield. Nissen then "tore a hole through right tackle 40 yards to the UW 20," the *Herald* said. "Rader went over on four successive bucks." Joe Halm "kicked a difficult goal" to make the final score 11-5.

> ". . . and when time was called at the end of the game, the telegraph told the tale of victory in Pullman and joy among the crimson and gray supporters knew no bounds!"

WSC clinched the Northwest championship at Walla Walla on November 28 by defeating Whitman College 16-8. Pullman's Cecil Cave had a big day, scoring two touchdowns, one on a thirty-five-yard run, and Halm kicked a field goal and two extra points.

St. Louis University had a good football team. Not only had it won the Missouri Valley title in 1907, the Bills had hammered Nebraska in a Thanksgiving Day game, 34 to 0. St. Louis cheerfully accepted an invitation—and an $800 guarantee or a split of the gross receipts—to play WSC at Spokane's Natatorium Park on Christmas.

The *Spokesman-Review* for December 26 told the story of the game:

> Proving themselves better mudlarks, stronger on defense and superior at the old style of play, Washington State College Wednesday took the full measure of the crack team from St. Louis university.

Touchdowns, both scored in the last half, one in the first three minutes of play and one in the very last minute, represented the Washingtonians' margin of victory. [The score was 11-0, with Rader scoring on a run and Herb Wexler, junior end from Pullman, recovering a fumble in the end zone. Halm kicked one conversion.]

It was Johnny Bender's finest hour. The little coach explained his game strategy to the press:

I think St. Louis' weak point was that she played her ends wide, putting the balance of too much weight on the tackles and giving our backfield a chance to get started. I played my ends exceptionally close, hence relieving the tackles and having them smash the interference before it formed completely. If the man got by, I had the halfback there to pull him down.

The *Review* estimated the crowd between 3,000 and 4,000 which, "despite the most discouraging weather conditions, filled the big Natatorium Park grandstand."

"The crowd," the *Review* writer contended, "was attracted by the intersectional importance of the contest rather than by any sort of college loyalty. It was Washington and the northwest against Missouri and the midwest. And the men from Missouri were 'showed.'"

The newspaper reported that gross receipts for the game "would approach $3,000," and added, "The St. Louis team will of course exercise its option on half the gross receipts instead of its $800 guarantee."

Defeated the men from St. Louis were, stupid they weren't!

In 1908 Johnny Bender moved on to become Athletic Director and Coach at the Haskell Indian Institute in Lawrence, Kansas. He took a similar position at St. Louis University in 1909, no doubt remembered there for his coaching job with WSC in 1907. Bender also earned a law degree while coaching at St. Louis, remaining at the school until 1912 when he was again "called" to Pullman to become Coach and Graduate Manager. Unfortunately, he was to prove an old adage: "You can't go home again."

"Joe Bunch"

His name was Joe Halm and he came from Prosser. In the years between 1904 and 1909 he became a sports institution at Washington State College.* Most people knew him better as "Joe Bunch" or "Bunchgrass."

A big, dark-haired kid who wore a benign smile in all his pictures, "Joe Bunch" was one of WSC's first great all-around athletes. How he acquired his nicknames is a guess now, but bunchgrass was the native vegetation in the Palouse when Joe played at WSC and it was the only thing resembling "turf" on Rogers Field, where he spent most of his time. Joe probably saw—and felt—a lot of bunchgrass down there as he competed in football, baseball, and track.

*The state legislature changed WAC's name to Washington State College in 1905.

●

Football scheduling was very "informal" in the early years. On September 25, 1908, Manager J. Houston McCroskey, *from Garfield, announced WSC's schedule for the 1908 season opening October 3. Gonzaga, Cheney Normal, Spokane YMCA, Montana, Montana School of Mines, Bremerton Navy, University of Washington, University of Idaho, Whitman, and, tentatively, the Carlisle Indians were on the WSC slate. As late as October 30 that year, the* Pullman Herald *quoted McCroskey as saying WSC was supposed to give St. Louis a return game (after beating the Billikens 11-0 in 1907), but he was trying to line up Notre Dame in Spokane instead. As it turned out, WSC did not play Carlisle, or St. Louis, or Notre Dame—or Gonzaga, or Montana or Montana Mines! All scheduling problems were forgotten, however, when WSC completed its season unbeaten in six games, tied only by Washington and Idaho.*

●

Joe Halm kicking a field goal during WSC's 38-0 victory over Montana on October 18, 1907. (Manuscripts, Archives, and Special Collections, Washington State University Libraries)

Current WSU football press books credit Halm with lettering four years, 1905-1908, in football as a guard. He pitched for five seasons, 1905-1909, and his twenty-two complete games still ranks fifth in the baseball record book. In track, Halm set new school records in the shot and hammer in 1907, and he was still competing and setting records in 1909. Matter of fact, Joe never did get around to graduating.

Halm was one of WSC's best kickers. He learned under Coach Everett Sweeley in 1905. Sweeley was the greatest punter of his day when he played for Michigan under "Hurry-up Yost." In the 1902 Tournament of Roses game at Pasadena, won by Michigan 49-0 over Stanford, Sweeley, an end, punted twenty-one times for an average of 38.9 yards! (He was at WSC in 1904-1905 and shortly thereafter retired from coaching to take up law. Sweeley had a distinguished career as an attorney and judge in Twin Falls, Idaho, returning to the WSC campus often to see games. In 1916 he went to Pasadena to watch his old team play Brown. Judge Sweeley died in Twin Falls at age seventy-seven in 1952.)

Joe Halm kicked his first field goal for WSC against the Spokane Athletic Club in the third game of the 1906 season. The twenty-five-yarder gave Washington State a 4-0 win. (Field goals counted four points until 1909). The following week he kicked a twenty-six-yard goal as WSC beat Idaho 10-0, and the week after that he had fielders of thirty-two and twenty-four yards to account for all the scoring in WSC's 8-0 win over the Spokane A.C. at Pullman.

On November 7, 1908, in Seattle, Halm played a key role in one of the weirdest football games ever played. After a scoreless first half, Halm

Coach J. Fred Bohler and Charles "Jit" Smith, his ace distance man in the 1909-1910 era. (Manuscripts, Archives, and Special Collections, Washington State University Libraries)

and Washington's Maxwell Eakins each kicked a field goal and WSC and Washington both scored safeties for a final score of 6-6. The tie ruined an otherwise perfect season for Washington's new coach, Gilmour Dobie. WSC also was unbeaten that year but was tied twice, the second time by Idaho, 4-4 at Pullman on November 14. (For some reason, John Foran, of Seattle, replaced Halm that day and kicked a fifteen-yard fielder to match an earlier thirty-five-yarder by Idaho's Rodney Small.)

Halm was a strong right-handed pitcher for WSC. He won sixteen of twenty-two starts and had one win in relief over five seasons. His best years were 1905 and 1907. He was 5-1 both seasons. In 1907, Halm and Merritt McCully, of Olympia, combined for eleven wins against just two losses as WSC went 16-3 under Coach Bender. Joe pitched only one game in each of his last two years, 1908-1909, apparently concentrating on the weight events in track. WSC won five of six dual meets those two years, losing only to Oregon, 62-60 in 1908. At the conclusion of his WSC career, Halm had school records of 40-11 in the shot and 139-8 in the hammer.

"Joe Bunch" was quite a guy.

There's a "Doctor" in the House

He never met a game he didn't like.

Fortunately for the thousands of young people whose lives he would affect in a very positive way by his instruction, his advice, his ideas, and his work, during a long and colorful career in higher education, John Frederick Bohler, better known as "Doc," chose the academic life over that of a professional athlete.

Bohler was a giant in physical education and athletics worldwide for nearly half a century. Happily, he wore the Crimson and Gray of Washington State for forty-two of those years.

Of all the people associated with intercollegiate athletics at WSU in its first century, none stands taller than Bohler. His contributions, as athlete, coach, trainer, teacher, administrator, were many; his story reads like a combination of Horatio Alger and Frank Merriwell—with some Huck' Finn thrown in.

Born April 18, 1885, in Mohnsville, Pennsylvania, a suburb of Reading named for his mother's family (Mohn), Bohler was of Swiss extraction, not "Pennsylvania Dutch" as so many have claimed. He had a pronounced lisp, and interchanged V's and W's as in the German. One night at Struppler's restaurant (in the Cordova Theater building) when he and other players on Buck Bailey's "Angels" dropped in for a snack after a game out at Johnson, Doc ordered a "wanilla" milkshake. Turk Edwards, the great Cougar All-American tackle in 1931, who also played with the Angels, told the waitress he'd like one of those "wanilla milkshakes, too."

Bohler spun around, grabbed Edwards by the throat and lifted the 230-pounder right off his stool.

"Don'thew mimic me, you thmart Alec!"

Turk laughed, but he also was surprised at the "old man's" strength.

John Frederick was the third of eight Bohler children, eldest of four boys, all of whom eventually had outstanding careers in athletics and physical education.

Fred (he didn't get the nickname "Doc" until he was at WSC and handling athletic training duties on top of all his other responsibilities) was big and exceptionally talented athletically at a very young age. He played first base for the Reading town team at age fourteen and at sixteen was on the Reading YMCA "Varsity" basketball team. He also began an apprenticeship in a hat factory about this time, often working ten or more hours a day, and at age sixteen was a skilled hat blocker.

Bohler attended Schuylkill Seminary (later Albright College), in Reading, and was outstanding in all sports. He was a fullback on the football team; played first and was the team's big stick in baseball; was an all-around competitor in track; wrestled, boxed, and was good enough in gymnastics (he was exceptional on the flying rings) that he seriously considered joining the circus as an aerialist. (This is no joke. A circus had winter quarters in Reading when Bohler was in college and he and a partner worked up an aerial act that brought them an offer to tour with the show.) After he came to WSC, Doc often was a featured performer on the rings and other "apparatus," or juggling flaming Indian clubs at "entertainments" staged by the Athletic Association to raise money for its programs.

In 1905-1906 Bohler organized a professional basketball team, the Reading Bears. The club won forty-two straight games, including one against the previous champions, the De Neir Club of Philadelphia, and claimed the "World's Professional Basketball Championship."

It was during this period that Bohler is credited with developing the one-hand push shot in basketball. He played center and scored 515 points for the Reading Bears. The opposition had 599 for the entire season of 1906.

Professionally, the three terms Bohler spent at the Chautauqua Summer School in Physical Education in New York were the most valuable experiences of his early life. Here he met and studied under some of the top people in physical education in the United States, Sweden and Germany, all of whom "represented different systems" (philosophies), he would say later.

William E. Heath, of Sumner, who wrote a splendid biography of Bohler for a Master's thesis in 1951, said Doc was "always open-minded and willing to hear the suggestions of his subordinates, particularly in regard to curriculum changes." Heath thought this might have been a result of Bohler's experiences at Chautauqua, where Doc said there was "continuous argument as to which [P.E. teaching philosophy] was best suited to American needs."

These annual sessions at Chautauqua drew as many as 10,000 people, and Bohler "won many awards for his performances in track and gymnastics," Heath noted. He also became an ardent admirer of Dr. Raymond Gustavus Clapp, professor of Physical Education and Director of Athletics at the University of Nebraska, who wound up offering Bohler a teaching assistantship at Lincoln in the fall of 1907.

"At Nebraska, Doc took classes, instructed activity classes and calisthenics, assisted with the gymnastics and basketball teams, had charge

•

Basketball was so new in "Doc" Bohler's first season at WSC (1908-1909) that the Pullman Herald *saw fit to explain in the WSC-OAC game story: "In the intercollegiate rules, blocking, dribbling in any form and shooting from a dribble is allowed." Bohler's first team finished 10-6. Starters were Captain C. F. "Andy" Anderson,* Napavine (later a long-time Pullman banker), *and* Eddie Holcomb, Snohomish, guards; *Ivan Putman,* Pullman, center; and *Tom "Bunk" Barnes,* Kent, and *Pat Crane,* Snohomish, forwards. *Bernhardt Torpen,* Montesano, and *Arthur E. Price,* Elberton, were the subs.

•

of the junior varsity track squad, and officiated in basketball and track in the area," wrote Heath.

That winter of 1907-1908, Doc had an offer of $300 a month—big money in those days—to play basketball in the Pennsylvania Professional League. He was all set to go, but on the advice of his mentor, Doctor Clapp, who urged young Bohler to "think about your future," turned down the pros.

A position at Washington State opened the following spring and Doc's "future" had arrived.

Bohler's appointment to replace Johnny Bender as Physical Director and Coach at WSC in the fall of 1908 has come to be regarded as the beginning of the formal programs in physical education and athletics at the college, even though others preceded him in those areas.

State Senator Asa V. "Ace" Clark, of Pullman, the Captain of WSC's first Rose Bowl football team in 1916, was a student when Bohler arrived at the college. When Ace was interviewed by Heath in 1951, he said:

> The people of the State College had no conception of Physical Education, and could not conceive of anybody taking play as serious as Bohler did. His enthusiasm, sincerity and drive soon became infectious, and began to spread through the student body and faculty.

Heath, who had researched Bohler's early history and knew his subject well, added:

> In view of the fact that Bohler's abilities and interests were so diversified, it is not surprising that each aspect of the program, namely varsity, intramural and interscholastic athletics, received adequate consideration. He began with that attitude, and held to it to the end.

Heath also told of how, as a student at Schuylkill, Bohler "created interest in a girls' [sports] program, promoted the same, and served as

WSC played its first "intercollegiate" basketball game on February 6, 1904, at Pullman against Whitman College and won 21-3. The lineup had Albert L. "Soapy" Smith, Steptoe, at center; Harry C. Robinson, Clarkston, and Jefferson H. Fulton, Asotin, forwards; Fred Thiel, Ritzville, and Barnard E. Smead, Blalock, Oregon, at guards. Fulton was the leading scorer with eleven points. Previously, only club and high school teams had been scheduled.

The Washington State College women's basketball team, circa 1907. (Manuscripts, Archives, and Special Collections, Washington State University Libraries)

coach of the girls' basketball team." He also started a basketball team made up of South American students at Schuylkill who had never seen the game before coming there.

"These two incidents," Heath pointed out, "serve to show that even at this early age Bohler was interested in sports for all, an interest that was to hold throughout his life."

Certainly he had help getting his ideas in place and his programs going at WSC, but as Heath noted, "Bohler again was the instigator, the promoter, and the driving force that assured a continual and healthy growth of the intercollegiate athletic program."

That is not an exaggeration. It might be an understatement. Doc Bohler often was a one-man-band promoting physical education and athletics at Washington State College in those early years. His energy and determination made it sound like a symphony.

Flyin' Jack

When Halley's Comet became visible in the Pacific Northwest in 1910, residents of eastern Washington viewed it with a yawn. They had seen the real thing—in person.

On May 29, 1909, a human comet by the name of Jack Nelson blazed down the cinder track at Rogers Field on the Washington State College campus and tied the world record for the hundred-yard dash at 9 and 3/5 seconds. Nelson was up against one of the best sprinters in the Pacific Northwest in this race, Bill Martin of Whitman College. The two dueled again in the 220, Nelson winning in a time of 22 1/5.

May 20, 1910, again in a dual meet with Whitman, this time on the newly constructed 220 straightaway at WAC, Nelson tied the world record in both the 100 and 220 with marks of 9 3/5 and 21 1/5.

Nelson's spectacular performances in the 100, 220, 440 and relay events, would dominate the Pacific Northwest track scene for two

•

Jack Nelson, *the WSC sprinter from Pueblo, Colorado (1909-1910), would have been great in any era, according to Cougar Track Coach* John Chaplin. *"His 100 time would have been 10.44 for 100 meters if clocked electronically, as now,"* Chaplin said in 1987. *"Remember, this was a dirt track, and they started from holes in the ground! If he were here now and running the times he ran in 1909-1910, he would be the best sprinter on my team."*

•

Flyin' Jack Nelson equaling the world record in the 220 at Rogers Field on May 20, 1910 in a meet with Whitman College. (Manuscripts, Archives, and Special Collections, Washington State University Libraries)

Captain Ivan Putman in 1909. Putman was one of WSC's best hurdlers in the early years. (Charles and Anne Morrison)

seasons—and his records stood for years. His spectacular finishes, lunging for the tape with both feet off the ground, arms flung wide, soon earned Nelson the nickname "Flyin' Jack." And what a flyer he was!

Track was one of the students' favorite sports at the college right from those very early years when the "Field Day" was the highlight of spring on the hilltop campus. Nelson's sensational marks in the seasons of 1909 and 1910 created new fans for the sport and focused more attention—this time nationwide—on Washington State College.

Coach Bohler was determined to give Nelson the best possible chance for good marks at WAC once the Colorado flyer had demonstrated his potential. Early in the spring of 1909, in a letter to the WSC Board of Regents, Doc recommended "immediate steps be taken for constructing a 220 straightaway track [on Rogers Field]...." The regents uananimously approved the idea at a meeting in Pullman on April 9 and the track was ready for Nelson's world record efforts in 1910.

Nelson's major triumph, however, and the thing that brought the college its greatest national exposure of the first two decades, was a great "double" on June 4, 1910, at the Western Conference (Big Ten) Intercollegiate Track and Field Meet at the University of Illinois, Champaign-Urbana. Nelson won both the 100 and 220 in the meet, which corresponded to the National Collegiate Championships (NCAA) today and drew most of the top athletes from across the country.

Sometime later, Nelson was divested of his victories in this meet because the Big Ten had a three-year Varsity rule. Since Nelson had competed in his freshman and sophomore years at Colorado Agricultural College in 1907-1908, he was ruled as having been ineligible for the Illinois meet. WAC and the Northwest Conference did not have such a rule.

Clarence Cooil, of Tacoma, the finest distance man WSC had produced to this time, ran the 880 and the mile at the Western Championships, placing fourth in the mile "after having set the pace for three and a half laps," the *Chinook* reported. Cooil at one time held the Pacific Northwest records in the 880, mile and two-mile while competing for WSC.

It is to Doc Bohler's everlasting credit that he recognized the importance of getting Nelson and Cooil to this meet. Faculty, students and business people contributed funds for the trip. Bohler gambled and won big on this occasion. He took quite a chance in pulling his two aces, Nelson and Cooil, out of the dual meet with Idaho, which also was scheduled for June 4. A loss to the Idees would not have been taken lightly at home—regardless of how the WSC athletes fared in Illinois.

Despite a valiant performance by Idaho's great all-around star, James Montgomery, who won the 100, 220, 440 and 220 hurdles, placed third in the shot put and anchored the winning mile relay team, WSC prevailed 76-64. John Dalquest, of Everett, was the leading point-winner for WSC, taking the discus at 106-7 1/2 and the pole vault, 11-2, and placing third in the high jump at 5-10.

One of the most satisfying victories of his short, two-year career at WSC, came in a special match race between Nelson and Idaho's great quarter-miler of the day, Clarence "Hec" Edmundson, later to achieve considerable fame as basketball coach at the University of Idaho and the University of Washington. An article in the Pullman *Herald* told of the race on May 1, 1909—and some "side benefits" for Jack's backers that day:

> Edmundson, Idaho's idol, who was thought to be invincible was defeated by Nelson in a special quarter mile sprint, in which Nelson made a new northwest record [50 1-5], lowering the time of Ben Williams, the Oregon wonder, by two-fifths of a second.
> Moscow people lost heavily on this race. So confident were the Moscow people that Edmundson was invincible that they offered big odds, some of the more enthusiastic offering five to one on Edmundson. A considerable amount of money was taken by Pullman people, but there were but few who had enough nerve or confidence in Nelson, who is admittedly a star, but his ability was not generally realized.

According to the *Chinook*, the race between Nelson and Edmundson was "a sprint from start to finish, Nelson leading by but a few inches until the final straight-away, when he sprinted away from Edmundson and finished easily thirty feet in the lead."

John William Nelson (he later changed it to "Nielson," the family name in his native Denmark) came to WSC from Pueblo, Colorado. The twenty-two-year-old transfer from Colorado Agricultural College (now Colorado State University, Fort Collins), enrolled on February 26, 1909, and was given credit for two years' work toward his degree in Chemistry, which he eventually took at WSC in 1911.

None of the area newspapers headlined Nelson's transfer. As the *Herald* indicated, the Pacific Northwest did not know his potential for stardom. Nelson had been Captain of the track team at Fort Collins in 1908, and, according to the *Silver Spruce*, the school yearbook, "The faculty presented Jack Nelson with a beautiful gold medal for breaking the state record in the 220-yard dash." He ran it in 22 1/5 that year.

In its preview of the 1909 track season, the Pullman *Herald* concentrated on Cooil, who headed up "perhaps the best bunch of (distance) men in the history of the school." Others listed were Everett Johnson, of Spokane; George Clarke, Sunnyside; and Otis Welsh, of Almira. Harlan Coe, of Plaza, star sprinter of 1906, was back after a two-year absence, the *Herald* noted, along with Ralph Lowry, of Republic, another sprinter; Joe Halm, "veteran weight man" (from Prosser); and Captain Ivan Putman, of Pullman, in the hurdles, jumps, and 440. Jack Nelson was not mentioned.

The Washington State track team of 1909 was one of the strongest ever assembled in the Pacific Northwest to that time. Coach Bohler undoubtedly did a good job in preparing his athletes, but in all fairness it should be pointed out that I. P. "Red" Hewitt, of Nebraska (he preferred I. P. over Irenaeus Prime for some reason), and Karl H. "Dutch" Kiesel, Wisconsin, provided excellent coaching in the 1907 and 1908 seasons, immediately before Bohler's arrival.

WSC swept through its dual meet season in 1909, posting easy wins over Whitman, Oregon Agricultural College and the University of Idaho. The State College then took the Conference meet at Seattle, scoring sixty-three points to thirty-two for runner-up OAC. The Univer-

"The Little Giant," Oscar Osthoff, in his Wisconsin letter sweater at Washington State College in 1909-1910. (Manuscripts, Archives, and Special Collections, Washington State University Libraries)

60   THE SECOND DECADE

Frank Jenne, of Coupeville, was Captain of the first WSC wrestling team in 1909. WSC met Spokane Athletic Club, Multnomah AC and Oregon Agricultural College, all on the road. Team members were Edward Cheely, *DeBeque, Colorado;* Fred Hunter, *Palouse;* Walter Ferguson, *Goldendale;* Fred Calkins, *Ellensburg; and* Cornelius Kruchek, *Waitsburg.*

sity of Washington entered only three athletes and finished last with five points. The Pullman *Herald* explained that the Alaska-Yukon-Pacific Exposition was being held on the UW campus, therefore classes had been dismissed two weeks early and the track team had disbanded for the summer.

In 1908, WSC did not own a single Pacific Northwest collegiate record in track and field. One year later, the State College had four of the top regional marks and shared two more. By 1910, WAC athletes owned five regional marks outright, three by Nelson: 100: 9 3/5; 220: 21 1/5; and 440: 49.3; and two by Cooil, who held the 880 at 1:59.4 and the mile in 4:31.1.

Everett Johnson, of Spokane, was a superb half-miler, and shared the Northwest record in that event with Edmundson of Idaho at 2:00 1/5 in 1909. Ralph Lowry, the big fullback, held the 220 mark jointly with Dan Kelley, of Oregon, at 22-flat. (Kelley was Oregon's first Olympian, capturing the silver medal at London in 1908 in the broad jump.) Cooil held the two-mile record at 10:17 2/5 in 1909, but Ed Stookey, of Creston, lowered this to 10:10.4 and then John McGuire of Oregon improved it to 10:05, both marks coming in the 1910 season.

Washington State lost only to Oregon in 1910, this at Eugene on May 27 by a score of 81 to 51. Nelson won three events, the 100 in 10-flat; the 220 in 22.3; and the 440 in 49.3, a new Pacific Coast record. Cooil, who was ill, managed to win the 880 in 2:02, but had to scratch from the mile. WSC's only other first place was shared by John Dalquest, of Everett, and Glenn Powell, of Oregon, Illinois, who tied in the high jump at 5-7 1/2.

Jack Nelson played one season of football at WSC and "made an enviable reputation as right half" on Coach Oscar Osthoff's 1910 team that posted a 2-3 mark. Nelson graduated in June of 1911 with a B.S. degree in Chemistry. He then went to Cal Poly, at San Luis Obispo, where he was a teaching assistant in Chemistry and continued his track work in preparation for the 1912 Olympics in Copenhagen. Nelson was considered a cinch to make the U.S. team in the sprints and relay events, but the serious illness of his wife that summer forced him to miss the qualifying trials.

John William Nielson received his M.D. degree from Stanford in 1919 and practiced medicine in the Los Angeles area until his death in 1965. He was elected to Washington State University's Athletic Hall of Fame in 1979.

E. T. "Curly" Humes gives WSC high jumper Morgan Moulton some sideline support at a meet on Rogers Field, circa 1908. (Manuscripts, Archives, and Special Collections, Washington State University Libraries)

The Second Decade, 1901-1910

Captain *John B. Evans*, Lewiston, Idaho, organized an athletic training table for his track men in March, 1901, in the "Crib." The *Evergreen* reported: "The track men live on regulation diet there, prepared by the skillful hands of *Mrs. Flanary.*"

•

Charles Proff, of Rosalia, is credited with being the first man to win three Varsity W's at Washington Agricultural College. *E. W. "Turkey" Thorpe*, of Dayton, captain of the 1904 baseball team and later owner of the Smoke House, a Pullman sports hangout, wrote in the *Evergreen* on March 28, 1911, that Proff lettered in football (halfback), track (discus and high jump), and baseball (outfield) in the 1899-1901 era.

•

Washington State College swept Washington, 4-3, 8-6 and 9-0 in the first baseball series between the schools. It was played at Pullman on April 24-26, 1901. *Roy "Curly" Thompson*, of Albion, pitched the first and third games, with *John B. Evans* winning the second.

•

No joy in Mudville! On November 1, 1901, the day WAC first defeated the University of Washington in football (10-0 at Pullman), *John Patrick Parnell Cahill*, a former baseball player familiarly known as "White Wings," and the original "Casey at the Bat," died in Pleasanton, California. (The story appeared in the same column as the WAC-UW game story in the Spokane *Spokesman-Review*. Do you suppose the editor had a sense of humor? Nah!)

•

Alvin Coon, of Asotin, played halfback on the 1902 football team, left school and later returned to complete his course in engineering and lettered in 1908 and 1909.

•

Engineering Professor *H. V. Carpenter* pitched a no-hitter for WAC on May 15, 1902, beating the Dayton town team 3-1 at Pullman. He struck out thirteen.

Stars of the 1902 track team included *William Kruegel*, of Pullman, later long-time WSC Bursar. Kruegel was WAC's first good miler. In 1903, while serving in the Orient as a yeoman aboard the *USS Wisconsin*, "In a mile and cross-country run on the Mikado's birthday, at Yokohama, he easily won from two Englishman. He said they were surprised to see a sailor 'lope in ahead of them.'"

•

Freshman *Roy Godman*, of Dayton, set a state record of 52 2/5 in winning the 440 against Whitman College in 1902.

•

"The WAC football team returned Sunday from Lewiston where they were engaged the day before [October 11, 1902] in a game of football with a team wearing the colors of the Lewiston Normal School, only three of whom, however, were members of that eminent institution of learning, the rest being recruited from Butte, the Nez Perce reservation and the byways of Lewiston. Our boys were badly bruised and battered [and lost 12-0] in this, the dirtiest exhibition of football ever seen in the West. . . ." (Pullman *Herald*)

•

Editorial by Associate Editor Eugene Person (Spokane) in the December 11 *Evergreen* noted that the Athletic Association had incorporated and issued $1,000 in bonds to liquidate its indebtedness. "The trustees have for sale a number of shares of stock at one dollar per share. . . . Every student should have at least one. . . . If you haven't a share, get one; frame it, hang it up in your room, and show it to your friend, and make him buy one. Make the possession of a share of stock a badge of loyalty to the WAC." (What a collector's item one of those certificates would make today. Especially if they are still drawing interest!)

•

"Curly" Thompson, a noted pitcher who could "throw a curve with either hand," the *Evergreen* declared, replaced *Bert Lougheed* as Baseball Coach early in the 1903 season and WAC finished 9-5 with a sweep of Lewiston (25-9 and 12-5), despite the absence of Captain *Frank "Cack" Barnard*, shortstop (studying for finals), and Captain-elect *"Turkey" Thorpe*, first baseman (too busy to go).

•

J. N. Ashmore, of Illinois, coached the WAC football team in the fall of 1903, finishing 3-3-2. He also coached the men's and women's basketball teams in the winter of 1903-04 (2-1 and 3-0), and the track and baseball teams in the spring of 1904 (3-0 and 10-2.) Ashmore went to the University of Colorado in 1905 and coached basketball and baseball in Boulder.

•

O. A. Thomle, of Stanwood, was Captain of the unbeaten WAC track team in 1904 and set a school record of 51 2/5 in the 440.

•

Fred "Jumbo" Hunter, of Palouse, was a sub on the 1905 football team and returned to letter three years in 1908-1910.

•

The mile relay team of *Ralph Cowgill*, Spokane; *Clare Ockerman*, Kelso; *Harlan Coe*, Plaza; and *Thomle* ran 3:34 in 1906.

•

William A "Bad Bill" Miller, of Goldendale, a tackle on the unbeaten WSC team of 1906, weighed 158 pounds, but sportswriters said he "outplayed *Dimmick*, Whitman's All-Northwest tackle, and "showed up" *"Piggy Lamb,"* the 220-pound tackle from St. Louis.

•

Philip "Chub" Cherry, of Astoria, Oregon, transferred to WSC from OAC in 1907 and starred at center for three seasons. Following WSC's 11-5 win in Seattle on November 21, 1907, in the first game of the series played on campus (Meany Field), UW officials questioned the eligibility of Cherry and backs *George Hardy*, of Waitsburg, and *Ralph Rader*, originally from Colorado. Hardy, who first enrolled in 1903, had been out of school a year and then re-enrolled in the fall of 1907. Rader transferred to WAC from Willamette that fall. Can't imagine the fuss.

•

Cheney Normal defeated the WSC women's basketball team 1-0 in a game at Cheney. The *Evergreen* reported on February 7, 1908: "The WSC girls were handicapped with a low ceiling, steam pipes and center posts which they could not knock out."

•

When WSC played Oregon in basketball on February 12, 1908, in Pullman, the halftime score was 7-7. "Then," the *Evergreen* noted, "ex-Yellmaster *F. F. "Jimmie" Nalder* took charge of the rooting, resulting in the most concentrated rooting that has been done this year." (Nalder was then Registrar. WSC won 15-12.)

•

Henry Judd, Kendrick, Idaho; *Earl "Dyke" Galbraith*, Spokan;, and *Mayberry Davis*, Pullman, won the Northwest tennis title for WSC in 1908, defeating Washington, Oregon, and Whitman.

•

Edward T. "Ned" Cheeley, De Beque, Colorado, and *Otto P. "Big" Deaner*, Sheldon, Illinois, transferred to WSC from Colorado Agricultural College in

1908. Cheeley entered in the spring and started at left half that fall. He also wrestled at 158 pounds. Deaner entered in the fall and played at tackle. Captain *Herb Wexler*, of Pullman, played every line position during the 1908 season.

•

Johnny Bender was referee and *W. S. Kienholz* umpire in one of the most unusual football games ever played, the 6-6 tie between WSC and the UW in Seattle, November 7, 1908. Both teams scored a touchdown (four points then) and a safety. (Bender was WSC coach in 1906-07 and again in 1912-14, and Kienholz was at WSC in 1909.)

•

WSC was penalized 145 yards to 45 for Whitman in the final game of the 1908 football season at Pullman. Johnny Bender again was the referee. WSC won 4-0 on a thirty-six-yard field goal by *Joe "Bunch" Halm.*

•

In tennis, *George Merrill*, Spokane, singles, and the doubles team of *Harold MacLeod*, Goldendale, and *"Dyke" Galbraith*, defeated Whitman College and the University of Washington in a tournament held in Seattle and won the 1909 Northwest title.

•

Pullman attorney *Frank Sanger*, a former pitcher at the University of Michigan, took over as Baseball Coach at WSC in April 1909 after Coach *W. S. Kienholz* was fired for football recruiting irregularities. Sanger coached two seasons, finishing 5-11 and 7-12. *Lyle "Paddy" Buck*, of Mount Vernon, was Captain both years.

•

Washington State won the National Intercollegiate Indoor Rifle Shoot title in 1909, besting seventeen of the nation's colleges in the telegraphic competition. Team members included *Manton Armstrong*, McMinnville, Oregon; *Jesse Kimm*, Pine City; *Arthur Stewart*, Republic; *Walter Cagle*, Davenport; *Jerry McGillicuddy*, Hoquiam; *Edward Emmick*, Walla Walla; *Ralph Davidson*, Reardan; and *Fred Morgan*, Oak Harbor. Davidson, an honor student as well as an excellent marksman, was the victim in a tragic shooting accident May 18, 1909 at the LaFollette home in Wawawai.

•

Daryl "Dud" White, of Cle Elum, came to WSC from Cornell and played halfback in the 1909 season. WSC lost only one football game that year, to Denver University 11-6 on December 4 in Spokane. It was only the second loss in four seasons for WSC. The teams did not meet until September 23, 1960, when Denver won, 28-26 at Denver, and celebrated by giving up football at the conclusion of the season.

•

The Tennis and Rifle Club for Collegiate Girls was organized in December of 1910 for the purpose of creating greater enthusiasm for outdoor sports. Indoor tennis was played at the Armory until the outdoor courts were ready. The club had a membership of thirty. *Grace Fancher*, of Mount Vernon, Iowa, was the first president.

•

Doc Bohler took an eleven-man squad to Oregon for track meets with Oregon and Oregon State, May 24-25, 1910. WSC lost to Oregon 81-51 (its only loss in four meets that season) but rebounded with an 82-45 win over the Aggies.

•

Charles North, of Punxsutawney, Pennsylvania, a track man, was named on a student committee evaluating dormitory food. He was subsequently discharged from his job in the campus dining room and in protest 150 students left the boys' dorm on April 12, 1910, and went downtown to eat. (The first protest against dorm food?)

The Third Decade, 1911-1920

The School Songs

WASHINGTON STATE HAS TWO OF THE BEST SCHOOL SONGS IN THE COUNTRY. THE Alma Mater, "Washington, My Washington," and the Fight Song rank with any, and they were written by Cougars!

Wherever Washington State University students and alumni gather, these songs bring back fond memories of college days, of the rolling hills of the Palouse country, golden with wheat in summer, snow-covered in winter, green with the new crops in spring, providing an ever-changing backdrop to the beautiful hilltop campus and its myriad red brick buildings.

How did these songs come to be written? Who were the people involved?

In 1913, Student Body President James A. Williams, of Palouse (he was one of WSC's best distance runners in 1912-1914), appointed a committee to conduct a song-writing contest to give the school some "rousing songs which belong solely to Washington State."

Many pieces were submitted, among them "The Crimson and the Gray," words by F. F. "Jimmy" Nalder, '01, and music by Professor W. B. Strong; "Hail to Our College," words and music by Gertrude Worthington, '14, of Hillyard; "Oh, Washington," words and music by Emory D. Alvord, '15, McGammon, Idaho; "For Washington's Praise," words and music by Paul Browder, '17, of Colfax; "Victory," words and music by Marie Simpich, '15, Spokane; "Football Rally Song," music by Leon K. Wiese, '15, Anacortes; "Tanglewood," music by Joe Shields, ex-'14, Spokane; "State College Alumni," words by C. C. Ockerman, '07, Kelso, music by J. DeForest Cline, ex-'09, Asotin.

"W.S.C. Color Song," by J. DeForest Cline, won first prize for Alma Mater Song, and "Washington Football War Song," by Emory D. Alvord, took first for Football Song.

Alvord, Captain of the WSC football team in 1914 and a varsity heavyweight wrestler, wound up with three prize-winners, and Cline, a music major, had two—plus, ironically, an honorable mention for the song eventually chosen as the Alma Mater, "Washington, My Washington."

In addition to his first prize, Alvord received a second for "Oh, Washington" and a third for "Hail! Oh, Washington," both in the Alma Mater competition.

Cline took a second prize for "Washington, My Glory, a Football Song." "For Washington's Praise" won fourth prize in the Alma Mater

OPPOSITE: *Asa V. "Ace" Clark, Captain and tackle on the championship team that beat Brown in the 1916 Rose Bowl.* (Manuscripts, Archives, and Special Collections, Washington State University Libraries)

Lester V. Cooke wins another 220, this one against Idaho at Moscow on May 17, 1913. The wiry little sprinter was one of the Pacific Northwest's best during the 1912-1914 era. Manuscripts, Archives, and Special Collections, Washington State University Libraries)

division for Browder. All of the songs were published in 1914 by Hinds, Noble & Eldredge, of New York City, in a book titled *Washington State College Favorite Songs*, which had a handsome Crimson and Gray cover and bore the official seal of the State College in gold.

As it turned out, both tragedy and triumph were connected with the song-writing contest. Charles J. Newland, '14, of Ritzville, who served as chairman of the contest committee, and Lee C. Lewis, '16, of Tumwater, a committee member, both became U. S. Army officers and died on battlefields in France in 1918, shortly before the end of World War I. Before his death, Lieutenant Lewis, a WSC cross-country man, had written to the Alumni Office that Mark Farnum, who played right tackle for Brown in the 1916 game against Washington State, was in his company and that the two of them had been coaching battalion athletic teams.

J. DeForest Cline was Chairman of the Department of Music at Cheney Normal (now Eastern Washington University) from 1915 to 1922 and later at Colorado State College, Greeley (now University of Northern Colorado), where he was an outstanding teacher and composer, writing many marches and college songs. Professor Cline died in 1952.

Emory D. Alvord stayed at WSC after receiving his B.S. in Agriculture in 1915 and earned a master's in Agronomy in 1918. Football was interrupted by World War I at the conclusion of the 1917 season and Coach Dietz went to Mare Island in California to coach the U.S. Marine team there. WSC did play two games in the late fall of 1918, however, after the Armistice had been signed. Alvord coached that team. WSC defeated Gonzaga 20-6 at Pullman on November 26 and lost 7-6 to Idaho on December 7.

Early in 1919, Alvord and his new bride (he was married December 31, 1918, in Seattle to Bernice Mapes) went to Africa as agricultural missionaries. They worked in Southern Rhodesia (now Zimbabwe), first at Mt. Silinda, a remote station in the southeast part of the country, and later at Salisbury, the capital. In 1926, Alvord was named by the

Women's field hockey was played on the area east of Arts Hall (now Murrow Center) in the early years. This action photo was taken circa 1914. Note the cupola on Ferry Hall in the left background. The structure has taken on new life as a gazebo situated about where this hockey match took place. (Manuscripts, Archives, and Special Collections, Washington State University Libraries)

government of Southern Rhodesia to become the first Agriculturist for Instruction of Natives, under the new Department of Native Agriculture.

Over the years, readers of the Pullman *Herald* and *Powwow* became familiar with Alvord's fascinating accounts of life on the "Dark Continent" through letters he wrote back to friends in Pullman. They are classics, describing the Alvords' trip to Mt. Silinda by steamer, train, and finally "trek wagon drawn by 16 little donkeys"; their lives as agricultural missionaries, complete with trials and rewards; big game safaris into remote areas of Rhodesia and Portuguese East Africa; deep-sea fishing off the coast of Natal (he once landed a 671-pound ratchet-tooth shark), as well as his work with the native population to improve farming methods and water storage to fend off the ever-present threat of starvation due to crop failure or drought.

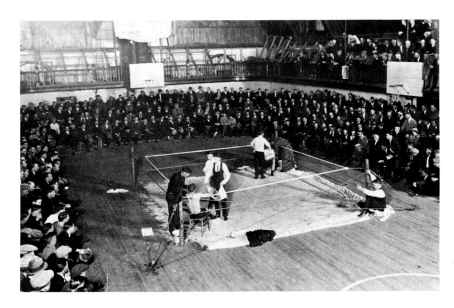

A boxing smoker in the old gymnasium. (Manuscripts, Archives, and Special Collections, Washington State University Libraries)

Lone Star Dietz in formal attire. The old coach was one of the real dandies of his day. (Manuscripts, Archives, and Special Collections, Washington State University Libraries)

The colorful and versatile old letterman died in 1959 at another African station, Waddilove Mission.

The Fight Song was written by Zella (Melcher) McMicken, of Spokane, and Phyllis (Sayles) Davis, of Fort Lapwai, Idaho, in 1919 when both were music students at WSC. Zella wrote the words and Phyllis wrote the music.

Mrs. McMicken, '19, was Music Supervisor in Chehalis city schools for a number of years after graduating from WSC. Sadly, she died of cancer in 1938 at age forty-one. Her son, Craig, starred as an end at Oregon State in the 1948 and 1949 seasons. Zella would have enjoyed seeing him play, but she probably would have been rooting for her beloved Cougars! Mrs. Davis, '22 (she attended Northwestern University, Evanston, Illinois, before coming to WSC), taught in the Los Angeles school system fifteen years after moving south in 1923. Phyllis died in Santa Barbara, California, in 1971 at age seventy-four.

"Lone Star"

In the late summer of 1915, a strikingly handsome, well-built man with the bearing and movements of a well-conditioned athlete stepped lightly down from a passenger train arriving at the Northern Pacific depot in Pullman, Washington. He was wearing a smartly tailored three-piece suit and a pearl grey homburg.

Edgar Muir walked up and asked the gentleman if he might be of assistance. Young Muir was driving dray for his father, George, owner of a livery stable in the town. One of Ed's duties was to meet all incoming trains. After some discussion with the new arrival, Muir took his horse and wagon around to the baggage room. He could not believe his eyes when he looked at the trunks and suitcases piled there, and his fare standing nonchalantly by.

Muir had to make two trips to get all that luggage up to the address on College Hill the man gave him. The landlady at the boarding house took one look and said there wasn't room in the whole house for all those cases and trunks, let alone in the small room she had reserved. So Ed took the man, and a good portion of his luggage, on up to the Men's Gymnasium to see if "Doc" Bohler might store a trunk or two there, temporarily.

That's the story of the arrival in Pullman of William H. "Lone Star" Dietz, soon to become a legend throughout the West as the football coach at Washington State College.

If Ed Muir thought he was looking at a dandy that day, imagine what he and other local folks must have thought when Lone Star really dressed up—which he did often, especially when some publicity photographs were needed. On those occasions Dietz would don pinstripe pants, spats, and a Prince Albert cutaway with a vest. He wore a silk top hat and yellow gloves and carried an ivory-topped walking stick with this outfit. At other times Dietz effected formal Indian dress, full-length eagle-feather headdress, beaded deerskin jacket and fringed trousers, elaborate necklaces, and fancy moccasins. Yet with his stoic manner and innate aplomb, he somehow never seemed overdressed, regardless of garb.

The story of Lone Star Dietz reads like pulp fiction.* His father, a young German civil engineer, was working with a railroad survey crew out on the plains when their camp was attacked by Indians. Dietz left the camp, unarmed and with only a little food, to try to reach Chief Red Cloud, leader of the warriors who had his party cornered. He was captured, but when taken before the chief Dietz stepped forward, hand outstretched in friendship. Instead of punishing his prisoner, Red Cloud assigned Dietz a lodge, and he took an Indian woman (a half-blood Oglala Sioux) to be his wife. Their second child was named Wicarhpi Isnala, "Lone Star."

Lone Star was a very talented artist. His principal subjects related to Indian lore, but he also did book and magazine illustrating and considerable graphic art work. He also taught for a time at the School of Applied Art in Philadelphia, and, later, with his wife, Angel De Cora, the most successful Indian artist of the early twentieth century, operated an art school.

It was Dietz's athletic ability rather than his talent for art that caught the eyes of college recruiters. He played football in high school at Rice Lake, Wisconsin, then, in 1903, at Macalester College in St. Paul, Minnesota, and the following year at the Chilocco Indian School in Oklahoma. In 1909, at age twenty-five, Dietz wound up at Carlisle, a 174-pound halfback playing alongside the great Jim Thorpe. Dietz played three seasons, his last year as the team's star defensive tackle.

Dietz stayed on at Carlisle as an assistant to Coach Warner in 1912-1914, then was recommended by Warner for the position at WSC in the spring of 1915 when Coach Johnny Bender was let go. He was hired in April, effective September 1, at a salary of $2,250 for the season ($1,500 to be paid by the college and $750 by the Associated Students).

Washington State football fortunes were at a low ebb when Dietz took over. The last winning season had been 1909, when William S. Kienholz, a former Minnesota player, came in and taught botany and coached WSC to a 4-1 mark. The only loss that year had been to Denver University, 11-6, in a post-season game in Spokane. But Kienholz was fired the following spring after questions arose concerning his recruiting methods. There were charges, not substantiated, that he had made monetary inducements to get a couple of veteran linemen, Otto "Big" Deaner, of Sheldon, Illinois, a transfer from Colorado Agricultural College, and Bill Miner, Pullman, to return to school the previous fall.

Oscar P. Osthoff, known as the "Little Giant" at the University of Wisconsin, took over in 1910. One of the most versatile athletes in Badger history, "Ostie" won eight varsity letters in four sports, football, track, gymnastics and swimming. He was not as successful as a football coach at WSC. His first team finished 2-3, and after a 3-3 performance in 1911 Osthoff was gone and the popular "Chief" Bender was brought back as Coach and Graduate Manager. Bender had been Coach and Athletic Director at Haskell Institute in Lawrence, Kansas, and at St. Louis University in the four years following his departure from WSC in

Lone star in full Indian regalia. (Manuscripts, Archives, and Special Collections, Washington State University Libraries)

---

*Dietz biographical information taken from an article by John C. Ewers in *Montana: Magazine of Western History*, Winter Issue, 1977.

1908. (He also had married Pearl Cassel, an instructor in Latin at WSC. When the couple returned to Pullman in 1912 they brought with them their fifteen-month-old son, John R. Bender, Jr.)

In his first two football seasons at WSC, in 1906 and 1907, Bender's teams posted marks of 6-0 and 7-1. Everyone looked forward with eager anticipation to the return of the school's most successful coach.

But things were not the same for Johnny Bender the second time around. (Although his baseball teams in 1913-1915 won three straight titles, and for five seasons, including 1907-08, he had a winning percentage of .758, still the best for any baseball coach at Washington State with five or more seasons.)

"Bender was the first Graduate Manager to assume the responsibility of conducting student affairs. . . ." the *Chinook* noted. In this newly expanded position Bender replaced both Coach Osthoff and the popular John Hugh Jones, the old 1902 football captain who in 1909 had become WSC's first "Graduate Manager." Jones received high marks for the three years he served, turning a good profit in football in 1910 and 1911 despite poor seasons. (He died tragically in 1923 trying to prevent the collapse of a power dam under construction on the Moyie River in northern Idaho.)

The WSC football team was 2-3 in 1912, Bender's first year back; 4-4 in 1913; and finished 2-4 in 1914. A 45-0 loss to Washington in the final game of that season finished him. The regents declined to renew Johnny's contract.

"Inter-fraternity quarrels" and "internal strife" were cited in Bryan's history as contributing factors, but Bender had been handed an impossible task. He not only coached football and baseball, but as Graduate Manager was charged with overseeing the activities program—including student government and the *Evergreen* and *Chinook*. Some of his problems undoubtedly stemmed from these added assignments. Coaches often have difficulty dealing with students. (It didn't take Dietz long to get this situation changed. The *Evergreen* reported in October of 1915 that "W. C. Kruegel, an accountant at the college [he later was Bursar],

•

"The greatest Conference Meet on record," the Chinook *called the May 29, 1914, track meet in Pullman. Lusker McCroskey,* Tekoa, *broke the NWC record in the 220 low hurdles with a mark of 24.3 and the WSC mile relay team of Captain Lester Cooke,* Ellensburg; *Carl Dietz,* Bremerton, *(fullback on the Rose Bowl team); McCroskey; and Leslie Schultz, Davenport, ran 3:22, three full seconds faster than the old mark set in 1913 by the same team. Cooke also won the 220. Five Conference records fell in that meet.*

•

"Coach Dietz giving his warriors a lecture between halves," the original caption of this photograph declares. It looks more like he's checking the walking wounded. Note the vegetation. This shot was taken just off to the side of the gridiron on Rogers Field. There was no such thing as turf in those days. WSC defeated Oregon 26-3 in this 1915 season opener. (Manuscripts, Archives, and Special Collections, Washington State University Libraries)

will hereafter perform duties required of the graduate manager. . . ." The paper said Kruegel's duties would include managing the College Glee Club, the *Evergreen* ". . . and other student and college enterprises. Athletic scheduling will be done by a committee consisting of Bohler, Kruegel and Dietz.")

Bender became Football Coach at Kansas State after leaving WSC, then went to the University of Tennessee in 1916 and produced another unbeaten team. His Vols had eight wins and a tie that year in nine outings. After wartime service as a physical director for the Army, Bender returned to Tennessee in 1919 and coached two more years, going 3-3-3 that year and 6-2 in 1920.

Bender left college coaching after this and took a position with the Knoxville school system. Johnny Bender died in 1928 at age forty-six.

Bender is the only coach in Washington State football history to lose three games to Idaho. His 1907 team was 7-1, its only loss a 4-5 squeaker to the Idees. When Bender came back in 1912, WSC succumbed 0-13, and in 1913 it was 0-3. Ironically, the only time a Bender coached WSC team defeated Idaho was in 1914, the year he was fired. A seventeen-yard field goal by Arthur "Bull" Durham, of Spokane, gave WSC a 3-0 victory.

That Team of '15!

Lone Star, Ace, Biff, Bull, Zim, Hack, Red, Fish, Rimrock, Digger. What great memories those names recall!

The Washington State football team of 1915—looking back on it after nearly three-quarters of a century—had all the elements for success; talent, leadership, heart, size (for those days), intelligence, speed, good coaching, and support from the student body and the community, important ingredients for any winning program, all came together in this team. It was a young club, academically, but the average age was twenty-two years. There were three seniors, three juniors, ten sophomores and six freshmen on the twenty-two-man squad. Three sophomores and two freshmen started!

•

What a difference a year—and a new coach?—sometimes makes. On that WSC team in 1914 were eight men who would start in the Rose Bowl a season later: Ray Loomis, *Captain* Asa V. "Ace" Clark, Harry A. "Hack" Applequist, Alf Langdon, Clarence Zimmerman, "Bull" Durham, "Biff" Bangs, *and* Carl "Red" Dietz, *plus several top reserves, including* Ray Finney, *and* Silas "Si" Stites.

•

Students and townspeople welcome the 1915 team back from Corvallis, where WSC shut out Oregon Agricultural College 29-0. (Manuscripts, Archives, and Special Collections, Washington State University Libraries)

WSC beat all its opponents and *the weather in that 1915 season, as this view of the kickoff of the Whitman game shows. Note that the playing field has been moved to the west of the old grandstand by this time.* (Manuscripts, Archives, and Special Collections, Washington State University Libraries)

Asa V. "Ace" Clark, of Pullman, was team Captain and played right tackle. In 1943, in an interview with L. H. Gregory, sporting editor of the *Oregonian*, Ace said that WSC had good material the previous season, 1914, but hadn't done much with it. Then Lone Star Dietz came to Pullman from the Carlisle Indian school in Pennsylvania and brought with him Glenn S. "Pop" Warner's single-wing offense. WSC had been using the old T-formation. ". . . we figured we had exhausted its possibilities under Coach Johnny Bender, so when Lone Star Dietz came out with the new-fangled single wingback that Pop Warner was using at Carlisle, man, were we happy!" Clark told Greg.

> Dietz had a natural. We were a pretty good football team. . . . All we needed was something to interest us veterans, and single wingback did it. Dietz was pretty smart, too—he didn't throw overboard Johnny Bender's stuff, just added the single wingback and his own stuff to it—and we were so interested that everything fitted in.

When Lone Star Dietz took over the coaching reins at Washington State in 1915 the school had not had a winning football team for five seasons. It didn't look too promising—except for the defense—when the varsity squeaked out a 3-2 win over an alumni team "on a well-placed drop-kick by 'Bull' Durham," in a pre-season practice game. (That "Alumni" team included some pretty fair country talent, as *Powwow* noted: "The regulars were up against a hard proposition when they met such combinations as Herbert Wexler, [Fred] 'Jumbo' Hunter, Bill Hinchcliff, and [Emory] Alvord, [Tom] Tyrer, [Howard] Sattherthwaite, [Dee] Gaddis, [Eddie] Kienholz, and Harry Wexler, all of whom played on some of the best teams Johnny Bender ever developed at W.S.C." *Powwow* neglected to mention the center on that team. It was none other than J. Fred "Doc" Bohler, recently promoted to the joint position of Physical Director and Director of Athletics at WSC, but on this occasion one tough hombre in the middle of that Alumni line.)

"One thing that bothered me . . . was that, somehow, we didn't seem to be working hard enough," Clark told Gregory. "I was used to the old system of scrimmage, scrimmage, scrimmage all the time—Dietz wasn't much of a scrimmager. He worked us into pretty good condition [at a pre-season camp at Liberty Lake, east of Spokane], then scrimmaged very little, and somehow it didn't seem right.

"When we won our first game, 28-3, from Oregon under [Hugo] Bezdek, I still wasn't convinced," Clark recalled. "Then we beat Oregon State 29-0, and I began to see the light. . . . Instead of leaving our football on the practice field, Dietz practiced us only enough to get the new stuff and to be in good shape, and when a game came up we were raring to go!"

Coach Dietz made some key position changes when he'd had a chance to watch his charges work out in their pre-season camp. Captain Clark, for example, a twenty-seven-year-old senior who had started out at fullback in 1911 under Coach Osthoff, was moved to tackle. Ace had laid out of school two years, working in the mines in Idaho's booming Coeur d'Alene district and in British Columbia, then returned in 1914 and made "All-Northwest" as the center on Johnny Bender's last team. As he proved later as an outstanding rancher/stockman and long-time state senator, Clark was a strong leader. Considering that Dietz was the third coach he had played under at WSC, and that he was being asked to play his third different position in three seasons, it is little wonder that Ace questioned the coaching. It is to his credit that he stayed and played, and played hard and well. He was just the sort of Captain the younger players on that team needed.

Clarence Zimmerman, of Everett, the starting right end on the team of 1915, was a sophomore who had played at guard the previous year. Dietz recognized his tremendous athletic ability—"best athlete on the team and one of the best I ever saw," Captain Clark often said—and put Zimmerman at a position where he could do more things to help the team, both offensively and defensively. In the first two games that fall, "Zim" intercepted passes and returned them for touchdowns, seventy yards against Oregon and sixty yards against Oregon State. He also ran seven yards on a reverse for another score in the Oregon game.

WSC had a number of excellent backs. Benton "Biff" Bangs, of Albion, Idaho, the only out-of-stater on the squad; Ralph Boone, from Cunningham, and Spokane's Dick "Rimrock" Hanley, were crackerjack halfbacks; and Carl "Red" Dietz (no relation to the coach), of Bremerton, a converted end, turned out to be the best fullback on the Pacific Coast that year. He was backed up ably by Basil Doane, of Spokane.

Quarterback "Bull" Durham was a crunching blocker and an excellent field goal and extra-point kicker. He drop-kicked five field goals during the season, three against Oregon State on that old sawdust field in Corvallis! Durham, later a Commodore in the U.S. Navy during World War II, was twenty-one for twenty-five on conversions.

The WSC line was quick and tough. Senior Harry A. "Hack" Applequist, of Marcus, was the strongest man on the team—and he could move! Hack shifted over to guard (from tackle the previous year) and teamed up with Fred "Fish" Fishback, a freshman from Olympia. They gave Dietz the pulling guards so important to the success of Warner's single-wing attack. Throughout that season, Washington State's "great

•

Ira Clark, *of Colfax, was one of the great Yell Kings of the early days at WSC. The 1914* Powwow *called Clark: "The great ex-Rooter King whose inspirational thunder from the sidelines succeeding generations of rooters have vainly sought to imitate. . . ."*

•

interference" was always prominently mentioned when coaches and sportswriters and fans talked football.

Captain Clark and Bert Brooks, a nineteen-year-old freshman from Everett were the tackles, and Alfred Langdon, a junior from nearby Palouse, took over Clark's old spot at center and played very well. He had been a guard previously. Ray Loomis, a sophomore from Seattle, played right end opposite Zimmerman.

Other squad members were Jack Finney, Olympia; Silas "Si" Stites, Puyallup; Donald Bartow, Vancouver; Carl King, Davenport; Walt "Fat" Herreid, Seattle; LeRoy Hanley (Dick's brother), from Spokane; Clarence "Digger" Boone and Frank Michael, both of Chehalis; and Fred Haupt from Ritzville.

WSC swept through its six-game schedule undefeated, with only a single touchdown scored by the opposition (by Montana on a blocked punt recovered in the end zone in a 27-7 WSC win at Pullman). The only other score against Washington State that entire season was a field goal by Oregon's great quarterback, Shy Huntington, in the season opener at Pullman won by WSC 28-3. (Huntington led Oregon through an unbeaten season the following year, including a 14-0 win over Pennsylvania in the 1917 Rose Bowl game.)

Washington State scored four shutouts in 1915, over Oregon State, 29-0; Idaho, 41-0; Whitman College, 17-0; and Gonzaga, 48-0. WSC might have poured it on a little in that final game against the 'Zags in Spokane on November 25. For one thing, Whitman and Gonzaga were the only common opponents the State College and the University of Washington faced that season. When the Sun Dodgers refused to play WSC in Pullman (after four consecutive trips to Seattle by Washington State between 1911 and 1914), WSC moved Gonzaga, considered a "practice" game at the time, from its opener to the Thanksgiving date in Spokane replacing Washington.

The "Dodgers" defeated Gonzaga 21-7 in Spokane and Whitman 27-0 in Seattle in the third and fourth games of their schedule. A lot was made of comparative scores in those days.

Another thing that might have inspired a super effort against Gonzaga was the fact that, almost two weeks before the final game of the 1915 season, WSC had received—and accepted—an invitation to play in the Tournament of Roses game at Pasadena on New Year's Day. The West's representative certainly wanted to look good to the eastern press in its final regular season game.

On Sunday, November 14, following WSC's 17-0 win over Whitman, Coach Dietz received the following telegram:

> Pasadena Tournament of Roses is arranging to bill football game between eastern and western teams for New Years Day. As chairman of sports committee am sure can secure invitation for Pullman. Occasion offers splendid opportunity to obtain national recognition. Earnestly urge you to come. Expenses for big squad assured. Quick action necessary. Get busy, consent to come and I will do the rest. Wire at my expense at once.
>
> [Signed] W. S. Kienholz.

•

Maybe this is where the term "Laugher" originated in sports. Lee Lewis, *of Olympia, writing in the* Evergreen *of the WSC-Whitman game at Walla Walla on November 30, 1916, recorded:* '[Bert] Brooks *pulled down a Whitman pass and started down the field. As he passed the WSC bench, Captain* [Benton] Bangs, *who had given way to* [C.C.] Digger Boone, *exclaimed admiringly, 'By Gobb, that's good!' and so stirred the risibilities of Bert that he failed to elude the Whitman safety and arose after being tackled still laughing." (WSC won the game 46-0.)*

•

The *Evergreen*, which had the entire story in its Wednesday, November 17, issue (including the fact that Brown University would be WSC's opponent), reported that Dietz and Athletic Director Bohler swung into action quickly. The proposition was put before the faculty committee on athletics and was approved, with the provision that the eastern team selected "must be of high standing." (WSC had hoped for "a stronger opponent," perhaps Cornell or Pittsburgh, the *Evergreen* added. Had Pitt come, Dietz would have been matched against his old mentor, "Pop" Warner, who left Carlisle for Pitt in 1915.)

A special meeting of the Athletic Council was held Monday afternoon, November 15, and Bohler sent off a telegram asking for additional information on guarantees and other pertinent considerations. By return wire he received reassurance on every count, including permission to bring a twenty-two-man squad, large for that day. (As it turned out, WSC used only fifteen players in the game).

So Washington State, 6-0, was off to Pasadena. There was wild jubilation among WSC students, alumni and fans, and considerable consternation in Seattle. The Sun Dodgers, 7-0 in 1915 and unbeaten over eight straight seasons (only twice tied) under Coach Gilmour Dobie, the sour Scot, were staying home—again!

The "Mystery Man"

Who was "W. S. Kienholz," the signer of that telegram inviting WSC to Pasadena in 1915?

The Pullman *Herald*, Spokane *Spokesman-Review* and the *Evergreen* reported at the time that it was "the former WSC coach." However, in his book on the Rose Bowl, sportswriter Rube Samuelsen says "Wayne S. Kienholtz" was Tournament football committee chairman the following year, 1916, and was instrumental in getting the University of Pennsylvania to come West for the New Year's Day game in 1917 to meet Oregon. There is a "W. S. Kienholtz" (note spelling) listed on the Tournament of Roses Board of Directors in 1915.

On the other hand, William Simms Kienholz, the old WSC football coach, definitely was in southern California in 1915. The Alumni magazines at WSC and the University of Minnesota, Kienholz's alma mater, carried items saying he was serving on the Tournament of Roses committee. "W. S. Kienholz (note spelling), Minnesota," also is listed in Samuelsen's book on the Rose Bowl as Referee of both the 1917 and 1918 Tournament of Roses games, and as Head Linesman for the 1921 game. For a number of years, "W. S. Kienholz," definitely the former WSC coach, was Director of Vocational Education in the Los Angeles School System.

The old WSC coach was something of a will-o'-the-wisp in the football coaching fraternity. In 1904, after graduation from Minnesota, Kienholz was Head Football Coach at North Carolina A & M (now North Carolina State), in Raleigh. His team posted a 3-1-2 mark. The next year, Kienholz moved on to the University of Colorado, and his team at Boulder went 6-2-1 in the fall 1905.

•

Lone Star Dietz *signed a contract for $4,000 for the 1916 football season. "Largest salary ever for a football coach in the Pacific Northwest," the Pullman* Herald *reported.* (J. Fred Bohler, *Professor of Physical Education and Director of Athletics, made $2,500 that year.*)

•

William Kienholz at Washington State College in 1909. (Manuscripts, Archives, and Special Collections, Washington State University Libraries)

"There are indications [from newspaper articles] which suggest that Coach Kienholz favored a looser interpretation of the rules on amateur athletics, or at least wanted to be on a par with other coaches who ignored the rules and recruited and paid athletes with university funds," wrote Colorado Archivist Cassandra Volpe tactfully, after some research into the coach's one season at Boulder.

In 1907, Kienholz showed up at Alabama Poly (now Auburn University). A shake-up in the Athletic program there following the 1906 season saw "Iron Mike" Donahue relieved after three years as Head Football Coach and Kienholz installed as Head Coach—with, get this, Donahue as his assistant! Alabama Poly posted a 6-2-1 record in 1907, but at season's end Kienholz was out and Donahue came back as Head Coach.

In 1908-1909 Kienholz was "Head of Calisthenics" at Spokane High School. He also coached Spokane to first place in the State Interscholastic Track Meet in the spring of 1909, then came to WSC that fall bringing with him two fine athletes from the Lilac City, a nephew, Edgar "Eddie" Kienholz, and Wes "Moose" Engelhorn, both of whom made the Varsity as freshmen. Engelhorn started for the WSC football team that fall and also for Doc Bohler's Northwest Conference championship basketball team of 1909-1910, and then transferred to Dartmouth in the Ivy League as a sophomore and starred there. Eddie Kienholz became a three-sport star at WSC, one of the early-day legends.

Coach Kienholz was at Washington State but one year. His 1909 team was unscored upon until the second half of the final regular season game against Whitman (and WSC defeated the Missionaries 23-6), but then lost 11-6 to Denver University in a post-season game in Spokane on December 4 to finish 4-1.

The following spring, just as he was preparing the 1910 baseball team for its season, Coach Kienholz was dismissed. The Pullman *Herald* for April 15 reported, in one long-winded sentence:

> The board [of Regents] took up the case of Coach Kienholz, which has attracted so much attention from the public press of late, and found that while the evidence was not sufficient to connect the coach of offering money to Otto "Big" Deanor [sic] and [Bill] Miner to play on the football team last fall that the language used in three letters written by Keinholz [sic] to Deanor was coarse and was suggestive of corrupt influences to induce Deanor to return to play football, and was unbecoming of a member of the faculty [he also taught Botany], and on account of these letters Mr. Keinholz would be relieved from any further duties or responsibilities in connection with the athletic teams or college classes.

In one of the letters in question, Kienholz had advised Deaner: "Don't take any of Rheiny's bull-con. . . . Hold them up and make them rattle their junk." (Kienholz obviously was referring to Walter "Rheiny" Rheinschild, who had preceded him as football coach at WSC in 1908, but what team Rheinschild might have been "recruiting" Deaner for is lost in the mists of time. "Rheiny" by this time was out of coaching and practicing law in Los Angeles.)

William S. Kienholz died in Seattle on September 20, 1958, at age eighty-two. In his obituary in the Seattle *Times*, Kienholz is identified as "the former football coach at Washington State" and the man who, "In 1916 [sic], as athletic chairman of the Tournament of Roses committee, invited Washington State to the Rose Bowl."

The old coach apparently held no grudges.

Roses are Red! The West Redeemed

The selection of Washington State to represent the West in the Tournament of Roses football game in Pasadena, California, on January 1, 1916, had many interesting angles, not least of which was the selection process itself.

Rube Samuelsen, in his book *The Rose Bowl Game*, said Tournament officials "naturally turned to the Northwest" where both WSC and Washington were unbeaten.

> Noting with pleasure that the Cougars [oops, Rube, not until 1919] had scored a 29 to 0 win over the Oregon Aggies [Oregon State], who had subdued the Michigan Aggies [Michigan State], 20 to 0, who in turn had beaten Fielding Yost's Michigan eleven, 24-0, an invitation to meet Brown was dispatched forthwith.

All of which brought this bit of doggerel from sportswriter Grantland Rice:

> How sad to think about the slump
> That's soaked the distant West!
> To think how far their teams have dropped
> Below the Laureled crest;
> To think that in the land along
> The old Pacific's rim
> They haven't any team at all
> From all their ragged hosts—
> Except a team that crushed a team
> That smashed a team of Yost's.
> Ah yes, it's sad to think about
> The old Pacific slump,
> The way the West has hit the chute
> And hit it with a bump;
> But when you speak of things like this,
> In a manner somewhat free,
> Don't mention it at Michigan
> Or up at M.A.C.;
> They haven't any stuff at all
> To call for autumn boasts
> Except a team that smeared a team
> That smashed a team of Yost's.*

Members of the Commercial Club in Wenatchee gathered around on January 1, 1916, to get telegraphic reports on the WSC-Brown game sent directly to the club. J. L. Miller and L. E. Swanson, of Pullman, dared each other to go to the WSC-Brown game in 1916. Two days before the game they hopped on the OWR&N and got to Pasadena just before the kickoff. Two days later they were back home.

After "Hurry Up" Yost's Michigan team dismembered Stanford 49-0 in 1902, the Tournament of Roses Association discarded the idea of a football game as a feature of its annual floral festival and in 1904 introduced—it could only happen in southern California—chariot

---

* Rice is better remembered for some lines he wrote nine years later: "Outlined against a blue-gray October sky, the Four Horsemen rode again." (Following Notre Dame's win over Army in 1924.)

Coach Lone Star Dietz and his crimson-robed "Warriors" of 1915. Dietz's Indian heritage carried over to his football teams at WSC, which were often referred to as the "Warriors" or "Indians" in the era before the "Cougar" became the college mascot. Coach Dietz, back row, left; and Trainer J. Fred "Doc" Bohler, back row, right. (Manuscripts, Archives, and Special Collections, Washington State University Libraries)

racing! (They almost killed the Tournament president in 1907; his horses spooked and ran away with the chariot as he was making like Ben Hur.)

In 1915, after everyone was sick and tired of the chariot races, now handled by professional drivers and "often 'fixed'," Samuelsen contended, Tournament officials looked around for another feature attraction to fill out the day's program after the Rose Parade. They decided to go back to football.

It was not surprising that Washington State got the nod over Washington. In that pre-television era size of viewing audience did not dictate choice. WSC was unbeaten and, as illustrated by those comparative scores in Granny's poem, had some "national" stature.

In addition, Athletic Director "Doc" Bohler and the colorful "Lone Star" Dietz clearly stood out over Washington and its dour Gilmour Dobie, one of the most unpopular coaches on the Coast.

Dobie's Sun Dodgers won fifty-eight games in nine seasons at the UW without defeat, which in itself made him easy to hate. His teams played forty-eight games at home; in only three seasons while Dobie was coach did Washington play two games on the road, and on two of those occasions his team was tied. Dobie never brought his team to Pullman. WSC and the UW met only once on the East side of the Cascades, in 1910 in Spokane, with Washington winning 16 to 0. Apparently, when Johnny Bender came back to WSC in 1912 as Graduate Manager and Football Coach, he was lured into signing a three-year agreement to play the UW in Seattle with assurances of big pay-days for the Pullman school.

When Bender was fired and Doc Bohler was appointed Athletic Director in 1915, he stood his ground and refused to play in Seattle as Dobie demanded. This insistence on the home field backfired on Washington. A game between the two Pacific Northwest powers in the 1915 season would almost certainly have determined the West's representative in Pasadena on January 1, 1916.

Rose Bowl historian Samuelsen notes that Washington State also got support from one of its victims in that 1915 season, the University of Montana.

"'We had the honor,' the Montana spokesman wrote (to the Tournament committee) 'of being the only team this year to score against Washington State. The Cougars [*sic*] are at least three touchdowns better than Washington.'"

A severe case of "Rose fever" broke out among WSC students and alumni following the announcement that Washington State had been selected to play in the New Year's game against Brown.

Frank T. "Cack" Barnard, the great old all-around athlete from the 1900-1903 era, was WSC Registrar at the time and he was appointed to coordinate the effort to "get the attendance of all former Washingtonians now living in California at the game."

C. C. Ockerman, a 1907 WSC graduate living in Long Beach, published a notice in several southern California newspapers notifying alumni in the area that a special WSC rooters' section was being arranged, and said he would serve as "Yell Leader for the old timers." The Pullman *Herald* reported that Ockerman was working on plans to secure a large attendance at the contest, with support from P. R. Feddersohn, of Puente, California, Class of 1915.

Walter M. Rheinschild, the WSC football coach in 1908, wrote to Doc Bohler from Los Angeles where he was practicing law asking for a list of college songs and yells "so boosters can practice." Doc told the press that "'Rheinie' will lead the LA delegation to the game."

On campus, the Pullman *Herald* reported that twenty-one team members had voted Carl Dietz, fullback, halfback and end, the "most valuable player and the man most inspirational to his teammates." Dietz edged out center Al Langdon by two votes and won a $30 suit from Essex Custom Tailoring of Rochester, New York. "David G. Kuehl of Thornton, well-known baseball player (he was a great catcher in 1912-1914), is local representative of the company," the *Herald* story added.

The WSC team and coaches, along with the official party headed by Athletic Director Bohler, who also served as Trainer, left Pullman December 21 by train for Los Angeles. Special automobile tours were arranged for the group during stopovers in Portland and San Francisco. The group arrived in Los Angeles on Christmas Day and the team was headquartered at the Hotel Maryland in Pasadena.

There are so many versions of the story about how Lone Star Dietz finagled jobs for his ball players as extras to provide football action scenes for a movie, *Tom Brown at Harvard,* rather than just working out twice a day before the game, it is difficult at this distance to separate fact from fiction. But the WSC players did do some scrimmaging for the movie cameras, and they were paid for it. Whether they took their earnings, pooled the money and bet on themselves against Brown and made a bundle, is anybody's guess now, since all those players, Dietz and Bohler are gone.

One yarn does hold up pretty well, and that's the story about how the WSC players double-crossed the movie director and laid out his star when they were supposed to let him run through them for a touchdown. Ace Clark often told that story, and Dick Hanley, a halfback on the WSC team, repeated it to author Rube Samuelsen for his book on the Rose Bowl. Clark and Hanley said the players did their bit and allowed the movie's "overstuffed hero" to get across the goal line, but then about four of them leveled on him. "When we hit him the ball squirted 30 feet into the air. . . ." Samuelsen quoted Hanley.

One thing is certain, Coach Dietz himself was smitten by the movie bug and later did try for some acting roles, apparently with little success.

The star of the Brown University team in 1915 was halfback Fritz Pollard, a splendid speedster who a year later became the first black to make Walter Camp's All-America team.

Another story about Dietz and his method of getting his players "up" for a game rings true because it comes from a variety of sources. One is Kenny Gray, of Pullman, who was still chuckling over the yarn in 1988 at age ninety-two.

"A day or so before the game, Dietz cornered every starter—individually—and told him that WSC's only chance against Brown was to stop Pollard. 'And I'm counting on you to do the job!'"

Gray said Dietz swore each player to secrecy because, he said, "he didn't want the others to know how much the coach feared Pollard."

As it turned out the weather and field conditions were ideal for Washington State, which played a power game, and just about the worst thing imaginable for Brown and the speedy Pollard. It snowed in Pasadena two days before the game, the first snow there in more than a decade, and New Year's Day dawned to rain.

The Tournament committee had brought in extra seating, raising the capacity of the old park to about 20,000. Shortly before game time less than 5,000 were in the stands. (To appreciate how Californians react to inclement weather, Coach Jim Sutherland liked to tell the story about taking a team down to Berkeley in 1960 to play California. It was

Doc Bohler was appointed to the National Intercollegiate Basketball Rules Committee in 1915.

overcast when the plane landed at the Oakland/Alameda airport and the first guy Suds saw when he got off the plane was Tom Gunnari, who was coaching at a high school just a few miles away. "What are you doin' here, Tommy? Don't you have a game?" 'Oh, yeah, Coach,' Gunnari said kinda sheepishly. 'We got rained out.' Then he laughed and said 'I never played on a day this good in four years at Kelso.'")

There's another story, and it does sound plausible, that tournament officials wanted to cancel that game in 1916, but Doc Bohler told the WSC players to go on out and start warming up.

Meanwhile, back in Pullman, a lot of folks started gathering at Thorpe's Smoke House down on Main street. The Pullman *Herald* had announced on New Year's eve that a direct wire from Pasadena to Pullman would bring local fans news concerning the progress of the big intersectional football game. "Excitement concerning the game is at a high point," the *Herald* said. Kickoff was scheduled at two o'clock and the first telegraphic report was supposed to arrive about 2:30, then they'd come in at five-minute intervals. When the game started, the place was packed and people were standing out in the street. The man who read the telegraph reports would read them once for those inside the Smoke House and then go out on the sidewalk and read them again to the rest of the crowd.

The first half was scoreless, although Brown held an edge and once penetrated to the WSC six before losing the ball on downs. The field, which was bad at the start, was a quagmire by halftime. It rained for much of the game.

After the intermission, Washington State's power game started to tell. Fullback Carl "Red" Dietz and halfbacks Ralph Boone and Benton Bangs did most of the damage on straight-ahead plunges behind the hard-charging forward wall composed of Clarence Zimmerman and Ray Loomis at ends; Clark and Bert Brooks, tackles; guards "Hack" Applequist and Fred Fishback; and Langdon at center. "Si" Stites and Jack Finney also got in the game at line positions, and Dick Hanley and Basil Doane played in the WSC backfield.

In the third quarter, after a fifty-yard punt by Dietz had put Brown deep in a hole, the defense held and WSC got good field position on the return kick. Boone ran twenty-one yards to set up the first touchdown and scored on a three-yard run. Quarterback Art "Bull" Durham drop-kicked the first of two straight extra points, an amazing feat in itself considering the condition of the field.

Seconds before the game ended, Dietz pounded over from four yards out for WSC's second score. He later was praised by Referee Walter Eckersall, from the University of Chicago, foremost official of the day, as the game's outstanding player.

WSC piled up 313 yards rushing, a total which stood as a Rose Bowl record for a number of years.

The Wild West was wild again!

"The largest and most enthusiastic athletic demonstration ever held in the Pacific Northwest was staged in Pullman and on the campus Thursday morning [January 6] when the returning Washington State players, conquerors of Brown university's team, were greeted by a wild,

Trivia Tricker: Who started the Rose Bowl? Clarence Zimmerman, *WSC end from Everett, kicked off to start the 1916 Tournament of Roses game, first in the continuing series which became the "Rose Bowl."*

Pullman welcomes Lone Star Dietz and his winning "Warriors" home from their 1916 Rose Bowl victory. (Manuscripts Archives, and Special Collections, Washington State University Libraries)

howling, cheering throng that overflowed the O. W. R. & N. [Oregon-Washington Railroad and Navigation Company, a subsidiary of the Union Pacific] station grounds and extended up Grand street at least a block," the Pullman *Herald* reported. "Classes at college were dismissed, the high school students were excused and all business houses closed, the hundreds of students, business men and residents flocking to the depot to witness the arrival of the conquering heroes and give vent to their joy over the victory."

Many of the businessmen, led by Mayor Harley Jackson, were dressed in full Sioux Indian regalia, complete with blankets and wearing feathers, and carried signs, some which read: "Lone Star! Lone Star! Yip. Yip. You! How We Love You! Oh, You Sioux!" Team members and coaches were loaded on a sled which was then pulled through the streets by 400 students, with another 600 persons following the entourage.

Noticeable by his absence was Coach Dietz. The Los Angeles *Express* reported that when the victorious Washington State team had left for home on January 2, Coach Dietz had stayed behind and "is going to be a movie actor. . . ."

Waiting in Spokane for the celebration to run its course, and to let the players and coaches—as well as departing President Bryan—"have their day," as he put it, was Ernest O. Holland, former Superintendent of Schools of Louisville, Kentucky, who, as of January 1, 1916, had become the State College's new President.

In another fourteen years, and four football coaches later, President Holland himself would be able to participate in a similar, though not quite as exuberant, celebration.

An Unexpected Casualty

Washington State's football fortunes continued to prosper under Coach "Lone Star" Dietz for two seasons after the great win over Brown in the 1916 Tournament of Roses renewal.

In 1916, WSC lost only to Oregon State, 13-10, and Oregon, 12-3, and Oregon wound up in Pasadena on January 1, 1917, representing the

West and defeating Pennsylvania 14-0. The loss to OAC in the season opener at Pullman was a heartbreaker. Whitney Gill recovered a fumble in the WSC end zone in the first quarter and the Aggies added two thirty-yard field goals by George Conn in the third and fourth periods. "Bull" Durham kicked a forty-yard fielder for WSC before the half and Ralph Boone ran in a fourth-quarter touchdown, but it was not enough.

Oregon quarterback Shy Huntington scored all his team's points in the 12-3 win over WSC at Portland. The game was tied 3-3 starting the fourth quarter. Huntington kicked a thirty-three-yard goal in the first quarter and Durham tied it for WSC in the third with a twenty-six-yarder. But Huntington added a touchdown and a thirty-yard field goal in the fourth period for the winning margin.

That game, on November 11, 1916, in Portland's Multnomah Stadium, marked the last loss for a Dietz-coached WSC team. Washington State won its final two games that season. Then, after a scoreless tie in the 1917 opener against a team of Army all-stars at Tacoma, WSC won six straight games. The only points scored against that 1917 team were on a fifty-three-yard field goal by Oregon quarterback Bill Steers as the Webfoots lost to WSC 26-3 at Pullman in the second game of the 1917 season on October 20.

Benton "Biff" Bangs put on a great show in that Oregon game, scoring all of WSC's twenty-six points. He ran for three touchdowns, returned an Oregon punt seventy-two yards for another score, and kicked two extra points!

Bangs, who also carried the nickname "Bing," was a great runner. Benton really never received the honors he was due. In the 1919 Tournament of Roses game, playing left half for the Mare Island Marines against Great Lakes, Bangs (with some help from right half Fred Glover, also from WSC) was tearing the Navy line apart with drives over tackle. With a first down on the Great Lakes eight yard line, and the Navy leading only 3-0, Mare Island quarterback Bill Steers, as one scribe put it, "begins to perform like a man from Marblehead, Vermont." (It's in Massachusetts, but those Los Angeles writers always were a little weak in geography.) Steers sent Bangs around end for a loss of two and then had him throw two straight passes, the second of which was intercepted.

Captain Cecil Cave leads the Washington State team down to Rogers Field from the dressing rooms in the old gym, far to the right. This photograph was taken in 1909, just prior to WSC's 38-0 win over Whitworth College. (Manuscripts, Archives, and Special Collections, Washington State University Libraries)

The 1918 All-Pacific Coast Service football team, selected by Coach Lone Star Dietz, *had* Clarence Zimmerman *and* Roy Hanley *at ends;* Fred Hamilton, *right guard;* Dick Hanley, *quarterback; and* Benton Bangs, *left half. All were from WSC and all except Hamilton, who played for the Army Air Corps team at Mather Field (Sacramento), were off Dietz's Mare Island Marines Rose Bowl team.*

That 1917 team at Washington State might have been Dietz's best. WSC routed Oregon, the team that just the year before had gone to Pasadena and beaten Penn, then shut out Whitman, Idaho, Oregon State, Montana, and Washington to finish 6-0-1. The only thing that kept WSC out of the Tournament of Roses game was World War I.

"Feelers went out to Michigan, Pittsburgh, Ohio State, and Georgia Tech, but none manifested interest," Rube Samuelsen wrote. "Washington State, considered as a Western representative, also demurred." Tournament of Roses officials decided on an all-service game and the Mare Island Marines wound up defeating an Army team from Camp [Fort] Lewis 13-0 at Pasadena on January 1, 1918.

WSC's 14-0 win over the Sun Dodgers in the final game of that 1917 season (in Seattle of course) was the last game "Lone Star" Dietz coached at Pullman. There's a sidelight to that game, unconnected with Dietz but nevertheless interesting considering a later happening in the series. Washington put up quite a pre-game fuss over the eligibility of C. C. "Digger" Boone, a WSC halfback from Chehalis. Shortly before the game Boone was drafted. (The *Evergreen* said he was at Camp Lewis but had not been sworn in, which hardly seems likely.) The Army gave him permission to play, but Washington's Faculty Athletic Representative— not acting entirely on his own initiative one would guess—filed a protest. Boone did not play, but WSC didn't need him. Washington didn't make a first down!*

At the conclusion of the 1917 season, as America's mobilization for war became total, Washington State gave up football and many of its players and coaches entered the service. Coach Dietz left for Mare Island, California, where, as a civilian, he coached the Marine Corps football team in the 1918 season—and right into the Rose Bowl on January 1, 1919! Seven WSC players were members of that Mare Island team which went through an eight-game schedule unscored upon: Clarence Zimmerman, Mike Moran, Benton Bangs, Fred Glover, Lloyd Gillis, and the Hanley brothers, Dick and LeRoy.

Since Mare Island had played in the 1918 Rose Bowl game, a certain inter-service jealousy developed among military higher-ups about a repeat performance. A post-season playoff was ordered and the Marines had to play two additional games. They proceeded to beat Mather Field 32-14 and Balboa Park Navy 12-7 to earn a shot at Great Lakes. Those additional games were costly, however.

The Marines lost several key players with injuries, and regular quarterback Dick Hanley was hospitalized with pneumonia just before New Year's Day.

Five former WSC players started for Mare Island against Great Lakes, and a sixth , "Biff" Bangs, did not start but nonetheless starred for the Marines in a losing (17-0) cause. The incomparable Paddy Driscoll, at

---

*History has a way of repeating itself. Washington's ace passer, Don Heinrich, was inducted into the Army about a week before the WSC-UW game in Spokane in 1952. Seattle *Times* writer Dick Rockne recalled in his book on Husky football: "It took a weekend pass issued by 'understanding' officers at Fort Lewis to 'spring' him for the game." Heinrich quarterbacked the Huskies to a 33-27 win.

quarterback, and George Halas, right end, were standouts for the winning Navy team.

"Lone Star" Dietz had been riding the crest of a wave of popularity which began with his first championship team at WSC in 1915 and continued through 1916, 1917 and well into 1918 as his teams at Washington State and Mare Island won game after game. The flamboyant Dietz was the toast of the West; whatever he did was headlined and he was idolized throughout the press. He was, as they say, "great copy!"

Following that unbeaten season of 1915, the WSC yearbook noted of Dietz: "He woke up the alumni, put the state college and the entire state on the football map to stay, and now has at least a life job open to him."

Short life!

Late in 1918, rumbles about Dietz's status with regard to the Selective Service System began to be heard. First it was learned that the WSC Athletic Council had withdrawn his name from consideration for the football post at Washington State for the 1919 season. Then, the Spokane *Review* used that dreaded word, "Slacker," in a headline and said that Dietz had registered for the draft as an "Indian, and not a citizen." It got rougher. The newspaper editorialized:

> [Dietz is] Now employed at Mare Island, and by the government, if you please, to coach a team of full blooded American boys, all of whom are true blue, otherwise they would not have enlisted.

Eventually the matter got into Federal Court. In February of 1919 Dietz was indicted by a Spokane grand jury on a charge of false draft registration, but on June 27, after a lengthy legal struggle, a jury there failed to reach a verdict. Polled, it stood 9-3 for acquittal.

It was a sad ending to a great coaching tenure. But WSC had not given up on Carlisle and hired Captain Gustavus "Gus" Welch, quarterback of Pop Warner's best Carlisle team (1911). Welch, an army officer who had seen considerable combat with U.S. forces in World War I, was still in France at the time of his hiring.

"Lone Star" Dietz went on to other head coaching jobs, at Purdue, Louisiana Poly, Wyoming, Haskell Institute and, ironically, Albright College, Doc Bohler's old school, and he coached frosh teams at Stanford and Temple for Warner. All told, Dietz had six unbeaten teams, his last at Albright in 1937. When the Pennsylvania school gave up football in 1943, during World War II, Dietz left coaching.

Early in 1956, when WSC was looking for a football coach to replace Alton S. Kircher, fired at the end of the 1955 season, who should show up in Pullman but "Lone Star" Dietz.

"Just paying a visit to an old friend" (his 1915 Captain, Asa V. "Ace" Clark, by this time a State Senator and prominent Whitman County farmer), the seventy-two-year-old Dietz said, but insiders knew he had approached Athletic Director Stan Bates about the WSC job.

It was sad, but Bates and President C. Clement French handled it well. The old coach was honored at a hurriedly-arranged luncheon at the Washington Hotel in Pullman, and he and Captain Clark sat side by side at the head table swapping stories of happier days.

Forty years after he directed WSC to victory in the 1916 Rose Bowl game, Coach Lone Star Dietz returned to the campus and was awarded the highly prized "Varsity W" blanket by President C. Clement French. (Manuscripts, Archives, and Special Collections, Washington State University Libraries)

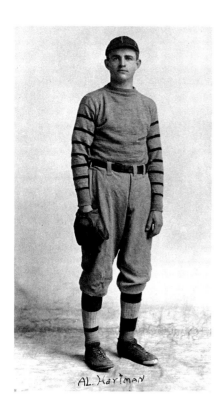

Al Hartman, greatest of the early-day pitchers at WSC. (Manuscripts, Archives, and Special Collections, Washington State University Libraries)

At halftime of the WSC-Oregon State basketball game in Bohler Gym on January 7, 1956, President French presented Dietz with the school's ultimate sports award, a Crimson and Gray Varsity blanket. It was something the old coach should have received in 1917 after three great seasons and an unsurpassed coaching record of seventeen wins and a tie in twenty games. No one since has even come close to his .895 winning percentage.

William H. "Lone Star" Dietz, nearing 80, died of cancer in Reading, Pennsylvania, on July 20, 1964. In 1983 he was elected to WSU's Athletic Hall of Fame.

Hartman and Moss

Greatest of the early-day pitchers at Washington State was Al Hartman, a crafty left-hander from Tacoma who pitched four seasons, 1913-1916. Hartman still is in the Cougar baseball record books for complete games pitched (career, thirty-one, and single season, fifteen) marks that very likely could stand for all time. He's tied with another left-hander, Elwood Hahn, of Billings, Montana (1958-1960), in shutouts with six, and ranks third in career wins, twenty-four, and fifth in games started, thirty-four.

Hartman was the first Washington State pitcher to throw a no-hitter. He achieved the pitcher's dream on May 2, 1916, in his senior season, beating Gonzaga University 8-0, in Spokane, and remains one of only two WSU pitchers to have hurled a no-hitter over a full nine innings, in college. Right-hander Eric Wilkins, of Seattle, who later pitched for Cleveland of the American League, no-hit Oregon State for nine innings on May 7, 1976, at Pullman, in beating the Beavers 1-0. Lefty Cliff Chambers, of Bellingham, who pitched for the Cougars in 1941-1942, threw a no-hitter for the Pittsburgh Pirates against Boston on May 6, 1951, winning 3-0.

Norm Moss, of Pullman, a strong right-hander, pitched with Hartman all four years, giving Washington State one of its all-time best mound duos. Moss also was a fine basketball player, having been Captain of Doc Bohler's championship team of 1916. Hartman and Moss pitched on WSC teams which won four straight Northwest Conference Eastern Divisions championships.

In their freshman year of 1913, Moss and Hartman shared pitching honors, accounting for all fourteen decisions in an 11-3 season! Moss was 7-2, Hartman 4-1. There was no playoff, but the *Chinook* claimed WSC won the Conference title on the basis of its .875 won-lost record, compared with .500 for both Oregon State and Washington.

As sophomores, Hartman and Moss again dominated WSC pitching, working in 16 of the 18 games played in 1914 and posting a combined record of 10-6. Moss was 5-2, Hartman 5-4 (but two of his losses were to professional teams, the Spokane Indians and the Chicago Giants, in exhibition games). WSC lost the Northwest title to Oregon in the play-offs at Eugene. Moss was beaten 2-1 and Hartman 4-1 on June 1-2. WSC lost third baseman Al Anderson, of Spokane, with a broken ankle two days before the play-offs began.

As juniors, Hartman and Moss accounted for seventeen decisions (and a rare tie) in 22 games. WSC and Gonzaga played to a 2-2 tie on April 24, 1915, at Pullman, but Gonzaga forfeited the game and it went into the record books as a 9-0 win for WSC because the Zags left after nine innings to catch a train. Hartman pitched the entire game and was credited with the victory. For the season, Hartman was 11-1 (his only loss being to the Spokane Indians of the professional Northwestern League), and Moss was 3-2 (he also lost a game to Spokane).

In the East-West play-offs at Pullman on May 31 and June 1 following the 1915 season, Hartman and Oregon State's William "Bickey" Williams pitched both games and Hartman won both. WSC catcher Dave Kuehl threw out four Oregon State base runners trying to steal second in the first game and WSC won 4-2. In the second game, Hartman and Williams battled twelve innings before WSC won 4-3.

Talk about your "Iron Men!"

Another hero of that series for WSC was Fenton Smith, of South Bend. A "sub," Smith hit a "slashing double" for two runs in the first game, and scored first baseman Fred Schroeder (San Diego, California) with another double in the second game to win it for WSC.

As seniors in 1916, Hartman and Moss again carried the pitching load as WSC won its fourth straight division crown. The pair had a combined record of 9-4-1 in eighteen games that season. The tie was Hartman's, 0-0 versus Oregon State in the season opener at Pullman on April 14, and again Hartman and Williams were mound opponents. The game was called after ten innings due to a prearranged time limit. The *Oregonian* termed it "One of the best baseball games ever played in college circles in the Pacific Northwest." (If this game were included among his career shutouts, Hartman would have seven. So it sort of balances out that "forfeit" from Gonzaga in 1915.)

Hartman was 5-2-1 in 1916, losing only to the Spokane Indians. He also led the WSC hitters with a stout .486 average in thirty-seven at-bats, including six doubles and two home runs. Moss was 4-2 on the season, and one of his losses was to the Spokane pros.

There was no East-West playoff at the end of the 1916 season. The *Chinook* says Oregon State "forfeited the championship" after Coach Bohler had made travel arrangements to go to Corvallis.

Johnny Bender was the WSC coach in the 1913, 1914, and 1915 seasons. Doc Bohler took over in 1916.

Some of the other stars of those championship seasons were Ross McElroy, Spokane, Captain and first baseman in 1913; Kuehl, who played outfield and caught (and hit .366 in 1915); Roy Bohler, shortstop; Eddie Kienholz, second base; Joe Lester, Spokane, 2B and SS; Cliff Casad, Bremerton, Captain and first base, 1914 (hit .395 and led Conference in stolen bases); Fred Schroeder, catcher; Al Anderson, Captain and third base, 1915; Lyman Passmore, Fortuna, California, outfield; Howard Satterthwaite, Everett, and Lyman Stenberg, Puyallup, infielders; Norbert Kulzer, Valley, pitcher, and Guy Tulley, Puyallup, outfield.

One player from this era will be remembered both on and off the diamond. That's Basil "Snooky" Jerard, of Spokane, a utility man who lettered as an outfielder in his senior season. Jerard made a "circus

•

WSC won National Intercollegiate Rifle Championships in 1913 and 1915, competing with the top teams in the nation. In 1913, WSC defeated nearest rival Michigan State by 100 points. Shooting was done in a range built by students in the attic of the Men's gymnasium (between Holland Library and the CUB). Members of the 1915 team were William E. Saupe, *Snohomish;* Roy W. Nash, *Ellensburg;* William L. McCredie, *Sunnyside;* Kenneth D. Ross, *Spokane;* John E. Geue, *Snohomish;* Glenn C. Farnsworth, *Pullman; and* Ted H. Farr, *Albion.*

•

catch" to save that 0-0 tie for Hartman against Oregon State. Later a prominent architect in Seattle, Jerard and his wife, Ella (Alexander), a 1916 graduate in Home Economics and long-time high school teacher in Seattle, set up a $400,000 endowment for the WSU English department in 1982 "to promote the teaching and learning of literature."

At the completion of his collegiate career, Al Hartman signed a professional contract and pitched with the Tacoma Tigers of the Northwestern League. During the next four years he was with Topeka, Kansas, of the Western League; Spokane (as a pitcher and outfielder), and Vancouver, British Columbia, of the Pacific Coast International League. (His old battery-mate Fred Schroeder caught for Spokane in the 1917 season.)

Norm Moss took his WSC degree in Pharmacy and worked in that field for fifty-four years, mostly in eastern Washington. He remained an avid Washington State fan, seldom missing a home game in either basketball or baseball, and he was present when his record of twenty-eight consecutive scoreless innings (set in 1916, against Montana, Idaho, Whitman and Idaho) was broken by WSU's Eric Snider, of Concord, Calif., in 1978. Snider pitched 29 1/3 shutout innings against Lewis-Clark State, Central Washington, Brigham Young, Boise State, and Valdosta (Georgia) State. During that span Snider had three shutouts, and after his consecutive string was broken he came back to pitch nine scoreless innings against Maine, winner of the Riverside (California) Tournament in 1978.

Moss lived in Colfax the latter years of his life. He cut quite a swath on the local scene buzzing around in his vintage Porsche, wearing a sporty cap and smoking a big ceegar. Norm said his main claim to fame was getting ticketed by the State Patrol for driving over his age—when he was in his eighties! The stalwart old WSC right-hander died in Colfax in 1981 at age eighty-nine.

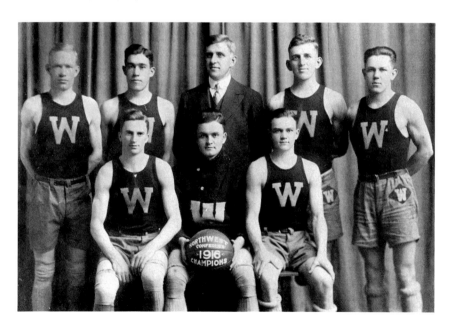

WSC's 1916 basketball team, the Northwest Conference champions that year. Front (left to right): Edwin Copeland, Norm Moss, Bob Moss. Back: Alvin Hildenbrand, A. Sorenson, Coach Bender, Roy Bohler, and Ivan Price. (Norman Moss)

Welcome to the PCC!

"When the Pacific Coast Conference comprising California, Oregon, Washington and O.A.C. (later called Oregon State University) was organized (in 1915), we hesitated to enter it, for we hardly felt equal to attain to their standard. . . ." Thus wrote Athletic Director J. Fred "Doc" Bohler in 1925, looking back over the first 33 years (of sports competition at Washington State College).

"In 1916 the question of our entrance into the Coast Conference came up again," Bohler recalled. "It was quite certain that Stanford would apply for admission. To stay out meant to eliminate ourselves from the group which had the standing and prestige and accept second rating. To enter meant a decided raise in standard. The [athletic] council decided in favor of applying for admission."

If there was hesitation on the part of the administration about entering the PCC, as Doc indicated, it was not apparent among the troops. Washington State fans were still basking in the euphoric afterglow of WSC's 14-0 victory over Brown, capping an undefeated football season for Coach "Lone Star" Dietz and his Crimson and Gray warriors. That win not only avenged the West, it sent WSC stock to an all-time high and got 1916 off to a "rosy" start throughout the Pacific Northwest.

The spectacular success of the WSC football team in the fall of 1915 was followed by the best basketball season in the school's history. Bohler's speedy quintet won eighteen of twenty-one games and captured the Northwest Conference title by sweeping two games each from Whitman College and Idaho in the final four contests of the season. Norm Moss captained that "home grown" team, which also featured two other Pullman boys, his brother, Bob, and Ivan Price, along with "Fast Eddie" Copeland, of Walla Walla; Al Sorenson, from Ellensburg; Alvin Hildenbrand, of Sunnyside; and Roy Bohler, of, uh, Reading, Pennsylvania. (Well, Roy really was a "local." He was Doc's younger brother, and lived with the Bohlers when he came out to Pullman in 1913 to enter college. Roy was a top-flight athlete, All-Northwest twice in both basketball, as a guard, and baseball, at shortstop.)

In the spring of 1916, pausing only to change uniforms, Doc Bohler directed the WSC baseball team to its fourth straight Eastern Division title with a perfect 6-0 record.

The "Harmony Doctor," as Bohler was dubbed early in his career at WSC by a grateful student body, missed a "Grand Slam" in coaching (championships in three major sports in one season) by one point when his 1916 track squad lost to Idaho 66-65. WSC won its dual meets with Whitman, Montana and the Spokane Athletic Club that spring to finish 3-1.

Imagine coaching basketball, baseball and track in the same year! Bohler did it from 1916 through 1920, while also serving as Athletic Director, Director of Physical Education, and Trainer for the football team! He also coached the wrestling team for a number of years. (Yet, in 1924, after three losing seasons in football, Regent A. W. Davis, a Spokane attorney, wanted Athletic Director Bohler fired—along with Football Coach A. A. Exendine. Ah, how soon they forget.)

•

Washington State runners dominated the Pacific Coast Conference two-mile between 1919 and 1953, winning the event nine times in twenty-three meets. "Jit" Smith *won the two-mile at the PCC meet the first two years it was held. He ran 9:59.4 in 1919 and 9:53.8 in 1920.* "Dixie" Garner *won the event in 1939-1940, running 9:22.1 and 9:12.5;* Noel Williams *won in 1941 at 9:23.8;* Bob Selfridge, *9:35.5 in 1948;* Bill Paeth, *9:29.3 in 1949; and* Al Fisher *won in 1952-1953, running 9:24.7 and 9:17.8.*

•

●

Katherine Ross, head of the Women's Department of Physical Education, named her selections for the 1919 Women's Honor Basketball Team: Agnes *and* Dorothea Sorenson, *seniors, Ellensburg;* Naomi Danielson *and* Roberta Houtchens, *both of Waitsburg, juniors;* Lois Comstock, *Alicel, Oregon, sophomore; and* Virginia Shaw, *Oregon City, Oregon, freshman.*

●

On December 2, 1916, at a meeting in Seattle, representatives of the four schools constituting the Pacific Coast Conference voted to admit Washington State and Stanford. There was some disagreement about Stanford because the Cardinal (it did not add "Indians" until 1930, and then dropped that nickname in 1972, about the same time the campus madness hit their marching band) had given up football in 1905 in favor of rugby. But Stanford agreed to resume football in 1918 and was voted in. The conference decided against admitting the University of Southern California at the same time WSC and Stanford came in. "Too far to travel," the PCC incumbents declared. USC entered in 1922, along with Idaho; Montana was added in 1924; and UCLA in 1928, rounding out the original ten-member Pacific Coast Conference.

If Washington State entered the PCC "hesitantly," it was not evident in the basketball scores that winter of 1916-1917. Rather, WSC "celebrated" its membership in the Pacific Coast's premier athletic organization by winning the conference basketball championship and recording the finest basketball season in the school's history.

Coach Bohler's team of 1917 posted a 25-1 record and was 8-1 in the PCC. The only defeat of the season came at the hands of the University of California, 28-20, in Berkeley. That loss was avenged the following night as WSC beat the Bears 32-29, and then went down the Peninsula and swept Stanford 36-18 and 23-15 at Palo Alto.

That great basketball team of 1917 was led by Captain Roy Bohler and Ivan Price, both All-Coast, with Bob Moss, Eddie Copeland and Al Sorenson, all five veterans of the Northwest Championship club of 1916, and newcomer Glenn Glover, another Pullman boy. An amazing statistic on that 1917 team is that it played eighteen of its twenty-six games on the road! This was no "home cookin'" outfit. Traveling by train to Oregon and California in early February of 1917, WSC won six of seven games played in the space of eleven days!

Of course the main reason that WSC was in a position to be invited to join the PCC in the first place was Bohler himself. In less than a decade after taking his first professional position out of college, the indefatigable Pennsylvanian had established himself as one of the top coaches and athletic administrators in the country.

In 1915, the same year the Pacific Coast Conference was born, Bohler was appointed by the National Collegiate Athletic Association to serve on the National Basketball Commission of the United States and Canada, a post he held through 1935. During this same period he also was the District Eight (Far West) representative to the NCAA, and for many years was a member of the Rules Committee of the National Intercollegiate Basketball Association and was "instrumental," according to biographer William Heath, in extending the end lines of the court beyond the backboard—two feet, and then four—which speeded up play greatly. Heath said Doc also was a key figure in the adoption of the ten-second (center) line in 1932.

J. Fred Bohler clearly was the man who put Washington State into the Pacific Coast Conference—"hesitant" though he may have been.

Bohler made all sports popular at Washington State. "Play the game!" was his motto, never mind whether it be at the intercollegiate, interscholastic, or elementary school level. Doc put all sports in the spotlight at WSC, and through innovative leadership and round-the-clock effort brought the school national exposure far beyond what might have been expected, considering its location and size.

At the end of his first year at Washington State, in the spring of 1909, Bohler organized and promoted the first statewide Interscholastic Track and Field Championship Meet. A "State" meet had been held at WSC as early as 1905, but it really was an East-side affair. Bohler's was truly statewide, with qualifying meets leading up to the main event in Pullman on May 22, 1909.

Broadway High School of Seattle walked off with the team title, winning ten of the fifteen events and collecting three second places. Sprinter Ira Courtney was the star of the meet, setting a state record in the 50 and tying the record in the 100.

Doc lived to see the Golden Anniversary of his state meet in 1960.

In 1910, Bohler introduced wrestling as an intercollegiate sport at WSC and coached the team for many years. He also started boxing and gymnastics and was the first instructor for both sports, in addition to coaching basketball and track and serving as the Trainer for the football squad. Bohler also was the WSC baseball coach for five seasons and was instrumental in getting a ski team started. His only failure, his son John said, was with lacrosse. "It just never caught on the way Dad thought it would."

Through all of this, Bohler never lost sight of the fact that a large majority of the students at any college could not compete at the intercollegiate level. He was the biggest booster there was for the intramural sports program at Washington State, one of the largest in the nation. Well into his fifties, Doc organized and played on the faculty teams in the intramurals. And when Bohler played he played fairly, squarely, and hard! And he always played to win.

They Won the Hard Way

When all the basketball records are posted, that team of 1917 has to be the most remarkable.

Eddie Copeland, looking back on that season at age ninety-four in 1989, said Doc Bohler's scheduling might have been the making of the team.

"Doc took us on a trip during the Christmas vacation that year. Might have been pretty good thinking on his part. It got us used to playing on strange floors," Copeland said.

WSC opened with Davenport High School on December 26 and played the Almira Athletic Club, Reardan A.C., Ritzville A.C., and Spokane A.C. on successive nights, winning all five games.

The starting lineup for WSC in all twenty-six games of the 1917 season had Roy Bohler at center (he was about five feet eleven inches, Copeland said, and the tallest man on the team); Ivan Price and Bob Moss forwards; and Copeland and Al Sorenson at guards. Glenn Glover was the sixth man and played in twelve games that season. Copeland said the team traveled with just six men.

•

Clement Phillips, of Spokane, a miler, was Captain of the 1919 WSC track team which posted a 2-0 season. "Jit" Smith and Eldon Jenne rated most of the headlines that year, but Overman Howell, of Wilbur, won the low hurdles in the Northwest meet and the highs in the PCC. Howell finished second to Stanford's Jess Wells in 15.4, but Wells was disqualified for knocking over too many hurdles!

•

"Price was an excellent shot and floor man," Copeland said, "I often thought of that when he went off to war (World War I) and was one of the first killed—how valuable he was to our team."

Copeland said he had a "trick" he used to get in position to grab the tip after each basket. (In those days, the center jump not only started each quarter, but was used after every basket.)

"I'd stick out my elbow so that it was just touching the man I was guarding. That way I could tell which way he was going to break."

Members of the Cougar Guard Chapter of the IKs, chained like a prison road gang to prevent the dreaded Sun Dodgers from stealing the stuffed cougar mascot they are carrying, march into Rogers Field just before a football game, circa 1920. (Manuscripts, Archives, and Special Collections, Washington State University Libraries)

They "Played Like Cougars!"

On October 25, 1919, an underdog Washington State College football team (under new coach Gus Welch, in his second game) went down to Berkeley and played the heavily favored, and unbeaten, California Bears to a standstill, winning 14-0. After that game a Bay Area sportswriter said the Pacific Northwest team "played like cougars!"

Back in Pullman, a jubilant WSC student body promptly picked this up and on October 28, 1919, officially adopted the name "Cougars" for its athletic teams.

At this time, the University of Washington athletic teams were known as "Sun Dodgers," a nickname that lasted until late in 1923 when UW teams officially became the "Huskies." Idaho teams did not become the "Vandals" until the 1920s. A sportswriter for the student newspaper, extolling the successes of Coach Hec Edmundson's basketball team, called them the "Heckers," which later became the "Wreckers." This then evolved into "Vandals." Oregon State's teams were the "Aggies" until about 1928 when the name was changed to the "Beavers."

Located in the rainy Willamette Valley, Oregon teams were called, appropriately, the "Webfoots" from a very early time. Newspaper headline writers found it difficult to handle and shortened it to "Ducks." But it was not until 1947 that Walt Disney's "Donald" was more or less officially adopted as the Oregon Duck. (Oregon sports press books still say "Ducks or Webfoots.")

It was nearly eight years after the nickname "Cougars" was adopted before Washington State had a live mascot. At least two stuffed cougars served as mascots between 1919 and 1927, and were the targets for several attempted cat-nappings, at least one of which was successful. In 1920, a group of University of Washington students, including Tom Martin, later to serve many years as Washington's Director of State Parks and State Treasurer, raided the WSC campus and snatched the symbolic Cougar out of its place of honor in the Gymnasium, then located between Holland Library and the CUB. This incident led to the formation of the "Cougar Guard," a group of students pledged to protect the WSC mascot. The group eventually became the Cougar Guard Chapter of Intercollegiate Knights at WSC.

On November 11, 1927, at halftime of the Homecoming football game with the University of Idaho, the first live cougar mascot was presented to the students of WSC by Washington Governor Roland H. Hartley.

The students first called their new mascot "Governor Hartley," in honor of its donor, but the governor (or a shrewd PR person acting for Hartley) gracefully declined the honor and suggested the name "Butch," for little Herbert L. "Butch" Meeker, of Spokane, the WSC football hero of the day. The name was quickly picked up by students and the cougar mascot became, first, "Butch Meeker," and then "Butch."

Butch I served as the WSC mascot nearly eleven years, dying on January 19, 1938, of infirmities of old age.

On September 24, at halftime of the 1938 season opener with Oregon, Governor Clarence D. Martin presented the student body with Butch II, a six-month-old cougar captured in the North Cascades. His was an ill-fated reign. WSC lost the game 10-2 (it was Oregon Coach Tex Oliver's inaugural), thereby ending the myth that WSC never lost a game at which a new mascot was introduced.

Butch II died on January 8, 1942, and Washington's new governor, Arthur B. Langlie, acted quickly to replace the deceased mascot. Just eleven days later, on January 17, at a WSC-Idaho basketball game in Bohler gym, the governor presented Washington State with twin cougar kittens, promptly dubbed "Butch III" and "Butch IV." Butch III served less than a year before he died. His twin proved to be the hardiest of all the mascots to that time, living to age thirteen.

During his reign, Butch IV traveled throughout the Pacific Northwest to games, served as the mascot for the battleship *USS Washington* during World War II, and kept alive the jinx over the University of Idaho football team that eventually reached twenty-eight years.

On October 23, 1954, Washington State lost to Idaho 10-0 at Pullman, ending a string of twenty-four consecutive wins begun in 1926 and interrupted only by ties in 1927 and 1950 and the war years of 1943-1944 when both schools gave up football. On December 19, less than three months after the traumatic loss, Butch IV was dead, from a broken heart many felt. But a post-mortem revealed that Butch IV, always referred to as "he," actually was "she," and WSC News Bureau Chief Denny Morrison promptly issued a bulletin changing the cause of death to "extended embarrassment."

In her thirteen years as mascot, Butch IV was involved in three "catnappings," with students at the nearby University of Idaho generally the culprits since she always reappeared on the Moscow campus, usually at a fraternity house. In the last of these incidents, in 1950, Butch was enticed into the back seat of a sedan (probably with some sort of "catnip") with only a cardboard partition between the animal and her abductors. After this episode, a burglar-proof cage was constructed with an alarm system wired into the campus police station.

With the death of Butch IV, Governor Langlie, back in office after a four-year hiatus between his first and second terms, presented Butch V during halftime of a basketball game with Oregon State on February 19, 1955. The Washington State basketball team, coached by Jack Friel, was so pumped up by the occasion that they handed the eventual Pacific Coast Champion Beavers their only conference loss, 68-66. (WSC was only 5-11 in the Northern Division that year.)

Butch V, described by keeper Elmer "Shorty" Sever, as "a downright mean cat," died in 1964, and six months later, in September of that year, his successor, Butch VI, was presented to the students by Governor Albert D. Rosellini.

In contrast to his predecessor, Butch VI was friendly and allowed students and children to pet him through the bars of his cage. Basketball coaches Marv Harshman and Jud Heathcote, neither known for exceptional courage, even entered the cage for publicity photos with Butch VI. Indeed, the animal was so tame that some students from Gonzaga University in Spokane cut a hole in the heavy wire cage (the alarm rang in the WSU campus police station but was deemed "another false alarm") and abducted the big cat. The Gonzaga students staged an elaborate ceremony at halftime of a basketball game with WSU in Spokane a few nights later and returned Butch VI.

"He was never the same," Shorty Sever always claimed. "After bein' up there with those Zags, he wouldn't eat meat on Friday. I hadda feed him fish!"

Butch VI, last in the sixty-one-year line of live cougar mascots, died August 24, 1978. He was fifteen years old, which Veterinarian Dr. John R. Gorham said translated to the human age of 105. Gorham, who treated the last three mascots, said Butch VI was suffering from arthritis and other ailments associated with advanced age and advised it be put to sleep. Butch did not go quietly.

WSU News Service Director Dick Fry prepared a release saying that Butch had been found dead in his cage. Fry then left the story with Assistant Manager Al Ruddy and went off to an Alumni Association meeting in Yakima. "Cut it loose when Gorham gives you the word," Fry said in parting.

Unfortunately, Gorham turned the euthanasia procedure over to an assistant who decided to remove the animal from its cage, haul him across campus to the Vet School and do the deed there. When the story came out that Butch VI had been found dead in his cage, the campus newspaper began to ask questions. Someone had seen the Cougar, alive, being taken out of the cage.

•

Glenn "Sap" Powell, '14, of Sedro Woolley, scored 101 points in the high jump, broad jump, and high hurdles in "three-plus" seasons on the WSC track team, and held the school record in the high jump at 5-9 3/4.

•

"Butchgate" the *Evergreen* headlined the story, and Fry, treed in Yakima, had to confess that the News Service release was erroneous.

WSU President Glenn Terrell, besieged by reporters, environmentalists, and a host of bleeding hearts, decided to conduct a poll of the student body to determine whether Butch VI should be replaced by another live mascot. Many alumni are still furious that 403 students (the number polled) could end such a long, and noble tradition.

Now, a student dressed in a "Cougar" suit and called "Butch" is present at sports events to assist the Yell Squad. Even the old landmark cougar cage which stood empty for a decade or so is gone, having been dismantled in 1987. At one time, Veterinary Dean Leo Bustad suggested putting domestic animals in the empty cage and having a "petting zoo" for children. The idea inspired no detectable enthusiasm outside Bustad's office staff.

The live animal mascot—with a few notable exceptions such as the Texas Longhorn, the Colorado Golden Buffalo, the Washington Husky (named "Sun Dodger," by the way), and, oh, yes, the University of Houston's cougar, "Shasta"—has become but a memory of a more innocent day in major college sports, a televisionless era of homecoming queens and parades, gigantic pep rallies with bonfires, games with set two o'clock kickoffs instead of "TBA," and athletes without scholarships playing on real grass for the cheers of their schoolmates and the glory of alma mater.

•

Captain A. L. King, *Entiat, 135;* (Oscar) Lincoln Cornwall, *Ellensburg, 158; and* Carl Pearson, *Trout Lake, 175, won Northwest wrestling titles in a tournament at Portland on March 20-21, 1914. WSC and the UW tied for the team title.*

•

A Cougar Vaults the Atlantic

"I was a proselyted athlete, but I didn't know it!"

Washington State isn't likely to be hauled up before the NCAA for illegal recruiting. The statute of limitations has run out on this one.

Eldon Jenne, WSC's first Olympic athlete, leaned back in his chair, smiled, and told the story of how it all happened back there in the spring of 1916.

"Strictly speaking, I was a professional before I went to college," the eighty-eight-year-old Jenne admitted in 1987.

"They used to have market days. First they'd be at Oak Harbor, and then Coupeville. There was jumping and running. Merchants would put up the money and the crowd would be there. I guess it paid off for everyone. I'd make $10 to $15 every Saturday. Never had any medals, just money. One Fourth of July, I won everything except the girls' baseball throw!"

Jenne grew up in Coupeville, on Whidbey Island. Just a few hundred people lived there in those days. His brother Frank, ten years older, went to Washington State and was a wrestler for Doc Bohler on the school's first team in 1910. Then he came back and was coaching at Mount Vernon when Eldon was a junior in high school over at Coupeville. Frank took out guardianship papers on his younger brother and "transferred me to Mount Vernon, where I could get more competition."

Eldon was a natural athlete. As a freshman at WSC in 1917-1918 he participated in football, basketball, baseball and track. He lettered four years in football and track and one year in baseball, giving up basketball "because it isn't very good for your legs if you're a jumper."

Eldon Jenne, greatest of the early-day vaulters. Note the bamboo pole. Imagine what Jenne could have done using one of today's "catapults!" (Manuscripts, Archives, and Special Collections, Washington State University Libraries)

But it's in track that Jenne is best remembered at Washington State. And it all started in a barn! Some of Eldon's friends out on Whidbey Island were vaulters.Used to cut their own poles in nearby woods.

"The place I really learned to get the vault form and get it correctly was in our barn. We put a rope down the center and there was maybe a hundred feet between the hay mows on either side. I'd stand up on a beam on one side and swing over on that rope and stand on the beam on the other side. When you stop and think about it, that was pretty much the pole vault form."

Jenne first attracted national attention in 1919 when he set a Pacific Coast Conference record in the pole vault at 12-10 1/8. The following year, at Stanford, Jenne improved the mark to 13-0 5/8, jumping with a pole borrowed from a Stanford vaulter. Two weeks later, in the Northern Division meet at Pullman, he improved this to 13-1, narrowly missing on a world record try at 13-3.

"There was always a problem with poles then," Jenne recalled. "We traveled by train and you couldn't take them into the Pullman with you. You just gave it to the baggage man and hoped it got there!"

Eldon Jenne vaulting in the Northwest Conference meet at Rogers Field in 1920. (Manuscripts, Archives, and Special Collections, Washington State University Libraries)

Jenne qualified for the U.S. Olympic team in 1920 at two meets, the Western Trials at Pasadena, which he won at 12-10, and the National Finals at Harvard, where he tied for second at 12-6. His WSC teammate, Charles "Jit" Smith, of Seattle, finest distance man on the Pacific Coast that year, was second in both the 5,000 and the 10,000 meters at Pasadena. For some reason, Smith entered only the 10,000 in the final Olympic Trials, finished sixth and narrowly missed qualifying for the team going to Antwerp, Belgium. Smith's time in the 5,000 at Pasadena was 14:59, 14 seconds behind the winner but still well below the American record, and about a minute faster than the winning times at Chicago and Philadelphia, where the other regional Olympic Trials were conducted. Why he chose to run the 10,000 in the finals is most puzzling. (Joseph Guillemot, of France, wound up winning the 5,000-meters at Antwerp in 14:55.6, only 3.4 seconds under Smith's time at Pasadena.)

One of the things Jenne remembered about the fourteen-day boat trip across the Atlantic was the small—about ten by fifteen feet—portable swimming pool set up on deck.

"They tied a rope around the swimmers, put 'em in the pool and they'd swim away there, but they couldn't go anywhere. The rest of us did some exercising and tossed medicine balls around," Jenne recalled, sixty-seven years later.

World War I had been over less than two years and the scars of battle—even some cannons—were still much in evidence in both Belgium and France. Jenne said the Olympic stadium at Antwerp was new, but the accommodations for the athletes weren't all that great.

"We stayed in a schoolhouse; bunked in one big room, a gymnasium I guess it was," Jenne said. "The ship that took us over was old and not very good. There was a lot of protesting, so the Olympic committee put us on a good ship coming home."

About twenty athletes competed in the pole vault at Antwerp. Frank Foss, of Cornell, won with a world record of 13-5. The U.S. won all three medals. Jenne was seventh.

Girls' Athletic Association changed its name to Women's Athletic Association in 1914.

"I had a bad day," Jenne said candidly. "It rained the day before and the runway was soft. They would smooth it off and roll it, and the first jumpers would have a pretty good track. But I was far down the list. Coming down on a soft runway, you don't have the speed. (Jenne had said he was not particularly fast, anyway.)

After the games, the U.S. team split up, one group going up into Scandinavia for a series of meets, the other, including Jenne, competed in Paris and London. He won in both cities at something over twelve feet.

"We were treated royally, banquets and shows. It was very nice," Jenne recalled. The athletes were in Europe about two weeks overall.

Some of the old Olympian's most vivid memories, however, six decades and more after the events, were connected with his football career at WSC rather than track, where he achieved his greatest fame.

"The first time we went down to California (in 1919) we got off the train at the Berkeley station and there was a whole flock of kids there. They had a chant: 'California's gonna beat the hell outta ya, California's gonna beat the hell outta ya!'"

"Well, we beat them 14 to nothing!" (That was the famous "Cougar" game.)

"We came back the next year and the same group was there with the same chant, and they did beat us." (And how! Andy Smith's "Wonder Team," with Harold "Brick" Muller, the All-America end and great passer, won 49-0. That was WSC's only loss of the season. It knocked the Cougars out of the Rose Bowl, put the Bears in, and they went on to beat Ohio State 28-0 on January 1, 1921 in Pasadena.)

"The sports writers (at California) had quite some slogans," Jenne remembered. "They'd write up different people, and I was one of those. They said I was 'as fast as a telegram,' Jenne laughed. "That's pretty fast!"

Jenne did all of the punting when he was playing at WSC and earned quite a reputation for his "coffin corner" placements.

"We played both ways, you know, offense and defense. I'd lose about ten pounds a game, but Monday it would all be back."

Washington State and Washington were feuding again in 1920, so athletic Director Bohler scheduled Nebraska at the end of that season. The teams met in Lincoln on Thanksgiving (November 25), and played one of the most exciting games in Cougar football history.

Nebraska scored in the first quarter on an eighty-one-yard pass, but WSC tied it when Lloyd Gillis plunged over and Frank Skadan, of

In the photo (handwritten): #4 The all important Relay. N.W. Conference Meet. W.S.C. Wins on this event.

Finish of the mile relay at the Northwest Conference meet at Rogers Field in 1919. (Ivan Shirrod)

Spokane, kicked the point. The Cornhuskers then scored thirteen unanswered points. Jenne remembered it as if it happened yesterday.

> I was playing safety. They didn't have a big stadium then; some of the fans watched from the sidelines. One fellow hollered at me, "You got a good team there," and I looked at him and said 'Are you kidding? We're 20 to 7 behind." "No, I think you've got a good team," the guy persisted.
>
> We beat 'em 21-20. Came up with a few passes. It was an amazing game.

And so it was. Gillis scored twice in the fourth quarter on runs of three and four yards, and Skadan kicked both points.

It was a landmark win for the Cougars and started a real "jinx" on the Cornhuskers. Nebraska still hasn't beaten WSU in three tries, all at Lincoln. Jim Sutherland's 1957 team bombed the Big Red 34-12, and Warren Powers began his brief coaching stay at Washington State with a major upset, 19-10 in 1977.

At 5-11 and 158 (he was a "slow developer," but went to 180 right out of college), Jenne had good upper body strength and strong legs, consistently winning points in the broad jump and high jump in addition to his specialty. He broke a leg in the UW football game on November 15, 1919 (both bones), and came back the following spring to make the Olympic team.

Pole vaulting in those years was "a world apart from the event now," Jenne noted.

> We had a [wooden] chute there with a foot end on it to bank the pole against. We landed on sand or sawdust. Once in a while the [bamboo] poles would break, and then you'd do a flip and wouldn't know where you were. [He had that happen in the Olympic Trials at Pasadena and still went on to win.] Now they don't care where they land; they've got these sponge rubber things [pits]. They can light on their head and it doesn't hurt them. We had to land on our feet. Had to be like a cat.

The pole of course had no zip to it. Nowadays the vaulters are about six feet higher than we did. We were doing thirteen and a little more, and now they go six feet higher and it's like an arrow going out of a bow! They really get the zip, and it boosts them up there, close to twenty feet now.

Jenne was a good tennis player, too, and the game was very popular when he was at WSC. He said he joined the Sig Eps because they had the only tennis court. "Right there by the house, a clay court." He could beat the players on the regular tennis team, but since the season corresponded with track he could not compete.

George Bohler, *Doc's younger brother, played at forward on the 1913 WSC team that won the Northwest Conference title with a record of 12-4.* Ralph Lowry, *Republic, was Captain, and* Vic Anderson, *Walla Walla, and* Laurence Sampson, *Oakland City, Indiana, were All-Northwest selections. The following year,* Roy Bohler, *youngest of the four Bohler boys, came out from Reading, Pennsylvania, and began his exceptional playing career at WSC. Roy lettered four years in basketball, playing on two Championship teams. He was Captain of the 1917 team which finished 25-1 and won the Pacific Coast Conference title. Bohler was an All-Northwest choice two years and All-PCC as a senior.*

We had very interesting baseball. Home plate was across from Lake de Puddle and you had to go over the bank when they hit one into right field. Whoever played right usually had a ball or two cached down there. Any ball hit over, well it came up again pretty fast. You know what I mean?

Jenne was a nominee for a Rhodes Scholarship but he was on the Olympic team when the exams for the prestigious award were conducted.

"I went through Oxford, though. In one day," he added with a sly grin. "On a trip up from London, when we were over there after the Olympics."

Eldon Jenne had a great career in athletics as a coach and administrator in the Portland, Oregon, school system. He coached at Washington High and then was Director of Physical Education for the entire Portland system for many years. (Portland had a flock of Cougars in those early years. Eric Waldorf and Len Gehrke were at Jefferson; Homer Hein was at Benson; and Gerald "Chief" Exley coached at Benson and Washington.)

Jenne relished a football win over Oregon in the 1919 season as much as anything in his sports years at Washington State.

"We beat them 7-0 (at Portland in front of a big crowd for those days, 12,000), and they went to the Rose Bowl and played Harvard." It was the only game Oregon lost during the regular season. Jenne kicked the extra point. (The Webfoots lost to Harvard 7-6 in the 1920 Rose Bowl.)

The Third Decade, 1911-1920

Leo Coulter, a junior halfback from Olympia, scored all of Washington State's points in 1912. WSC was shut out by Idaho 13-0 in its opener on October 18 in Pullman. Coulter ran for a touchdown and kicked the extra point in the first quarter of the game at Eugene on October 26 as WSC shut out Oregon 7-0. The following weekend, on November 1 in Pullman, Coulter scored a touchdown and kicked the point in the first quarter, then, with Oregon State leading 9-7 in the fourth quarter, he kicked a twenty-five-yard field goal from a very difficult angle to give WSC a 10-9 victory.

That was the end of the scoring for WSC that season. Whitman shut them out on November 9, and *Johnny Bender's* beleaguered troops ended the year with a 19-0 loss to Washington in Seattle on Thanksgiving Day, November 28.

•

With less than a minute to play in the WSC-UW game at Pullman on February 13, 1915, the campus photographer exploded a flash to get an action picture of the teams on the floor. A sensational shot by Roy Bohler from about mid-court was not allowed as Washington said they thought the flash was the signal that the game was over. *Victor Anderson*, of Walla Walla, led in scoring and WSC won 29-28.

•

WSC-Brown Rose Bowl stats: Rushing, WSC 329, Brown 99; First Downs, WSC 22, Brown 4; Punting, WSC 36, Brown 25; Passing Yardage, WSC 0, Brown, 12; Interceptions, two by each team; Penalties, WSC 5-45, Brown 2-10.

•

President *E. O. Holland* found out what football fans are really like on October 28, 1916, when he arrived in Missoula to attend the WSC-Montana game. "Upon my arrival in the stronghold of the Bruins (Grizzlies?)," he wrote later, I was astonished to find a large number of familiar faces on the street. Most of these young men spoke to me, and looked suspiciously like certain well dressed young men I had once seen in Pullman; but their garb, in Missoula, suggested that a large delegation of I.W.W.'s [Industrial Workers of the World] had invaded Missoula. . . . I was surprised again when I learned that the I.W.W.'s from W.S.C. were enjoying the hospitality of the fraternity houses at Montana University; that the overflow from the fraternity houses were enjoying free entertainment in Missoula's best hotels on the generosity of the Missoula Chamber of Commerce." (Now that's hospitality!)

•

Harold Merrin, of Spokane, won the 1917 Pacific Northwest Swim Meet for WSC single-handedly. Merrin won the 220, 440 and 880 freestyle events and was second in the 100 at Spokane's Natatorium Park

•

The letter "W" for women was initiated in the 1917-1918 college year. First winners of the award were *Vernon Barnes*, Silverlake; *Dorthea Sorenson*, Ellensburg; *Kate Argo*, Spokane; *Nancy Hughes*, Lind; *Emily Babcock*, Pullman; and *Marie Cave*, Pullman. In 1918-1919, *Mildred McMaster*, Vancouver, was recommended for a "Varsity Sweater for Women," and *Louise Stilke*, Tacoma, "Varsity W for Women."

"Crimson W" was introduced in 1918-1919. Winners were *Ameila Hedges*, Pullman; *Dorthea* and *Agnes Sorenson*, both of Ellensburg; *Beryl Wadsworth*, Richland; and *Angeline Ward*, Toppenish.

"Crimson W sweaters" came in 1919. Winners were *Ward, Sorenson, Hedges, Leita Brandt*, Spokane; *Frances Lincoln*, North Yakima; *Argo; Gladys Beck*, Walla Walla; *Marjorie Duffin*, Camas, and *Josephine Vogler*, Hatton

•

A wartime casualty at WSC was the old "Give 'em H___" yell. The Pullman *Herald* reported on April 26, 1918: "Never again will the State College campus ring with the yell 'Give 'em H___ , Washington,' a phrase which has been used to cheer athletic teams on to victory since time immemorial in the annals of State College athletics . . . the yell finally succumbed to the vote of the student body yesterday, when 229 students voted their disapproval of the objectionable yell, with 166 supporting it. The opposition to the yell was led by Miss *Bernice Oliphant*, a student from Easton. . . ."

•

The game nobody saw! On January 18, 1919, Washington State defeated Spokane University 59-17 in a basketball game in Bohler gymnasium. Due to the Spanish flu epidemic, no public gatherings were permitted. *Doc Bohler* locked the doors to all spectators. *Pink McIvor* was high scorer with 24 points and *Chick Rockey* had 21.

•

Here's another one for the books. In the WSC-UW basketball game at Pullman on March 1, 1919, timer *Glenn Glover*, of Pullman, pulled the trigger three times but his gun failed to fire as time expired. By the time Glover notified Referee *Hunter* of Idaho that the game was over, Washington forward *Clinton Sohns* "slipped in a field goal" and won the game 25-24.

An argument ensued between the timers and scorers, which was done away with by *[Doc] Bohler* who conceded victory to the University. Bohler said the rule specified that action continued until a gun sounded or officials were notified the game was over. The lineup for WSC: *Pink McIvor* and *Chick Rockey*, forwards; Captain *Julius "Jazz" Hollman*, Wenatchee, center; and *Martcil Kotula*, Pe Ell, and *Harland Burgess*, Pullman, guards. WSC won the first game of that series 28-17 on February 28.

•

The Sun Dodgers had more to celebrate than their 13-7 win over WSC at Pullman on November 15, 1919. They stole a Cougar! The Pullman *Herald* related "a tale of the smooth duplicity, so characteristic of the denizens of large cities and the sublime innocence of the unsophisticated frosh who hail from the farms and small towns of the state."

> Both cougars [WSC had acquired two stuffed cougars a month previous when the 'Cougar' was adopted as the college mascot] were used to grace the stage and arouse enthusiasm at the big rally in the college auditorium Friday evening. After the rally they were placed in charge of a body of frosh. . . . Shortly after, a big automobile, containing two honest looking men wearing W.S.C. fezes, drove up. . . . One of them said in honeyed tones: "Boys, Doc Bohler wants one of the cougars at the gym, so let's take it up in the car."
>
> Hypnotized by the glad rags and suave tones of their visitors, the guards stood aside and permitted the helpless stuffed cougar to be carried away and placed in the machine. . . .
>
> The machine dashed to Moscow, Idaho, where the cougar was securely boxed, brought back to Pullman Saturday and kept in the automobile until the University special was pulling out at 2 o'clock Sunday morning, when the auto drove up to the baggage car and the box was slipped aboard.
>
> That is how the cougar happened to grace the triumphant procession of the U. of W. students through the streets of Yakima and Seattle; why a lot of W.S.C. frosh have been going about with hanging heads and chastened spirits, and why so many students are mournfully humming:
>
> 'Cougar, Cougar, poor lost cat,
> How we wonder where you're at?'

As a matter of fact, the cougar was "residing" at the Sigma Nu fraternity house at the UW and would be a source of irritation to WSC students at every football game played in Seattle from 1920 until 1932, when it was "rescued."

(Note: After this catnapping incident, the remaining cougar was named *Old Coug* and was guarded by a group of students calling themselves the "Cougar Guard" which eventually became the Cougar Guard Chapter of Intercollegiate Knights, national service/honor group.)

•

Doc Bohler was negotiating for a game with the Haskell Indians in Lawrence, Kansas, on the same trip WSC took to the Midwest to play Nebraska in 1920. (Doc's brother-in-law, *Fred W. Leuhring*, was Athletic Director at Nebraska when WSC played the Cornhuskers at Lincoln on November 25.) Bohler also tried to get a game with Notre Dame, to be played on New Year's Day, 1921, in the Tacoma stadium. On December 12, 1920, the *Pullman Herald* reported: "Negotiations came to an end when Bohler was notified of the death of Halfback *[George] Gipp*, whose serious illness had caused the long delay in negotiations."

•

Here's a point spread to think about. In 1920, Montana beat Mt. St. Charles College of Helena 133-0. WSC beat Montana 31-0.

•

Mike Moran, halfback, and *Roy Hanley*, end, were benched for "insubordination" by Coach *Gus Welch* following WSC's 49-0 loss to California on November 6, 1920. (The loss eliminated the Cougars from the Rose Bowl race). Welch's action was backed by Athletic Director Bohler. In its next game, on November 13, WSC trounced Oregon State 28-0 at Pullman and the Cougars ended the year by upsetting Nebraska at Lincoln 21-20 on November 25.

•

"Dutch" Dunlap, center; *Fred Hamilton*, guard; and *Lloyd Gillis*, fullback, made the PCC All-Star team picked by George Varnell of the Seattle *Times* following the 1920 season. This is made more interesting by a subsequent incident recorded by *Rube Samuelsen* in his book, *The Rose Bowl Game*. Just prior to the 1921 Rose Bowl, Cal Coach *Andy Smith* had picked his All-Coast team for 1920 and named his entire Golden Bear lineup. When called on it, Samuelsen says Smith retorted, "I doubt if California could be improved by substituting a man from any other Coast team, with the possible exception of *[Cornelius] Righter* of Stanford, center; *[Bill] Steers*, halfback, and *[Lloyd] Gillis*, of Oregon; and *[Fred] Hamilton*, tackle, Washington State." (Hey, Rube! Gillis played fullback for Washington State. Give the Cougars two spots on that All-Star club.)

Mel Hein

The Fourth Decade, 1921-1930

Last of the Carlisle Coaches

THE "CARLISLE ERA" AT WASHINGTON STATE, WHICH BEGAN WITH FRANK SHIVELY in 1898, ended with Albert A. Exendine, who coached the WSC football teams from 1923 through the 1925 season. "Exey" followed Gustavus "Gus" Welch, who, in turn, had replaced William "Lone Star" Dietz when WSC resumed football after a one-year hiatus during World War I.

Three of these men had been stars at Carlisle under Glenn S. "Pop" Warner. Exendine made Walter Camp's All-America (second team) at end in 1907, and Dietz played tackle and Welch quarterback on the great Carlisle team of 1911 which featured the nonpareil Jim Thorpe at tailback. Sports Historian John McCallum, the old Cougar, wrote in his excellent book, *College Football U.S.A. 1869-1971*, that there were many who felt Exendine belonged on the first team All-America.

Gus Welch was half Chippewa. He had been an Army officer in World War I and served with distinction in combat in France. In fact, he was in France when he accepted the WSC job in 1919 and came directly to the campus for the start of football practice on September 15.

Welch had good success his first two seasons. He had excellent material in 1919. The older Hanley brothers, Dick and LeRoy, who had been in two bowl games, with WSC in 1916 and with Dietz and Mare Island in 1919, were back, along with a younger brother, Harold (Bones). Fullback Lloyd Gillis, of Ritzville, and halfback Mike Moran, Republic, also had played for Mare Island. Gillis was a star for the Marines in that game against Great Lakes and still ranks as one of WSC's all-time best backs. Moran, another hard-running back, also was an outstanding baseball player. (Jack Friel said he saw Moran hit a line-drive back through the pitcher's legs one day, "and it went over the centerfielder's head!")

WSC opened in 1919 by beating the Multnomah Athletic Club of Portland 49-0 in Spokane. The Hanley brothers had a field day in their hometown. Dick scored three times, twice on ten-yard runs and once on a twenty-one-yard pass from Eldon Jenne, and kicked four extra points. LeRoy blocked a MAC punt and scored, and Harold ran twenty-five yards for another touchdown. It was the first time—and only time to date—that three brothers have played together in one game for Washington State. (If you are thinking of the Heins, Lloyd played in

OPPOSITE: *WSC's all-timer, Mel Hein. Hein is listed as the center on every all-time All-America team; he is a charter member of both the College and Professional Football Halls of Fame.* (Manuscripts, Archives, and Special Collections, Washington State University Libraries)

Ready to go! The Cougars charge out onto Rogers Field from one of the two little "houses" at the east end of the field built for pre-game and halftime pep talks. There was a building for the visitors. (Myron Huckle)

1926-1927; Mel, 1928-1930, and Homer, 1931.) Interestingly, WSC had three sets of brothers on that 1919 team. In addition to the Hanleys, there were Robert and Rufus Schnebly, a set of twins from Ellensburg, and Carl and Raymond King, of Davenport. All four were linemen, and Carl King had been a squad member on the bowl team of 1916.

WSC followed up its opening win with a stunning 14-0 defeat of California at Berkeley (the "Cougar" game), then went on to score shutouts against Idaho and Oregon the following two weeks.

The Idaho game at Pullman on November 1 was memorable for several reasons. WSC won 37-0, the first time a State College team had played as "Cougars." The game also was a first for the new turf on Rogers Field. Carved out of a hillside in 1892 and leveled for athletics, Rogers Field was not planted to grass until the spring of 1919. "White clover and bluegrass," the Pullman *Herald* said, "a change from the Palouse dust and mud which is hailed with delight." (It really must have been awful in those early years playing in that bunchgrass and dirt. No wonder the Sun Dodgers didn't want to leave their dung hill.)

The win over Idaho was costly. Quarterback Dick Hanley was injured and had to sit out the important Oregon game the following week. Hanley's injury was only the first in a series for the Cougars, who were unbeaten and unscored upon heading into the Oregon game at Multnomah Stadium in Portland on November 8.

Washington State's 7-0 win over Oregon turned out to be the high point of that 1919 season. It was the only loss for the Webfoots during the regular season. They lost 7-6 to Harvard on New Year's Day at Pasadena.

"Curley" Skadan started in place of Hanley against Oregon, but suffered a broken ankle early in the game. Another sophomore, Milo "Pink" McIvor, of Pullman, was thrown into the breach and demonstrated the poise that eventually, in 1921, would make him the first winner of the J. Fred Bohler Inspirational Award.

Gillis made the only score in that Oregon game, plunging over from two yards out in the third quarter after he and Moran had pounded the

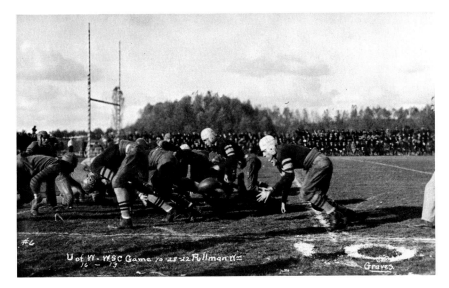

Getting close to that Purple and Gold line! WSC's Vern Hickey taking the snap in the 1922 WSC-UW game on Rogers Field. Note that the center is the end man on the Cougar line. There were no "hash marks" in those years. Washington won 16-13. (Manuscripts, Archives, and Special Collections, Washington State University Libraries)

ball steadily down field behind great blocking by the Cougar line. Roy Hanley, Bert Brooks (Everett), Walt "Fat" Herreid (Bangor), Fred Hamilton (Chehalis), the King brothers and the Schneblys, Earl "Dutch" Dunlap (Dayton) and Arnold Ellwart (St.John) all performed well in the line for the Cougars. WSC gained 234 yards, Oregon 241 in the hard-fought game.

Victorious but badly battered, WSC came home on November 15 to play Washington. The Homecoming game at Pullman marked the first time since 1903 that the Sun Dodgers had ventured into the Palouse. The teams met in Spokane in 1910; the eight games after that all had been in Seattle.

Washington prevailed 13-7 in another tough football game. Although WSC clearly had the edge in yardage gained, 250 to 125, the Sun Dodgers scored on a five-yard run by Art Theisen in the first quarter and Ray Butler scored the winner from three yards out in the fourth. The Cougars' lone score came in the third quarter on a two-yard plunge by Gillis.

The first loss of the season was a particularly bitter one for Coach Welch and his team, made even more so by the fact that the Cougars lost star punter Eldon Jenne for the season with a broken leg in this game. The following Saturday, back at Multnomah Stadium again, Washington State lost to Oregon State 6-0 on a pair of Carl Lodell field goals (thirty-eight and twenty-eight yards) in another bitterly contested game.

WSC ended its season with a 42-14 win over Montana at Missoula on Thanksgiving. Gillis and Dick Hanley were the stars for Washington State. Gillis scored three touchdowns and Hanley had an eighty-yard scoring run.

Coach Welch had another star-crossed season in 1920, missing the Rose Bowl by one game, albeit it a one-sided 49-0 loss to California. The Bears went on to Pasadena and whipped Ohio State 28-0 on January 1, 1921. WSC was unbeaten in three starts going into that Cal game.

Washington State rebounded, however, and finished the season like champions, whomping Oregon State 28-0 at Pullman the following weekend and then edging Nebraska 21-20 at Lincoln in the season-ender to finish 5-1. The Cougars and Sun Dodgers did not meet in 1920. Washington would not agree to a 50-50 split in gate receipts, as provided by PCC rules, so Athletic Director Bohler reached into the Midwest and signed the Cornhuskers.

Gus Welch ended his coaching tenure at WSC with a 4-2-1 season in 1921, giving him an overall record of 14-5-1 with the Cougars. He later was Athletic Director at Randolph-Macon College, Ashland, Virginia; Haskell Institute in Kansas; and at American University in Washington, D.C. He also was at the University of Virginia as lacrosse coach. Welch died at Bedford, Virginia, in 1970.

A. A. Exendine, an Arapahoe Indian, came to Washington State from Georgetown University in Washington, D.C., for the 1922 season. He had considerably less success than Welch and Dietz, but, before he left, Exendine too enjoyed his "day in the sun."

On November 26, 1925, in Los Angeles, Washington State beat a good Southern Cal team 17-12. That was the day USC got its first look at sophomore quarterback Herbert "Butch" Meeker. Mostly, the Trojans saw Meeker's heels—and his right toe. Los Angeles sportswriter Frank T. Blair summed up the game: "No score in a season marked by grid upsets provided more of a form reversal than yesterday's sensational victory of the lowly Cougars over the U.S.C. machine, second in the country in the little matter of scoring points on the gridiron this season. The Trojans were outfought and outplayed by a team that came down from the North with the inglorious record of having failed to score a touchdown on an opponent to date during the 1925 season." (After five games WSC was 1-4. All of its points had come on field goals, two by Meeker and one by Bill Kramer in a 9-0 win over Montana at Missoula in the season opener, and two more by Meeker in a 6-7 loss to Idaho at Pullman the following week.)

The first WSC-California game played in the Pacific Northwest was on October 29, 1921, at Portland's Multnomah Stadium. Cal won 14-0. WSC first played Cal at Berkeley on October 25, 1919 (the "Cougar" game), and won 14-0. For trivia fans, Cal did not come to Pullman until October 1, 1938, when they beat WSC 27-3.

A. A. Exendine, last of the Carlisle football coaches at WSC, with his staff in 1923. From left to right: H. A. "Hack" Applequist, Roy Bohler, Asa V. "Ace" Clark, Exendine, and Doc Bohler, Athletic Director and Trainer. (Manuscripts, Archives, and Special Collections, Washington State University Libraries)

How then did Washington State beat Southern Cal?

"Meeker, a 142-pound quarterback of the Cougar team, was the shining light in Washington State's spectacular victory," wrote Blair. "This diminutive star was a host in himself, tearing off neat gains through the line and around the ends, tossing passes, kicking a placement goal from the 34-yard line and playing a whale of a defensive game. He also piloted the Cougar eleven in faultless fashion."

Meeker startled the Trojans immediately, grabbing Brice Taylor's opening kickoff and running it back forty-six yards, "a sparkling return," Blair wrote. Then halfback Bill Kramer, of Colton, threw a short pass to fullback Eric Waldorf, of Kennewick, who broke away around right end and went fifty yards to score WSC's first touchdown—of the season!

It was no cakewalk. USC led 12-10 at the end of three periods.Then halfback Bill Sweet, of Winona, passed to end John Parkhill, of Wenatchee, who ran thirty-five yards to give WSC its first-ever win over Southern Cal.

The Cougar team that had left Pullman in such disarray the previous week returned home to a heroes' welcome. Students were let out of class to go to the Union Pacific depot the following Tuesday morning to meet the players' train when it arrived from Los Angeles. Players and coaches were paraded up to the campus amid much cheering and celebration. (Fullback Eric Waldorf, who became one of the Pacific Northwest's finest prep coaches at Portland's Jefferson High, commented on that 'Welcome Home' years later saying, "You'd have thought we had won the Rose Bowl!")

WSC finished its season—and Exendine's career at the State College—with two games in the Hawaiian Islands over the Holidays. The Cougars defeated the Honolulu All-Stars 24-7 on Christmas Day and lost to the University of Hawaii 20-11 on New Year's.

Exendine later coached at Otterbein College, Westerville, Ohio; Occidental College in Los Angeles; Northeastern State, at Tahlequah, Oklahoma; and Oklahoma State University. He was elected to the National Football Hall of Fame and, in 1968, was named Indian of the Year by the Council of American Indians, in Tulsa. Albert A. Exendine died in 1973 at age eighty-eight, the last survivor of the four WSC Indian coaches from Carlisle.

"Froggy"

Between 1925 and 1946 no one at WSC, with the possible exception of President Ernest O. Holland, had a greater sphere of influence—and got more done—than Graduate Manager Earl V. Foster.

Foster entered WSC at age twenty-three in 1919, having served in France with the 39th Infantry. He had enlisted right out of Wenatchee High School, where he was a good football and baseball player, took part in four major battles and was gassed in the Argonne. He was discharged with the rank of lieutenant.

At WSC, Foster played baseball and lettered three seasons as an outfielder under coaches Frank Barber and "Hack" Applequist. (He was known to his old teammates and cronies as "Froggy." Foster's upper

Milo "Pink" McIvor, of Pullman, senior halfback, was the first recipient of the J. Fred Bohler Award presented at the conclusion of the 1921 football season to the player deemed "most inspirational" to the team. A gold medal, designed and presented by the Hoxsey-Lambert company of Spokane, will go to the winner each year. Morris Hoxsey, ex-'14 Kappa Sig, and Fred Salt, '17 Sigma Nu, of Hoxsey-Lambert, set up the award.

Earl Foster, Graduate manager of Washington State from 1925 to 1946. (Daily Evergreen)

eyelids drooped, giving his eyes a hooded look, much like a frog's.) He started out in Civil Engineering but graduated in General Studies. When he returned to the campus in 1925 to become Graduate Manager, Foster replaced Harry Chambers, '13, who had been holding down three positions, as Graduate Manager, Alumni Secretary, and Editor of the alumni magazine. (Chambers later was Registrar at the college for many years.)

Foster had an empire that included athletics and all student activities except those directly under the Dean of Men or Dean of Women. Student government and student publications, including the *Evergreen* and the *Chinook*, came within Foster's purview, along with just about every event on campus not handled directly by departments. He obviously came into his position with some clout, and he knew how to use it. More importantly, perhaps, he earned the confidence of the students and used their backing to gain support for programs he administered, including intercollegiate athletics.

Jennie Thomas Harold, '44, of Prosser, first woman president of the student body at WSC (1943-1944), said years later of her working relationship with Foster: "He was my mentor." Many other student leaders, including Edward R. Murrow, president in 1929-1930, might have said the same about Foster. (Murrow and Foster became fast friends, and it was on a salmon-fishing trip to Neah Bay with Murrow in 1957 that Foster suffered the heart attack which claimed his life.)

Whether it was the time, the man, or a combination of both, the athletic program made giant forward strides during Foster's twenty-one years as Graduate Manager. Among other things, WSC acquired a great set of coaches, the equal of any on the Pacific Coast, and Foster's shrewd management and imaginative financing gave the college one of the finest athletic complexes in the nation in this period.

Without question, Bohler had laid a solid foundation for a successful athletic program, but Doc was a "doer," a hands-on man who took on more and more jobs because someone had to do them. Foster, on the other hand, was above all a financial genius. ("Tighter'n a bull's ass in fly-time," Buck Bailey used to say when "Scotty" Foster reluctantly doled out travel money to his team.) Foster also was a superb administrator who knew how to use the strengths of other individuals and groups to achieve a goal, whether it be a stronger athletic program, better student services, or more and better staff and facilities for both.

When George "Blackie" Blakkolb, '34, MeKenna, Washington, and Mildred (Perry) Applequist, '23, Spokane, wrote letters nominating Foster for the WSU Athletic Hall of Fame in 1979, they pointed out that, in addition to hiring (with Doc Bohler) all those famous coaches in WSC's "Golden Age," just about every facility in the school's athletic plant was a direct result of Earl's efforts. Foster also encouraged expansion of the marching band, was a "collaborator" in developing the first electric scoreboards to appear on the Pacific Coast, and "pioneered" sports broadcasting over KWSC radio. (If you've wondered what those orange cages hanging from the ceiling of Bohler gym are, they're broadcast booths, built under Foster's egis in an era before sportscasters moved themselves down to courtside where they could coach, smell jockstraps, and *be seen.* WSC had the first on the Pacific Coast.)

The fine Italian hand of the Graduate Manager was very evident in 1927 when, as Professor William Landeen wrote in his history of the Holland administration, ". . . the Associated Students proposed to the Board of Regents through Graduate Manager E. V. Foster" that they be permitted to inaugurate an Associated Student Building Fee of five dollar per month per student each semester, in addition to the $6.50 student body card fee already in place. "Said building fee to create funds for a permanent building program, either through accumulated monies or by bond issue."

In "their" proposal to the regents, students said needed improvements included:

Fireproof hospital	$75,000
Completion of women's athletic field	3,000
Additional playfields	5,000
Pay off indebtedness on Rogers Field grandstand	12,000
Additional tennis courts, etc.	8,000

"The Associated Students estimate that annual receipts from the new fee would total $228,000, which would make it possible to liquidate the first program in five years without recourse to the accrued profits from Associated Students business operations," Foster wrote to President Holland in February of 1927.

It did not take Holland long to see the possibilities of such a plan, if in fact he had not worked the whole thing out with Foster beforehand. But it sounds more like Foster; he usually was the students' representative in dealings with the administration.

As historian Landeen so aptly put it, "The Holland administration was fortunate to have during most of its tenure the services of only one graduate manager of the ASSCW, Earl V. Foster. Mr. Foster was an able financier, a staunch supporter of all forward-looking enterprises on the

•

The Women's Athletic Association (WAA) was reorganized in 1922 under the direction of Mary R. McKee, *head of the Women's Department of Physical Education, making it possible for WSC to qualify for membership in the Athletic Conference of American College Women.*

•

A student foursome tees it up on the new WSC golf course shortly after it opened in 1926. Notice the sand "tee" under the ball. (Myron Huckle)

The steel framework for Hollingbery Field House went up in the summer of 1929. (Manuscripts, Archives, and Special Collections, Washington State University Libraries)

campus, and a community-minded citizen as well. He managed student finances with a view to achieving important and lasting objectives.

During Foster's term as Graduate Manager the WSC stadium was enlarged (both by improving the south stands and adding a press box and by building the north, "student" stands, and completing the horse-shoe end); Bohler Gymnasium was built; the Field House constructed; the baseball field was moved from what is now the Intramural Field behind Bohler to a site down along the willow trees where Jack Mooberry Track was later built; the women's playfield across Colorado Street was laid out; the nine-hole golf course got new, grass greens (in place of the original ones of sand), and the Stadium Way loop was completed around the campus.

A building fund for a student union at WSC was another of Foster's accomplishments. Unfortunately, some have said, the Union was not completed until 1952, six years after Foster's departure from campus. By that time, practically none of the students at WSC remembered Earl Foster, so the building was named for Wilson Compton, the recently departed president. (Students quickly shortened it to the "CUB," for Compton Union Building. As someone said later, even if Earl had been remembered by the students, they couldn't very well have named it the "Foster Union Building"—and had it become the "FUB."

Pullman *Herald* Editor Paul Stoffel, Jr., writing Foster's obituary in 1957, summed up the old Graduate Manager's style:

> A Scotch instinct for thrift, combined with broad vision and firm management soon brought the start of many changes and lasting improvements to the WSC campus. . . . Some of these improvements were made during depression years with the aid of WPA federal grants, but they were made possible because canny Earl Foster always had the necessary "matching funds" tucked away somewhere, ready when opportunity knocked.

Babe Hollingbery demonstrates his punting ability on Rogers Field shortly after taking over the Cougars' coaching reins in 1926. He was a fine all-around athlete, playing all the backfield positions and end for the San Francisco Olympic Club. (Manuscripts, Archives, and Special Collections, Washington State University Libraries)

"Babe"—The Un-College Man

The name Orin Ercel "Babe" Hollingbery is still the best known in all Washington State University athletic history, although he coached his last Cougar football team nearly a half century ago.

It lives in such tales as this one written by Art Rosenbaum of the San Francisco *Chronicle* as the old Cougar coach lay dying in 1973—the first time he had missed the East-West game since he coached the West team in the series opener in 1925:

> . . . In his day he stood with Knute Rockne, Pop Warner, Andy Smith, and Slip Madigan, both as personality and coach. . . . Inspiration was a big item with the Babe. In those days the "fight talk" was always believable and this man delivered one of the most torrid.
>
> They tell a story of how his Washington State Cougars of 1941 upset the then mighty University of California 13-7. WSC had lost three fullbacks to injury and was "hurting all over." A late fumble cost them a game to UCLA.
>
> "California," Hollingbery had said, "was ticking like a forty-dollar watch." [Remember, this was 1941.] They should have

beaten patched up WSC 60-0. Hollingbery told them in an impassioned pre-game session that he had never known a team to have such bad luck, that they had already been whipped as much as ordinary folks could stand but, when those big 'uns from Berkeley knocked them down, if they would just get up again and keep going, forget the score and fight, why, they would take home from the game a lesson that would live with them forever.

More than a year later he got a letter from a bomber pilot stationed in England who had been a member of that 1941 team. It said in part . . ."on this mission over Germany my copilot was dead, my gunner dead, radio operator dead, instrument panel riddled, and me full of holes and bleeding and I remembered, just kept repeating what you had said before the Cal game, Babe, that I had taken about as much as ordinary folks could stand but if I didn't give up they couldn't whip me. In my mind I kept getting up like you said and I made it back, I pancaked in."

Members of Babe Hollingbery's first team at WSC in 1926 might have longed for the "good old Exendine days" by the time they finished pre-season workouts. Fall practice began on September 15 and Babe worked his players out six hours a day until just before the opener on October 2 against College of Idaho. At the end of fall practice, Hollingbery took the entire squad on a six-mile hike into the Palouse countryside!

Hollingbery was born in Hollister, California, in 1893, graduated from Lick High School in San Francisco. He was an all-around athlete there, competing in football, track, baseball, basketball, and swimming. An end, quarterback, and fullback in his football playing days, he stood six feet tall and weighed 175 pounds. He went to work as an insurance company safety engineer out of high school and began playing football for the Olympic Club and coaching his prep alma mater.

After serving in the Army Air Corps in 1918-1919, he went back to the Bay Area, where he kept busy with a string of four service stations his family had acquired and as coach of three teams. In those days Babe had a motorcycle, and scheduled practices so that when one was over he could bike to the next. One year he found that two of the schools he was commuting between, Lick High and Bates Prep, were scheduled to play. He coached half the game on one side, half on the other. Hollingbery said later he hoped for a scoreless tie, but the Bates boys surprised him by scoring and won 6-0.

But it was his success with the Olympic Club football team that attracted wide interest. In 1925 the Winged-O under Hollingbery had its finest season, going unbeaten and ending the fifty-victory string of Andy Smith's "Wonder Team" at California. At just this time, Washington State was looking for a replacement for the last of its Carlisle coaches, A. A. Exendine, whose record had fallen to 6-13-4 over three seasons.

Naturally, Hollingbery's success at the Olympic Club interested WSC officials. There was one sticky wicket. Babe was not a "college man." (Nor was his assistant, Buck Bailey, as it turned out, although Bailey had been "exposed" to academe at no fewer than three institutions of higher learning.) Hollingbery also had a noticeable speech impediment, a pronounced stammer. The lack of a college degree appears to have been more of a concern at the time, however. The newspapers harped on this fact, and years after he took the WSC job and was a great success, Babe was identified in practically every story written about him as "the college coach who wins without a college degree." (In an article for *Collier's*, November 20, 1937, Richard L. Neuberger observed: "He is the only one of 227 major football coaches recently listed by the Olympic Athletic Foundation who never attended college. . . ." And again in the same article: "Although he is the solitary big-time football coach in America without a higher education, he plasters the walls of the Washington State locker room with stirring quotations from great statesmen and philosophers." (How's that for a jim-dandy non sequitur!)

Fortunately for WSC, Athletic Director Bohler and Graduate Manager Foster did their homework and recommended to President Holland that Hollingbery be hired. All three lived to see Babe make them look very, very good as judges of "un-college" talent.

Babe Hollingbery was as solid a football coach as ever paced the sidelines. His teams were fundamentally sound, played tough defense, and always had solid kicking games. A disciple of conservative, single-wing, "go through 'em five yards!" football, Babe occasionally shocked the opposition with trick plays verging on the bizarre. He favored the run over the pass and his offense was built around the ground game. But when Billy Sewell came along in 1939, Babe opened up his offense to take advantage of the Tacoma sophomore's great arm. Old "Single-Wing" Hollingbery's Washington State team led the nation in passing in 1940 with Sewell winging them.

Herb Godfrey, who played for Babe in 1942 and again in 1946-1947, was Head Football Coach at Whittier College in California in 1962 when he wrote this to his old coach:

> Your life has been filled with more than one man's share of successful accomplishments and grateful friends. You have earned these because of your fine character, hard work, and high intelligence.
>
> Coaching terminology may have changed, but the game hasn't. Your basic pattern of a stout defense and good kicking game is still the key to success today. We talk of 'tackle dominance' as being essential for victory. It seems to me that you prescribed to this theory when you went off-tackle on that tailback cutback play.
>
> We talk about 'reading the blocker'—you called it "fighting the pressure." We still use the term "EPOY"—every play over you—on short-yardage situations.
>
> Yes, you could start coaching tomorrow, Babe—and win.

When Babe Hollingbery brought his "Hup-ti-ditty" to Washington State in 1926, it did not take Cougar fans long to realize they had a legend in their midst!

"Echa Pelote!"

It was one of the greatest bargains in sports history. Washington State College hired "Babe" Hollingbery and got "Buck" Bailey in the same deal.

No figure in Cougar sports history is remembered with such affection and delight as Arthur B. Bailey, the big, colorful Texan. Bailey came to WSC as Hollingbery's line coach and scout, and he remained that for seventeen years, but it was as Cougar baseball coach for thirty-two years that most people remember him. And what a baseball coach he was!

"Buck Bailey's Circus Coming to Town," the *Oregon State Barometer* headlined in the mid-1930s when the big fellow led his Cougars into

• Wrestling was switched from a major sport to minor in 1926 and Harold Berridge, Monroe, PNA Champion at 175 and Heavyweight, took over as Student Coach. Al Polenske, Edwall, won the PNA title at 135. •

Never a dull moment when WSC's Buck Bailey, right, and Forrest Twogood of Idaho got their baseball teams together in the Palouse. (Note the "Groucho Marx" character in the background.) (Manuscripts, Archives, and Special Collections, Washington State University Libraries)

Corvallis for a crucial series. And so it was all over the Pacific Northwest. No college baseball team drew like Bailey's Washington State nines. Everyone turned out when Buck came to town because it was going to be a great show—regardless of how the game went, or who won. You didn't have to be a baseball fan to enjoy one of Buck's performances. He was worth the price of admission. If he wasn't kicking the water bucket in disgust at an error of "O-mission" by one of his players or scattering the bats to get a Cougar rally started, then he would be baiting the umpire, or out on the mound on his hands and knees piling dirt and trying to settle down a wild left-hander. Then he'd leap off his coaching bench by the Cougar dugout and let out that high-pitched, blood-curdling scream, "ieeeee!" to move an outfielder into position, or, with a bellow that would invoke a sonic boom, he'd order a coach to "Put a ring in that guy's nose!" when he thought a base runner was leading too far off first. Whatever he did, he did it colorfully—and loud.

The story goes that when Babe Hollingbery accepted the head football job at Washington State in early 1926 he told Buck they'd come for a season to see how it went. "Maybe we won't like it, or maybe they won't like us," Babe is supposed to have said to Bailey when they came up from the San Francisco Olympic Club. It makes for good story-telling, but anyone who knew either of those determined gentlemen would know they came to win, and they came to stay!

A giant of a man (for those days), Buck was better than six-feet and weighed—depending on the menus he'd been enjoying—anywhere from 230 to 250 in his prime. He had arms that made a gorilla's look skinny by comparison, and when he wrapped his big paws around a baseball bat—or even better a golf club—look out!

Buck was not quite thirty years old when he first appeared on the WSC campus for spring practice in April of 1926. He made an immediate impression on those football players, who had been used to the gentle approach of the old Carlisle Indian, A. A. Exendine, the previous three seasons. Buck dearly loved to get down in the "trenches" with his linemen. He was big and he was quick; he also liked to hit people. But, having said that, it must be added that he could be the gentlest of men. It all depended on the setting—and the situation.

"If I'm spittin' at a crack, I'm spittin to win!" was one of the big fellow's favorite expressions. He meant it. When Buck competed, it was all out. When he was having fun, nobody had more —unless it was those around him, and he always attracted a crowd.

Arthur B. Bailey—the "B" stood for "Buckner," so his nickname was not a description, as many have believed—was born deep in the heart of Texas, at San Saba, in 1896.

"I was born in jail!" Buck liked to say. His father was Sheriff of San Saba County and the Bailey family was living in the jail house when Buck was born. (It's an interesting coincidence that Babe Hollingbery's father also was a sheriff at one time, of San Francisco County, California.)

Buck grew up playing baseball. He usually was the catcher. "Wore the tools of ignorance," he'd say with a certain pride. The family had moved from San Saba to Eldorado, out in west Texas, when Buck was very young, and he always considered Eldorado his hometown. Big for his age, he was playing ball for the town team there by the time he was fourteen.

After high school, Buck went to Texas A & M, planning to play baseball. But football coach Dana X. Bible saw the big fellow and decided he'd make a good addition to the Aggie gridiron squad. As the story goes, Bible sent some of his regulars over to Buck's dorm room and they "persuaded" him—with the assistance of some Sam Brown belts—to play football.

"I played in the first football game I ever saw," Buck used to say, with that million dollar smile. Apparently this was true. He played two years at A & M and then went into the Army during World War I.

After the war, Buck and some of his buddies enrolled at Hardin-Simmons College over in Abilene, but there was some mix-up on eligibility so they transferred across town to Abilene Christian. AC promptly won its first football championship.

When someone asked him why he left Abilene Christian for Bethany College in West Virginia after just one season, Buck gave a typical answer: "The hours were shorter and the pay was better."

Buck was at Bethany one year and then went to California to play on a semi-pro team under an old A & M and Carlisle gridder, Vic "Choc" (for Choctaw) Kelley, who was coaching at Selma in the American Legion football league in the Fresno area. (Kelley was the father of longtime UCLA Sports Information Director Vic Kelley.)

On Armistice Day, 1923, Selma went up to Stockton and beat a team made up of alumni off some of Cal-Berkeley's "Wonder Teams." Shortly thereafter, Buck got an offer to play for the Olympic Club in San Francisco. That's where he hooked up with Babe. The stories of Buck's prowess as a football player are not exaggerated. He was a gridiron

●

"Exey, Exey, Good old Exey; we all love you next to Prexy," the 1925 Chinook *chanted. That fall, Exendine's team finished 3-4-1 and "Exey" exited. But not before his Cougar team visited Hawaii for a pair of games with the Honolulu All-Stars and the University of Hawaii, the latter before a record crowd of 13,000. The WSC-UH game was recreated by radio station KGO, Oakland, California. W. C. Prindiville, described by the* Pullman Herald *as a "local radio fan," sent a petition signed by 1,500 persons to KGO requesting that the station broadcast the game. "Persons who pick up KGO are requested to mail postcards to the station expressing their appreciation of the service," the* Herald *added.*

●

legend before he got to Pullman. Buck was the Captain and guard (or center, depending on what they needed most) of the Olympic Club team that won thirteen straight games and ended Andy Smith's fifty-game unbeaten string at California, 15-0, in 1925. At the conclusion of that season, Buck played in the first East-West Shrine game on December 26, 1925, leading the West to a 6-0 win over a favored East team coached by "Navy Bill" Ingram at old Ewing Field in San Francisco. Buck intercepted Ingram's pass in the final moments of the game to stop an East drive and preserve the win for the West.

In his history of the Shrine game, *Football's Finest Hour*, Maxwell Stiles says Bailey was "one of the standout players of the game." In 1940, when a group of sportswriters got together to pick an "original All-Star team" for the Shrine classic, Ed Slaughter, of Michigan, a guard on the East team in that first game, was selected ahead of Buck. Stiles wrote: "There appears to be evidence that Buck Bailey of the Texas Aggies, later the Olympic Club, was equal to or superior to Slaughter . . . ."

Virginia Shaw, of Oregon City, Oregon, received the Final Emblem Award in 1923. (Professor Shaw served on the WSC faculty in Physical Education from 1929 until her retirement in 1962. She died in 1987 at Panorama City.)

On January 24, 1926, "Buck Bailey's Tigers," a team of former collegiate and club stars Buck organized, defeated George Halas' Chicago Bears 14 to 9 at Kezar Stadium in the first professional football game played in San Francisco.

Most of the folks attending that game had come out to see Harold "Red" Grange, the immortal "Galloping Ghost," who had just been signed off the University of Illinois campus by Halas for the unheard of sum of $100,000. In an effort to recoup some of the money he had invested in Grange, Halas took him on a nationwide exhibition tour. But it was Bailey and his "Tigers" who carried the day, with Buck a standout on both on offense and defense in what he often described as "the toughest football game I ever played in."

Ed R. Hughes of the San Francisco *Chronicle* wrote: "Buck Bailey was happy as a schoolboy over winning the game. That big boy will never lose his enthusiasm and he hugged his players after the game." How typical. He never lost that love of winning!

The following day, Halas called Buck down to the Palace Hotel where the Chicago team was staying and offered him a contract.

"But he didn't want to pay me $100,000, like he'd paid Grange," Buck recalled later on many occasions, rubbing a big paw across his face and grimacing. "He offered me some cash, but mostly he wanted me to take stock in his team. I don't like to think what that would be worth now!"

Players at Washington State heard Buck bellow "*Echa pelote!*" for the first time in the spring of 1927. Even those who had played football the previous fall and were somewhat accustomed to his bellowing must have been a little puzzled. "*Echa pelote?*" They soon learned this was Bailey pidgin Spanish for "play ball!"

Buck succeeded "Hack" Applequist as baseball coach at WSC and won the championship of the Northern Division in his first outing. As *Chinook* sports editor Lloyd Birkett, of Spokane, pointed out, "He nearly lost his hair in the series with O.S.C. for the title. . . ." (That didn't leave him much for the subsequent thirty-one seasons!)

Buck's contributions in that season of 1927 amounted to more than coaching. He also proved his "recruiting" mettle by bringing in two old boys from Texas, catcher Festus Sebastian, of Moody, and center fielder Roy Aubrey, of Crowell, who were key players in that championship season. (Both survived only one semester, striking out in the classroom.)

It's a wonder Buck made it through his first game. WSC used four pitchers in its opener at Pullman on April 11 in a 9-2 win over the College of Idaho. Duane Shelby, of South Bend, pitched five shutout innings "in grand style," reported the Pullman *Herald*, and got the win. Rudy Becker, of Tacoma, and Howard "Lefty" Damon, Vancouver, followed and allowed but two hits between them in the next three innings. But Henry Riggs, of Rosalia, passed two men in the ninth and allowed two runs on two hits. That was the first—and last!—appearance young Riggs made on the mound for Coach Bailey, and no doubt marked the first time at WSC that Bailey uttered his immortal words: "Those bases-on-balls will kill ya!"

Bailey's infield provided the power in that first win. First sacker Arthur Berg, of Tacoma; second baseman Guy DiJulio, Seattle; and third baseman Ted Rohwer, Spokane, each hit for the circuit.

Washington State won the Eastern division title with a 6-2 mark and took on Oregon State, winners of the West, in the play-off series at Pullman beginning May 31. Hoquiam sophomore Erwin McDowell hurled the opener, surviving four errors by his teammates to win 5-2. (Oregon State made six boots!)

Buck used three pitchers in the second game, Jimmy Highton, of Renton; Kenny Adams, Spokane; and Becker, with Adams taking the loss as Oregon State prevailed 8-7 in a 21-hit slugfest. Again, errors dominated the game, OSC committing six and WSC five. Sebastian, the big WSC catcher from Texas, had a homer, triple, and double in a losing cause.

Regardless of what name he happened to be using, Ike Deeter was one tough middleweight in the mid-1920s, when this picture was taken. (Myron Huckle)

Lefty Elbert Mitchell, of White Swan, hurled the deciding win for WSC in the third game, with relief help from Highton. Oregon State had the tying runs on in the ninth, but Highton got the final OSC hitter on a pop-up to Sebastian.

It was a great start for a great Cougar. He'd have many more before hanging up his spikes after thirty-two seasons at Washington State.

"Mr. College Boxing"

Isaac Ferguson "Ike" Deeter came to Washington State College in 1923 to play football. He stayed to become "Mr. Boxing."

Ike had been a 160-pound fullback at North Central in Spokane, but a knee injury in his freshman year at WSC ended his football aspirations. Thanks to Doc Bohler, who got him a job around the gym, Ike stayed in Pullman for sixty-six years—so far.

Deeter was a good fighter before he arrived in Pullman. He lived in the same neighborhood in Spokane as WSC's famous Hanley brothers and put on the gloves at an early age. The Spokane Elks had a club boxing program in those years and it wasn't long before Deeter was one of the best young mitt-slingers in town. In the summer of 1922, Ike and Don Jones, a classmate at North Central, were "recruited" by the

Recreation Director at Elk River, Idaho, to fight a couple of bullies who'd been making life miserable for the folks in the little lumber town. They were given jobs at the mill (four-bits an hour, plus expenses) as a cover, and when the Fourth of July came around the boys were matched against the trouble-makers.

"We did a pretty good job on 'em," Ike recalled. "Jones hit his guy on the bridge of the nose and just split it. Years later, I was in the barber shop at the Senator Hotel in Sacramento and the barber says 'Hi, Ike. Remember me? (It happens to Deeter all over the world.) I was in Elk River in the summer of 1922 when you and that other kid took care of the town bullies.'

"Word of that episode got back to Spokane pretty quick. We almost lost eligibility for our senior year," Ike said.

Deeter pretty much fought his way through high school and college. He didn't often get paid for his fights, but the sponsors would give him "merchandise slips" and Ike would have a friend cash them in on a fifty-cent tie and give him the change, say for a twenty-five-dollar slip.

Deeter was Pacific Northwest and Pacific Coast amateur champ as a middleweight while at WSC. In Portland one time for a fight, he discovered he had a bye into the finals of the 160-pound class, so he entered the light-heavy division, too. Ike won the middleweight title and went to the finals with the 175-pounders.

All Ike's battles weren't in the ring. John Bohler, son of the former Athletic Director, likes to tell the story of an incident (it occurred in 1925 at Moscow) when his father was still the trainer for the football team.

"Dad had Ike down on the sidelines as a 'gofer.' A fight started at one end of the field and he sent Ike down to stop it. A few minutes later he looked up and saw that the brawl looked bigger. Dad went over and there was Deeter right in the middle of the fight swinging away.

"'Gee whith, Ike,' Dad said with that lisp of his, 'I thent you down here to ththop thith fight, not thtart it!'"

Deeter remembered the incident well—sixty-three years after—but with a twist.

> Yeah, he grabbed me and give me a kick in the pants and told me to get up in the stands. But about then a couple guys from Idaho jumped Doc. So I ran back and pulled one of 'em off. I've got him down and am poundin' him when Doc turns around, sees me and yells, "Deeta! I thought I told you to get up in the thtandth." And he grabbed me by the coat collar, kicked me in the tail again and gave me a shove toward the stands.

Deeter and Bohler made a great combination. John said his Dad and Ike were "real buddies."

Only Ike and Bob "Punch" Eldred, Pacific Coast Golden Gloves champion and Captain of the WSC boxing team in 1931, know how close Eldred came to missing that season over a little "eligibility" problem. Eddie Quinn, a Spokane fight promoter called Deeter in the summer of 1930 and told him that Eldred was fighting over in the Wenatchee area under the name of "Battling Shugrue" and they'd run out of opponents for him. He offered Ike $60 for the fight, quite a sum in that Depression year, and Deeter accepted. Only hitch was, Quinn

told Eldred that Deeter was coming over but neglected to mention that Ike was going to be his opponent.

When Ike arrived in Wenatchee he went right to a hotel so he wouldn't be seen. Eldred showed up shortly and said, "Gee, Ike, nice of you to come over. You can be in my corner tonight."

"Well, we talked it over," Ike said, "and decided we could give the folks a good fight.

> When we crawled into the ring that night over at the old Labor Hall there was a packed house, including a bunch of WSC alums and students. Joe Burks, [Jack] Mooberry, [Lisle] Garner and "High Tone" Lucas were there, I remember. They let out a real howl when I was introduced as "Bob Ross."
>
> We gave 'em a good fight, knockdowns and everything. Fought six, two-minute rounds. My nose started to bleed and when Quinn started to clean me up between rounds I told him, "Don't do that, Eddie. They like that blood."
>
> At the start of school that fall, Doc Bohler got word of the fight and he was really mad. Said we almost lost Eldred's eligibility.

Boxing was not a recognized intercollegiate sport at WSC when Deeter arrived on campus in 1923, but Bohler was a real booster for the ring sport. Next to basketball, it might have been Doc's favorite, and he promoted it heavily in the intramural program. In 1926, Glenn "Brick" Johnson, of Spokane, a senior who'd won the Pacific Northwest Amateur heavyweight title, served as coach and Paul Ryan, of Spokane, and Deeter won PNA titles at 147 and 165 pounds.

Ike served as student-coach two seasons and after graduation in 1928 stayed around for another year as boxing coach and teaching assistant in physical education. In 1929 he was offered two jobs, one at North Central high as an assistant football coach, at ninety dollars a month, the other as director of the Potlatch (Idaho) Athletic Club, at $200 a month.

> I asked Babe [Hollingbery] what I should do.
> "Put your pride in your pocket. Go get that dough!" Babe advised.

Deeter stayed at Potlatch for a year. The PAC had teams in practically every sport for the 300 men who worked at the big Potlatch mill in those years. Deeter coached everything and was assistant football coach at the high school. That's where he ran into a tough little kid named Roy

Karl Schlademan, Cougar Track Coach 1927-1940.

"Pooch" Petragallo. In 1937, "Pooch" became WSC's first National Champion.

Bohler invited Ike back to Washington State in 1931 to become the school's first fulltime boxing coach and instructor in P.E. Except for Navy service in World War II, Deeter never left, and he built one of the nation's strongest college mitt programs.

Ike's team at WSC won the Pacific Coast Intercollegiate (PCI) team title in his first season as coach in 1932.* Three of his boxers, Clarence "Bud" Taylor, of San Francisco, at 135; Ed Prisk, of Bremerton, 145, and Kenov "Red" Lokensgard, Columbia Falls, Montana, 175, won individual crowns for the Cougars. That 1932 season was the start of an amazing record for Deeter's boxers. Ike had at least one PCI titlist every year from then on.

WSC won only one PCI title in 1933, but it was a fight Deeter will never forget.

> "Lambie" [George Theodoratus] was up against [Milo] Mallory, a big football player from California who'd won the heavyweight title the year before. The fight was in Sacramento, Lambie's hometown, but there were a lot of Cal fans there—and they were loud. The guy kinda' roughed Lambie up the first round and I told Lambie to go out and get all over him.
>
> When the bell rang, Lambie walked right over and hit him in the belly with a right and then dropped him in his tracks with a left hook. The place went crazy.
>
> Every Greek in Sacramento was in the ring. They were tryin' to get Lambie on their shoulders and Lambie didn't want to get on their shoulders. So we had another—unscheduled—bout among all the Greeks in Sacramento!
>
> They celebrated for three days. Half the restaurants in town were closed.

In 1934, Bud Taylor won his second PCI title at 135 pounds, and the following year Washington State took four individual crowns and gave Deeter his second PCI team championship. Titlists in 1935 were Roy Petragallo, at 115; Bert Johnson, Colfax, 155 (an "agony fighter" Deeter calls this counter-puncher); Al Pechuls,** Huntington Park, California, 165, and Theodoratus, heavyweight.

In 1936, when the Cougars began their long and great dual match series with the Wisconsin Badgers, Athletic Director Bohler decided that he had better make the trip to Madison with the boxing team.

"You know how exthited Deeter geth. I betta go along to keep an eye on him," Bohler told Graduate Manager Foster.

There were nearly 15,000 rabid boxing fans in the old Camp Randall pavilion that night. The Badgers loved college boxing.

Hal Jones, of Spokane, was fighting at 165 for Ike and Jones was a good one. Hal won the Pacific Coast Intercollegiate middleweight title later that year.

---

* Mike Burke, 135, of Cheney, was WSC's first PCI Champion, in 1930.

**Brigadier General, Chief of Materiel for the U.S. Air Force in Europe when Deeter and Gonzaga's Joey August went over in 1960 to conduct boxing clinics for the Armed Forces and assist with the U.S. team at the Rome Olympics.

"Hal got a terrible decision that night in Madison," Ike says. "It wasn't even close. The referee gave it to Wisconsin. After the bout the ref kind of walked over and was in our corner. The next thing I know, Doc jumps up and reaches over the ropes and grabs the guy by the throat and starts chokin' him.

"'Gol dang it, you call 'em right!' Doc screams at the ref. I had to get up there and pull him away.

"The next mornin' at breakfast Doc said, 'Ike, you tell thoth kidth not to take any paperth back home." The sportswriters had given Doc a pretty good goin' over for grabbin' the ref.

"'I don' want the prethident [Holland] to get ahold of any of thoth paperth, Ike. He might call me up on the green carpet.'"

WSC and UCLA tied for the PCI team title in 1936, with Bob Bates, Stanwood, 147, and Jones claiming individual crowns.

The Relay Man

Karl Schlademan came to Washington State from Kansas in 1926, at the start of the "Golden Age," to replace Doc Bohler as head coach in basketball and track and to serve as frosh football coach. Schlademan had been head track coach for the Jayhawks and was a founder of the Kansas Relays, a premier cinder event of the era.

He didn't have much luck with the Cougar basketball team, going 11-10 in 1927, his first year at the helm, and then sinking to 7-17 the second. His teams won just four of sixteen Conference games those years and Schlademan was replaced by Jack Friel in 1928. (In Schlademan's defense, he inherited Bohler's basketball team in 1927, and Doc had won just nine of twenty-six games in the 1925-26 season, only one in Conference play.)

Track was Schlademan's sport, and relay teams his specialty. Within a few years he had Washington State in the national spotlight at track carnivals such as the Kansas and Drake Relays. Building on a solid foundation left by Bohler, and concentrating on the sprints and middle-

Ken Driskill, of Hillyard, PNW champion at 158 and one of the best wrestlers ever at WSC, was appointed Wrestling Instructor in 1929. (Driskill took his degree in 1930 and stayed on as wrestling coach through 1933.)

The greatest distance man of his era, Johnny Divine breaks the tape in record time in the two-mile in the WSC-Idaho meet on Rogers Field May 14, 1925. (Manuscripts, Archives, and Special Collections, Washington State University Libraries)

Field Hockey Champions of 1925. (Note the "mascot".) This photo is from the Women's Athletic Association scrapbook in the WSU Archives. Unfortunately, the players are not identified. (Manuscripts, Archives, and Special Collections, Washington State University Libraries)

distance events, Schlademan put together some of the most exciting teams in Cougar history. WSC won eight straight Northern Division meets between 1932 and 1940. (There was no Northern Division meet in 1936, probably due to the Olympic Trials and a shortage of travel funds in that Depression year.)

An all-around athlete at DePauw University in Indiana, Schlademan won nine letters in football, baseball and track as an end, pitcher and hurdler. Following graduation from DePauw, he coached at Missouri Wesleyan, University of Arizona, and Baker University (Baldwin City, Kansas), before landing at KU, in Lawrence.

"I could always tell when things were going well with Dad," Sarah Schlademan Hall said. "He'd cock that hat on the back of his head. It was a signal that we'd won!" (Mrs. Hall, a 1941 WSC graduate now living in Everett, was in Pullman in 1987 with her brother, Dr. Ramsay Schlademan, a Fort Wayne, Indiana, physician and a Golden Graduate with the Class of 1937.)

Sarah and Ramsay also knew when things weren't going so well for their father.

"Dad had a habit of scuffing his feet when he was disturbed or disgusted, but when he was preparing to be angry he would twitch his nose—sort of sniff," Sarah said, and her brother nodded. "I must have gotten into more trouble than Ramsay. I remember that habit of Dad's vividly."

The Schlademans agreed that relay events were their father's favorites.

"I believe Dad's teams won every relay event at the Drake Relays at one time or another over the years," Dr. Schlademan said. "Even the shuttle hurdles."

Washington State was involved in three fantastic finishes in 1927, Schlademan's first track season at Pullman. At Eugene on May 7, Oregon

Court Champs of 1926. Don Williams, John Wilcox, and Fred Tucker. (Manuscripts, Archives, and Special Collections, Washington State University Libraries)

edged the Cougars 66-65. At Pullman the following week, WSC reversed the procedure, squeaking by Idaho 66-65. On May 20, at Pullman, WSC defeated Montana 67-64. Three meets decided by a total of five points!

The Montana meet was a thriller, going down to the final event, the mile relay. The WSC quartet of Rowland Newman, Thorp; Ray Williams, Eatonville; Captain Glenn McGillivrae, Bremerton; and True Ouillette, Bellingham, won in 3:27.8.

WSC's track program, as well as football and baseball, got a real boost with the completion of the huge Field House next to Bohler gymnasium in 1929. Athletes in all events could work out there, even javelin and discus throwers. The WSC Indoor Meet was inaugurated and proved an immediate success, eventually drawing athletes from throughout the Pacific Northwest. Hollingbery moved his spring football practice sessions indoors to get away from the chancey weather in the Palouse at that time of year. Mel Hein, the all-time great Cougar center recalled those early spring sessions in the Field House. "That's where you made Babe's team—if you made it," Hein said. "It was tough in there in that dirt!"

Schlademan had some great sprinters in those early years. Wes Foster and Jack Mooberry, both out of Wenatchee; Bob Barnard, Pullman, son of the old Cougar star Frank "Cack" Barnard; and Paul Swift, of Spokane, were perhaps the greatest of those on his early teams.

Coach Schlademan took his first team to the Drake Relays in 1930 and in 1931 WSC was represented at both the Drake and Kansas events. Swift (and swift he was!) won the 100 in 9.5 at Lawrence in 1931 and set a Kansas Relays record, and Lloyd "Rosy" Hein took the javelin at 199-9 in the Drake Relays at Des Moines. (He threw 200-1/2 for second at Kansas.)

Schlademan recorded his first dual meet win over the Huskies in 1933 (72-59). It was the first for the Cougars over their cross-state rival since

Wes Foster, *Wenatchee, and* George "Jo-Jo" Martin, *San Francisco, won National Junior titles in the 220 and the broad jump in a meet at Chicago during their Frosh year at WSC.*

1914. After Schlademan broke that jinx, his teams won five of the next six meetings with the Huskies, losing only in 1938, when WSC failed to win a dual meet in three starts. (And then came back and won the Northern Division Meet!)

Like Hollingbery and Deeter of the "Golden Age" group, and Jack Mooberry later, Schlademan was one of those coaches athletes thought of as second fathers. Ken Leendertsen, of Spokane, a good middle-distance man in 1934-1936, told of dropping the baton in a crucial mile relay at Eugene as a sophomore in 1934.

"Retrieving the baton cost us the lead and the race through disqualification," Leendertsen recalled.

Imagine his "shock and surprise" the next day on the train trip back to Pullman when his teammates elected him Captain for the following season. Team members may "elect" a Captain, but Leendertsen knew who had approved their choice.

"I know from his coaching course in Track that he felt the needs of the individual track athlete took precedence over those of the team and the need to win meets," Leendertsen wrote later of his old coach. "His program was not the hard driving professionalized kind we see today. . . . I suppose one could look back and wonder what might have been had we been motivated to work a little harder. On the other hand, I hope today's athlete gets as much enjoyment from his efforts as we did."

Lawrence Giles, of Pullman, was a good high jumper for Schlademan, but he was "shocked, heartbroken and angry" when the coach laid him out of a Conference meet because he got too involved in activities and his work on the *Evergreen* in 1936 and let his grades slide.

"He looked at more than points. He was teaching me what slacking off might mean later on, and of course it was one of the great lessons of my life," Giles said fifty years later on his Golden Grad weekend in Pullman.

Glenn Taylor, of Long Beach, California, a great hurdler for WSC in the 1934-1936 era, called Schlademan "a great gentleman—but you knew who the boss was." Taylor came to WSC from Long Beach Poly Junior College to play football for Babe Hollingbery. He was a good end. Schlademan learned that Taylor also was a crackerjack hurdler—and he had three varsity seasons of eligibility left in track, only two in football. Just before the football team left for Montana to open the 1934 season, Hollingbery "released" Taylor to Schlademan. Another example of the spirit of cooperation which existed among Cougar coaches in that great era.

Schlademan had one of the greatest Cougar track stars on his teams in the mid-1930s in Lorin "Bill" Benke. Sarah and Ramsay said Benke's failure to make the 1936 U.S. Olympic team in the 400 meter hurdles was one of their father's biggest disappointments.

"Dad thought a lot of Bill Benke," Sarah said, and her brother nodded agreement. "He always believed Bill would have made the 1936 Olympic team if he'd been at the Trials."

"Benke drew an outside lane in the finals of the 400-meter hurdles" (at Randall's Island, New York), Dr. Schlademan noted. "Dad said Bill could not judge the pace from that lane."

The Athletic Department, apparently hurting for money in that Depression year, did not send Coach Schlademan to the final Olympic Trials with his ace hurdler and Benke lost out in the last race.

Karl Schlademan left WSC for Michigan State after the 1940 season and continued a great track coaching career in East Lansing, winning several IC4A titles and sending a number of his athletes to the Olympics. He retired in 1958 and died in Fort Wayne, Indiana, in 1980 at the age of ninety.

Wes Foster, right; Jack Mooberry, left, and Roland Newman run 1-2-3 in the 220 for Washington State against Idaho in 1930. Foster's time was 21.3. (Manuscripts, Archives, and Special Collections, Washington State University Libraries)

Wenatchee Wes

Wes Foster was the first great black sprinter at Washington State. He set a WSC and National Freshman sprint record in 1927, running the 220 in 20.8. (Converted to 20.94 for 100 meters by Coach John Chaplin in 1988, the mark ranks eighth best in Cougar track annals.)

Foster won three individual events, set new state records in each, and anchored the Wenatchee 880 relay team to victory in record time in the State Interscholastic Meet at Pullman on May 16, 1925. His 5.3 in the 50-yard dash that day was a world high school record, erasing the 5.6 by E. C. Jessup of St. Louis on July 4, 1904. That 5.3 is still in the books for the State meet. The event was discontinued after the 1925 meet.

Foster's 9.8 in the hundred lasted thirty-seven years. Charles Greene of Seattle's O'Dea High School ran 9.6 in 1963. Spokane's Paul Swift broke Foster's 220 record of 21.7 in 1929 when he ran 21.3 at the State meet for Lewis and Clark High School.

The 880 relay mark of 1:32.8 that Foster and his Wenatchee teammates set in 1925 fell in 1928 to an all-star Northwest District team which ran 1:32.1.

*An overflow crowd at the WSC-
Idaho game on Rogers Field in the
mid-1920s.* (Manuscripts, Archives,
and Special Collections, Washington
State University Libraries)

In his first season at WSC (1927), Foster set the national freshman record in the 220 (straightaway) at a championship meet in Chicago. As a sophomore, he set an unofficial world record for 175 yards with a time of 16.6. The previous record of 17.4 was set by Charlie Paddock, Southern California's great Olympic sprinter (1920, 1924, 1928). It was not unusual in those years to clock the event within the 220. On this particular day, all four watches caught Foster in identical time. Another fine WSC sprinter, Glenn McGillivrae, was second in that race.

Foster won both sprints at the Pacific Coast Conference Meet in 1928, taking the 100 in 9.9 and the 220 at 21.6, thus becoming WSC's first PCC sprint champion. He eventually won five individual Pacific Coast titles for WSC, and a sixth as a member of the winning mile relay team in 1929 with Ken Kelly, San Bernardino, California; Jack Mooberry, Wenatchee; and True Ouillette, Bellingham.

Wes Foster lost only three races in his collegiate career, all to Crosby Pendleton of the University of Washington. But he caught up with the great Husky sprinter in his senior season, defeating Pendleton in both the 100 and 220 in the Northern Division meet of 1930.

Wes Foster was inducted into the WSU Athletic Hall of Fame posthumously in 1981.

"The New Spirit"

The *Chinook* for 1927 had as its theme "The New Spirit." It was appropriate. WSC did have new spirit in that 1926-1927 school year, exemplified by its new football coach, Orin E. "Babe" Hollingbery, and his big, colorful line coach from Texas, "Buck" Bailey.

As if by magic the pair lifted the college from the athletic doldrums of 1925 and headed it into a "Golden Age" for athletics.

John Gannon, who ran the City Club in those years, remembered when Babe came to town in 1926:

> You gave us all a lift. . . . You gave the average man about town the feeling he belonged as far as the Athletic department was concerned.

Pullman dentist Dr. Fred Johnston, who became a great admirer of Babe and Buck, said that in no time at all Hollingbery knew everybody in town.

> He'd come into the office and say, "Fred, we're goin' to need an extra, uh, $100 this year. Gotta get some kids who can, uh, beat those city slickers." Everybody'd dig down for Babe.

Jack Friel, who was coaching at North Central High School in Spokane when Hollingbery came to Pullman, said, "I well remember the early 1920s when WSC football was at a low ebb. When Babe came to Pullman he brought just what the doctor ordered in the way of coaching ability, aggressive leadership and cooperation."

Doc Bohler's son John, writing in 1962, remembered Babe's arrival from a very personal standpoint.

> When you . . . came into our lives, the Bohlers' spirits were at a low ebb. Poor seasons in both football and basketball had left a cloud of uncertainty over the Athletic Director's head and Dr. Holland had made it clear that it was very important the new football coach had to be a strong man with winning ways. So, if ever there came an answer to our prayers, it was in your person.

Starting with a team which had won a total of six games in the previous three seasons, only three in Conference play, Hollingbery took his first team at Washington State to within one game of a Rose Bowl bid. The Cougars were 6-1, their only loss coming at the hands of the powerful (8-2) Trojans of Southern Cal in Los Angeles on October 9 by a score of 16-7.

Washington State scored four shutouts in 1926 and defeated Enoch Bradshaw's University of Washington Huskies 9-6 in Seattle. Washington lost only to WSC and Rose Bowl-bound Stanford that year.

Herbert "Butch" Meeker, the diminutive quarterback for whom the school's Cougar mascot would be named the following year, opened the Hollingbery Era at Washington State by running thirty-eight yards for a touchdown on the first play from scrimmage in WSC's 35-0 win over College of Idaho (Caldwell) on Rogers Field, October 2, 1926. Ted Rohwer, Spokane; Carl Gustafson, Ellensburg; and Franz Joseph "Joe" Koenig, Olympia, also scored for the Cougars in that game.

The starting lineup for Washington State in Hollingbery's first game had John Parkhill, Wenatchee, and Gerald Exley, Colville, ends; Harold "Ox" Hansen, Tacoma, and Harry Speidel, Seattle, tackles; John Smith, Sprague, and Fred "Fritz" Kramer, Colton, guards; Jack "Brick" Graham, Spokane, center; Meeker, quarterback; Koenig and Rohwer, halfbacks; and Lloyd "Rosy" Hein, Burlington, at fullback.

Babe's team won all five of the games played in the Inland Empire that inaugural season of 1926, but he and his players must have been

WSC defeated the touring Meiji University baseball team of Tokyo 6-3 on April 22, 1924, in Pullman. Harold "Bill" Weingarten, of Tacoma, got the win with relief help from Munyo Maeda, of Puyallup. WSC won the Northwest Conference title that year, edging Oregon State. In a crucial series at Pullman on May 26-27, Weingarten won the opener 10-8, and Bill Nollan, Kirkland, and Weingarten shared pitching duties the following day as the teams battled to a 9-9 deadlock in twelve innings. (Called by darkness.)

water-logged by the end of the year, and the home season, unbeaten though the Cougars were, was a disaster at the gate. It rained 7.03 inches in Pullman between August 1 and October 22 of 1926.

"When old Jupiter Pluvius tipped over his water bucket on the football fans assembled on Rogers field Saturday [October 22] to see the W.S.C.-Montana game, he left [sic] loose of .67 inch of moisture," the Pullman *Herald* reported.

> A downpour of rains has greeted the Cougar team on both of its home appearances this year, cutting down the attendance to a minimum. It is estimated that the game Saturday attracted less than 2,000 [only 1,500 had seen the home opener against College of Idaho], most of them college students. . . .

Herald news editor Karl P. Allen warned that unless the weather improved for the Homecoming game with Oregon on November 3, "the athletic department may run out of funds and the fans out of patience."

It didn't get better. Graduate Manager Foster predicted the Oregon game would draw a record crowd of 12,000. Only 8,000 showed up to witness the 7-0 WSC victory. (Rohwer scored on a one-yard plunge in the second quarter and Meeker kicked the PAT.)

Herald sportswriter Sherman MacGregor,'29, of Hooper, noted in his story of the Oregon game: "The oozy field and wet ball hampered the Webfooters in their strongest form of offense, passing."

Even the (to be) Ducks were grounded in 1926!

Despite the inclement weather, the season was a huge success for Hollingbery and his gridders. Actually, the highlight came midway of the schedule, on October 23, when WSC defeated Washington 9-6 in Seattle. "Butch" Meeker figured in all the Cougar scoring. His field goal attempt in the second quarter was short, but UW safety man George Guttormsen, "using reverse English on his bean," the *Alumnus* reported, "took the ball on the one-foot line and grounded it in the end zone for a safety!"

Washington led 6-2 into the fourth period, but then WSC fullback Carl Gustafson drove the ball thirty-four yards in five plays to the UW thirteen, and Meeker, after a double-fake to Gustafson and then Rohwer, circled the Washington end to score. Butch kicked the extra point to make it 9 to 6 and give the Cougars their first win over the "Huskies." (Washington athletic teams were called the "Sun Dodgers" until 1923, and the last Cougar win over the UW had been in 1921.)

The following week, Meeker kicked field goals of 30 and 18 yards, both in the first quarter, to give WSC a 6-0 win over Idaho, ending the longest Vandal win string in the series at three. WSC had not beaten Idaho since 1922, but Hollingbery started a new tradition. His teams never lost to the Vandals.

Gene Dils, of Seattle, was a junior center on that first Hollingbery team. Interviewed at his home in San Marcos, California, in 1987, Dils said Babe established himself—and his principles—early.

They had what they called a "Campus Day" in those years, sort of a work/play day where the students would build sidewalks or provide some other improvement on campus. Apparently, some would have a beer or two along the way.

"Babe threatened to resign right there, when he saw some athletes drinking and misbehaving during the annual Campus Day," Dils said. "He said, 'I'm not going to have anything to do with a bunch of drunks.' That never happened again, I'll tell you that!"

Dils also recalled "Butch" Meeker.

> He was tough! He was an egotistic little monkey, but if you ever saw him play, when there was a pileup he somehow would come up on top of everybody, like a little rooster. He'd just squirm up, and there he was on top of all these men—with the ball! They wouldn't try to tackle him around the legs (he was only 5-4 and had very short, strong legs), it was always up high, and he got his face pretty well beat up. I remember in Missoula [in 1925] he broke off a couple teeth. When the team went to dinner, he went to the dentist's office. [He also kicked field goals of twenty-six and twenty yards in WSC's 9-0 win. Bill Kramer booted the other one, twenty yards.]

Following the 1926 season, "Fritz" Kramer was named to the West squad for the second East-West game on January 1, 1927, and was a starting guard as Hollingbery and Bailey coached and the West edged the East 7-3. Fritz long has been acknowledged to be the first WSC player to participate in the classic.

"Not so," says Marion [Blanchard] Hickey, '24. "Vern was!"

Marion is correct. Her husband, Vernard B. Hickey, of Everett, was an outstanding halfback and end for the Cougars in the 1921-1923 seasons (Captain in 1923). Hickey was coaching at Fort Bragg (California) high school in 1925 and played at end for the winning West team in the first East-West game on December 26, 1925.

Vern later coached at Santa Rosa Junior College and then went on to coach and be athletic director for many years at the University of California, Davis. The Vernard B. Hickey gymnasium at UC-Davis is named in his honor. Vern died in 1987.

By year's end, all the Cougar fans were emulating Babe's hustle yell, "Hup-ti-ditty!," and describing how he'd pace the sidelines in his lucky green suit, exhorting his Cougars to "Go through 'em—five yards!"

On November 27, 1926, it was announced that Babe and Buck had signed three-year contracts to remain at Washington State.

"Wild applause greeted the news" when Graduate Manager Foster announced the signings at a meeting of boosters in the Egyptian room of the Dessert Oasis hotel in Spokane, the *Alumnus* reported.

The Gentle Giant

Washington State athletic teams have been blessed with great trainers over the years, beginning in 1908 with "Doc" Bohler who came to the college as Physical Director and did double-duty as trainer for all the teams through 1925.

The first full-time, professionally schooled athletic trainer at WSC was Dr. Wilbur Harrison Smith Bohm, of Edwardsville, Illinois, one of the real pioneers in the field. One-time National AAU Champion in the discus and a graduate of the American College of Osteopathy in Kirksville, Missouri, Bohm joined the WSC faculty in 1926. Doc's

The long and short of Cougar football in 1925 is personified by center Gene Dils, 6-5, and quarterback Herbert "Butch" Meeker, 5-4. (Manuscripts, Archives, and Special Collections, Washington State University Libraries)

WSU football staff 1922(left to right): Hack Applequist, Head Coach Gus Welch, Athletic Director Fred Bohler, and Frosh Coach Eldon Jenne. (Manuscripts, Archives, and Special Collections, Washington State University Libraries)

professional ability, combined with his genial personality, rapidly earned the gentle giant (he was 6-4 1/2 and weighed 260 in his prime) the respect and admiration of everyone he worked with and made him one of the best "ambassadors" the school ever had. Doc was well acquainted with the Palouse country even before he joined the WSC faculty. He'd been at the University of Idaho in 1915-17 as a student athlete, competing in track and playing some football.

Bohm knew his stuff. He was one of the early advocates of calisthenics, seeing the regimen as a way of cutting down on injuries, and he wrote extensively on that subject and others related to athletic training methods.

"Coaches nowadays are beginning to see the absolute necessity for calisthenics as a part of the training work, both to build up general physique and to get the muscles in supple condition before the actual workouts begin, . . ." the *Alumnus* quoted Bohm in 1926. The magazine reported that:

> . . . . the Cougars this year set a new pace in the line of injury reducing. . . . Down at Pullman they are inclined to give much of the credit for this showing to their new trainer, the gigantic man who carries the name of Dr. Wilbur Bohm. . . . Dr. Bohm was on the job at all times, scorning assistance when a player had to be recovered from the field, and picking the casualty up in his arms to carry him off like a baby.

They don't make 'em like that any more!

Doc Bohm was an unforgettable character. A very large man, particularly for those years, his size was exaggerated by rolls of tape, jars of analgesic, cans of resin, towels, and other impedimenta, carried in bulging pockets of his pants, coat and overcoat, along with notebooks, newspapers, pens, and pencils, usually a sandwich, and always a supply of postcards that would have lasted the average man three lifetimes. (Bohm was the greatest postcard-sender of all time. If you never received a postcard from Doc Bohm, then he hadn't met you.)

"Just the greatest, the greatest man," 1934-1936 Cougar All-American Ed Goddard said of the old Trainer.

> I used to get cards from him from all over the world. That was one of his things. He always had a pack of [post]cards in his pocket. Something'd happen and he'd sit down, write a card and send it off to somebody. [Goddard said Bohm also carried dextrose tablets in his pocket—along with all that other stuff— and he'd sidle up to a player on the sideline and slip him one of those, for a little extra energy.]
>
> I didn't have any money for my folks to come to graduation, so I went to Doc and asked if there was any way he could loan me a hundred dollars. "Well, we can go to the bank," he said. I went back to the Chicago All-Star game that summer and we got $150. Doc came to that game and I signed my check over to him. He sent me back the $50. He paid the interest on my loan.
>
> Yep, Doc Bohm was the greatest!

Bohm had remedies and cures for every athletic injury or ill. Many of his antidotes were secret concoctions known solely to the Trainer. Cougar middle-distance ace Ken Leendertsen recalled one:

> A pickup cross-country team from WSC was invited to meet a UW team on the morning before the annual football game in Seattle. Our roommates at the Meany Hotel were members of the football team. Lambie Theodoratus was my roomie, and he had been treated for some minor injury with one of Doc Bohm's famous concoctions that contained a high percentage of a red dye-like substance. When Lambie showered, the hotel tub, shower walls and towels became what must have appeared to the hotel's maid service a real murder scene!

Doc fought a continual battle with weight, and lost every round. He'd wear one of those rubber suits in the training room to sweat off pounds, and when he wasn't treating someone he'd get the athletes to throw a medicine ball at his ample midsection. Then, at the end of the day, he'd retire to the dining room at the Washington Hotel and go through a couple of steaks—with all the trimmings. When the Cougars got to San Francisco on a football trip, Doc would really hit his gastronomic stride. He was a legend at Fisherman's Wharf.

Bohm and Buck Bailey, the twin behemoths of the athletic department from 1926 to 1943, "batched" in a small room at the Washington Hotel in Pullman from the time the hostelry opened in 1928 until Buck got married in 1939. One big, very sturdy bed occupied most of the floor space, and Doc had the walls completely "papered" with photos of famous athletes. The place looked like a sports museum. He knew most of the stars of the day and all the photos were personally autographed. (Clarence Bohm gave some of the photos to the University after his brother died, and recently built a special room at the family home in Edwardsville to display thousands of others that Doc collected over his lifetime.)

"Doc" Bohm was a familiar, and welcome, sight on the athletic fields at WSC from 1926 through 1943. The great trainer is pictured here midst the paraphernalia of his trade, pouring out resin to fullback Hal Gus Smith on a cold, wet day on Rogers Field. Also identified are Bob Campbell, 18, guard; Chris Rumburg, 46 (number hidden by Campbell's elbow); John Klumb, end, facing camera; Manager John Noel; Hal Harrison, 35, end; and Bob Grimstead, 32, tackle, between Bohm and Smith. (Barbara Jean Clark Collins)

"Never had a cross word with old Buck," Doc said in 1969 on his last visit to Pullman. "We had an agreement. If we argued about something, one of us would just take a walk. I got a lot of exercise and a lot of fresh air in those years. Yessir, old Buck and I never had a cross word."

Bohm worked tirelessly throughout his professional career to improve athletic training methods. In 1942, shortly before he left WSC, the great Trainer conducted an experiment with Kirk Gebert, one of Coach Jack Friel's basketball players, to determine how much distance a player covered during a given game. Bohm strapped a pedometer to Gebert during a WSC-Idaho game. He reported in an article in the *Athletic Journal* for March 1942 that Gebert, a guard who played less than half of this particular game (under Friel's "Platoon System," used for the first time that season), ran slightly over 3 1/4 miles. In a footnote to this article that was typically Bohm, Doc wrote:

> We give a standing invitation to all high school trainers and coaches to submit to us any questions they may have and, if at all possible, we send off the reply by return mail. At times we have sent our replies by telegram.

After leaving WSC in 1943, Doc was a trainer for the Cincinnati Reds and the Washington Redskins, and later worked winters and through spring training with the St. Louis Cardinals' baseball club. He also was with the Washington Senators, Calgary Stampeders and the New York (football) Giants.

Bohm was perhaps the best known and best liked Trainer in the country during his working life. Doc attended a number of the Summer Olympic Games, Los Angeles in 1932, Berlin, London, Rome, Tokyo and Mexico City, among others, and on several occasions was a working consultant with the U.S. team. During the 1960 Games in Rome, Bohm and Dr. T. K. Curaton of the University of Illinois surveyed the diet and training practices of the athletes for a book they were writing.

In 1965, when WSU was playing Iowa at Iowa City, Doc was a halftime guest with Bob Robertson on the Cougar Football Network. When word got around that "Doc Bohm is here," a dozen or more athletes who'd known Doc in college or in the pros came to the pressbox to pay their respects to the grand old man and swap some stories.

"Dr. Wilbur Bohm was a huge man with a heart to match," said Cougar gridder Rod Giske.

Thousands of people all over the world who knew and loved the old trainer would say "amen" to that.

Dr. Wilbur H. S. Bohm died in 1971 at the age of seventy-seven. He was elected a charter member of the WSU Athletic Hall of Fame in 1978.

Washington State has had only nine trainers through its first century of athletics. Doc Bohler served from 1908 to 1926 (except for 1917, when Leslie J. Clough came up from the Multnomah Athletic Club for one year); Bohm, 1926-1943; Jack Mooberry, 1945-1949; Vernon "Bucky" Walters, 1950-1955; Edwin B. "Eddie" Lane, 1956-1960; Dick Van-dervoort, 1960-1971; Dick Melhart, 1971-1978; and Mark Smaha, who replaced Melhart in 1978, is the ninth. Bohm, Vandervoort, and Melhart all served on the Board of Directors of the National Athletic Trainers' Association, and Smaha was national president of the NATA, 1988-1989.

An Old Star Comes Back to Shine

John Bryan Friel (he went by his middle name for some time, then "John" and later, inevitably, "Jack") came over to Washington State College in 1919 from Waterville. He was older than the average freshman, and had seen a little more of the world. When Jack finished high school in 1917 the U.S. had just entered World War I. A year later he was in France with a field artillery outfit.

Friel lettered three years at WSC in both basketball and baseball. He played at a forward spot for Doc Bohler in the 1921-1923 seasons, making Bohler's All-Coast second team as a junior. Pitching for Frank Barber in his sophomore and junior seasons, and for "Hack" Applequist as a senior, Friel posted a sparkling 15-1 mark in 18 starts and had nine complete games. Jack had a crackling good curve and was "sneaky fast," as they say.

During the summers, Friel played in the Timber League for Kelso and for two Bellingham teams. After graduation he also managed and pitched for Spokane in the old Idaho-Washington League.

Friel got his degree in Economic Science and History in 1923 and coached at Colville High School for two years before moving to Spokane's North Central. In 1928, Jack took the Indians to the State Championship. That summer the WSC basketball job opened up and Friel returned to Pullman.

"You know how Jack Friel got the Washington State job, don't you?" Mary Maude (Hungate) Buckley, '29, asked the crowd at Jack's Hall of Fame induction in 1978.

Archie [Buckley]* was on the Athletic Council. He played for Jack in high school at Colville. When Archie heard that no WSC

Jack Friel, Basketball Coach from 1928 to 1958.(Manuscripts, Archives, and Special Collections, Washington State University Libraries)

grads were being considered for the coaching position, he got Teddy Rohwer and a couple of other athletes and went to see Doc Bohler. They told Doc that if WSC grads weren't going to be considered for coaching jobs at their alma mater they were going to transfer out of the Physical Education department. That's how Jack got the job.

Friel's first team in the 1928-1929 season dedicated Bohler gymnasium by beating Lewiston (Idaho) Normal 62-18 on December 15, 1928, the first of Jack's 495 victories in a thirty-year coaching career at WSC. The starting lineup for Washington State in that first game in Bohler Gym had Leonard Mitchell, of Renton, at center; Erwin "Eddie" McDowell, Hoquiam, and Jim Gilleland, Pullman, at guards; and Archie Buckley, Colville, and Bob Van Tuyl, Yakima, forwards. Other letter-winners on Friel's first team were Gene Endslow and Ted Rohwer, both of Spokane; Carl "Tuffy" Ellingsen, Yakima; and Phil Pesco, Ilwaco.

Jack Friel, Waterville, and W. B. "Red" Reese, Pullman, teammates on Doc Bohler's 1923 Cougar basketball team, posted quite a three-year coaching record at Spokane's North Central High in 1928-30. Friel took the Indians to their first State basketball championship in 1928, then moved on to WSC as Head Coach. Reese, who'd been coaching at Cashmere, took over at North Central, finished second at State in 1929 and won it all again in 1930.

The Fox of the Palouse

It is amazing how much Jack Friel accomplished in such a short time after taking over as head basketball coach at Washington State in 1928. Friel had never coached a college game, and he inherited a team which had won only seven of twenty-four starts and was 1-10 in the Conference the previous year. In just three seasons Jack established himself as one of the top basketball coaches on the Pacific Coast.

Friel started turning the WSC program around immediately. True, his team lost six of its first seven games in that 1928-1929 season, but after that the Cougars went 8-8 and gained an even split in ten Conference starts, sweeping both Oregon and Oregon State in the process, something a Washington State team had not done since Doc Bohler's PCC championship season of 1917 (and did not do again until George Raveling's 23-7 team in 1983 took the Webfoots and Beavers twice each. Marv Harshman's 1969 club swept the Oregons in Conference games, but lost the Far West Classic title to the Ducks 80-78 in a chiller.)

After a 9-14 start that first year, Friel posted seasons of 14-12, 18-7 and 22-5, losing the ND title in 1932 by a single game. Sophomore Huntly Gordon, of Mount Vernon, began a brilliant varsity career that season, leading the Cougars in scoring and being selected to the All-Coast team at center. Claud "Bull" Holsten, of Fairfield, and Art McLarney, Port Townsend, were the only seniors among the starters in 1932. (McLarney was All-Coast at a guard spot as a sophomore in 1930 and twice was named to the All-Northern Division team.)

The Cougars won their first Northern Division title under Friel in 1937. It was a roller-coaster season with a fantastic finish. WSC fans still talk about it, and the play-off series with Stanford which followed.

Washington State had a good mixture of seasoned veterans and talented newcomers that season. The center, Conference scoring leader Ivar Nelson, of North Bend, was one of the seniors, along with Captain Bill Dahlke, from Waterville; Orville "Tini" Johnson, Tacoma; Frank

---

*Lieutenant Archie Buckley, USN, was killed in action in 1945 while serving aboard the aircraft carrier USS Saratoga during the battle for Iwo Jima.

Watch those Idees! Members of the Cougar Guard chapter of IK protecting one of WSC's first stuffed Cougar mascots at a game in Moscow in 1922. (Manuscripts, Archives, and Special Collections, Washington State University Libraries)

Hooper, from nearby Johnson, and Sewell "Swede" Carlson, of Hoquiam. Clyde "Corky" Carlson, of Renton, was a junior, and Friel had a great quartet of sophomores in Albert "Pete" Hooper, Frank's younger brother; Ed Kerpa, from Buhl, Idaho; John Kosich, of Wilkeson, and Cassius Dolquist, Yakima.

The Cougars won eleven of twelve non-Conference games, including their first-ever matchup with UCLA, 33-23 in Pullman on December 14. But the Conference race was wild!

After WSC lost both ends of a crucial series with the Huskies in Pullman on February 19-20, some of the wobblers dropped off the Cougar bandwagon. In its February 26 issue, the Pullman *Herald* told readers just how desperate the situation was:

> State's only chance for the pennant now depends on the possibility of both Washington and Oregon, the two first-place teams, losing a game. Should Oregon and the Huskies split their two-game series in Seattle, Washington State win their remaining three, and Oregon take their fourth win over Oregon State, the conference would end with a three-way tie for first [at 11-5].

Miracle of miracles, it happened just that way! But the Cougars still were deep in the woods. Oregon drew the play-off bye and Washington State had to play the Huskies in Seattle.

On March 12, Friel took his team back into Edmundson Pavilion and beat the Huskies 36-33. Trailing 30-23 with ten minutes left, the Cougars put on a sixteen-point charge—big for those days—while holding Washington to a field goal and a free throw for the entire second half!

There was not an inch of unoccupied space in Bohler gymnasium on the night of March 20, 1937. Crowd estimates ranged as high as 6,500, probably a thousand or 1,500 over capacity. The Cougars did not disappoint their fans.

WSC led 16-15 at the intermission after a "feeling out" first half. That was a good Oregon team. "Slim" Wintermute, Wally Johansen and Bobby Anet, all members of the "Tall Firs" who would win the first NCAA National Basketball Tournament for Coach Howard Hobson two years later, were starters, and another future great, Laddie Gale, was a

Carl Ellingsen, WSC Football, 1929-1930.

sub. The Cougars and Webfoots had each won two games in their meetings during the regular season.

Friel's team came out in the second half and blew Oregon away 42-25. The Webfoots went nine minutes without scoring as the Cougars built a 29-15 lead. Nelson wound up with sixteen points and Dahlke had eleven.

Angelo "Hank" Luisetti was the magic name on everyone's lips for the next week as Friel and his Northern Division champions prepared to meet the Southern Division winners from Stanford. The man who stunned the New York sportswriters with his running one-hand shots in Madison Square Garden the year before, earning unanimous All-America honors, was coming to Pullman to match his offensive wizardry with one of the all-time great defensive strategists in the game, the "Fox of the Palouse."

Stanford won, 31-28 in the first game and 41-40 in the clincher, but, as any Cougar fan over sixty will tell you when this great series is mentioned, "Ivar Nelson outscored Luisetti!"

Ivar did, nineteen to eighteen in the two games. The following year, when Stanford played Oregon for the PCC title, Luisetti scored forty-six points in two games and "dominated play."

Friel did what he had to do, "doubled" Luisetti and made Stanford win with its other talent. Coach John Bunn and the Indians had just enough board power to do that.

If you don't think Angelo Hank was nervous in that second game, look at the play-by-play. In the final thirty seconds, with the score standing 41-40, Luisetti was fouled twice and missed both free throws. The Cougars failed to capitalize.

In his excellent history of athletics at Stanford, *The Color of Life is Red*, long-time Sports Information Director Don Liebendorfer wrote of this series:

> The Indians had all they could handle in Pullman . . . to beat Washington State . . . in two straight squeakers.

Four years later, same place, same opponent, Friel would write a different ending to the script.

Back to Pasadena

"Good? They should'a been," he growled around the battered cigar that invariably stuck out of the corner of his mouth at a forty-five-degree angle.

"We beat the hell out of 'em for three years."

The gravel voice and cigar were Al Flechsig trademarks, but the old Cougar knew whereof he spoke. He played on three of Babe Hollingbery's early teams, one of his worst and two of his best. As a senior, Al was a starting guard on the 1929 club, the only Washington State football team, to date, to win ten games in one season. That was the outfit that beat the hell out of the team that eventually made it to Pasadena on January 1, 1931.

Flechsig, a long-time engineer for Westinghouse Corporation, always swore that it was the beatings those guys took in practice for three years that made them great in 1930.

As so often happens with championship teams, especially at the smaller schools in a powerful conference like the PCC, or now the Pac-10, everything just comes together, and a great season is the result. That's what happened for Hollingbery and the Cougars in 1930. As Flechsig said, some of the guys who didn't get to the Rose Bowl made important contributions, too.

Washington State had an unbeaten frosh team in the fall of 1927.

"The greatest bunch of athletes ever to come to Pullman," apprised Maynard "Swede" Lundberg, of Port Orchard, sixty years after he'd left his hometown to enroll at WSC. "Swede" was a 145-pound sub quarterback on that team, which scored 203 points to six by its opponents. Twelve men who played in the 1931 Rose Bowl were on that Frosh club, seven were Rose Bowl starters: Ends Sam Hansen, Tacoma, and Lyle Maskell, Spokane; tackle Harold Ahlskog, Spokane; center Mel Hein, Burlington; quarterback Bill Tonkin, Southworth; and halfbacks Carl "Tuffy" Ellingsen, Yakima, and Porter Lainhart, Goldendale. Five others off that Frosh club also played in the Rose Bowl: Ends George Hill, Dayton, and John Hurley, San Francisco; guard Harold Yap, Honolulu; center Howard "Huck" Morgan, Elma; and halfback Oscar "Stub" Jones, Chehalis. Hill, Hurley and Jones could be considered "starters" because Hollingbery platooned them with Hansen and Maskell and Lainhart all year.

"John Hurley was one of our great ends, but he'd get so excited before a game that Babe would never start him," Mel Hein said. (Hurley, later a pro end with the old Cleveland Indians, was killed while serving with the infantry in Italy during World War II. He'd earlier won the Silver Star in Sicily and is cited in Ernie Pyle's *Brave Men.*)

How often does a team have three legitimate All-Americans? That 1930 club did. Glen "Turk" Edwards, of Clarkston, and Ahlskog were named to tackle spots, and Hein was an All-America choice at center. Edwards was the first Washington State player to make the Associated Press first team All-America. Elmer Schwartz, of Port Orchard, made

With Coach Babe Hollingbery and Athletic Director J. Fred Bohler flanking President Hoover, the Pacific Coast Conference Champions of 1930 pose on the grounds of the White House for this picture taken on Dec. 1, two days after WSC had defeated Villanova 13-0 in Philadelphia to end its regular season 9-0. (T. Myron "Mike" Davis)

several second and third All-America teams at fullback that year. (Schwartz played at guard as a sophomore and moved to fullback as a junior in the 1929 season.)

Three players on that Rose Bowl team actually enrolled at the University of Washington as freshmen and then transferred to WSC, Schwartz, tailback "Tuffy" Ellingsen, and Bill Goodwin, of McKenna, a reserve tackle and end (who later became a WSU regent and then a federal judge).

Ellingsen left Seattle for Pullman before the UW Frosh season started in 1927 and wound up as the triple-threat star for the Coubabes. He scored two touchdowns and did some great passing and punting in WSC's 27-6 win over the UW Frosh in Wenatchee on Armistice Day. Miffed, the Huskies blew the whistle with the Conference and "Tuffy" was ruled ineligible for football as a sophomore. He became eligible at the end of the first semester, however, and promptly made Jack Friel's first basketball team.

Mel Hein figures in another of those "things that happen" to make championship teams. Rated by many as the finest two-way football lineman the game has ever seen, collegiate or professional, Hein grew up thinking he'd be rowing for the University of Washington crew. His father operated the power plant at Clayton Bay, near Bellingham, and Mel used to spend all his spare time down there in a rowboat strengthening his arms and legs so he could row for Washington. He said he came to WSC "because my older brother, 'Rosy' (Lloyd), was at Pullman and bragged me up to Hollingbery."

Mel was only the number three center on that unbeaten Frosh team in 1927 and very nearly did not return in 1928. Actually, he was better at basketball and track in high school. He was 6-2 and weighed 175 when he came to WSC (and played at 6-3, 198 as a senior on the Rose Bowl team). He ran the 440 and threw the discus in the State Meet as a senior at Burlington. (Mel still laughs about how he "joined" Sigma Nu that spring of 1927 as a high school senior. He stayed at the frat during the State Meet weekend and Jack "Brick" Graham and Melvyl "Meg" Dressel, Livermore, California, a couple of varsity linemen, hung a pledge pin on him and introduced him to the "brothers.")

Evergreen sportswriter Ron Broom, '31, later Sports Editor and Associate Editor of the Spokane *Chronicle*, related shortly before his death in 1987 how Hollingbery came to the Phi Delt house one night after a tough practice to visit with a rookie who'd performed poorly. A great psychologist, Babe seemed to know what all his players were thinking, all the time. The player Hollingbery came to see was in the process of packing up to go home.

"Babe just said to the kid, 'I think you ought to, uh, stick around,'" Broom recalled.

"The kid" didn't help much the next two seasons, but in 1930 Bill "Sarge" Tonkin was WSC's starting quarterback and a real sparkplug on the Rose Bowl team. (Hollingbery was a great one for nicknames. He called Tonkin "Sarge" because Bill had attended Culver Military Academy in Indiana.)

Washington State got to the Rose Bowl in 1931 the old fashioned way; they earned it!

Hollingbery had built solidly and well after taking over the coaching reins at Pullman in 1926. He switched from the Warner system WSC had played under four Carlisle coaches to a single-wing, with some short punts thrown in to utilize the quick-kick, which he employed with great success. ("Tuffy" Ellingsen blames a trick knee he developed fifty years after playing for Hollingbery to quick-kicking sideways out of that formation.)

Babe's teams were always fundamentally sound, strong defensively, and excelled in the kicking game. Heading into the 1930 season, WSC teams under Hollingbery had shut out seventeen opponents and allowed just seven points or less to ten others in a total of thirty-seven games. Hollingbery had not had a losing season; 1927 was a little shaky, 3-3-2, but Babe recruited his best crop of freshmen that year and the Cougars were 7-3 and 10-2 the following two seasons. WSC was unbeaten on Rogers Field from Hollingbery's first game in 1926 through the third game of his tenth season (1935).

Washington State did not have an easy schedule in 1930, but the tough games were spaced well as it turned out. WSC opened with a 47-12 win over College of Idaho at Pullman, and then jumped right into the Conference schedule, whipping California at Berkeley 16-0 on a pair of touchdown passes by Ellingsen (to John Hurley and Sam Hansen) and a thirty-one-yard field goal by reserve quarterback Mentor Dahlen, a sophomore from Spokane. It was a particularly sweet win for Hollingbery, his first in the Bay Area since leaving the Olympic Club in 1926, and further enhanced his image as the "Fightin' Friscan."

The Washington State-Southern Cal game, played on Rogers Field October 11, 1930, is still remembered as the greatest football game the Cougars ever played. (USC finished 8-2 that year, losing only to WSC and Notre Dame.)

"We used 14 men in that game," Mel Hein recalled fifty-seven years later, sitting in his home at San Clemente, California, and looking as if the season had ended yesterday. (What an amazing specimen he is! Mel played fifteen pro seasons with the New York Giants after leaving WSC, was All-Pro eight straight years, and in 1938, the year the Giants won the World Championship by beating Green Bay, was voted the Most Valuable Player in the National Football League. He is a Charter member of both the College and Professional Football Halls of Fame.)

> We had four ends that were about equal, so they divided the [playing] time. "Stub" Jones and Porter Lainhart divided the time at right half. There were no other substitutions. Tonkin played the whole game [at quarterback]; our fullback [Schwartz] played the whole game; "Tuffy" Ellingsen played the whole ball game, and the whole line, except for the ends, was in there sixty minutes.

Washington State scored in the first quarter on a one-yard run by Lainhart after a sustained drive. Maskell kicked the extra point. The game was scoreless thereafter until the fourth quarter when Marger Apsit scored for SC on a forty-seven-yard pass from Orville Mohler. John

Baker was back to kick the point but the snap was low and wide and Mohler couldn't get it down before the Cougars swarmed all over him.

"It was a very hot day," Hein recalled. "I really think if we'd had more men or it had been cooler, we'd have beaten them two or three touchdowns. But they wore us out. I remember that last quarter. They had a big squad and they had sophomores and juniors that were just as good as their seniors. That last quarter they had a fellow—I can't think of his name right now but he turned out to be an All-American at USC later, he was a sophomore at that time, and they put him in there that last quarter and he ran wild. (It was Mohler, one of SC's greatest, and he far out-shone the Trojans' senior quarterback, Marshall Duffield, that day.)

> I think they were down on about our twenty-yard-line when the game ended. [It was the twelve, actually. That was where "Stub" Jones made his game-saving, open-field tackle of Mohler. The gun sounded before SC could get off another play.]
> We were really tired out. If that game had lasted five or ten more minutes they may have beaten us. We were completely exhausted. I know I had the worst headache I ever had after that game. I perspired so much that even the next day I had a terrible headache.
> My older brother and I were batchin' out and I wanted to go home and go to bed, but he had a date and he wouldn't let me use the room. I had to go up to the fraternity house and go to bed.

The estimated attendance at that WSC-USC game was 22,000. Not bad considering the old stands on Rogers Field would only hold 21,500, jammed. (At least 50,000 people have sworn at one time or another over the years that they saw that game!)

Washington State defeated Gonzaga 24-0 the following week in Spokane and then romped over Montana 61-0 at Pullman.

During the course of the 1930 season Hollingbery's Cougars picked up the nickname "Red Devils" because of the red (Crimson?) uniforms. Sportswriters seemed particularly enamored of the name, but it rankled quite a few Alums. Floy Beeman, '13, of Spokane, wrote to *Alumnus* Editor Harry Chambers: "Won't you please refuse henceforth to include the term 'Red Devils' in the *Alumnus*? We don't like it—and 'Cougars' quite suffices. . . ." Editor Chambers agreed and pointed readers to another letter in the same (February, 1931) issue from Lynn Keyes, '16, Yakima: "Can anyone give a . . . reason for changing from 'Cougars' to 'Red Devils' as a cognomen for WSC athletic teams. . . ? We trust the use of the term 'Red Devils' is just one more freshman prank to be quashed by further deliberation."

A good Oregon State team (the Beavers were 7-3 that year) gave the Cougars a scare in Portland on November 1 before a crowd of 32,600 in Multnomah Stadium. It was the first Shrine hospital benefit game played in the Pacific Northwest. One-third of the $75,000 gate went to the Shrine hospital.

"Tuffy" Ellingsen, a great coffin-corner kicker for the Cougars, dropped one out on the Beaver three-yard line early in the game. When OSC's big guard, Coquille "Chief" Thompson, tried to kick the Orange out of trouble, Ahlskog charged in, got a piece of the ball and Schwartz recovered on the OSC nine. Four plays later, Ellingsen scored on an end run from four yards out and Maskell kicked the point after touchdown.

There was no more scoring until the fourth period when Oregon State tied it on a thirty-six-yard pass from Floyd Root to Ralph Buenke and Thompson booted the extra point. The Beavers tried to mount a last-gasp passing attack but WSC end "Spud" Hill deflected one of Buenke's tosses into the hands of Turk Edwards and the big tackle rumbled twenty yards for the clinching touchdown. Dahlen kicked the point to make the final score 14-7.

WSC waltzed over Idaho 33-7 at Moscow the next week, setting up the big game with Washington in Seattle on November 15.

As some said later, "That game was like a Joe Louis fight. If you got there two minutes late you missed it!"

Washington State kicked off (as Hollingbery so often chose to do, although in this case Washington won the toss and elected to receive). Merle Hufford fumbled the return and Schwartz recovered for WSC on the Husky twenty-eight.

The Cougars ran three plays for little or no gain and Maskell kicked a field goal, variously reported as 43, 45 and 48 yards in length. (WSU records list it at forty-three yards.) Only two minutes had ticked off the game clock.

Spokesman-Review Sports Editor Eugene Russell said Maskell scraped a couple of big chunks of mud out of his cleats and tossed his helmet aside before he kicked. Hein made a perfect pass to holder Ellingsen and Maskell kicked the ball, from a slight angle, low and "with just distance enough," Russell wrote.

"FUMBLE, FIELD GOAL AND COUGARS BEAT HUSKIES," the Seattle *Post-Intelligencer* bannered in its Sunday edition.

Maskell's kick was all there was. WSC won 3-0 and was on its way to the Rose Bowl—via Philadelphia.

Not to take anything away from Lyle Maskell; he was a great clutch kicker in that 1930 season. His toe provided the margin of victory in both the USC and Washington games. But Lyle had his moments. He was only 11 for 20 on extra-points that season.

On November 29, Washington State made its first gridiron appearance in the East and subdued a stubborn Villanova team 13-0 on a bitter cold day at Franklin Field. Schwartz scored in the first quarter on an eleven-yard run and Lainhart punched over for another score in the fourth period.

All-America tackle Harold Ahlskog, writing to Coach Hollingbery in 1962, recalled an incident from the game: "Some disgruntled fan, after watching our offense bog down on the frozen field, yelled out, 'How in the world did you beat USC?'"

"You turned with your index finger lifted, 'By one point.'"

What happened to Oregon that year? Why didn't WSC play the Webfoots?

Spokane *Chronicle* Sports Editor Bob Johnson wondered the same thing, so he turned the sleuthing over to Spokane sports historian Kent

●

"The tackles [Harold Ahlskog *and* Turk Edwards] *and* Mel Hein *at center are supermen," Rose Bowl Coach* Lone Star Dietz *said after watching the 1930 Cougars play Idaho at Moscow on November 8. Dietz was out west with his Haskell Institute team.*

●

Brennan. Brennan got the answer from L. H. Gregory, sporting editor of the *Oregonian*, and Johnson related the story in his column, "My Nickel's Worth," for December 22, 1967.

> "I can tell you why, because I was right there when it happened," Gregory wrote. "In [John J.] Cap McEwan's first year at Oregon [from West Point] in 1926, Oregon played at Washington State. It was also Babe Hollingbery's first year at Pullman.
>
> Cap, an Army man, was a great stickler for coaching protocol. The home coach was supposed to visit and welcome the visiting coach. . . . Babe, with an Olympic Club background, knew nothing . . . about this protocol and cared less. . . . He did not visit Cap to greet him and welcome him to the campus.
>
> The railroad parked the special Oregon car behind a warehouse and it rained, rained, rained. No movies, no nothing. It still rained the next day and Babe won (7-0) in the mud; at least on a very wet field for Washington State had the best turf in the conference, and still does, I believe.
>
> Cap left Pullman all burned up and vowing that while he was coach Oregon would not play Washington State again. And it didn't, and beyond that period. Cap's last year at Oregon was 1929, but the embargo continued . . . to 1936."

Johnson phoned Hollingbery in Yakima and Babe hooted at Greg's story.

> I remember that when Oregon arrived for the 1926 game McEwan demanded that a telephone be installed on the bench and that we put a lot of straw around the bench to help keep the players warm. We got him all the straw he needed. But we didn't install a telephone. And in those days we didn't have one on our side of the field either.

In 1930, the Webfoots were unbeaten (under Coach C. W. "Doc" Spears) going into their eighth game. The weekend Washington State beat Washington, Oregon State shut out Oregon 15-0 in Corvallis and knocked the Webfoots out of the Rose Bowl race. (In fairness to Oregon, who had beaten the Huskies 7-0, they were without their great back, John Kitzmiller, in the OSC game. He'd suffered an ankle injury against Washington. The Webfoots also lost the following week to St. Mary's 7-6, again without Kitzmiller.)

Next Time

The eighteen-year-old freshman bounded onto the porch at 505 Campus Avenue, opened the front door and burst into the house.

"Dad, a bunch of the guys at the house are going to the Rose Bowl. What do you think about me going?"

The Sigma Nu house was right across the street and they'd just pledged the freshman. What a thrill, to be in the same house with All-American Mel Hein!

"Well, son," his father put the evening paper down and peered up, his eyes narrowing a bit. "I don't know. Your grades weren't all that good at mid-term. Better stay home over the Christmas holidays and study.

"You can go next time."

In 1981, Cliff Wexler was sixty and still waiting. Washington State was getting ready to play Brigham Young in the Holiday Bowl at San Diego and a sportswriter phoned Cliff to see if he was going to the game.

"Dad said I could go next time, and I'm going," Wexler answered. Good thing he did. Cliff died in 1982. He couldn't have waited another year.

Beauty and the Beasts? Well, it's Cougar Captain Elmer Schwartz (right) and Alabama Captain Charles "Foots" Clement (left) with Irene Dunne, a reigning movie queen of the day, prior to kickoff at the 1931 Rose Bowl game. (Manuscripts, Archives, and Special Collections, Washington State University Libraries)

Rose Bowl II

"We didn't scout Alabama, but they sure scouted us!"

"We couldn't stop them in the air."

Carl "Tuffy" Ellingsen and Mel Hein should be well qualified to tell what happened that day long ago in Pasadena, California, when Alabama defeated Washington State 24-0 in the 1931 Rose Bowl. Ellingsen, the Cougars' triple-threat halfback, and Hein, an All-American at center, had played major roles in getting Washington State to Pasadena. Both were seniors, both played practically every minute of every game for WSC that year, including the Rose Bowl.

Washington State came out with new uniforms for the game. Dubbed the "Red Devils" during the 1930 season, the Cougars lived up to their billing by wearing red—lots of it, red helmets, red jerseys, red pants, red sox and red shoes.

"Their faces matched their uniforms when it was over," one wag wrote.

Ellingsen recalls that the shoes had been painted red.

"I had to scrape the paint off my right shoe to get a good feel of the ball," the Cougars' great punter remembered more than half a century after the fact. "I wore what they called a 'featherweight' shoe, with a soft toe, and kicked off the instep for better feel of the ball.

All-America tackle Glen "Turk" Edwards, *of Clarkston, and* Jack Parodi, *a guard from Stockton, California, were the only non-senior starters for WSC in the 1931 Rose Bowl.*

"Bill Tonkin had played at Culver Military Academy [in Indiana] and was the only one who knew about those 'two-piece' uniforms we wore in the Rose Bowl" (the hip pads were separate, not built into the pants), Ellingsen said.

One thing for sure, a team of Hollingbery's never wore those uniforms again. Babe saw to that.

"Word got around that Babe burned those uniforms," Hein said. "I don't know how big the bonfire was, or how much smoke was raised. Actually, I think he burned 'em in secret because he always kinda denied that he did it."

And they never again called the "Cougars" the "Red Devils."

Although the game is remembered by Washington State players and fans as a disaster, actually the Cougars had nothing to be embarrassed about. Alabama was a great football team, maybe as good as Wallace Wade had coached, and he'd had some good ones. Alabama was in its third Rose Bowl game in six years, so playing in front of 65,000 people was nothing new to the Tide.

Coach Wade knew all about losing teams being "embarrassed." He played at a guard position on the Brown University team that lost to Washington State 14-0 in the 1916 Rose Bowl. This game was "different" right from the opening kickoff. Wade, up against a recognized master psychologist in Hollingbery, pulled a little "psych" of his own. The Alabama coach started his second string, except for Captain Charles "Foots" Clement at a tackle (he wore an unheard of, in those years, size fourteen shoe, and his football shoes were custom made), and J. B. "Ears" Whitworth at one guard. After a scoreless first quarter, Wade threw his regulars into the fray and the Crimson Tide wasted no time limbering up its air arm. In just six minutes Alabama had three touchdowns.

End Jimmy Moore passed to wingback John "Flash" Suther for a sixty-two-yard touchdown and set up another touchdown with a forty-yard pass to End Ben Smith. Although most people seem to remember Alabama's aerial attack in that game, those were the only passes the Tide completed (in nine attempts), but they were devastating!

The next time 'Bama got the ball, Halfback Johnny "Monk" Campbell broke loose for forty-three yards and another score. It was 21-0 at the half.

Except for "Ears" Whitworth's thirty-yard field goal in the third quarter, the second half was scoreless, and Washington State might have had a slight edge.

"They didn't make too many yards running the ball, and we made pretty good yardage," Hein recalled. "But we couldn't stop them in the air with our defense."

Washington State marched to the Alabama one-yard-line late in the game. Porter Lainhart's thirty-seven-yard run and two passes from George Sander to John Hurley and George Hill being big plays in the drive. But Elmer Schwartz fumbled, Campbell recovered for the Tide on the six and WSC's scoring opportunity went begging.

Little was said about the part injuries and illness played in determining the outcome of the game, but the Cougars suffered from both. All-

America tackle Harold Ahlskog, one of the steadiest of the Cougar defenders, sprained an ankle in pre-game practice and quarterback Bill Tonkin, usually a demon punt-returner, was operating on one wheel.

"[John] 'Sugar' Cain, a left-footed punter, hit 'em low and let them roll," Ellingsen remembered. "This bothered Bill, who played safety." Tonkin's injury also made the Cougar secondary even more vulnerable to the Tide air attack, coming as it did off a run threat, Tuffy pointed out.

Coach Hollingbery, a "near-pneumonia victim" according to Rose Bowl historian Rube Samuelsen, was far from his usual fiery self, bundled in an overcoat on the sideline. Sick as he was, Babe ignored the advice of Trainer Doc Bohm and exhortations of family and friends and attended the post-game session with the press.

"I might not have, uh, gone if we'd won," he said later.

It had taken Hollingbery just five years to pick up a program that was staggering and bring it to the top of the Pacific Coast Conference. Despite the loss to Alabama, few would have bet that day that Babe and his Cougars wouldn't be back in Pasadena.

Mel and Turk

Mel Hein and Turk Edwards. Two names that will live forever in football histories and the memories of those who were honored to see them play in the twenties, thirties, and forties.

Hein is considered the finest center ever to play the game. He was named a charter member of both the College and Professional Football Halls of Fame and is on practically every all-time team.

In 1969, when Edwards was being inducted into the NFL Hall of Fame, Hein called his old Washington State teammate "the greatest tackle who ever played," and added, "In my opinion, he never has received the praise he was due." The *Biographical Dictionary of American Sports* says:

> [Turk] Edwards' pro career spanned seventeen years [nine seasons as a player and eight as a coach, three years as head coach of the Redskins], during which time he earned accolades such as "the greatest football lineman of them all."

The publication noted further:

> During the 1930s Edwards proved the preeminent NFL lineman. . . . On both offensive and defensive lines, he displayed overwhelming strength and power.

Turk was All-NFL four times in the 1930s.

Hein and Edwards played their entire careers with two organizations. Hein played for the New York Giants from 1931 to 1945. Edwards started with the Boston Braves in 1932, moved to Washington with the franchise in 1937 and finished his career with the renamed "Redskins" in 1940.

Hein, tabbed "Old Indestructible" after fifteen seasons with the Giants (his only injury of consequence was a broken nose), was an All-Pro center eight straight years (1933-1940) and in 1938 became the first interior lineman to be voted Most Valuable Player in the National Football League.

Glen "Turk" Edwards, All-American tackle, 1930-1931. Teammate Mel Hein called Turk "the greatest tackle who ever played." (Manuscripts, Archives, and Special Collections, Washington State University Libraries)

Giant fans don't even like to think about how close Mel Hein came to wearing another uniform all those years he played. But it's true.

Early in 1931, while a senior at WSC, Hein signed a contract with the Providence (Rhode Island) Steamrollers for $125 a game. Two days later Mel learned from Ray Flaherty (an old New York Giant who was coaching football at Gonzaga) that the Giants had mailed him a contract calling for $150 a game.

> I knew the Giants were a more stable ball club [the Steamrollers, for whom Butch Meeker played in 1930-31, folded after the 1931 season], and twenty-five bucks was a lot of money in those days, so I asked Ray what to do. He suggested I go to the postmaster in Pullman and see if he would send a telegram to the postmaster in Providence. Maybe I could get that letter intercepted.
>
> The next day I went to see the postmaster in Pullman but he said he wouldn't send a telegram for me. "Why don't you send it," he suggested. So I did.
>
> In about 7-8 days here comes that letter. They had intercepted it and sent it back to me. It wasn't until sometime later that I learned it was against the law—or at least against the rules, what I'd done. Maybe the fellow felt sorry for me. I did say it was very necessary that I get that letter back, that I'd made a mistake.

Mel said he made $1,800 for (twelve games) that 1931 season with the Giants, $100 more than he had been offered to coach football at Raymond (Washington) High School.

Mel Hein and Turk Edwards had something else in common, other than being Cougars and great Pro stars. Both married their WSC sweethearts, Mel married Florence Porter, of Pullman, and Turk wed Bonnie Beaudry, of Spokane.

The Golden Age

The gloom that descended on Washington State's athletic program after World War I only served to prove that Longfellow knew his stuff when he wrote: ". . . the nearer the dawn the darker the night. . . ."

Doc Bohler's fear that WSC might find it difficult to compete on an equal footing in the powerful Pacific Coast Conference, expressed at the time the school was invited to join the PCC in 1916, appeared to have been justified as the Cougar athletic program slid downhill following the glory years of Lone Star Dietz. And it was not only football that hit the skids. Doc's basketball program, which had made such a splash winning the PCC in that first season of 1916-1917, also went into decline.

The rosy glow started to fade following the war when the PCC schools resumed full schedules. By 1925, all the major sports at the College were in trouble. Coach Exendine posted his third straight losing season and was released. Bohler's basketball team slipped from 25-1 in 1917 to 7-12 the following year, and did not have another winning season until 1923. In 1925, the Cougars were only 2-8 in Conference play.

Similar slumps were occurring in baseball and track. After six straight first-place finishes between 1913 and 1918, WSC took only one dia-

Ted Danielson, of Spokane, Ik Duke, and Chris Crossman, Long Beach, California, led a successful drive for funds to take WSC's mascot to the Rose Bowl game in 1931.

The Washington State College Coaching Staff in 1929, the "Golden Age" group. Front (left to right):Bill Bond, swimming; Ken Driskill, wrestling; Ike Deeter, boxing; Jack Friel, basketball; H. H. "Shanty" House, physical education; Back row: Doc Bohm, trainer; Buck Bailey, baseball; Babe Hollingbery, football; Doc Bohler, athletic director; Karl Schlademan, track. (Manuscripts, Archives, and Special Collections, Washington State University Libraries)

mond title in the next six years, that in 1924 when the Cougars won both the Northern Division and the Northwest Conference Championship. In 1925, the Cougar nine dropped to fourth in the ND and was fifth in the final year of the old Northwest Conference.

Although Bohler had an unbeaten track team in 1924, defeating Oregon, the PCC Champion, 66-65 at Eugene, WSC lost every one of its six meets with cross-state rival Washington between 1915 and 1925, and in that last year lost to Montana for the first time in history. (The Grizzlies also took a four-way meet with WSC, Idaho and Gonzaga in 1926, but that, combined with the win in 1925, was the extent of their track successes over the Cougars.)

Regent A. W. Davis, a Spokane attorney, began to urge drastic changes in the entire athletic program at the State College. In the winter of 1924-1925, Davis called for the removal of both Director of Athletics Bohler and Football Coach Exendine. It was, Doc's son John said later, a time when "the Bohlers' spirits were at a low ebb."

President Holland stood by Bohler, however, and a majority of the Regents supported the president. But Davis continued to call for Bohler's scalp even after Exendine was fired early in 1926 and the "drastic changes" the regent had called for in the Athletic Department were well underway.

Among the few seeing light on the horizon was George H. Gannon, '15, a Pullman banker who later served as one of the college's most effective regents. Gannon was president of the WSC Alumni Association in 1925, and in April of that year helped hand-pick Earl V. Foster, a 1923 graduate from Wenatchee, for the newly expanded Graduate Manager's

position. It proved to be another "turning point" in the history of athletics at the college.

In an editorial headed "A Forward Looking Move," in the April 1925 issue of the *Alumnus,* President Gannon wrote: ". . . the athletic coaches and instructors have been laboring under some serious handicaps. One of these has been too much detail work aside from the particular branch of sport or sports for which they are accountable. The new graduate manager should relieve a large part of this difficulty."

In 1926, a year after Foster came in as Graduate Manager, there was a major reorganization of the Athletic Department. The heavy overload that Director Bohler had shouldered since his arrival in 1908 was lifted. Doc was relieved of all coaching and athletic training duties so that he might more effectively concentrate on administration as Director of Physical Education and Athletics. A move was made to give each sport its own coach, and, for the first time, coaches were hired on a year-around basis rather than by season. It was the start of a totally new look in athletics at WSC.

Cougars, particularly those old enough to remember the era, often refer to the years between 1926 and 1942 as "The Golden Age" of athletics at Washington State. That's when "Babe" Hollingbery, "Buck" Bailey, Jack Friel, "Ike" Deeter and Karl Schlademan were turning out great teams and had all those stars; the incomparable "Doc" Bohler was Director of Athletics and Physical Education; Graduate Manager Foster kept an eagle eye on the finances; and "Doc" Bohm, the gentle giant with the healing hands, was the Trainer.

There may never be a more compatible, colorful—and winning!—group of coaches and administrators than those who made WSC's athletic program a model for success during those three decades of the twentieth century.

It *was* a "Golden Age" of course, and what made it so were the people involved. They were great human beings and they also happened to be excellent coaches and administrators. They wanted to win—and win they did!—but they also were interested in helping each other succeed. In the "Golden Age," everyone worked together, played together, and *stayed* together.

The Fourth Decade, 1921-1930

Doc Bohler's Greenhouse was the name students gave the structure around the old reservoir (where the CUB is), erected in 1921 at a cost of $1,200 to serve as an "indoor" track. A covered, 500-foot cinder track with a sixty-yard straightaway and banked turns, enabled athletes to start workouts regardless of weather.

•

The Pacific Coast Conference broke up in December of 1921 and was succeeded "for scheduling purposes" by "The Big Three" (California, Stanford and Washington). About all it amounted to, after a lot of "newspaper fighting," was that football schedules were disrupted for the 1921 season and WSC wound up playing USC instead of Stanford (on December 3 in Pasadena) and losing the first game in the series 28-7. The UW *Daily* hailed the news that WSC and the UW were getting together again after their "spat" in 1920 over gate receipts: "This news is received with joy by the students who would like to see Washington play her traditional rival from Pullman in the big game. . . ."

•

The *Bohler Brothers* pretty well dominated Pacific Northwest athletic administration at this time. Doc, of course, was Athletic Director and Chairman of Men's Physical Education at WSC; George was Athletic Director at the University of Oregon; and Roy was AD at Willamette University in Salem, Oregon. George later became head football coach and athletic director at Alabama Poly (Auburn), and Roy went to Beloit (Wisconsin) College and then Chico (California) State, where he spent the rest of his life.

•

"William H. 'Lonestar' Dietz, former football coach at Washington State College and present coach at Purdue University . . . today [January 27, 1922] admitted in part that he made offers of financial assistance to *Glen Carlson, Harold Britt*, and *George Wilson* of Everett High School, *Stendall* of Sedro-Woolley high and *Abe Wilson* and *Walter Dailey*, university freshmen, if they would matriculate at Purdue next fall. "President *Henry W. Mashall* of Purdue University told Dietz that he and his recently-signed assistant coach, *Dick Hanley*, former W.S.C. star and coach at Pendleton, Oregon, high school, would not be employed next year." (Seattle *Times*)

•

Captain *Ford Dunton*, Spokane, a tackle, and *Vernard Hickey*, of Lowell, halfback, were chosen on the 1922 All-Coast team. Longtime college architect *Harry Weller*, '23, of Tacoma, told a great story about *Ford Dunton*. Seems *Rudolph Weaver*, chairman of the Department of Architectural Engineering, was "moonlighting" as architect for the new Sigma Nu fraternity house. Dunton was Sigma Nu president in 1922. The two had a disagreement over some plans and Dunton hit Weaver in the eye, giving him a "lovely shiner," Harry said. "Didn't bother Rudy a bit; he wore it as a badge."

•

WSC and Oregon State played to a 3-3 tie on November 17, 1923, in the first PCC game played in Tacoma. *Vern Hickey* kicked a twenty-five-yard field goal for the Cougars, matching a thirty-five-yard fielder by *Luke Gill*, both in the first quarter. (WSC never won a game played in Tacoma; has never scored a touchdown there! Other scores in Tacoma were 0-0 with the 392nd Infantry in 1917; 0-7 with Texas A & M in 1941; and 0-7 with Penn State in 1948.)

Johnny Divine, of Sacramento, California, was the best distance man in the Pacific Northwest in this era (1925-27). The diminutive, perpetual-motion running machine won the two-mile at the 1926 National Championships in Chicago in 9:32.8, becoming the first PCC runner to win a distance event in the NCAA. Earlier, he had clipped ten seconds off the PCC record with a mark of 9:36.9 in the dual meet with Washington, and on May 22, 1926, ran his best-ever, 9:22.8, in WSC's 77-57 win over Idaho.

•

Washington State had a string of small quarterbacks beginning in 1920 with *Moe Sax*, 5-6, 148. Then, in 1925, came *Butch Meeker*, 5-4 and 145; followed by *Ray Luck*, Spokane, 5-6, 130; *William Linden*, Everett, 5-8, 146; and *Archie Buckley*, Colville, 5-8, 150. *Bill "Sarge" Tonkin*, Southworth, who quarter-backed the 1930 Rose Bowl team, wasn't exactly a giant at 5-8, 157.

•

Gene Dils, of Langley, a center for the football teams of 1925-1927 recalls: "We took a piano out of the Theta Chi house—I think we were pumped up with some artificial energy—and ran it up Thatuna to give the Alpha Chis a little sere-nade. (The Alpha Chi Omega sorority house was where the Koinonia House is now.) About half-way, the hulk of *Dean [Carl] Morrow* loomed up and the piano was abandoned, right in the middle of the street!" Gene swears Morrow weighed 485. That might be a little high, but you can still see his *two seats* in Bryan Hall. They removed the armrest and made two into one for the ample Dean.

•

ASSCW Golf Course opened April 23, 1926. "Family membership" was twenty dollars for the year. Graduate Manager *Earl Foster* drove the ceremonial first ball, then a foursome of *Fred C. Forrest* and *W. L. Greenawalt*, Pullman businessmen; *Harold Brackett*, a student from Olympia; and Athletic Director *Bohler* teed off to christen the course. Forrest hooked into the ditch along number one (which paralleled North Fairway Drive, across from the Perform-ing Arts Coliseum); Greenawalt sliced one into the road that runs up through the middle of the course; Doc Bohler hit one 200 yards down the middle, and Brackett also got off in good shape. Brackett wound up medalist with a 47 and his partner, Bohler, had 53. Forrest and Greenawalt combined for a 107.

•

H. O. "Fritz" Crisler, later a great coach at the University of Michigan, was interviewed on the WSC campus in 1926 for the head football job succeeding *A. A. Exendine*. At the time, Crisler was at the University of Chicago as an assistant to the immortal *Amos Alonzo Stagg*.

•

WSC's *"Butch" Meeker* starred in the West's 16-6 win over the East in the Shrine game played December 26, 1927. "Butch, a terrific broken-field runner, twisted and squirmed his way back twenty-five yards [with a free kick] to set up the West's final score. . . . So legendary a figure is Meeker in the traditions of Washington State that the live Cougar mascot of the Pullman school is named after him," wrote *Maxwell Stiles* in his history of the game, *Football's Finest Hour*. (Meeker got HIS nickname because his father owned a butcher shop in Spokane.)

•

Johnny Bender, the old WSC coach (1906-1907 and 1912-1914), was at the University of Houston in 1927 when the school was a junior college. It was Bender who suggested to Houston students that they adopt the "Cougar" as their mascot.

•

Forrest "Coop" Curry, of Spokane, was a living legend around WSC in the 1926-1929 era. The big, handsome end somehow met, was introduced to, or had a date with (the stories vary) *Clara Bow*, the "It" girl, when the Cougs were in Pasadena for a game with USC. Miss Bow, so it is told, subsequently phoned

Curry at the SAE house. Promoter that he was, Coop arranged for the "brothers" to listen in on extensions—for one dollar an ear!

•

During the early years, *Doc Bohler* was instrumental in bringing many of the nation's leading coaches to WSC summer sessions as guest lecturers for his physical education courses. Among these were such household football names as *Fielding "Hurry Up" Yost*, of Michigan; *Glenn S. "Pop" Warner*, Stanford; *Howard Jones*, USC; and *Bob Zuppke*, Illinois; and basketball coaches *Ward Lambert*, of Purdue, and *Dr. Robert E. Meanwell*, Wisconsin. *Amos Alonzo Stagg* taught a summer session course at WSC in 1917, but President *E. O. Holland* always claimed *he* talked Stagg into coming.

•

The Field House (now Hollingbery Field House), measuring 125- by 300-feet with an overhead clearance of sixty feet, was opened in 1929. Even the old-timers cheered. *"Turkey" Thorpe* told how, one bleak April day, "the men took off their shoes, rolled their pants above their knees and waded into the swamp called the athletic field to dig ditches to drain it in preparation for spring training." Those days were gone forever!

•

WSC's first "Fireman"? Sophomore *Oscar "Stub" Jones*, of Chehalis, pitched in seventeen of twenty-three Cougar games during the 1929 season (including nine in a row at one stretch) and posted a 4-0 record, with seven "saves." In his WSC career, 1929-31, Jones was 12-1 with eight saves. His only loss came on May 4, 1931, in the last game Stub pitched for old WSC. (Either his arm gave out or Buck couldn't stand his jokes.) Stub was one of the all-time great pranksters among Cougar athletes. The old timers still talk about the "faculty movie" Stub put on one night in Seattle for a Cougar Club gathering. It was promoted straight, but turned out to be an African wildlife film which Stub narrated and gave faculty IDs to the various animals as they appeared. Everyone remembers the hippopotamus ambling in: "Ah, and here's *Dean Morrow*," Jones cracked. He somehow survived that one, but when he turned a bunch of pigeons loose in the new Washington Hotel at another gathering, Alumni Director *Joe Caraher* got a scathing letter from the humane society and old Stub's days as program chairman were over.

•

The Oakland, California, *Tribune* reported in its November 15, 1930, issue that Stanford might drop Southern Cal from the schedule because: "1. Subsidizing of athletes; 2. Academic laxity permits longer and better practice hours for the Trojans; 3. Use of a loophole in the 'triangular agreement' (USC, Cal and Stanford) to get poor scholars on the U.S.C. varsity."

•

Did it actually happen? *Stub Jones* told *Royal Brougham* of the Seattle *Post-Intelligencer* it did. When WSC was in the East to play Villanova at the end of that great 1930 season, the team was invited to the White House to meet President Hoover. Everyone was standing around in the reception room waiting when, finally, Mr. Hoover arrived. The president and Coach Hollingbery looked at each other for an embarrassed moment, each trying to think of something to say. The president eventually spoke: "Well, Mr. Hollingbery, what are you doing now?" Whereupon Babe replied (and remember, this was during the Great Depression and Hoover was being criticized from all sides), "I'm winning football games, Mr. President; what are you doing?"

The Fifth Decade, 1931-1940
Doggone Those Dogs!

WASHINGTON STATE CAME CLOSE TO THE PROMISED, PASADENA LAND IN THE 1932, 1934, and 1936 football seasons, but in each of those years the arch-rival Washington Huskies put the nip on the Cougars' chances.

In 1932, WSC still had a slim chance at the Conference title when it came into Seattle with a 6-1 record. The Cougs had lost only to USC, that in the second game of the season, and subsequently had won five straight, allowing their opponents only eight points in that span. Washington was 5-1-1, having played a scoreless tie with Oregon and losing to Cal 7-6.

On November 12, 18,000 of the faithful sat through sixty minutes of steady rain to watch the Cougars and Huskies maul each other from goal line to goal line with nary a point put on the board.

The most exciting part of the game came at halftime when members of the "Big W" Club at Washington started their biennial parade around the track in front of the WSC rooting section, taunting the Washington State fans with the stuffed Cougar mascot they'd stolen off the Pullman campus years previously. This time they were jumped by several hundred *real* Cougars, and the battle was joined! When police finally broke it up, the mascot was missing one leg and most of its fur—and still was better off than many of the combatants.

WSC had the best scoring opportunities in that 1932 game, moving the ball to the Husky five in the second quarter and to the two in the third. Both times Coach Hollingbery chose to go through the line rather than over it.

"He [Hollingbery] prayed as [Johnny] Eubank dashed up and down the sidelines, warming up," George Varnell of the Seattle *Times* wrote of the first Cougar scoring threat.

Babe endured lots of criticism for not going for the field goal against the Huskies, but he had statistics on his side. WSC was only 8-for-21 in extra points going into the Washington game that year, and Eubank, at best, was 2-for-5. Stats were not accurately reported in that era, so Eubank could have missed more. Seven extra-point attempts that season were listed simply "Kick missed," and the fact that Hollingbery used George Sander, "Lambie" Theodoratus, Ollie Arbelbide and Eubank—and perhaps others—for conversion tries, indicates a decided lack of confidence in any of his place kickers. Most game summaries in that era also failed to list field goal attempts. WSC made only one that year. But what a one it was!

OPPOSITE: *Three-time Cougar All-American, Ed Goddard, 1934-1936.* (Hilltopics)

When the Cougars were playing away from home, WSC students gathered in Bryan Hall to follow telegraphic re-creations of the games. This large "Grid-o-Graph" was set up on the stage and the position of the ball, gains and losses, were shown by a flashlight held behind the screen. This one was set up for the WSC-UW game in 1925. (Manuscripts, Archives, and Special Collections, Washington State University Libraries)

The second-guessers really went after Babe following WSC's game against UCLA in the Coliseum on November 24. In that one, Eubank earned himself a spot in Robert Ripley's "Believe it or Not" by kicking a forty-seven-yard fielder to beat the Bruins 3-0 as the final gun sounded!

Lee Wiggins, '42, of Pullman, tells a great story about that one. They used to have what they called a "Grid-o-Log" in Bryan Hall and students and townspeople would gather there to follow a game. Reports came in over a telegraph ticker. An announcer with a flashlight stood behind a large sheet with a football gridiron marked on it. He'd tell fans what was going on and trace the progress of the ball up and down the field with the light.

"The announcer said 'Eubank will try a field goal!'" Wiggins recalled. "The next thing we saw and heard was the light going up in the air in circles and a loud crash!

"Everybody knew Eubank'd made it. The announcer got so excited when he read the tape that he fell off the ladder. He went ass-over-teacup and threw the flashlight up in the air."

Eubank, a transfer from Glendale (California) Junior College, also won the 1931 Idaho game for WSC, 9-8, with a twenty-four-yard field goal in the fourth quarter. Wes McCabe, '43, recalls that in 1933 Eubank got his first coaching job at Tekoa high. "He used to suit up at halftime of the games and put on a field goal-kicking exhibition. The folks loved it!"

The 1936 WSC-UW game also ended in a scoreless tie. If anything, it was even duller than the 1932 struggle, and it ruined both teams' chances for the Bowl.

The Cougars, who had beaten USC 19-0 in the second game of that 1936 season, wound up 4-0-1 in Conference play. Washington finished

Rodger "Batman" Dougherty, 34, flies in to keep the bad guys away from "Robin" (Ed Goddard, 28) in this 1934 action on Rogers Field against Oregon State. (Manuscripts, Archives, and Special Collections, Washington State University Libraries)

6-1-1. Stanford's "Vow Boys" went to their second straight Rose Bowl with a 5-0 mark.

The thing most remembered by the record crowd of 38,000 at that game on November 24 in Seattle was the great punting duel between WSC's Ed Goddard and Washington's Elmer Logg, both sophomores. Goddard won, averaging 43.4 yards to 39.3 for Logg. This in a steady drizzle! Goddard got off a sixty-five-yard quick-kick in the first quarter. The ball sailed over Logg's head (he was playing safety) and rolled to the UW nine.

Washington State lined up for a twenty-five-yard field goal attempt in the fourth quarter, but it was a fake. Goddard, holding for kicker Mel Johansen, of Enumclaw, took the pass from center and threw a pass to quarterback Rodger Dougherty, of Portland, Oregon, in the flat. The Huskies' Byron Haines knocked it away.

Perhaps because so many interesting things happened to the Cougars that season before they got to Seattle, the 1936 game is the one Cougars remember most in that frustrating series. On October 3, 1936, WSC played Stanford for the first time. The game was memorable for many reasons. It was a perfect autumn day in Pullman, there was a record crowd of 23,000 in attendance, and they were dedicating the newly enlarged stadium. (The horseshoe end was added that year, and the press box expanded.)

The Cougars squeaked out a 14-13 win in a highly controversial game. WSC got both its scores on Goddard passes, forty-one yards to Dougherty in the second period and six yards to end Floyd Terry, of Exeter, California, in the third. Stanford's William Luckett missed the tying point in the fourth quarter after tackle Pete Zagar recovered Goddard's fumble in the Cougar end zone to make it 14-13.

The controversy came in the final seconds when Referee Bobby Morris, of Seattle, ruled that Stanford's Sam Brigham was stopped short

*The first Cougar-head monogram,
painted on an agronomy division
truck in the summer of 1936 when
artist Randall Johnson was working
a summer job in Pullman. Randall
changed "C" in the Cougar's "jaw"
to a "U" "WSU" when the college
became a university in 1959.*
(Randall Johnson)

of the goal line—"by an inch," the *Spokesman-Review* reported. The beef continued into the next week with the Bay Area papers carrying a story that Referee Morris not only had deficient eyesight but was guilty of "advising Goddard on his play-calling." (Now there's one you don't hear every day.)

On October 14, WSC and USC played to a scoreless tie in Los Angeles. It rained, and the *Evergreen* said WSC was at a disadvantage because it had been two years since the Cougars had played in the wet. Sunny south. Humbug!

On October 31, at Berkeley, WSC defeated California 14-13 in a game that is remembered for several things other than the score. WSC's second and tying touchdown came late in the final period.

Trailing 13-7, Goddard took the Cougars the length of the field on a couple of passes, one to Carl "Moon" Littlefield, of Sutter Creek, California. Then, with the ball on the Cal four, the Cougar drive stalled.

"We ran three plays and were still on the four," Goddard recalled at his Golden Grad reunion at WSU in 1987.

The *Evergreen* reported that Goddard dropped back ten yards and then dove over the top for the score. Old timers who saw the game have sworn for years that the Cougars went into punt formation that day on the Cal goal line.

Goddard said both versions are correct.

> Rog [Dougherty] said, "What'll I do?"
> I said, "Go into punt formation." I figured from there I could pick out something. With only four yards to go, wsshhhtt! I just dove over the top," Goddard said, laughing.
> "Hollingbery was going crazy on the sidelines!"

But Goddard's touchdown only tied the game. So Babe grabbed big George Rowswell, a sub tackle from Centralia, and shoved him out onto the field. (Rowswell had tried only one extra point that season—against Idaho on October 10. He made it.)

For some unexplained reason, Rowswell apparently thought the coach needed assurance that he had made the right decision. After running out onto the field a few yards, Rowswell stopped, turned and yelled to an astounded Hollingbery, "Don't worry, coach, I'll make it."

Witnesses said Hollingbery's mouth was still agape when the ball went through the uprights. You can bet he would have killed Rowswell had the kick missed.

On October 24, Washington State and Oregon ended their ten-year hiatus and renewed the series at Eugene. Ironically, WSC won 3-0 on a twenty-seven-yard field goal by quarterback Dougherty, who'd played football at Jefferson High School in Portland under the old Cougar, Eric Waldorf, '26. (If you don't think that didn't burn some tailfeathers!)

On November 7, in Pullman, it was another of those "underdog wins" games with Oregon State. The Beavers, going nowhere en route to a 4-6 season, upset unbeaten WSC 16-6 on two long passes by Joe Gray and a field goal by Prescott Hutchins.

On November 14, WSC tackle Dwight Scheyer, of Granger, scored his second career touchdown (both occurred in the Los Angeles Coliseum), as the Cougars overwhelmed UCLA 32-7.

As a sophomore in 1934, subbing for "Lambie" Theodoratus late in the fourth quarter of WSC's 19-0 win over USC, Scheyer picked off a Cotton Warburton pass deflected by end Harold Hawley, of Spokane, and returned it twenty-seven yards for a score.

In 1936, against UCLA, Scheyer ran over Bruin blocking back "Izzy" Cantor, blocked a punt, and returned it forty-four yards for a TD.

The win over the Bruins was costly, however. WSC lost three guards, starters Al Hoptowit, of Wapato, with a broken leg, and Bud Jones, of Spokane, along with sophomore Dick Farman, Kent. (If you've enjoyed "Farman's Pickles," that's Dick's company.)

So the Cougars came into Seattle on Thanksgiving Day, November 26, with their guards down, so to speak. "Babe was so intent on going to the Rose Bowl again—if we won that game we were in the Bowl he told us, I think we over-trained for the damn thing," Goddard said fifty-one years after. "The kids bet a lot of money on themselves. It was a terrible humiliation. But we really didn't have the same ball club. After we played UCLA and got those guys hurt, we were through."

The Huskies scored early on a five-yard run by Al Cruver, climaxing a seventy-three-yard drive. Newlyweds Joe and Marcella Caraher were sitting in the Cougar section.

"Watch those Cougars, Marcella; they'll come back," Joe reassured his bride.

But they never did. The Huskies put their second score on the board in short order, Cruver scoring again, this time from fifteen yards out.

Reserve lineman Bob Walters had a front-row seat on the Husky bench that day. He said later, "I never saw him (Coach Jimmy Phelan) like that, before or after. He was beside himself. He just wanted to keep scoring."

Score they did. It was 20-0 at half and the Huskies scored twenty more to make the final 40-0. It was by far the worst drubbing a Hollingbery-coached team ever received. Little wonder that the discouraged Cougars lost to a good Gonzaga team 13-6 in Spokane in the season-ender on December 5. By then, few paid attention to the fact that WSC finished 6-3-1 that season, a strong second in the PCC at 6-2-1.

Ed Goddard was one of the finest athletes ever to wear the Crimson and Gray. He played both football and baseball for the Cougars between 1934 and 1937 (as a tailback and catcher/outfielder) and still is the only WSC player to be selected All-America three straight years. You won't find that in the Cougar pressbooks, but it's true. The only first-team All-America honor listed for Goddard, a real "triple-threat" back, was in 1936 when he was picked by United Press. But in all three of his varsity seasons Goddard was named to *Liberty* magazine's All-America. *Liberty* asked players to name their All-Americans, and Goddard was on everyone's list.

After graduation, the "Escondido Express" played both pro baseball and football for a couple of seasons and then turned to coaching and spent "thirty-five very happy years in education in Orange County [California]."

Dead heat! Bill Nolf and Ken Wills join hands as they break the tape in the mile run against Washington. It was May 20, 1933, and the Cougars beat the Huskies 72-59 on Rogers Field. Nolf and Wills ran 4:27.4. (And here's one for the books. Just a year later, May 19, 1934, Nolf, Herb Redfield and Roy Carriker ran a dead heat in the mile in 4:32.9 as WSC defeated Oregon—get this— 72-59, on Rogers Field.) (Manuscripts, Archives, and Special Collections, Washington State University Libraries)

Scott Fiscus cuts off a Husky at first base in a series at Pullman in 1931. Note that the game is being played on the old diamond up by Smith and Bohler gyms. (Manuscripts, Archives, and Special Collections, Washington State University Libraries)

Coaches and Cars

Americans have been chided by most of the rest of the world for their love affairs with the automobile. In the cases of Buck Bailey, Doc Bohler and Babe Hollingbery it seemed more of a love-hate relationship. They loved cars but drove like hell.

Buck is famous for his driving exploits. "Sixty miles and hour," he used to say when questioned about his speed. That may have been true, but Buck drove sixty at all times!

Bailey knew the distances between every hamlet on the routes he traveled from Pullman to Spokane, Seattle, San Francisco and Eldorado, Texas, and he judged his speed not by the speedometer but by the clock.

Every generation of Cougars, from 1926 through to 1961, had a Bailey "driving" story to tell. Most of them were far-fetched. Almost all were true.

Babe Hollingbery drove only green cars. But he hardly could have considered them lucky, as he did the green suit he wore to every Cougar game he coached.

"He was the Green Streak!" one of his old ball players said of Babe's driving.

On one trip to Sacramento to see the PCI boxing tournament, Babe left home with a new car, hit some ice down around Klamath Falls and rolled it over. (He told Hazel he wasn't driving. "Got sleepy and turned the wheel over to a passenger.")

Babe ordered a new car, green of course, out of San Francisco and continued on to Sacramento. A few days later, on the way back to Pullman, "he became drowsy, due to the slow driving necessary in a new car," the *Alumnus* reported in its May 1935 issue, hit a bridge abutment and a steel railing went through the windshield, grazed Babe's right side and exited the rear window.

"Luckily, a young fellow riding with the coach [probably a recruit] had just lain down on the rear seat to sleep. . . . Hollingbery received a broken collar bone and numerous cuts and bruises, not to mention that his right ear was practically torn off," the *Alumnus* detailed.

Three cars on one trip. Not a record, as the guy said, but a helluv'n average!

Buck's and Babe's driving was better publicized, but Doc Bohler's was at least as good—or bad.

"Cars were scarce in those days [1916]," John Bohler recalls. "Dad went to Montana with the track team and when he came back from Missoula he had this old Model T Ford that had been converted into a racer. Some guy had apparently run out of money and for ten dollars or so he'd sold dad his car and dad drove the dang thing home. You can imagine the reception he got from my mother. She really laced it to him.

"Next morning, Dad went out to look at his prize acquisition. The tires were flat!

"Dad used to take the family to Lewiston once in a while for Sunday dinner. One summer evening we were coming home and there'd been a gully-washer out there around Uniontown. Water was going across the road like crazy. Cars were lined up on both sides of the road and people were looking at the water. Dad comes tearing along, sees those cars and throws on the brake. Nothing happens. So he turns into the opposite lane and WHOOSH! water flies everywhere.

"Dad just shifts her into second gear and we go right on through. Never stopped.

"Once we were out around Vantage. There was no bridge across the Columbia in those days. You had to be ferried across. Depending on the time of year, you either got out on the other side where the road continued, or, if the river was low, you had to drive up a long track in the riverbank to get where the road was.

"You drove up as far as you could go, and then when you got stuck a man with a team of horses was there and for a fee he'd pull your car on up to the road.

"My mother and brother and I were walking up that west bank and dad was in the car in a long line waiting his turn to start up the bank on this one-way track. It was a real tricky drive and nobody had made it all the way without sliding off that track.

"When dad's turn came he really roared up that hill—made it farther than anybody had—and it looked like he was going to make it. But he couldn't resist bragging a little, so he toots the horn and turns to wave at somebody. *Zap!* Down he goes into the mud, and out came the horses." (What John did not learn until years later was that the guy who owned the horses used to sneak out at night and water down that hill so the cars couldn't make it up!)

"I think my dad was the first person who ever drove from Pullman to Spokane and back in one day," John said. "Before that, it was like the four-minute mile, nobody could break it.

Steve McNeil, *of Hoquiam, who became one of America's favorite magazine fiction writers, played basketball and baseball for the Cougars. In WSC's 33-27 win over the Huskies on February 9, 1935, in Seattle (first Cougar win since 1920), McNeil held the Huskies' high-scoring* Bobby Galer *to a single point. In 1962, McNeil sold his 100th story to the* Saturday Evening Post.

"There was a funeral up there and dad and some of his associates felt they had to attend. He said 'C'mon, we'll go up and come back!'

"'Think you can do it, Doc," one fellow said. "'Thure,' dad said. You know how he lisped.

"Well, I sat in the back seat and there was some fellow from out of town sitting back there with me. I remember because he'd never been over the road, which was gravel then and very narrow and crooked. Up near Steptoe the road paralleled the railroad tracks, which were up on a fill, and then there was this trestle and the road went under the tracks and made a ninety-degree jog to the left and then immediately ninety degrees back to the right. Those underpasses were really built for wagons. They weren't much wider than a car.

"We came charging up there—dad had been there many times of course, but this stranger had no idea of what was coming. Dad makes that left turn, goes under the tracks and whips 'er back to the right.

"This man was scared to death. After we'd gone a little way he said, 'I only had that feeling once before in my life. That was when I was in World War I and I was looking across No-Man's Land at all those Germans!'"

Buck's favorite driving story was one where he actually, so he said, was a passenger. (There were quite a few "passengers" on this one, so just take it as a good story.)

L. H. Gregory, long-time sporting editor of the *Oregonian,* was one of the all-time great drivers. (He absolutely refused to fly.) Buck claimed he popped into the *Oregonian* one night as Greg was finishing his column and the gravel-voiced sportswriter asked in his abrupt manner, "You like chili?"

"Ever see a Texan who didn't!" Bailey responded.

"I know where they serve the best chili in the world," says Greg.

"You're on," says Buck.

Buck said they must have driven for hours, talking sports all the time. He finally fell asleep.

"When I woke up we were in Pendleton! That's gotta be a coupl'a hundred miles from Portland."

The two walked into a diner and Greg ordered two bowls of chili "and lots o' crackers."

"So help me," Buck would say, raising his right hand, "the guy reaches up and pulls two cans of chili right off the shelf!"*

National Champs

The year 1937 is one that Cougar boxing fans remember. Washington State won it all that year, the Pacific Coast Intercollegiates and then the U. S. National Intercollegiate Tournament, both at Sacramento, California.

---

*Author's note: years later, I asked Don McLeod, executive sports editor of the *Oregonian,* if that story were true. I'd heard it so many times by then. "Naw," Don said, shaking his head and pausing for effect, "it was The Dalles."

Roy "Pooch" Petragallo became Washington State's first National Champion, winning the opening bout of the USNIT Finals at 119 pounds on April 3, 1937.

A stubby, strong, perpetual motion type of fighter, Petragallo hit surprisingly hard for his weight class. (He always had trouble making the weight, too. Loved that spaghetti!)

Petragallo, who'd won his second PCI just before the Nationals (he won at 115 in 1935 and 119 in 1937), scored a TKO over George Takayanaigi of San Jose State in 1:58 of the opening round of his first fight. Pooch then won a close decision over Frank Jenkins of South Carolina in a great fight to claim WSC's first individual National Championship.

Ed McKinnon decisioned Rex Williams of South Carolina in his opening bout; scored a TKO in 1:32 of the second round over Maynard Harlow, of Virginia, then decisioned Steve Wilkerson, of Mississippi, for the National title at 155 pounds.

Paulie Waller, 139, of Carbondale, Illinois, and Bob Bates, 147, Stanwood, won two fights each in the Nationals for the Cougars but lost close decisions in the finals. Their points helped the Cougars pile up a winning total of twenty-five, however, beating out runner-up Duke with fifteen.

McKinnon, nicknamed "Deadpan" because of a rather deceptively innocent expression which never changed, no matter how furious the action became, was perhaps the finest boxer Deeter coached in his long career at Washington State. A tall, slender man with very long arms, McKinnon was a powerful puncher with either hand. When Eddie won his National Championship at Sacramento in 1937, Petragallo hollered, "You owed me that one, McKinnon!"

In 1933, when Pooch was a freshman at WSC, Deeter took a bunch of his boxers down to Kamiah, Idaho, to meet some local lads tutored by "Diamond Billy" Carter. (A tavern owner in Kamiah, Carter sported a diamond in one front tooth. He was a great fight fan and often drummed up a bus load to come up to Pullman when Deeter's team was fighting at home.) As Petragallo tells the story of his first—and only—trip to Kamiah, he fought first, and won.

"So I was feelin' pretty good when I came back out to sit at ringside. When they announced the fight between Bob Eldred and McKinnon, some guy behind me says, 'Watch this guy. He'll beat this college kid.'

"I grabbed the only dollar I had and laid it out there and said, 'I'll take Eldred!' Then I scrambled around and collected all the money I could from the rest of the guys and bet that too. Those hicks didn't know Eldred was the Pacific Coast Diamond Gloves champ!"

McKinnon proceeded to knock Eldred down a couple of times and beat him rather handily. Long before it was over, Petragallo was looking for a place to hide.

"Those guys [his teammates] wanted to kill me. Those were depression times, you know. That probably was their meal money for the month I lost!"

Idaho kept WSC from making it four straight PCI team titles for Deeter in 1938 by edging the Cougars 30-26, but Andy Tidrick, of Seattle, at 125, and Bob Bates, 145, gave Washington State two individual titles that

Ed McKinnon. (Manuscripts, Archives, and Special Collections, Washington State University Libraries)

Roy "Pooch" Petragallo.
(Manuscripts, Archives, and Special
Collections, Washington State
University Libraries)

year. And the Cougars were back in the throne room again in 1939. Harris "Ben" Drake, 155, of Tracy, California, and Mckinnon, 165, won their divisions.

In 1940, Les Coffman, Troy, Montana, fighting at 135 pounds, won WSC's only PCI title.

Washington State had four individual champs in 1941, Byron Hostetler, of Asotin, at 127 (his twin brother, Bruce, also fought for Ike that year, at 132); Coffman won again at 135; Drake took his second title at 155; and Fred Spiegelberg, of Omak, won at 175 as WSC waltzed to its sixth PCI team title under Deeter with thirty-five points to runner-up California's seventeen.

"I remember our boxing team leaving Pullman in two station wagons, Ike driving one and Doc Bohler the other," Spiegelberg remembered forty-six years after. "We were all reluctant to ride with Doc as he did not pay too much attention to the road, talking and gesturing with both hands off the wheel and burning up the road, as Buck Bailey did."

> I recall dividing up the boxers by weight to balance out the car loads. A lot of the fellows had to watch their weight, like Les Coffman and the Hostetler twins. I felt sorry for them when it came to meal time and Ike restricted their diet. Fortunately for me, I had no trouble making 175. I ate good!
>
> After Sacramento, the winners and Ike headed for [the Nationals at] Penn State, by train. WSC was represented by Coffman, Ben Drake and myself. [Byron Hostetler suffered a cut lip in the PCI finals at Sacramento and had to miss the Nationals.] It was a three- or four-day trip and Ike would have us work out at every opportunity. When the train stopped he had us off running up and down, and then we'd go to the baggage car and shadow-box until we about dropped. The motion of the train, keeping our balance as we rounded those curves, probably helped our footwork.
>
> Another week passed. No school. We brought along books, but there were far more interesting subjects along the way than studying.
>
> After the Nationals—I was second and heartbroken—we headed for Wisconsin for a dual match.* The rest of the team from Pullman met us at Madison. [Wisconsin beat the Cougars 5 1/2-2 1/2.]
>
> Ike and Doc Bohler had purchased new cars in Detroit and we drove back to Pullman in them. We were gone from the campus over three weeks, missing all those classes, which some professors did not appreciate.

In 1942 at the PCI tournament in Sacramento, Merle Vannoy of Clarkston won at 120 and Spiegelberg repeated in the light-heavy division. That 1942 tournament was one to remember.

WSC led San Jose State 22-19 going into the final bout between heavyweights Frank Manini of the Spartans and Idaho's Veto Berllus. A tall, pale kid, Berllus looked absolutely skinny alongside Manini, the wide favorite, a swarthy brawler who went about 215. A win by the San Jose fighter would give his team the championship.

---

* Deeter swears to this day that Spiegelberg "was robbed!"

"Ike said he'd give Berllus a WSC letter if he won," Spiegelberg said.*

Berllus, about 6-6 and long-armed, kept a left jab in the swarming Manini's face most of the way and won a unanimous decision. Washington State took the team title, Deeter's seventh.**

Shortly after that 1942 season, Deeter and many of his "boys" left for the service. Ike, as he has done for so many years since, tried to keep in touch. Stationed at the Navy's Pre-Flight center at St. Mary's College in California, Lieutenant Commander Deeter picked up *Life* Magazine one day in 1944 and saw a picture of wounded servicemen being returned to the U.S. from the fighting in Italy. He recognized Army Captain Harris "Ben" Drake, his two-time PCI champ at 155, in one of the pictures. Ike made some calls, learned that Drake had lost a leg in combat and was being sent to a base in Texas for treatment. He phoned Drake, and when the nurse who took the call handed Ben the phone Deeter growled: "Don't slug! Don't slug! Go out there and box!"

"Aw, coach," Drake blurted out, and started to cry.

Deeter got in touch with Jess Watson, '42, and "Red" Lokensgard, '33, two of his former fighters who were stationed at a tank base in Texas, and they visited Drake.

"Took him out on the town a couple of times," Ike said. "Little morale building."

Any wonder Ike's fighters, to a man, love the guy.

A World Record!

On May 29, 1937, in the Pacific Coast Conference meet in the Los Angeles Coliseum, the Washington State mile relay team composed of the Orr brothers, Jack and Lee, from Monroe; Harry Nettleton, South Bend; and Bill Benke, Los Angeles, set a world record of 3:12.3.

Their time broke the previous record of 3:12.6 by the Stanford team of Maynor Shove, the Hables brothers, Ike and Abe, and Ben Eastman, set in 1931.

Two world record teams, both with brother combinations!

Jack Orr was the lead-off man in that world record effort, Nettleton ran second, Lee Orr third, and Benke was the anchor. After two laps, WSC trailed by one yard. Lee Orr, running against Stanford's Jack Weiershauser (yes, he coached track at WSC in 1941), made that up and gave Benke a yard lead on the final exchange.

That race between Benke and Stanford's great quarter-miler Ray Malott remains a classic. Benke had finished second to Malott by inches

Harris "Ben" Drake. (Manuscripts, Archives, and Special Collections, Washington State University Libraries)

---

*Spiegelberg served as a rifle company commander in the ETO during World War II, earning two Bronze Stars and the Purple Heart. He then had a marvelous coaching career at Medford, Oregon, High School from 1948 to 1982, thirty years as head coach of the perennial champion Black Tornado football teams. Fred remembers his old coach as so many of Deeter's boxers have: "Ike was a second father . . . always treating us with respect and encouraging us. . . . Anyone who ever fought for Ike loved him. He was a great influence on my life." (Spiegelberg was inducted into the WSU Athletic Hall of Fame in 1983. Deeter, still living in Pullman with his college sweetheart, Claire Rose Deeter, '27, was a charter member of the Hall of Fame in 1978.)

** The story has a tragic postscript. Lieutenant Veto Berllus, USMC, died March 1, 1945, of wounds suffered at Iwo Jima.

Coach Schlademan and Lee Orr, in 1936, just before Lee made the Canadian Olympic team and went to Berlin. (Manuscripts, Archives, and Special Collections, Washington State University Libraries)

in the 440 earlier in the meet. This time it was to be reversed, Benke out-chesting Malott at the tape, and the Cougars had set a world record!

In Berkeley two weeks later, at the NCAA championships, Benke and Malott met again and Benke avenged his loss in the 440 at Los Angeles, edging the Stanford star in 47.1.

Benke and Orr

Lorin "Bill" Benke and Lee Orr were two of the greatest athletes in Washington State track and field history. How great? After fifty years, their times still rank in the top ten in the 200 and 400 meters and the 400 meter hurdles. Between them, Benke and Orr kept the Cougars in the sports headlines for the better part of seven seasons between 1934 and 1940. They won a total of eighteen Northern Division, Pacific Coast Conference and NCAA individual titles and ran on four winning mile relay teams in Conference championships.

Benke came to WSC from Los Angeles in 1934. A blond Adonis, he was dubbed "curlilocks" by a disparaging Bay Area sportswriter. It didn't bother Bill; he kept right on running and jumping—and winning for the Cougars.

Ironically, Orr, who entered WSC from the little northwest Washington high school in Monroe in 1935, was the first of the college's great athletes to compete for another country in the Olympic Games. Born in Saskatchewan, Canada, Orr ran under the Maple Leaf in the games in Berlin in 1936.

Benke and Orr competed in the sprints and 220 low hurdles, an event which subsequently was discontinued, and Benke ran the intermediate hurdles and broad jumped. Both were powerful runners, Orr the heavier; he lettered in football in 1939 for Coach Babe Hollingbery as a halfback.

Former WSU Athletic Director Stan Bates used to enjoy telling how Orr "made me a great coach." Bates, just out of college in 1934, took his first teaching-coaching job at Monroe. Orr was a senior that year. Bates took Lee to the State Meet at Pullman in the spring of 1935 and he won the 100 and 220.

"Lee came over and asked if I wanted him to broad jump. I thought he must be tired, so I said, 'Why don't you skip it.' He probably could have won the State meet all by himself." (The broad jump was won at 21-5 1/4 in 1935, well within Orr's reach.)

Stan "coached" Orr to a 9.9 hundred that day, and Lee set a new state record in the 220 at 21.2, breaking the mark of 21.3 by Paul Swift of Spokane's Lewis-Clark High in 1929, a national interscholastic record at the time. Orr's 21.2 in 1935 stood as a state record in the 220 until 1963 when Charles Greene of O'Dea High School in Seattle ran 21.0.

In 1936, Benke broke the Northern Division long jump record, was second in the PCC in the low and intermediate hurdles, and was an All-American in the 440 hurdles with a fourth place finish in the NCAA finals. He barely missed making the Olympic team in the 400-meter hurdles.

Orr was a freshman at WSC in 1936 when he made the Canadian Olympic team in the sprints and relay. He wound up fifth in the 200 meters at Berlin. Lee won one heat, finished second in another, and was second in the semi-finals. Not bad for a 19-year-old kid who hadn't even had a chance to win a Varsity letter.

Benke did not let missing the trip to Berlin bother him. As a senior and team Captain in 1937 he anchored the Cougar relay team which set that world record at 3:12.3 in winning the PCC at Los Angeles. Earlier that season, Bill set a new Northern Division record at 46.9 in the quarter-mile, and he later won the NCAA 440 at 47.1. His career "bests" also include a 24-8 long jump.

Lee Orr won eight Northern Division titles, taking the 100 twice, the 220 three times, the 440 once and the 220 low hurdles twice. He also won the 220 in 1937 and the 440 in 1940 in the PCC vs. Big Ten series. Oddly enough, WSC never won the mile relay in the Northern Division while Lee was running, but he was on two mile relay teams that won in the PCC meet and two winning 440 relay teams in PCC versus Big Ten meets, 1937 and 1938. Orr won four individual PCC titles, the 220 twice, the 440 once (he equalled Benke's 46.9 winning time in 1940), and the 220 low hurdles. In 1940, he won the NCAA 440 in 47.3.

Lee Orr and Lorin "Bill" Benke are both in the WSU Athletic Hall of Fame.

•

Nora Hall, Republic, and Elizabeth Anderson, Tacoma, were winners of the Final Emblem Award in 1936. (The award appears to have been discontinued after this year. "We had some wonderful teams in those years," Miss Hall recalled fifty-two years later. "Much to the disappointment of some of us, we had no 'intercollegiate' competition.")

•

Jack Orr, left, hands the baton to Cougar anchor man Bill Benke in the mile relay on Rogers Field. That's Bob Mattila, '34, timing. (Manuscripts, Archives, and Special Collections, Washington State University Libraries)

Professor Covington

Athletes remember professors for many reasons, but memories of N. G. Covington seem to be particularly vivid among those who wore the Crimson and Gray.

Covington was in the College of Veterinary Medicine at WSC from 1927 to 1945, but he also taught Phys. 3, a course in human physiology required for all physical education majors. A Czech, Dr. Covington had retained much of his native accent, and it became particularly pronounced when he was confronted by someone in his classroom wearing a letterman's sweater.

"I geeve you flonk!" he would scream at some offender, at times adding vehemently, "I geeve you dobble-flonk!"

Fulton Imbert "Mickey" MacMillan, a 112-pounder from Neppel, came over to Washington State in the fall of 1935 to box for Ike Deeter and promptly ran afoul of Dr. Covington. Mickey was on a boxing trip and missed an exam in Covington's class. At Deeter's suggestion Mickey went to see the prof and asked if he could take a makeup test.

After some dire threats and much harumphing about "atleets alvays lookink for spashul tritment," Covington told MacMillan he'd give him the test the following Friday before the regularly scheduled class. In his nervousness, Mickey forgot that the frosh were leaving that same morning for a Golden Gloves tournament in Seattle.

Come Friday, MacMillan was up early and over in Covington's office. No prof. He waited around until about 6:30 then went over to the apartment house where Covington lived and beat on the door. After repeated knocking, a sleepy, surprised Covington, clad in pajamas, peered out the door.

"Vot you doink, Meekie?" he demanded.

"I came to take that test," MacMillan answered. "The team's leaving for Seattle this morning."

Cords were in for golfers in 1938!
Coach Ray Hall, center, with one of
his good teams of the 1930s:
Clement Kalitowski, Mearle Miller,
Fred Campbell, Northern Division
medalist, and Howard Welch.
(Manuscripts, Archives, and Special
Collections, Washington State
University Libraries)

"Meekie, Meekie, you g'wan home," Covington wailed. "I geeve you
Cee." And he shut the door.

He did give MacMillan a C, but Mickey didn't stick around for the
second semester. It wasn't worth it, having to take classes like Covington's and spar with Ike's ace 119-pounder Roy "Pooch" Petragallo.
MacMillan decided to be a jockey.

Bunky Outwits 'em

Billy "Bunky" Holmes was one of three Holmes brothers from
Marysville who played football for Babe Hollingbery at Washington
State between 1936 and 1941. Bunky, '40-41, and Dale, '40, were
halfbacks, Charles (Chub), who played in the 1936-1938 era, was a
guard.

Against Idaho in 1940, Bunky lost a front tooth and loosened about
three others. The college arranged for him to get a bridge and everything
seemed O.K. until the three teeth that had been loosened began to turn
black in the spring of 1941. Doc Bohler wasn't too sure the school owed
Bunky for those.

Over at the Theta Chi house the night before the spring game in 1941,
with teammate Jim Rainbolt, of Everett, holding him down, and Bob
Kennedy acting as "dentist," the three dead teeth were removed.

The following day, Bunky awaited his chance. He finally got in at the
short, up back, on a punt return. The kick was short and Bunky grabbed
it—with one hand and a fist. He ran it back a few yards and dove head-
first into a gang of oncoming tacklers.

When the bodies unpiled, up jumped Bunky, bleeding from a cut lip.
He headed straight for Hollingbery on the sideline.

The Fifth Decade, 1931-1940

Paul Swift, WSC sophomore sprinter from Spokane, became, according to "Ripley's Believe It or Not" the first man to equal a world record twice in one day. Swift did it at the Kansas Relays in 1931, running 9.5 in the 100-yard dash prelims and repeating the performance in the finals. (Shortly after this great effort, Swift suffered a muscle injury in a truck accident and never again was the super sprinter he was in 1930-1931 at WSC. Paul's marks at Lawrence, Kansas, were not world records, by the way. WSC and Kansas Relays records, but not world marks.)

•

Washington State and Oregon State have had some real barnburners over the years—in all sports. In 1933, when the Beavers won their first PCC basketball title, the best they could do with the Cougars was a 2-2 split, WSC winning the fourth game 34-31, at Corvallis, in overtime! In 1941, when *Jack Freil* had his best WSC team, the Cougars won the Northern Division with a 13-3 mark. All three losses were to Oregon State. Then, in 1955, when *Slats Gill* had his finest Beaver team and went 15-1 to win the Division, the only loss was—yep, to WSC, 68-66 at Pullman.

•

In 1936, the WSC football team was unbeaten in six games, only a scoreless tie with USC spoiling the record. Oregon State came up to Pullman on November 7 and shocked the Cougars 16-6.

•

The WSC-Oregon State football upset most remembered by Cougar fans took place on October 25, 1941, at Pullman. Quarterback *Billy Sewell* scored on a four-yard run in the first quarter, *Joe Beckman*, of Tacoma, kicked the point and the game ended 7-0. That, of course, was the year of the "transplanted" Rose Bowl. The Beavers went on to win the PCC and defeat Duke 20-16 at Durham, North Carolina, on New Year's Day, 1942.

•

One more for the trivia buffs: Who refereed that 1942 Rose Bowl game? You can look it up in the program. It says "*Jack Friel*, Washington State."

•

Another upset! It wasn't Friel. PCC Commissioner, ex-G-Man *Edwin Atherton,* wouldn't let Jack fly to North Carolina, and he couldn't afford to be away from his ball club for the two weeks it would take to make the train trip. So *Lee Eisan* replaced Friel as Referee of the only Rose Bowl game not played in California.

•

Barbara Robertson, of Tacoma, was the recipient of the Final Emblem Award in 1933.

•

Here's one that reads like fiction, sad fiction. *Harry E. "Ed" Goldsworthy*, '36, Rosalia, tells it:

> *Stan Colburn*, Spokane, had a tendency to fumble and it got to be an obsession with him. Against UCLA one day [it had to be the 1933 game, November 30 in Los Angeles], Stan was almost unstoppable. In fact, he was selected by the UCLA players on their All-Opponent team on the strength of his performance that day. As the game neared the close, the Cougars were a touch-down behind. On the final drive, *Phil Sorboe* kept calling Stan's number and they marched down to the UCLA goal line to come up with a fourth and a yard or so. Phil called Stan's number again, but as they came out of the huddle Stan pushed [*Henry*]

Bendele over into his position. Bendele didn't make it. The
specter of a fumble in that crucial situation got in Stan's way.
Shortly before his death in 1987, Phil confirmed my recollection
of that incident.

•

Washington State was unscored on in Conference games in the 1934 season.
The Cougars defeated Montana 27-0, USC 19-0, Oregon State 31-0, and Idaho
19-0. WSC was tied by the UW 0-0. But the Cougars lost to three non-conference
opponents that season, Gonzaga 13-6; St. Mary's 9-6; and Detroit 6-0. All three
of these teams used the "Notre Dame" offense.

•

Hank Hayduk, Chicago, and *Frank Stojack*, Tacoma, were known as the
"Watch-charm Guards" when they were starring for the Cougars in 1932-1934.
Tough and quick, the pair made up for its lack of size (they weighed 184 and
186) with 100 percent hustle and fight. Hayduk, a Shell Oil executive, died at
age fifty-five shortly before the start of the 1969 football season. Just weeks
before, Hank had written WSU Coach *Jim Sweeney*: "I want to live to see the
Cougars beat the Huskies one more time and make it three in a row." [WSU
defeated the UW 9-7 in 1967 and 24-0 in 1968. But the Huskies won 30-21 in
1969. The Cougars were only 1-9 that season. That would have killed old Hank.]
Stojack played football with the old Brooklyn Dodgers and then was in
professional wrestling for eighteen years, eventually claiming the World Light-
heavyweight title. He later was Sheriff of Pierce County. Frank died in 1987.

•

Bob Neilson, Pullman, '42, tells one on Stojack. When *Bob Neilson, Sr.*, came
to WSC in 1934 to be the Wrestling Coach, Stojack was a student coach. He'd
hold tryouts for the week's matches on Thursday nights. Neilson, Sr., wanted
to change this, but Stojack balked. Neilson challenged him to a match, winner
gives the orders. "He pinned Stojack in thirty-three seconds," says Bob, Jr.

•

Jean (Joanna Leonard) Emerson, '35, knows football players aren't all "He-
Men." Jean needed five subjects for an "out-of-doors" blood drawing for *Doctor
Brice's* Bacteriology class. *Phil Sorboe* and *Stan Colburn* told her they'd send
along some football players. Came the day, and as the subjects approached her
needle, each in turn "bit the green grass by 'Hello Walk' and I, dejected, took
my little vials back—empty. It must have been the waiting," Jean said, kindly.

•

What was the closest score recorded in a Pacific Coast Conference track
meet? WSC 65 3/5, Oregon 65 2/5 on May 4, 1935, at Pullman. (Not counting
the 65 1/2-65 1/2 tie between WSC and the UW in 1950, of course.) Washington
State, after trailing all afternoon, got its winning margin in the final event, the
mile relay, when the Cougar team of *Jack Schneller*, Walla Walla; *Harry
Nettleton*, South Bend; *Ken Leendertsen*, Spokane; and *Lorin "Bill" Benke*, Los
Angeles, won in 3:26.2.

•

How did they come out with such an odd fraction score? There was a five-
way tie for first in the high jump at six feet. *Lawrence Giles*, Pullman, and *Ted
Christofferson*, Honolulu, tied with three Webfoots and the nine points were
divided five ways.

•

Babe Hollingbery once said he thought *Henry Bendele*, a 170-pound
running back in the 1931-1933 era, was a slow learner. "But I realized later that
he really wanted to learn the game!" Babe said. And Bendele learned it well. In
his first coaching job, at Spokane's John Rogers High School in 1935, Bendele
took the Pirates to their first ever City League title. Then they went to Portland
on Thanksgiving and beat *Eldon Jenne's* Portland City Champs at Washington
High 6-0. In 1938, Bendele returned to Ballard, his old high school, and in 1940

took the Beavers to their first title since 1923, when he was a member of the team. He had six championship teams at Ballard and was unbeaten in 1947 and 1951. Bendele died in 1962.

•

Levi McCormack, of Clarkston, a Nez Perce Indian, played one year of football and baseball for the Cougars in 1935-1936, then signed a pro contract with Seattle of the Pacific Coast League. Levi played on two Western International League pennant winners with Spokane in 1940-41 and had a career batting average of .313 in five seasons. He was on the bus that went off Snoqualmie Pass on June 24, 1946, killing nine members of the Spokane baseball club. McCormack survived with knee and hip injuries. Levi died in 1974.

•

"'What's in a name?'" The *Alumnus* for March, 1936, asked, and then answered its own question: ". . . to one junior at Washington State a certain name happens to be worth $20,000."

•

"When attorney *George Nethercutt* of Spokane was killed in an accident in December [1935] his will revealed that if *George Tiefel*, his protege, would change his name to Nethercutt, the estate would provide his education through law school and would give him the principal of the trust fund when he is 40 years old. . . . Tiefel or Nethercutt, as he is now, who is managing editor of the *Chinook* and a varsity baseball player [a shortstop, and All-Northern Division George was], said 'yes' to the terms of the will. . . ."

•

New grass greens were planted on the WSC course and used for the first time in the spring of 1936, replacing the old, original sand greens. (Retired WSU Agronomist *Al Law* has been cursing those greens for years. "They put down 6-8 inches of cinders and clinkers from the old heating plant, covered this with six inches of Palouse soil—loess, and planted the grass atop that," Law says. Since water will not move from fine soil to course, Al explains, they've had a terrible time ever since with those greens hardening.)

•

Remember *Tabut?* The huge clock (sixteen feet in diameter) on the twenty-four by twenty-five-foot scoreboard at the west end of Rogers Field was installed just before the WSC-Stanford game, October 3, 1936. The second hand was ten feet long and the minute hand eight-and-a-half feet. It was donated by the Tidewater Associated Oil Company, which sponsored most of the football broadcasts on the Pacific Coast in those days, and was constructed by *W. F. Taylor* and *L. C. Butts*, Pullman jewelers. "It is the largest on the Coast and perhaps in the nation," the *Chinook* said. That winter, the 9-foot clock in Bohler gym, invented and patented by jeweler Watts, was installed. The power was in the end of the second hand, rather than on the axis, and the clock was said to be accurate to 1/64th of a second. (It also was confusing. Several times, visiting teams not familiar with the clock threw up last-second shots only to discover there was another full minute to play.)

•

They had quite a celebration when they dedicated the expanded Rogers Field stadium on October 3, 1936. *Randall Johnson*, '37, Pullman (who designed the famous Cougar-head WSC logo that same year), was in charge of the big halftime pageant at the game. There were actors in costume and a huge (twenty- by thirty-foot) "book" was brought out and the history of the college was depicted as the pages turned. Johnson and a large crew of students had worked on the show in the Field House for weeks. Student Body President *Marion "Tex" Brotherton*, of Walla Walla, presented the newly enlarged stadium to President *E. O. Holland*, and he in turn gave it to Governor *Clarence D. Martin*, who accepted on behalf of the state of Washington.

Jess Willard, Jr., son of the former Heavyweight Champion, was a top-flight hurdler for Coach *Karl Schlademan* at WSC in 1937-1939 and also boxed for *Ike Deeter.* "Great guy," Ike said. "Too bad the papers wouldn't stay away from him. He won a couple of fights but they expected too much because of who he was, so he quit boxing. I sure didn't blame him." Willard was Northern Division high hurdle champion in 1937. He came to WSC from Glendale (California) Junior College.

•

"This is the story of the game nobody saw," *Braven Dyer* of the Los Angeles *Times* wrote on October 30, 1937: "Sounds crazy, doesn't it, but it's the gospel truth. Everybody knew when the battle started because they heard [referee] *Bob Evans* blow his whistle. And all of us were pretty sure the game had ended because we heard the final gun go off."

•

Johnny Carpenter, doing the play-by-play for a Spokane radio station that day, took his microphone down to the sidelines—and still couldn't see! Once, when the play went away from him, Carpenter told his listeners: "There they go—but they'll be back."

•

Well, that was *one* of the famous WSC-USC "fog" games, but sportswriter Dyer made it a little worse than it was. Actually, the fog lifted just after the teams left the field at halftime and most of the second half was played under clear conditions. "The scoreless tie was almost an exact duplication of last year's battle fought in Los Angeles," Dyer admitted late in his story. "Southern California had a big edge in first downs and yardage but the Cougars came nearer to a touchdown." (WSC got to the USC eight in the first quarter, but Hollingbery chose not to go for the field goal, although *Joe Sienko,* of Pe Ell, had beaten UCLA 3-0 the previous week in Los Angeles with a twenty-yarder in the fourth quarter.)

•

In case you missed it, the starting lineup for WSC in that famous "fog" game had *Paul Bates,* Albany, Oregon, and *Harold Harrison,* Monroe, at ends; *Dick Farman* and *Bob Grimstead,* Tacoma, tackles; *Chuck Semancik,* Tacoma, and *Al Hoptowit,* Wapato, guards; and *Chris Rumburg,* Millwood, at center. In the backfield were *Joe Angelo,* San Francisco, at quarterback; *Carl Littlefield,* Sutter Creek, California; and *Sienko,* halfbacks, and *Eddie Bayne,* Billings, Montana, fullback. (Old Buck Bailey used to tell a wonderful story about Eddie Bayne. Seems when Bayne was a sophomore, he questioned something *Babe Hollingbery* told the backs. Eddie said, "In high school we . . . ." Hollingbery turned to the youngster and said, "Uh, yeah. What was the score when you played USC?")

•

Forrest "Twogie" Twogood coached basketball and baseball at Idaho from 1936 to 1941, and he and *Buck Bailey* put on some great shows for the folks over on the old diamond by the Field House. One day Twogie sent his pitcher, *Earl Gregory* (later with the Boston Red Sox) up to the plate without a bat. Buck let out a howl and charged umpire *George Clink,* from Spokane. "He can't do that!" Buck bellowed. "Show me in the rule book where it says a player has to have a bat," Twogood responded. It was a close game and Idaho had a runner on with nobody out. Twogie figured Gregory, a non-hitter, would at best strike out, or, worse, hit into a double-play. Poor old Clink didn't know what to do. Finally, Twogie laughed and handed his pitcher a bat. (He struck out.) *George Clink,* the umpire who loved pitchers and hated walks, died in late December of 1961 in Hot Springs, Montana.

•

Dick McCroskey, of Pullman, a great Cougar sports historian, recalls that Coach *Jack Friel* introduced the "double pivot" in 1938 "when Jack had some real bulls around," like *John Kosich, Jack Jennings,* Centralia, and *'Pete' Hooper.* "Yeh, Friel laughs, I used Pete in the post once in a while. He was strong; liked to get some of those panty-waist forwards in there and knock 'em around!"

•

This game is important in sports history because it marked the beginning of the *Idaho Walk* tradition. *Bill McGowan,* sports editor of the *Argonaut,* the U of I student newspaper, challenged *Loyd Salt,* of Neppel (Moses Lake), sports editor of the *Evergreen,* the loser to walk the eight miles to the other's campus the Monday following the game. McGowan's timing didn't look too bad. WSC was 1-6 going into the Idaho game. In his column, "Grains of Salt," the *Evergreen* editor implored the Cougar team to win, even promising to "shine the players' shoes" at the Bookie the following Monday. The Cougars won and McGowan, and some of the Argonaut staff and a few Idaho students walked the eight snowy miles to the WSC campus. Salt had his stand set up at the Bookie, but McGowan did the honors. He shined some of the WSC players' shoes, and a tradition was born! It lasted through the 1974 game, and only three times in that 36-year span did the Cougars walk.

•

"Cougar Charlie" Hatley, Pullman, sports editor of the *Evergreen,* wrote: "Something new in sports broadcasting for KWSC will be tried on Friday [May 31, 1940] when the Cougars and Idaho tangle in Moscow. Telephone reports will be reconstructed into a play-by-play account of the game." (The first "recreation" done by KWSC.) *"John Jarstad,* Bremerton, and *Jim Scott,* of Hay, regular baseball announcers from KWSC, will give the play-by-play. . . ." As it turned out, Idaho won a thriller, 6-5, Lefty *Cliff Chambers,* Bellingham, taking the loss for the Cougs.

•

(Stanford) Stan Johnson, Enumclaw, was named "Player of the Week" by a radio station in LA for his great defensive play and two extra-points in WSC's 14-14 tie with USC on September 28 in the Coliseum. WSC produced two thrilling TDs in that game. *Les Mclennan,* of Escondido, California, started into the line, flipped a lateral to *Billy Sewell* who ran downfield and, as he was being tackled, lateraled to *Dale Holmes,* of Marysville, a halfback, who scored on the thirty-six-yard play. USC was leading 14-7 in the fourth quarter when Sewell passed sixty yards to *Felix Fletcher,* of Everett, and Johnson kicked his second extra point to tie.

•

The biggest ovation at this game, however, was for *Cecil "Hippo" Wetsel,* former WSC guard from Peshastin, who was introduced as "Public Hero Number One." Wetsel ran a sawmill in California. He had made a daring capture of the kidnapper of three-year-old *Marc de Tristan, Jr.,* and was the toast of the country. "Hippo" sat on the WSC bench during the USC game, and, on October 19, 1940, was an honored guest at WSC's Homecoming game in Pullman versus Stanford.

•

Only bright spots in the 33-9 loss to the Huskies in Seattle on November 30, 1940, were the blocked punt (resulting in a safety) by *Nick Susoeff,* of Los Angeles, and an eighteen-yard run by *Billy Sewell* off a "sucker play" which put the Cougars ahead 9-6 in the first quarter. *Evergreen* sportswriter *John Jarstad* described the play in his column, "Cougar Pause": *"Don Greeley* [Okanogan] called a reverse from the UW eighteen and *Felix Fletcher,* near out of bounds, came in, picked up the ball and 'scooped it' to *Billy Sewell* who ran untouched to score." Here's one for the books: The WSC frosh football team tied every game it played in 1940, 13-13 with Moffett Field Flyers (Sunnyvale, California), Gonzaga, 0-0; UW, 7-7; and Idaho 6-6. The team was coached by *Buck Bailey* ("officially," but actually a group of graduate assistants, *Ken Devine, Dick Emerson, Earl Ross,* and *Joe Angelo* handled the squad).

The Sixth Decade, 1941-1950

Those Train Trips

ALL THE LONG DISTANCE TRAVELING BY ATHLETIC TEAMS BEFORE WORLD WAR II WAS done by train. Pullman had good train service, the Union Pacific (it was the O W R & N, Oregon-Washington Railway and Navigation Company, up until late 1941) went south and southeast, the Northern Pacific went to the coast, north and east.

Every old athlete has stories about those train trips. Some of the yarns overlap, and there are differing versions of quite a few, but all are fascinating, especially to the generations too young to remember train travel.

"The Cougs always traveled by train, whether it was to Spokane to play Michigan State or Los Angeles to play the Trojans," says old Cougar guard Rod Giske, who played for Babe Hollingbery in 1941-1942 and for Phil Sorboe in 1945.

> We kept the same two cars all the way to San Francisco when going south. Then we'd catch the high-speed "Daylight" to L.A., arriving in time for a late afternoon workout. After the game, the same two cars would be waiting for us back in San Francisco on Sunday.
>
> The place all the Cougs would remember is Wallula (Ayer) Junction. We always had to wait there for hours on a siding for a 'local' to pull us on into Pullman. It was a learning experience to listen to the coyotes wail in between the gusts of cold wind that swept through that miserable place. The only thing you could be sure of, was that nobody was sleeping!

Giske has a marvelous touch for telling about those trips. Rod was a "city boy," from Tacoma, but it was a different age then; even city boys appreciated some of the little things that have made those memories last, vividly, nearly half a century.

"Departures," Giske says, "were always fun. No more three-hour turnouts for the rest of the week. Trips to Los Angeles were Tuesday evening departures. Lots of pretty pep staff and other girls and friends to see the team off. We won a lot more than we lost in 1941 and 1942, so the 'welcome back' crowds were usually large, too."

> But with all good things there was the in-between. The long days on those two green monsters. "Rattle, rattle, toot, toot,"— stop here, stop there. If the stop was for over five minutes you could be sure Babe would have us out on the siding doing calisthenics to help keep us tuned up. He saw to it that we

OPPOSITE: *Cougar Guard Rod Giske in 1941–before those train trips and the grid wars aged him.* (Manuscripts, Archives, and Special Collections, Washington State University Libraries.)

*Shrine spine tingler!
Quarterback* Dick Renfro, *of
Glendale, California, got
behind Penn State's* Aldo
Cenci, *took a thirty-five-yard
pass from* "Squirmin' Herman"
Wedemyer *of St. Mary's and
ran thirty yards for the tying
touchdown as Coach* Babe
Hollingbery's *West team tied
a highly favored eleven East
13-13 in the annual Shrine
game January 1, 1944, in
San Francisco's Kezar
stadium.*

stayed "regular" also. The chocolate and candy man who walked all the trains many times each day got a real fast escort through our two green monsters. We remember Babe's favorite expression: "That chocolate will plug you up ever time, fellas!"

We had a lot of serious football players as far as gaining an education. A lot of textbooks came aboard and you would see Joe Beckman, Jim Woody, Bill Gustafson, Jim Wright, George Dyson, Bill Remington and others doing class assignments. Buck Bailey hosted most of the sessions in sophomore to senior poker.

Babe worked hard at group sessions in defensive strategy. These were mandatory. He didn't have much trouble getting volunteer sessions going with the likes of Dale Gentry, Nick Susoeff, Bill Ward, Felix Fletcher, Dick Renfro and [Hjalmer] "Jelly" Andersen, who just loved to upend people on Saturday afternoon. [Giske didn't miss too many of these sessions.] They all paid off. I imagine the defensive records set in 1941 and 1942 probably still stand. [Indeed they do, Rod. Nine single season defensive records set in 1942 are still in the Cougar record book, along with three more set in 1941.]

Veterinarian Dr. Bill Gustafson, who played tackle on those 1941-42 teams [all 205 pounds of him!], took the "Cougar" train from Seattle to Eugene in 1986 for the WSU-Oregon game. In conversation with the most elderly-looking porter, Bill asked if he remembered how passengers [and Cougars] took a ferry from Oakland to San Francisco to catch the Daylight in those long-ago years. The fellow looked at Bill and said, "You really go way back!"—but he remembered.

On those ferry rides, Babe would attract quite a following as we circled the deck and he explained all the sights.

After playing in the Bay Area at Stanford or Berkeley, the squad always got a few hours to ourselves in San Francisco. Babe would have us all around him and he'd tell us where to go. Such advice as "Take a cab to the wharf and have a crab cocktail." Once I fell in with Nick Susoeff's group. About nine of us shot across the street and into a cab. We all got in OK and the cabbie said, "Where to?" "Top of the Mark," says Susoeff.

"No dice," the cabbie said, in no uncertain terms, and we all started getting out. Babe sees this and runs across the street to ask the cabbie what was wrong.

"I'm not takin' all these guys up that hill!" the cabbie tells him, and Babe says, "uh, hell, there's no hill to Fisherman's Wharf!"

"These guys want to go to the Top of the Mark, not Fisherman's Wharf!" the guy answers.

All nine were now split into about three groups going different directions, which couldn't have been too thrilling, as I don't remember where we ended up. [Rod recalled with a laugh.]

One of the great "games" people played in those train travel days was to try to sneak aboard. Lots of students did it. George "Blackie" Blakkolb, who was sports editor of the *Evergreen* back in 1931, recalled that he and Wally Halsey, of Asotin, a yell leader, were "smuggled" aboard for the USC trip that year.

Carl "Tuffy" Ellingsen tells about his brother-in-law-to-be, Dr. George Kuhn, '30, stowing away on the train and riding to Philadelphia with the team in 1930. Tuffy and Harold Yap, a guard from Honolulu, would

Wilbur "Doc" Bohm reads—what else—The Sporting News! *in the room he and Cougar Baseball Coach Buck Bailey occupied in the old Washington Hotel in downtown Pullman. Bohm was the Cougar Trainer from 1926 until 1943. Many of the thousands of autographed sports pictures Bohm collected during his lifetime now are in WSU Archives; others, his brother Clarence has installed in a special memorial room at the family farm in Edwardsville, Illinois.* (Hilltopics)

switch Kuhn from one bunk to another when the conductor came around.

Walt Wyrick, who was a Senior Manager for Babe in 1929, made a trip or two as an "extra" passenger. "You'd roll under the made-up bunks and stay there until the train crew stopped counting heads," Walt remembers. "It was close under there—and those steam pipes were hot. The ball players would bring back snacks, so you got some food."

Wyrick recalled one memorable stowaway when he was Manager and the team was going to Hawaii over the Christmas Holidays in 1929.

"Babe left Jack Parodi home. Took Frank Mitchell along as the last guard. Parodi asked me to pack his gear, which I did. He got on the ship OK, and ate in [Emmett] 'Mutt' Shroeder's place. Mutt got sick even before we got into the open sea and never left his bunk.'"

The railroads often used many of the same porters and dining car personnel trip after trip in those years. Bill Buford was a man the fellows all came to like on the U. P., Wyrick said.

"Babe and Earl [Foster] took us all to dinner in downtown LA one time," Wyrick remembered. "Outside the restaurant a fellow was selling 'radio sets' for a couple bucks. Great music, but he warned buyers not to plug them in a wall socket. Ray Luck and John Hurley fell for his line and bought one. When we got back to the Huntington Hotel [in Pasadena] the thing wasn't working, so Luck plugged it in up in his room and must have blown out every light in the place—and the radio too!

"When we got back to Pullman, Bill Buford had shined all the shoes and dusted down our clothes. Everybody handed him some change as they left the train. Everybody except Luck. When Ray went by, Bill stuck out his hand and Ray said, 'You got your dough.'

"Buford grinned and said, 'I'd like some more—so I could buy a radio.'"

1941 basketball team. Back (left to right): Coach Friel, Dosskey, Butts, Harrington, Sundquist, Hunt, Mahan, and Doc Bohm. Front: Gebert, Hooper, Gilberg, Lindemann, Zimmerman, Gentry, Akins, and Manager Wainscott. (Manuscripts, Archives, and Special Collections, Washington State University Libraries)

Love Those '41 Cougs!

Washington State didn't fall off much after that Northern Division championship season in 1937. Friel's team won nineteen games the very next year and then posted twenty-three-win seasons back-to-back in 1939 and 1940, leading up to that great 1941 season.

The Cougars won thirteen Conference games in a row in 1941, a Northern Division record. Oddly enough, WSC lost its first two Conference starts that year, to Oregon State at Corvallis on January 7-8, and then, beginning January 10 against Oregon at Eugene, were unbeaten until March 8, the night after they clinched the Northern Division pennant at Pullman against Oregon State. (They did lose a game in that stretch, to Signal Oil, an AAU team, 47-37 in a game at Longview on February 11.)

During that long march to the title, Friel's team took four games from the Washington Huskies. It was the first time Washington State had swept the University of Washington since 1917, and the first time ever under the Northern-Southern Division PCC format adopted in 1923. It is interesting to note that Friel had dominated Oregon State 29-13 in meetings between 1929 and 1940, yet the Beavers took three games out of four with the Cougars in that championship season.

"We did not have much speed on that team," Friel recalled nearly half a century after. "We tried to break and we kept the pressure on by using a lot of players. [Eleven Cougars played in twenty-nine or more of WSC's thirty-two games that season.] I think we ran Arkansas down a little in our semi-final game. And we were a pretty good shooting team. But our forte was all-around defense."

The 1941 Cougars had four seniors, Paul Lindemann, of Cowiche; Dale Gentry, Walla Walla; Captain Ray Sundquist, Hoquiam; and Vern Butts, Stanwood; four juniors, Kirk Gebert, Longview; John Hooper, Johnson; Jim Zimmerman, Yakima; and Al Akins, Spokane; and four sophomores, Marv Gilberg, Spokane; Owen Hunt, Highline; Phil Mahan, Bremerton; and Chuck Dosskey, North Bonneville.

Lindemann, the center, "6-6 7/8 and I suppose 240," was the biggest man Friel coached in the pre-World War II era. "Pig" Gentry, 6-2 1/2,

200, a big end off Hollingbery's football team, and Butts, 6-2, were the starting forwards. Friel was ahead of his time by about thirty years. He used Gilberg, 6-2, "as a sixth man [for Butts] to sort of liven things up." Sundquist, 6-1, and Gebert, 5-10, were the starting guards.

After Washington State defeated his Vandal squad, winning its twelfth straight Northern Division game, Idaho Coach Forrest Twogood was asked by *Evergreen* sportswriter Bob Boyer to rate individual players in the league.

"Cougar Captain Ray Sundquist, in my opinion, is the outstanding ball player in the Northern Division," Twogood responded, adding, "He always seems to come through in the clinches." ("Twoogie" also predicted that WSC would win the Pacific Coast title.)

The Cougars were underdogs to Stanford in the PCC play-offs at Pullman on March 14-15 but swept the Indians 46-43 and 44-40. Washington State trailed 13-20 at halftime of the opener, "But from that time on the smaller Indians saw the greatest display of fight and courage they have ever seen," *Evergreen* sports editor John Jarstad wrote in his game story.

There wasn't much doubt about the championship game. WSC jumped out front by six at the half and led by as many as twelve in the second period. Lindemann topped all scorers with fourteen. Bill Cowden, a floor leader for Coach Everett Dean the next year when Stanford won the NCAA title, led the Indians with nine.

Rod Bankson, covering the series for the *Spokesman-Review*, wrote:

> The true tale of the entire series . . . lies in the one simple fact that ten good Washington State players could and did wear down six good Stanford men. [Friel went to full "platoons" in the 1942 season.]

The NCAA had an East-West championship format at Kansas City in 1941. Washington State was matched against Creighton in the Western semis and shot down the Blue Jays from Omaha 48-39, with Lindemann getting twenty-six. The following evening, Friel's team upset favored Arkansas 64-53. Lindemann, Gebert and Butts all were in double figures, scoring fourteen, twelve, and eleven respectively, as the Cougars blew away the Southwest Conference champs.

In the East, Big Ten champion Wisconsin edged Dartmouth 51-50 in the semis and then beat Pittsburgh 36-30 to move into the finals opposite the Cougars.

Looking back, Coach Friel remembered that Wisconsin "sagged on Lindemann, so we concentrated on our weave and tried to free up our outside shooters.

"Gebert was the only one who hit well that night," Friel recalled. (Kirk did indeed. He had twenty-one points and led all scorers. Wisconsin's high man was Center Gene Englund, with thirteen.)

"It was tough to get the ball in to Lindeman, but maybe we didn't do it enough," the eighty-nine-year-old coach added quietly, still thinking about that game and remembering in 1987 as if it had been last night. Jack sounded as if he might try that "next time."

Frank Herron, '42, Port Angeles, long-time "Voice of the Cougars" on football and basketball broadcasts, began his sportscasting career in Portland in 1946 with Rollie Truitt doing Portland Beaver baseball in the Pacific Coast League.

WSC led 12-9 early, but trailed 21-17 at the intermission. The Cougars closed to 24-22 early in the second period, but never could catch up. The Badgers defeated Washington State 39-34 in that NCAA Championship game on March 29, 1941, at Kansas City.

But you had to love those 1941 Cougs!

Crimson and Gray Goes Red, White, and Blue

What were you doing when you heard about Pearl Harbor?

"Recovering from the Texas A & M game," many WSC students and alumni answer. The Cougars lost to the Aggies 7-0 on December 6, 1941, in Tacoma. It was a bitter loss; a win could have meant a Cotton Bowl bid. But all feelings soon were washed away in the tidal wave of war news which engulfed the nation that weekend.

Looking back, 1941 was one of those "landmark" years—even before Pearl Harbor.

Cougar fans will always remember it because of Jack Friel's great basketball team, runner-up for the NCAA title that year. But hardly had the cheers died away for the basketball team when a new, young track coach had everyone talking about the Cougar cinder squad.

Jack "Blackie" Weiershauser, well known to all Pacific Coast track buffs as one of the premier sprinters in the West, had come up from Stanford the previous fall to take over when the veteran Karl Schlademan left for Michigan State. That in itself was a landmark; Schlademan had been at Washington State since 1926 and had made the Cougars a recognized name in track across the country. When he left in 1940, all eyes were on his twenty-six-year-old replacement, who was making his coaching debut in the big time. Weiershauser's 1941 team—his only one at WSC as it turned out—was unbeaten in dual meets with Idaho, Montana, Oregon and Washington, and won the Northern Division title as well. That made it nine straight for the Cougars, who had won the previous eight Northern Division crowns under Schlademan. The 1941 Cougars also finished a solid third in the PCC meet.

Captain Bill Dale, of Victoria, British Columbia, overcame early season injuries and finished strong with a meet record 1:52.9 half-mile against the Huskies. Dale then improved on that, winning the PCC in a record 1:51.7.

Sophomore Pat Haley, of Trail, British Columbia, "blossomed into the fastest man on cinders in this part of the country," the *Chinook* said. Haley ran twenty-one flat against Oregon to break Lee Orr's dual meet record of 21.1, and also won the low hurdles in the PCC meet.

Noel Williams, of Pullman, had a good year in the distances, highlighted by his win in the two-mile at the PCC.

When fall came, everyone was expecting great things from Babe Hollingbery's 1941 football team. Another Rose Bowl? Could be. WSC had been one of the nation's most exciting teams in 1940 with junior quarterback Billy Sewell as the NCAA passing champion.

But 1941 was one of those star-crossed seasons. The Cougars dropped three of their first four, two by identical 7-6 scores on missed extra points to UCLA and USC. WSC beat a good Cal team 13-6 on October 4 at

The Air Corps flew the WSC baseball team to Mountain Home, Idaho, in a DC-3 on May 8, 1945, and the Cougars defeated the airmen 19-8, with Darroll Waller, *of Spokane, getting the win. He was 4-0 that season.* Adrian "Dutch" Jorissen, *Lynden, was 4-2 with one save.* Buck Bailey *used to rant and rave, stomp and scream at Jorissen: "How can you be so wild so young!" Leading hitters in 1945 under Interim Coach* Jack Friel *were* Bob Anderson, *cf, Spokane, .465, and* Ray Johnson, *2b, Tacoma, .400.*

Pullman, but the following week disaster struck again. Leading the Huskies 13-0 in the second quarter on Rogers Field, Sewell was trapped in the end zone for a safety and WSC never regained its momentum. The Huskies scored twenty-one unanswered points in the second half to win 23-13.

Then, in typical Hollingbery fashion, the Cougars rallied and shut out three straight opponents. They beat Oregon State, 7-0; Oregon, 13-0; and Idaho, 26-0, leading up to the game with the defending Rose Bowl Champions, the Stanford Indians, on November 15 at Palo Alto. It's a game thousands of WSC fans remember—for two big reasons: Gentry and Susoeff!

Dale "Pig" Gentry and Nick Susoeff hounded Stanford's All-American quarterback, Frankie Albert, all afternoon. Every time Albert went back to pass, he had company. The play of Gentry and Susoeff in that game still is remembered as one of the best defensive efforts by a pair of ends in the history of West Coast football.

In the end it was a missed extra point—by a shaken Albert—that was the difference. WSC scored on a fourteen-yard run by Billy "Bunk" Holmes, of Marysville, and on a four-yard plunge by fullback Bob Kennedy, of Sandpoint, Idaho. Sewell kicked the first extra point and Joe Beckman the second. WSC won 14-13.

The following weekend the Cougars shut out Gonzaga 59-0, and the Spokane school gave up football.

Washington State-Texas A & M drew the largest crowd ever to see a WSC football game in Tacoma, 26,000. The only score came in the second quarter on a thirty-eight-yard "bomb" from Leo Daniels to Cullen Rogers.

Less than twenty-four hours later, real bombs started falling on Pearl Harbor. Before another football season began many WSC students and fans who saw that game would trade cords and jeans (or short dresses and bobbysox) for the olive drab of the Army or Navy blue.

The Crimson and Gray was going Red, White, and Blue for the next three years.

The End of an Era

The military already was making inroads on the campus before the track season of 1942 got under way, little more than three months after the U.S. entered World War II.

Track Coach Jack Weiershauser went into the Navy and was replaced for the 1942 season by one of his old Stanford coaches, W.B. "Bill" Ellington. With a thin, young squad, WSC lost the Northern Division meet for the first time in ten years, but still managed to defeat Oregon in their annual dual, while losing to Washington and Idaho. Captain Noel Williams and Pat Haley were mainstays of the team in the distances and sprints and hurdles. Frank Londos and Pete McRae, both of Tacoma, scored consistently in the shot and broad jump.

Boxing Coach Ike Deeter guided his WSC team to another PCI title, his seventh in eleven campaigns, before accepting a commission with the Navy's physical fitness program at St. Mary's College in California.

•

Les Liebel, '44, of Kennewick, Cougar middle distance man, had four coaches in four years beginning with Karl Schlademan. *Then, in 1941,* Jack Weiershauser, *great Stanford sprinter, came to WSC to replace Schlademan. Weiershauser went into the Navy shortly thereafter and was followed by* W. B. "Pop" Ellington, *also of Stanford, in 1942, and* Babe Hollingbery *in 1943. "Babe did a good job," Liebel said of the old football coach, who was making his first start as a Track Coach. "He got the eight returning lettermen to recruit prospects on campus and we wound up with a squad of fifty-seven. Turned out to be a pretty good team. Babe kept a little black book with best times and distances, and he ran time trials each week."*

•

Lefty Cliff Chambers in the Crimson and Gray. Chambers, who pitched for WSU in 1941-1942, was the first Cougar to hurl a no-hitter in the Major Leagues. (Hilltopics)

Buck Bailey's baseball team missed the Division title by one game and finished with a 23-11 record in the spring of 1942, the big fellow's last before following Deeter into the Navy at St. Mary's.

George O'Malley, Seattle, .370; George Davison, Twin Falls, Idaho, .346; Ernie Bishop, Walla Walla, .327; and George Dyson, San Francisco, .324, were the Cougars' leading hitters in 1942, and Glenn Hursey, Selah, 7-3, and Lefty Cliff Chambers, Bellingham, 6-4, were the top pitchers.

Swimming Coach Bill Bond departed for the Army after the 1942 season and was replaced by Doug Gibb, of Bellingham, a Cougar swim ace during the years 1939-1941. Doug did such a good job he stayed on at WSC for thirty-eight years, retiring in 1980.

Super retriever Merwin Miller, of Santa Monica, California, retained his Northern Division tennis title, defeating the Huskies' Bob Odman again, 6-4, 4-6, 6-3 and 10-8, and the Cougars were second in team standings.

Football enjoyed a final fling in the fall of 1942. Babe Hollingbery had one of his best-ever teams, a big, solid outfit loaded with lettermen and outstanding sophomore talent. The Cougars boasted All-Coast players in fullback Bob Kennedy; end Nick Susoeff; guard Bill "Smiley" Ward, of Sequim; and center Bill Remington, South Bend. They also had a triple-threat halfback in big Jay Stoves, of Centralia, and a fine two-way player in quarterback Dick Renfro. Hjalmer "Jelly" Andersen, of Seattle; Max Dodge, Fall City; John Godfrey, Bill Gustafson, Rod Giske, and Frank Londos, all of Tacoma; George Dyson; Wally Kramer, Toppenish; and Earl Brenneis, Onalaska, saw lots of action.

Whether Hollingbery saw the handwriting on the wall is difficult to say; surely Babe must have suspected that football would be a likely wartime casualty in the sparsely populated Palouse after the 1942 season. The big Navy/Marine officer training program at the University of Washington would keep the Huskies well stocked with players, but the Army Specialized Training Program which brought Air Corps and Signal Corps personnel to WSC made no provision for intercollegiate athletics.

WSC opened the 1942 football season with three straight wins, back-to-back shutouts of Stanford and Oregon (6-0 at Palo Alto and 7-0 at Pullman), and a 68-16 lambasting of Montana on Rogers Field.

The Cougar-Trojan meeting in Los Angeles on October 17 was a wild one. WSC opened with a fifty-six-yard scoring pass from Stoves to Frank Akins, of Spokane, and USC answered with a twenty-yard run by Mickey McCardle. It was 6-6 at the half, but McCardle broke a fifty-one-yard punt return and Bob Musick hit Joe Davis with a forty-one-yard scoring pass in the third period for the Trojans.

Washington State got the only score in the fourth quarter on a two-yard blast by fullback Kennedy to make the final 26-12.

The Cougars almost exactly reversed the favor the following week in Portland as they put it on Oregon State 26-13 and the *Oregonian's* L. H. Gregory asked rhetorically, "How did this Washington State team ever lose to USC!"

The Cougars again opened with the bomb, fifty-six yards from Stoves to Brenneis, but Oregon State scored twice before WSC got on the board again with a six-yard pass from Kennedy to Stoves. It was 13-13 at the half. Kennedy kept blasting away at the Beaver line and punched over scores in the third and fourth quarters to seal the victory.

On November 7 in Spokane, WSC met Michigan State for the first time and defeated the Spartans from East Lansing 25-13. Kennedy again was the workhorse. He scored three times on runs and threw a thirty-six-yard pass to Susoeff for another Cougar touchdown.

After a 7-0 squeaker over Idaho at Moscow on November 14, the Cougars were back in Spokane on November 21 to meet the Second Air Force, a team of college all-stars coached by W. B. "Red" Reese, the old Cougar, Class of 1925.

The first half was scoreless, but in the third period Dyson blocked a punt by Hal Van Every, former Minnesota star, and Remington recovered in the end zone. Dyson blocked two punts that day.

Second Air Force evened it in the fourth on a five-yard pass from Washington's Randall "Rink" Bond to Albert Bodney, of Tulane. And that's the way it ended, 6-6, both teams missing extra points. (If you are wondering about the seeming inability of teams to kick extra points in these years, remember, substitution was limited. For most of these years, if a player left the game he could not return until the following quarter. There weren't any specialists to speak of. You had to be able to *play* as well as kick.)

The Second Air Force lost only one game in 1942, and went on to defeat Hardin-Simmons 13-7 in the Sun Bowl at El Paso, Texas.

Washington State and Washington met in Seattle on November 28 with a Rose Bowl bid at stake for the Cougars. WSC went in with a 5-1 record in conference play. UCLA, also 5-1, was playing Southern Cal in Los Angeles. A win by the Cougars would put them in Pasadena by virtue of a superior overall record, 6-1-1 to 7-3 for UCLA (also figuring a win by the Bruins). WSC had another game remaining, with Texas A & M, but it would make no difference in the overall standings if the Cougars beat the Huskies.

They still call it the "$100,000 miss," the pass that slithered through the arms of Nick Susoeff in the fourth quarter and preserved a scoreless tie for the Huskies. Nick lived with that the remainder of his life, although he went on to a successful pro career with the San Francisco Forty-Niners.

Photos of the play don't back up statements that "Susoeff just dropped it!" Game action photos—and there were a lot more of them, and better in those days—in both the Seattle *Times* and *Post-Intelligencer*, clearly show that the big Cougar end was twisted backward in an attempt to take the ball thrown almost directly over his head. And two Washington players were up in the air flailing their arms vainly trying to bat the ball away, effectively—and legally—blocking Susoeff's vision.

It would have been one helluva catch!

After nearly half a century, there remains a humorous postscript to that heart-rending season. Sophomore guard Rod Giske tells the story:

•

Marv Gilberg, *who led Lewis-Clark High School to three straight Spokane City League basketball titles in 1937-1939, played on WSC's NCAA runner-up in 1941 and was the second leading scorer and an All-Northern Division choice at forward for Coach* Jack Friel's *Cougar team in 1942.* Gale Bishop, *of Blaine, led the Cougars in scoring in 1942 with 150 points. Gilberg had 149. Marv had another season of eligibility but had been accepted by the University of Oregon Dental School and Friel told him he'd better not pass up the opportunity. Gilberg enjoyed a long and successful career in dentistry in San Francisco. His son, Mark, played at guard on the Stanford basketball teams in 1972-1974.*

•

A down-hearted group of Cougars left Seattle [by train, after the tie that took them out of the Rose Bowl] in order to get back to Pullman for Monday classes. Monday evening we entrained again for San Antonio, where we were to play Texas A & M.

We worked out in snow and ice at brief stops in Montana, then on to Denver and a full workout, and back on our two "green monsters" [cars the Cougars always traveled in on the Union Pacific], which were on a siding.

About two a.m. we were all awakened as they jockeyed the two cars into the "San Antonio Rose," which was the swift train down into the heart of Texas.

Our first major stop was at Amarillo. As we rolled into the crowded station [wartime train travel was heavy], just about everyone stopped and looked up at our cars. What did they think? Two old cars in the middle of a streamliner; maybe they knew the Cougars were coming through and wanted to check out this gang. . . .

Our puffed up pride retreated rapidly when we got off for our usual few minutes of exercises.

When the cars had been pulled out of the siding the night before in Denver, the train crew forgot to lift off the buckets under the urinals and toilets. The offerings of about fifty Cougars were scattered over the length of two cars!

We had, indeed, arrived in style. You never saw two cars split off a train and sent into the yard for steam cleaning so fast.

WSC had an undefeated wrestling team in 1942 under Coach Bob Neilson, winning all its dual meets and the three-way tournament with Idaho and Washington. Letter winners were Walt Rohde, Monroe; Leighton Wallace, Snohomish; Don Bennett, Spanaway; Henry Brown, Tacoma; Chet Gisselburg, Cathlemet; Ryomi Tanino, Bellevue; and Alex Ryncarz, Tacoma.

About that game, Rod says "the lackluster Cougars didn't perform well. We lost to a team we really should have beaten." A fumble in the end zone in the second quarter seemed to open the gate. The Aggies got one score there before the half and two more in the third quarter. WSC lost 21-0.

"The loss of the Rose Bowl bid, plus a telegram from the college that Babe read to us on Friday night stating we were to entrain home to Pullman after the game took away most of what was left," Giske recalls. "The couple of days of fun activities the San Antonio Chamber of Commerce had for us never materialized."

Many said they were staying over but the only one who made it was "Jelly" Andersen. They took him in royally, buying him western clothes, cowboy boots, hotel fare and flew him home the next week.

Somewhere along the line we got off the train [probably Pendleton, Oregon] and finished on a bus. Babe had left us in Denver; Buck led us on home.

"Smiley" Ward picked up a can of sneezing powder and blew it out on the bus ride.

It was a sad end to a great season. It would have been sadder had those players known that when Babe Hollingbery left them in Denver he never again would ride the old "green monsters" with a Cougar team.

As late as mid-June, things looked promising for a season in 1943. PCC representatives met in San Francisco and the four Northern schools worked out a nine-game, home-and-home schedule. WSC was set to open on October 2 against Washington in Pullman and close with the Huskies in Seattle on November 27. Coach Hollingbery started workouts September 9 and on September 17 the Pullman *Herald* said Babe reported the thirty-five-man squad was "looking good."

On September 24, 1943, in a joint announcement with Idaho, Oregon and Oregon State, WSC officials cancelled football "for the duration."

Hollingbery was retained as Track Coach in 1943. There was some bickering about his salary—"No Rift, Just a Misunderstanding" the *Herald* said in a front page editorial on June 4. Babe's salary was reduced to $7,000 (from $10,000) between 1942 and 1943, and in 1944 he was granted "leave without pay." It wasn't official until 1945, of course, but a great era in Crimson and Gray sports history had ended.

Babe Hollingbery compiled a 93-54-14 record at WSC, highlighted by the Pacific Coast Conference title in 1930 and the 1931 Rose Bowl game. His teams finished second in the PCC in 1932, 1934, 1936, and 1942, and tied for second in 1926 (with Oregon State) and in 1941 (with the University of Washington). In his total coaching career, including high school, club, college and all-star (East-West) teams, Hollingbery had 203 wins, seventy losses and eighteen ties.

It is worth noting that Hollingbery's tenure at WSC is almost twice that of any other football coach in the institution's first 100 years. Jim Walden, with nine seasons between 1978 and 1986, is second to Hollingbery's seventeen. And the Babe's won-lost record at WSC is better than all except Forest Evashevski (in the modern era). Evy was 11-6-2, but he never beat a California conference school, and he stayed only two years (of a five-year contract signed in 1950).

Psychologists at Work

Babe Hollingbery was one of the great psychologists in football. The men who played for him will testify to that.

Rod Giske and "Black Tom" Parry saw him give one of his finest performances. It was on October 24, 1942. The scene was Portland's Multnomah Stadium. Oregon State was coming off a Rose Bowl season and had an excellent team. Washington State had one of Babe's best clubs. The game promised to be a bruiser.

Giske and Parry tell this story:

> The Cougars are suiting up and the Equipment Manager passes out Crimson jerseys. Somebody questions that, but Hollingbery says, "Thu . . . that's OK. Red and Orange [Oregon State wore orange at home] won't clash."
>
> WSC no sooner gets out on the field to warm up than Oregon State comes out. Coach Lon Stiner takes a look at the Cougars and orders his team off the field. So Babe waves WSC off and back to its dressing room.
>
> By the time the players get there, Hollingbery is in the center of the room standing on one of the old steamer trunks they used to haul the uniforms in and he's rantin' and ravin', callin' Stiner all sorts of things. Says Oregon State told us to bring our Crimson jerseys and now they won't let us wear em. Then he yells at Buck and Doc Bohler and tells them to go get us some White jerseys somewhere.

Mel Hein *joined the coaching staff of the Los Angeles Dons of the newly established All-America Football Conference in 1946. Mel said the most he ever made as an NFL player was $5,000. When the AAFC came along, the era of big player salaries in professional football was born.*

Pretty soon, Doc comes back with a couple of bales of T-shirts and a bucket of black paint. He tells us to put the shirts on over our Crimson jerseys and then he and Buck proceed to "paint" numbers on the T-shirts.

"We were a mess; photos of the game show that," Parry said.

All this time, Hollingbery is yelling about the "rotten trick," and saying, "They did it just to make you guys look bad out there!"

"I got so excited in the pre-game goings on I forgot to take off my watch," Giske recalled. "In the second quarter, I noticed it, but all that was left was the metal case that had held the works."

On several occasions during the game, Giske and Parry said, time had to be taken while a new T-shirt was brought out for a Cougar player and Doc Bohler did a quick renumbering job on the sideline.

"It was an exciting game and we won 26-13, despite Earl Brenneis getting about two or three TDs called back," Rod said.

In 1941, when WSC was in Palo Alto to play Stanford, Giske says Hollingbery picked up one of their season ticket folders. It listed all the home game ticket prices, which ranged from Cal at ten dollars down through USC, eight dollars; UW, seven dollars and fifty cents; San Jose State, six dollars, to WSC at four dollars.

He brought that card into the locker room before the game and really laid it on us.

"Uh, you see these ticket prices for the Stanford games?" And he listed 'em off one by one, very dramatically, ending with "And here's Washington State, clear down here at the end of the list. Four bucks! You see what they think you guys are worth!"

Most exciting? The 26-26 tie played by WSC and Oregon State on November 6, 1948, rates high on the all-time list. Spokane's Jerry Williams *scored three times for the Cougars, once on a twenty-nine-yard pass from* Frank Mataya*, and* Ken Carpenter *threw three TD strikes for the Beavers. But the thriller of the day was a ninety-two-yard kickoff return—by three Beavers! Carpenter took the ball on the eight and ran it to the WSC twenty-five where Williams corralled him. But Carpenter flipped the ball to lineman* Rudy Ruppe*, who took a couple of steps before unloading it to halfback* Don Samuel*, who scored standing up.*

Bill Moos, long-time director of the Cougar Club at WSU and an All-Coast lineman for the Cougars in 1970-1972, says Jim Sweeney was known to pull a "Psych" or two himself.

The Cougars had beaten Stanford 24-23 in the biggest upset of the 1971 season, so when the Cardinal came into Pullman the next year old Jim was looking for a way to get his club up.

Stanford came in on Friday and was taking a workout in the stadium. WSU players were waiting to go on and the Cougar Marching Band was practicing on the field next to the stadium. The band's show that weekend was a salute to Walt Disney. Just as Stanford finished its workout and the Cougars started to go on the field, the band was playing the theme from the "Mickey Mouse Club."

"Naturally," says Moos, "some of the Stanford players were humming and whistling the catchy tune, and some were singing along: 'M-I-C, K-E-Y, M-O-U-S-E.'

"'Did you guys hear that!' Sweeney screams. 'Those guys think you and your facilities are Mickey Mouse! Are you goin' to take that? Are you goin' to let them get out of here thinkin' you're Mickey Mouse? I wanna know, are ya?'

"He called off our workout right there and let us think about it overnight. Next day, before sending us into the stadium, he reminded us again." Moos is still laughing.

Washington State beat Stanford 27-13 on November 11, 1972. The "Mickey Mouse" game it's known as.

John Bley, of Spokane, who played at a tackle for Babe in 1933-1935, remembers the game with St. Mary's in San Francisco's Kezar Stadium his senior year.

"San Francisco was Babe's town, you know, and that game was something special for him. The day before the game, the whole team was paraded up and down Market Street, players, coaches, managers, led by Babe and Buck, and that evening there was a dinner at the Olympic Club in Babe's honor," Bley remembers.

> Hollingbery loved to give a fight talk and then announce the starting lineup just before the game. But on this day we noticed it was quarter to two and nobody said anything, nobody was moving. Finally, Babe got up and named the lineup and said, "Get out there and warm up." We looked at each other and out we went.
>
> Well, I went out to meet the St. Mary's Captain and we tossed to see who was going to get the call. We won. We always kicked off in those days, so I went back to the team and said, "We're going to kick." Hollingbery said, "Fine," and started to say something and then started to cry. He walked out of the huddle and went back to the sideline.
>
> I looked at the team and said, "Well, fellas, you know what we gotta do today!"
>
> We kicked off and I think eleven guys hit the ball carrier on the ten-yard line. And the whole game went that way. St. Mary's was lucky to get out of there with a tie [7-7].
>
> I remember going to the St. Mary's Captain, if there was a tie you usually flipped to see who won the game ball. He looked at me and said, "I'm not goin' to flip for this ball. I'm givin' it to you. You guys whipped us today."
>
> Of course Babe was delighted because the odds had been that we would lose by a couple of touchdowns. That team came way beyond its capabilities that day.

Bley also recalled another, not-so-happy time, in 1934 when the Cougars were upset 13-6 by Gonzaga in Spokane the week after WSC had beaten USC 19-0 in the Los Angeles Coliseum. John's father and mother came out to see him as he was getting on the bus to go back to Pullman after the loss to Gonzaga. Bley said he wasn't talking.

> Dad wrote me a letter that week, one of the few he ever wrote to me, about not losing the fighting spirit, and to forget last Saturday and look forward to playing Oregon State. He had quite a little pep talk in it.
>
> I thought so much of the letter that I showed it to Hollingbery. He read it and said, 'Do you mind if I read this to the team before you go out on the field Saturday?'
>
> So he read it and we won rather handily [it was 31-0], and played a good game. I kinda like to think that my dad helped.

Heroes

Two of the great stories of World War II involve former Washington State athletes. Ross Greening, '36, of Tacoma, who threw the javelin for the Cougars, was with Gen. Jimmy Doolittle on the famous *Thirty*

•

Jerry Williams, halfback; Laurie Niemi, tackle; and Dave Swanson, Tacoma, end, played in the 1949 East-West game. (East won 14-12.)

•

Seconds Over Tokyo raid in 1942, and Jerry Sage, '38, Spokane, a tackle on two WSU football teams, became known as "the Cooler King," the man no German prison camp could hold.

Greening and Sage were prominent campus figures in the 1930s. A Fine Arts major whose work was seen regularly in the *Evergreen*, Greening was Art Editor of the *Chinook* and was named to Crimson Circle scholastic and service honorary as a senior. Sage was a pre-law major, active in student government, and was named Phi Beta Kappa. He was one of the leaders of the student strike in 1936.

Greening was a Captain in the Army Air Corps when he participated in Doolittle's raid on Tokyo by sixteen B-25s flying off the aircraft carrier *USS Hornet* on April 18, 1942. Captain Greening assured himself of immortality by designing the "twenty-cent bombsight" used on that raid. (The Norden bombsights were taken out of Doolittle's planes because they were still top-secret and the odds were overwhelming that most of the planes would fall into enemy hands—and did. Only one got down whole, and it landed near Vladivostok, in Russia. The Norden bombsights would have been useless anyway at the tree-top altitude Greening and his mates flew on that one-way mission.)

After completing the historic raid on Tokyo, Greening parachuted to safety when his plane ran out of fuel over China. Guided by friendly Chinese, he walked hundreds of miles through enemy-held territory to safety in Chungking, the wartime capital. From there he was flown to India and eventually back to the United States, to be honored by a grateful and admiring nation with the Distinguished Flying Cross.

Shortly thereafter, Major Greening took command of a B-26 medium bomb group operating out of North Africa. On a mission against a German airfield at Naples on July 17, 1943, his plane was shot down and Greening parachuted into Italy, landing on the slopes of Mt. Vesuvius. He was captured, but subsequently escaped and dodged German patrols for six months in the winter of 1943-1944 before being recaptured and sent to *Stalag Luft 1* in Barth, Germany. Assigned a barracks, Greening entered, found what appeared to be an empty lower bunk and asked, "Anybody using this?" A man lying in the upper bunk rolled over and Greening found himself staring at his old Theta Chi roommate, Lieutenant Colonel Loren McCollum, '37, of Ritzville, whose plane had been shot down earlier over Europe.

During his internment, Greening started sketching—and painting when he could find or manufacture something to paint with. He also taught art classes and put on art and crafts shows, encouraging fellow prisoners to use their talents to relieve the tedium and provide entertainment. (Some of Greening's art work during this period was later collected and put into a book, *Not as Briefed*, published in a limited edition by Brown & Bigelow, St. Paul, Minnesota. It's well worth a look.)

Colonel Charles Ross Greening died March 29, 1957.

Sage was dubbed "the Cooler King" (in *The Great Escape*, a movie that starred Steve McQueen), and became the subject of many postwar stories in adventure magazines (such as "The Slippery Giant of the OSS" and "He Never Stopped Trying").

WSC tackle John Godfrey played with a West All-Star team that split two games with Island teams in Hawaii following the 1947 season, and Cougar Co-Captains "Black Tom" Parry, Seattle, guard, and Fran Bacoka, Everett, end, played for the West in the 1948 East-West Shrine game. (The East won 40-9. Babe's worst whomping in the Shrine classic.)

Sage's odyssey began early in 1943 when, as a major in one of "Wild Bill" Donovan's OSS units, he was captured while on a mission behind General Erwin Rommel's lines in North Africa.* From then until 1945 when he made his final escape from the notorious Nazi prison camp *Oflag 64*, Sage was a constant threat to escape.

After a career in the Army, Sage retired and turned to teaching in Columbia, South Carolina. In 1978 he was named South Carolina Teacher of the Year. Then, in 1985, he wrote *Sage* (released by Banbury Books), an autobiographical book which recounted some of his war-time experiences.

Many Washington State athletes served in World War II, a number gave their lives. Among those who gave "the last full measure of devotion" were Major John J. Hurley, Lieutenant Archie Buckley, Captain Bill Dahlke, Lieutenant Colonel Chris Rumburg and Lieutenant George Davidson.

John Hurley was a football letterman at end in the 1928-1930 seasons and played in the 1931 Rose Bowl game. He was killed in 1943. Hurley had earned a Silver Star for gallantry in action during the campaign in Sicily, and was mortally wounded later in Italy leading his men to safety through a minefield, for which he was awarded the Army's Distinguished Service Cross.

Archie Buckley was an all-around athlete at WSC in 1927-1930. He earned three letters in football, quarterbacking the Cougar teams of 1927-1930; lettered three years in basketball; and won two awards in baseball during his WSC athletic career. He died in 1945 in action in the Pacific as a naval officer aboard the *USS Saratoga* during the battle for Iwo Jima. Lieutenant Buckley was awarded the Bronze Star posthumously.

Bill Dahlke played basketball for Coach Jack Friel in the 1935-1937 seasons at WSC and was Captain of the 1937 team. He was killed in 1945 near Ormont, Germany, while serving as a Captain with the 347th Infantry, and was awarded the Bronze Star posthumously.

Ira Christian (Chris) Rumburg, '38, of Spokane, was the center for the Cougar football teams of 1936-1937 and Captain of the 1937 team. He was drowned in the sinking of a troop transport in the English Channel in 1944. Wounded, Lieutenant Colonel Rumburg perished while helping others into lifeboats. He was cited posthumously for heroism for giving up his lifejacket to one of his men.

Lieutenant George A. Davidson, Twin Falls, Idaho, a basketball letterman in 1943, was killed in action serving with the infantry in the European theater of operations in 1945.

The Cougar swim team finished 6-1 in dual meets in 1948 and was second in the Northern Division under Coach Doug Gibb. Bob Fuller, Battleground, breaststroke, and Bob DeVleming, Pomeroy, freestyle, were co-captains.

* There is some disagreement over this particular event. In his book, Sage says he was captured "while carrying out clandestine operations of sabotage." In *OSS*, by R. Harris Smith (Berkeley: University of California Press, 1952) another Intelligence officer, a Yalie named Donald Downes claims that, under his protest, his men were sent on "ordinary combat intelligence missions" under Sage, whom Downes described as "a nice, big jolly college boy who had distinguished himself on the Washington State football team."

Starting Over

Babe Hollingbery and Washington State College officially parted company on July 1, 1945, when Babe turned down an offer of $6,000 to return to the job he left in 1942 making $10,000.

"There is no such thing as 'part-time coaching,'" Hollingbery said in response to a story out of Pullman that the college had offered him the football job again in 1945 on a "part-time basis."

By this time, of course, Babe was pretty well established as a hops broker and with other business enterprises in the Yakima area. Whether he and the college could have come to terms over a coaching contract is doubtful. There was a lot of comment in the sports pages, and some of the alumni expressed bitterness over the treatment of Hollingbery, but Babe remained a faithful friend of the college the rest of his life. He was always "Mr. Cougar" in Yakima and remained active in the Cougar Club and other programs connected with athletics at WSC. As late as 1971 he served as "Honorary Chairman" of the drive to replace the burned-out Rogers Field stadium.

Babe was not the only Hollingbery to leave WSC at this time. Son Orin E. Jr., "Buster," a letterman center in 1941-1942, concluded his playing career in 1945 at Oregon State under Coach Lon Stiner.

Graduate Manager Earl Foster has taken most of the heat over the years for the failure of the college to bring Hollingbery back after the war. It's true that Foster was a demon for economy, and there was acrimony between the two on occasions, but Foster could not have been totally responsible for Hollingbery not returning as Football Coach.

In less than four years after World War II, WSC lost three Graduate Managers, Foster, Loyd Bury, and Scott Witt. Foster, who practically invented the position on the Pacific Coast in 1925, resigned August 1, 1946. Bury had been a student assistant in Foster's office as an undergraduate at WSC, and, except for Navy duty during the war, a regular Assistant Graduate Manager since 1929. Loyd took over when Earl resigned in 1946, but lasted little more than two years, resigning (officially) November 10, 1948.

Witt, a good basketball player for Jack Friel in the 1942-1943 era, had worked in the Graduate Manager's office with Foster and Bury as a student. After Army service he returned to campus and took over briefly (really just to handle the three football games remaining on the Cougar schedule that fall after Bury resigned, Cal, Michigan State and Penn State, in Tacoma. Scott resigned right after that 1948 season.)

All three of the men who'd served in the Graduate Manager's post were exceptionally talented individuals and astute businessmen, as borne out by their success after leaving WSC. Foster, who became the prototype for Graduate Managers in that era of athletics beginning in 1925, made a bundle in the lumber business at Gold Beach, Oregon, and retired less than ten years after leaving the college. Bury and Witt both became highly respected vice-presidents of large firms, Bury with Murphey-Favre, Inc., an investment company, and Witt with Weyerhaeuser.

The state of Washington boasted the three top scorers in basketball in February of 1945: Cougar Gale Bishop, then playing for Fort Lewis, was the nation's leading scorer; Vince Hanson, of Tacoma, at WSC, led the major college scorers; and Jack Perrault, of Eastern Washington College, was number one among the independent colleges. (Perrault came to WSC the next fall as a quarterback and scored the winning touchdown as the Cougars beat the Huskies 7-0 at Pullman on November 24.)

Four great ones. Left to right: Ralph Coleman, OSC baseball coach ; Dixie Howell, Idaho football coach; Buck Bailey; and Guy Wicks, Idaho baseball coach, on the first tee of the Moscow Elks course in 1947.
(Kenny Jordan)

Howard Greer, '27, who had been one of the early Sports Information Directors on the Coast (second only to Don Liebendorfer at Stanford), and served also as Publications Advisor at WSC in Foster's organization from 1927 until World War II Navy service intervened, was another who resigned in this period. Greer's resignation statement to the *Evergreen* gives a bit of insight on the situation: "I am voluntarily resigning (December 6, 1948) because of the confusion and turmoil which has overtaken the administration of the Cougar athletic set-up."

Two others who departed the athletic scene in this period of turmoil were Carl Christensen, the office manager in the Graduate Manager's office and Harold "Tobe" Saunders, Athletic Equipment Manager.

WSC President Wilson M. Compton was not an athletics-oriented person, and he certainly had a lot of other things on his mind, taking over as he did in 1945 just as the war was ending and the "GI Bulge" of enrollment started to hit the college.

"You really couldn't get his [Compton's] attention," one official at the college at that time recalled. "He was not supportive of Athletics; he seemed to feel it was something to be tolerated."

The years, too, had taken their toll on Doc Bohler, the grand old man of Physical Education and Athletics. Bohler was in his thirty-seventh year at WSC as World War II ended. All those years of double- and triple-time were beginning to show, and athletics was entering a new and high-pressure era where sport was secondary and money was the name of the game.

Babe Hollingbery's tenure at WSC really ended with the 1942 football season. He never coached another college football team, and his active coaching days with the West team in the annual East-West Shrine Game in San Francisco ceased with the game on Jan 1, 1946—a 7-7 tie.

Northern Division Champs in 1949-1950. Front(left to right): Ed Werner, Mel Olson, Benner Cummings, Rich Larsen, Bill Demastus, and Hugh Van Liew. Middle: Jim Shattuck (Co-Captain), Roland Elledge, Coach Doug Gibb, Jim Sherrod, Pat Canning. Back: Don Duncan, manager; Robert "Doc" Fuller, Dick Hannula (Co-Captain), Jack Morelock, Paul Sellin, and Will Dolphin. (Manuscripts, Archives, and Special Collections, Washington State University Libraries)

Although he continued to be a vital part of the Shrine Classic until his death on January 12, 1974, at the age of eighty, that 1946 game ended Hollingbery's coaching career. From then on, the staffs of the competing teams in the Shrine classic changed from year to year.

Two of Babe's old players at Washington State, Rod Giske (1941-1942) and Max Dodge (1942), have the distinction of playing in the last college game Babe coached (versus Texas A & M on December 5, 1942 at San Antonio) and in that final Shrine game (January 1, 1946, at Kezar stadium in San Francisco). Giske had returned to WSC after the war and played his final season in 1945 under Phil Sorboe. Dodge, a big end, finished up at the University of Nevada that year. (The colorful—and outspoken—Buck Bailey once told Dodge, who had some trouble giving Buck his undivided attention: "I could put a dress on a broomstick and lead you right out of town!")

Phil Sorboe, of Tacoma, a football and baseball star at WSC in 1931-1934, returned to his alma mater as Head Coach in 1945 to succeed Hollingbery. Sorboe had played professional football as a back with the Chicago Cardinals and Brooklyn Dodgers in 1934-1936, and also played some baseball in the high minors with Kansas City and Des Moines. Phil coached at Aberdeen and was Director of Physical Education at Central Washington College in Ellensburg during the war. He had taken Lincoln High School of Tacoma to the mythical state title in football the season before coming back to WSC.

Sorboe was signed to an eleven-month contract at a salary of $4,000, which pretty well illustrates that Foster still had that condition which Buck Bailey described so graphically years before. Phil was raised to $6,000 on January 1, 1946, after a 6-2-1 record his first season—which turned out to be his best, by the way.

Another Cougar, Jack Mooberry, also returned to his alma mater at this time. A great high school sprinter, Mooberry came to WSC in the late 1920s from Wenatchee. He was outstanding, particularly in the 220, until a severe leg injury ended his career. Jack was Athletic Director and Track Coach at John Rogers High School in Spokane in 1945 when he accepted the position as Head Trainer at WSC. Jack replaced another of the "Golden Age" group, Wilbur "Doc" Bohm, who had been part of the wartime exodus in 1943.

The Track program had limped along during the war years under four coaches: Jack Weiershauser in 1941; W. B. Ellington in 1942; Hollingbery in 1943; and, after a year's hiatus in 1944 when the program was given up completely due to the scant supply of male bodies on the campus (386, to be exact), Bob Campbell in 1945. (Campbell was still in the Air Corps at the time.)

WSC had been holding the track job open for Weiershauser, but in 1946 when he left the Navy "Blackie" was offered the track coaching position at Stanford, his alma mater, and he accepted.

Mooberry was appointed Track Coach in 1946 and continued to serve in a dual capacity as Track Coach and Athletic Trainer until 1950 when Vernon N. "Bucky" Walters, a 1950 WSC grad from Garfield, was named Trainer.

Boxing Coach Ike Deeter; Baseball Coach Buck Bailey; and Wrestling Coach Robert Neilson were out of the service and resumed their positions. (Neilson only stayed on until the end of the school year, then resigned to enter private business as a contractor in Pullman.) Bill Bond, who had been Swimming Coach from 1926 until he entered the Army in 1942, did not return to the college after the war. Doug Gibb, who had replaced Bond in 1942, remained.

On December 9, 1948, the Board of Regents created a "Department of Intercollegiate Athletics" at WSC and introduced a new Graduate Manager, soon to become "Director of Athletics." He was Robert Brumblay, no stranger to Cougar fans and one of the leading high school coaches in the state for many years. Brumblay played basketball for WSC in the 1927 and 1928 seasons under Coach Karl Schlademan. Actually, Brumblay was already on the WSC staff when he was named Graduate Manager. He had joined the Office of Admissions as "Information Director" a few months previous. Bob came back to his alma mater from North Central High School in Spokane, where he had led the Indians to the State basketball title in 1947-1948 and been named "Coach of the Year" by the media.

Brumblay's tenure at WSC was short.

"The two guys I helped hire got me fired," Bob reminisced wryly some years later.

•

Darroll Waller was a great all-around athlete at WSC in 1945-1948. He pitched, competed in the pole vault, hurdles, and high jump, and was a quarterback on the football team.

•

Back on the Gridiron

The shrill blast of the referee's whistle sounded across the Palouse hills for the first time in three years on September 29, 1945, when Washington State and Idaho teed it up in Moscow in the 46th renewal of the "Battle of the Palouse."

Doc and his boys. Lefty Cliff Chambers (left), who no-hit the Boston Braves on May 6, 1951, and Ted Tappe, who hit a home run in his first major league at-bat (September 14, 1950, for Cincinnati, off Erv "Bo" Palica, of Brooklyn), with Trainer Doc Bohm at spring training in Tampa, Florida, in 1954. (Jean Chrey)

A goodly number of those facing each other across the line of scrimmage that day in Neale Stadium had been facing much tougher enemies for much higher stakes. Many of the players were fresh out of the service and some carried real battle scars—not football inflicted.

It was a great opening game for new Cougar Coach Phil Sorboe and his staff, which consisted of Buck Bailey and three former Cougar gridders, Bob Campbell, '38; Dick Farman, '40; and Felix Fletcher, '42. WSC's new Trainer was Jack Mooberry, '31.

The Cougars played a nine-game schedule that first year after the war, around the horn twice with Idaho, Oregon, Oregon State and Washington, home-and-home, and a trip to Berkeley for a game with the Golden Bears on November 3.

Fans really got their money's worth in that opener with Idaho! The Cougars and Vandals matched each other quarter-for-quarter through the first three periods. The scoring went: 0-6-6 on both sides. It was tied at 12-12 entering the fourth quarter. Then, *Bloooooie!* Washington State scored five times to win 43-12. That's still a modern record for points in one quarter by a Cougar team.

Fullback Dick Abrams, of Bellingham, scored the first postwar touchdown for Washington State on a one-yard plunge in the second quarter. Quarterback Jack Perrault, of Connell, ran forty-four yards for another score in the third period.

The fourth-quarter deluge started when Perrault threw nineteen yards to halfback Bill Lippincott, of Wenatchee, for the tie-breaking TD. Then it got wild!

One of WSC's best, halfback Don Paul in action on Rogers Field in the late 1940s. Paul had a long pro career with Cleveland as a defensive back. (Manuscripts, Archives, and Special Collections, Washington State University Libraries)

Halfback Bob Ross, of Carbonado, flipped a lateral to his old high school teammate, freshman center Andy Lazor, of Buckley, and Andy rumbled thirty-one yards to score.

The next three Cougar scores all were the result of pass interception returns—another school record. Guard Elwood Sturdivant, of Montesano, a forty-two-yard return; quarterback Dean Eggers, of Walla Walla, a fifty-five-yard return; and halfback Frank Miyaki, of Spokane, an eighty-nine-yard return (which still ranks third on the all-time list). During the afternoon, WSC intercepted six Idaho passes (a school record, tied later that year against Washington), and returned them 193 yards (still a record). Miyaki's two interceptions for ninety-six yards also is a single game return record that has held up.

WSC played some sparkling football in that 1945 season under Sorboe, taking two each from Idaho and Oregon State, splitting with Oregon and Washington and playing to a 7-7 tie with Cal at Berkeley. It was never that good again for Phil.

After a good effort against Southern Cal in the Coliseum in the 1946 opener (the Cougars lost 13-7 on a fumble in the end zone in the fourth quarter), WSC managed only a win over Idaho and a scoreless tie with Oregon at Eugene and finished 1-6-1.

Prior to the 1947 season, Coach Sorboe had his named legally changed to Sarboe. It didn't help much in the win column. The Cougars were 3-7 that season. The only wins came against Idaho, Portland and Oregon State, but that Idaho victory settled a "family feud."

It was Jerry versus Billy on October 4 at Neale Stadium in Moscow. The Williams brothers, Jerry at WSC and Billy at Idaho were in the spotlight. It was billed as a real grudge match since Jerry had enrolled at Idaho before the war and transferred to WSC when he came out of

Vince Hanson. (Manuscripts, Archives, and Special Collections, Washington State University Libraries)

service. The Cougars won 7-0 on Jerry's six-yard run (and Lippincott's conversion) in the second quarter.

The largest gathering in the history of the Gem State (23,500 the papers said) witnessed the game. The Williams brothers served as Captains of their respective teams. Jerry was a real "iron man" for Washington State that year. He played 479 out of a possible 600 minutes during the 1947 season.

Washington State had some outstanding individuals during the Sarboe years. Somehow they did not go together to make winning teams. Jerry Williams and Tacoma's Don Paul were long-time defensive stars in the National Football League for the Los Angeles Rams and Cleveland Browns, and Cougar linemen La Vern Torgeson, of La Crosse, and Laurie Niemi, Clarkston, both played for the Washington Redskins. "Torgeson intercepted three passes and was all over the field on both offense and defense" one story on the WSC-Penn State game in Tacoma in 1948 said. Niemi was named National Lineman of the Week for his play in WSC's 10-0 win over the Huskies in Pullman the same year.

At the conclusion of the 1949 season, after three consecutive losing years, WSC and Sarboe parted company. Phil later went to Humboldt State at Arcata, California, and had an outstanding record with the Lumberjacks.

He Shot Up a Gale!

Gale Bishop is generally credited with being the finest scorer in Washington State basketball. Had his career not been interrupted by World War II, Gale's records—and the Cougars'—would have been even better.

Bishop came to Washington State from tiny Sumas, up on the Canadian border in northwest Washington, and promptly started re-writing the school's basketball scoring records. In 1942-1943, his sopho-more season, Gale set a Northern Division scoring record with a third-place team. He had 224 points in only fourteen games, two short of the full Conference schedule. (He was called up for Army duty before the season ended.)

In the Army, as player-coach for the Fort Lewis Warriors in 1943-1945, Bishop continued his record-smashing, once setting a National AAU scoring record with sixty-two points in a tournament game.

Much to Coach Jack Friel's regret, Bishop was not released from the Army until only ten games remained of the 1946 season, his senior year at WSC. He nevertheless scored 185 points and lost the Northern Division scoring title by only nine points to Oregon State's "Red" Rocha, who played in the full sixteen games.

Bishop was an All-America choice at forward in 1943 and was named on the all-time Pacific Coast Conference team selected by sports editors and broadcasters in 1948.

Gale was elected a charter member of the WSU Athletic Hall of Fame in 1978.

Big Vince

Vince Hanson set all sorts of basketball scoring records at Washington State in 1945-48 as the first really big center Coach Jack Friel had.

The 6-8 Hanson, out of Tacoma's Lincoln High School, led the nation's scorers in 1945 as a sophomore with a record 592 points. His point total and 242 field goals remained school records until Don Collins broke them in 1980 with 647 and 253, but Vince still ranks second in these departments.

Hanson also set a new PCC scoring standard in 1945 with 253 points in sixteen games, breaking the mark of 224 set by Cougar great Gale Bishop in 1943. On February 10, 1945, in Bohler gym, Hanson had thirty-four points in leading WSC to a 65-43 win over the Huskies. It was a school single game record and tied the ND mark at the time.

In his three-year career (he played only two games as a frosh and scored only one point), Hanson also set WSC records for total points, 1,153; field goals, 460; and Conference scoring, 625, which still rank him among the top ten in those departments.

The big fellow also competed in baseball and track, lettering two years as a first baseman and a high jumper.

Hanson won All-America honors for his play in 1945. Vince was named to the WSU Athletic Hall of Fame in 1986.

"Clutch"

Bill "Clutch" Tomaras came to WSC as Wrestling Coach in 1948 from Illinois and founded a dynasty. He also is recognized as the "Father of High School Wrestling" in the State of Washington.

Tomaras, the ace 121-pounder for the Illini before and after World War II, coached his first team at WSC in 1948-1949. The Cougars were unbeaten in dual meets and won the Pacific Coast Intercollegiate title. Coast champs on that team were Hirashi "Sosh" Watanabe, 121, and Rich Clark, 128, both of Tacoma; Bob Closs, 145, Lake Mohawk, New Jersey; and Captain Harry Gust, 165, Tacoma.

Between 1949 and 1955, Tomaras's teams won three PCI championships, were co-champs on two other occasions and finished second twice. WSC wrestlers had a string of twenty-three consecutive dual match victories broken in 1955 in a 16-14 loss to Oregon State.

While all this winning was going on Tomaras still found time to initiate the State High School Wrestling Tournament. The first event was held in 1953 and drew fifty contestants. Bill's "baby" grew so fast that within three years they had to have District tournaments to cut the State field to manageable size.*

Tomaras had 21 PCI champions in ten seasons at WSC. He left in 1959 to become Head Coach at Cal-Berkeley, then was Athletic Director at Western Washington University in Bellingham.

In 1973, Dr. William Tomaras was named to the Helms Hall Amateur Wrestling Hall of Fame. It was a proud time for Bill, but what made it

Gale Bishop scored 185 points in only ten games to lead all WSC scorers as the Cougars and Oregon tied for the Northern Division title in 1945. In the play-offs, Oregon won the opener 51-41 in Pullman; WSC took the second game 53-48 at Eugene; and Oregon won the clincher at home, 39-37.

* Tomaras lettered three years at Illinois before and after World War II. He was third in the NCAA at 121 pounds in 1946 after three years of Army service in the ETO.

Wounded winners! This is Coach Bill Tomaras's first Pacific Coast Championship team, 1949. Front (left to right): Harry Gust, Tom Baker, Gordon Evans, and John Lawson. Back: Coach Tomaras, Rich Clark, Charley Jackson, Bob Closs, Rob Clark, and Sosh Watanabe. (Manuscripts, Archives, and Special Collections, Washington State University Libraries)

even sweeter was that one of his former Cougar Champions, Vaughan Hitchcock, a 177-pounder in 1954-1956, long-time wrestling coach at Cal Poly-San Luis Obispo and former U.S. Olympic Coach, went into the Hall with Bill.

Tomaras rates Watanabe, Closs and Hitchcock, along with Delance Duncan, 137, Nespelem; Byron Nelson, 147, Richland; and Del McGhee, 167, Longview, as some of his all-time best at Washington State. Duncan, Klamath Falls; and David Douglas, Portland; Nelson, Mountlake Terrace; and McGhee, Longview, all had long and distinguished coaching careers in high school wrestling.

An Expensive Recruit

Gene Conley was one of the most sought-after athletes in the West in 1948-1949, his senior year at Richland High School. So much so that three Pacific Northwest schools were fined heavily for illegal recruitment of the baby-faced giant.

Jack Friel enjoys telling the story of how Conley wound up at Washington State.

> I got a call from Fran Rish [WSC, '42, who coached football at Richland many years]. He asked me if Washington State was interested in Conley. I told him we sure were.
> "Well then you better get over here. Finley ["Cheerful Chuck" Finley, the Idaho basketball coach] is practically sleepin' at the kid's house!"
> So I went in to Bury's office [Loyd Bury was the Graduate Manager at WSC at the time] and said, "I'm goin' to Richland and get that Conley. You can worry about the fine!"

Friel took a lot of heat when the Conference fined WSC $3,720 in the Conley case, but he was quick to point out that Idaho was fined $4,010 and Washington $5,500.

"And we got him!" Jack always added emphatically.

Only a portion of Washington's fine involved the recruiting of

Conley. The Huskies topped the PCC infractions list in both 1948 and 1949 with fines totaling $9,000, a lot of money in those days. In fact, WSC's fine, in today's dollars, would amount to about $30,000.

Was Conley worth it?

"Every dime," Friel says.

"Conley was a great athlete. I never saw anybody learn to hook shoot the way he did in just one season," Friel says. "He was a natural."

The 6-8 Conley was only the second really big man Friel had at Washington State. The first was Vince Hanson, in 1945-1948. Jack had Conley only one Varsity season, 1949-1950. But in that one year Conley was a major factor in WSC winning both the Northern Division basketball and baseball titles. He played the pivot for Friel and pitched for Buck Bailey.

Gene Conley's story reads like Frank Merriwell. He led Washington State in scoring in that 1949-1950 season with 426 points, and topped the Northern Division with 220. (Ed Gayda was runner-up with 200.)

A right-handed pitcher for the Cougar baseball team, Conley had a 5-2 record with two saves for the WSC team that won the Northern Division, knocked off Stanford in the Coast play-offs and finished second in the College World Series.

M. A. "Doc" Northrup, '33, left, former Cougar and greatest of the San Francisco Olympic Club wrestlers. Northrup suited up for a little workout when he returned to the campus in 1954 and was greeted by Cougar Coach Bill Tomaras. (Center is Chuck Gottfried of the University of Idaho, who was refereeing the Cougar matches this day.) (Manuscripts, Archives, and Special Collections, Washington State University Libraries)

Conley signed a professional baseball contract with the Boston (later Milwaukee and now Atlanta) Braves after his sophomore season. He also played professional basketball with the Boston Celtics and is one of the few players in history to play on championship teams in two professional sports. He was with the Celtics four seasons, including their World Championship years of 1959-61, and pitched for the Milwaukee Braves in two World Series, in 1957 when they defeated the Yankees in seven games, and in 1958 when they lost to the Yanks in seven.

Every Cougar old enough to remember that 1949-1950 season recalls it like yesterday. With Conley at center, Friel had the veterans Ed Gayda, Hoquiam, and Bob Gambold, Longview, at forwards, and Ted Tappe, from Bremerton, and Leon Mangis, of Marysville, at the guards. Tappe, at 6-3, a big guard in those years, had played for Olympic College in the National Junior College tournament the previous year and transferred to WSC in the fall of 1949 as a sophomore.

Friel had great depth for his "platoon" system that season and forced everyone in the league—including John Wooden of UCLA in the Coast playoff series—to substitute along with him. George Rosser, Bellingham; Eric Roberts, Hollywood, California; Gordy Brunswick and Ron Button, both of Tacoma; Lloyd Schmick, Colfax; Frank Mataya, Cle Elum; and Jim Howell, St. John, played a lot that season as WSC won the Division by three full games over the Huskies.

The play-offs were in the south that (even) year, so the Cougars met UCLA at Westwood.

"They trapped us in a handball court," Conley reminisced in 1979, when he was elected to the WSU Athletic Hall of Fame.

UCLA's gymnasium seated only 2,500 (and that was like saying Bohler held 6,000!). It was the smallest on the Coast, tinier even than Stanford's old crackerbox at Palo Alto.

He wasn't that *tall, but 6-8 Gene Conley must have looked it to Cougar opponents in 1950 when he led Washington State to the Northern Division title.* (Hilltopics)

"It was a howitzer explosion heard from LA to Pullman," one sportswriter declared. Ralph Joeckel, a Bruin forward, threw in a fifty-foot shot at the gun to give UCLA a 60-58 win over Washington State in the first game of the play-offs on March 10, 1950. The following night, with the tiny gym bulging with Bruins, UCLA clinched its first PCC title under Coach Wooden in another nailbiter, 52-49.

"Jack Friel had the misfortune of having the playoff series in the south the year he won the Northern Division," Wooden said later. "Had it been otherwise, his team might very well have won. The home court was a big advantage in those years." (Still is.)

Wooden knew whereof he spoke. His team won the Southern Division in 1949 and had to go to Corvallis, Oregon, where the Bruins lost two out of three to Oregon State. And in 1951, the year following the WSC-UCLA series in Westwood, the Bruins again won in the South and the play-offs were in Seattle. Washington beat Wooden's team two straight.

Friel retired from coaching in 1958, exactly thirty seasons and 495 wins after he'd come back to Washington State to take over as Head Basketball Coach. One can't help but wonder what might have been had Conley and Tappe (Ted signed with the Cincinnati Reds as a first baseman after that 1950 season) stayed around two more years.

Friel won three Northern Division titles at WSC and tied for a fourth. His Cougars finished second on five other occasions.

Forrest "Phog" Allen, the legendary coach at Kansas, once called Jack Friel "the finest Coach in the Western section of the nation, if not anywhere at any time, during the development of the game of basketball into a national sport."

Friel may best be remembered for the brilliant defensive strategies he designed, but Jack was no slouch at the offensive end of the floor. As cagey a basketball coach as ever worked the sidelines, Friel seldom lost two games on a weekend. If his team lost the opener, more often than not Jack would find a way to win the rematch. His "platoon" substitution system (first used in 1942, although Jack always substituted liberally), earned Friel nationwide recognition. When he had representative talent, Jack forced opposing coaches to platoon along with him, whether they wanted to or not. Friel's theory, backed up by research, was that players regained almost 100 percent of their starting energy level after a two or three-minute rest. So Jack would bench his entire starting unit when he figured it was tiring. Often as not, the "shock troops" Friel sent in were so fired up they'd play over their heads.

Friel is one of the truly great students of the game. At age ninety he was still predicting to friends at WSU games, or those watching television with him, what coaches would do or should do in a given situation, and invariably being right.

A pioneer in the development of the one-and-one free-throw rule, Jack was instrumental in getting the Pacific Coast Conference to put it in on a trial basis in the 1950s.

Friel was a marvelous teacher, not just in basketball. He taught just about every sport during his four decades in the Department of Physical Education at WSC. Jack coached some of Buck Bailey's frosh baseball

Cougar Ron Bennink bedazzles Oregon's Phil McHugh, 51, and Jim Loscutoff, 53, for an easy two. (Manuscripts, Archives, and Special Collections, Washington State University Libraries)

teams during that period, and in 1943-1945 took over for the Bucko when the big man was in the Navy winning World War II. Gene Conley credited Friel with helping him develop a good curve ball in 1949-1950. Chuck Brayton played for Jack as a freshman in 1944 and said Friel gave him some good hitting instruction. Friel coached the Cougar golf team for years, and also ran the Intramural Program, one of the nation's largest and best.

Although he mellowed a lot in later years, Friel still is remembered for the "vivid" language he used from the sidelines, addressed equally to his players and the officials. Michigan State Coach Jud Heathcote, who played for Jack in the 1948-1949 seasons, recalled one night in Madison Square Garden when the Cougars were warming up to play Manhattan. Two rather mature ladies carrying Crimson and Gray pennants arrived and seated themselves immediately behind the WSC bench.

"We got up a pool on how long the ladies would last in those seats once the game started," Heathcote said. "They were gone before the first timeout. Jack was in good voice that night."

Although sportswriters called him "The Fox of the Palouse," and, when his dark, curly hair began to grey, "The Silver Fox," most of his players in the later years picked up son Wallie's nickname for his father, "The Prune." Time and coaching did wrinkle Jack a bit.

Without doubt the most erudite of all the coaches of WSC's "Golden Age," Friel got himself in dutch with some of the conservative element when his name appeared in a newspaper ad supporting Henry Wallace in the 1948 Presidential campaign. WSC officials did a lot of dancing around on that one until Jack explained that, although he considered his political views to be "my own goddamn business," he had not authorized the use of his name in the ad.

Most of the criticism—and critics—disappeared when Jack's teams had a winning season in 1949, and then won the Northern Division in 1950.

While Jack gave up coaching in 1958, he remained on the Physical Education faculty at the college until 1963 and coached the Cougar golf team during most of that time. And when he retired from the University he did not stay retired long. For two years Jack was Northwest Supervisor of Basketball Officials for the Pacific Intercollegiate Officiating Bureau (PIOB), which provided officials for PCC games and those of several other conferences in the West.

In 1965, Big Sky Conference officials saw just the man they needed for Commissioner of their newly-formed loop. They came and got Friel. For the next six years, Jack did a great job of getting the Conference off the ground. He is accorded much credit for the subsequent success of the eventual six-state (Washington, Idaho, Montana, Arizona, Utah, Nevada) Big Sky Conference.

When he retired for the third time in 1971, Friel immediately was snapped up by the (now) Pac-10 as an "observer" of basketball officiating, a position he still holds (in 1989)—at age ninety.

At the opening of the 1977-1978 basketball season at WSU, the playing floor in WSU's Performing Arts Coliseum was named "Friel Court" in honor of the great old Coach, and a superb portrait of Friel done by former WSU Museum of Art Director Harvey West was hung in the concourse. (West also was a fine tight end for the Cougars in 1959-1961.)

In 1978, Jack Friel was named a charter member of the WSU Athletic Hall of Fame.

Since Doc joined W.S.C. in 1908, he has coached...

BASKETBALL, BASEBALL, TRACK, BOXING AND WRESTLING

DR. J. FRED BOHLER

Bohler is one of Pullman's favorite citizens... He's mayor of the city and the W.S.C. men's gym is named for him...

HOWDY, JUNIOR

HI, POP!

MEN'S GYM

WHO RETIRES AS ATHLETIC HEAD AT WASHINGTON STATE COLLEGE THIS YEAR AFTER MORE THAN 40 YEARS OF SERVICE WITH THE COUGARS..

A Legend Says Goodbye

On August 1, 1950, after forty-two years of devoted service to the institution, J. Fred "Doc" Bohler retired as Chairman of the Department of Physical Education for Men at WSC.

Bohler did it all at Washington State. He joined the college faculty in 1908 when physical education and intercollegiate athletics were in their infancy. He built both programs, equally and well, making them models that would be admired and copied for years. His interest, his ability, and his drive created a "togetherness" at the institution that made WSC the envy of schools throughout the Pacific West.

In his book *E. O. Holland and the State College of Washington*, Professor William A. Landeen cited the impressive continuity of the coaching at WSC from 1926 up to World War II and asked, "What held these coaches to the institution?

Off to the slopes! Athletic Director J. Fred Bohler, who introduced skiing as an intercollegiate sport at WSC, takes another team to a Pacific Northwest meet. (Manuscripts, Archives, and Special Collections, Washington State University Libraries)

. . . We surmise that J. Fred Bohler, director of physical education and athletics during all these years, played more than a common part in holding the members of this large and fine staff together, in times of defeat and in times of victory. . . ."

Bohler created a "togetherness" between physical education and athletics that very likely could not have been achieved by any lesser mortal. It required total commitment, and Doc gave it his all for forty-two years. He coached every sport, officiated at every game, lined every field, handed out equipment, taped ankles and treated all sorts of injuries, and never turned down a chance to play any game, anywhere, any time.

He represented the departments at interminable meetings, always working to achieve improvements for his faculty, but always fairly and with consideration for the total institution. Doc was WSC's representative at meetings all over the country; served on local, state and national committees concerned with physical education and sports; and was a leader in all of them. He was as totally committed to the community as he was to the college. He led the drive for a community swimming pool and even served as Mayor of Pullman. He was prominently involved in the formation of Kamiak State (now County) Park, and as President of the Chamber of Commerce in Pullman worked with his old footballer, "Ace" Clark, to develop the area around the butte for family recreation.

His family life—and he was a great family man—still revolved around his work. His son, John, recalls that sometimes, even occasionally in the middle of the night, his father would get a call from President Holland or his housekeeper asking Doc to come over—the Bohlers lived just across the street there on Campus Avenue.

"Dr. Holland couldn't sleep, or he had neck pain, or tension, and needed a massage," Bohler said. "Dad would get dressed and go over;

he might be there an hour or more, and then come home and try to get a few hours of rest before going to work."

Bohler Gymnasium, for which Doc worked so long and hard, was named in his honor in 1946. That same year, Bohler was elected a charter member of the National Football Hall of Fame. He served from 1915 to 1936 as a member of the National Intercollegiate Basketball Rules Committee, and was on the U.S. Olympic basketball committee for the games in Berlin in 1936. He was elected to the Helms Hall of Fame for college basketball in 1955. After his retirement, the Bohlers continued to live in Pullman, of course, and he was active as ever in all sorts of community and college affairs. Doc served briefly as Manager of the new Albi Stadium in Spokane when it opened in 1950, and saw the opportunity for the college to benefit by playing some of its games in the larger facility. He pointed out, correctly, that both Oregon and Oregon State were playing games in Portland because of the larger Multnomah Stadium there, and that WSC had played games both in Portland and Tacoma in earlier years. (Albi stadium seated nearly 35,000 in 1950, compared with 23,500 for Rogers Field at the time.)

J. Fred "Doc" Bohler died July 12, 1960, at age seventy-five. Friends, colleagues—admirers all—came from many parts of the West for his service.

"It was the hottest day in the history of Pullman," John Bohler said. "112 degrees!"

> Joe Burks [Class of 1925, former football player and later a prominent insurance man in Yakima] paid the greatest tribute to my Dad that day that I ever heard.
>
> I said, "Joe, it's sure marvelous of you to come all the way from Yakima in this terrible heat."
>
> "I'd do anything for your Dad, because he did *everything* for me," Joe answered. "When I started college, I wasn't doing very well; things were kinda crosswise for me and I decided to heck with it, I'm goin' to give it up. So I went up to your Dad's office and told him I was goin' to quit.
>
> "Joe," he said, "I think you should quit! You haven't got the guts to go to college. You haven't got the guts to play football. You're a loser; why don't you quit!"
>
> That made me so mad. I was goin' to prove to that old goat that I knew I could play. And I stuck with it, finished school and had a successful career.
>
> If it hadn't been for your Dad, I could easily have been a bum!

"I guess Dad just knew how to challenge Joe Burks—and a lot of other guys," John Bohler said. "I thought that was a real tribute."

"Doc" Bohler was elected a charter member of the WSU Athletic Hall of Fame in 1978.

•

Andre Paul "Joe" Nebolon, *of San Pedro, California, finished second to Jamaica's* Herb McKenley *in a world record 46.3 quarter-mile at Berkeley in 1946.*

•

The Sixth Decade, 1941-1950

On November 22, 1941, *Ed Pillings*, of Ellensburg, had one of those days every player dreams about. The 165-pound sophomore, a second-string halfback, scored on runs of twenty-four and twenty-six yards and picked off a Gonzaga pass and went seventy-five yards for another TD as WSC defeated the Zags 59-0. Those were the only points Pillings ever scored in his collegiate football career. He came back after World War II and was a sprinter on three of Coach *Jack Mooberry's* undefeated track teams at WSC in 1947-49. Eddie eventually joined *Earl "Red" Blaik* as Head Trainer at West Point and was at the Academy from 1957 until he retired in 1981.

•

Merwin Miller, of Santa Monica, California, won the Northern Division singles title and led WSC to a 5-2 dual meet season. Miller was awarded a Major "W" award for his Division title. He also won the Ohio singles championship at Columbus in the summer of 1941. Other players on the Cougar net team in 1941 were *Bob Guitteau*, Olympia; *Bill Klein*, Port Orchard; *John Rankin*, Pullma;, and *Harry Bussard*, Spokane.

•

Bob Kennedy, fullback, and *Nick Susoeff*, end, were voted to the All-Shrine game team following the 1943 game in which the East defeated the West 13-12 (then at March Field). "At the end," wrote Prescott Sullivan in the San Francisco *Examiner*, "the West could claim most everything but the most points. It had a wide statistical edge and it produced the afternoon's finest individual performer—*Bob Kennedy* of Washington State". Kennedy returned to the Shrine game in 1945 and had another great day, but was overshadowed by the performance of UCLA's *Bob Waterfield*. Still, Kennedy scored one TD and flipped a lateral to Waterfield who ran twelve yards for the winning score. (In a chapter titled "Babe's Blue Ribbons," which he wrote in 1950 for *Football's Finest Hour*, the history of the East-West game, *Babe Hollingbery* noted that Kennedy had played both halfback and fullback in the Shrine game and "was a one-man show at tailback." For the All-Time halfback spot opposite Cal's *Hank Schaldach*, Babe wrote: "If it were only my club, I'd take Kennedy. . . ." Hollingbery also selected *"Turk" Edwards* at a tackle spot saying, "Edwards was every bit as good in this game as he has always been, and he is known as one of the great professional tackles of all time."

•

Gale Bishop scored a record sixty-two points (twenty-eight field goals and six free throws) for Fort Lewis in a game against Hoxie, Kansas, at the 1945 National AAU Tournament in Denver. Bishop led the nation, scoring 1,085 points in forty-three games as Player-Coach of the Army team.

•

Cougar gridders *Wally Kramer*, a fullback from Toppenish; *Al Akins*, Spokane, halfback; and *Bill "Smiley" Ward*, a guard from Sequim, started for the Washington Huskies in the 1944 Rose Bowl game versus USC. All had been at WSC before the war and were sent to Washington under the Navy/Marines officer training program. Another Cougar, tailback *Jay Stoves*, of Centralia, also played for the Huskies in 1944 but was transferred and missed the Rose Bowl game. (The Huskies lost to USC 29-0.)

•

Veteran guard *Gene Arger*, of Tacoma, arrived on campus three days before the October 13, 1945, game with Washington, worked out and made the twenty-eight-man travel squad. A letterman in 1941-1942, Arger had been in Italy with an Airborne outfit for thirty-three months in World War II.

•

Mary "Pete" Peel, of Burke, Idaho, won the National Women's Downhill at Sun Valley, Idaho, and was rated one of the best skiers on the Pacific Coast during the 1946 season.

Bud Roffler, of Spokane, had one of the greatest days ever in the Seattle vs. State all-star football game on August 28, 1948. Roffler returned Seattle's opening kickoff 88 yards, then scored from the two. He also caught two touchdown passes, eighteen yards from *Don Heinrich*, Bremerton, and twenty-eight yards from *Leo Gilnett*, of Longview. State won 26-12.

•

Cougar freestyler *Brian "Pat" Canning*, Colville, won the 220 and 440-yard and 1,500-meter freestyle events in the 1949 and 1950 Northern Division meets, the first time anyone had ever won three events in the championships. WSC also won the 330-yard medley relay with a team of *Canning, Wilford Dolphin* (what a great name for a swimmer!), of Spokane; *Dan Bigger*, Tacoma; and *Jack Morelock*, Anacortes. Canning represented WSC in the NCAA at Chapel Hill, North Carolina, and Columbus, Ohio, in 1949 and 1950. He was fifth in the 1,500 meters at Ohio State in 1950.

•

The WSC Golf team won the 1949 Northern Division title. Players were *Ivan "Duke" Matthews*, of Olympia (Duke later was the pro at Seattle's Broadmoor Country Club); *Bob Lyons, Dick Olson*, and *Bob Benjamin*, all of Spokane; *Ray "Spike" Beeber*, Klamath Falls, Oregon; *Bill Teufel*, Wenatche;, and *Jerry Colkitt*, Tacoma.

•

Coach *Ringnell "Ring" Thorgerson's* WSC Ski team was one of the strongest in the nation in 1949 with Norwegians *George Thrane* and *Lars* and *Tormod Forland*. Thrane was among the world's best jumpers at the time. Coach Thorgerson was from Seattle, a WSC graduate in physical education in 1940.

•

They never listen! Long-time WSC P. E. Professor *Vic Dauer* had coached for two years at Springfield (Massachusetts) College before coming to WSC in 1949 and had scouted Yale, coached by *Howie Odell*, four times during the 1948 season. Lo and behold, who's coaching at the UW when Vic arrives in Pullman, *Howie Odell!* Dauer offered his scouting notes to Cougar Coach *Phil Sarboe* and got a nice smile—but "Thanks, no thanks." One particular play WSC had to look out for, Dauer warned, was a fake pass off the old Statue of Liberty. "The first time they used it, *[Hugh] McElhenny* ran forty-eight yards for a TD," Vic recalls. "No one laid a hand on him!" (The Huskies won 34-21 at Seattle on November 19, 1949.)

•

Washington State won the Northern Division Swimming Championship for the first time in 1949 and also took the Inland Empire AAU meet, defeating Washington for the second time. *Dick Hannula*, Aberdeen, and *Jim Shattuck*, Vancouver, were Co-Captains. *Roland Elledge*, Spokane; *Paul Sellin*, Tacoma; *Morelock*; and *Canning* represented WSC at the 1950 NCAA meet in Columbus, Ohio.

•

Idaho fullback *King Block* gained seventy-five yards in a seventy-three-yard drive (another back lost five) and lifted the Vandals into a 7-7 tie with WSC at Pullman on October 28, 1950. Block joined *Bert Clark's* coaching staff at WSC in 1964, and thereby hangs a tale. Somehow, Kinger got *Larry Broom's* name on his "recruiting" list after a trip to southeastern Washington and sent the 1939 grad a scholarship form. Broom and Waitsburg *Times* Publisher *Tom Baker* collaborated on a resumé for Broom, complete with pictures of a portly, forty-ish insurance man in various football poses, and sent it to Block— with the signed scholarship agreement. They also distributed copies liberally among friends. King's sense of humor was severely tested when fellow coaches learned of his gaffe. (Too bad Larry didn't live to see the story of his "recruitment" in print. The great old Cougar died in June 1988.)

The Seventh Decade, 1951-1960

Evy Shakes 'em Up

The alumni? When I'm winnin' I don't need 'em; when I'm losin' they can't help me!*

OLD COUGARS DIDN'T KNOW QUITE WHAT TO MAKE OF FOREST EVASHEVSKI WHEN he first came to Washington State in early 1950 to replace the deposed Phil Sarboe as football coach. When Athletic Director Bob Brumblay took him around the state on a "Meet the Coach" trip shortly after his arrival, Forest shook up some of the old guard.

"You just get me the money. I'll get the kids—and do the coaching," he told 'em in that tough-talking way he had. But he delivered. Evy ran the football program the two years he was at Washington State. He also ran the Athletic Director off, and, some say, was at least partially responsible for the departure of President Wilson Compton in 1951.**

Every real football fan knew Evashevski, at least by reputation, long before he got to Pullman. Evy was the highly publicized "front man" for Old 98 for three seasons at Michigan. Many said it was Evashevski's blocking that made Tom Harmon an All-American. He proved to be as tough a coach as he was a blocker.

Evy and his assistants, Al Kircher, Bob Flora and Ed Frutig (plus Dan Stavely, a holdover from the Sarboe staff), installed the Wing-T offense at WSC in the spring of 1950. It was a combination of Single-wing and "T" and Evy generated a lot of power out of it. He also had a good passing game, as WSC's statistics in the 1950-1951 seasons reveal.

The Cougars didn't pull off any miracles in Evy's first season—although they came close to one in a 20-20 tie with USC at Pullman on October 7. He won the games he was expected to win and, except for a 42-0 pasting from UCLA, looked pretty good in the ones he lost. (Evy had a helluva time with Idaho, though. The pesky Vandals tied him 7-7 at Pullman in 1950, and WSC prevailed only 9-6 the following year at Moscow, coming back from an 0-6 deficit with nine points in the second quarter.)

---

* In a history term paper by Dan C. Peterson, '82, Ike Deeter is quoted as saying Evy included "reporters" in this statement.

** Former History Chairman Ray Muse, in an oral history interview in 1986, said, ". . . He [Compton] was not in very good favor with the football coach at the time of his resignation."

OPPOSITE: *Clem Eischen, Cougar Olympian.* (Hilltopics)

Evy and his staff. Left to right: Dan Stavely, Ed Frutig, Forest Evashevski, Buck Bailey, Al Kircher, Bob Flora. (Manuscripts, Archives, and Special Collections, Washington State University Libraries)

The low point in Forest Evashevski's two years at WSC occurred on the weekend of November 24-25, 1950. WSC and the UW were scheduled to dedicate Spokane's new Joe Albi Stadium. The night before the game, Bob Torgeson, brother of the Cougar Captain and great center La Vern Torgeson of La Crosse, died of asphyxiation in his car outside the stadium. Bob and some other WSC students had been spending the night in their cars in order to get in early the next day and get seats in the Cougar section.

Captain Torgeson did not play in the Washington game. The Huskies won 52-21 and bragged later they had "given" WSC its final touchdown so that Washington quarterback Don Heinrich could have the opportunity to set an NCAA passing record. (He did.)

The game every Cougar fan remembers from the Evashevski years was the battle with number one-ranked California in Pullman on October 13, 1951. Evy and Lynn "Pappy" Waldorf's teams traded touchdowns all afternoon, sometimes in great gobs!—and Cal finally won it 42-35, but only after the Cougars gave them an awful scare. WSC was going for the tying TD on the final play, a pass from Bud Roffler to Wayne Berry, which was knocked away on the Cal 13.

That was the Cal team with one of the Bears' all-time greatest running backs, Johnny "O" Olszewski, and their best-ever linebacker, Les Richter. Cal had been to the Rose Bowl the year before, and they wound up 8-2 in 1951, barely missing a return visit.

It's worth going over the highlights of that 42-35 donnybrook. Johnny "O" opened the scoring in the first quarter with a twenty-eight-yard gallop. WSC countered in the second period with fourteen quick points on a twenty-four-yard pass from sophomore quarterback Bob Burkhart, of Kellogg, Idaho, to Don Steinbrunner, of Wickersham, and a fifty-three-yard pass interception return by Spokane halfback Al Charlton. Cal interrupted the Cougar onslaught with a TD of its own on a six-yard run by fullback John Pappa, but WSC tied it 21-21 just before halftime when "Bye-Bye" By Bailey, of Seattle, went fifty yards on a great run. (Every extra point in this game was successful; Cal's Richter made six and Roffler made five for WSC.)

Fans went out at halftime totally spent. It's a wonder they survived the final two quarters!

Cal scored twenty-one unanswered points in the third period. It was 42-21 as the fourth quarter opened. Then WSC broke loose, again. By Bailey scored from the one after a good drive, and Burkhart hit sophomore halfback Wayne Berry, of LaGrande, Oregon, for the Cougars' final score with a pass from the two, ending a sixty-seven-yard drive.

WSC had a big margin in passing yardage, 161 to 62; Cal was awesome rushing, 389 to 149. The Cougars had the edge in first downs 15-13. Bailey was WSC's leading rusher with 17 for 93 yards.

The *Spokesman-Review's* Sunday morning lead summed it up pretty well:

> The magnificent Crimson Cougars of Washington State College fought the nation's No. 1 team, California's Golden Bears, to a standstill here today, losing 42 to 35 after 60 minutes of terrific football.

The tilt stayed in the news for several days, partially because of a post-game quote attributed to Evashevski which forever endeared him to Pappy Waldorf: "Well, a blind hog gets an acorn once in a while."

The other game Cougar fans warmly recall in that season was the finale with the Huskies in Seattle on November 24. Washington State defeated Washington 27-25, capping a 7-3 season for the Cougars and sending the Huskies reeling to their sixth defeat.

WSC fans did not have long to celebrate, however. Evashevski had signed a five-year contract with Washington State when he came to Pullman in 1951. Now, it appeared, Forest was unhappy with some things at the institution and wanted to renegotiate. Which he did from a position of strength, as you can well imagine, after that 7-3 season.

Dave "Trees" Nordquist, of Lake Stevens, who was President of the Student Body in 1951-1952 and for some years now has been Director of General Services at the University, played some football under both Sarboe and Evashevski. He remembers Evy as more of a force to deal with than Sarboe.

"You *feared* Evy," Dave says, but adds, "I was impressed. He took charge, inspired confidence in his players, and was a master at getting teams up for a game—and at bringing them down when they had their heads in the clouds! He was a good [football] administrator. He had a good staff, and he knew how to use his assistants. Great psychologist!"

Nordquist was in an interesting position in *l'affaire Evashevski*. Dave gave up his football scholarship prior to his senior year, after he was elected ASSCW President, and when Evy made his "demands" at the end of the 1951 season—one being that he wanted complete control of the football budget, Nordquist was on the Athletic Council and right in the middle of it all.

There was some talk of a student strike if the administration didn't salve Forest. Of course the students had no way of knowing that

•

Coach Lars Forland's *1951 ski team won the Northern Division and finished second in the National Intercollegiate meet, winning the jumping and cross-country events at the nationals.* Allan Fisher *took all but one cross-country race during the season, and* Torbjorn Falkanger, *of Norway, won every jump. Other team members were* William Noble, *Kalispell, Montana;* Robert Brown, *Bremerton; and* Ben Parsons.

•

Evashevski was playing games, with the Iowa job in hand, and there was a good bit of alumni "sympathy" with the coach as well. After all, he was winning and the Comptons had lost. President and Mrs. Compton had already departed the campus and Dr. William A. Pearl, chairman of Mechanical Engineering and Director of the Institute of Technology, was Acting President.

"Evy was about twenty minutes late [for a meeting with Dr. Pearl and the Athletic Council to discuss his *demands*]," Nordquist recalled. "He walked in cool as could be; said he'd taken his son sledding."

Bill Pearl played it cool, too. He was telling a story when Evy came in and he kept right on—in fact stretched it out a bit.

Someone asked Evy about his plans. He said it reminded him of his last game in college, when they were trailing Michigan State in front of 102,000 fans in Michigan stadium at Ann Arbor.

"We went back to the huddle, and I was the only one in that stadium who knew what the next play was going to be." He paused briefly, then added, "And that's the way it is now, gentlemen." [One wonders, if a 21-one-year-old kid was calling Michigan's plays, what Coach Herbert O. "Fritz" Crisler was getting paid for. Maybe it's just as well WSC hired Hollingbery rather than Crisler in 1926.]

Nordquist called a special meeting of the Board of Control and Dean Golden Romney of the College of Physical Education and Athletics came and outlined Evashevski's demands.

"After we heard them," Dave said, "everyone realized it was impossible to meet them all. So we asked for a special edition of the *Evergreen* to let the students know what the score was. That meeting changed student views and solidified their support for the administration," Nordquist said. "He [Evy] must have had a firm offer in his pocket."*

Evashevski went back to Iowa and the Big Ten and proved that he was a great football coach, in any company. He took the Hawkeyes to two Rose Bowl games, in 1956 (against Oregon State) and in 1959 (against Cal), and won both games.

Wouldn't it have been something if the ball had bounced a little differently in that '58 season and Washington State instead of California had been Evy's Pasadena opponent on January 1, 1959.

It was, oh, so close!

The "Kiss of Roses"

Shortly after he arrived in the midwest to take over the job at Iowa, Forest Evashevski was quoted in the national press as saying he'd left a Rose Bowl team at Washington State.

Whether that was an accurate quote, or a sportswriter's version of what Evy said in pointing out that he'd gone 7-3 with a young team at Washington State in 1951 and was trading that for the 2-5-2 team at Iowa

WSC was undefeated in dual meets during the 1951 wrestling season, won the Northwest AAU team title and was co-champion with Cal in the PCI. Sosh Watanabe was Captain and team members were Jim Jennings, Yakima; Gordon Evans, Colfax; Dan Bigger, Tacoma; Erv Graber, Vancouver; Bob Ratfield, Bow; Jerry Holt, Fairfield; Irv Dahlberg, Tacoma; Bob Closs; and Jim Dolle, Tacoma.

---

* "The demands Evy made . . . revolved around four basic areas: (1) the Athletic Council had to be abolished; (2) Evy would have a free hand in developing the football budget; (3) the Regents would underwrite the football budget, agreeing to cover any deficits; and (4) Evy and his assistants would get new contracts calling for substantial raises." (From a term paper by Dan C. Peterson, with points from a Pullman *Herald* article.)

left him by Kenny Raffensperger, no one will know. But when the "quote" reached the West Coast it put the kiss of roses on Evy's successor, Alton S. Kircher.

A great all-around athlete at Michigan State, Kircher won letters in football, basketball, and baseball at East Lansing. He had come to WSC as Evy's Offensive Coordinator, working upstairs during the games, calling plays and passing along advice to the defense. When Evashevski pulled up stakes, Kircher was persuaded to stay on.

Kircher was a popular choice. After all, astute observers loudly proclaimed, "Al wasn't only Evashevski's 'Eye-in-the-Sky,' he was his 'brains, too!'" Kircher signed a five-year contract offered by Acting President Bill Pearl—at the direction of the Regents, of course.

The bloom fell off the Roses, so to speak, in Kircher's first game. USC took the Cougars apart 35-7 in the Coliseum on September 19, 1952. And the following week, despite two touchdowns by Dwight Pool, of Pasco, a wraith with bad knees, WSC lost to Stanford 14-13 in Pullman and the Rose bush died.

Al Kircher (Hilltopics)

Washington State finished 4-6 in the 1952 season, recording wins over Oregon State, Oregon, Idaho and Oklahoma A&M. (In light of subsequent opening seasons for Cougar coaches, that wasn't at all bad. Jim Sutherland, Bert Clark and Jim Sweeney all went 3-6-1 in their first years, and Jackie Sherrill, the blithe Spirit of '76, later the gold-plated coach of the Texas Aggies, was only 3-8 in his first—and only— campaign.)

But 4-6 wasn't good for a "Rose Bowl team," and Kircher never was able to build on the momentum that Evashevski had started. He went 4-6 again in 1953 and 1954, 1-7-2 in 1955 and it was all over.

There are several things about those years which should be recorded, however.

In 1954, C. Clement French stepped into the athletic picture for the first time. French had come in from Texas A & M in 1952 to replace Wilson Compton as WSC President. Dr. Golden Romney was running the Athletic Department at that time as Dean of the College of Physical Education and Athletics. He had succeeded the retiring J. Fred "Doc" Bohler as Chairman of the Men's Physical Education department in 1950 and took over the Athletic Director's duties when Bob Brumblay departed in 1951.

French soon realized that Romney was not suited for the Athletic Director's job. A Mormon, Romney neither smoked nor drank, and was uncomfortable in the presence of those who did.*

Since much of the business of intercollegiate athletics is conducted in an atmosphere more closely resembling the smoke-filled rooms of politics than the halls of ivy, Romney was never comfortable in the Athletic Director portion of his position.

President French remedied the situation in the fall of 1954. He appointed Stan Bates, a widely known and highly popular coach and school administrator at Snohomish, as Athletic Director.

---

* Dr. Helen Smith, long-time chairman of Women's Physical Education at WSC and a smoker, said Romney objected to her smoking in staff meetings. "I detested the man!" Dr. Smith once declared.

•

Bill Parnell, *competing for his
native Canada in the 800
and 1500 meters at Helsinki
in 1952, became the sixth
Cougar in the Olympics. The
others at that time were* Eldon
Jenne, *Coupeville, pole vault
in 1920 at Antwerp, Belgium;*
Lee Orr, *Monroe, fifth in the
200 meters and the 4 x 100
relay for Canada at Berlin in
1936;* Clem Eischen,
*Vancouver, Washington,
1500 meters, USA;* Leo
Roininen, *Canada, javelin;
and* Pete Mullins, *sixth in the
decathlon for Australia at the
London Games in 1948.*

•

Bates, who had been a great all-around athlete at the College of Puget Sound in Tacoma in the early thirties, happened to be on the Pullman campus, having come in as Associate Director of Admissions in 1953. (By coincidence, Bob Brumblay also had stepped from the Admissions Office into the AD job. Bates was to have a much lengthier—if at times just as trying—tenure.)

"I wondered what I'd gotten myself into those first two weeks!" Bates has recounted on many occasions how he took over as AD on September 15, 1954, and, on September 19 in the football season opener with USC in Los Angeles, big Ed Fouch, a Trojan tackle, delivered a double forearm shiver to Cougar guard Doug Leifeste's face. The Sunnyside gridder suffered a broken jaw, lost two teeth, and had had both knees dislocated. The incident was all over the sports pages and drew an angry, and official, protest from Bates and President French to the USC President and the PCC office, as well as to SC Coach Jess Hill, who subsequently wrote a letter of apology.*

The shouting, threats and recriminations had hardly died away before WSC was back in the headlines.

"I got a phone call from Dana Bible (Athletic Director at Texas) the week after the USC game," Bates recalled. "He sort of hmmed and hawed around a little, and then said, 'Ah, Stan, I understand that you have a black player on your team this year.'"

"That's right," Stan replied. "Duke Washington, our fullback. And he's a good one."

"Well, ah, Stan, you know we don't have black players in Texas, and we'd like you to leave him home when you come down here. It might be better all around."

Bates assured Bible that if Washington State came, fullback Talmadge "Duke" Washington, of Pasco, most assuredly would be on the travel squad. Then Stan headed up to President French's office and told him storm clouds were building over Texas.

"Dr. French never hesitated," Bates says. "He picked up the phone, called Austin and told the Texas president he backed my decision one hundred percent. If Duke Washington couldn't play, Washington State wasn't coming."

Washington went, and played. He ran seventy-three yards for the first Cougar score in a 40-14 loss to the Longhorns.

Writer Willie Morris recalled the event in his autobiography, *North Toward Home* (New York: Houghton Mifflin, 1967). Morris gives a feeling for the time and the situation that is worth noting:

> As for me, I began to see many of these things [education, politics, racism], but mainly through a prism. It was only later that I directly faced these aspects of Texas society and found them tawdry and suffocating. What I mainly noticed then were the boorish remarks of Regents, who could make the most reflective and charitible monk in the most isolated cloister want

---

* Joe Koenig, the great old Cougar halfback, says the Men of Troy were using that forearm shiver as far back as 1925. "My ears rang for a week after that game," Joe recalled. It was worth it. The Cougars prevailed 17-12 in the upset of the 1925 season.

Talmadge "Duke" Washington packs his equipment before joining the West team for the 1955 East-West game in San Francisco. Assisting Duke is E. E. "Pete" Ingram, left, long-time Athletic Equipment Manager. (Manuscripts, Archives, and Special Collections, Washington State University Libraries)

to bite back, the mindless self-satisfaction of most of the students, and, politically, the general hardening of the arteries after the Supreme Court decision of 1954. It also was during this time, as a foretaste of later years, that a second-team halfback named Duke Washington broke away on a touchdown for Washington State against Texas. A large part of the Texas student section, myself included, stood up to applaud the first Negro ever to play in Texas Memorial Stadium." [A couple of notes to Willie: Duke was *first team* all the way, and he was the Cougar *fullback*. For the record, Hugh "Pete" Toomey, of Visalia, California, scored the other WSC touchdown, on a fifteen-yard run. Mert Purnell, of Ellensburg, and Frank Sarno, of Somerville, Massachusetts, kicked the extra points.]

Now an art teacher in the Seattle school system, Washington says he was not really aware of the tempest surrounding this game.

"We had four blacks on the team in 1952 when we played at Waco [against Baylor; they were Duke, ends Bill Holmes and Howard McCants,

WSC won the Northern Division in track in 1953 and placed fourth in the PCC meet as Allan Fisher *defended his two-mile title and* Howard McCants, *of River Rouge, Michigan, tied for first in the high jump at 6-6.*

and halfback Rudy Brooks]. I don't recall that there was anything made of that," Duke said three decades later.

In 1954, at Austin, Washington stayed at the home of a local family, while the team checked into a hotel. He doesn't remember any special arrangements being made for him and his teammates at Waco or in Stillwater, Oklahoma, in 1952 when WSC played Baylor and Oklahoma A & M.

Two other games, altogether different, also are memorable from Al Kircher's four seasons at WSC.

On October 23, 1954, Washington State lost to Idaho 10-0 at Pullman. It was the first time a WSC football team had lost to the Vandals since 1925. The traditional "Idaho Walk," started in 1938, became a "WSC Walk." Hundreds of WSC students participated, with *Evergreen* sports columnist Bob "Yogi" Harris, of Vancouver, and Student Body President Dale Boose, Seattle, leading the way, along with the Cougar Pep Band.

WSC News Bureau Manager Denny Morrison slipped a picture of the "walk" to *Life* magazine, which printed it in a two-page spread in the November 15 issue under the title "The March on Moscow."

Kircher's 1955 team defeated Idaho 9-0, only victory of that season, and the Vandals again started walking. WSC students walked twice more before the regular WSU-Idaho series ended in 1978. Bert Clark's 1964 WSC team lost to Dee Andros and the Vandals at Moscow, and in 1965 Bertie again lost to the Vandals, this time coached by Steve Musseau, "the Great Pumpkin" had moved on to Oregon State.*

The other unforgettable game in the Kircher Era was played on November 12, 1955, at Pullman. Through the shrewd machinations of Athletic Ticket Manager Bob Smawley, '52, of Pullman, and Sports Information Director Don Faris, the game has become popularly known as the "Refrigerator Bowl." It was played on a frozen field with the temperature right around zero. This game is always included in sports trivia books as the college football game where only one ticket was sold!

An arctic front hit the Palouse on November 11, bringing extreme cold and heavy snow. WSC Groundskeeper Elmer "Shorty" Sever scraped snow off the field prior to the game and built fires in large incinerators placed alongside the players' benches. Timers moved down from the pressbox and sat in a car parked near the field. The WSC band showed up but their instruments soon froze and the musicians gave up and went home. It was scheduled to be "High School Band Day," but they called that off.

In the press box, Professor Maynard Hicks, working with the stats crew, could not get his ditto machine to work in the extreme cold, and Herb Ashlock, '33, of the Spokane *Chronicle*, said his typewriter keys "froze half-way to the paper." Most of the sportswriters (all of those up from San Jose!) went over to the CUB and watched the game from the second-story ballroom windows.

---

*Harry Missildine, Sports Editor of the Spokane *Spokesman-Review*, is credited with hanging this moniker on Coach Andros. WSU Coach Bert Clark, one of Andros' teammates at Oklahoma, countered: "He looks more like a mobile A & W stand to me."

Most of the players wore gloves of some type—cotton, wool, even rubber. Just before the game, San Jose State Coach Bob Bronzan and Trainer Lincoln Kimura bought all the cotton work gloves Guy Allen had in stock at his hardware store on Main Street in downtown Pullman.

Fred Merrick, who covered the game for the *San Jose Mercury-Herald*, said later that several Spartan players told him they suffered chilblain for years after, any time their hands were subjected to cold.

Quarterback Bobby Iverson, of Puyallup, scored both of WSC's touchdowns in that game, which ended, appropriately some superstitious folks thought, 13-13.

Although Smawley sold only one reserved seat ticket, students, season ticket holders and general admissions swelled the actual attendance to an estimated 1,600, most of them heavily bundled or cocooned in sleeping bags.

Smawley later identified the lone ticket buyer as Chuck Moore, a high school student from Harrington, Washington, and refunded the young man's $3.00 at halftime of the WSC-Oregon State basketball game in Bohler gym on January 7, 1956. (WSC won 58-52.)

Washington State bought up the remaining year on Al Kircher's contract at the end of the 1955 season. Al took the money and he and Dorothy bought Dick Holdgraf's Hilltop Motel & Steakhouse in Pullman. The Kirchers expanded the dining facilities and for years operated the best steak house in the Palouse country—if not all of eastern Washington—and Kirch presided at the grill.

Timing is Everything

On October 24, 1953, Washington State met UCLA in the Los Angeles Coliseum. The Cougars were heavy underdogs, but they took the opening kickoff and marched straight down the field and scored on a six-yard option pass from halfback Wayne Berry, of LaGrande, Oregon, to end Howard McCants, of River Rouge, Michigan. It looked *sooo* easy.

Gordon Oman, '39, in from Palmdale, California, to watch his alma mater, was sitting in the WSC rooting section. When the Cougars scored and led 7-0, Oman stood up, turned in the general direction of the UCLA fans and bellowed: "How'dja like that, Lemonheads!"

Final score, WSC 7, UCLA 44.

In the Scout Box

Mike "Mo" Scarry came up from the University of Santa Clara in the fall of 1954 to be Line Coach for Al Kircher. Mike was a good football man. He also was about 220 pounds of solid muscle. Scarry had been Captain and played center for years with the Cleveland (LA) Rams of the NFL. He later went with Don Shula to the Miami Dolphins and coached there until he retired in 1987.

Scarry worked upstairs in the scout box for "Kirch" and he was one of those very intense guys. Big and easy going off the field, a great family man, but all business when football was involved.

The Cougars were at Eugene on November 13 to play Len Casanova's Oregon team. WSC got out in front 14-7 on a couple of touchdowns by

Coach Bill Tomaras's Cougar wrestling team was undefeated in the 1953 dual meet season and won the PCI for the fourth time in five years. Eight WSC grapplers reached the finals of the PCI and all ten men on the squad scored. Coast Champs were Rich Gibson, 123, Richland; Captain Delance Duncan, 137; Byron Nelson, 147, Richland; and Del McGhee, Longview, 167.

Janet Harman, '52, has won just about every honor offered in Bowling. Here she is with the 1964 Southern California All-Star Team Award. (Janet Harman)

Bobby Iverson, of Puyallup, but quarterback George Shaw had the Ducks marching as it came down to halftime.

The scout box at old Hayward Field was up on top of the north grandstand and you reached there via a series of wooden ladders. Scarry was getting anxious about how long it would take him to get down and over to the Cougar dressing room in MacArthur Court at halftime.

As the clock ran down, Scarry got more nervous. He was yelling defensive calls down to the sideline and at the same time trying to collect all his notes and charts for a quick exit.

At this critical moment the door to the scout box opened and a short gentleman in overcoat and hat stepped in. Scarry caught the movement out of the corner of his eye and immediately thought "spy."

His attention still riveted on the field, Mike reached back with one big paw and pinned whoever it was to the wall of the booth.

"Get him! Get him!" Scarry stood up and screamed as the Cougars chased the elusive Shaw. In the next breath, without turning, he yelled "Who the hell are you?"

"I . . .I'm . . . K.Kem. . . ."

Just then Shaw broke loose from his pursuers and looked as if he were going to run instead of pass. The Cougar safety hesitated just long enough for big Leroy Campbell to get behind him. Shaw uncorked a mighty heave and the ball arched far downfield into the outstretched arms of the rangy Oregon end.

"Shit!" Scarry yelled, let go of whatever it was he had in his left paw, swept up the rest of his papers and headed out the door.

Dr. Kemble Stout's legs were a little shaky. The Chairman of WSC's music department sat down to compose himself for a moment before getting ready to announce the halftime program by the Cougar Marching Band.

Hall of Famer

When someone mentions "Hall of Fame" in connection with Janet Harman, the next question is, "Which one?"

Harman, of Walla Walla, a 1952 WSU graduate in Physical Education, was inducted into the Women's International Bowling Congress Hall of Fame in 1985, that's the top honor that can be accorded a woman bowler in the U.S. Previously, Harman had been honored by the Oregon and Northern and Southern California bowling Halls of Fame.

An all-around athlete her entire life, Janet grew up in Walla Walla where her father was a golf professional and later owned a bowling alley. She became adept at both sports early.

At WSC, Janet played all sports but was a standout in field hockey and a member of the first Bowling Club. In 1949, at the annual Pacific Northwest Hockey Conference in Corvallis, Oregon, she played center-forward on the WSC team that defeated Washington 1-0 and played a 1-1 tie with Oregon State. She scored the Cougars' only goal in a 5-1 loss to the University of Oregon Evergreens, one of the top teams in the fourteen-team NW Conference.

Janet won the inaugural WIBC Queens Tournament in 1961 with a three-game series of 794. She won two other National titles, the Professional Women Bowlers Association National Championship in 1963, and the bowling Proprietors' Association of America National Doubles in 1965 with another WIBC Hall of Famer, Donna Zimmerman. In 1958-1959, bowling in a Portland, Oregon, league, Janet had a 300 game and led the nation's women bowlers with a 197 average.

A long-time teacher in the Vancouver, Washington, system and in California, she now lives in Cerritos, California (And is a fifteen-handicap golfer.)

Northern Division Champs of 1947. First row (left to right): Arnie Torgerson, Ward Rockey, Don Aries, Bing Dahl, Bill Faller, Chuck Brayton, Tom Marier, Tiz Miller, Wally Kramer, John Wilburn. Back row: Bob Ellingsen, Wayne Brock, Bobby McGuire, Jud Heathcote, Gary Paré, Lefty Foster, Henry Jorissen, Joe Hemel, Larry Orteig, Coach Buck Bailey. (Manuscripts, Archives, and Special Collections, Washington State University Libraries)

Buck and Moob Go on a Roll

It took Buck Bailey only one season to get his Cougar baseball club back atop the Northern Division after he got out of the Navy in 1945, but then Buck had a pretty good man watching the store while he was away. Jack Friel paved the way for Buck's re-entry with winning seasons in 1944 and 1945 despite a dearth of players.

Washington State won four straight Northern Division pennants beginning in 1947. Chuck "Bobo" Brayton, of Hamilton, made the All-American team at shortstop that year. Bobo was WSC's first All-American in baseball. (Joe Caraher swears that Art McLarney made it in 1932, also at shortstop, just before Art signed with the New York Giants. The records don't show it, and since 1947 was the first year the College World Series was played it figures that might also have been the first year for college baseball "All-Americans.")

WSC lost the playoffs to California, winner of the Southern Division, in a one-game "series" at Berkeley. The Bears won the rain-soaked opener 6-1 and the second game was rained out after only four innings with the score tied 4-4. Sunny California? Hah!

Cal then went on to win the first College World Series ever played, beating Yale 8-7 in the championship game.

Leading hitters for the Cougars in that 1947 season were John Wilburn, Spokane, the catcher, at .333, and Brayton, .323. Wally Kramer won eight games against only two losses and had two saves.

In 1948, the Cougars were 21-7 and lost two heartbreakers to USC, 7-5 at Pullman on May 28 and 6-3 on May 31. An interesting sidelight was

A sixty-mile-an-hour blizzard hit Stevens Pass during the Northern Division ski meet in 1956. WSC finished second with Bard Glenne, Mads Danielson and Otto Coucheron, all of Norway, placing for the Cougars coached by Don Wells of the WSC Philosophy department. Glenne was first in the four-way.

American end, Dr. Harold "Brick" Muller, operated and Bill recovered completely, but missed the 1957 season.)*

Rallying from the terrific psychological and physical loss of their All-American End, the Cougars thumped Nebraska 34-12 on September 21 at Lincoln to open the 1957 season. Newman threw three TD passes to Fanning in that game, still a WSU single game record. (Tied by two other great Cougar receivers, Hugh Campbell in 1960 versus Arizona State, and Mike Levenseller in the 1976 Washington game.) WSC then came home and beat Cal 13-7 in a very physical football game and headed for Stanford to try to avenge the 40-26 defeat in Sutherland's opener in Spokane in 1956.

Many stories have been told about the WSC-Stanford game at Palo Alto on October 12, 1957. Here are a couple.

With Stanford dominating WSC in every department, leading 18-7 and marching deep in Cougar territory with less than five minutes to play, President and Mrs. Wallace Sterling excused themselves to Clement and Helen French and left the President's box, saying they had to get home and get ready for a post-game party.

"You know how to get to the house, Clement. We'll be expecting you and Helen right after the game," Sterling said to French.

Stanford went for a first down instead of the field goal and lost the ball to the Cougars on downs on the WSC 13 with 3:45 to play leading 18-7. On the first play, Newman hit Fanning with a pass over the middle and Jack split the Stanford safety men and ran eighty-seven yards for a touchdown. (It's still the longest touchdown pass play in the Cougar books.) Newman then booted the extra point and everyone in the stands got ready for the obvious onside kick attempt to follow.

About this time back in Pullman, Dr. Dorothea Coleman, Professor of Physical Education for Women, stopped pacing in front of her radio, went out to the utility room, got a bucket of hot water and a large sponge and in a burst of nervous energy started washing her living room walls.

"A neighbor came over on a church call, and I'm afraid I was just plain rude to her," Dort recalled years later. "I told her I just could not talk then because I was listening to the football game!"

Cougar tackle Gene Baker, from Buckley (or as Bill Boni of the *Spokesman-Review* invariably wrote, "Gene Buckley from Baker"), had never tried an on-side kick. Gene sidled up to the ball, laid the side of his foot on it and sent it spinning down the field like a top. Over the fifty it went—which made it legal, and then back it came, to be fielded by a diving, sliding Phil Mast, a halfback from Spokane, on the WSC forty-seven.

Newman went to work again and in a few plays had the Cougars on the Stanford eighteen. From there he flipped a pass to Ellingsen and WSC won 21-18.

---

*Quarterback Bobby Newman, who was swimming with Steiger when he suffered his paralyzing injury, went to see Bill in the hospital right after his surgery. Nobody told Newman what they'd done to Steig to relieve the paralysis, so when he walked into the room and saw Bill stretched out there in traction, with those holes drilled in his skull, Newman keeled over in a dead faint.

Janet won the inaugural WIBC Queens Tournament in 1961 with a three-game series of 794. She won two other National titles, the Professional Women Bowlers Association National Championship in 1963, and the bowling Proprietors' Association of America National Doubles in 1965 with another WIBC Hall of Famer, Donna Zimmerman. In 1958-1959, bowling in a Portland, Oregon, league, Janet had a 300 game and led the nation's women bowlers with a 197 average.

A long-time teacher in the Vancouver, Washington, system and in California, she now lives in Cerritos, California (And is a fifteen-handicap golfer.)

Northern Division Champs of 1947. First row (left to right): Arnie Torgerson, Ward Rockey, Don Aries, Bing Dahl, Bill Faller, Chuck Brayton, Tom Marier, Tiz Miller, Wally Kramer, John Wilburn. Back row: Bob Ellingsen, Wayne Brock, Bobby McGuire, Jud Heathcote, Gary Paré, Lefty Foster, Henry Jorissen, Joe Hemel, Larry Orteig, Coach Buck Bailey. (Manuscripts, Archives, and Special Collections, Washington State University Libraries)

Buck and Moob Go on a Roll

It took Buck Bailey only one season to get his Cougar baseball club back atop the Northern Division after he got out of the Navy in 1945, but then Buck had a pretty good man watching the store while he was away. Jack Friel paved the way for Buck's re-entry with winning seasons in 1944 and 1945 despite a dearth of players.

Washington State won four straight Northern Division pennants beginning in 1947. Chuck "Bobo" Brayton, of Hamilton, made the All-American team at shortstop that year. Bobo was WSC's first All-American in baseball. (Joe Caraher swears that Art McLarney made it in 1932, also at shortstop, just before Art signed with the New York Giants. The records don't show it, and since 1947 was the first year the College World Series was played it figures that might also have been the first year for college baseball "All-Americans.")

WSC lost the playoffs to California, winner of the Southern Division, in a one-game "series" at Berkeley. The Bears won the rain-soaked opener 6-1 and the second game was rained out after only four innings with the score tied 4-4. Sunny California? Hah!

Cal then went on to win the first College World Series ever played, beating Yale 8-7 in the championship game.

Leading hitters for the Cougars in that 1947 season were John Wilburn, Spokane, the catcher, at .333, and Brayton, .323. Wally Kramer won eight games against only two losses and had two saves.

In 1948, the Cougars were 21-7 and lost two heartbreakers to USC, 7-5 at Pullman on May 28 and 6-3 on May 31. An interesting sidelight was

The Cougar gymnastics team won the Northwest AAU and Pacific Northwest College Invitational meets in 1955 and defeated California. Team members included Roger Richert, *Shelton;* Dale Steindorf, *Walla Walla;* Matt Brislawn, *Pullman;* Roy Wellman, *Seattle;* Noel Brown, *Mead;* Clinton Glover, *Clarkston;* William Monlux, *Everett;* Obe Healea, *Moses Lake;* Al Trout, *Mazama;* Jerry Deuker, *El Cerrito, California;* James Thurston, *Lake Stevens;* Neal Wood, *Pullman;* Karl Hansen, *Denmark, and* David Weatherly, *Clarkston.*

that USC flew into Pullman on a Western Airlines plane, which then loaded up Jack Mooberry's Cougar track team and returned to Los Angeles for the PCC meet there. (Pullman International had opened to air traffic in 1947.)

Buck had to bite his tongue about "that lousy California weather." It rained hard in Pullman that weekend. The first game was delayed almost a half hour between the seventh and eighth innings, and then was called in the bottom of the ninth when the Cougars had men on second and third with nobody out!

The Pullman *Herald* said "fans swarmed out of the stands in protest, but umpire Turple stood by his decision." Bobo Brayton, who played in the game, recalls that "Coast League umps" (he still says it with a sneer), were brought in for the series.

After a two-day rain delay, the Trojans prevailed 6-3 in the series decider. Again, the team that beat the Cougars for the Pacific Coast title went on to win the College World series. USC beat poor old Eli Yale 3-1 for the championship.

Ward Rockey, of Olympia, had six wins and a save, and Dick Stiles, Coulee Dam, was 5-1 and had two saves. Gordy Brunswick, Tacoma, .462, and Russell "Tiz" Miller, Kelso, .415, led the WSC hitters in Conference play.

Washington State came even closer to the promised, World Series land in 1949, finally losing in three games to USC in Los Angeles. Ward Rockey, who was 9-0 on the season, beat SC 15-2 in the opener of the playoff series. Dick Stiles, 12-1, suffered his only loss of the season, a 2-1 decision in ten innings, as USC evened the series on Saturday and went on to clinch a World Series berth with a 9-2 win in the third game. Arnie Torgerson, of Everett; Russell "Lefty" Foster, of Palouse; and Gerald Compton, Spokane, pitched, with Torgerson taking the loss.

Following the advice of that old saw, "If at first. . . ." Buck finally made it to Omaha in 1950 with what had to be his best team. WSC had a 32-6 season mark and beat Stanford two straight on the "new" Bailey Field (what is now the north end of Mooberry Track), which was dedicated on May 13, 1950. Lee Dolquist, of Yakima, beat the Indians 3-2 in the playoff opener and Lefty Foster picked up the win in relief of Gene Conley, Richland, as the Cougars prevailed 6-5, to clinch the NCAA District Eight title, on their fourth try in as many years.

In the College World Series at Omaha, Washington State won three straight games before bowing to Texas. Dolquist beat Tufts 3-1; Conley won over Alabama 9-1; and lefty Rod Keogh, of Kent, pitched a 3-1 win over Rutgers.

In the final two games, Texas beat Dolquist 12-1, Lee's only loss that season, and Keogh bowed 3-0. The second place finish in the World Series by that 1950 team is the best by the Cougars in the CWS to date.

For the season, Dolquist was 9-1 with two saves; Keogh 6-1; Conley, 5-2 with two saves; Foster 4-1 with four saves; and Earley Denton "Sonny" Galloway, Exeter, California, was 4-1 with two saves. Jorissen was 3-0 and had two saves.

The Cougar hitters were led in Conference by Ted Tappe, Bremerton, .372; Bob McGuire, Tacoma, .364; and Terry Carroll, Seattle, .362.

The pro scouts were "thicker'n flies around honey" during that 1950 season, Buck said. After the World Series, Conley signed with the Boston Braves (later Milwaukee), and Tappe, the Cougars' first sacker, signed with Cincinnati. (Jack Friel rightly predicted that baseball would lift the lid on bonuses, and advised Conley to wait a year, but Gene went in 1950. Probably cost himself a ton of money.)

Buck said the scouts at Omaha were more interested in Cougar third sacker Don Paul than they were in either Conley or Tappe. But Paul, who was a great back for the Cougars in 1947-1949, was set on pro football, and of course he went on to a fine career as a defensive back with Cleveland, so who's to know what might have been.

Loss of the talented sophomores was a big blow to two Cougar programs. Conley and Tappe had been starters and stars in both basketball and baseball and had two years of eligiblity remaining. Even without the pair, Buck only missed the Northern Division crown by a single game in 1951 as catcher Clayton Carr, of Bellingham, hit .355; right fielder Bill Mayberry, Seattle, .354; shortstop Eddie Coleman, Seattle, .350; and Lefty Keogh was 5-1 (and hit .378 in 37 at-bats!)

Jack Mooberry took over the Cougar track program starting with the 1946 season. After an opening loss to Idaho, Mooberry's teams won eighteen straight dual meets before losing to Oregon 75 1/2 to 55 1/2 in the second meet of the 1950 season. Then they put together another string of eight before the Ducks stopped that, 67 1/2 to 63 1/2 in 1952.

Andre Paul "Joe" Nebolon, of San Pedro, California, became Jack's first All-American, in 1947. Nebolon had a best of 46.8 in the quarter in the Big Ten meet at Berkeley in 1948 to tie Lee Orr's 1940 mark. In 1948, Clem Eischen and Dick Paeth, both of Vancouver, earned All-American honors at 1500 meters, and Eischen went on to the Olympics at London as Mooberry's first protege to make the U.S. team. Bill Parnell, of Vancouver, British Columbia, and Peter Mullins, the Australian, both of whom later competed for Mooberry at WSC, also were in the London games, Parnell in the 800 and 1500 meters and Mullins in the decathlon. Bob Selfridge, Ketchikan, Alaska, won the PCC two-mile for the Cougars in 1948.

Paeth won the PCC two-mile in 1949 and Fran Polsfoot, of Montesano, an excellent football end of this era, lowered the WSC high hurdle mark to 14.4 in winning the Northern Division.

The Cougars had a lock on the shot put in the Northern Division for about twenty-five years. Beginning in 1933 with Hal Dunker, of San Francisco, and continuing with "Lambie" Theodoratus in 1934-1935; Bob Cox, of Bridgeport, 1939; George Rowswell, 1939; Frank Londos, 1941-1942; Frank Mataya, Roslyn, 1948; Joe Widman, Rosalia, 1949 and 1951; Bob Swerin, Forks, 1950; and Burl Grinols, El Cerrito, California, 1955-1957 (he tied in 1956). The Cougars won the shot twelve times in twenty-two meets.

Mooberry was an able coach from a technical standpoint and maintained almost a parental relationship with many of his athletes. With a very limited track budget, Jack always was on the lookout for help from other sports. One day in the fall of 1949 he spied a slender young fellow

Peter Mullins, left, races Olympic decathlon champion Bob Mathias in the 100 meters at the London Games in 1948. Mullins later was an outstanding track and basketball player at WSC, graduating in 1953. (Manuscripts, Archives, and Special Collections, Washington State University Libraries)

running in a plowed field near the campus and asked the kid what he was training for.

"When I told him I was getting in shape for the ski season, he said he'd give me some training sweats and better shoes if I'd go in a cross-country running race that Saturday," said Al Fisher, of Rossland, British Columbia. Fisher, who had never competed in track in high school, ran and finished third. He was on Mooberry's track team from then on, eventually becoming a two-time Pacific Coast Conference Champion in the two-mile—as well as an outstanding skier on a National Championship team at WSC in 1953.

Some thirty-five years later, as the Executive Vice President of an international consulting engineering firm in his native Canada, Fisher wrote of Mooberry: "He not only taught me a lot about running, but also a lot about what I could expect out of life."

With three straight unbeaten dual meet seasons behind him, Mooberry was working his team out in the WSC Field House on March 27, 1950, in preparation for the opening of the outdoor track season when he walked into the path of a sixteen-pound shot and was hit solidly on the right side of his face and critically injured. Bob Campbell, of Pullman, the old Cougar weight man who'd been acting coach in that wartime season of 1945, stepped in while Mooberry was recovering.

The coach's injury, and one of the rarest of all track happenings, a dual meet tie that ended with a dead-heat in the final event, the mile relay, made that 1950 season one no Cougar track fan will ever forget.

On May 13, 1950, on Rogers Field, the Cougars and the Huskies duelled to a 65 1/2-65 1/2 deadlock. The only meet record that day was the 6-5 1/2 high jump by the Cougars' Eric Roberts, of Hollywood, California. But the event everyone remembers was the mile relay.

Running for the Cougars in that historic race were Chuck Millard, of Yakima; John Higgins, Mount Vernon; Glenn Wiese, Graham; and Clem Eischen. The Husky team was composed of Ken Morgan, Jim Johnson, Fred Bush and Jack Hensey. The time was a respectable 3:18.8.

Unfortunately, the names of the judges were not recorded. Maybe Cougar fans lynched 'em. Should have.

A Cougar Bags a Russian

You can look all day for his name in WSC boxing records—and come up empty.

What? The guy who licked the Russian in the Olympics and then fought for the World Championship in his first professional fight? He had to be one of Ike Deeter's boys if he went to Washington State.

Well, yes. Pete Rademacher was one of Ike's boys. Except he couldn't fight for Ike.

Tieton, Washington's favorite son came over to WSC in 1950 after two years at Yakima Valley College. Pete played football for Forest Evashevski as a guard and lettered on both of Evy's teams in 1950 and 1951. He also gave baseball a try. But Pete couldn't fight for Deeter because he'd had Golden Gloves experience. That automatically disqualified him for intercollegiate boxing in those days.

Three-time NCAA Champion Gordy Gladson, left, and 1956 Olympic Heavyweight Champion Pete Rademacher get ready for a little friendly sparring under the eye of Coach Ike Deeter at WSC in 1952. (Manuscripts, Archives, and Special Collections, Washington State University Libraries)

Rademacher did fight at WSC, but in exhibitions and in some Golden Gloves tournaments. He won the Pacific Northwest Golden Gloves Heavyweight title twice, and later was National AAU champion. A broken hand ended his hopes for an Olympic team berth in 1952.

Pete received his B.S. degree in Animal Husbandry from WSC in 1953, was commissioned in the Army and, in 1954, assigned to Fort Benning, Georgia. He continued his training in the Army and when the Olympic year of 1956 rolled around Pete was ready for a try at the U.S. team. In August of that year he fought his way to the finals of the Olympic Trials in San Francisco where he defeated Hal Espy of Idaho State to claim the heavyweight spot on the U.S. team headed for Melbourne, Australia.

Pete suffered a ruptured muscle in the bicep of his right arm in training less than two weeks before leaving for Australia. There was a question as to whether he'd be replaced on the team almost up to the day it left for Australia. When the plane left, Rademacher was on it. He'd convinced his coaches he would be ready to give it his best.

Rademacher knocked out his first two opponents at Melbourne, setting the stage for his match with the Russian Heavyweight Champion, Lev Mouhkine.

Nine thousand spectators were jammed into Melbourne Stadium for the final matches in the Olympic boxing competition. It was more than a tournament, it was a war, at least as far as the heavyweight match was concerned. It was Russia versus the United States of America. There could not have been more drama involved if TV had scheduled the finals.

The American and the Russian sized each other up. Pete moved sideways, then in and out, keeping his feet under him and close to the mat. He was following his own advice: "Don't dance, don't bounce. A bouncing fighter doesn't have much punch," Pete says. (Sounds a little like Ike, wouldn't you say?)

Less than two minutes into the fight Rademacher saw an opening and shot out a straight left. Boom! The Russian was down. The crowd went wild!

"Pete always carried his left hand lower than I like to see it, but he got a lot of leverage that way," Deeter said. "And he could always hit. Make no mistake about that!"

Mouhkine got up. Rademacher was all over him.

Down went the Russian again!

The referee stepped in after the third knockdown and raised the American's hand. It was all over in two minutes. The U.S. had beaten Russia!

Pete said he was so emotionally involved in that fight it was frightening.

"It was wonderful, but it was horrible," he said.

Pete Rademacher, Class of 1953, was Washington State's first gold medalist in the Olympic Games. A replica of Pete's medal hangs in the athletic trophy case at the University.

A year after his Olympic triumph, on August 22, 1957, in Seattle's Sick Stadium, Rademacher became the first man in the history of the sport to fight for the Heavyweight Championship of the World in his first professional bout.

Pete had Champion Floyd Patterson on the deck in the second round of their fight, landing a solid right to Patterson's jaw. The Champion took a three-count, but he got up and came back.

Patterson KO'd the challenger in the sixth round, after flooring Rademacher seven times.

For many years now a successful businessman in Akron, Ohio, Rademacher ended his professional fight career in 1961 at age thirty-three with a ten-round decision over Carl "Bobo" Olson. Pete's Pro record was 17-6-1, and he won six of those by KO.

"Suds"

Jim Sutherland was a genius in his use of the forward pass in football. He did things with his offense at Washington State beginning in 1956 that they were calling "new" and "innovative" into the 1970s—even in the pro game. It's difficult to believe that Sutherland learned his football as a blocking back under Howard Jones on those run-oriented USC teams of 1934-1936.

Sutherland came to WSC to replace Al Kircher. He'd been at Washington with Johnny Cherberg for two turbulent seasons. But Jim earned his reputation, and a nickname, at Santa Monica High School in California, where he had an .847 winning percentage in nine seasons ending in 1951 and was labeled Samohi's "Super Suds."

Sutherland was involved in considerable controversy before he landed at WSC. Controversy—and some downright rotten luck—followed Jim through his eight-year stay in Pullman.

After nine seasons at Santa Monica, Jim joined "Pappy" Waldorf's staff at Berkeley in 1952. Sutherland's great Samohi quarterback, Ronnie Knox, arrived at Cal about the same time and of course there was talk of a "package deal." (It didn't work; Knox left Cal for UCLA and Sutherland went up to Washington.)

At Washington, in 1954-1955, Suds walked into a panic situation. He was pretty much thrust upon Head Coach John Cherberg by some of the powerful Husky boosters who felt "Cowboy Johnnny's" offense needed some updating. Jim soon made the headlines when it was reported that, working with the Husky quarterbacks, he'd changed the snap-count, unbeknownst to Head Coach Cherberg.

Sutherland often said that Royal Brougham, sports editor of the *Post-Intelligencer*, didn't exactly help the situation.

"The day I got to Seattle," Suds said, "Brougham wrote that 'The man who would some day like to be Head Football Coach at the University of Washington arrived in town today.'"

To his dying day, Sutherland hated Seattle—and distrusted Brougham. (He had a lot of company there. The old Ephrata pharmacist "Cougar Ed" Jones and some of his buddies got together and wrote to Brougham that because of his long, loyal and unwavering support of Washington State athletics in the *P-I* they were naming the booster group in Ephrata "The Royal Brougham Chapter of the Cougar Club." (It still is.)

"The old bastard really went for it," Cougar Ed used to say, and then roar with laughter.

In his first season at WSC, Sutherland turned the Cougars into the best passing team in the Pacific Coast Conference. While winning only three games and tying a fourth, WSC set a new Conference passing yardage mark with 2,068 yards through the air. Quarterbacks Bob Newman, of El Cerrito, California, and Swinton "Bunny" Aldrich, of Honolulu (via Compton Junior College, which he'd led to the "Little Rose Bowl" title in 1955), pitched for 2,068 yards to receivers Bill Steiger, of Olympia; Don Ellingsen, Don Gest and Jack Fanning, all of Spokane; Dick Windham, North Hollywood, California; and others.

Steiger, a running back for two years at WSC, became an end under Sutherland. He caught thirty-nine passes (second in the NCAA) for 607 yards and five touchdowns and made *Look* magazine's All-America team at the end of that 1956 season.

The Cougars had everyone excited heading into the 1957 season. Steiger was back, along with the two quarterbacks who had piled up all that passing yardage in 1956, Bobby Newman and "Bunny" Aldrich, plus all those receivers and a sophomore who looked like a prospect, Gail Cogdill, of Spokane. (He was Rookie of the Year for the Detroit Lions in the NFL in 1960.)

Then just a couple of weeks before the season started, Steiger dislocated his neck in a diving accident in California and was partially paralyzed. (A team of Bay Area surgeons, including the old Cal All-

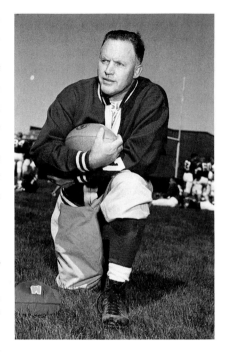

Jim Sutherland, Head Football Coach, 1956-1963. (Manuscripts, Archives, and Special Collections, Washington State University Libraries)

A sixty-mile-an-hour blizzard hit Stevens Pass during the Northern Division ski meet in 1956. WSC finished second with Bard Glenne, Mads Danielson *and* Otto Coucheron, *all of Norway, placing for the Cougars coached by* Don Wells *of the WSC Philosophy department. Glenne was first in the four-way.*

American end, Dr. Harold "Brick" Muller, operated and Bill recovered completely, but missed the 1957 season.)*

Rallying from the terrific psychological and physical loss of their All-American End, the Cougars thumped Nebraska 34-12 on September 21 at Lincoln to open the 1957 season. Newman threw three TD passes to Fanning in that game, still a WSU single game record. (Tied by two other great Cougar receivers, Hugh Campbell in 1960 versus Arizona State, and Mike Levenseller in the 1976 Washington game.) WSC then came home and beat Cal 13-7 in a very physical football game and headed for Stanford to try to avenge the 40-26 defeat in Sutherland's opener in Spokane in 1956.

Many stories have been told about the WSC-Stanford game at Palo Alto on October 12, 1957. Here are a couple.

With Stanford dominating WSC in every department, leading 18-7 and marching deep in Cougar territory with less than five minutes to play, President and Mrs. Wallace Sterling excused themselves to Clement and Helen French and left the President's box, saying they had to get home and get ready for a post-game party.

"You know how to get to the house, Clement. We'll be expecting you and Helen right after the game," Sterling said to French.

Stanford went for a first down instead of the field goal and lost the ball to the Cougars on downs on the WSC 13 with 3:45 to play leading 18-7. On the first play, Newman hit Fanning with a pass over the middle and Jack split the Stanford safety men and ran eighty-seven yards for a touchdown. (It's still the longest touchdown pass play in the Cougar books.) Newman then booted the extra point and everyone in the stands got ready for the obvious onside kick attempt to follow.

About this time back in Pullman, Dr. Dorothea Coleman, Professor of Physical Education for Women, stopped pacing in front of her radio, went out to the utility room, got a bucket of hot water and a large sponge and in a burst of nervous energy started washing her living room walls.

"A neighbor came over on a church call, and I'm afraid I was just plain rude to her," Dort recalled years later. "I told her I just could not talk then because I was listening to the football game!"

Cougar tackle Gene Baker, from Buckley (or as Bill Boni of the *Spokesman-Review* invariably wrote, "Gene Buckley from Baker"), had never tried an on-side kick. Gene sidled up to the ball, laid the side of his foot on it and sent it spinning down the field like a top. Over the fifty it went—which made it legal, and then back it came, to be fielded by a diving, sliding Phil Mast, a halfback from Spokane, on the WSC forty-seven.

Newman went to work again and in a few plays had the Cougars on the Stanford eighteen. From there he flipped a pass to Ellingsen and WSC won 21-18.

---

*Quarterback Bobby Newman, who was swimming with Steiger when he suffered his paralyzing injury, went to see Bill in the hospital right after his surgery. Nobody told Newman what they'd done to Steig to relieve the paralysis, so when he walked into the room and saw Bill stretched out there in traction, with those holes drilled in his skull, Newman keeled over in a dead faint.

"Just shows you how much luck there is in the game," Newman said years later. "That was a terrible pass. My hand slipped and I threw a real knuckle-ball. But the guy covering Donnie fell down and he was all alone in the end zone."

When President and Mrs. French arrived at the home of President and Mrs. Sterling, they were surprised to find they were the first ones there.

"Come in, come in," Dr. Sterling said, smiling. "Sorry about the game, Clement."

"But *we won!*" French said, and watched Dr. Sterling's mouth drop wide open. He had not even bothered to turn on the radio after leaving the stadium.

In Pullman, Dr. Coleman finished off her cleaning, spruced up a bit and walked over to her neighbor's home and apologized.

The road from Colfax to Pullman that night looked like Broadway; there were that many people out there in cars with headlights on to greet the Cougars when they bused in from Spokane.

If there is one game in the Sutherland era at Washington State more talked about than that one at Stanford, it's the one the following week, on October 19, played in Pullman against Oregon. The famous—or infamous—"goal-post game."

Oregon led 14-0 in the fourth quarter, but WSC shoved across a score on a one-yard run by fullback Eddie Stevens, the "Cunningham Comet," and then got another with little more than a minute to play on a two-yard sneak by Newman. Decision time!

There was hesitation on the Cougar sideline, and then Stevens trotted out onto the field. People have assumed for years that Sutherland sent Eddie in to try the extra point and that Newman waved him off.

"When Ed came in I asked him if he was supposed to kick," Newman said later. "He said, 'I dunno.' So he stayed in and blocked and I kicked."

The ball hit the left goalpost upright and Oregon won 14-13. The way the rest of the season went, even a tie with Oregon that day would have put the Cougars in the Rose Bowl.

"Coach [Len] Casanova came right into our dressing room and found me in the shower after that game," Newman said in 1988. "He told me he knew exactly how I felt because the same thing had happened to him as a player. I've always appreciated his saying that to me." (Casanova was a class guy in every respect. In 1958 at Eugene, after WSC had beaten the Ducks 6-0 in a real grinder for Cas and his staff, the Cougars went to the airport only to learn that their plane, which was also shuttling Idaho somewhere that weekend, was delayed by fog. Within a half-hour, Cas and three or four members of his staff came to the airport and spent the next two to three hours visiting with the WSC staff while they waited on their plane.)

Of course the Monday morning quarterbacks had a field day with Sutherland's decision—or lack of decision—on that extra point, but, looking back on it, Suds had a problem. Washington State had used five different PAT kickers up to that time. Remember, there was limited substitution then. But the trouble Suds had with that extra-point wasn't anything compared with what was ahead. In 1958 they put in the two-point rule. Sutherland never did figure that one out.

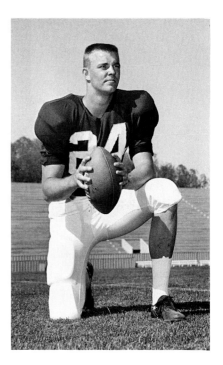

Bob Newman, quarterback. (Hilltopics)

"He almost threw it into the Gulf of Mexico," one writer noted, but somehow Gail Cogdill ran under this pass from Quarterback Mike Agee and hauled it in for a WSU touchdown against Houston in 1959. The following year, Cogdill won Rookie of the Year honors in the NFL playing for the Detroit Lions. (Houston Post)

Washington State did not dwell very long on that painful loss to Oregon. The Cougars bounced back the following week with a one-point win of their own, 13-12 over Sutherland's old alma mater, USC, in the Los Angeles Coliseum. The Trojans missed both extra points in that one, and Ellingsen, who'd suffered a broken nose early in the game (another one of those forearm shivers Joe Koenig described in 1925), returned the second half kickoff eighty-nine yards for a touchdown to go with Newman's eleven-yard pass to Ted Gray, of Seattle, in the first quarter. Angelo Brovelli's PAT was the difference.

The Cougars finished 6-4 in 1957, winding up with a picture-perfect passing exhibition at Seattle as they defeated the Huskies 27-7. It was the widest WSC victory margin in history at the time, and it ended Jim Owens' first season 3-6-1.

Bill Steiger was back for the start of the 1958 season and scored WSC's first touchdown in a 40 to 6 rout of Stanford.

Maybe the worst thing that ever happened to Suds was when the Cougars went for—and made—a two-point conversion after Steiger's touchdown. Newman passed to Cogdill and made it look soooo easy!

Suds must have looked the other way on the other attempts. The Cougars missed on four out of the next five two-pointers they tried. (It cost them against Northwestern the very next week at Evanston. WSC scored first and went for two, missed, and never got back in sync. Ara Parseghian won his first start with the Wildcats, 29-28.)*

Another thing happened in—or rather after that Stanford game which came back to haunt Sutherland. Some jolly idiot, celebrating WSC's one-sided victory, sent a postcard to new Stanford Coach "Cactus Jack" Curtice with a four-word message: "Welcome to the PCC." The Card was signed: "Jim Sutherland."

Suds was shocked—and saddened—when Curtice phoned him the following week madder'n hell, accused Jim of sending the card. Which of course he hadn't.

As it turned out, Cal and WSC came down to the final weekend of the 1958 season running one-two in the Rose Bowl race. A WSC win over Washington and a Stanford win over Cal would put the Cougars in. Washington State did its part, beating Washington 18-14 in Spokane. But Cal squeaked by Stanford 16-15 at Berkeley on a highly controversial call. Stanford went for two points after its second score and completed the pass, but an official ruled the receiver was out of the end zone.

On Sunday, Sutherland received a phone call from Curtice.

"Suds!" Curtice hollered up the phone line from Palo Alto, "the referee made an honest man of himself. He reversed that call. We won! You're in the Rose Bowl!"

"Hey, Jack, that's wonderful!" Suds responded.

After a pause Curtice said, "Now we're even for the postcard."

"Whattaya mean?" Suds asked.

"They didn't change the call. We lost," Curtice said, and hung up.

A lot of bad things happened in the Pacific Coast Conference in 1958.

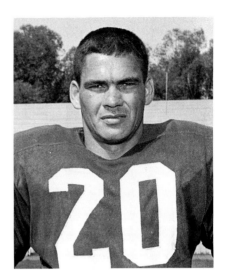

Bunny Aldrich, 1956-1957. (Hilltopics)

Bunny

Swinton "Bunny" Aldrich, from Honolulu, was twenty-seven years old, married with a couple of children, had been in the paratroops and led Compton Junior College to the Little Rose Bowl title in 1955, all this before he came to WSC in the fall of 1956 to play quarterback for new Cougar Coach Jim Sutherland.

Bunny had supreme confidence in his ability and was a fine passer. On November 2, 1957, Washington State was playing at old Bell Field in Corvallis and was trailing Oregon State by a touchdown midway of the second quarter. The Beavers were preparing to kick the ball to the Cougars and Coach Sutherland called Aldrich over.

"Let's go for it, Bunny!" Jim said, patting Aldrich on the back and sending him onto the field as the Cougars took over the ball.

The Cougars lined up on their thirty-five, Aldrich called signals and sent flanker Dick Windham on a quick out pattern right in front of the

---

* Cogdill set an NCAA pass reception yardage record in this game. He caught seven for 252 yards. It stood for years.

WSC bench. Bunny delivered the ball perfectly; it looked like a sure completion.

But out of the defensive backfield came Oregon State's great halfback, Joe Francis. In full flight, Francis reached in front of Windham, plucked the ball right out of Dick's hands. He had nothing but forty-nine yards of muddy turf to the goal line.

Aldrich took off his helmet, walked to the sideline, shrugged his shoulders and said to Sutherland: "Live by the pass, die by the pass."

Jim was speechless.

Jay Eliason, of Clarkston, set a new PNW record in the rope climb in 1959 and again in 1960. Eliason was the Cougar Captain in 1960.

Donnie

"Pound-for-pound the best all-around athlete at Washington State," old Coach Dan Stavely said of Spokane's Donnie Ellingsen.

The son of great Rose Bowl tailback Carl "Tuffy" Ellingsen, Don was a wide receiver and pole vaulter for the Cougars in the 1956-1959 era. He was 5-9, never weighed more than 165. What he lacked in size, Ellingsen more than made up in athletic ability, smarts and courage.

In three varsity seasons, Ellingsen caught eighty-six passes for 1,166 yards and seven touchdowns. He led the Pacific Coast Conference as a junior with forty-five catches. An intelligent, tough safety man, Donnie also contributed defensively with five interceptions, ran back eighteen punts 118 yards, and returned twelve kickoffs for 336 yards (twenty-eight-yard average) and a touchdown.

Against USC in the Coliseum in 1958, Donnie caught a Trojan forearm with his face in the first quarter, breaking his nose. He had trouble breathing and seeing the rest of the game, but he managed to run back the second half kickoff eighty-nine yards to give the Ellingsen family its second one-point win over USC. (His father's 1930 team beat the Trojans 7-6 in Pullman.)

Donnie shared pole vaulting honors during his career with Spokane Rogers High School teammate Jack Fanning. Both held the school record on occasion. Ellingsen's best vault was 14-3 1/2.

In the classroom, nobody touched him. Don's 3.85 grade point average in the pre-med program made him the number one man in his graduating class in 1959. Don and brother Bruce, '62, a Cougar quarterback in 1959-60, are practicing ophthalmologists in Spokane. Brother James, '57, a Cougar golfer in 1955-1957, is a dentist in Spokane. Mom Ellingsen (Virginia Kuhn, Pullman, '31,) also is a Cougar.

Don Ellingsen was named to the WSU Athletic Hall of Fame in 1984. He and his father, who was elected in 1978, are the first father-son combination in the WSU Hall.

The Russian Veto

Washington State was picked by quite a few people to win the strife-ridden Pacific Coast Conference in 1958 and go to the Rose Bowl. USC, UCLA, and Washington all were ineligible for the Pasadena classic due to rules infractions, but the Cougars had earned their pre-season ranking off a solid, 6-4 performance in 1957 which included wins over two of the "eligibles," Stanford and California.

The Cougars made the pickers look pretty good in that 1958 opener against Stanford, and even though they blew the game with Northwestern the following week NBC Television selected WSC for its National Game of the Week against Cal at Berkeley on October 4. The Bears had been less than spectacular in their first two games, losing to College of the Pacific 24-20 and Michigan State 32-12.

Joe Kapp and his California teammates put it all together against the Cougars. WSC drove deep into Cal territory three times in the opening quarter, but came up empty on each occasion. After that, it was all Cal. Hank Olquin ripped off a thirty-nine-yard run late in the first quarter, and the Bears added two more scores to go up 22-0 before WSC managed to get on the board on a twenty-five-yard pass from Newman to LaRoy Rath, of Grandview. (It's worth noting that Cal's Pete Elliott hadn't quite figured out the new two-point rule either. He went for two after that opening score. Kapp made Pete look like a genius when he ran it in.)

Washington State lost only three games in 1958, despite the fact that quarterback Bobby Newman was injured in the fourth game and missed most of his senior season. Backup quarterback Dave Wilson, a senior from Olympia who had not played enough to letter in two previous varsity seasons, came on and did a spectacular job. Wilson completed forty-three of sixty-three pass attempts (.683) for 641 yards and eight touchdowns, with only two interceptions.

Another key game that season was the meeting with USC in Spokane on October, 25. Sutherland tried Newman at quarterback to start, but his injured knee gave out early and Wilson came in. Davey directed WSC to a first quarter touchdown, with fullback Chuck Morrell scoring from a yard out. Again, WSC went for the two-point conversion—and failed. This one didn't backfire as others had, however. The Trojans' Don Clark (acting like that "Man from Marblehead, Massachusetts," as the old sportswriter said) showed even less understanding of the new rule. USC scored the tying touchdown in the second quarter and also went for two! Willie Wood's pass attempt failed.

With the score 6-6, Washington State lost its second quarterback. A charging USC lineman stuck a finger in Wilson's eye and Dave went out of the game with double vision. Defensive back Geoff Price, who had been a quarterback at Everett Junior College, was called on for emergency duty, but the Cougar offense was severely limited from there on.*

WSC and USC battled through the third period and down to the three-minute mark of the fourth tied 6-6. Then, with the ball deep in his own territory, Trojan quarterback Willie Wood dropped back to pass.

"Their tight end [Mike McKeever] came out and ran a P-hook," Price remembered years after. "The split end [Hillard Hill] came off with him, veered in and then took off down the middle. Donnie [Johnston, who was playing at a safety] came across to pick up McKeever and as I turned to go after Hill we collided."

---

* Geoff is the older brother of Mike Price, named on March 14, 1989, to succeed Dennis Erickson as Head Football Coach at WSU.

Up in the President's box at Albi Stadium with President and Mrs. French that day were, among other guests, the wives of the Cougar coaches. When Price and Johnston collided, long-striding Hillard Hill broke into the open and was easily ten yards behind the nearest Cougar when Wood let go with his pass.

As the ball sailed far downfield toward the outstretched arms of USC's speedy receiver, Maxine Niemi, Laurie's wife, let out a shriek.

"Sheeeeeeeeeeeeeeeeeeeeeeeeeeeeit!"

The pass and run was good for seventy-seven yards. No one paid much attention to the fact that USC, now leading 12-6, again went for the two-point conversion. The only reason it wasn't a completely stupid move is that Wood ran it in, and the Trojans won 14-6.

Washington State won four straight after that loss to USC and finished with what would be Sutherland's best record, 7-3. The Cougars beat UCLA 38-20 in the Coliseum a week after losing to USC. (It was WSC's first win over the Bruins since 1937, when Joe Sienko, of Pe Ell, kicked a twenty-yard field goal in the fourth quarter to give Babe Hollingbery's team a 3-0 victory.)

The Cougars had one last fling at glory in that 1958 season. The Sugar Bowl in New Orleans queried Athletic Director Bates about WSC's interest in meeting Louisiana State University on New Year's Day. President French, stating that "WSC has always abided by Conference rules and will continue to do so," even though the league was to all intents and purposes dissolved, requested permission of the PCC to accept the Sugar Bowl bid. USC and UCLA voted "Nyet."

Since unanimous approval by PCC schools was required, WSC told Sugar Bowl officials it would not accept their bid.

Trouble in Paradise

When the Pacific Coast Conference broke up in 1958 the most surprising thing was that it hadn't happened years before.

The PCC was born out of controversy. In 1915, when Stanford and California fell out over whether freshmen should be eligible to compete—Stanford said yes, California said no—Cal went looking for schools that felt the way it did and hooked up with Washington, Oregon and Oregon Agricultural College to form the Pacific Coast Conference.

In 1916, Washington State and Stanford were invited to join, Stanford having decided to go along with the "freshman rule." But even more important, the administration down on the farm had agreed to give up rugby and start playing "American football," as Cal had done the previous year. The northwest schools had been playing "football" since before the turn of the century. (As it turned out, Stanford did not compete in football in the PCC until 1919.)

The University of Southern California had applied for membership in the PCC in 1916, but had been turned down, ostensibly because of "travel difficulties." USC was the only school that did not have a regional "partner." Cal had Stanford, Oregon had OAC, and Washington had Washington State. UCLA was not even established until 1919, and then only as a two-year "Southern Branch" of UC-Berkeley.

In 1922, USC was admitted, along with Idaho. (A natural regional opponent?) Southern Cal had played all of the member schools except Washington in football (first game in 1923) prior to entering the PCC, and began a short-lived (seven-game) series with Idaho in 1922, the year the two schools came into the conference.

The University of Montana joined in 1924 and UCLA was admitted in 1928, bringing Pacific Coast Conference membership to ten schools scattered over five large Western states. All thoughts of "travel difficulties" apparently had vanished from the minds of the Conference elders. It's about 1,500 miles as the crow flies from Los Angeles to Missoula. In 1928, that would be a three- or four-day train trip, one-way, and only Doc Bohler was getting to Missoula by car in those days!

The ten-member conference started to disintegrate almost immediately. USC played Montana only four times in football, the last game being in 1935, and met Idaho for the last time in 1929. UCLA's first PCC football victory was over Montana (14-0 in 1929) and the Bruins and Grizzlies played on only six other occasions over the next seventeen years. The Bruins also played seven games with Idaho, beginning in 1928 (Idaho won 20-6 for its only victory), and the series ended in 1948.

Within five years after its admission to the PCC, Montana had dropped out of the "Northern Division" in both basketball and baseball. Washington played the Grizzlies only sporadically in football after 1932, as did Oregon State. Oregon played Montana only three times between 1928 and 1940.

The PCC "family" had many squabbles over the years, and in 1937 retained a former G-Man, Edwin N. Atherton, as a "fact finder." (Only in Academe!) At the end of one year, Atherton had turned up so many irregularities that the PCC extended his contract, and in January of 1940 the conference hired him as its first Commissioner. At a meeting in Sun Valley, Idaho, in June of 1940, the PCC leaders wrote what one sportswriter described as an "impossible" conference code.

In the next four years, up to his death in 1944, Atherton exerted total control over the athletes, coaches, alumni—anyone involved whatsoever in intercollegiate athletic activity at PCC schools. He was, in the words of veteran San Francisco *Chronicle* Sports Editor Bill Leiser, "the most powerful 'czar' ever employed by any association of universities."

"On May 5, 1941," Leiser wrote, "after no conference meeting, no hearing, no nothing, he [Atherton] calmly called in the press and personally announced that, by the authority vested in him, he had disqualified twenty-five athletes at Oregon, Stanford, Oregon State, Washington and WSC." Four freshman football players at WSC were banned from varsity competition under this edict: Keith Carr, center, Bellingham; Fred Small, guard, Mead; Don Prentice, halfback; and Bob Simpson, end, both of Spokane. (Not the same Bob Simpson, from Edwall, who lettered at WSU in 1965-1967.) All four players had been starters on the 1940 frosh team at WSC, the *Evergreen* reported.

Victor O. Schmidt, an attorney whom Atherton had hired as his assistant, succeeded to the Commissioner's job in 1945 following

Commenting on Forest Evashevski's *appointment as Athletic Director at Iowa in 1960,* Spokane Chronicle *Sports Editor* Bob Johnson *wrote: "Well, Evy retained his title as the heavyweight ouster of Athletic Directors when he won out in his feud with* Paul Brechler, *the previous AD for the Hawkeyes. Forest scored his first victory with the top brass of the Athletic department when he succeeded in getting* Bob Brumblay *to quit at Washington State some years back. The question now is who will Evy fight with next? It can't be with an AD unless he picks a scrap with himself. The guy is fresh out of opponents." (But he had one later, and that one got him— Iowa Football Coach* Ray Nagel, *in 1970. Nagel later came to WSU as Athletic Director.)*

Dorsett V. "Tubby" Graves, long-time baseball coach at the University of Washington and frosh football coach of WSC's Buck Bailey at Texas A & M, died January 17, 1959, in Seattle. Husky AD Jim Owens wired Bailey: "We'll fly you over for the service."

"For Tubby, I'd walk!" Buck responded.

Atherton's death.* Although roundly blamed in many quarters for actions—or lack of action—which led to the eventual breakup of the conference, Schmidt "was foremost in advocating 'liberalization' of that old code," Sports Editor Leiser contended in 1956.

The astute Leiser also wrote that same year:

> Much invective today is being directed to Dean Orlando J. Hollis of Oregon, and he is made to appear the man who invented the present code and the man who would force it down everyone's throat. If he is responsible for the rules of today, then he has liberalized the code, for the provisions and rules that came out of the Sun Valley PCC meeting in June, 1940, were far more strict than anyone would dare dream of enforcing today.

The year 1956 was critical for the Pacific Coast Conference. In February it was revealed that the University of Washington had a "slush fund," some of which came from receipts of a pro football game played in the UW stadium. The following month, UCLA was charged with under-the-table payments to a former football player. In the late spring and summer of 1956, the PCC levied major penalties, including probation, against Washington, UCLA and USC. (In fact all conference members, with the exception of Washington State, received some sort of penalty or fine. Cal was fined $1,550; Idaho $1,000; Oregon State, $650; Oregon, $350; and Stanford, $250.)

It was about this time that the United Press wire carried a story out of Los Angeles quoting a UCLA alumnus to the effect that he was "sick and tired of Washington State sitting up there looking so lily white in all this, when I know for a fact that a WSC alum gave Bob Miller [a Cougar halfback from Canoga Park, California] twenty-five acres of wheat land to go to Pullman to play football."

"Twenty-five acres!" chortled KWSC News Director Burt Harrison when he tore the story off the wire. "Hell, he'd have to lather it to harvest it!"

WSC had a major "player" in all of this action. He was Emmett B. Moore, Chairman of the Department of Civil Engineering at the college and three-time president of the PCC. ("The only guy dumb enough to accept that job three times!" Emmett said shortly before his death in 1986. He didn't add that his boss, WSC President C. Clement French, was one of those who insisted Emmett serve a third term. Moore had been appointed WSC's Faculty Representative by French's predecessor, Acting President William A. Pearl, in 1951.)

"We spent all our time on violations," Moore recalled, "debating, determining guilt, and assessing penalties. Never anything constructive. There wasn't time. I always felt the Big Ten did a better job because they had time to do things that were constructive.

"When I came in as Faculty Representative [replacing Dr. T. H. Kennedy of the Department of Sociology], the first thing I got from

---

* E. G. "Pat" Patterson, former WSU Alumni Director, was "abated" from recruiting in 1950-1951 after it was disclosed he had been violating PCC rules by driving prospects to campus from the Seattle area, where he resided at the time.

[Commissioner] Schmidt was a ten-page, single-spaced report listing offenses WSC had committed," Moore said.

President French, interviewed in retirement in 1986, said Oregon Law School Dean Hollis was "the intransigient one. He insisted that every i be dotted, every t crossed. Emmett would have conceded some things."

At age eighty-five, French remained the realist.

"It was the same old story. They claimed we were getting the same share as everyone else and were not producing our share of the income to the conference. They [USC and UCLA] felt we were a drag. Long trip, no gate. That was then—and is today," said the old president, shrugging his shoulders and smiling.

They played out the 1958-1959 schedules, although dissolution of the Conference had been agreed at a meeting in Portland, Oregon, in early August of 1958. It was a "lame duck" football season that fall, with USC, UCLA and Washington ineligible for the Rose Bowl, and some players banned for all or part of the year. As it turned out, those three schools won only ten games among them and would not have been in the Rose Bowl race even if eligible. But USC did help kill the Cougars' chances, and, together with UCLA, enjoyed one last parting shot at Washington State.

The Pacific Coast Conference, age forty-three, breathed its last on June 30, 1959.

Washington State played as an "Independent" in the 1959-1961 seasons, along with the other Pacific Coast Conference castoffs, Oregon, Oregon State and Idaho. Bates scheduled a home-and-home series with Oregon and added the University of Houston to fill open dates in the 1959 football schedule when USC and UCLA cancelled games with the Cougars. Cal, Stanford and Washington remained on the WSU schedules throughout this three-year "Independent" period (although Cal did not play WSU in basketball in 1961).

President French confirmed in 1986 that WSU had received a "feeler" from the Western Athletic Conference in the early 1960s but decided that its future was with the Pacific Coast schools. He revealed also that a group of schools which later formed the Big Sky Conference queried WSU at this time regarding possible interest in a new league.

"I did not feel there was any backing (for leaving the Pacific Coast schools), either from the alumni or within the institution," French said.

Stanford President Wallace Sterling was French's "confidante" when WSU had no conference affiliation, and Stan Bates maintained a good relationship with his old friend Al Masters, the Athletic Director at Stanford.

"Wallace said to be patient, that we were going to get back in," French said years later. "He also told me he had his own problems with the southern California schools."

Dr. French recalled that Sterling had said to him on several occasions, "Give me time. You belong with us."

"Sterling was on our side—to the extent that he could do something," French said. "He told me, 'Your way of doing business is our way.' We always understood each other."

Ray Hobbs, Cougar fullback in 1950-1951 from Sheridan, Wyoming, coached the only unbeaten major high school football team in Washington in 1954 at Pullman. His Greyhounds won thirty-five in a row between 1954 and 1956.

Stanford had been a rather reluctant signee in the Athletic Association of Western Universities, the five-school league comprised of Cal, Stanford, USC, UCLA and Washington which superseded the PCC. (It often was referred to in the press, particularly in Portland, as the "AAUW.") Stanford's alumni magazine urged the school to stand pat and not be wooed by the so-called "Big Four" (USC, UCLA, Cal and Washington) when the dissidents were organizing. The magazine referred to the proposed league as the "Western Union," because it's held together by (telegraph) wires.

Good fence mending, primarily by Sterling, ably assisted by Masters, his AD, and patience and understanding on the part of WSU, paid off. On June 13, 1962, at a meeting in Victoria, British Columbia (which one wag said made it illegal, since the action was taken outside the continental limits of the U.S.), Washington State became the first of the four schools left out in the cold when the PCC broke up to be invited into the new AAWU. The loop was dubbed by some as the "Big Six," but became the "Pac-8" in 1963 when Oregon and Oregon State were invited to join.

Idaho was the only member of the old PCC left out when the reorganization took place, leading to the comment: "They went through all that just to get rid of Idaho?"

Washington State had two more winning seasons under Sutherland. Jim's 1959 team, playing an independent schedule which included home-and-home games with Oregon, went 6-4, and WSU was 5-4-1 in 1962 after starting out 4-0-1. Sutherland's old two-point conversion Jonah jumped up again in a game with Pacific at Stockton that season. His thinking in this instance was even more puzzling. Pacific scored first and missed the extra-point kick. WSU then scored on a pass from Dave Mathieson to Hugh Campbell and "essayed the two-point conversion and failed," wrote a puzzled Harry Missildine in the Spokane *Spokesman-Review.* WSU then scored again, on a twenty-seven-yard run by fullback George Reed, to lead 12-6, and again went for two and failed. COP won the game, as it turned out, in even more unorthodox fashion. Halfback Kenny Graham, of Santa Monica, California, blocked a Tiger field goal attempt in the second quarter, only to have COP halfback Greg Stikes retrieve the live ball behind the line of scrimmage and run it in for a touchdown.

WSU never regained its poise after this loss, losing three of its last four, including a 26-21 heartbreaker to the Huskies in Spokane.

The Jim Sutherland era at Washington State ended in 1963 just as it had begun eight years before, with a 3-6-1 record. Sutherland was let go at the end of the season and WSU again reached across the state and picked an assistant coach from the University of Washington. This time it was Bert Clark, an old Oklahoma linebacker who had been an assistant in Jim Owens's highly successful Husky program since 1957.

Little Davey

The 1958 pressbook player profile read:

DAVE WILSON, 5-9, 170, Sr., Olympia. Heady quarterback
who has played two years in the shadow of [Bob] Newman and

the now departed Bunny Aldrich. Directs club well and is fine runner and good passer. Will be number one replacement for Newman this fall.

That, of course, meant that as long as Newman was able to play, Wilson would retain his seat on the bench, right where he'd been for two full seasons.

It happened in the fourth game of that season. Punting against Idaho, at Moscow, Newman was side-swiped by Vandal fullback Kenny Hall and went down with a knee injury. In came Wilson.

The pressure was on little Davey right from the start. Idaho had a good football team (they wound up beating Utah, Arizona, Utah State and Montana, and lost a 14-10 toughie to Missouri), and they were locked in a scoreless tie with the Cougars.

Late in the fourth quarter, Wilson threw an eight-yard pass to Donnie Ellingsen for the only score of the game. (It was low and behind him, but great competitor that he was, Ellingsen slid to the ground, reached back and pinned the ball between his shoulder pad and the side of his helmet.) WSC won 8-0.

Dave Wilson was Washington State's quarterback most of the rest of the 1958 season and the Cougars won five of their final six games, finished 7-3, the best by a Jim Sutherland team at WSU, and, except for a "Russian Veto" by USC and UCLA (as the Pullman Herald headlined), should have gone to the Sugar Bowl.

When "Little Davey" got his chance, he showed 'em he was a Cougar!

Dave Wilson, 1958. (Hilltopics)

They Can't Measure Heart

Bill Berry came out of Pullman High School in 1957 covered with athletic laurels. He'd been named "Outstanding High School Wrestler" in the state two years running. In football he was voted "Outstanding Lineman," "Outstanding Blocker" and "Most Inspirational Player" on three of Coach Ray Hobbs' championship teams—teams that had won twenty-seven straight games!

WSU Wrestling Coach Bill Tomaras offered Berry a scholarship, because Cougar football coaches weren't interested. But Berry insisted on giving football a try.

As a sophomore in 1958, Berry was a starting guard on offense and played tackle on defense (in the two-way football of the day). He was named to an All-Coast team at guard on the Cougar team that posted a 7-3 mark. He lettered three years in football and wrestling.

Berry came into college standing 5-6 and weighing 157 pounds. By the time he was a sophomore and playing on the varsity he was 5-7 and weighed 165. During the winter months when he was wrestling for Tomaras, Berry got down to 147. He won two Pacific Coast Intercollegiate titles at 147 and barely missed a spot on the 1960 U. S. Olympic team in Greco-Roman.

In 1963, Lieutenant Bill Berry of the U.S. Air Force (he was commissioned in 1961 through the ROTC program at WSU) was named to the U.S. Wrestling Team for the *Conseil international du sport militaire* Championships in Cairo, Egypt. He was Captain of the Air Force

Bill Berry, 1958-1961. (Manuscripts, Archives, and Special Collections, Washington State University Libraries)

Hugh Campbell, 1960-1962.
(Manuscripts, Archives, and Special Collections, Washington State University Libraries)

Wrestling Team, and in 1964 was runnerup for the Olympic team.

Too little? They can't measure heart.

The Rose Garden Defense

Ask a Cougar football fan about the Denver game in 1960 and the reaction will be, predictably: "Oh, that's the game where Hugh Campbell caught ten passes and started his record-breaking career." That's correct.

Or the answer might be: "Oh, that's the game where the Cougars ran and passed for all those yards and still lost." Right again.

But only those who were there know about the "Rose Garden Defense." That wasn't in the papers.

Washington State had not been impressive in its first outing that season, barely squeaking by Stanford 15-14. Somehow, Coach Jim Sutherland attributed that shakey start to defensive lapses, although the Cougar offense caused most of the problems in that game and it was the defense (Garner Ekstran's forty-yard touchdown interception and Bob Hoien's last-minute interception of another Dick Norman pass) that turned the tide. That was the same game where Pat Crook set the all-time distance heave for a center, propelling the ball at least thirty yards— fifteen yards over punter Keith Lincoln's head. Then, the practice week was short. The Cougars played Stanford on a Saturday night and had to fly to Denver on the following Thursday for a rare Friday night game with the Pioneers.

Anyway, Suds was very edgy, and on Friday called a special squad meeting to go over the defense. He wanted to do more than just put chalk on a board so he took everyone out into the rose garden at the old Park Lane Hotel in Denver and proceeded to install a new defense— much to the chagrin of his staff, particularly those charged with that phase of the game plan.

Washington State had a great night offensively against Denver, 514 yards. The Cougars passed for 307 yards, ran for 207 more; never lost the ball on downs, never punted. And lost the game 28-26.

The Rose Garden Defense proved thorny only to the Cougars. Denver quarterback Ramiro Escandon thew TD passes of fifty-nine and thirteen yards to end John Hayhurst in the third quarter and Denver hung on for the win.

Oh, another thing. Denver University gave up football after the 1960 season. In their trophy case are two old pigskins, one marked "Denver 11, WSC 6, 1909," the other. . . .

Moose of the Palouse

"A big moose from the Palouse was turned loose on the field here this afternoon and the result was thirty-six points for Washington State to nineteen for the Stanford Red."

That's how the "Moose of the Palouse" legend began.

"The moose," wrote Bill Leiser, veteran Sports Editor of the San Francisco *Chronicle*, "was a 205-pound six footer named Keith Lincoln who went all the way from Monrovia, California, to play football at

Mr. Lincoln goes to Houston. Escorted by Guard Ron Green, 62, and End Ed Shaw, Washington State's Keith Lincoln, 22, sets off on a long gain in WSU's 32-18 win over the University of Houston in Rice Stadium, Houston, in 1959. (Houston Post)

Pullman, Washington, and so far as the Indians are concerned, he could just as well have stayed home."

It was October 17, 1959, and the locale was Stanford Stadium in Palo Alto. Lincoln had a big day against the Cardinal, rushing thirteen times for eighty-four yards, completing three straight passes (for sixty-one yards and two touchdowns), catching one pass for twenty-seven yards, and punting twice for a 46.5-yard average. Keith also passed for a two-point conversion and, when he was in there, kicked off for the Cougars! (Both of Keith's TD passes went to halfback Don Ellersick, of Newport, one for twenty-six yards, the other seven.)

As great a day as he had at Stanford, Lincoln is better remembered for another—even greater—day, which also spawned a legend.

January 5, 1964, in old Balboa Stadium in San Diego, California, Lincoln led what came to be known in pro football lore as "The Boston Massacre."

Playing for the San Diego Chargers in the American Football League Championship game against the Boston Patriots, Lincoln rushed thirteen times for 206 yards, caught seven passes for 123 yards, and completed a pass for twenty yards. He accounted for 349 yards in total offense and scored two touchdowns in the 51-10 rout.

That performance earned Lincoln another nickname, "Golden Boy of the AFL."

Sid Gillman, Lincoln's old coach at San Diego, and one of the most astute minds in football, once called his all-purpose back "the best all-around player in pro football." In addition to rushing and passing for the Chargers, Lincoln occasionally saw action as a defensive back. He also was San Diego's backup punter and place-kicker, and in the 1964 season booted a forty-seven-yard field goal against the New York Jets. He was twice named to the AFL All-Star team.

Keith set career records in rushing (1,501 yards) and punting (40.3) in his three seasons at Washington State, 1958-1960.

Lincoln was elected to the WSU Athletic Hall of Fame in 1979.

Good "Coverage"

The Seattle Cougars were pretty mad at *Post-Intelligencer* sportswriter Mike Donohoe after WSC's 18-14 win over the Huskies in Spokane on November 22, 1958. Mike wrote: "The Cougars were lucky as hell."

Those Cougars might like this story better.

WSC used to get a lot of static about its old wooden press box, in the days before Martin Stadium. But Stanford's (and Cal's for that matter) was worse. At Palo Alto, the press box seating sort of melted in with the paying customers. Donohoe was there this day to cover an Indian-Husky titanic. Unlike his brother Ed, of whom Harry Missildine of the *Spokesman-Review* once wrote: "He could buy a $300 suit at Littler's, wear it around the block and look like he'd ridden the rods in from Omaha", Mike was always a picture of sartorial splendor. This particular day he had on a beige gabardine suit that must have set him back at least $300.

Mike was sitting in his "press box" seat just before game time when a kid carrying a hot dog ran up the aisle, tripped and draped the mustard-laden "dog" over the shoulder of Mike's suit coat.

"You little bastard!" Donohoe yelled, reaching for the urchin.

Whereupon the youngster's mother, seated nearby, reached out and zonked Mike on the head with an umbrella.

All of the action took place *in* the Stanford press box.

Haste Makes . . . Brrr

Steve Belko brought his first Oregon basketball team into Pullman on January 25, 1957. The Ducks came in on the Union Pacific out of Portland and were supposed to get in at 8:30 in the morning.

"Just a nice overnight hop and everybody would be rested and we'd have time for a workout before lunch," Steve said.

It didn't exactly work out that way.

An arctic cold front hit the Northwest shortly before the Webfoots left Portland. By the time they reached Pullman—at 3:30 on Friday afternoon, seven hours late, it was minus twelve. Steve's club barely had time to get over to the Washington Hotel, check in and get to their pre-game meal.

"Washington State's hustling, harrying, scurrying Cougars fought their way to an 87-81 Coast conference basketball victory over Oregon tonight as the temperatures of 20 below held attendance in Bohler gymnasium to 1,654," the *Spokesman-Review's* Bill Boni wrote.

Belko was steaming, about the loss, about the way his team lost. Charlie Franklin set an Oregon single game scoring record of thirty-six points and had an Oregon and Bohler gym record 18 for 21 at the line,

Keith Lincoln *was the ninth ranked punter in the NCAA in 1959 with a school record 43.4-yard average.*

but the Ducks also might have set a school record for turnovers, and the officiating!

Belko bolted into the Oregon dressing room after the game and hollered: "Get on the bus and get back to the hotel!" Then stormed out of the gym and started to walk to town.

"I hadn't gone a block before I realized I'd made a terrible mistake," Steve said later. "From then on it was just a matter of survival. I was too cold to be mad."

The whole weekend turned into a disaster for the Webfoots—and Charlie Franklin.

On Saturday night the Cougars won again, 74-67, for their first PCC sweep since 1953. Larry Beck hit 21 of 26 free throws, erasing Franklin's one-day-old record and setting a new PCC mark as well. The Cougars "held" Franklin to twenty points.

"(Jimmy) Ross' ball-handling and ball-hawking were highlights of the game, as well as the all-around play of Beck and long-shooting of Mert Kennedy," the *S-R's* Danny May wrote of the game.

It was twenty-six below zero in Pullman Saturday night. Belko went back to the hotel on the team bus.

Marv Harshman, Head Basketball Coach, 1959-1971. (Manuscripts, Archives, and Special Collections, Washington State University Libraries)

Marv and Jud

Marv Harshman came over to Washington State in 1958 from Pacific Lutheran College in Parkland to take over the Cougar basketball reins when Jack Friel retired.

A great all-around athlete at PLC (and football All-American in 1941 along with his old quarterback, Tommy "Tommygun" Tommervik), Harshman had been coaching the Lutes for thirteen seasons and was one of the most successful hoop mentors in the country.

Marv came to WSC when the Cougars were entering the doldrums of "independence." The Pacific Coast Conference was in the process of breaking up and the future of the college's athletic program was uncertain. He had the reputation of being a winner, but it took him a while to get things going. The Cougars were 10-16 Marv's first year, and a respectable 13-13 the second. Then the program went into a tailspin and hit bottom in 1963-1964 with back-to-back years of 5-20 and 5-21. Marv lost several good guard prospects in this period—Doyle Wilson, George Henningsgard and Howard Thoemke to name three, prompting sportswriter Harry Missildine to label the Cougars "a Brinks team." (No guards.)

Harshman operated at WSU without a full-time assistant for the first six seasons, and the penuriousness of the program made it very difficult for him. Help arrived in 1964-1965 in the person of George "Jud" Heathcote, a former All-State player at South Kitsap High School and one of Jack Friel's defensive specialists in the late forties. (Jud and Washington's Sammy White were "flagged out" of a game at Pullman in 1948 "for roughness," and the Cougars won 62-58 in two overtimes. Friel got the better of that trade. White was the Huskies' second-leading scorer with fifteen. Heathcote had three points.)

Bob Gary, finest of the WSC sprinters in the 1950s, is so far ahead of the field all the interest seems to be on the race for second place. (Manuscripts, Archives, and Special Collections, Washington State University Libraries)

Jud came back to WSU from West Valley High School in Spokane where he had turned the Eagles' program around. He promptly directed the Cougar frosh through an unbeaten season (22-0), with Jim McKean, a 6-9 center from Tacoma, and zippy little guard Ray Stein, of Richland, leading the way. Three other players off that frosh squad, Blaine Ellis, Everett; Doug Kloke, Burlington; and Dick Watters, Ballard, also made good contributions to the Cougar varsity the next three seasons.

WSU picked up the Mutt and Jeff combination of 6-8 Ted Wierman and 5-9 Lenny Allen from Yakima's Davis High in the 1966 season and the Cougars' resurgence in basketball was underway.

Had more progressive thinking been abroad at the time, at both the NCAA and Conference levels, Washington State and other good teams in the Pac-8 very likely would have made it to post-season tournaments while UCLA was dominating the national basketball scene. The Cougars were 18-8 (11-3 in Conference) in 1969 and 19-7 in 1970 and played some of the most exciting basketball in the West. Harshman's teams were second in the Pac-8 in 1967, 1969 and 1970, and a strong third in 1968. None made it to the NCAA, which had a static format in those years, and short-sighted Pac-8 rules made it impossible to go anywhere else. (It was the same in football. PCC, and later Pac-8, Athletic Directors were afraid to challenge the Rose Bowl and send their teams to other Bowl games, thus losing millions in potential revenue for their schools.)

It was during this era that John Wooden, the "Wizard of Westwood," told Spokane *Chronicle* sportswriter Bruce Brown: "Marv Harshman comes closest to getting the maximum potential from his players of anyone I know. And I've said that for years."

WSU broke a thirteen-game domination by Oregon State on January 16, 1965, serving notice of things to come. Ted Werner got eighteen points and eighteen rebounds in the 64-53 win at Bohler gym, and forward Darrel Peeples, of Renton, checked OSU star Charlie White to three points. Then on March 5, in Seattle, the Cougars beat Washington 78-74 in two overtimes. Bud Norris sent the game into overtime by picking up a loose ball and pumping in a twelve-footer with six seconds left. The game was tied 70-70 at the end of the first overtime period, but Dennis Kloke made a clutch one-and-one to seal the win in the second extra period. Werner had twenty-three points and seventeen rebounds and set the career rebounding record in this game, moving ahead of the 827 by Charlie Sells in 1960-1962.

The Cougars' biggest win in their turn-around year of 1966 was the 84-83 thriller over UCLA, followed two nights later by a 75-62 thrashing of USC. Forward Dennis Koke went to the line to shoot a one-and-one with seven seconds left and the Cougars trailing the defending National Champion Bruins 82-83. He got 'em both. But it was Birdsview's Bud Norris "who lit the fuse" for the Cougar rally that won it, one sportswriter noted. Norris, whose deep-dipping outside shot was described by Assistant Coach Heathcote as the "Birdsview Pump," got thirteen of his sixteen points in the second-half Cougar surge. Tommy Tommervik led WSU in that one with nineteen points; Stein and Kloke also had sixteen; and McKean eleven. In the win over USC, Kloke popped in twenty-two; McKean had seventeen; and Stein fourteen.

Washington State closed out the year with an 81-74 win over the Huskies and began Harshman's five-year peak production period (1966-1970) when the Cougars were 83-46.

In the 1966-1967 season, WSU started a six-year run of opening-round upsets in the Far West Classic at Portland by knocking off nationally-ranked West Virginia 92-86. In succession, the Cougars then beat Princeton, 82-75; Syracuse, 86-68; Illinois, 59-58; Indiana, 83-80; and Michigan, 81-67, the last one in 1971 under Coach Bob Greenwood in his only season at WSU.

Standout players for the Cougars in these years included Gary Elliot, of Sandpoint, Idaho; Randy Stoll, Bellevue; Terry Ball, Seattle; Marv "Tommy" Tommervik, Tacoma; Ted Werner, Lake Stevens; Dennis Kloke, Burlington; Charlie Sells, Seattle; Bud Norris, Sedro Woolley; Dwight Damon, Spokane; Jim Meredith, Anaconda, Montana; Dennis Hogg, Berkeley, California; Rick Erickson, Vancouver; Dan Steward, Nampa, Idaho; John Maras, Spokane; Byron Vadset, Seattle; Jimmy Ross, Warren, Oregon; Mert Kennedy, Aberdeen; Jim Walton, Richland; and Dale "The Whale" Ford.

The Cougar record book still shows some evidence of players from Harshman's era, which ended nearly twenty years ago. Center Jim McKean (who has earned a national reputation as a poet and teaches English in college) came to WSU largely unrecruited, a skinny, immature kid out of Tacoma's Wilson High, and became the three-year career scoring and rebounding leader. He's still in second place with 1,411 points and 844 rebounds in 1966-1968, trailing only Steve Puidokas in those three-year stats. McKean's scoring average (18.2) puts him in third place all-time, and his 18.3 scoring average for Conference games was still tops as of 1988. McKean had six games in which he scored thirty-one points or more, the best being a thirty-five-point effort against Nebraska at Lincoln in 1966, his sophomore year.

Guard Terry Ball (1960-1962) set a single game scoring mark with thirty-seven points against Montana State in Bozeman in 1960 (since broken), and still ranks fourth in career scoring (1,169) and third in scoring average (15.8) among three-year players.

Center Ted Werner (1963-1965); forward Charlie Sells (1960-1962); and center John Maras (1958-1960) rank second, third and fourth respectively among three-year career rebounders, and only Puidokas, a four-year man, and McKean rank above them all-time.

Byron Vadset, a guard in 1962-1964, ranks first in free-throw accuracy. Using the old underhand style, a la Rick Barry, By hit 255 of 309 attempts for a career 82.5 percent.

Dan Steward, another three-year man, had 277 career assists, ranking behind only Keith Morrison (1983-1986) and Marty Giovacchini (1974-1977), a pair of four-year players.

Ted Werner was the workhorse for the Cougars in the tough years, 1963-1965, and set a career rebounding record of 837, which still ranks him third all-time.

Gary Elliot takes one giant step for mankind—and the Cougars—as he races down the old Bohler gym court to score in the 1970 season when he was starring for Coach Marv Harshman's best WSU team. (Lewis Alumni Centre)

*Pacific Northwest Gymnastics
Champions, 1951-1952: Dave
Chilson, Preston Shepherd, Rex
Davis, Jake Monlux, Coach Hubie
Dunn, Dick Olson, Jim Sullivan,
Dick Loren, and Richal Smith.*
(Manuscripts, Archives, and Special
Collections)

Rick Erickson probably was the finest all-around guard Harshman
had at WSU for shooting, floor work and defense, and, teamed with
Steward in the 1970 season, gave the Cougars an awesome front end to
their fast-break. The Ray Stein-Lenny Allen tandem also was about as
exciting as any to watch on the break.

The Seventh Decade, 1951-1960

Coach *Hubie Dunn's* gymnastic team was undefeated in dual meets in 1951 for the second straight season. Team members included *Rex Davis*, Richland; *Myron Bostwick*, Spokane; *Jim Sullivan*, Clarkston; *Lyle Pugh*, Spokane; *Jake Monlux*, Everett; *Wayne Aeschliman*, Colfax; *Ken Savage*, Independence, Missouri; *Preston Shepherd*, Selah; *Dick Loren*, Tacoma; and *Jack Olson*, Everett.

•

The WSC Women's Bowling Club was started in 1950-51 with *Mary Ellen McKee* of Women's P.E. as coach.

•

Dan Stavely was an assistant coach and ace recruiter at WSC under four coaches from 1949 to 1958: *Phil Sorboe, Forest Evashevski, Al Kircher,* and *Jim Sutherland.* "He'd bring tears to the eyes of the kids' mothers," *Jack Friel* said of Stavely's recruiting technique. Now retired in Colorado, where he was inducted into the Sports Hall of Fame recently, Stavely said of recruiting for Evy: "'If you go after a guy and he can't play, it may cost you your job,' Evy used to say. 'If there is a guy in your area who you overlook and he turns out to be a player, you for sure will lose your job!' Didn't leave a guy much room for error."

Stavely's greatest recruiting "coup" at Washington State was in 1954 when he got All-American *Bill Steiger* and *Ray Taipale, Bill Bugge,* and *Terry Yeager* off Olympia's Championship team.

"Mrs. Steiger called me about ten days before the lads were scheduled to come to campus and said the Huskies were really putting pressure on the kids and she wasn't sure they'd be able to hold out. I called *Bob Templin* at Coeur d'Alene and Bob said he had just the place for the boys—a cabin across the lake that was only accessible by boat. I called those kids and suggested a ten-day vacation where they could fish and swim and loaf. They left Olympia that day and drove to Coeur d'Alene and had a great week or so and then came down and enrolled at WSC, which made 'em ineligible to transfer. Washington never knew what happened!" All four players stayed and graduated. Three lettered, and *Steiger* was an All-American in 1956.

•

Ed Barker, of Sunnyside, set a national pass receiving yardage record in 1951 with 853 yards. That broke the record of 820 yards in 1941 by *Henry Stanton,* of Arizona. Barker's forty-six receptions for 853 yards also broke the PCC records by Stanford's *Bill McColl* in 1950 of thirty-nine catches for 671 yards.

•

Sam, were you looking? When *Forest Evashevski* left WSC for Iowa at the end of the 1951 season, he had three years left on a five-year contract. *Spokane Chronicle* Sports Editor *Bob Johnson* asked: "Why not write the contracts in such a way that the coach can quit but must reimburse the school, just as the school must reimburse him if he's canned?" In 1977, when *Warren Powers* jumped ship to Missouri, Athletic Director *Sam Jankovich* had him by the contract. Powers had to pay the school $55,000 for the time remaining on his contract.

•

Cougar Trivia: Who was the first Cougar boxer to fight *Floyd Patterson?* You say *Pete Rademacher?* Sorry, *Gordy Gladson,* of Bremerton, three-time NCAA Champion, lost a first-round TKO to Patterson in the 1952 Olympic Trial finals at light-heavyweight.

•

Ed Barker, starting seven yards back, caught Washington's *George Black* and threw him out-of-bounds on the WSC seven in the final game of the 1952 season. A touchdown would have given Black the PCC scoring title. As it was, Barker won with forty-four points, to forty-two for Black. (In 1958, *Chuck Morrell*, of Downey, California, broke loose behind a great block by *Gail Cogdill*, Spokane, and ran eighty-seven yards, only to fall down on the College of Pacific eleven yard line. Morrell lost the PCC rushing title that year to Cal's *Joe Kapp*—by ten yards.)

•

Bob Gary, of Seattle, won the 100 at the PCC meet in 1952, becoming the first Cougar sprinter to win that event since *Wes Foster*, Wenatchee, in 1928. Gary also won it in 1955, and he took the 220 twice, in 1954 and 1955.

•

Buck Bailey lost two good left-handers when first baseman *Ed Bouchee* and pitcher *Jack Spring*, a pair of Spokane freshmen, signed pro contracts at the end of the 1952 baseball season with the Philadelphia Phillies. Spring made it up to the big club in 1955 and eventually stayed in the majors eight seasons, compiling a 12-5 record and 4.26 ERA with six different teams, three in each league. Jack was 9-5 in relief and had eight saves. Bouchee was in the running for Rookie of the Year in 1957 with the Phillies when he hit .293, with thirty-five doubles, seventeen homers and seventy-six runs batted in. Ed stayed in the National League seven years and had a career batting average of .265.

•

The famous "Look Sharp" march, written by 1923 WSU grad *Mahlon Merrick*, of Centralia, made its debut on the Gillette "Calvalcade of Sports" in 1953. After a brief try at teaching, in Redmond, Merrick decided on a career in music. He played saxophone at the Italian Gardens in Spokane's Davenport Hotel and then went to Hollywood where he was associated with a number of popular television shows, including "George Burns and Gracie Allen" and the "Bob Cummings Show." Merrick was musical director for Jack Benny for thirty years. In September, 1966, he made a guest appearance at WSU for the first performance of the "Cougar Fight Song," which he composed for his alma mater. (Not to be confused with the "WSC Fight Song," written in 1919 by Zella Melcher and Phyllis Sayles.) *Mahlon Merrick* died August 7, 1969, at age sixty-nine.

•

Bob Patrick, of Entiat, representing Pi Kappa Alpha fraternity, appeared before the Board of Control in January, 1955, and sought permission for the frat to pledge Butch V, the WSC mascot. ASSCW Vice President *Barry Jones*, Spokane, said that "because no one at WSC knows for sure whether Butch is male or female it could not properly be pledged by either a fraternity or sorority." Board went on record opposing the pledging, ruling that "Butch belongs to the entire student body."

•

"Mo" Winter, of Las Vegas, Nevada, great first-sacker on *Buck Bailey's* last College World Series team in 1956, saw his baseball career literally blown away in 1957 in Louisiana. Mo was playing with Lake Charles in the Evangeline League when Hurricane Audrey ripped through the Bayous. "That was the end of the Evangeline League—and they still owe me $250," Winters said. Mo gave up baseball and spent the next twenty-eight years in the Army, retiring in 1987 as a Lieutenant Colonel—and one of the best lefthanded golfers in the armed forces.

•

On February 21, 1957, Cougar Basketball Coach *Jack Friel* was quoted in the Spokane Chronicle: "Some teams just lower their heads, run somebody off the court with their shoulders and go to the free throw line. . . . I don't care if the officials stand on their heads in the ticket booth as long as they have good judgment. Officiating is knowing enough about the game to know when a guard has done his job and is entitled to protection under the rules." (Nothing changes.)

Washington State finished second in the Northern Division baseball race in 1958 with a 10-6 mark and three sophomore pitchers—all from Billings, Montana—figured in all of the decisions. *Elwood Hahn* and *Dick Montee* were both 4-2 and *Bob Bolingbroke* was 2-2. Hahn and Bolingbroke were lefthanders. Billings did not have a high school baseball team, but former Cougar great *Eddie Bayne* coached the American Legion program there for years and turned out tremendous teams. Other "Billings Boys" who starred for the Cougars in baseball were *Bob Fry*, centerfield; *Wally Lito*, third base; *Dale Scilley*, shortstop; and *Ray Moline* and *Joe McIntosh*, pitchers.

•

After the 1958 High School All-Star football game in Seattle, Cougar assistant coaches *Laurie Niemi* and *Bob Gambold* headed for Othello to watch a promising young lineman by the name of *Larry McCourtie* play for the town team against the neighboring air station. They had the kid's number, but their attention soon was drawn to a big old boy playing fullback for Othello who was running over everybody. "Who's that 45," Niemi asked a sideliner. "That's McCourtie," came the answer. "I thought he was 66," Laurie persisted. "That's Larry; 45's his Dad," the guy says. And sure enough it was, *J. R. McCourtie*. "Wonder if he's got any eligibility left," mused Niemi.

•

Duane Ranniger, Spokane, had one of those nights on January 3, 1959. He scored 19 points in 27 minutes as WSU defeated UCLA 71-54 at Pullman. It was only his second start for the Cougars in two varsity basketball seasons.

•

Things Are Tough All Over department. When *Perry Overstreet*, Spokane, qualified for the NCAA championships as a member of the WSC golf team in 1959, he went in to see Athletic Director *Stan Bates* to ask whether he could go to the tournament at Eugene, Oregon. "Sure," said Stan. "Just bring in the five-dollar entry fee."

"Imagine what he'd have said if my Dad hadn't coached against him in high school, and my father-in-law (Dr. *Milt Durham*) hadn't been on the Board of Regents!"

•

When Coach *Ike Deeter* greeted his frosh boxers in 1959, he saw a couple of familiar faces. "Our Dads boxed for you," said *Daryl Click*, of La Crosse, and his buddy, *Phil Rhodes*, Omak, nodded. Click was the son of *Glen Click*, of Latah, a 126-pounder for Deeter, and Rhodes' father, *Wally Rhodes*, Pomeroy, fought for Ike at 145 in the mid-thirties.

•

WSC and Oregon played two games in 1959, the first year after the breakup of the Pacific Coast Conference. The first game, on October 3 at Eugene, was a "no-counter." Oregon won 14-6. At Pullman, on November 14, they played the "counter." It's better known now as the "tennis shoe game," and was played on a frozen field. The day prior, the WSU frosh, with the backs and ends wearing tennis shoes, had beaten the Ducklings 44 to 6 on the field below the CUB. Coach *Jim Sutherland* phoned Oregon Coach *Len Casanova* in Spokane where the Duck varsity was staying and told Cas about the field conditions. Casanova promptly bought a supply of tennies for his backs and the Ducks waddled to a 7-6 win next day on icy Rogers Field.

•

Cougar end *Garner "Cow" Ekstran*, of Bow, who enjoyed wearing vests, came back from Stanford in 1959 wearing *two*. He won the extra from former WSU assistant *Dan Stavely*, then an assistant at Stanford. They bet on the game. WSU won, 36-19.

The Eighth Decade, 1961-1970

Buck Goes Out a Winner

BUCK BAILEY WAS FEUDING WITH THE PROS THROUGH MOST OF THE FIFTIES. THEY signed his sophomore stars, Gene Conley and Ted Tappe off that championship team of 1950, and snatched a couple of freshmen, Jack Spring and Ed Bouchee, both of Spokane, off the 1952 club.

Ron Koeper, of Pine City, a freshman catcher on that 1952 club (he later changed his name to Carlon), was grabbed off by Pittsburgh, and in 1955 Buck lost junior pitchers Wes Stock, of Shelton, and Ron Webb, of Lewiston, Idaho, to Baltimore and St. Louis "respectably," as old Diz used to say.

Buck maintained a good relationship with all the scouts, and just about everyone in baseball knew him and liked him, but he did get upset when the pros would swoop in and pick off a freshman or sophomore. It was more than just losing a good prospect and hurting his team; perhaps because he never finished college himself, Buck hated to see a kid miss an opportunity to get that "insurance" (a degree) before taking a chance on a career in baseball, where so few really were able to make a living out of it.

Buck's mind never was very far away from baseball, no matter what time of year it was. Bob Bucklin said Buck came over to a King County Cougar Club meeting once in the fall and someone asked him what the outlook was in eastern Washington for the upcoming bird hunting season.

"Never saw so many pheasants, partridge and quail in my life drivin' over," Buck replied.

"Any chukkars, Buck?" asked Bucklin.

"Yeah," Buck growled, "but they're just a bunch of green sophomores!"

Everyone who ever played for Buck Bailey had a story about the great man. Jerry Bartow, of John Day, Oregon, who was Captain of the 1956 team, the last one Buck took to Omaha, was a sophomore in 1954 when the Cougars went to Eugene to play Oregon. He'll never forget it.

> Ernie Cecaci is on first and Gordy Hersey hammers one over George Shaw's head in center. "Maybe an inside-the-parker" Gordy is thinking, and rounds first with his head down. Just as he passes second, he also passes Cecaci. There's a close play at third, but Hersey is safe with a triple!

OPPOSITE: *Gerry Lindgren*

All the guys start to laugh and Buck is going crazy trying to quiet them down. "Shhhh! Maybe they won't see it," he says.

Schlosstein, the Oregon first baseman, is from Tacoma and was a high school teammate of Hersey's. He calls time and Coach Don Kirsch comes out. Something's wrong.

Buck is out there with his all-innocent face on, nodding, nodding. "Ummm, hmmm. Oh? Ummm, hmmm."

Then they call Hersey out and Buck goes crazy. He was always after Hersey for one thing or another. Tore the end off the dugout down at Yakima goin' after him. Then he turns on Cecaci. "What are you doin' all this time! Don't you ever look at the coach wavin' you on? You run like old people. . . !" [Buck used to say he'd time Cecaci with a sun dial.]

•

The Cougar tennis team defeated Washington, Oregon and Idaho and won the Far West division of the NCAA in 1961. Team members were Jim Norland, *Klamath Falls, Oregon;* Joe Kleitsch, *Seattle;* Tom Buchanan, *Pullman;* Dave Ringler, *Friday Harbor; and* Dallas Edwards, *Parma, Idaho.*

•

Buck hated sophomores. Hated to play 'em because they were "always making sophomore mistakes!"

Bartow, a left-handed pitcher and a pretty fair hitter, pinch-hit against Washington in 1954 and got a hit. Feeling pretty good, he was dancing around off first and got picked off. Before he could get to his feet, Buck had him by the back of the uniform near the neck and was dragging him back to the dugout shrieking in that high voice he always effected when in severe emotional pain.

"I was never picked off again," Bartow said.

Every one of Buck's players also has a story about his driving.

"We were going over to the Tri-Cities to play an early-season game against CBC," Bartow remembered, "and Buck was late getting started. Out around Kahlotus we ran into a paving crew and a flagman was stopping traffic. Buck said, 'I don't have time. We're late!,' and drove right through that flagman and right over the new blacktop, scattering workers and picking up great hunks of hot macadam on the tires. They would 'thunk, thunk' inside the fender wells as he ripped along muttering about 'being late already, and now this!'"

Bob "Squirrel" Noel, from Kennewick, was a utility man and left-handed pinch hitter for Buck in the late fifties.

"I hit a pop-up down the third base line at Oregon State and of course Buck screamed 'Swing and look up!'" Noel remembers. "The third baseman stretched that restraining rope way back and made the catch.

"Buck went after the ump. When he lost that argument he went over and stretched that rope so tight that if anybody'd run into it they'd been shot like an arrow over the right field fence!

"We went on over to Eugene and we had those same umps. Somebody hit a dribbler over to Buck and he picks it up and gets into a little discussion with the same ump who'd made the call at Corvallis. I was in left field and the next thing I know the ball is on top of MacArthur Court (the University of Oregon gym). He threw that ball clear out of the park! And he was in his sixties!"

That 1956 team was one of Buck's all-time favorites. Maybe he knew it was going to be his last Championship team. (Although his last two teams, in 1960 and 1961, won the Northern Division, they failed to get to Omaha.) That 1956 club had four Northern Division All-Stars in catcher Bill Rich and third baseman Bill Mashburn, both of Yakima, and Hersey and Bartow. Ron Foisy, Seattle, was the shortstop. Pretty good

"Hey, we're goin' ta Omaha!" a delighted Buck Bailey hollars after his 1956 Cougars took two straight from USC in the Pacific Coast Conference playoffs on Bailey Field. Left to right are outfielder Jack Hardman; Ron Aiken, who pitched the series clincher; and Bill Rich, catcher, who drove in all of the Cougars' runs in the 5-4 win. First sacker Mo Winter cheers in the background. (WSC photo)

pitching too. Ron Aiken, from Raymond; George Plummer, Vancouver; John Freeman, Zillah; Bruce Boldt, Colfax; and Don Nieland, Bonners Ferry, Idaho. Joe Trembly, Kelso, and Jack Hardman, Seattle, were the regulars in center and left, and Ron Overby, Kalispell, Montana, and Henry Legge, Spokane, shared time in right.

That was the year Buck was out with Shorty Sever checking on the infield the day before the play-off series with USC and found a rock about the size of an egg.

"Lookie here, Shorty," he says, "Whattaya want me to do with it?"

"Well, either sit on it and see if it'll hatch or throw it ta hell outta here," Sever answered in his usual gracious manner.

Buck harrumphed, whirled around and flung the offensive rock over the fence—right into the windshield of his own car!

When the Trojans arrived in Pullman for the play-offs on June 1-2, rumor had it they already had their plane reservations on to Omaha for the College World Series. Coach Rod Dedeaux supposedly asked Buck: "How d'ya get to Omaha from here?" To which Buck replied, putting that big paw on Rod's shoulder, "Well, Sonny Boy, I'm not sure you can get there from here—unless you can beat us."

The Cougars shocked SC two straight. Bartow beat 'em 5-2 in the first game and Aiken won 5-4 in the clincher. Catcher Bill Rich knocked in all five runs for Aiken with a three-run homer and a double.

WSC had tough luck in Omaha, losing two squeakers. Bartow lost to Bradley, 5-4, and New Hampshire beat Aiken, 6-4.

In 1960, Buck won the Northern Division for the tenth time. The Billings, Montana, pitching trio of Dick Montee, Elwood Hahn, and Bob Bolingbroke—good ol' Eddie Bayne's contributions to Buck's Welfare

Chris Marker, Cougar All-American in the 1960-1964 era, was one of Coach Doug Gibb's best swimmers. (Hilltopics)

Plan—won twenty-four games that year as WSU posted a 29-6 record. Montee, the right-hander, won ten; Hahn and Bolingbroke, both lefties, nine and five. Top hitters were Arnie Pleasant, of Cowiche, .395; Gary Wyche, Vancouver, .380; Nick August, Spokane, .330; Marv Marchbanks, Kennewick, .315; and Arley Kangas, Tacoma, .313.

In the District 8 play-offs at good old Bovard Field, USC's crackerbox, the Cougars beat the Trojans 8-7 in the opener. First sacker Paul Tomlinson, of Seattle, got WSU off winging with a grand-slam homer in the first inning, but reserve catcher John Gallagher won it in the ninth with a pinch-hit single. Montee got the win in relief, but Buck had to use all three of his starting pitchers and USC bounced back the next day to sweep both ends of the doubleheader, 8-3 and 10-5.

Buck went out just the way he wanted it—a winner!

The crusty old Cougar guided his 1961 team to the Northern Division pennant, winning his twelfth and final title on the last day of the season. Over thirty-two seasons, Buck won 603 games and posted a winning percentage of .649.

Woodrow "Pat" Crook, of Richland, was Buck's catcher in that last season. He says the 1961 team wasn't given much chance of winning the Division.

"We were mighty low after we'd lost both games to Oregon State at Corvallis (May 3-4)," Crook said. "But old Buck he said 'That's all right, Sonny Boys. They still gotta come up to our dung hill.'"

And of course Buck called it. His Cougars won both of those games, 9-8 and 3-2, with Boyd Swent, of Endicott, getting the win in the opener in relief of starter Mike Carlon, Yakima; Bernie Keller, Centralia; and Harold Haddock, Walla Walla. Old Buck used "Our Gang" to win that one! Ray Moline, of Billings, Montana, went all the way for the win in the pennant clincher.

Then WSU had to play USC in Pullman for the NCAA District 8 title.

"My Dad came up from Richland for that series," Crook said. "Buck had a ritual he went through before every practice and every game at home. He had an old four-wheel cart with two handles. He'd load it up with all the equipment and, in that bow-legged way, push it out to old Bailey field.

"My Dad met Buck there at the gate. 'It's gonna be tough today, huh, Buck? We're gonna play those Trojans.'

"Buck kinda squinted and he says, 'You know, we weren't supposed to get this far, were we? Just goes to show, when you poke a frog you never know how far he's going to jump.'"

That was vintage Buck Bailey.

When Buck announced that he would retire at the end of the 1961 season, athletic director Stan Bates didn't waste much time looking around for a replacement. He went right over to Yakima Valley College and got Chuck Brayton, Buck's old All-American shortstop. Brayton had monopolized the Northwest Junior College baseball conference, winning ten titles in eleven seasons.

"Ol' Charlie's the man I'da picked," Buck said when he heard Bates' choice. "He'll do a great job!"

On a collision course! Cougar fullback George Reed heads upstream in WSU's 6-0 win over Oregon on old Hayward Field at Eugene in 1958.

Too bad Buck couldn't have stayed around longer to admire his prediction. He only got to enjoy three years of his retirement. Buck and his wife, Frances, were killed in an automobile accident near Albuquerque, New Mexico, on October 28, 1964, while returning to their home in Spokane from a visit with relatives in Texas.

Buck Bailey was elected a charter member of the WSU Athletic Hall of Fame in 1978.

Jesse Gets Even

Edward F. "Bill" Denton, '50, long-time News Director at KREM-TV in Spokane, often came down to the campus and worked with visiting TV crews doing Cougar basketball games in the 1960s when Marv Harshman was coaching at WSU. On the way home, Bill and his cronies usually stopped at the tavern in Garfield for a beer.

On this particular Saturday, KREM for some reason delayed the Cougar telecast. When Denton arrived in Garfield, a full hour after the game ended, it was still in the first quarter on television.

WSU trailed badly in the early going, and some of the locals, particularly Don "Stonkey" Davis, were loud in their criticism of the Cougars and were taking their gall out on owner-waitress Jesse Rompel.

Denton motioned Mrs. Rompel over and whispered that he'd just come from Pullman, the game was over, and the Cougars had gone on to win big.

"Take all the bets you can get and give ten points," Bill advised.

As he left the tavern, Denton heard Stonkey and his cohorts hooting as they lined up to get their bets down.

"We're gonna own this place, Jesse!"

The Phantom

He was the most unlikely looking All-American you ever saw.

His muscles, such as they were, didn't bulge. He was about six feet tall, but looked 5-10 because he always slouched. They listed him at 185 pounds in the program, but he usually weighed less than 175, and he moved in a loose-jointed amble, as if he was running uphill—on sore feet.

Scouts used to watch him, shake their heads and say, "Don't know *how* he does it, but he sure *does* it!"

Hugh Campbell came to Washington State in the fall of 1959 from Saratoga, California. He'd been both a quarterback and a receiver at Los Gatos High School, but the Cougars had plenty of QBs on that frosh team (including Dave Mathieson), so Campbell played at wide receiver. He demonstrated early that he had a knack for getting open and could catch the football, but quarterbacks Mathieson and Donnie Knight, of Portland, Oregon, got most of the ink that fall, along with a little speed-burner out of Spokane, Mel Stanton.

Coach Jim Sutherland, a pretty fair judge of receivers, was not impressed with the herky-jerky sophomore during two-a-days preceding the 1960 season. To Suds, Campbell seemed always to be running at half-speed. (Maybe Jim had been watching Gail Cogdill too long. He always said Cogdill was the most graceful athlete he ever coached. Gail played the three years before Campbell and Suds always seemed to be looking for those same, gazelle-like moves from Hugh.)

Assistant Coach Bob Gambold, who'd recruited Campbell, asked Suds to withhold judgment when the 1960 season started. "He'll fool ya," Gambold advised.

Washington State opened the 1960 season in Spokane against Stanford and had a terrible time beating the Indians. Campbell caught one pass, but it was erased by a penalty. Gambold had to talk Suds into putting him on the travel squad for the next game.

At mile-high Denver, Colorado, on Friday night, September 23, 1960, the Phantom of the Palouse hit center stage and began a three-year run as the nation's top pass receiver. It was, you might say, the first Rocky Mountain high!

Campbell tied the all-time WSU pass receiving record against Denver, catching ten for 195 yards and two scores. His first touchdown came on a twenty-two-yard pass from Mel Melin, of Olympia, in the second

Don Bertoia, of Rossland, British Columbia, set a WSU record in the mile at 4:04.7 in the Far West meet at Eugene, Oregon, and tied the school record in the 880 at 1:51.3 versus Oregon State in Pullman in the 1962 season. Wayne Wilson, Spokane, set a new vault record of 14-7 1/2 in that OSU meet, and Eilif Fredriksen triple-jumped 50-4 3/4 against Washington for one of the best marks in the nation.

quarter and put WSU ahead 20-14 at halftime. In the fourth quarter, he caught another scoring pass, this one on an eighteen-yard option toss from halfback Keith Lincoln.

The rest is history. Hugh Campbell caught sixty-six passes for 881 yards and ten touchdowns in his sophomore season. At year's end he owned NCAA records for receptions and total yardage.

Campbell's greatest game—among many—might have been his performance against Arizona State in the third game of that 1960 season. Coming off a ten-catch night at Denver, Hugh was a marked man when WSU went into Tempe to meet the Sun Devils. He not only repeated his record night against Denver with ten catches, but caught three touchdown passes, to tie another Cougar record.

Many fans would say Hugh's catch and run in the final seconds of a game in Spokane on October 20, 1962, against Indiana was his finest "pressure" catch. WSU was trailing 14-15 in the final seconds and was fifty-one yards from pay dirt. Campbell somehow got behind Hoosier defensive back Nate Ramsey, later to play years in the NFL, and Mathieson lofted the ball to him.

The guy who couldn't run suddenly found a way to out-leg one of the game's faster defensemen. Hugh caught the ball, zigged to throw Ramsey off a half-stride, and then stepped right in front of the charging Indiana safety and let Nate's speed and weight knock him the last three yards into the end zone for a 21-15 Cougar win.

Slight though he was, as football players go, Campbell was very durable. He played hurt on a number of occasions, but never missed a start after once breaking into the lineup. All the old Cougars remember the "tennis shoe game" at Laramie, Wyoming, on September 30, 1962. Hugh had a tender ankle and aggravated it in the first half and gave way to Mike Abbott, of Seattle. At the intermission, Campbell traded his cleats for a pair of tennis shoes, which he said enabled him to run and cut with less pain. He then proceeded to catch six passes, two for touchdowns, and WSU won 21-15.

Campbell's three-year career stats at WSU show 176 receptions for 2,452 yards and twenty-two touchdowns. His receptions and yardage were NCAA records, not only for three-year careers but four as well. As for school records, Hugh owned four single-season marks and three career. He was shut out only twice, in that opener in 1960 and again against Stanford in his senior season. In that 1962 game, a press box wag said "Campbell's got more Indians around him than Custer at the Little Big Horn!" (While Stanford chased Hugh, Gerry Shaw, the Calgary Stampeder, caught the only four passes the Cougars completed that day. But Suds fooled 'em, he ran, and WSU won its sixth straight game from the Cardinal, 21-6.)

Hugh had four ten-reception games at WSU. Those two against Denver and Arizona State in 1960 and a third in the final regular season game of his career versus Washington in Spokane on November 2, 1962 (ten for 178 yards and a touchdown). The fourth was in the 1962 Shrine Game in San Francisco.

The San Francisco Forty-niners drafted Campbell, but Hugh didn't get much of a look, even after that great performance in the East-West

Lightning doesn't strike twice? Bill Gaskins would testify that it did. Two years after that "Lost Down" game at Iowa, on October 30, 1965, at Corvallis, WSU was hanging on to a 10-8 lead in the face of a desperation passing effort by Oregon State. Another set of officials, this time from the Pac-8, got confused and gave the Beavers a fifth down. While Coach Bert Clark was trying to stop play to recheck the downs, OSU's Paul Brothers unleashed a mighty heave downfield toward a streaking Beaver end. Guess who made the interception? Yep, Bill Gaskins, now a senior—and aging fast. (Gaskins decided if you can't beat 'em, join 'em. He's now a Pac-10 official.)

game, where he caught ten passes (a record at the time) for 152 yards and two touchdowns. (The East won 25-19 after Hugh had tied it at 19-19 in the waning minutes on a pass from Sonny Gibbs of Texas Christian.)

So Campbell went up to Canada and joined two old teammates, fullback George Reed and defensive tackle Garner Ekstran, with the Saskatchewan Roughriders. The Roughies promptly went to three Grey Cups and won it all in 1966.

The old Phantom of the Palouse switched from playing to coaching in 1969, first as an assistant to Jim Sweeney at WSU, then as Head Coach at Whitworth College in Spokane. He went to Edmonton of the Canadian Football League in 1977 and led them to five Grey Cup titles before returning to the States as Head Coach of the Los Angeles Express of the short-lived World Football League in 1984. Hugh coached the Houston Oilers in 1985-1986 in the NFL and then moved back to Canada as General Manager at Edmonton.

He was elected a charter member of the WSU Athletic Hall of Fame in 1978.

•

Jim Sweeney, former Ohio State gymnast, took over as Coach of the Cougar gymnastics team in 1963 replacing *Hubie Dunn,* who started the intercollegiate program at WSU in 1947 and also originated the State Interscholastic meet in 1958. Dunn left WSU to become Head Coach at Northern Illinois University in DeKalb.

•

Football's All-timer

"Worst football leg injury I ever saw," WSU Team Physician Dick Morton said. "His leg was broken cleanly. They said it sounded like a rifle shot when it happened. The ankle was badly dislocated."

Fifteen years after that terrible injury, George Reed hung up his cleats as the greatest running back in professional football history. His 16,116 yards rushing for the Saskatchewan Roughriders of the Canadian Football League in thirteen seasons between 1963 and 1975 was an all-time professional football record–Canada or the U.S.

That mangled leg was not the only thing Reed had to overcome on the road to success and membership in five sports Halls of Fame on both sides of the border. Nor was it the most painful.

In 1959, his sophomore season at Washington State, Reed and Perry Harper were the only blacks on the Cougar team. When WSU played the University of Houston on Thanksgiving Day in Houston, to end the 1959 schedule, Reed and Harper could not stay with their teammates in the Texas State Hotel in downtown Houston. (This was five full years after the Supreme Court decision declaring segregation unconstitutional.) They had to stay in a dormitory at Texas Southern University, a black school in Houston.

As he did so often throughout his career, Reed rose above that blatant discrimination. Indeed, he turned prejudice into victory–not only on the football field, but in his life. WSU defeated Houston 32-18 and after the game, while attending a gathering at Texas Southern, George met Angie Levias, a student at the university, who later became his wife.

Reed's thirteen-year career with the Saskatchewan Roughriders included eleven seasons where he rushed for 1,000 yards or more. He led the CFL in scoring five times. Saskatchewan reached the Western Con-

ference playoffs in each of his thirteen seasons and George made the All-Canada team nine times, the All-Western Conference team eleven times. He played in four Grey Cups (Canadian Super Bowls) and led the Roughriders to their first ever Canadian Football League Championship in 1966.

In 1965 he received the Schenley Award as the Most Valuable Player in the CFL. He was the first recipient of the Tom Pate Memorial Award in 1976, recognizing sportsmanship, contributions to team, community and the CFL Players Association, of which Reed was president. He was member of the association from 1972 until 1980, five years after his retirement as an active player. In 1978, he was awarded the Order of Canada Medal by the national government.

Active throughout his playing career in organizations to help physically and mentally handicapped children, Reed spearheaded formation of the George Reed Foundation in 1975 to raise and distribute funds for these youngsters. In 1981, the University of Regina conferred an honorary Doctor of Law degree on Reed for his outstanding contributions to the advancement of disabled persons within society.

For a number of years, Reed has been a District Sales Manager for Molson Breweries, LTD., in Alberta, Canada. In 1978 he was elected a charter member of the WSU Sports Hall of Fame.

•

Dick van Hersett won the Tumbling and Trampoline titles at the Pacific Northwest Open and Stu Rehnstron was tops in All-Around. Bob Olds *completed three varsity seasons undefeated on the Side Horse in 1963.*

•

The Whale

William Dale Ford, better known to Cougar sports fans as the "Whale," was one of the finest all-around athletes ever at Washington State University. He might have been the last (in men's athletics) to win varsity letters in three sports.

Ford earned eight letters at WSU, three each in baseball and basketball and two in football, between 1963 and 1966, an era in which freshmen were not eligible to compete on Varsity teams. It has been nearly forty years since anyone matched or exceeded Ford's letter numbers. Frank Mataya won nine Varsity letters in the four major sports between 1947 and 1951 and Dale "Pig" Gentry garnered eight in football, basketball and baseball in 1938-1942. There were other multi-letter winners earlier, of course, but these two are the most prolific of the last forty-seven years. Ford and Gentry both are in the WSU Athletic Hall of Fame. Mataya should be.

"The Whale" was 6-3 and 210. In a basketball uniform, he rather resembled the other famous Cougar, Dale Gentry. Both were prototypes of what they now call the "power forward," barrel-chested, beetle-browed and tough!

Ford set an NCAA home run record with seventeen round-trippers in the 1966 season and made All-American. He is one of only two collegians (the other was Grimm Mason of Oregon State in 1958) to hit a ball completely out of the old Bailey Field, where Mooberry Track is now. (That was in 1966 against Washington.)

Ford was a quarterback in football in 1962-1963. In '63, when Jim Sutherland's team was struggling along at 2-5-1 going into the Stanford game at Palo Alto, it appeared as if Sutherland's six-game win string against the Indians was in serious jeopardy. WSU was coming off a discouraging 7-21 Homecoming loss to Oregon.

Going over films the week before the game, Cougar coaches detected a couple of soft spots in first-year Stanford Coach John Ralston's wings. Suds secretly worked up a little option attack with Ford at quarterback. Dale had been playing some at left half as well as being the backup to starting signal-caller Dave Mathieson.

Washington State ran Stanford into the ground the following Saturday. Ford, Clarence Williams and Johnny Browne had a field day around and over Ralston's ends off that option. "The Whale" rushed twelve times for forty-seven yards and scored twice on runs of one and three yards. He also was 7 for 12 passing for 117 yards. Clancy averaged 6.5 yards on thirteen carries.

"Whale Plays WSU Hero in 32-15 Upset Victory," the headline read on Sunday, November 17, 1963.

Dale Ford was elected to the WSU Athletic Hall of Fame in 1983.

Ike Hangs up His Gloves

Ike Deeter has been around WSU as long as bunchgrass, someone once said.

"Well, maybe not quite that long," Deeter would say, in his best Hartline drawl. (He was born out there in the coulee country.) "It only seems that way to some folks."

But when Ike returned from Navy duty in 1946, he was picking up a Cougar career that began as a student in 1923. He did not turn out as many championship boxing teams after World War II as he had in the glory years (1932-1942), but he had a flock of individual champions in the PCI, and twelve NCAA titlists in the final fourteen years of the sport at WSU.

The 1954 team was Ike's last PCI winner, and it came against one of the largest fields in the history of the tournament at Sacramento– eleven schools. The Cougars edged perennial rival San Jose State for the team title, with Eddie Olson, Colfax, 125; Gil Inaba, Wapato, 132; and Gordy Gladson, Bremerton, 165, winning individual crowns.

College boxing started its decline in the mid-1950s when schools began dropping the sport because of financial strain. In the Pacific Northwest, Gonzaga, then Idaho, two former powers in the college mitt game and WSU's natural regional rivals, dropped their teams. The Cougars' nearest opponent then was Idaho State, at Pocatello, 600 miles distant, or Nevada-Reno, an even longer haul.

"If it hadn't been for Ike, we'd have given up boxing well before we did," said WSU Department of Athletics Business Manager Glenn Oman.

In 1960, following the death of Charles Mohr, a University of Wisconsin boxer, a number of schools, including WSU, dropped the sport.

"It was a shame it had to go out that way," Deeter said. "It's a great

WSU won the West Coast AAU and Pacific Northwest cross-country meets and was undefeated in eight meets during the 1964 season. John "Prince" Valiant, *of Victoria, British Columbia, was first in all eight races. Other top finishers for the Cougars were* Chris Westman *and* Vic Bennet, *both of Seattle;* Jan Bentzon, *Norway;* Fred Miller, *Manson;* Mike Evans, *Vancouver, British Columbia; and* Jim Colpitts, *Wenatchee.*

Ike's Champions in the post-war years:

Pacific Coast Champions

1947—Jack Melson, Seattle, 125
1948—Ralph Campbell, Pullman, 112, and Jack Melson, 125
1949—Jack Melson, 125, and Eldon "Nip" Long, Cheney, 145
1950—Ev Conley, Everett, 135, and Hubert "Hub" Christianson, Twisp, Heavyweight
1951—Jack Melson* 130; Ev Conley, 135; Hub Christianson, Heavyweight
1952—Ev Conley, 132, and Gordy Gladson, Bremerton, 165
1953—Gil Inaba, Wapato, 132, and Chuck Morgan, Omak, 165
1954—Eddie Olson, Colfax, 125; Gil Inaba, 132; Gordy Gladson, 165
1955—Eddie Olson, 125, and Gordy Gladson, 178
1956—Willard Ira, Portland, 112, and Dick Rall, Seattle, 132
1957—Dick Rall, 132, and Jesse Klinkenberg, Seattle, 156
1958—Dick Rall, 132, and Jim Keys, Spokane, 147
1959—Bob Cornwell, Detroit, Michigan, 125
1960—Bob Cornwell, 125

National Champions

1951—Ev Conley, 135, and Jack Melson, 130
1952—Ev Conley, 132, and Gordy Gladson, 165
1954—Gordy Gladson, 165
1955—Gordy Gladson, 175
1956—Dick Rall, 132
1957—Dick Rall, 132
1958—Dick Rall, 132, and Jesse Klinkenberg, Seattle, 156
1959—Bob Cornwell, 125

college sport." Hundreds of men who boxed for Ike would agree, along with thousands of students who witnessed those great matches in Bohler gym.

Deeter always enjoyed plunking around on a banjo, and in the 1950s he was a member of what they called "The Bull Moose Quartet," made up of Ike, Buck Bailey, Jack Mooberry and Dan Stavely. (Ike on banjo, Stavely on piano, Mooberry played harmonica, and Bailey? Well, Buck played the Jew's harp, he said.)

In 1958, at the PCI tourney in Reno, Ike would see that his athletes were all tucked in at the Holiday Hotel and then he'd take his banjo and head on up to Virginia Street where most of the clubs were. When the hour got late, and the crowds thinned out, some of the bands would invite Ike to sit in. He loved it!

After the PCI, it was the plan that the losers go back to Pullman and Ike and the winners would go on to Sacramento for the NCAA tournament. Eddie Cole, the old Athletic Director at College of Idaho, had been

---

*Jackie Melson was one of only two collegiate boxers to win four Pacific Coast Intercollegiate titles. The other was Herb Carlson, Idaho's great middleweight in 1947-1950.

*Neither snow nor cold kept Gerry
Lindgren from his appointed
rounds, and rounds. . . .*
(Manuscripts, Archives, and Special
Collections, Washington State
University Libraries)

refereeing at the PCI, and when he learned there would be space in one of the cars headed back to Pullman he asked Deeter if he might catch a ride as far as Caldwell.

At 4:30 in the morning on the following Sunday, Cole showed up in the lobby of the Holiday with his suitcase. When he saw Ike there, in sport coat and tie, talking with the team members who would be heading back to Pullman, Cole was overwhelmed.

"Can you imagine any other coach in the world getting up at 4:30 to see a bunch of losers off?" Eddie wondered out loud. "Deeter, you are the greatest!"

Nobody had the heart to tell Cole that Ike was just coming in from one of his banjo gigs.

After the demise of boxing, Ike stayed on at WSU until 1965, teaching boxing and other courses in the physical education program (including fly fishing). He and his college sweetheart, Claire (Rose, Spokane, '29), still live in Pullman, and Ike gets out whenever he can get away from Claire's "Honey-do list," to fish and hunt a few birds. And, oh yes, he also keeps up on his correspondence and phone conversations with hundreds of his old proteges in "the manly art of aggravated assault," as Deeter lovingly refers to his favorite sport.

Ike Deeter was named a charter member of the WSU Athletic Hall of Fame in 1978.

The Running Machine

"It was," said many who witnessed the event, "the most dramatic sports happening of the twentieth century in America."

That, of course, was Gerry Lindgren's victory in the 10,000 meters in the United States-Soviet Union meet at the Los Angeles Coliseum on July 25, 1964.

A little more than a month after he graduated from John Rogers High School in Spokane, the 5-6, 128-pound Lindgren shocked the sports world. He was not only the first American to beat the Russians in a long-distance race, no other American had even finished second at that distance!

That one race—and the revelation by the skinny, freckle-faced youngster that he trained by running up to 200 miles a week!—triggered a revolution in running that is still going, still growing, a quarter of a century later.

Gerry Lindgren entered Washington State University in the fall of 1964 after competing in the 10,000 meters at the Olympic Games in Tokyo. Four years and eleven NCAA Championships later, he left as the greatest distance runner in collegiate history. Lindgren won the NCAA three-mile and six-mile events in each of his first two varsity seasons, then won the NCAA 5,000 and 10,000 meter races as a senior when the events were changed to the metric distance. This record will never be matched.

Gerry also won the NCAA Indoor two-mile in 1966 and 1967 (his only collegiate defeat coming in the NCAA Indoor two-mile in 1968 at the hands of Jim Ryun, of Kansas), and NCAA Cross-Country titles in 1966,

1967 and 1969. His American record of 12:53 in the three-mile at Seattle in 1966 stood for years.

In the fall-winter of 1965-1966 when he was a WSU sophomore, Lindgren ran five indoor races in five weeks against some of the world's best. During that stretch, he ran an 8:31.6 two-mile, third fastest in history. And remember, Lindgren never considered himself good at that distance; he preferred 10,000 meters.

After a two-week layoff from competition (although he was still running eighty to a hundred miles a week across the frozen tundra around Pullman to keep in trim), Gerry won his first NCAA Indoor title, holding off John Lawson, of Kansas, in the two-mile at 8:41.3 with a great kick down the stretch. (Lindgren had a sore foot going into that race.)

Gerry's 10,000 at Tokyo in 1964 turned out to be his only appearance in the Olympic Games. He sprained an ankle in a workout just prior to the race, but ran anyway and was tenth. In 1968, an ailing stomach—he had an ulcer—kept him out of the Games in Mexico City. (It was not enough to keep him out of the Service, however. WSU Team Physician Dr. R. E. Morton diagnosed Gerry's ulcer and sent X-rays of his condition to the Spokane Draft Board. But Lindgren was drafted anyway, and had to give up a teaching-coaching position he'd accepted with a school district in northwest Washington. Within a few months, the Army discharged Lindgren. He was diagnosed as having—of all things—an ulcer!) In 1972, bothered by a bad knee, Lindgren didn't make it to the Games in Munich.

In 1965, in the face of a threat of ineligibility (the Pac-8 had voted not to permit its track and field athletes to compete in "open" meets sanctioned by the AAU), Gerry went to Washington, D.C., and testified before a Congressional committee investigating the power struggle between the AAU and the U.S. Track and Field Federation. He came away unscathed and WSU drew much favorable editorial comment for his courageous stand.

Twenty years after he completed his career at WSU, one of the nation's premier track and field schools, Gerry Lindgren is still ranked in the Cougar top ten in five events, and his 12:53 three-mile remains a school record. Gerry ranks fourth in the 5,000 meters with 13:20.8 (number one is Henry Rono's old world record of 13:06.2); sixth in the mile at 4:02.4 (to Rick Riley's 3:59.2); eighth at 10,000 meters in 28:10.3 (to Rono's former world record, 27:22.5); ninth at 3,000 meters (behind Rono's former World Record, 7:32.1); and tenth at 1,500 meters in 3:44.3 (to Olympic steeplechase silver medalist Peter Koech's 3:38.1).

Sportswriter Bob Payne knows Gerry Lindgren better than any writer in the country. Payne was with the *Spokesman-Review* in Spokane and wrote about Lindgren from his earliest days as a high school competitor. Now with the Tacoma *News-Tribune,* Payne was on hand in May of 1988 when Lindgren returned to his hometown to run in the annual Bloomsday event. Bob wrote: "A majority of the 53,000 [entrants] . . . never had heard of Gerry Lindgren. Almost half of them hadn't even been born when Lindgren was traveling the world rewriting records—and revising the image of American distance running."

Little Gerry was the greatest "running machine" this country ever saw.

All-weather surfaces were laid on Rogers Field for field events in 1965. The surface was a mix of ground-up tires and asphalt. In 1967, WSU's entire running track was weatherized under a $36,000 contract

Don Bertoia, left, set a Pan-American Games record winning the 800 meters in 1:49.4 in 1962 at Sao Paulo, Brazil. The former Cougar was trailed by Seig Ohlemann, right of Oregon (and Canada), and Ernie Cunliffe, Stanford (U.S.). (AP Wire photo)

Jack and the Near Miss

Jack Mooberry had a great coaching record at Washington State. His teams won 118 dual meets against 50 losses (and that unusual tie with the Huskies in 1950), and took the Northern Division five times. Jack coached seventeen individual NCAA champions and his teams placed in the top ten in the National Championships fifteen times in twenty-eight seasons.

The thing that pleased Moob most, however, as former Sports Information Director Mike Wilson pointed out at Jack's retirement in 1973, was the number of athletes who came to Washington State unheralded and left as NCAA All-Americans and school record holders. He singled out Jim Allen, Seattle, a 16.4 hurdler who became second best in the world in the intermediates; Clem Eischen, a 4:33 high school miler who represented the U.S. in the 1948 Olympics at 1,500 meters; Jim Precht, Omak, first Cougar to vault sixteen feet (16-5 1/2 eventually), who went only eleven feet in high school; and Don Bertoia, Rossland, British Columbia, a 2:00 half-miler who later won the 800 meters in 1:48.3 for Canada in the 1962 Pan American Games.

There were many others. Al Fisher, for example, did not even compete in track in high school at Rossland, British Columbia. After Mooberry got him to put away his skis and put on track shoes, Fisher won the PCC two-mile twice, in 1952 and 1953. Bill Henry, from tiny Skykomish High School, who long-jumped 25-6 for a new school record in 1969, was another, and Clint Richardson, of Auburn, also one of Mooberry's walk-ons, set a school record in the triple jump in 1952 and was third in the NCAA. Jack took enormous pride in the achievements of athletes such as these, and of course their successes reflected his great teaching talents.

Washington State has always been well represented in track and field, whether in competition with its Pacific Northwest neighbors or on a Coast-wide or national level. In years when the Cougars struggled in

other sports, they managed to have champions in track. Jack Mooberry coached more than his share of them.

Bob Gary, Seattle, was the premier sprinter on the Pacific Coast in the 1950s for Washington State. He took the 100 at the PCC in 1952 and 1955 and won the 220 back-to-back in 1954-1955. Gary won the 100 four straight times in the Northern Division meet (1952-1955) and only teammate Clint Richardson kept Bob from a four-year sweep in the 220. Clint won the furlong in 1952.

Among the outstanding performers for the Cougars in the 1950s were Howard McCants, the big football end from Michigan, who tied for the PCC high jump in 1953 at 6-6 (after his famous "snooze" through the Idaho meet the year before); Bill Link, of Mead, who won the 880 at the PCC in 1954 in 1:53.4; Darrell Pearson, Mount Vernon, with a school record 225-1 1/4 javelin in 1956; Burl Grinols, El Cerrito, California, 54-0 1/2 shot put in 1957 (to erase "Lambie" Theodoratus's 1935 mark); Walter "Spike" Arlt, Ritzville, 14.1 in the highs, 23.1 in the 220 lows, and 52.9 in the 440 intermediates in 1958 (and barely missing the Olympic team in this event in 1960); and Don Maw, of Vancouver, ran a 20.8 220 in 1958, tying the earlier marks of Wes Foster, Lee Orr and Bob Gary.

Northern Division champs in this era included Gordon Farrar, Bremerton, and Clint Richardson in the broad jump in 1951 and 1952; Elmer Messenger, an All-Coast tackle from Centralia, who won the discus in 1952 and 1953; and Alan Torgerson, Spokane, high hurdles, and Carl Strom, Seattle, discus, in 1955.

Both the 440 and 880 relay marks fell in 1959. A team of Dave Kerrone, Tacoma; Perry Harper, McKeesport, Pennsylvania; Arlt; and Maw took Mooberry and his 1930 teammates off the books. Dick Rubenser, of Starbuck, won the PCC javelin at 229-9 1/2.

Stars of the 1960s included Wayne Wilson, Spokane, second in the 1960 NCAA pole vault, and Hank Wyborney, Port Angeles, 6-11 in the high jump. Arlt set a school record 13.8 in the highs and Bertoia ran 1:49.8 in the 880 in 1961. Norwegian Eilif Fredriksen was second in the NCAA triple jump and had a best of 50-6 3/4 in 1962, and John Chaplin, Pasadena, California, won the Northwest AAU 220 in 20.8 at Everett in 1963.

The Cougars moved into the AAWU (revamped PCC) in 1962 and triple-jumper Fredriksen became WSU's first track/field champion in the new loop in the spring of 1963. (The WSU wrestling team won the AAWU for Coach Roger James in 1962, the first tournament the Cougars were in.) Nels Siverson, Otis Orchards, was WSU's first vaulter over 15 feet with 15-1/8 at the ND meet. AAWU champs in 1964 were Buck Kipe, Cincinnati, Ohio, in the javelin; Allen in the 440 hurdles; and Chris Westman, Seattle, first of the great distance runners of the 1960s, with a Conference record 13:55.1 in the three-mile. Bob Keppel, Spokane, was second in the NCAA high jump and John Valiant, Victoria, B.C., set a school record 8:57.1 finishing fourth in the 3,000 steeplechase at the 1964 NCAA, the first time he'd attempted the race. WSU's fifth place finish in the 1964 NCAA was Mooberry's best to that point.

1965 has been called the "Year of the Cougar" (WSU was 7-3 in football, Bobo went to the College World Series, Heathcote had an

Sixteen of the twenty-four records in the WSU Track and Field books in 1965 were held or shared by athletes of foreign birth. Canadian Lee Orr had the 440, shared the 100 and 220, and was on the best Cougar mile relay team (World Record of 3:12.3 in 1937); Canadian Don Bertoia, 880; Canadian John Valiant, mile, steeplechase, 5,000 and 10,000 meters, and six-mile; Norwegian Eilif Fredriksen had the long and triple jump marks; Chris Westman, born in France, owned the two- and three-mile marks; and Norwegian Harald Lorentzen had the shot and discus records. (Sixteen of the 24 records were set in the three years prior to 1965.)

Smilin' Jack Mooberry and his great discus thrower John Van Reenen, 1968-1970. (Lewis Alumni Centre)

unbeaten frosh basketball team, and Harshman beat the Huskies twice), and Mooberry's athletes certainly did their part. Washington State defeated USC 81-65 on April 24, handing the Trojans their first Conference dual meet loss in thirty-five years. Other track highlights of that year included the 100-yard dash win by Dick Hickman, of Los Angeles, in the Pac-8 meet at Pullman; a sixth place NCAA team finish; and Bob Yard, of Trail, British Columbia, won the pole vault at the first NCAA Indoor championships at Detroit.

Freshman Gerry Lindgren made his presence known in 1965 by setting a world record in the National AAU six-mile at 27:11.6, and an American record in the three-mile at 13:04, among other American and national freshman marks. Gary Benson, Okanogan, and Westman became WSU's first Cross-Country All-Americans, and Harald Lorentzen, Norway, broke the sixty-foot barrier in the shot with a heave of 61-3 1/2.

Lindgren won WSU's first NCAA Cross-Country title in 1966 and he and Westman ran 1-3 in the NCAA Indoor two-mile. Gerry salvaged the 1967 season for Moob by winning the NCAA Cross-Country again, the Indoor two-mile, and the outdoor three- and six-mile titles.

Mooberry got his first full-time assistant in 1968 when John Chaplin, his great sprinter of 1961-63, came back to WSU from Oregon State, where he'd been an assistant.

The year all Cougar track fans remember was 1968 when Jack's team missed the NCAA championship by a single point, losing 58-57 to Southern Cal in the meet at Berkeley on June 15. Few remember that WSU was third in the NCAA the following year and second again in 1970, a great three-year run for Mooberry.

Highlights of the "near miss" in 1968 included Gerry Lindgren's come-from-behind victory in the 5,000 meters to complete his third "double" in NCAA distance events.

"Gerry Lindgren, scoring surely the most exciting and courageous victory of his NCAA championship career, ran from far back in the last 330 to smash the field of 5000 meter ambushers for his sixth straight outdoor title and, with Thursday's 10,000, his third championship double—a fantastic close to a fantastic career," wrote the *Spokesman-Review*'s Bob Payne. (Gerry ran a meet record 13:57.2 in the 5,000 and said later that he "felt lousy all the way. . . .")

South African John Van Reenen won the discus and was second in the shot in 1968, and Carl O'Donnell, of Wenatchee, "the guttiest competitor in the field," Payne wrote, "unloaded the greatest series of javelin throws in his life to win one of the meet's most stunning upsets" at 258-11. (O'Donnell had a bad elbow throughout the 1968 season.)

"And Boyd Gittins (Bellevue), a junior intermediate hurdler of less than spectator's credentials just three months ago, fought down the stretch to take second behind England's and Boston University's Dave Hemery in one of the meet's wildest finishes," Payne noted. (Gittins' 50.6 was a personal best at the time.)

"For the record," Payne concluded, "this will have to go as the finest NCAA without doubt. Some 18,000 spectators . . . saw five meet records broken [in the finals], and depth of performance that was unprecedented."

Mooberry, who had suffered a severe heart attack in 1964, died on August 1, 1978, just five years after retiring as Head Track Coach, a post Jack held for twenty-eight years.

Payne paid Moob his finest salute:

> Mooberry was a lot more than a great track coach, although that he was. What endures with the hundreds of athletes he coached is not so much the marks they achieved and honors they won but the man they met, the friend they kept.

Bobo Goes to Omaha

It took Frederick Charles "Bobo" Brayton only four seasons to get his Washington State Cougars to the College World Series after he took over the baseball coaching reins from Buck Bailey in 1962. Nobody who knew Bobo was surprised.

Brayton came over to WSC in 1943 from Birdsview, a hamlet up in Skagit county—"Tarheel country," Bobo says—and, except for a brief hitch in the service at the tail end of World War II, never left eastern Washington.

Brayton started having a nationwide impact on college baseball as soon as he got to Washington State. For one thing, in 1962 college coaches weren't allowed on the coaching lines—and no, the rule was not put in to keep Buck Bailey on the bench. Bobo not only wanted to get out there where the action was, he wanted to direct it! So he got that rule changed.

He also was instrumental in making it mandatory for players to wear protective helmets. Brayton nearly lost his life when he was hit on the side of the head with a line drive while pitching batting practice at Yakima Valley College. Jerry Reimer, a big left-handed hitter, scalded

•

Bobo Brayton *received the NCAA District 8 Coach of the Year Award in 1965 from* Stan Musial *at a ceremony in Washington, D.C. Bobo was a finalist for National Coach of the Year. The Cougar coach also was present to see his old coach,* Buck Bailey, *inducted into the National Collegiate Baseball Coaches Hall of Fame posthumously.*

•

A sell-out (and then some!) crowd witnessed the WSU-Stanford NCAA District 8 playoffs in 1965 on old Bailey Field. The Cougars beat the Cardinal two straight, 2-1 and 13-3, and went to the College World Series in Omaha, where they finished third. (Bob Bullis)

one back through the middle. The ball hit Bobo on the side of the head and crushed his skull. Dr. Dick Stiles, the old Cougar pitcher, was one of the physicians who operated on Bobo and saved his life. Right then, Brayton decided that he—and all his players—would wear helmets. Of course Bobo was just years ahead of the game, as he has been so often.

In 1965, his fourth season at WSU, Brayton had a ball club he had recruited and coached. The Cougars won the Northern Division handily with a 14-4 mark. Bob Salisbury, senior lefthander out of Bellingham, was 7-1 on the season with a spectacular 0.85 ERA, even though he came up with a sore arm later. Right-hander Danny Frisella, a junior college transfer from San Mateo, California, also was 7-1, with a 1.48 ERA, and Mike Avey, a lefthander from Whittier, California, was 6-1 and 1.22. (Avey had an exceptional move to first base; the best he's ever seen in the college game, Bobo says.) The Cougar pitching staff had a combined earned-run average of 2.37 for forty-one games and WSU won thirty-three of them.

Bobo had a good hitting team in 1965. The Cougars were led by their All-America catcher and Captain, John Olerud, of Federal Way, with a .336 average, and left fielder Dale "The Whale" Ford, of Lacey, at .331. The pair tied in RBI with 35. Bob Fry, of Billings, Montana, speedy centerfielder, hit .313 and stole eighteen bases. Hal Brunstad, of Kennewick, a left-handed hitting first baseman, hit .310 and was third in RBI with twenty-six. (Tri-Cities *Herald* sports editor Charlie Van Sickel, while praising Brunstad as a player, always said his mom, Helen Severance Brunstad, Pullman, '36, was better—and faster!)

As good as that 1965 team was, and as well as it did in the play-offs and the World Series, Bobo will always wonder what it could have been had Frisella been available for post-season play. Danny was ineligible due to a junior college transfer rule. (He also was a strong, left-handed hitter, with two home runs, a triple and a double and hit .250 in thirty-two at-bats in 1965.)

In the NCAA District 8 play-offs at Bailey Field, Avey four-hit Stanford in the opener and Brunstad drove in both runs in the 2-1 win with a 413-foot double against the centerfield fence in the Cougar eighth. WSU blasted the Indians 13-3 to win the play-offs. Lefty Joe MacLean, of Puyallup, got the win, with four innings of one-hit relief from Paul "PT" Taylor, of Kirkland.

Bobo got some revenge for old Buck in the World Series opener at Omaha in 1965. Texas, perennial Southwest Conference champ and winner over the Cougars in the finals of the 1950 Series, was pretty well shut down by Avey's left-handed slants and Cougar hitters had a field day against Longhorn pitchers in the 12-5 win. Brunstad doubled for two runs in the first inning and WSU was never headed. Olerud was 4-6, Brunstad had three RBI and Fry had three hits, drove in three runs, and set a World Series single game record with four stolen bases. He stole home on one of two double-steals Brayton engineered in that game.

Going over the hitters. All-American catcher John Olerud, captain of the 1965 Pacific Coast Champions, goes over some strategy with Coach Bobo Brayton. (Manuscripts, Archives, and Special Collections, Washington State University Libraries)

The second game was quite a reversal. Ohio State hammered WSU 14-1, and the Cougars barely survived a losers' bracket game the following night, edging Connecticut 3-2 on a double by Wally Lito, of Billings, Montana, in the eighth. Ed Fiskland, of Spokane, relieved Salisbury in the fifth and got the win, while Avey earned a save pitching the ninth.

The Cougars and Buckeyes went at it again in the fourth game. It was a complete turnaround from their first meeting. The two teams battled through fourteen scoreless innings before Ohio State won it, 1-0, in the fifteenth with an unearned run. But that was almost an anticlimax.

In the bottom of the thirteenth, Dale Ford led off with a 400-foot triple off the top of the centerfield fence at Rosenblatt Stadium. Buckeye pitcher Steve Arlin—later a great hurler for the San Diego Padres, but never greater than on this night—then intentionally loaded the bases with nobody out, bringing up Dale Scilley, a sophomore from Billings, Montana, playing right field.

What happened next still interrupts Bobo's sleep, almost a quarter of a century later. Scilley, trying to get out of the way of a high, inside fastball, inadvertently tapped the ball back to Arlin for the 1-2-3 double-play. Arlin struck out the next hitter, one of 20 Ks he had that night, and Ohio State was out of the inning. MacLean pitched 6 1/3; Fiskland 2 2/3; and Avey went six and picked up the loss, his only defeat that season against six wins.

Washington State's battle with Ohio State tied the World Series record for innings played set in 1962 by Santa Clara and Michigan.

Despite the loss of Olerud, Fry, Salisbury, Lito, and infielders Duane "Duey" Rossman, Clover Park, and Larry Schreck, Spokane, the Cougars were right back knocking at the World Series door in 1966. They had very strong pitching, perhaps the strongest ever, and Ford tore up the league, batting .390 and hitting an NCAA record 17 home runs, driving in forty-six runs in forty-three games while winning All-America honors.

WSU waltzed through the Northern Division with a 15-1 mark and wound up 35-8 for the season. Frisella was 10-0; Doug Lukens, of

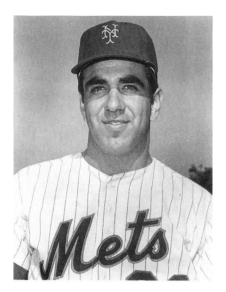

One of WSU's greatest pitchers, Dan Frisella was at the peak of his Major League career when he died in a dune buggy rollover in 1976 during the off-season. (Lewis Alumni Centre)

Richland, 5-1; Avey, 5-2; Taylor and Joe Karp, Bothell, both at 3-0; Tom Brown, Spokane, 3-1; MacLean, 4-3; and Fiskland, 2-1.

The NCAA District 8 play-offs were scheduled for the lighted Long Beach, California, municipal stadium, but, somehow, wound up in USC's home park, quaint Bovard Field, with its 289-foot right field screen, gerrymandered center field, and no lights.

Four teams were involved, the Cougars, Fresno State, Cal Poly-Pomona, and the Trojans, coached by Raoul "Rod" Dedeaux. The evening before the tournament opened, Fresno State Coach Pete Beiden, who was disgusted with the stadium venue change, had dinner with Bobo.

"Y'know what's goin' to happen don't you, Bobo," Beiden said, not expecting an answer. "We're gonna kill each other off and that SOB is gonna wind up in Omaha!"

Pete Beiden was never more right.

Frisella and Fresno's Larry Gonsalves hooked up in a classic pitching duel. It went eleven innings to a 2-2 tie (Frisella hit a two-run homer in the fifth), and was called because of darkness. USC and Cal Poly had staggered through ten innings in the first game before the Trojans prevailed 11-7 on a grand slam homer by their sophomore catcher, Steve Sogge. It was smogdusk before WSU and Fresno State got started.

The following morning, the Cougars and Bulldogs resumed at ten o'clock. WSU scored three unearned runs in the top of the thirteenth and won 5-2. Neither starting pitcher from the previous day could continue, of course, so the Cougars used Joe Karp, of Bothell, and Avey, with Avey getting the win.

Fresno State stayed right on the field and played Cal Poly in a losers' bracket game. It was another nail-biter, and Brayton began to wonder where Pete Beiden got his crystal ball. Fresno State finally won 5-4.

At one in the afternoon, still in their uniforms from the morning game and beginning to look a little shopworn in the eighty-degree heat and ninety percent humidity, the Cougars took on USC, at home, fresh uniforms, same old umps (Cece Carlucci and Pat Orr, ex-Coast Leaguers).

Big Tom Brown pitched a splendid game and had a three-hitter going into the eighth, with WSU leading 3-1. But the Trojans exploded for three runs in that frame and won it 4-3.

The Cougars stayed on the field to play Fresno State in a loser-out game in the double-elimination tournament. They went 10 innings to a 1-1 tie. Game called by darkness!

Doug Lukens had pitched splendidly in that game, but gave way to Frisella the next morning and Dan went five more innings, gave up only three hits, and got the win, 2-1 in the fifteenth. (As fate would have it, Gonsalves, who had pitched so well against Frisella in the opener, took the loss in this game in one inning of relief.)

Dirty, bone-tired, but still fightin', the Cougars stayed on the field to meet the freshly laundered, rested Trojans. (Later, the reason given for playing the tournament at Bovard was that USC was in finals that week and the players couldn't get to Long Beach and back to meet their finals' schedules.)

Lefty Joe MacLean started for WSU in the final game, but the Trojans got to him in the second for six runs. Karp finished up and held SC scoreless the rest of the way in the 7-4 loss.

Washington State had played forty-six innings of baseball in a little more than forty-six hours, spread over three days.

Great guy that he was, Pete Beiden went back to Fresno and never once said to Bobo, "I told you so!"

A very sad postscript to this story is that Danny Frisella, after ten Major League seasons, mostly as a top-flight relief pitcher with the New York Mets, Milwaukee/Atlanta Braves and San Diego Padres, was killed in a dune-buggy rollover on December 31, 1976.

Frisella was 17-1 in his two seasons at WSU, struck out 191 and walked only 46 in 162-2/3 innings, and had a 1.48 earned run average.*

The "Cardiac Kids"

Bert Clark inherited a "tradition" when he took over the football reins at Washington State from Jim Sutherland in 1964. WSU had won seven straight games from Stanford under Suds, beginning with that 21-18 stunner in 1957.

As fortune would have it, Clark's opener as Head Coach at WSU was with Stanford. It was in Spokane on September 19, 1964, another date Cougar football fans have indelibly etched in their memories.

Trailing 16-23 with 3:23 to play, Washington State scored, went for two—and was stopped short.

At this point, the "Palouse Jinx" started to work on Stanford. With little more than a minute left, quarterback Terry DeSylvia passed complete to flanker Dick Ragsdale for a first down. But Cougar halfback Clarence Williams, of Renton, wrenched the ball from Ragsdale's arms and returned it to the WSU thirty-seven. Stanford not only lost the ball but also picked up a fifteen-yard penalty on the play when Ragsdale was flagged for venting his frustration after tackling the "thief."

Quarterback Tom Roth, of El Cajon, California, guided WSU forty-eight yards and scored with seventeen seconds left. Bill Ebel, of Moses Lake, kicked the extra point and WSU had a 29-23 win, its eighth straight over the Cardinal.

Fortunately for Stanford fans back in the Bay Area, they missed the worst part. Somewhere in Oregon, a farmer working a back-hoe cut the coaxial cable and the telecast lost its picture just before Clancy stole the ball and started the Cougars' winning drive. Sportscaster Chick Hearn (yep, the Lakers' veteran announcer) was doing the telecast that day. When Chick learned he was off the air for that exciting finish, he was almost as frustrated as Ragsdale—and Coach John Ralston.

That was the most exciting moment the Cougars of 1964 gave their fans that season, finishing 3-6-1. But the following fall it really got wild!

Pac-8 leaders turned down the request of basketball coaches (for the third time) that the runnerup team be permitted to play in the National Invitation Tournament (NIT) if invited. Their reasoning? It might create a precedent for football. Horrors! Meanwhile, the Southeast, Southwest and other conferences were hauling in much needed funds by sending second, third, and fourth place teams to bowl games.

---

*Both Frisella and Ed Fiskland, who were juniors in 1966, signed professional contracts after that season. It was tough on Bobo and the Cougars. The Pac-8 instituted a round-robin schedule the following year and WSU wound up sixth, but only 4 1/2 games out of first in a very tight, six-team race.

Don't look back, Clancy! WSU's Clarence Williams scampers for yardage vs. Arizona in the Cougars' 7-2 win over the Wildcats in Spokane in 1963. Williams won it for WSU with a 75-yard run in the second quarter.

Washington State opened the 1965 season by defeating Iowa 7-0 at Iowa City on a twenty-yard pass from Roth to tight end Rich Sheron, of Beaverton, Oregon, in the last minute of play. Tough defense, particularly the play of tackle Wayne Foster, of Port Orchard, and some great punting by left-footed sophomore Jim "Tiger" Engstrom, of Arlington, kept Iowa at bay all afternoon.

The next weekend, the Cougars scored again in the final minutes and halfback Bill Gaskins, of Spokane, kicked his second extra point to beat Minnesota 14-13 at Minneapolis in another big upset. Minnesota had opened its season with a 20-20 tie against highly rated USC the week before. The extra points Gaskins kicked in this game were his first attempts at WSU. He was subbing for Foster, the regular kicker, who was bothered by a tender ankle. (Wayne nevertheless earned the Associated Press's National Lineman of the Week for his play against Minnesota, and WSU picked up its nickname of the "Cardiac Kids" from Spokane *Chronicle* Sports Editor Bob Johnson.)

There is a good story behind the story of that win. Aaron Brown, 6-8, 250-pound Gopher end who later starred professionally with the Kansas City Chiefs, was noted for his "clothes-lining." Brown would come downfield on a kickoff, extend an arm and level an unsuspecting opponent. The Cougars had seen him do this in the USC game film.

"Yeah, we know about Brown," assistant coach Joe Marvin said shortly before the game. "Keep your eye on him on the kickoff."

Minnesota kicked off to the Cougars and WSU fullback Larry Eilmes, leading the blocking wedge, appeared unaware that Brown was bearing down on him. At the last moment, Eilmes turned into the big fellow and lifted him right off his feet and over backward with a double-forearm shiver under the chin strap. Brown was not a factor against WSU that day; a post-game x-ray showed he had a hairline jaw fracture.

Washington State figured to beat Villanova on October 9 in Spokane, but late in the fourth period the Wildcats were leading 14-10. Then, like lightning, the Cardiac Cougars struck on a 78-yard scoring pass-run from Roth to Bob Simpson, of Edwall. Seconds later, Gaskins picked off a Villanova pass and returned it forty-one yards for another touchdown and the final score was WSU 24, Villanova 14.

In their third game that season against Big Ten teams, on October 23 at Bloomington, Indiana, Washington State trailed the Hoosiers until time had run out, then scored on a rerun when Indiana was offside on a pass interception. The touchdown came on a five-yard pass from Roth to Doug Flansburg, of Palouse. Roth then calmly hit halfback Ammon McWashington, of Conroe, Texas, with a two-point conversion pass and the Cougars won it 8-7. The last two plays were run after time had run out!

That win gave the Cougars a first. Washington State became the first team (outside the Big Ten) to defeat three Western Conference teams on their home fields in one season.

The Cougars even lost excitingly that year. Idaho beat WSU 17-13 and Arizona State squeaked by Clark's team 7-6 at Tempe on two very close calls. WSU fullback Larry Eilmes was stopped short (they ruled) of the Sun Devil goal line in the third period, and WSU's successful two-point conversion after its fourth quarter touchdown was nullified when the Cougars were called for too much time in getting the play off.

When Harry Missildine of the *Spokesman-Review* learned that the official timing the play was using a sweep second-hand watch, he wrote: "WSU was beaten by the 'Night Watchman of Tempe.'"

The "Cardiac Kids" went 7-3 in 1965 and narrowly missed a Rose Bowl bid. UCLA got it with a 7-2-1 record.

That 1965 season was Clark's best at WSU. His teams were 3-7 and 2-8 the next two years and Bert was let out at the end of the 1967 season after he criticized his players following a bitter 31-10 loss to Stanford at Palo Alto. WSU led the Indians 10-0 in the first quarter of that game, saw Stanford tie the score before halftime and then score twenty-one unanswered points in the second half. The loss ended the "Cougar Jinx" over Stanford which had reached eight games and extended back to 1957.

Halfback Clarence Williams and fullback Larry Eilmes set new WSU rushing records in this era. Williams, who made the AP All-America team as a defensive back in 1964 and was a first round draft pick of the LA Rams, averaged 4.9 yards per rush in his varsity career (1962-1964).

Eilmes, playing in the 1963-1965 seasons, set a single game rushing mark with 194 yards against Villanova in 1965; a single season rushing record of 818 yards, also in 1965; and career marks for total rushes and most rushing yards, 369 and 1,597.

Clark ended his four-year stay at Washington State on a high note. The Cougars beat Washington in Bert's final game. Mike Cadigan, of Seattle, the quarterback he'd banished to the secondary after a season-opening 21-6 loss to Cal in 1966, returned and led WSU to a 9-7 win in Seattle.

He's a Cougar!

Number one Cougar football fan?

It's not even a contest. Attorney Bob Burks, '54, of Bellingham, wins hands down.

Burks, who has been collecting clippings, programs and action photos of Cougar football games since he was a youngster, has the most complete record of WSU football to be found anywhere. His collection comprises six fourteen-by-seventeen-inch bound volumes of about 100 pages each. Some of the material dates back to the early 1900s.

You can ask Burks the scores of the WSC-Cal games in 1921, 1931, or 1941 and he'll tell you 0-14, 7-13 and 13-6 faster'n you can look 'em up in the Cougar pressbook. The guy has a photographic memory where Cougar football is concerned—and he remembers details of the games as well.

Burks came by his love of Cougar football naturally. His father, the late Joe Burks, '25, was a letterman at center for WSC in 1923, and for years after was one of the Cougar Alumni stalwarts in the Yakima Valley.

Barrister Burks isn't just a cut-and-paste Cougar fan. He's a football addict! He's probably seen more WSU games than anyone. In 1965, Burks took a position with the Internal Revenue Service in Milwaukee, Wisconsin. Sure, he likes beer, but that's not why he went to Milwaukee. It happened to be the nearest Internal Revenue Service office to his center of operations that fall. As you may recall, the Cougars played Iowa at Iowa City; Minnesota at Minneapolis; and Indiana at Bloomington in 1965. Burks saw 'em all. (Old Harry "Misinterp" Missildine used to sneak Burks into the pressbox as his "stats man." He crashed so many boxes they began to call him "One-eye Connolly.")

When he wasn't following the Cougars that fall, Burks was in Milwaukee or Green Bay watching the Packers, who were having a pretty good year, too.

The Cougars had such fantastic success in 1965 that Burks couldn't bear to leave them, so he moved his headquarters to Tucson, Arizona, the following year.

When the 1966 football season began, Burks had his vacation schedule all set. He drove up to Salt Lake and took in the Cougar-Utah game on October 15; then cruised on up to Pullman for the WSU-Idaho and WSU-Oregon State games the following two weekends; down to Eugene for the Oregon game on November 5; and back to Tucson in time to catch the Cougars against Arizona on November 12.

•

Tony Tenisci, *of Trail, British Columbia, threw the hammer 180-1 as a WSU freshman in the spring of 1969 and broke a record that had been on the books sixty-one years, set by* Joe "Bunch" Halm, *of Prosser, in 1908. (The hammer was discontinued about 1910 and did not come back until 1969.)*

•

For some years now, Burks has been practicing in Bellingham. He still keeps an eagle-eye on the Cougar football schedules and sees most of the games in Pullman—and of course all of those on the West side, in Seattle, Corvallis and Eugene, and Berkeley and Palo Alto if the Cougars are worth watching. He usually manages to sneak in another college game, depending on the schedules, and there's always the pros on Sunday. In 1988, Burks was in Champaign for the Cougar opener against Illinois, then hustled up to catch Northwestern that night in Evanston and the Bears the next day in Chicago. Of course he saw the Cougars at Minnesota the following week, and then managed to squeeze in a Viking game the next day before heading back to Bellingham for a couple days' work. He was back in Pullman on September 17 to see the Cougars' home opener with Oregon.

Yep, Burks is WSU's number one fan, and he has the scrapbooks and mileage to prove it.

The "Bethlehem Babe"

John Van Reenen cuts loose with a record throw in the discus at Rogers Field in 1982. Note the large crowd in the old North stands. The big South African later set a world record in the discus. (Lewis Alumni Centre)

John Van Reenen was 6-8 and weighed 275 pounds when he came to Washington State University in the fall of 1967 from Bethlehem, South Africa.

Van Reenen was such a perfectly proportioned athlete that he did not look his size. When Cougar Track Coach Jack Mooberry laid eyes on the big guy and saw him throw the discus, he could not believe his good fortune. Football Coach Jim Sweeney drooled when he looked at Van Reenen.

Professor T. H. Kennedy, WSU's long-time Faculty Athletic Representative and former Chairman of the Department of Sociology, was responsible for Van Reenen coming to WSU. An old weight man at Abilene (Texas) Christian College as an undergraduate back in the late twenties, T. H. was on some sort of sociological boondoggle in Africa when he happened to read in a local newspaper about a young giant up in Bethlehem, Orange Free State, who was throwing the shot and discus record distances at every outing. Dr. Kennedy just naturally gravitated up that way and used some of his southern charm on the Van Reenens, extolling the virtues of an educational experience in the Palouse.

From the time he enrolled at WSU in the fall of 1967, Van Reenen was a record-setter. By the time he graduated, the big South African was a three-time NCAA Champion in the discus and held school records in both the discus and shot. His discus record of 208-10 at Rogers Field in 1970 is still the best in the Cougar books, and a mark of 65-0 in the shot, made at Bethlehem that same year, ranks second. (He probably would have thrown the discus farther at WSU had it not been for the limited landing area on Rogers Field in those years. John got gun shy after throwing a few over the old snow fence Mooberry erected to protect runners on the track from flying discuses.

In 1975, Van Reenen held the world discus record for a time at 224-8. Unfortunately, due to the apartheid policies in his native South Africa, that nation's athletes were barred from Olympic competition, so John never was able to compete in the games. He also holds the unofficial world indoor record for the discus at 181-9 1/2, set in the WSU Field House in 1967.

A talented artist, Van Reenen has been a book illustrator (his special field is children's books) and now teaches art at Stellenbosch University in Capetown.

Sweeney finally got John into a football uniform and used him at fullback in the final minutes of the UCLA game in Spokane on October 11, 1969. Van Reenen scored a touchdown on a two-yard plunge. Jim always said the big South African would have made a great tight end or defensive tackle had he concentrated on football.

The Penguin

He played only one varsity baseball season at Washington State but Cougar fans will never forget the "Penguin."

Ron Cey, who had a career at third base for the Los Angeles Dodgers from 1973 to 1982, jumped into the starting lineup at the hot corner as a sophomore at WSU in 1968. He led the Cougars in the Pac-8 that season, hitting .369 (led the league in home runs, four, and triples, three; was third in RBI with 13; and sixth in overall average).

Those were the days of wooden bats, and old Cougars still remember the "Cey sound." When the sturdy (5-9, 185) righthanded hitter from Tacoma smashed one at old Bailey Field you could hear the CRACK! echo off the Field House. (Dodger Manager Walter Alston saw Cey go 6-for-9 one day against Cincinnati and said, "nine of the hardest-hit balls I've seen consecutively from one man.")

Ron had a Major League bat at WSU, and he was an excellent fielding third baseman as well. On the Cougars' first road trip to California in the 1968 season, WSU opened against Stanford in the sunken diamond at Palo Alto. Cey doubled home Greg Schubert, of Edmonds, in the seventh, and won the game 7-6 with a line shot home run to left in the ninth. Lefty Rick Austin, of Tacoma, got the win with relief help from fellow Tacoman Donald "Skip" Gillis, and Norm Angelini, of Half Moon Bay, California.

The following day, across the Bay at Berkeley, the Cougars played one of the most memorable double-headers in WSU baseball history. Joe Karp, of Bothell, had four-hit the Bears in the seven-inning opener, but Cal got two aboard in the final inning after two were out. Cey made a marvelous backhand stop of a smash down the line, stepped on third for the force and Karp had his shutout, 1-0.

In the second game, with starting lefthander Angelini still going in the tenth, Cal loaded the bases with one out. The crafty Angelini pitched high and tight to Dave Texdahl and the big Bear hitter, trying to squeeze, popped one up. Angelini caught it, flipped to Cey and the threat was ended.

In the twelfth, another miracle play saved the Cougs. With two on and one out, Gillis, a right-hander, relieved Angelini.

"I remember cheating in a little because I didn't have a great arm and I thought I might have a better chance of cutting off the winning run on a base-hit," said Cougar left fielder LeRoy Miller, of Spokane.

WSU won the 1966 Inland Empire AAU gymnastics title and had a 7-1 dual meet season. Coach Jim Sweeney resigned following the 1966 season to return to Ohio State, his alma mater. Rex Davis, Cougar gymnast in 1951-1953, returned to WSU as Gymnastics and Tennis Coach in 1967. Davis had been coaching at Columbia High in Richland.

Ron Cey, the "Penguin." (WSU Sports Information)

To this day, every Cougar who saw what happened next has trouble believing it. The Cal hitter drove a ball halfway to Emeryville. It was gone—or at least so far over Miller's head that the winning run could walk home.

"I did get a pretty good jump, but the wind must have caught the thing," Miller recalled. "I just kept running, put up the glove and 'Pop!' there it was, right at the fence."

Coach Bobo Brayton still says it was the greatest catch he's seen in a Cougar game.

Austin, who'd started at Stanford the day before, came on in place of Gillis and struck out the next batter to end the twelfth.

In the thirteenth, Cey led off with a triple and first baseman Steve Dickerson, of Richland, singled up the middle to score Ron.

Austin got the Bears on two popups and a strikeout in their half to collect his second win in two days, 5-4.

The Cougars then moved on to Los Angeles where they split with UCLA, losing the first 4-3* and winning the second 10-6 in the tenth on a grand slam home run by senior catcher Jim Hannah, of Ferndale.

Cey had five hits, including a homer, in that UCLA double-header, and Austin got his third win in four days in the second game.

WSU ended its five-day, six-game road trip against USC. Although they outhit the Trojans 14-11, the Cougars lost 4-3 in fourteen innings. Cey had two hits. Rick Austin, in relief of starter Jeff Clark, of Vancouver, took the loss.**

During his career with the Dodgers, Cey set both hitting and fielding records for the LA club. In April of 1977, Ron enjoyed the greatest start of his career, batting .425 for the month and driving in twenty-nine runs. He had nine home runs that month, just two short of the Major League record. That 1977 season Cey had thirty homers and 110 runs batted in and fielded .977, all three top marks for a Dodger third baseman.

Ace lefthander Rick Austin hurled two no-hitters for the Cougars, in 1967 and 1968, and pitched in the Majors with Cleveland after graduation. (Hilltopics)

The Smilin' Irishman

Jim Sweeney's coaching record at Washington State belies his popularity at the school. Sweeney posted an unexceptional 29-59-1 mark at WSU and had only one winning season in eight years. Yet he could have owned the school—and most of the sportswriters on the Pacific Coast, if he'd wanted 'em—because of a ready wit and Irish charm that usually disarmed even his most severe critics. (And he had a surprisingly good record against the Huskies, 3-5; it should have been 4-4, but that's getting ahead of the story.)

---

* Bobo protested the first game because UCLA had two staff coaches on the lines and only one was permitted in those years. It was a cut and dried violation. The Pac-8 office said it had "no machinery set up to handle a protest." Later, USC protested a call in a game at Stanford and it was upheld.

** The Cougars used six pitchers on this trip and they hurled a total of 60 innings in five days. Jeff Clark started both the second game against UCLA and the USC game. Gillis started the first UCLA game and was relieved by Karp and then Scott Doman, of Oak Harbor. Austin was 3-1; Karp 1-0; and Skip Gillis 0-1. Angelini had a save.

All-Americans Chris Westman *and* Gary Benson, *of Bridgeport, led the Cougar cross-country team to its third straight unbeaten season in 1966.*

When President Glenn Terrell announced Sweeney's hiring on January 17, 1968, he said the coach from Montana State so inspired him (in their first interview) "that I wanted to suit up!"

Sweeney replaced Bert Clark at WSU after the 1967 season. Clark was a tough coach, who ran a tough program, but got himself fired for criticizing his players after a 31-10 loss at Stanford that year and telling the press that maybe WSU didn't belong in the Pac-8. But mainly because he lost. Bert was 15-29-1 in four seasons.

It took Jim Sweeney all of one appearance—at halftime of a basketball game in old Bohler gym—to win over the student body as no football coach at WSU had since Babe Hollingbery. When he peeled off his coat, revealing a "Sweeney Red" Cougar tie, and yelled "Gimme a Ceee!," he had the students—and most of the rest of the crowd—right in his pocket.

Sweeney was thirty-nine years old when he came to WSU from Montana State. He was 3-6-1 his first season, and the Cougars didn't look bad. They got hammered by Arizona State, 41-14 at Tempe, but were very respectable in a 31-21 loss to UCLA (matching the Bruins 14-14 in the fourth quarter), and surprised everyone by tying Stanford 21-21.

When Sweeney resurrected senior quarterback Hank Grenda, of Burnaby, British Columbia, from the discards and beat Washington 24-0 in Spokane to end that 1968 season, the future looked rosy indeed. Grenda really had a day against the Huskies. He ran three yards for WSU's opening score, kicked a twenty-six-yard field goal, threw touchdown passes of sixty-four and twenty-four yards to flanker Freddie Moore (Washington, D.C.) and halfback Glen Shaw (Yakima), and kicked all three extra points!

The luck o' the Irish continued into the 1969 opener. WSU beat Illinois 19-18 at Champaign on some fourth-quarter magic. Tailback Bob Ewen, of Portland, passed twenty yards to Tacoma's Ed Armstrong to make it 18-16. Then, after the two-point conversion to tie failed, the Cougars stopped the Illini, took over and drove down for a twenty-nine-yard field goal attempt by defensive back Mike Monahan, of Portland, who'd kicked a twenty-four-yarder in the first quarter. It was blocked!

But Illinois was called for holding and Monahan got another chance from the twelve. Mike booted this one right through for the win.

All of Jim Sweeney's Irish luck apparently was used up in that game. The Cougars did not win another in 1969, and lost 10 in a row before defeating Idaho 44-16 in Spokane on September 19, 1970, in the "Displaced Bowl."

Both WSU and Idaho were without home fields in the 1970 season. Washington State's stadium (the south stands and pressbox, built in 1926) burned in a fire on April 4, 1970. Idaho's Neale Stadium had been condemned the year before. The Vandals played their 1969 schedule at Rogers Field and had planned to play there again in 1970. After the "Sweeney Fire" (so-called because the smilin' Irishman cheered the demise of the old wooden stadium), both WSU and Idaho played their "home" football games in 1970 in Spokane's Albi Stadium. Idaho moved into its "New Idaho Stadium" (now roofed and re-named "Kibbie Dome") in 1971, but WSU's new Martin Stadium was not completed until 1972. The Cougars played all of their "home" games in Spokane in 1970 and 1971, returning to dedicate "Martin Stadium and Academic Center" against Utah on September 30, 1972. ("It was all 'academic,'" one wag said after Utah beat the Cougars 44-25 in the dedication game.)

After those horrendous seasons of 1969 and 1970 when his teams went 2-19, Sweeney began to turn the WSU program around in 1971. Jim found a game-breaker in Bernard Jackson, a little sprinter out of Pierce Junior College in Los Angeles, and Ty Paine, his junior quarterback from Billings, Montana, was beginning to feel at home in Sweeney's option offense. Those two, along with Ken Grandberry, of Tacoma, and Ken Lyday, Wichita Falls, Texas, operating behind some Pac-8-quality linemen such as Jim Giesa, Coeur d'Alene, Idaho; Bill Moos, Edwall; Buzz Brazeau, Pullman; Wallace Williams, Bakersfield, California; Mike Johnson, Wenatchee; and Mike Talbot, San Leandro, California, gave the Cougars a solid ground game.

WSU surprised Minnesota 31-20 at Minneapolis in the third game of the 1971 season. Then, after a painful 24-23 loss to California in Spokane, the Cougars turned in the upset of the year by beating Stanford, the Pac-8's two-time Rose Bowl representative (in 1971 and 1972), 24-23 on a twenty-seven-yard field goal by Don Sweet, of Vancouver, British Columbia. (Sweeney always had the right crack at the right time for the media, and they loved him. After this game, one of the great nail-biters in Cougar football history, where WSU had driven eighty-five yards in the final 1:40 and Sweet kicked the winning goal as time ran out, Sweeney walked into the pressroom and said, "Well, there never was any doubt, huh?")

The following week, in Spokane, Sweeney pulled the old hidden ball trick on Oregon and Jackson ran forty-six yards out of punt formation for what proved to be the winning score in a 31-21 chiller. Even some of the fans who saw that game still disagree about what actually happened.

With fourth down and seven, and trailing 21-17 in the fourth quarter, the Cougars sent Jim Dodd, of Seattle, into "punt formation." The ball was snapped by center Mike Hill, of Santa Clara, California, and Dodd kicked. The ball, however, had been snapped short, to fullback Ken Grandberry. Grandberry, still bent over in blocking position, shoved the ball ahead, between Bernard Jackson's legs as he, too, stood crouched as if to block. Then Grandberry faked a hand-off to flanker Don Transeth, of San Jose, California, coming around from the left side.

Oh, it was complicated! Too complicated to work, really.

As the Cougars executed the play, an Oregon tackle stepped across the line of scrimmage, put his hand on Jackson's helmet momentarily and looked for the ball. The Cougar linemen peeled off as if in kick coverage, Jackson hesitated a count, and then sneaked down the east sideline forty-six yards to score.

Sweeney got that gee-whiz play from Stanford's John Ralston.

In the Rose Bowl game on January 1, 1972, Ralston finally got to use his own play—and it worked again, enabling Stanford to come from behind late in the fourth quarter and defeat Michigan.

Jim Sweeney works up another of his great one-liners as he watches his Cougars in action. The "Smilin' Irishman" was an all-time favorite with fans and the media for his colorful quotes. (Lewis Alumni Centre)

All-America running back Bernard Jackson had a record season in 1971 with 1,189 yards rushing and 14 touchdowns. (Lewis Alumni Centre)

Sweeney had his best season in 1972, going 7-4 and chalking up wins over Kansas, 18-17; Arizona, 28-6; Idaho, 35-14; Oregon, 31-14; Oregon State, 37-7; Stanford, 27-13; and Washington, 27-10. For the first time in Cougar football history, WSU played a "home" game in Seattle—in Husky Stadium on November 4—and lost to USC 44-3, the only Cougar points coming on a record fifty-yard field goal by Joe Danelo, of Spokane.

WSU slipped to 5-6 in 1973 and wallowed in a 2-9 morass in 1974 (including a 42-7 loss to Ohio State in another game played in Husky Stadium, and a 54-7 thumping from USC in Spokane), but Sweeney maintained his effervescence and was as popular as ever.

Two opening wins on the road in 1975 had the old smilin' Irishman positively beaming. WSU beat Kansas 18-14 at Lawrence and hammered Utah 30-14 at Salt Lake City. But then the Cougars dropped seven straight, hitting bottom in a 54-14 loss to Stanford at Palo Alto.

In the Washington game, the Cougars came to play, looking like the team that had opened the season with two wins. Washington State dominated the Huskies in every department for three quarters while piling up a 27-14 lead. With 3:01 remaining and apparently driving for another score, the Cougars came up fourth and one on the Husky 14. Indecision. Timeout!

After a sideline conference, Quarterback John Hopkins huddled the Cougars and came out in running formation (no field goal, that is). But it was a pass, one of those quick, "look-in" jobs, intended for tight end Carl Barschig, of Pico Rivera, California. Barschig never got to the ball. Washington's Al Burleson stepped in front of the Cougar end, picked off Hopkins' toss and ran it back ninety-three yards for a touchdown. The conversion made it 27-21.

With only 2:47 left, WSU was alert for an onside kick, but the Huskies kicked it deep and the Cougars got the ball on their twenty. Three plays gained eight yards and then Gavin Hedrick did his job—punted the ball forty-five yards to the Huskies' Pedro Hawkins, who lost a yard on the runback attempt and was stopped at the UW twenty-two.

Warren Moon, a sophomore who had replaced the ailing Chris Rowland at quarterback for some of the first half and all of the second, was 3 for 21 passing at this point and had been roundly booed by his own fans much of the afternoon. Now he was in an obvious passing situation again.

On first down from his own twenty-two, Moon lofted a long one and, as the Seattle *Times'* Dick Rockne wrote, "it appeared his twenty-second throw was to be at best an incompletion."

Two Cougars were in good position to defend against the pass, and they swatted Moon's Moon-shot—not away, but directly into the hands of Robert "Spider" Gaines, a Husky wide receiver. Gaines scored untouched on the seventy-eight-yard play.

There's an even more ironic—or tragic—ending to this story. Steve Robbins' kick to break the tie appeared to have missed! Rowland, the holder, grabbed his head in despair. But an official signalled the kick good. The Huskies won 28-27, and Coach Don James was a winner in

Rick Simon, left, and Mark Kaufman bid on and won the broadcast rights for WSU football and basketball in 1970 when both were seniors in Radio-TV. Their timing was not good, at least for football. Jim Sweeney's team went 1-10 that year. Once during the season, Sweeney cornered Kaufman and said he'd been hearing a lot of complaints about the broadcasts. "That's OK, Coach," Kaufman shot back, "we've been hearing the same thing about your coaching." (Lewis Alumni Centre)

his first season at Washington, with a 6-5 record instead of the 5-6 he'd been staring at all afternoon.

"Sweeney went to see [President] Terrell the day after that game," Dr. Edward M. Bennett, a history professor and WSU's long-time Faculty Athletic Representative, recalled. "Jim was really low. He blamed himself for the loss, of course, and wanted to quit. Terrell talked him out of it. They sat down and talked about what could be done to help the program.

"By the time he got to the office on Monday morning, Sweeney was all charged up and ready to get started on his recruiting," Bennett said. "But whoever it was that usually opened the mail didn't show up that morning, so Sweeney opened it himself," Bennett recalled, shaking his head. "There was some real 'hate stuff.'"

After Sweeney read those letters, he just sat down and wrote out his resignation.

Jim might have tumbled out of WSU, but he landed on his feet at Fresno State. His old boss at Montana State, Gene Bourdet, had moved to the San Joaquin Valley and was in need of a football coach. Sweeney signed on, and he and the Bulldog fans have lived happily ever after.

"Shorty"

Elmer "Shorty" Sever was the groundskeeper for the WSC Athletic Department from 1928 until his retirement in 1969. And a great groundskeeper he was!

As part of his assignment, Shorty ran the work program under which athletes had to put in so many hours a month to qualify for their scholarships. Unofficially, and without tenure of course, he taught Sex Education 101 for years. His classroom was the little building behind the north stands of Martin Stadium with the sign that read:

Shorty's Shack—Built at No Expense to the State

It was really Sever's toolshed, but in addition to groundskeeping equipment it also contained a marvelous collection of pictures, pasted, glued, tacked and otherwise affixed to its interior walls, and, on occasions, served as a screening room for the movies used in Shorty's "classes."

"Tickled to meetcha" Sever would say, extending a horny (from hard work) hand of greeting. It always came as a shock to the uninitiated when he'd scratch his forefinger across their palm.

Sever was the all-time, "All-Time Groundskeeper" of the Pacific Coast Conference. The turf he built and maintained on the WSU athletic fields was admired by the great and small.

In 1955 after the WSC-UCLA game, members of the Fourth Estate gathered around UCLA Football Coach Henry R. "Red" Sanders for some post-game wisdom. Red mused, reflected on the 55-0 thrashing his Bruins had just handed the WSC Cougars, and opined: "Best turf we ever played on."

Some folks said it was the only kind thing Red could have said about that game. Shorty preferred to think of Sanders' words as a testimonial to his professional efforts. (There is no truth to the story Shorty invited Red to his class as a guest lecturer.)

The life of a groundskeeper is fraught with pain, especially when he's working in a climate where the elements are as unfriendly as they are in Washington's Palouse country and all he's got for help is "Brother" and a bunch of athletes whose main purpose in life is avoiding all sorts of work. Shorty's brother, Harry, known universally as "Brother," drove a mower at WSC for years. Nobody ever saw Harry get on that tractor or off it; he was always just riding around, wearing his bib overalls and a big straw hat. Looked a lot like that over-fed southern deputy sheriff on television.

Fertilizer was costing the Athletic Department a ton of money back in the late fifties and early sixties, so Shorty worked out a deal to get sludge from the Pullman sewage treatment plant. He found a 500-gallon tank, mounted it on an old truck and rigged up a system for spraying the stuff on the fields. "Brother" drove the truck.

One day when Harry was sludging down the field below the CUB the outlet got plugged and Shorty waved him to a stop. A rope extended from the back of the tank up to the cab and all Brother had to do was trip it and the spray mechanism would start shooting that stuff out. Shorty was back there working on the outlet valve and happened to glance up to see Brother's hand reaching for that rope.

"No! No!" he yelled, but it was too late. Brother let him have it.

"He finally got me," Shory told Athletics Business Manager Glenn Oman. "I was covered from my chest to my feet with shit."

Other than that little mishap, the system worked fine and it saved the Department of Athletics quite a bit of money.

"Only problem was we had some peculiar 'grass' on some of those fields the following spring," Oman recalled. "Looked a lot like tomato plants."

●

WSU's win over Illinois in 1969 was the Cougars' sixth straight over the Big Ten (counting the 14-14 "lost down" tie at Iowa in 1963).

●

$\mathcal{T}$he Eighth Decade, 1961-1970

University of Missouri Coach *Dan Devine* phoned *Jim Sutherland* in the summer of 1961 and said he'd like Suds' team to wear its crimson jerseys for the game with the Tigers at Columbia on September 23. "The folks here never get to see our opponents in their home colors," Devine sweet-talked Suds. It was about ninety and the humidity was the same when the Cougars in their horse-blanket crimson jerseys came out to play at Missouri. *Pat Crook*, Cougar guard from Richland, remembers the game. "I don't know how hot it was, but *[Tom] Erlandson* started hallucinating in the second half and they had to get him out. (Erlandson, of Bellingham, played center and linebacker for the Cougs.) I think I lost twenty pounds that day," Crook said. The Cougars had just finished two-a-days, so Crook probably started out at less than 195.

•

Johnny Browne, a great broken-field runner from San Bruno, California, tore up his knee in the Husky game in Seattle in 1961 and they flew him directly into Spokane for surgery the next day. On Monday, Assistant Coach Bob Gambold went up to check on Browne and the nurse said he wasn't feeling very well. "I looked at the doctor's note and thought it said 'Get him up.' I did and he fainted." When the doctor came in he explained. The note said "Give him 7-Up!" Johnny came back to play a lot for the Cougs and later had a long and successful high school coaching career in California.

•

Bobo Brayton's first Cougar baseball team was 18-12 and third in the Conference in 1962, but WSU was *numero uno* in the Knife and Fork League. On a trip to California that spring, the Cougars pulled up to a little mom and pop smorgie in Madras, Oregon, just as the proprietor hung out the "Open for Lunch" sign. Brayton's locusts swarmed into the place and within a half-hour—and before the regular lunch trade arrived—the poor guy turned the sign over: "Closed."

•

WSU scored three touchdowns and made three, two-point conversions in a 24-24 tie with Arizona State at Tempe on October 6, 1962. ASU scored three TD's, kicked three points, and made a field goal for its 24. As the game ended, *Dale "The Whale" Ford*, passed to *Hugh Campbell*, who flea-flicked it to *Clancy Williams*, who was finally knocked out of bounds on the ASU 20. "We won the tie!" exuberated Cougar sportscaster *"Frantic Frank" Herron* up in the broadcast booth at Sun Devil stadium.

•

Bob Gambold, '52, of Longview, all-around Cougar athlete and later assistant football coach, hated lefthanders. After he left *Jim Sutherland's* staff in 1961, Gambold went to Oregon State, where *Tommy Prothro* was switching his offense from the single-wing to accommodate the talents of *Terry Baker*, a lefty, and needed Gambold's "T" expertise. Baker won the Heisman Trophy in 1962, the first West Coast athlete to win the nation's premier collegiate football award. Gambold loved Baker. Still hates lefthanders.

•

Jack Friel, after retiring at WSU, was named Commissioner of the newly formed Big Sky Conference in 1963. The "Big Sky" may be the only conference named by a sportswriter. *Harry Missildine*, Sports Editor of the Spokane *Spokesman-Review*, suggested the name, from author A. B. Guthrie's novel, *The Big Sky*, which was set in Montana.

•

Remember the famous "Lost Down" game? That was the one at Iowa on September 28, 1963. After trailing the Hawkeyes 0-14 at half, WSU rallied with a touchdown pass from *Dave Mathieson* to *Dennis Kloke* in the third quarter and a twenty-three-yard run by *Clancy Williams* in the fourth to tie. Then, late in the game, backed by a thirty-mile-an-hour wind, the Cougars mounted a drive to the Iowa 24. In the noise and confusion, the Head Linesman, one *F. Gus Skibbee*, from the Big-10, got confused and turned the down marker ahead on an Iowa penalty. When WSU ran a play on third down to get in position for a *Clete Baltes* field goal (he'd already kicked two PATs, and with that wind behind him had only a flip for a winning field goal), Skibbee ruled the Cougars had run out of downs and turned the ball over to Iowa. Everyone in the press box—including the Iowa stats crew—was hollering that it was only fourth down coming up, and coach *Jim Sutherland* ran out on the field. But the referee signalled play to start and Iowa quarterback *Gary Snook* dropped back and threw downfield to halfback *Paul Krause*. Cougar sophomore Bill Gaskins made a game-saving tackle on Krause as the game ended.

•

"You were robbed!" yelled Betty Wilson, wife of Iowa Sports Information Director *Eric Wilson*, to WSU's *Stan Bates*. Stan had been sitting in Iowa Athletic Director *Forest Evashevski's* box watching the travesty. Betty was so right.

•

Cougar All-American *Chris Marker* was undefeated in the 100 and 200 freestyle in dual meets and won the Pac-8 title in both events in 1964. Marker was fourth in both and sixth in the fifty at the NCAA championships and qualified for the Olympic Trials. Other standouts for the Cougars in that 1964 season were *Bob Browning*, McMinnville, Oregon; *Paul Gibb*, and *Dave Spencer*, both of Pullman; *Bill Pascual*, Redwood City, California; and *Ed Urban*, and *John Bayless*, both of Los Altos, California.

•

What do those coaches know! QB *Dave Petersen*, Wenatchee, tells this one. "In the game against San Jose State at San Jose on October 17, 1964, Coach *[Bert] Clark* had certain plays he wanted run. *Clancy [Williams]* came back to the huddle and said, 'The quick pitch is open.' I told him it wasn't on the list Coach gave. 'Well, all I know is it's open,' Clancy shrugged. So we ran it and he went sixty-five yards and scored."

•

It was one of those seasons. *Bill Gaskins* knocked down *Mike Brundage's* two-point conversion pass at Eugene on November 7, 1964—right into the lap of *Ray Palm*, Oregon wide receiver, who had fallen and was sitting on the ground. It gave the Ducks a 21-21 tie.

•

They'll manage—somehow. *Nick August*, Spokane, and *Bob Stephens*, Seattle, a couple of ex-Cougar diamond stars, were coaching the WSU frosh for *Bobo Brayton* on April 15, 1965, against North Idaho College in Coeur d'Alene. The Coubabes were trailing 4-3 in the seventh and it was getting dark. Stephens turned to *Ken "K.O." Moos*, of Moses Lake, and told him to "Get a bat; we might need you." *Gary Johnson*, of Hoquiam, was the next scheduled hitter and had singled the last time up. All of a sudden, August, who was coaching third, looked up and K.O. is standing at the plate. Nick ran over to the dugout and hollered at Stephens, "Did you send Moos up there?" "Heck no," said the Kingfish. "Well, you better get him outta there then," says Nick, and turns around just in time to see K.O. hit the first pitch over the left field fence.

•

Washington State defeated Southern Cal 81-65 on April 24, 1965 in the first dual meet between the two schools in Pullman. It marked the first time since 1932 that USC had lost a Conference dual meet. Nationally ranked on Coach Jack Mooberry's team that spring were *Chris Westman*, distances; *Buck Kipe* in the javelin; *Bob Yard*, Trail, British Columbia, and *Bill Self*, Spokane, pole vaulters; *Bob Keppel*, Spokane, high jump; *Kent Swanson*, Centralia, triple jump; and *Bill Bleakney*, Vancouver, hurdles. *Dick Hickman*, Los Angeles, won the 100 at the AAWU meet in Pullman, becoming the first Conference sprint champ from WSU since Seattle's *Bob Gary* won both the 100 and 220 in 1955.

When Idaho beat WSU (17-13 on October 2, 1965, at Pullman), Cougar and Vandal alums had their traditional "walk" bet on—only these alums were on Kwajalein, in the Marshall Islands, and listened to the game on Armed Forces Radio. When the Vandals won, five Cougars walked the length of the island (a mile and a half). Making the losers walk were *Darrell Westover*, '58, of Portland; *Phyllis Moore*, 58, Spokane; *Betty (Nelson) Gill*, '61, St. John; *Pat Gill*, '60, Olympia, former senior football manager; and *Nancy (Giardi) Burke*, '62, Bellingham. All were employees of Global Associates and were teaching and working on Kwajalein, a U.S. missile test center.

•

Cougar pitcher *Dan Frisella* failed to make the 1966 NCAA District 8 All-Star team. Frisella was 10-0, had a 1.08 ERA and struck out 108 in ninety innings. (Almost as big an oversight as *John Olerud, Jr.*, of Bellevue, being left off the 1988 Olympic team. Olerud was 15-0, with a 2.49 earned run average and hit .464 with twenty-three home runs and eighty-one runs batted in [all school records.] A sophomore, Olerud was named to the All-America team in 1988 as a pitcher *and* first baseman.)

•

Washington State played in the first football game in Houston's new AstroDome on September 23, 1966, and it was a memorable event—for several reasons. It was the first college football game played on AstroTurf, both teams were nicknamed "Cougars" and both teams had live cougars as mascots, although the puny puma the Houston Cougars had on the sidelines that night wouldn't have made one good meal for Butch VI, WSU's brawny mascot. Early in the second half, with the score tied 7-7, Cougar punter *Jim Engstrom* lofted a fifty-two-yarder and an unidentified Cougar grounded the ball on the one-inch-line. No one in the press box saw who grounded the ball, and it soon became academic. Houston QB *Bo Burris* brought his team out, barked signals and handed the ball off to fullback *Dickie Post* diving into the middle. At least that's what 36,104 fans, everyone in the press box and WSU's defensive secondary thought—until Burris stood up and lofted a pass over the middle to flanker *Warren McVea*, who was streaking for the WSU goal line. McVea took the ball about the twenty-five and ran untouched seventy-five yards for the score. At game's end, writers covering WSU still were grousing to Houston Sports Information Director *Ted Nance* to get the name of the player who had grounded the punt. So Nance sent a runner to the WSU dressing room. The fellow stuck his head in and yelled "Hey, who grounded that punt on the goal line in the third quarter?" Without a moment's hesitation, tackle *Bob "Trigger" Trygstad* looked up and answered: "You mean the play that set up the touchdown?" Even in defeat (21-7), everyone laughed—except Coach *Bert Clark*. (For the record, it was *Dave Thomas*, WSU center from Culver City, California. It's still the longest touchdown pass-run in NCAA books. They called it the "Ivory Soap touchdown"—99 44/100 yards.

•

March 4, 1967, WSU trailed Oregon by eight points with 1:02 to play. *Mike Fels*, reserve guard from Central Valley of Spokane, tied it with two seconds left and the Cougars beat the Ducks 82-79 in overtime in Bohler gym. "We'd had a better chance [of winning] in Communist China," Oregon Coach *Steve Belko* said of the officiating.

•

Bert Clark and his entire WSU staff went to Houston to observe Coach *Bill Yeoman's* "Veer" offense in the spring of 1967. Clark then installed the Veer at WSU and put quick flanker-back *Johnny Davis*, of Wichita Falls, Texas, at quarterback in the option offense. The day after WSU lost to USC 49-0 in its 1967 opener, Spokane emcee *Dick Pratt* cracked: "Bert's Veer was more like 'near veer.'"

•

Laurie Niemi died of leukemia February 19, 1968. Laurie, who came to WSC from Clarkston, was an All-America lineman in 1948, played on the West team in the 1949 Shrine Game, was with the Washington Redskins and B.C. Lions, and coached at Montana, WSU and with the Philadelphia Eagles. Laurie was on *Jim Sweeney's* WSU staff when he died.

●

Here are some marks to think about: In the 1968 Northern Division meet at Corvallis, *Foss Miller*, Wenatchee, won the javelin at 258-2; *John van Reenen* took the discus at 198 feet; and *Gerry Lindgren* won the three-mile in 13:16.2. All three were the best by collegians at that time that year.

●

Coach *Marv Harshman* tied paddles to the hands of a couple of his players to give the rest of the team a look at what it was going to be like to play against UCLA's *Lew Alcindor*. Didn't help much. UCLA won 101-70 on February 26, 1968, in Bohler gym. But Alcindor only got twenty.

●

Sure and the Irish have a way with words. Spokane UPI Bureau Manager *Bobbie (Roberta Tucker) Ulrich*, '50, of Pullman, interviewing Cougar Football Coach *Jim Sweeney* the day after his appointment in 1968 asked what sort of offense he was going to use. "Three yards and a cloud of blood!" retorted Sweeney, and Bobbie wrote it. (Bobbie covered all the Cougar home games in the late fifties and sixties and nobody ever complained about the "woman in the press box!" or thought it was unusual. Bobbie was a real pro.)

●

Feathered friends? Don't you believe it. WSU's *Boyd Gittins*, of Bellevue, running for a spot on the U.S. Olympic team in the 400 meter hurdles in the summer of 1968, had finished third in the Pac-8 and second in the NCAA and was in the finals of the National AAU meet in Los Angeles. As he came into the last turn, a flight of pigeons swept low over the stadium. Plop. Right in the eye! Gittins, nearly blinded and minus a contact lens, staggered, stumbled, and dropped from first to fifth. After examining the evidence, meet officials gave Gittins a reprieve into a consolation race and he made the Olympic team. Alas, although he ran 49.1 (still a Cougar record) at the Olympic training camp at South Lake Tahoe, Gittins pulled a muscle at Mexico City and was unable to run in the games.

●

Ted Gerela, of Spokane, played fullback and was WSU's first soccer-style placekicker in the 1965-1966 era. Gerela developed huge calf muscles in his legs—and it paid off. He set an all-time field goal record with the B.C. Lions of the CFL, kicking thirty fielders in the 1968 season. His kicking shoe was bronzed and is in the British Columbia Sports Hall of Fame.

●

Washington State was down by sixteen points with 7:58 to play on February 22, 1969, and rallied to beat Stanford 69-68 on a twelve-foot jump shot by Rick Erickson, of Vancouver, off a Cougar fast break with forty-eight seconds left. *Blaine Ellis* was the comeback leader. He scored thirteen points in those final seven minutes.

●

During what they called the "student unrest" period at WSU in 1969, someone phoned the Athletic Department and said a bomb had been planted on Rogers Field. So, *Bruce Rutherford*, head of Buildings and Grounds (now Physical Plant) got together with WSU Groundskeeper *Elmer "Shorty" Sever* and went out to have a look. Sure enough, right in the middle of Shorty's prized turf, someone had cut out a section and then carefully replaced it. Sever very carefully removed a couple pieces of sod to reveal—a toilet seat cover. Fearing a booby-trap, a wire was looped around the lid and then a rope was tied to the wire and investigators got back twenty yards before raising it. "It gave a little, then nothing," said Rutherford. "So they crept back up with their flashlights and looked in. The toilet seat lid was up and they were looking down at an entire commode, planted upright on the fifty-yard line. There was a roll of paper inside, along with a note indicating that it was a 'gift' from some architectural engineers."

●

Just prior to the 1969 baseball season, *Bobo Brayton* and English Professor *Howard McCord* had an interesting exchange. After reading that Bobo was making his players cut their hair and shave off long sideburns and beards before the start of the baseball season, McCord wrote to the *Evergreen*: "I think Professor Brayton's requirement is a dandy idea. It's a good device for creating and reinforcing a positive image of themselves among his students. . . ." McCord said he was going to try the "pedagogical device" in another discipline, English 452 (Creative Poetry), which he taught. "I am requiring that male students allow their hair and/or beards and sideburns to grow to suitably poetic lengths . . . following the hirsute tradition of such poets as Walt Whitman, Ezra Pound, Allen Ginsberg . . . and many more," McCord declared.

●

M. A. "Doc" Northrup, '33, was inducted into the Helms Athletic Hall of Fame in 1969. Northrup, from Heisen (sometimes spelled Heisson), Washington., lettered in wrestling at WSC in 1932-1933 while completing his degree in Veterinary Medicine (with Highest Honors). Northrup was one of the all-time greats in AAU wrestling, winning national titles in 1943, 1944, and 1945, and again in 1955 (at age forty-six) for the San Francisco Olympic Club. He was still wrestling competitively at age sixty in 1969!

●

Rick Riley, who ran in the shadow of Gerry Lindgren through some of his career at WSU, won one of the most dramatic mile races in Cougar track history in the Pac-8 championships at UCLA in 1970. Riley caught Stanford's *Duncan MacDonald* in sight of the tape, than overhauled the favorite, former record holder Roscoe Divine of Oregon (and Vancouver, Washington) in the last stride to win in a record 3:59.2. It's still the WSU mile record.

●

Another memorable incident in Cougar football history was the tackle *Terry Smith*, of Richland, laid on Stanford's *Eric Cross* just as Cross was completing a twenty-five-yard TD run against the Cougars in Spokane on October 17, 1970. Why memorable? Smith came out of the student stands to apply the stopper. "Hardest hit I got all day," said Cross, after he and his teammates dismembered WSU 63-16 at Albi Stadium. (Students took up a collection and bailed Smith out of jail after the game—and had enough left over for a keg.)

●

The Cougars lost a great booster in 1970 when *C. K. "Pete" Graham* died. Pete played for Jack Friel at North Central in Spokane when they won the State title in 1928 and again at WSC in the early thirties. But hundreds of younger Cougars remember him as the guy who always met the teams when they came through the Spokane airport. Pete would be there and he'd hop on the team bus and give a cheer—if they won—or a word of encouragement after a loss. One late night after a particularly rousing Cougar victory, Graham pulled up in his car, trotted over to the team bus—just before it pulled out for Pullman he thought—jumped aboard and hollered "Way to go, gang!" Then, as he said later, "I looked around and didn't recognize a soul. It was the Idaho bus, and they'd just lost.

"I was lucky to get out of there alive."

$\mathcal{T}$he Ninth Decade, 1971-1980

Sports Go Co-ed

FROM VIRTUALLY A STANDING START—FIELD HOCKEY WAS THE ONLY SPORT BEING contested on an intercollegiate basis prior to 1970—women's athletics sprang full grown onto the sports scene at Washington State University in less than two decades between 1971 and 1988.

The change is even more dramatic in terms of dollars. In 1973, only $23,599 was spent on women's athletics at WSU. By 1979, women's sports were receiving $406,132. That's an increase of more than 1,600 percent in six years. It was only the beginning. The budget for women's athletics at WSU in 1988-1989 called for the expenditure of $1,610,300 including $413,500 for scholarships.

In 1983, women's basketball was budgeted $173,000. Five years later this had risen to $255,000. In 1988-1989 it was up to $302,000. Volleyball went from $117,000 in 1983 to $276,000 in 1989; track, $149,000 to $258,000 (which is more than the men's program received that year); and swimming, $64,000 in 1983-1984 to $135,000 in 1989.

Is WSU's situation different? What has been the experience of other schools across the country? A former university' assistant attorney general wrote:

> The progression-regression of women's athletics at WSU has
> been clearly comparable to the athletic movement nationwide.

As had been the case with men's athletics in the early years, two and three sport stars were the rule in the 1970s when intercollegiate athletics really got rolling for the women. As performances improved, competition got tougher, the demand for better athletes and better teams increased, and there were fewer multi-sport stars.

A look at the record book for women's track makes the point graphically. In 1988, the oldest record was the javelin throw of 178-3 in 1979 by Jeanne Eggart, of Walla Walla, an All-American in two sports at WSU in 1977-1982. Only five marks pre-dated 1986.

Eggart, who placed fourth in the Olympic javelin trials in 1980—and still holds a handful of basketball records, including the all-time scoring mark—was just a super athlete, far ahead of her time.

Field Hockey

Field hockey was introduced at WSC early on as an intramural sport, but the first regular coach of the sport was Carrie Brown, of Hanover, New Hampshire, who came to the Department of Physical Education for

OPPOSITE: *Karen Blair was one of WSU's best middle-distance runners in 1980, but she will remain in Cougar sports history forever because of the landmark discrimination suit that bears her name.* (Lewis Alumni Centre)

WSU's Cathie Treadgold gives teammate Sharon Hecker a high "High Five" after scoring against California in the Invitational Field Hockey Tournament at Martin Stadium in 1981. Jennifer Davis (7) shares in the celebration. (Lewis Alumni Centre)

Women in 1929 and brought her extensive playing and coaching experience. Brown coached until 1943. Dr. Mildred Wohlford, Dr. Dorothea Coleman and Dr. Madge Phillips coached into the sixties. Marilyn Mowatt took over in 1967 when the sport was starting to go "intercollegiate."

Field hockey competition in the early years was largely intramural, with intercollegiate matches limited to "Field Days" or the annual Pacific Northwest Hockey "Conference."

"WSC's group of fifteen players looked sharp in their maroon shorts and sweat shirts," Dr. Coleman wrote in a 1950 departmental newsletter, telling of the 1949 Conference at Corvallis, Oregon, where 300 women representing fourteen schools met for a field hockey tournament.

"WSC defeated the University of Washington Golds 1-0 on a well-hit shot by Bernadine Van Tine, center halfback [of Garfield]. The game with Oregon State ended in a tie, 1-1. M. J. Larimer, right wing [Snohomish], scored WSC's goal from near the edge of the striking circle. The University of Oregon's Evergreens beat WSC 5-1. Janet Harman, center forward [Walla Walla], made our goal."

At the start of the intercollegiate era, WSU won ten straight matches to close out the 1973 season and give Coach Mowatt her best record at 13-2-1. Goalies Karen Reed, Seattle, and Denise Peterson, Granger, shut out twelve opponents that season. In the fourteen-team Northwest tournament at Portland, WSU beat Marylhurst 3-0 and Oregon College of Education, Oregon and Central Washington, all by 1-0 scores. For the season, WSU scored forty-five goals to six by the opposition. Marcia Walter, Wenatchee, was the leading scorer with eighteen goals. (She had twenty-two in the 1975 season.)

WSU highlighted its 1977 season by winning the Northwest Collegiate Women's Sports Association tournament in a fourteen-team field at Burnaby, British Columbia. Kathy Smith, Tacoma, was the leading scorer. WSU was 12-7-3 on the season.

In 1978, coach Mowatt's last year as coach, WSU went 17-4-1 and goalie Marilyn Parish, of Kirkland, recorded ten shutouts. Ann Zachwieja, Port Angeles, was a good defender, and the top scorers were Smith, with twenty-seven (the single season record), and Cathie Treadgold, Kelowna, British Columbia, with twenty-four.

Another star of this era (1975-1978) was Linda Kays, of Tacoma, who also excelled in track as a middle-distance runner and in basketball. Kays scored a "hat trick" (three goals) in a 3-0 WSU win over Oregon State in 1976.

WSU went to the AIAW (Association for Intercollegiate Athletics for Women) national tournament for the first time in 1979 under Coach Sandy Moore, who came out from Exeter, New Hampshire, and took over from Mowatt after the 1978 season. WSU had a 15-8-3 record, including a 1-0 win over thirteenth ranked Oregon at Pullman.

Many of the good players at Pacific Northwest schools came from Canada where the sport had a long tradition. Treadgold, the leading player of this era, holds the single game record of four goals and the career scoring mark of 67 set in 1978-1981. She was one of seven players from Kelowna on the 1981 team. The "Kelowna Connection"—Donna McIntyre, Sharon Hecker, Helena van Staalduinen, Debbie Nicholson, Jane-Marie Davis, Dayna Geddes, and Treadgold—was no coincidence. Hank Grenda, the old Cougar quarterback (1966-1968), was Athletic Director up there.

Other good field hockey players for the Cougars in the 1970s-1980s included Beverly Kissoon, Guyana, and Margaret Frost, Mountlake Terrace.

WSU went to the AIAW Nationals three straight years beginning in 1979 and was ranked eighteenth in the nation in 1981. The Cougars took the Colorado State Invitational that year in Fort Collins. After an opening 4-1 loss to Stanford, WSU defeated CSU 3-2; Denver 1-0 in overtime; North Dakota 3-1; and Colorado 5-0.

WSU put together a nine-game win string in 1981 en route to the nationals. The Cougars earned a spot in the AIAW finals by beating California 3-2 in overtime in Berkeley.

In the Nationals, WSU lost to third-ranked Iowa 2-1 in two overtimes followed by two stroke-offs and finally a sudden-death period. Pam Monroe, of Newmarket, New Hampshire, had a school record twenty-seven saves in goal for WSU in this game.

WSU defeated Dartmouth 2-1 for the Cougars' first post-season tournament win, and then lost to Cal 1-0 in overtime for fifth place. The sixth-place finish by the WSU team was the highest ever by a women's team in a national event at the time.

Three WSU players were named to the All-Championship team: Monroe, the only goalie to make the sixteen-member squad; Grace McCarley, of Irvine, California; and Donna McIntyre. Treadgold received All-America mention, the first Cougar player to be so honored.

Just when women's athletics really began to hit its stride, field hockey was dropped (after the 1982 season). The situation was very similar to

•

Dr. Carol Gordon, Chair of the Department of Physical Education for Women at WSU, was President of the Association for Intercollegiate Athletics for Women (AIAW) in 1973. (The organization was the equivalent of the NCAA.)

•

that of boxing in the late 1950s. Schools began dropping field hockey and it became increasingly difficult to find enough regional opponents to draw up a practical schedule. In its final season, only one home hockey event was scheduled, a four-team tournament involving Stanford and two Canadian teams.

Women's Basketball

Basketball has been one of the most popular women's sports at Washington State from the time the girls caromed the ball off the low ceiling and dodged pipes playing in the dining room of Stevens Hall or shook the floors of the old Ad building, sometimes upsetting inkwells on workers' desks in offices below. It was the first "intercollegiate" sport for women, dating from February 20, 1902, when WAC defeated Cheney Normal 10-8 at Cheney.

The modern era of women's baskeball—full court as opposed to the old "zone" version—began with the 1970-1971 season under Coach Dorothea Coleman. WSU played twelve games, all but two at home, against intercollegiate opponents and won eleven, capturing the Northwest Regional title in the tournament at Pullman. WSU defeated Montana 46-27; Simon Fraser (of Burnaby, British Columbia) 40-37; and Western Washington 35-32.

"JoAnn [Washam] was our field general and playmaker," Coach Coleman said later, recalling that season. "It was her coolness that won the 1971 tournament for us. She sank two free throws with less than ten seconds left in the championship game (versus Western)."

"I called it her $10,000 putt," Coleman laughed. (Washam joined the Ladies Professional Golf Association tour after graduating from WSU in 1972 and became one of the leading money-winners in women's golf. Hence Dr. Coleman's reference to the "$10,000 putt.")

Sue Durrant, a veteran coach on the WSU Physical Education faculty, took over basketball in the 1971-1972 season and, except for a sabbatical leave during 1972-1973, coached through the 1981-1982 season.

WSU posted an 11-4 record in Durrant's first season, winning five straight games in the Northwest Regional tournament and going to the National AIAW tournament for the first time. At Normal, Illinois, the Cougars lost to Northern Illinois 50-43, despite having a 34-30 margin in field goals, and to Utah State 54-37. Durrant credited her predecessor, Coach Coleman, with setting up the 1972 season with her earlier work with the women's team.

Two of the leading players on that first AIAW team were sophomore point guard Marda McClenny, of Walla Walla, and 6-6 freshman center Jennifer Gray, of Puyallup, nicknamed "Big Bertha" by her teammates. McClenny was picked to attend the U.S. Women's Basketball Tryout Camp in 1974 as a senior, and as of 1988 still held the WSU single season record for field goal percentage at .529, set in 1971 when she was a freshman. She also is listed among the career leaders in steals, scoring average and total scoring.

Gray, dominant in rebounding and scoring in the 1972-1975 era, still leads all Cougar women in career field goal percentage (.480) and

Cougar golfers won the Northern Division title in 1973 under coach Bob Doornink. John Beutler, *Clarkston, and* Jeff Urban, *Falls Church, Virginia, tied for second in the tourney at the Clarkston Country Club. Winning team members were* Lawson Abinanti; Paul Felts, *Richland;* Bill Ratcliffe, *Yakima;* Neal Nelson; Mike Halvorson, *Seattle;* Jerry Curtis, *Wenatchee; and* Chris Repass, *Walla Walla. Beutler shot 66 in the final round to wipe out a four-stroke Oregon lead.*

Northwest Regional Basketball Champions in 1972. Back (left to right): Coach Sue Durrant, Christy Gregory, Anne Fruechte, Jennifer Gray, Judy Howe and Manager Betty Young. Front: Linda Dunston, Kay Williams, Jan Guenther, Marda McClenny, JoAnn Washam and Diane Byrnes. (Hilltopics)

rebounding average (9.6), and ranks among the leaders in four other categories. Jennifer's twenty-three rebounds against an AAU team in 1975 is still a record, as are her 294 rebounds and per game average of 14.7 in her senior season of 1975. She was nominated for the Kodak All-America basketball team that year.

Other team members on that first AIAW tourney team from WSU were Christy Gregory, Oakesdale; Ann Fruechte, Spokane; Judy Howe, Otis Orchards; Linda Dunston, Marysville; Diane Byrnes, Sultan; and Washam.

Linda Hackbarth replaced Durrant for the 1972-1973 season and WSU went 11-2, narrowly missing a berth in the Nationals on a 48-46 loss to Western Washington in the Northwest Regionals.

Ann Fruechte had an 8.7 rebounding average in 1974 and shot free throws at an .810 clip that year, both still among the best in the WSU record book.

WSU was 29-11 in 1975 and Dee Coffin, Spokane, led all scorers with 204 points. (She also was a good tennis player.) Katie Gray, Renton, played basketball and volleyball and participated in track in the 1974-1978 seasons. She played on three winning basketball teams in that era and the Cougar volleyball squads of 1976-1977 went 31-10 and 36-9. Katie was a long-jumper in track.

Laurie Turner, of Puyallup, called the "Too Tall Guard" (at 5-11), and top rebounders Janet Kusler, Snohomish, and Mary Danielson, Othello, were seniors on the 21-5 team in 1979, the high-watermark year of Durrant's ten seasons at WSU. Kusler still ranks second (as of 1988) in rebounding and blocked shots. Laurie Turner became Women's Basketball Coach at the University of Idaho.

Cougar forward Jonni Gray stretches for a rebound against the Idees in 1987 action. At right is WSU guard Penny Bowden. (Spokesman-Review photo by Linda Seeger)

The dominant player in women's basketball at WSU in these years was Jeanne Eggart, a freshman on Durrant's best team in 1979. Eggart still leads in six career statistical categories.

Holly Bertus Zapel, 6-4, of Lewistown, Montana, was an outstanding frosh player on the 1982 women's team and is still the career leader in blocked shots with 146 between 1982 and 1985.

Harold Rhodes, from Florence, Alabama, a WSU basketball star in 1976-1977, replaced Durrant as women's basketball coach in the 1983 season after serving as her assistant for five seasons. During her ten years as head coach, Durrant posted an overall record of 134-99 and was 66-47 in Conference games.

Jonni Gray, of Auburn, a two-time All-Pac-10 selection, completed her WSU career in 1989 by moving into second place in scoring behind Eggart with 1,500 points. An all-around player, Gray's 688 career rebounds put her third in this category. She set marks of 111 games played and 106 starts.

Marcia Miles, of Portland, Oregon, an All-Conference forward who played in 1983-1986, ranks with Eggart and Jennifer Gray and Jonni Gray as a dominant player of the era. Through the 1989 season, Miles was third in career scoring (1,485) and scoring average (15.0), and was WSU's most accurate free thrower, converting 78.9 percent of her tosses in a four-year career.

Cassandra Overby, of Inglewood, California, who played in 1981-1984, was the career rebounding leader with 875, and Karen Brown, of Bickleton (1979-1983) was second in games played, 108.

Penny Bowden, of Los Angeles, set a single season assist record in 1987 with 141, breaking the mark of 115 by Linda Wulff, of Bend, Oregon, in 1985, and then improved this to 166 in her senior season of 1988. Bowden also set a single game assist record of fourteen against Oregon State, breaking the record of twelve by Cheryl Mariani, of Portland, Oregon, in 1974, also against OSU.

WSU moved out of the AIAW in 1982 and into the NCAA, and in 1987 left the NorPac Conference for the Pac-10 in women's sports. The Cougars got their first Pac-10 win in women's basketball over Arizona. Lynda Clegg, of Spokane, scored the go-ahead basket and Bowden had nineteen points, eight assists and five steals in the 67-60 win.

Two of the biggest wins for Coach Rhodes' team came in 1988 when WSU defeated UCLA 53-52 and two days later upset nationally-ranked Southern Cal 77-60.

Sophomore Angie Miller, Red Bluff, California, led WSU in scoring with 499 points in the 1989 season and moved into second place behind Eggart on the single-season scoring list. Miller's 17.8 scoring average put her fourth all-time and her .841 free throw shooting percentage was a single-season record, besting the .824 by Miles in 1986.

Women's Track

The women's track program got its official start at WSU in the spring of 1974, having been a club sport since 1971. Jeanette Marsh was the first women's coach, in 1972, and guided the teams through the 1975 season.

Dot Dobie (1976-1978) and Kelli Koltyn (1979-1982) coached the women's teams until 1983 when the program took on major status and Jessica and Rob Cassleman came in from Illinois as coaches of the Track and Cross Country teams respectively.

In 1974, Katie Hale, of Wapato, a freshman, qualified for the National AIAW meet in Denton, Texas, and placed third in the pentathlon with 3,158 points. (The event, consisting of the 100 meter hurdles, shot, high jump, long jump and 200 meters, was won with 3,257.)

In 1975, Marcia Walter, Wenatchee, placed sixth in the javelin at 149-4, a school record at the time. Marsha Kinney, of Ephrata, was fifth in the AIAW pentathlon at Corvallis with 3,392 points and set a school record at 5-5 in the high jump.

Laura James, who competed for her native Trinidad in the Munich Olympics in 1972 at age sixteen, was a top sprinter at WSU in 1980, setting records in the 100 and 200 meters which still rank in the top ten, as does the 1500 mark by Lisa Woodcock, of Kent, that year.

Karen Blair, of Bellingham, set records at 400 and 800 meters and ran on several good relay teams in 1980. Her 800 mark of 2:10.2 is still in the top ten, and Wendy Tyus, of Tacoma, one of the best of the early sprinters (1977-1981), remains ranked at 100, 200 and 400 meters. Cheryl Byers, of Pullman, who competed in the sprints, 400 meter hurdles, long jump and both relays, still is ranked in those events from 1979-1982.

The WSU women's track team scored its first dual meet victory in 1981, defeating Idaho 69-58 and Montana 94-26 on the same afternoon at Jack Mooberry track. Theresa Lenardon, Vancouver, British Columbia, was fifth in the National Track and Field Association heptathlon at Corvallis that year.

Joan McGrath, of Vancouver, British Columbia, set a 10,000 meter record in 1983 that lasted until 1988 when Cary Schwartz, of Yakima, broke it early in the season and then saw Lisa Braun, of Cashmere, improve her mark to 35:21.2 in the Pac-10 meet. Braun also lowered her own school record in the 5,000, running 16:37.62.

Cheryl Livingstone, of Edmonton, Alberta, holds the 3,000 record at 9:22.69, set in 1985 when she won the "Y" award as WSU's outstanding woman athlete.

Conny Eckl, of West Germany, placed third in the NCAA heptathlon in 1985 with 5,637 points, and then improved that to 5,718 and second place in 1986. She owned the WSU record for that event, along with the 100 meter hurdles (13.86) and long jump (20-2 1/4). In the 1988 season, she set her fourth school mark, 48-9 in the shot, one-quarter of an inch better than the record by Lisa Merrill, of Pullman, in 1987.

Other fine performers include Camille Rivard, of Yakima, 1500 meter record holder at 4:08.10 (1986); Lynn Saalfeld, Kent, who owns the triple jump mark at 38-4 1/4 (1985); and Janice Farwell, Long Beach, California, whose 58.51 in the 400 meter hurdles in 1986 was still a record through 1988. Farwell also was a member of the record 400 meter relay team (with Helen Caffee, Tacoma; Amy Moore, Seattle; and Pam Qualls-Reynolds, Sacramento, California) which ran 45.78 in 1986.

Harold Rhodes, WSU head coach, during 1983 Dial Classic game. (Lewis Alumni Centre)

Too little, too late! WSU's Marcia Miles draws a pained expression from her Oregon State opponent as she flips in a basket in this 1986 action. (Lewis Alumni Centre)

Rivard was second in the 800 meters at the NCAA Indoor in 1985 and was fourth at 1500 meters in 1986 with a school record 2:44.80, bettering her own mark of 2:45.0. WSU finished tenth in the NCAA in 1986, had a 6-1 dual meet season and was runnerup in the NorPac.

The most outstanding performers for WSU nationally have been Laura Lavine, two-time NCAA outdoor champion in the discus (1987-1988), and Mary Moore, two-time NCAA Indoor winner in the high jump (1984-1985). Both are from Issaquah. Lavine, one of the great clutch throwers in WSU track history, won the Pac-10 title in 1987 at 186-2 (a Conference record) on her next to last throw, and retained her NCAA crown in 1988 by throwing 188-1 on her final effort. Her 189-7 in 1987 is the school discus record.

Moore jumped 6-0 to win the NCAA Indoor in 1984 (WSU's first National women's title), and improved that to a school record 6-3 in taking the title again in 1985.

Qualls-Reynolds and Celestine N'Drin, of the Ivory Coast, made 1986 a record-breaking year at WSU in the sprints. Reynolds set new marks in the 100 (11.61) and 200 meters (23.36) and N'Drin improved the 400 record to 54:04 and the 800 to 2:03.10. Reynolds also ran on the record-breaking 400 and 1600 meter relay teams that year and N'Drin was on the 1600 meter quartet. In 1987, N'Drin set a Pac-10 record at 2:04.61 in winning the 800 meters.

A team of Lisa Braun, Camille Rivard, Karri Jonassen (of Woodinville), Cheryl Livingstone, Linda Spaaragen (Daly City, California) and Joan McGrath was the first to represent WSU at the NCAA Cross Country Championships at Bethlehem, Pa., in 1983. At the NCAA District 8 meet in Eugene, Oregon, that year, Braun, Livingstone, Rivard, McGrath, Jonassen and Spaaragen all placed in the top twenty-five runners from a field of nine West Coast schools.

WSU finished seventh in the NCAA Cross Country championships at Milwaukee, Wisconsin, in 1985, with Spaaragen the top finisher for the Cougars. Other team members were Jonassen, Braun, Rivard, Livingstone, Zenny Koehler, of Alexandria, Virginia, and Mary Reed, Kansas City, Missouri.

The Cougar women defeated Washington for the first time May 10, 1986, at Pullman, by a score of 82 2/3 to 51 1/3 under Coach Rob Cassleman.

Rob and Jessica Cassleman came to WSU in 1983 from the University of Illinois. Jessica, a former hurdler and pentathlon athlete on the National team in her native Chile, was Head Women's Track Coach at WSU in 1983 and 1984 and then took over as Head Cross Country Coach and Rob became Head Women's Track Coach. He was an outstanding middle distance man and 400 meter hurdler at Michigan State in his undergraduate years.

Volleyball

Washington State began regular intercollegiate competition in volleyball with the 1973 season under Coach Sue Durrant. That team posted a 14-12 record and finished ninth in the Northwest Collegiate

"Oh, no you don't!" holler Cindy Baker, 6, and Deirdre Runnete, 4, as an Idaho player tries a kill. (Daily Evergreen)

Women's Sports Association, one of four volleyball leagues in which the Cougars have competed.

Durrant was followed by Judy Novine (1976); Marie Matsen (1977-1978); Kay Wilke (1979); Cindy Laughlin (1980-1981); Jim Coleman (1982-1984); Kaprice Bray (1985); Karen Lamb (1986-1988); and Cindy Fredrick (1989-).

WSU's first championship season came in 1977 under Coach Matsen. The Cougars went 36-9, won the NCWSA by dethroning three-year champion Portland State, in Portland, and played in the National AIAW tournament at Provo, Utah, finishing 1-4 with a win over Ball State. Jean Purdy, Seattle, was named to the All-Tournament team in Region Nine of the NCWSA as a middle blocker.

Mandy Kister, of Spokane, was a standout on the 1978-1979 teams and also triple-jumped for the WSU track team.

The Cougars moved into the Northwest Women's Volleyball League for two seasons beginning in 1980; competed in the Northern Pacific Athletic Conference (NorPac) in 1982-1985; and then joined Pac-10 competition in 1986 when that conference established a volleyball loop.

Single season statistical leaders for the Cougars include Kathy Jentoft, of Seattle, kills, 350 (1981), and hitting percentage, .274 (1979); Nancy Lust, Yakima, service aces, 68 (1980); Laurie Van Diest, Sumas, solo blocks, 38 (1986), and block assists, 96 (1986).

Individual match records include twenty-nine kills by Chani Phillips, of Yakima, in 1981 versus Washington; seven service aces and eight block assists by Margy Robinson, Federal Way, in 1981 versus Washington; twenty-eight digs by Sue Geppert, Tacoma, in 1985 versus Washington; and best hitting percentage, .750 by Kelly Bohart, Seattle, in 1980 versus Lethbridge, British Columbia (nine kills, zero errors, in twelve Attempts).

Jan Cunningham, of Seattle, was one of the most versatile athletes of the 1970s at WSU. Winner of the "Y" award in 1978, Cunningham played

Super mermaid Beth Platte held a flock of individual marks and was a member of record-setting relay teams in her swim career at WSU in 1985-88. (Lewis Alumni Centre)

on the 1974 volleyball team that went 29-11; captained the Alpine ski team; and participated in track.

Yvonne Velasco, of Seattle, was a standout on the 1977 team that went to the Nationals in volleyball and, as a senior in 1978, was co-captain and was voted to the All-League team.

Women's Swimming

Beth Platte, of Yakima, holds many current records and in 1988 won the YMCA award. Teri Leonard, Bellevue, went to the Nationals in diving in 1976 and 1977, and in 1988 still held WSU records in one- and three-meter diving she set in 1977. Leonard and Tami Stewart, of Kalispell, Montana, are the only WSU swimmers to hold Gibb Pool records at WSU. Stewart set hers in the 100 butterfly at 58:97 in 1981.

WSU qualified four swimmers for the Nationals at Tucson, Arizona, in 1975. Theresa Butt, Lynnwood; Sandy Ragsdale, Bothell; Glenda Kotulan, Tacoma; and Dawn Kuntz, Bothell, represented WSU in the 100 freestyle, 50 butterfly, 50 backstroke and 200 medley. Butt was voted Outstanding Swimmer that year and Ragsdale won the Inspirational Award.

Coach Wilma Harrington's 1976 team broke seven school records and posted a 5-1 dual meet mark. Record-breakers were Dawn Kuntz; Gloria Sherfey, Kennewick; Marianne Berry, Tacoma; Kathy Pflueger, Seattle; and Cindy Watson, Tacoma.

WSU placed fifth in a nineteen-team field at the Regionals in 1976. Top placers were Kuntz, individual medley and butterfly; Laurie Grantham, Kirkland, backstroke; Lynn Gourley, Vancouver, 200 and 500 freestyle; and senior diver Teri Leonard, who qualified for the Nationals at Providence, Rhode Island.

Record setters for Coach Debbie Pipher in 1979 were Caroline Greer, Boise, Idaho, 200 backstroke and individual medley; Linda Trueblood, Bellevue, 50 backstroke; and Barbie Black, Moses Lake, 100 butterfly.

Other outstanding swimmers in the 1970s included Dede Rowland Boone, Pullman, in the breaststroke and butterfly. Boone and Kathy Hitsman, Seattle; Carol Cutler, Moses Lake; and Sue McDougall, Gig Harbor, swam in the relay events and set four WSU marks in 1974. Julie Haugseth, Mercer Island, and Kathy Hermann, Edmonds, posted top times in freestyle events.

As a freshman in 1980 Tami Stewart took three Regional titles and the WSU women's swim team grabbed third place in the NCWSA championships. Stewart won the 50, 100 and 200 meter freestyle events and set a school record in the 50.

In 1981, freshman Sarah Emard, of Ketchikan, Alaska, set school records in the 50, 100, 200, 500, and 1650 freestyle, 400 meter individual medley, and was a member of five record-setting relay teams. At the end of 1988, Emard's 100 freestyle mark set in 1985 was intact, but Platte had broken all the others and was on three record-setting relay teams.

Stewart won the butterfly at the NCWSA Regionals in 1981 and Tami Hansen, of Moses Lake, qualified for the Western Zone Diving Championships. In 1982, Lisa Bertocci, Los Altos, California, qualified for the Nationals in the breaststroke and during her senior season broke four individual school records, the 50 breaststroke (31.32); 100 breaststroke (1:09.04); 100 individual medley (1:02.07); and 50 freestyle (24.88). She also was a member of five record-setting relay teams.

Twyla Porter, Spokane, held WSU records in three individual medley events in 1983, the 100, 200 and 400.

Theresa Goetz, of Seattle, a four-year letter winner in swimming, Phi Beta Kappa with a 3.96 grade point average, and a double major in political science and communications, was named to the Academic All-American first team in 1984. She also was first alternate for a $2,000 NCAA post-graduate scholarship. During her WSU career, Goetz set a record in the 200 breaststroke. She won the "Y" Award in 1984.

1984 was a top year for Coach Pipher and her WSU women swimmers. They finished second in the Pac-West Championships and set seven new school records in the process. Platte; Karen Seresun, Seattle; Ellie McIntosh, Bellevue; Emard; and Mary Ann Unger, Kirkland, all were named to the Pac-West All-Conference team. WSU placed fourth in the Nor-Pac Championships at Salinas, California, that year.

Women's Gymnastics

In 1974, Lisa McKuen, of Auburn, became the first WSU woman gymnast to qualify for the AIAW Nationals. She went in floor exercise. Diane Albright coached the team from 1966 through the 1977 season, when Al Sanders took over the reins.

Stars included Nanette Thomas, Aiea, Hawaii, in 1976; Kathy Kortier, Mercer Island, 1979; and in the 1980s Patty Warner, of Boise, a record-holder in all-around, vaulting, bars and beam. Warner was fourth at the Regionals as a sophomore in 1981 with a school record 36.00 and went to the Nationals in Salt Lake City. Kortier placed first in the Regionals in 1979 as a freshman and just missed making the Nationals.

WSU finished fourth in the NCWSA/AIAW Regional championships in 1980, best ever by a Cougar team, and Coach Sanders was named Co-Coach of the Year in the Region, in his third year at WSU. Robin Boasen, Richland, was fourth on the uneven parallel bars at the Regionals.

Kim Rogers, Corvallis, Oregon, won the all-around title and the uneven bars at the AIAW Regionals in 1982 and led WSU to the Nationals at Memphis, Tennessee. It was the first time WSU sent an entire team to the National AIAW Women's Gymnastics Meet. Coach Sanders took Joan Carbaugh, Spokane, all-around; Warner and Rogers on the bars; and Lesa Stark, Kent; Lisa Onweiler, McCall, Idaho; Linda Spears, Spokane; Linda Femling, Woodinville; and Kirsten Jensen, Oak Harbor. WSU placed eleventh at Nationals.

Coach Sanders, an All-American at George Williams College in Chicago in his undergraduate years, was named NorPac Coach of the Year in 1984.

Among other top gymnasts through the 1980s were Tammy Baker, Redwood City, California; Suzy Sawyer, Boise; Sarah Larson, Great Falls, Montana; and Kathy Bovaird, Santa Clara, California. Bovaird received the Outstanding Senior Woman Athlete Award in 1987 and also won the Pac-10 Scholar-Athlete Award the same year.

Kim Rogers looks pleased with her performance in floor exercise, an event in which she excelled at WSU. (Lewis Alumni Centre)

Celestine "Tina" N'Drin won the Pac-10 title in the 800 meters and held the WSU record in both the 400 and 800. (Lewis Alumni Centre)

The women's gymnastics program was discontinued after the 1987 season due to overall financial problems in the athletic program.

Women's Skiing

Julie Newnam, of Mercer Island, a top cross-country skier at WSU through her senior year in 1980, went on to national honors in the Biathlon, an event which combines cross-country skiing and rifle marksmanship. In her sophomore and junior years, Newnam helped WSU to ninth and tenth place finishes in the cross-country relay in the AIAW Nationals after cleaning up in the individual cross-country.

Dick Domey, of Pullman, well known Biathlon coach, suggested Julie try that event. In 1980, she was among the thirty-eight athletes selected to the U.S. Biathlon team, and in 1984 in the World Championships in France, she was twenty-sixth in the ten-kilometer competition and twenty-second in the five-kilometer. In 1985, as America's top-ranked woman Biathlon competitor, Newnam won a World Cup five-kilometer event in Italy, finished the U.S. Biathlon National Championships in second place in the 10K, and was third in the 5K event. She was named Athlete of the Year in the Biathlon in 1985 by the U.S. Olympic Committee.

Jeanette Marsh coached the WSU Women's Ski Team in 1972-1975. In 1975, Mara Haase, South Lake Tahoe, California, alpine; and Terah Reagan, Arlington, cross-country, were WSU's top skiers.

Coach Bente Kjoss-Hansen, from Northern Colorado, took over the women's ski team in 1976. WSU was third in alpine and second in cross-country at the NCWSA Regionals that year.

Alpine skiers Karin Buchstatler, Auburn, and Jean Young, Metaline Falls, and cross-country skiers Alice Goodwin, South Paris, Maine, and Julie Newnam were the top athletes on the WSU team that made it to the AIAW Nationals at Northern Michigan University, Marquette, in 1979 and finished ninth.

WSU was tenth at the 1980 AIAW Nationals in Middlebury, Vermont. Led by Nancy Korte, Ottawa, Canada, WSU won the AIAW Region 9 title at McCall, Idaho. Korte placed first in the slalom for Coach William "Bucky" Zietz's team.

WSU won the Northwest Collegiate Ski Conference title in 1982 and 1983 and qualified six athletes for the AIAW National Championships at Stowe, Vermont, in 1983, with two placing in the slalom, Lisa Edmonds, Pembroke, Ontario (in her third appearance in the Nationals), and Carole Hill, Seattle. (Hill won the giant slalom for WSU in 1984 and 1985.)

Some of the outstanding skiers of the late 1970s and early 1980s at WSU were Christine Heikkila, Sudbury, Ontario; Judi Richardson, North Bay, Ontario; Trisha Ruby, Reno, Nevada; Kelli Lee, Rossland, British Columbia; Sharon Hecker; Mary Evans, Anchorage, Alaska; Cindy Shane, Edmonds; Jane Schaller, Seattle; and the Rust twins, Amy and Libby, of Seattle.

The Rusts were versatile in sports and tops academically. Both ran cross-country as frosh, Lib was field hockey manager her sophomore and junior years, and both participated in Fish Fans. They were on the WSU ski team from 1978 to 1981 and participated in three National meets.

Women's skiing was discontinued as a team sport by the Athletic department after the 1982 season.

Tennis

Sue LaLonde, Vancouver, Washington, won the consolation bracket at the NCWSA tournament in Corvallis in 1974 after losing her opening match. LaLonde played tennis at WSU in 1973-1976, and in 1975 was ranked fifteenth nationally in women's racquetball, placing second in the World Open.

WSU went 16-3 in 1975 under Coach Linda Hackbarth. Allison Cone, Ellensburg, and Dee Coffin were 12-2 in doubles and WSU won the nine-team NCWSA Regional in Seattle. Cone and Coffin won the Regional doubles crown. Cone was WSU's No. 1 singles player in 1975 and placed third in the Region. Jo Montgomery, Spokane, was fourth in number four singles.

WSU finished second at the Regional tournament at Ashland, Oregon, in 1977 and had a 14-2 dual meet season under Coach Bente Kjoss-Hansen. The Cougars tied for second in the NCWSA tourney in Seattle and Marlaine and Elaine Dickson, Spokane twins, qualified for the National Women's Tennis Tourney at Salisbury, Maryland, by defeating teammates Rhonda Panattoni, Ellensburg, and Ann Sugars, Roseburg, Oregon.

Dr. Carol Gordon, Marsh, Hackbarth, Kjoss-Hansen, Bette Harris and Terry Coblentz served as tennis coaches from the 1960s, when intercollegiate competition began at WSU, until Rex Davis took over as Men's and Women's Coach in 1983.

Athlete of the Year for 1985 in the Biathlon was Julie Newnam, 1980 WSU graduate in Forestry Management. (Hilltopics)

Two-time NCAA Indoor Champion Mary Moore flops over the bar at Mooberry track. Moore won the NCAA Indoor in 1984 as a freshman and defended her title successfully in 1985. (Hilltopics)

Conny Eckl, one of WSU's all-time bests, finished third in the NCAA Heptathlon in 1985 as a sophomore. (Hilltopics)

Erin Young, of Lynnwood, played number one in 1981 and made the All-Region team as a freshman with a 14-7 record.

WSU posted a 20-4 record in 1984 under Coach Davis and Erin Majury, freshman from Mercer Island, finished the season unbeaten in eighteen straight matches.

YMCA Award

The YMCA Award, given annually through the Athletic Director's office at WSU, goes to the student-athlete considered most outstanding for academic achievement and contributions to the highest values of athletics. Winners have been:

> 1978—Jan Cunningham, Seattle (Volleyball, Track, Skiing)
> 1979—Yvonne Velasco, Seattle (Volleyball)
> 1980—Karen Blair, Bellingham (Track)
> 1981—Jeanne Eggart, Walla Walla (Basketball, Track)
> 1982—Cathie Treadgold, Kelowna, B.C. (Field Hockey)
> 1983—Patty Warner, Boise, Idaho (Gymnastics)
> 1984—Theresa Goetz, Seattle (Swimming)
> 1985—Cheryl Livingstone, Edmonton, Alberta (Track)
> 1986—Marcia Miles, Portland, Oregon (Basketball)
> 1987—Kathy Bovaird, Santa Clara, California (Gymnastics)
> 1988—Beth Platte, Yakima (Swimming)
> 1989—Phelicia Sperrazzo, Spokane (Volleyball)

The Throwin' Samoan

Talk about smiling through adversity.

Jack Thompson had a knee operation in pre-season before his freshman year at Washington State, a shoulder operation prior to his senior season, and four different Head Coaches in five years—and still became the most productive passer in collegiate football, made All-America, had his jersey, number "14," retired and was the third player chosen in the 1978 NFL draft.

Thompson, who was born in American Samoa, came to the U.S. at age five. He attended Seattle's Evergreen High School before entering WSU in 1974. Jack earned the very apt nickname "Throwin' Samoan" for his accomplishments passing the football for the Crimson and Gray during the 1975-1978 seasons.

Considering his unfortunate start in 1974, he tore up a knee in practice before the first game that season, and the fact that he did not become a regular until the fourth game of his sophomore season (1976), Thompson's accomplishments verge on the miraculous.

When Jack was pronounced fit for duty at the start of the 1975 season, he found himself number three on Coach Jim Sweeney's quarterback depth chart behind John Hopkins and Wally Bennett. Thompson did not play in WSU's opener, an 18-14 win at Kansas, and made a very inauspicious 0-4-1 passing debut in a 30-14 win over Utah at Salt Lake in the second game.

Thompson made only four appearances in 1975, but was quite effective, completing twenty-six of fifty passes for 351 yards and three touchdowns, two of those against UCLA in a 37-23 loss.

Jackie Sherrill, who became Thompson's second coach at WSU in the 1976 season, brought the youngster along slowly. (A credit to Jackie who lost his first three games, to Kansas, Minnesota and Wisconsin, all on the road, and certainly was looking for help. Sherrill told Sports Information Director Rod Commons he was not going to start Thompson until the Cougars played at home because he did not want to take a chance of hurting his confidence.) Thompson threw fifty-one passes in the losses to Kansas, Minnesota and Wisconsin, completing thirty-two, five for touchdowns, and had two intercepted.

Jack Thompson made his first college start at Martin Stadium on October 2 against Idaho. It was the opening chapter in the saga of the "Throwin' Samoan" at Washington State. He completed nineteen of twenty-five passes for 265 yards and led WSU to a 45-6 win, tying the school record with three touchdown passes. Thompson was the starting quarterback for the Crimson and Gray from that day until he completed his career in 1978.

The statistics say Thompson's greatest passing day at WSU was against California, at Berkeley, in the 1976 season. Jack completed twenty-eight of fifty-two for 391 yards and again matched the record for touchdown passes with three. But WSU lost 23-22 when Thompson was blind-sided going for the two-point conversion after rallying the Cougars valiantly in the waning moments.

Thompson had three other 300-yard passing games in his career, against USC in Seattle and Oregon State in Pullman in that same 1976

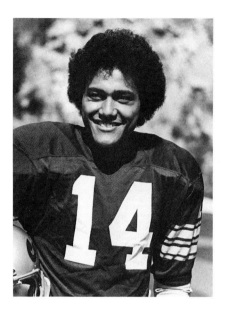

Jack Thompson, the "Throwin' Samoan." The man with the golden arm and the million-dollar smile. (Lewis Alumni Centre)

*Athletic department fund raiser
Sam Jankovich brought "Victory,"
the wrestling bear, to WSU in 1974
and promoted a "match" at the
WSU-USC basketball game in the
Coliseum. Sam, his assistant Bill
Moos, and wrestling coach Roger
James, pictured here, were billed as
Victor's opponents.*

*"Sam got in there first," said
Moos, "and, naturally, he made
Victor mad. By the time Roger and I
got to wrestle, Victor was rubbing
that leather mask in our faces and
trying to bite!"*

*Said James: "That bear had awful
breath!"* (Lewis Alumni Centre)

season, and against Michigan State at East Lansing in 1977. But the game most Cougars think of when Jack Thompson's "great days" are mentioned is the Nebraska opener in 1977. Thompson led Washington State to a monumental upset, completing eighteen of thirty passes, two for touchdowns, and did not have an interception in the 19-10 Cougar win.

He could have signed after the 1977 season because his class had graduated, but when the NCAA granted him another year (due to that injury in 1974), Thompson stayed and played out his senior season under new coach Jim Walden. He took a chance on missing out on a lot of money by doing it, but that was Jack Thompson. (The same Thompson who answered the phone one day in his apartment in Pullman and said, "Sure I'd like to come to your birthday party," when 10-year-old John McFadden called. And he went!)

Thompson finished his career in 1978 as the most prolific passer in the history of the National Collegiate Athletic Association—7,818 yards. He was only the fourth quarterback in NCAA history to pass for 2,000 yards or more in each of three seasons.

The Throwin' Samoan set Pac-10 and WSU career records for passes attempted (1,086), passes completed (601), and total plays (1,345). He tied the Conference record for touchdown passes (53) and touchdowns responsible for (63).

Washington State retired Jack Thompson's number "14" at the conclusion of the 1978 season. Only Mel Hein had been so honored in Cougar football annals, forty-eight years previously.

Thompson was elected to the WSU Athletic Hall of Fame in 1987.

Movin' On

There was lots of "movement" in the WSU Athletic department in the early seventies. Jud Heathcote, who had joined Marv Harshman in the Cougar basketball program in 1964, was announced as the new Head Coach at the University of Montana on April 1, 1971.

Jud's departure was a shock, but no surprise. Those who followed basketball knew he'd be a prize catch for some school. They always rather hoped that school would be WSU, his old alma mater. But Harshman was too young to retire, so no one blamed Jud for jumping over to Missoula.

A bigger surprise came on April 6 when it was announced out of Denver, Colorado, that Stan Bates had accepted the position of Commissioner of the Western Athletic Conference. Bates was a seventeen-year veteran of the Cougar front office, second only to the tenure of Doc Bohler (1908-1950), and tying the longevity of Earl Foster, Graduate Manager (1925-1942). Bates had turned down an earlier offer to become Commissioner of the more prestigious Pac-8.

When Ray Nagel, ex-football coach at Iowa and former UCLA star (1947-1949), was announced as Bates's replacement, there was considerable speculation on just what had happened to Harshman. That question was answered shortly when the University of Washington announced that Marv had accepted its offer to become the Huskies' Head Basketball Coach. Denny Huston, the graduate assistant who had just been named to succeed Heathcote as Marv's assistant, then moved on to Seattle with Harsh.

There was wonderment at the time, and still is, about the timing of all of these moves. Heathcote knew when he left for Montana that Bates had been offered a position, so he stipulated that if the WSU job opened he could still be a candidate. Harshman also knew Bates was leaving, but Marv hadn't thought of giving up coaching to be Athletic Director. Even so, a number of people in the Athletic and Physical Eduction departments urged him to be a candidate.

It soon became moot. When Nagel was named to succeed Bates on May 19, he brought Bob Greenwood, an assistant coach at Iowa, in as the new Cougar basketball coach.

Greenwood lasted only one season, going 11-15, and Washington State then hired George Raveling, from Maryland.

Heathcote, Harshman and Bates all were successful in their new locales.

Jud made Montana a winner in short order. He took the Big Sky title in 1975, a first for Montana, and then won the first NCAA playoff game held in WSU's Performing Arts Coliseum, beating Utah State. (The Utags must have wondered about the "neutrality" of the WSU site when they heard the reaction of the Pullman crowd to Heathcote's underdog Montana team.) Shortly thereafter, Jud moved on to Michigan State where, in 1978, he worked a bit of "Magic" (Johnson) and became the first Washington State graduate to coach a championship team in the NCAA basketball tournament.

Harshman had great success at Washington. He won the Pac-8 in 1984 and 1985 and took the Huskies to five post-season tournaments before retiring after the 1986 season.

Bates found the WAC office to be a place where he could put his considerable NCAA connections to work effectively. He helped bring the Western Athletic Conference into national prominence and was a leader in getting both the Fiesta and Holiday Bowls established. When Bates retired in 1980, he and Mildred returned to Pullman to make their home.

Early in 1972, Sam Jankovich left his position as Defensive Coordinator with the WSU football program and became Assistant to Athletic Director Nagel. Sam's forte was fund raising and he did a good job. When Nagel resigned in 1976 to take the AD job at Hawaii, Jankovich was named WSU's Athletic Director.

WSU Lets George Do It

George Raveling arrived at Washington State as Head Basketball Coach just in time to drop the curtain on old Bohler Gymnasium (in 1973) and open the university's new, 12,000-seat Performing Arts Coliseum (in 1974).*

---

* It subsequently was named the Wallis Beasley Performing Arts Coliseum, honoring the long-time WSU Executive Vice-President and Faculty Athletic Representative. In 1979, the playing floor was named Friel Court in honor of Jack Friel, basketball coach at WSU from 1928 to 1958.

Debbie Rolph, of Richland, holds the U.S. Twirling Association trophy she won while at WSU in the mid-1970s. She performed with the Cougar Marching Band. (Hilltopics)

"Thanks, Sammy!" George Raveling gives Cougar guard Sammy Miller a victory hug after WSU defeated Louisiana State 80-78 in the dedication game of the Performing Arts Coliseum in 1974. (Lewis Alumni Centre)

Raveling was the first black to be a Head Basketball Coach in the Pac-8 Conference. He had played at Villanova and came to WSU from the University of Maryland where he'd been an assistant to Charles "Lefty" Dreisell for three seasons.

Raveling had the reputation of being a top-flight recruiter. He lived up to that billing, and also proved to be an indefatigable worker—and a winning coach. George was much in demand on the rubber chicken circuit as an emcee and after-dinner speaker. He also wrote a weekly column of sports notes which was syndicated and carried by a number of newspapers around the country.

Raveling had seven winning seasons out of eleven at WSU, and took the Cougars to NCAA tournaments in 1980 and 1983 when his teams finished 22-6 and 23-7.

WSU opened its new $8.5 million coliseum on December 1, 1973, with a basketball game between the Cougars and the Bayou Bengals of Louisiana State University. LSU was coached by Dale Brown, who had been an assistant under Bob Greenwood at WSU in 1972. The Bengals were a pre-season pick by some to win the Southeast Conference that year.

The starting lineup for WSU in that first game in the Coliseum had Brad Jackson, Vancouver, and Edgar Jeffries, Youngstown, Ohio, at guards; Steve Puidokas, Chicago, center; and Sammy Miller, Norwalk, Connecticut, and Ricky Brown, St. Louis, at forwards. Jeffries led all scorers with twenty-five points and the Cougars won 70-68 in a game that was close all the way. (Louis Soriano and Dan Sherwood were the officials.)

Puidokas, a 6-11, 255-pounder who almost re-wrote the Cougar record books in the 1974-1977 seasons, and Don Collins, a muscular 6-6 forward from Toledo, Ohio, who played in 1977-1980 and became WSU's second all-time scorer, were the outstanding players of the Raveling era at WSU.

Puidokas's strong play at both ends of the court helped Raveling to his first winning season (19-7) in 1976. Steve scored 450 points and grabbed 264 rebounds that year. He followed this up with 431 points and 230 rebounds in 1977 when the Cougars went 19-8. In his four-year career, Puidokas had 1,894 points and 992 rebounds, still Cougar records. He also holds career marks for field goals (734); field goal attempts (1,499); and minutes played (3,592).

Steve Puidokas's number "55" was retired at the end of the 1977 season. He was the first Cougar basketball player to be so honored.

Collins moved into the number two scoring spot in 1980 with 1,563 career points and led the Cougars to the NCAA playoffs. WSU finished third in the Pac-10 with a 14-4 mark. The Cougars lost to Pennsylvania 62-55 in the NCAA Midwest Regionals played at Purdue.

In 1983, WSU finished second in the Conference with another 14-4 record, despite losing top scorer Guy Williams fifteen games into the schedule. The Cougars defeated Weber State 62-52 in the NCAA Far West Regional at Boise, Idaho, and then lost narrowly, 54-49, to Ralph Sampson and the Virginia Cavaliers in a great effort.

Standouts for WSU in that 1983 season included Craig Ehlo, a hustling 6-6 guard from Lubbock, Texas, who later played in the NBA; Steve Harriel, Compton, California; Aaron Haskins, Tacoma; Bryan Pollard, Detroit; Chris Winkler, McMinnville, Oregon; Ricky Brown, Dublin, Georgia; Mike Wurm, Hazelwood, Missouri; and Keith Morrison, Los Angeles.

1983 was an amazing season. The Cougars were unbeaten at home that entire year, a feat they'd accomplished only once previously, in 1917 with their 25-1 PCC championship team under Doc Bohler. The 1983 Cougars won eight of their nine home conference games by four points or less; one by one point, and four by two points.

Two home games stand out for Cougar fans in the Raveling years. On February 16, 1980, fourth-ranked (nationally) Oregon State came into Pullman and the Cougars knocked them off 69-51 in front of a record Coliseum crowd of 12,327, including about 300 standees. Collins had twenty-six points and Bryan Rison, of Mount Morris, Michigan, twenty. At the end, when OSU was battling desperately to get back in the game, the Cougars hit twelve of fourteen free throw attempts, ten of them by Rison. Terry Kelly, Spokane, had fourteen for the Cougars in that game.

In the final home game of the 1983 season, on March 7, Raveling's Cougars faced the toughest possible barrier to their goal of an unde-

Not too many people got by Oregon State's Lonnie Shelton intact, but WSU's Steve Puidokas laid this one in for two and lived to tell about it. Shelton went on to become one of the NBA's best "policeman." WSU retired Puidokas's "55" at the end of his great career in 1977. (Photo by Roy C. Woods, *Lewiston Tribune*)

Brian Pollard celebrates his tip-in that gave WSU a 70-68 win over UCLA at the buzzer in 1983. Delirious teammates—and Coach George Raveling—awarded Pollard the net AND the rim after the game. (Hilltopics)

feated home season—the UCLA Bruins. George pulled out all the stops to get the home crowd charged up for that game, including Aaron Haskins' saxophone rendition of the National Anthem. Aaron really had 'em jumpin.'

With the score tied at 68 after 39:58 of play, Cougar guard Chris Winkler jumped up a shot from deep in the right corner. The ball hit the back rim, bounced over. At exactly that moment, Bryan Pollard soared, caught the ball in one hand and rebounded it through for a 70-68 Cougar win.

In the ensuing melee, Pollard hyperventilated and fainted, and the glass backboard exploded as hundreds from the record crowd of 12,422 swarmed onto the court to get at the net.

George Raveling left WSU at the conclusion of the 1983 season to become Head Coach at the University of Iowa. He moved back into the Pac-10 in 1987 as Head Coach at Southern Cal.

Outstanding players of this era at WSU also included James Donaldson, Sacramento, California, the Cougars' first seven-footer, who later played in the NBA; Harold Rhodes, Florence, Alabama, present Coach of the Cougar women's basketball team; Stuart House, Detroit; Marty Giovacchini, Salt Lake City, Utah; Ron Davis, Phoenix, Arizona; and Tyron Brown, Raleigh, North Carolina.

Title IX Takes Hold

If Bohler gymnasium had been hit by an earthquake registering ten on the Richter Scale it could not have caused more concern to athletic department officials there than *Title IX*, when its ramifications were explained to them shortly after Congress passed the act in 1972.

Greatly simplified, and applied to athletics, *Title IX* said men's and women's programs must be supported equally in any institution receiving Federal assistance. Of course WSU, with all its Land-Grant responsibilities in research and extension, is a big recipient of Federal funds.

Women's athletics at WSU—and at virtually every college or university across the country—had operated pretty much within the Department of Physical Education for Women. Competition was almost entirely "intramural" rather than "intercollegiate." Even when the women's basketball team played a few off-campus games, in the early 1900s, the opposition was high school or "academy" teams in the area. The only truly "intercollegiate" games included one with the University of Washington, in 1903, which WAC won 4-2, and a couple against Cheney Normal, one of which WSC lost 1-0.

In those early years, largely because of the prevailing thought regarding "physical limitations," women's sports consisted mainly of "exercise" or "physical culture" activities, and the competition was kept on the campus between teams representing classes, living groups, departments or colleges. (Pharmacy had a women's basketball team at one time.)

"Play Days" were held regularly, again mostly on the campus, with an occasional event at a regional school. Even as late as the 1960s, "intercollegiate" competition for women was pretty much limited to field hockey, basketball and volleyball, and this took place at tournaments or "Field/Play Days."

Helen Smith. (Women's Athletics)

The Crimson W, an athletic award for women, was established in 1918 and was based on the accumulation of 700 "points." Points being awarded for participation in various sports.

A Physical Education major for women was initiated at WSC in 1919. Five years later almost half the P.E. majors in the college were women. Doc Bohler's faculty was composed of five men and four women, and the Women's Athletic Association (WAA) had become affiliated with the Athletic Conference of American College Women.

The "Final Emblem Award" for the outstanding woman in the WAA was established in 1921 and presented for the first time in 1922. Lois Comstock, of Alicel, Oregon, and Amy Kelso, Kiona, shared the honor, which the *Chinook* said "corresponds to the Bohler Award" for men.

There is some argument as to when Orchesis, the modern dance company, began at WSC. Some say as early as 1923, when Hazel Wright is listed in the *Chinook* as "instructor in charge of women's athletics and interpretive dancing." But it definitely was operating by 1926 because Maurine Hall, a faculty member in physical education from the University of Wisconsin, was its adviser and initiated an annual "Dance Drama."

Doc Bohler was instrumental in getting the Physical Education program split into three divisions—men's, women's and men's athletics. In 1924, Genevieve Barber, from Columbia University in New York, became the first Chairman of the Department of Physical Education for Women, holding the position until 1928 when she took leave and Helen Smith, of Oberlin College (for whom Smith Gymnasium at WSU is named) became Chairman. Dr. Smith held the post until her retirement in 1962.

When interviewed by Professor Joanne Washburn of the Department of Physical Education, Recreation and Sport in 1983 for WSU's Oral History Program, Dr. Smith described herself as "one of the low ceiling

Dorothea Coleman. (Manuscripts, Archives, and Special Collections, Washington State University Libraries)

graduates." She said she played basketball in the days when "gym ceilings were so low you had to carom shots off them to score." She said she also played "center ball," a version of basketball in which players stood in circles and could not go out. "It was dumb!" Helen said.

Dr. Smith gave a good picture of the conditions under which Women's Physical Education operated in the early days at WSC. Faculty members' "offices" were scattered over the campus, she said, her own office being in the original campus bookstore, a wooden building near where Community Hall is now.

"We moved into this small building and my office was in the display window of the old book store, with two or three showers and a. . . ." At this point interviewer Washburn interrupted in a startled voice, "The showers weren't in the display window!" and Dr. Smith broke up in laughter. "No! No!"

When Duncan Dunn Hall was built, the women were given the dining room as a gym.

"It had a low ceiling—and windows. You couldn't do anything. It was what you might call 'a very limited program'—good old dumbbells and wands and exercises and folk dancing." Helen said she felt she was back where she came in, in 1925!

> I'm sure the reason President Holland was anxious to get us out of the Ad building was because whenever we did dancing or anything that shook the floor it spilled the ink on the desks of the Agricultural Extension [office] which was on the floor below us, and even the President's desk, which was below that.

When Bohler gym was built in 1928 the women "inherited" the men's old gym. "That was a palace as far as I was concerned," she declared. "We even had a running track [around the balcony], but we couldn't use it because it jiggled."

Chairman Smith had just completed a Summer School at Columbia University in the mid-thirties and was planning a short vacation before returning to WSC. Dr. Holland telegraphed her to come back immediately because he had received funds for a women's gym.

"I was always grateful to the person who advised me to 'Get the swimming pool, because if you don't you never will. There's one in the men's gym!'"

Even when "completed," however, much of the interior of the women's gym remained bare into the early days of the Compton administration, she said, noting that the top floor activity room was "unusable." Dr. Smith praised President Compton for finally getting the women's gym finished.

"He loved wood, you know; used to be a lobbyist for the Forest industry. He got money to finish the gym and we wanted to have wood cabinets all along one side, because that was to be the dance studio, and we wanted a rail along the windows and good flooring. We got all of it!"

Holland was a great one for interrupting people on vacation or holiday, or, as mentioned previously, thought nothing of calling poor old Doc Bohler in the middle of the night to give him a massage when he couldn't sleep. Dr. Smith told a story about a "command performance" golf game she was forced into with Holland one time.

"He had his 'chauffeur' act as caddy. I think the chauffeur became the Chief of Police of Pullman many years later. [Right, Helen, Archie Campbell.] Anyhow, this boy lugged my clubs as well as President Holland's, and along came two or three women whom we all knew, and he invited them to join us, and that boy carried five people's clubs! No wonder he became Chief of Police. He deserved it."

In 1927, WSC started hiring women's coaches for a full year, the same as in men's athletics, which had made that move only two years before, and by 1929 women's athletics had acquired a new look.

"The uniforms were positively modern, and bare legs abounded," wrote Patti Guerin of the WSU Attorney General's office in 1980 in "A Very Short History of Women's Athletics."

Women's sports listed in the *Chinook* for 1929 were hiking, hockey, swimming, volleyball, softball, basketball, field and track, tennis, apparatus, dancing, posture, and rifle.

"Fish Fans," the synchronized swim group at WSC, was organized in 1929 by Lois Carrell, a physical education instructor, and has survived to this day. Dr. Agnes McQuarrie was the adviser in 1944-1962; Sue Durrant from 1962 to 1968, when the current adviser, Diane Albright, took over.

Carol Gordon. (Manuscripts, Archives, and Special Collections, Washington State University Libraries)

When women's teams did participate in off-campus events, transportation and expenses usually were taken care of by the individual participants or with monies raised by the women in their WAA or WRA (Women's Recreation Association) activities. Coaches often provided the cars and drove, sometimes buying the gas or sharing costs with their students until the days when "State" cars became available. They also officiated, kept score, acted as trainers, swept the gyms, and, when playfields needed lining or preparation, did the groundskeeping. It had to be a labor of love and dedication on the part of these faculty members; they certainly weren't getting paid for all this extracurricular activity.

Dr. Carol Gordon, Chairman of Physical Education for Women at WSU in 1962-1982, put things into perspective. "Women Coaches have gone through the same evolutionary process as the men, only more recently. We drove the cars, swept the courts. You talk about women not having the 'endurance' for athletics. Ha! On 'Sports Days' you'd drive, play Friday night, all day Saturday, sometimes 2-3 back-to-back full games, and when you weren't coaching you'd have to officiate another game, and then drive home and be ready for class and a full teaching load on Monday!"

Carol pointed out that a strong women's sports organization existed in the Pacific Northwest, including all the four-year schools in Washington, Oregon, Idaho and Montana (with a separate organization for the Jaycees), and that competitive athletics was strong on a regional basis up here before there were any comparable organizations nationally.

Dr. Dorothea Coleman was a leader in the competitive athletic program.

"She coached hockey, volleyball, basketball, tennis, the year around, and it wasn't until the younger group came in that she gave up some of these," Dr. Gordon noted.

WSU had its best ever NCAA finish in gymnastics in 1974 under Coach Bob Peavy. Dubi Lufi *was second on the parallel bars (best ever by a Cougar);* Bob Dickmeyer *was seventh in vaulting; and* Gene Johnson, *Westminster, California, fifteenth on rings. WSU finished fourth in the National AAU meet that year, with Lufi second on parallel bars and Johnson third on rings.* Jim Holt *won the National YMCA Senior Men's Rings in Seattle.*

Dr. Coleman, professor of physical education for women at WSU from 1949 until her retirement in 1975, coached just about every sport at one time or another during her long career. Now living in Arizona, "Dort" recalled the "endurance tests" teacher-coaches went through for the sake of the sport.

"I never thought of refusing to coach a sport. If somebody asked, I'd say 'Sure, I'll do it.' I suppose my age group had so much to prove—not like the young people today who'll say: 'I'll do this much and that's it!' But I don't regret that. It was another era."

Coleman drove all over the Pacific Northwest conducting officiating clinics in basketball and volleyball, "sometimes driving twelve or thirteen hours to get some place in Montana and coming home in a snowstorm," she says. Dort says field hockey was the toughest sport she officiated.

Dr. Coleman was perhaps the women's P.E. faculty member most interested in intercollegiate competition for women, and, as a member of the National Rules Committee, helped pioneer the "unlimited dribble" in women's basketball.

"The belief that women did not have the stamina or endurance to dribble the ball the full length of the court and play was one of the stupidest ideas we women ever entertained—and men supported us in this, I think."

Coleman said there was a tendency among both women and men, even those professionally trained in physical education and athletics, to cling to old beliefs about what women could and could not do.

"I'm so glad I lived to see the day when a girl who throws the ball like a boy isn't ridiculed for it!"

It has not been easy for women trying to run sports programs. All sorts of obstacles and problems, unrelated to funding, arise from time to time. Marilyn Mowatt, Associate Professor of Physical Education at WSU and long-time Field Hockey Coach, told of the time she went through all the proper channels well in advance to be sure the field in Martin Stadium would be lined and ready for an important match. As game time neared, she discovered the field had not been prepared and the crew in charge had left for the day.

Desperate because the teams were about ready to take the field, she went into the laundry room in Smith Gym, filled a bucket with detergent, located a measuring tape and lined the field herself, drawing the striking circles and sidelines with the white soap powder.

It worked perfectly, and Mowatt, who was scheduled to attend a conference in Portland, left town right after the game. It rained that night.

"There was a high school football game scheduled in there Friday night," Mowatt said, but the stadium was full of suds. "They told me it took ten guys to hose down the field and get rid of all that soap.

"But you know, I didn't hear one word about it from (Athletic Business Manager) Glenn Oman."

Nora Hall, '37, of Republic, was one of the last winners of the Final Emblem Award. She and Elizabeth Anderson, Tacoma, shared the honor in 1936. Now retired in Puyallup after a long career in education, Miss Hall said with a twinge of regret, remembering back to the days before there was much intercollegiate competition for women, "It's wonderful to see all these girls getting a chance to compete in sports. We had some great athletes at WSC in the years I was there, you know."

Title IX opened the way for equality for women in athletic programs in America's colleges and universities. A group of WSU coaches and athletes helped speed up the process.

The Cougar Crew gets in a workout on the Snake River near Wawawai, eighteen miles from the WSU campus. (Lewis Alumni Centre)

The Palouse Navy

Crew? At Washington State?

It's true. The program, officially designated as the WSU Rowing Club, was initiated by a group of thirty students in the 1970-1971 school year and workouts started on Lake Bryan (named for President Enoch A. Bryan), above Little Goose Dam on the Snake River, about eighteen miles southwest of Pullman, in the spring of 1971. Two practice shells were donated to the club by the University of Washington.

Two former UW oarsmen, WSU Assistant Vice President for Business Ken Abbey, and Bob Orr, a doctoral student in Education at WSU, served as the first coaches. In the spring of 1972, Ken Struckmeyer, a former University of Wisconsin rower who had joined the WSU faculty in Landscape Architecture, took over the coaching chores.

In 1985, the rowing course was moved upriver to the lake behind Lower Granite Dam, near Wawawai. It's one of the most spectacular crew courses in America, sitting in the Snake River canyon below the towering, layered cliffs of the prehistoric Columbia basalt flows.

Crew racing on the river was made possible following completion of Little Goose and then Lower Granite Dam by the U.S. Army Corps of Engineers in the early 1970s. Lower Granite is the most easterly of eight dams on the Columbia-Snake River system between Lewiston, Idaho, and Portland, Oregon.

The rowing program at WSU has had considerable success—and more than its share of problems. Palouse weather dealt the fledgling

club a cruel blow in late January, 1972, when winds gusting to seventy-five miles per hour up the Snake River canyon toppled the club's new shellhouse and destroyed the entire fleet of the Palouse Navy. The University of Washington again came to the rescue and "loaned" WSU three shells. Rowing club members mounted a major fund raising drive and kept the program afloat.

In 1976, the women's crew bought its first shell in Seattle and was hauling it across the state atop a truck. Just outside Pullman, a gust of wind lifted the shell off its moorings and the boat was badly damaged. After many fund raising projects, including a twenty-mile "row-a-thon" by such notables as athletic director Sam Jankovich, football coach Jim Sweeney, basketball coach George Raveling, and others, followed by another, sixty-mile row-a-thon, the shell was repaired and Kristi Norelius, of Stevenson, stroked the WSU Women to a fifth-place finish in the Open Weight Four at the Northwest Regionals.

The WSU Men's Eight finished fourth in the Pac-8 regatta in 1977; it's biggest win was over UCLA. The Women's Lightweight boat was second at the Western Invitational Championships in Redwood City, California.

Coach Struckmeyer was voted "Coach of the Year" in 1978 after WSU finished fourth in the Pac-10 regatta, and on June 2, 1979, in a borrowed shell, WSU won the Four-oared Boat with Cox at the Intercollegiate Rowing Association (IRA) regatta at Syracuse, New York. In that boat were Rich Ray, Tacoma; Doug Engle, Lacey; Chris Gulick, Bellevue; and John Holtman, LaConner; with Al Fisher, Seattle, as coxswain. Brown University loaned WSU a shell so they wouldn't have the expense of shipping one across country, and team members paid their own way to Lake Onondaga.

Savoring the win, Coach Struckmeyer said, "When we started crew at Pullman, a Seattle sportswriter said we'd need a sail and would have to have a warning light when we crossed the finish line (it would be so dark!). We've always remembered that."

In 1980, John Holtman and Rich Ray, with Kerin McKellar of Vancouver as coxswain, won the Varsity Pair with Cox at the IRA regatta, again on Lake Onondaga at Syracuse.

The WSU's Women's Crew took first place in the Lightweight Division in both the Pac-10 and Northwest regional meets in 1981.

The biggest boost for the WSU program came in 1984 when two alums won Gold Medals at the Olympic Games in Los Angeles. Kristi Norelius, '76, rowed with the winning U.S. Women's Eight and Paul Enquist, '77, teamed with Bradley Lewis of Corona del Mar, California, to win a gold in the Double Sculls.

The Blair Case

A decade has passed since fifty-three coaches and athletes in women's sports at WSU filed suit charging the university with discrimination against women in athletics, in what is commonly known as the Blair Case.

The suit was filed October 26, 1979. Eight years passed before a State Supreme Court decision finally settled it on August 6, 1987. The two years which followed have been notable not only for WSU but the state of Washington and the nation. The case has achieved landmark significance. By mid-1988 WSU had emerged as a national forerunner on the road to true sports equity for women.

The name of Karen Blair of Bellingham, a 400- and 800-meter star on the Cougar women's track team, and one of forty students among the plaintiffs, was the first listed on suit documents which were entitled simply "KAREN BLAIR, et al., Plaintiffs, vs. WASHINGTON STATE UNIVERSITY, et al., Defendants."

A sudden philosophical change in women's athletics, which had emphasized participation for all but not intense competition, plus changes in attitudes about women and sports, and national and state women's rights legislation, was marked and sudden. Meanwhile, the WSU sports program for women grew rapidly in the 1970s, program costs going from $23,599 in 1973 to $841,145 in 1981; and scholarships from zero in 1973 to $236,000 in 1982. This did not include substantial support for offices and activities funded by the men's program. However, women's demands for better intercollegiate sports opportunities found WSU at first poorly equipped to finance them.

There remained many differences between men's and women's programs, and growing dissatisfaction culminated in the suit, for which Sue Durrant, then women's basketball coach, was the moving force.

The *Daily Evergreen* in an October 30, 1979 story quoted Durrant: "Our basic thrust is to reduce the inequality of opportunity that exists now.... We hope the law suit will be a positive thing. When people hear the word litigation, they usually think of something bad, but we hope

•

The Washington Legislature at its 1989 session passed three bills to help universities achieve sex equity in their intercollegiate athletic programs. The most significant of these was Substitute House Bill 2020, in which legislators acknowledged for the first time–in the State of Washington–that it is justifiable to use state funds to support intercollegiate athletic programs. The legislature made a direct appropriation of $300,000 to WSU for 1990-1991 to help the university achieve equity in its athletic program, as mandated by the Washington State Supreme Court decision in BLAIR vs. WASHINGTON STATE UNIVERSITY in August of 1987. The legislation also will allow state institutions of higher education to waive tuition and fees for athletes up to a total of one percent of the total tuition and fee collection at the school.

•

The new look in Hollingbery Field House, after the Tartan surface was installed in 1985. (Hilltopics)

this can be something good. We hope the university will move toward the direction of equity."

The case went to trial January 6, 1982, in Colfax before Superior Court Judge Philip H. Faris. It served up vitriolic exchanges, humorous interludes and a long parade of witnesses. Among the witnesses were university officials ranging from President Glenn Terrell to Director of Development Connie Kravas; women's and men's coaches; student athletes such as Amy Cox, from Brewster, a field hockey player who was a plaintiff and one of the most active students in the case; Pamela Jacklin, former WSU Affirmative Action Director; Donna Lapiano and Christine Grant, women's athletic directors at the University of Texas and University of Iowa respectively; former WSU Basketball Coach Jack Friel; Kenneth Foreman, former Seattle Pacific College women's track and Olympic coach; and Margaret Dinkle, former *Title IX* consultant—to name a few.

Testimony continued until February 24, and on March 10 Judge Faris delivered his findings in the case orally. (He did not issue the final written judgment and decree until January 3, 1983.)

Despite the growth of the women's program, Faris found the university overall continued to treat the men's program more favorably. The discrepancies in the programs violated Washington's Equal Rights Amendment and the State Law Against Discrimination, the judge ruled.

Although women athletes were found to be receiving equitable treatment in many areas, the court concluded the program continued to receive inferior treatment in publicity and promotions, scholarships, scheduling of practice and competition facilities, locker room facilities, coaching and instruction, and administrative staff and support, and that expenditures of donated funds, gate receipts and service and activity fees were not equitable.

He found that women coaches were discriminated against in office space, shared services, and summer sports camps, for which injunctive relief was ordered. But he rejected claims for damages in a dozen areas.

The judge decreed damages be awarded student athletes who did not receive various letter awards, practice clothing and tennis uniforms, and to twelve coaches of women's teams who had not been given complimentary automobiles, such as some men's coaches were provided. The total damages—most of it $58,600 for the complimentary cars, came to $85,000 in all, $124,000 with interest. The plaintiffs had asked nearly $1,500,000 in specified damages. They had also sought $1,067,153 for alleged inadequate coaching salaries and student scholarships, which claims were denied, as were unspecified damages for emotional distress and a $7,000,000 athletic facility.

Judge Faris designed complex formulas involving funding, participation and scholarships in order to achieve equity (not a 50-50 split for women), with which the university was ordered to comply. This would mean increasing women's opportunities until the percentage of women athletes equalled that of women undergraduates.

The crucial point was that he excluded football from the calculations, ruling:

> Football is "unique" in such areas as the number of participants, scholarships, coaches, amount of equipment and facilities, income, media interest, spectator attendance and publicity generated as a whole for the university. Because of the unique function performed by football it should not be compared to any other sport at the university. Because football is operated for profit under business principles . . . football should not be included in determining whether sex equity exists. . . .

Ironically, at the time of the decree WSU was allocating more funds to women's sports than was required under Judge Faris's formula.

Faris ordered 37.5 percent of the university's financial support of the athletic program was to be allocated for women in 1982-1983, and that the support increase by two percent each academic year until reaching a level representing the same percentage as women in the total undergraduate count, then put a cap on the formula. Athletic scholarships would be considered separately, on the same percentage basis.

The judge ruled that in determining university financial support of athletics, basically composed of "state funds"—appropriations and student fees—for purposes of formula calculation, the revenue generated by a specific sport or program would not be included. This self-generated money comes from gate receipts, at home and away, guarantees, the lucrative conference revenues including the Rose Bowl and other TV shares, sales of media rights, concessions and novelty sales, work projects, and donations attributed to a sport or a program. Each sport could keep the revenue it brought in. That provision basically recognized that different sports have different costs—exhibit number one being football, with by far the biggest income, and biggest expense.

Under Faris's decision, however, the bulk of contributed funds—such as those used for football and basketball—would be dealt with separately, in order to channel an equitable share of them quickly to the

•

John Ngeno, *of Kenya, won the three- and six-mile events for WSU in the NCAA and the Cougars finished ninth in 1974. Ngeno's time of 13:22.73 for the three-mile broke the BYU stadium record. Ngeno also led WSU to the Pac-8 cross-country title in 1975, and a second place finish in the NCAA.*

•

Gymnastics coach Al Sanders was named Co-Coach of the Year in the Pac-10 for his work in his first season with the WSU Women's Gymnastics team in 1980.

women's program rather than wait for the creation of separate fund raising structures. The money was to be allocated on a per capita basis, increasing yearly, and would be counted in determining the overall level of university financial support for women's athletics.

The plaintiffs appealed and on August 6, 1987, the Washington State Supreme Court reversed Judge Faris's ruling on the exclusion of football from equity calculations but upheld his decree on self-generated revenue.

The high court said:

> To exclude football, an all-male program, from the scope of the Equal Rights Amendment would only serve to perpetuate the discriminatory policies and diminished opportunities for women. . . .
>
> It is stating the obvious to observe the Equal Rights Amendment contains no exception for football. . . . The exclusion of football would prevent sex equity from ever being achieved since men would always be guaranteed many more opportunities than women. . . ."

On the retention of self-generated revenue, however, the high court said it "provides a solution which does not violate the Equal Rights Amendment and encourages revenue development for all sports while accommodating the needs of the sports programs incurring the greatest expenses at this time."

Surplus football funds have always been used to help finance other sports and continue to be.

The high court ruled that Washington law does not require state colleges or universities to put all revenue generated by each sport into a common athletic scholarship fund. Had they found otherwise, it would have been a fatal blow. Football would have been crippled by lack of funding, and its beneficiaries in both men's and women's sports would have lost the revenue it provided.

The university set to work immediately to comply with the Faris mandates of 1983, and, until the Supreme Court ruling, had met or exceeded the standards of equity set by the judge. It had fulfilled his order that women's opportunities be increased until the percentage of women athletes equalled that of women undergraduates—approximately forty-three precent.

Excluding the ninety-five football scholarships that Division 1-A schools such as WSU are allowed, the equity percentages were fifty-seven percent for men and forty-three percent for women, with approximately forty-three percent of the undergraduate students being female. But the figures became obsolete when football entered the picture. Counting football, the figures would have gone up to sixty-eight to thirty-two percent had the seven men's and seven women's teams at WSU (the NCAA minimums for Division 1-A) been funded to NCAA scholarship limits.

So it was start over—add forty-six full women's scholarships or eliminate seventy-four current men's scholarships. But because of the NCAA minimum sports requirement (seven—which is WSU's total), WSU did not have the option of making that cut and still offering a viable program. So a multi-year approach was adopted. It was anticipated that it would put WSU in compliance with the Supreme Court ruling at the end of a four-year period. Scholarships were increased by fifteen full-time equivalents (some athletes receive fractional scholarships) for 1988-1989. An additional sport for women was to be added in 1989-1990, a second the next year and the third in 1991-1992 to complete the plan. Soccer, softball and crew were among those being considered.

Costs related to the Supreme Court decision were estimated to be $336,000 for 1989-1990 and $564,000 for the following year, a biennial increase of $900,000. The next biennium expenditures would come to $1,739,000 ($811,000 for 1991-1992 and $928,000 for 1992-1993).

It brings WSU's spending for women's sports far from the totals of the early 1980s ($855,000 in 1981-1982). Including scholarships and financial aid, funding had jumped to $1,465,000 by 1987-1988. The budget for 1988-1989 was $1,610,000. Projections for the following four years, 1988-1989 through 1992-1993, were $1,801,000; $2,029,000; $2,276,000, and $2,393,000.

Financially, it means an additional expense with little opportunity to reduce costs in other areas—this for an already underfunded athletic program whose operating budget is lowest in size among Pac-10 schools and which already has been forced to drop seven sports during the 1980s.

"It is ironic, almost unfair, that the Cougars, already in debt, must shoulder a burden other more wealthy schools do not. Because the courts say they must, the Cougars are in the process of putting women on scholarship with money they don't have," wrote Blaine Newnham of the Seattle *Times* in August 1988. He then quoted WSU Athletic Director Jim Livengood: "But we think it is right, and although it is difficult now, we may be on the road to solving the problem when most schools are just starting to face it."

Additional money had to come from some source, and while WSU officials were actively pursuing new and expanded sources of income in the areas of contributed funds, gate and concession receipts and marketing plans, they were also building a case for state funding.

As President Sam Smith pointed out, since the state ordered the change in athletic participation, the state should pay for it. "It's only logical to me, that if the state mandates new programs we should ask for help in funding those mandated programs."

The WSU Board of Regents in August, 1988, approved a 1989-1991 biennial budget request that included the $900,000 necessary to fund the first two years of the compliance program.

"There is no doubt the rules of the game have been changed and a broader, more encompassing definition of equity in intercollegiate athletics has been established," Marcia Saneholtz, Senior Associate Athletic Director at WSU, told a special 1988 panel from the state House Higher Education and Education committees studying athletic opportunities open to young women, the impacts of the court decision in the WSU case on other colleges and universities, funding, and related issues.

1980 was the first season for the new Northwest Collegiate Conference for Bowling. WSU men's and women's teams were the defending regional champs, and in 1980 they placed second in the National Holiday Tournament where eighty-three teams and 712 bowlers from twenty-five states participated. WSU's Don Knight, *of Edmonds, led men's competition, and* Kathy Davis, *Seattle, and* Yvonne Ling, *Richland, were the top women keglers.*

"From my perspective, the Blair case as it related specifically to WSU is really behind us. . . . The implications of the decision are for all state institutions, not just WSU," Saneholtz added.

> Washington universities and colleges have been asked to achieve a standard of equity in intercollegiate athletics that the rest of the country is not being asked to fulfill at this time.

"The Supreme Court decision of 1983 set a standard . . . for WSU that we have fully met. Now we must all look to the future and work together to achieve full equity in intercollegiate athletics in the state of Washington as defined by the State Supreme Court decision of August 1987," Saneholtz declared.

Justifiably, in the long, warm summer of 1988, athletic officials throughout the country were on Uneasy Street as they pondered the Blair case's implications for their schools.

Des Moines *Register* writer Tom Witosky, who visited WSU for a series on the status of college women's athletics, quoted WSU officials as saying the case is "a time bomb for college athletics." And WSU Athletic Director Livengood warned that other Division 1-A schools could face problems like WSU's.

One writer said no school in the country could comply with such guidelines as were ordered for WSU by this state's Supreme Court. And Newnham of the Seattle *Times* sounded a warning: "While the decision was just, it was not wise, and it will, in some situations, mean less for both men and women as programs fold under the mandate."

The case, in addition to attracting national press coverage, is already a legal landmark. Female athletes at Temple University, a public institution in Philadelphia, brought a discrimination suit against the school in 1988. The WSU case was cited in the proceedings. An out-of-court settlement resulted in increased scholarship and financial support for the women's programs, and addition of at least one new sport. The suit was brought under Pennsylvania's Equal Rights Amendment and the Fourteenth Amendment.

The movement could grow. More than a dozen states, in addition to Washington and Pennsylvania, have equal rights amendments to their state constitutions; two others have similar provisions in their original charters. All states have some sort of anti-discrimination laws.

It is possible that additional cases could be brought under a newly rejuvenated *Title IX.* The 1988 *Civil Rights Restoration Act* put teeth back in the measure which bars sex discrimination at schools receiving federal money.

Nicknames

Nicknames have always been a part of sports. They usually originate with teammates or coaches and often stem from physical characteristics or descriptions of players. Among the early players given nicknames were Arthur "Prexy" Bryan (President E. A. Bryan's son, who played in 1906-1908); Jerry "The Dane" Nissen; Milo "Pink" McIvor; Walter "Fat" Herreid; the Harter brothers in 1910-1913, Joe "Wide" and George

"Short" (Joe, a guard, indeed was wide, but George, one of the better centers of the era, was over six feet). And of course there was the immortal Joe "Bunch" Halm in 1905-1908. The list is long.

Glen "Turk" Edwards, the first Cougar to be tabbed All-American by the Associated Press (1930), picked up his nickname as a sophomore in 1929 while the Cougars were in Hawaii for two post-season games.

"Turk very seldom was on time," Bonnie Beaudry Edwards, '32, recalled. "They were having a team meeting and he wasn't there.

"'Where is that terrible Turk anyway?' Babe (Hollingbery) wanted to know. "Turk" had those high cheek bones, and he was swarthy," Bonnie said.

Edwards was "Turk" from then on. And what a great one he was.

"Tad" Richards was a good baseball player for the Cougars in the 1924-1926 seasons. His full name was Addison Whitaker Richards and he came up to Pullman from Claremont, California. Later, Richards became a well-known actor, on the stage and in the movies. His most memorable role was as the demented Lieutenant Crofton in the 1940 classic *Northwest Passage*, starring Spencer Tracey and Robert Young, much of which was filmed in Idaho.

"We called him 'Leapin' Tuna,'" said contemporary Bob Bucklin, remembering the old WSC first baseman. "He really got up in the air for those throws."

How did Chuck "Bobo" Brayton come by his nickname?

"I used to get so sick on those [basketball] train trips. I'd curl up on a seat and try to sleep while the other guys were playin' cards," Brayton said. "Bobby Rennick ['45, Portland, Oregon], would come by and start that old carnival chant: 'It's way past Bobo's feeding time. Bobo the dog-faced boy. He walks, he talks, he crawls on his belly like a snake!'"

In his own right, Brayton is one of the all-time Cougar best at handing out nicknames. There's some argument as to whether Bobo or Tommy Lasorda, then at Albuquerque, gave Ron Cey his "Penguin" label, but "The Buffalo" (Tom Niedenfuer) is all Bobo. Brayton hung that one on the hulking big relief ace from Redmond because of his huge shoulders and large head.

Most athletes accept their nicknames; they usually don't have a choice. Bobo tagged catcher John Sullivan "Marmot Man," back in the late sixties. Sullivan, who came from Washtucna, thought Bobo was calling him "Marmes Man" (for the 10,000-year-old remains WSU archaeologist Roald Fryxell uncovered near Washtucna in the mid-1960s).

When he learned that Bobo was saying "Marmot Man," Sullivan queried Brayton: "Hey, the dictionary says a marmot is a long-bodied, short-legged rodent."

Bobo looked at the long-waisted, stubby catcher standing in front of him and said, "Umm-huh."

Tom "The Buffalo" Niedenfuer at work in the Dodger livery in 1984. He picked up his nickname while pitching for the Cougars in 1978-80. (Los Angeles Dodgers)

The Ninth Decade, 1971-1980

WSU opened a drive for a new football stadium shortly after the old stands were destroyed by a fortuitous fire on April 4, 1970. *Orin E. "Babe" Hollingbery*, of Yakima, was named Stadium Drive Chairman. When the drive ended successfully early in 1972, helped immensely by a $250,000 gift from *Dan* and *Charlotte Martin* of Los Angeles, WSU President *Glenn Terrell* phoned Hollingbery. "He said he had some good news for me," Babe recalled. "I thought they were going to name the stadium for me. The 'good news' was that the Martins had given a quarter-million, so, naturally, they were going to name it 'Martin Stadium.'"

•

Shortly before the start of the 1971 football season, WSU Education Professor *Jerry Milligan* was back in Kansas visiting relatives and, football fan that he is, naturally dropped by to watch the Jayhawks work out. As he walked along the practice field, he saw a familiar, stocky figure ahead. "I very nearly blurted out, 'Hello, Walt,' but then I stopped. What was *Walt Cubley* [Cougar Assistant Football Coach] doing back here when the practice season had started at WSU? And what was he doing in a pair of shorts and a T-shirt, wearing a visor and carrying a big notebook with a KU sticker on it?" (What Cubley was doing, of course, was his job. Walt's title on Sweeney's staff was "Chief Scout." We tell this story now because it's harmless. The NCAA statute of limitations has run out and, heck, Kansas beat WSU 34-0 that year. Obviously Milligan was mistaken. Cubley *couldn't* have scouted Kansas.)

•

After a 31-20 win over Minnesota in Minneapolis in 1971, Coach *Jim Sweeney*, speaking to the Spokane Cougar Club, said: "When the Victory Bell [atop WSU's College Hall] rang, we ruined what was becoming a bird sanctuary." (WSU had lost eleven straight over two seasons going into the Minnesota game.)

•

On the same weekend that WSU defeated Minnesota, Idaho beat Montana (35-7). Local statisticians rushed to their records and determined it was the first time since September 25, 1965, that the two schools had won on the same weekend, and, guess what, WSU's victim that Saturday was—Minnesota! 14-13 at Minneapolis. (Idaho beat San Jose State, 17-7 at Moscow.)

•

It could only happen to a smilin' Irishman. At the end of the 1971 season *Jim Sweeney* was named Coach of the Year in NCAA District 8—with a 4-7 record! But he had four players on the Pac-8 All-Star team: halfback *Bernard Jackson*; *Steve Busch*, offensive guard; *Don Sweet*, placekicker; and *Ron Mims*, Pasadena, California, defensive back.

•

Dick Vandervoort, trainer at WSU since 1960, resigned in 1971 to become Head Trainer of the San Diego Rockets of the National Basketball Association. (By the time Vandy got to San Diego they'd moved the team to Houston, Texas.) He was Trainer and Traveling Secretary for the Rockets until his unexpected death July 4, 1987, in Maryland at age fifty-one.

•

L. H. Gregory, great old Sporting Editor of The *Oregonian*, retired in 1973 at age eighty-nine. "Greg" stories abound. He had a bulky old overcoat he always wore to games in Pullman. Called it his "Palouse Coat." One particularly cold day in that old wooden press box atop the Rogers Field stadium, Greg had some newspapers wrapped around his chest inside the overcoat. "Sports pages, no doubt?" cracked a fellow sportwriter. Greg believed in "hard money." He carried an ample supply of silver dollars at all times, and the pockets of his suit pants were double-lined to handle the extra weight. Greg always ate at the Oriental Restaurant when in Pullman, to visit with his old friend *Tommy Eng* and to enjoy his favorite dish—German-fried potatoes. When Oregon played in the Cotton Bowl at the end of the 1948 season, Greg naturally went along (on the train, he *never* flew, always drove to Pullman). At the big Cotton Bowl luncheon preceding the game, Greg was introduced as from Portland, Ory-*gone*. Not expected to speak, Greg bounced to his feet and bellowed: "It's nice to be here in Tex-*ass*!"

●

On May 18-19, 1973, when WSU met USC in the District 8 baseball playoffs on old Bailey Field, *Al Hartman* and *Dave Kuehl*, the Cougars' battery in 1913 and 1915 were on hand to start the festivities. Hartman pitched for WSC in 1913-1916 and held the record for wins (twenty-four), and complete games (thirty-one). Kuehl played five seasons between 1912 and 1919. Hartman's career record for wins fell in that 1973 season to *Joe McIntosh*, of Billings, Montana. Joe wound up with thirty-four wins, still a record.

●

That was the same year an Assistant Dean of Women was stopped at the Bailey Field gate bringing in a six-pack. "Great school. Great traditions!" said SC coach *Rod Dedeaux*, who observed the hit.

●

John Delamere, Cougar long-jumper from New Zealand, introduced his "somersault" jumping technique in 1973. Delemere jumped 25-6 3/4 doing a complete forward somersault which, he contended, put his feet farther ahead of his center of gravity on landing, and also cut down on wind resistance.

●

Only four home runs were hit out of old Bailey Field (where Jack Mooberry Track is now) in its lifetime (1950-1980.) *Grimm Mason* of Oregon State hit the first one on May 14, 1959, off WSC's *Dick Montee* in the ninth with WSC leading 10-3. Montee had relieved starter *Bob Bolingbroke* in the third with OSC leading 3-1 and shut the Beavers out for five innings until Mason launched his rocket. *Dale Ford*, great Cougar slugger of the mid-sixties, hit the second one out of Bailey on May 20, 1966, against the Huskies en route to an NCAA record seventeen. Could you name the others? They were hit on the same (windy) day, April 10, 1974. *Roy Howell*, of the Spokane Indians, hit a grand slam off the Cougars' *John Bush*, of San Gabriel, California, and on the very next pitch *Pete MacKanin* hit one out.

●

In May of 1974, USC Football Coach/Athletic Director *John McKay* expressed displeasure over WSU's announcement that it would play Ohio State in Seattle that fall, and USC in Spokane. "We draw more people in Los Angeles to watch us huddle than we'll draw in Spokane to watch us play," McKay grumbled. (The game drew 32,000; WSU-Ohio State drew 50,000 in Seattle.) On another occasion, McKay was in Pullman for a Conference meeting and was invited to be a guest at the Goodfellowship Club. When his host took him to Bill's Welding Shop owned by *Hartman Gearheiser*, one of the "Goodfellows," McKay snorted and walked out. "So it ain't the Century Plaza," admitted Gearheiser.

●

A rubberized surface was put over the dirt floor of Hollingbery Field House in 1974 at a cost of $150,433. This completed a five-year renovation project which included steam heating and mercury vapor lights, five tennis courts, a running track and areas for baseball, volleyball, badminton, field hockey and soccer.

●

When WSU's *George Yarno* faced Idaho's *John Yarno* across the line of scrimmage in 1976, was it the first "brother" confrontation since *Jerry Williams* of WSC faced brother *Billy Williams* of Idaho at Moscow on October 4, 1947? Nope, WSC's *Hal Lokovsek* and Washington's *Leo Lokovsek* met in Spokane on November 25, 1950, in Spokane.

•

The *Babe Hollingbery* Award was established by San Francisco Shriners in 1976 to honor "a former player or coach who has distinguished himself in American life." First winner was *Gerald R. Ford*, center for Michigan, who played for the East in the 1935 Shrine game. (Babe beat 'em 19-13, with help from *George "Lambie" Theodoratus* and *Frank Stojack*.)

•

Not everyone cheered—when Arizona and Arizona State were invited to make the Pac-8 the Pac-10. "Pac-8 'expansion' is profit without honor," Seattle *Times* Sports Editor *George N. Meyers* headlined his column, "The Sporting Thing," following entry of the Arizona schools on July 1, 1978.

•

"*With the Honor* that is becoming the hallmark of college athletics, Arizona and Arizona State are walking away from commitments with fellow members of the Western Athletic Conference, so they can join the Pacific-8—and make more money," the usually calm, cool, collected Meyers wrote, adding: "*Stan Bates* [WSU Athletic Director, 1954-1971], commissioner of the Western Athletic Conference, speaks of suing the defecting Wildcats and Sun Devils, and I, for one, hope he takes 'em for their last sweatsock and jockstrap."

•

Mixed emotions! *Gene Dils*, played at center for the WSC football teams of 1925-1927 and he was Dean of Men at the College in 1945-1948, but he busted a few buttons when grandson *Steve Dils* pitched Stanford to a 43-27 win over WSU in Martin Stadium in 1978. Young Dils completed thirty-two of fifty-one passes for 430 yards and five touchdowns—with no interceptions! He set a new Conference record for total offense, 438 yards, breaking that of Stanford's *Jim Plunkett* against Purdue in 1969. (WSU's *Jack Thompson* didn't have a bad day. Jack was twenty-four of thirty-four for 274 yards and two TDs, and he had only one intercepted.)

•

Debbie Rolph, of Richland, international baton-twirling champion, thrilled Cougar football crowds in the 1975-1979 era with her sparkling routines.

•

Doug Gibb retired in 1980 after thirty-eight years at WSU, thirty-two as Swimming Coach. Doug was a leader in collegiate and AAU swim circles and had served as President of the National Collegiate Swimming Coaches Association.

•

The largest crowd in Inland Empire basketball history, 12,327, watched WSU defeat nationally-ranked Oregon State 69-51 on February 16, 1980, on Friel Court. *Don Collins* led all scorers with twenty-six.

•

Two great Cougars died in 1980. *Roger James*, 48, resigned following the 1980 season after seventeen years as Wrestling Coach at WSU. On March 27 at Sheridan, Wyoming, he took his own life. That last year had been difficult for Roger. In the fall of 1979 while the two were hunting birds down on the Snake River, a gun discharged accidentally killing his son, Bret, 19. *Jim Sutherland*, WSU football coach from 1956 to 1963, died June 21, 1980, at his home at Hayden Lake, Idaho. He was sixty-five.

The Tenth Decade, 1981-1990

The Golden Willows

SAM JANKOVICH WAS SELDOM AT A LOSS FOR WORDS—OR ACTION. HIS SEVEN YEARS as Athletic Director at Washington State were, without question, the most turbulently productive in the history of the school. Sam got it done, but it usually was done his way!

Sam left his mark on the Pullman campus in the form of new facilities as no one had since Earl Foster, and the two could not have been farther apart in their management styles.

Jankovich came to WSU in 1968 from Butte, Montana, to serve on Jim Sweeney's football staff. Sam worried himself into an ulcer in four years as Sweeney's defensive coordinator (the Cougars gave up an average of twenty-five points a game in 1968-1971), and in 1972 applied to become an Assistant to Athletic Director Ray Nagel. Nagel made Sam chief fund raiser for the Athletic Department. Someone said it was a logical appointment since Sam was used to dealing in big numbers (having been responsible for Sweeney's defense). But he did the job; raised contributions to the athletic department to an all-time high.

When Nagel resigned in the summer of 1976, Jankovich was his logical successor. Anyone else might have approached the job with some trepidation. Not Sam. He jumped right in, and two coaches later (he inherited Jackie Sherrill, but hired Warren Powers), turned Powers's departure into a $55,000 bonus for an athletic program under great financial stress.

Jankovich's biggest coup however, and the thing for which he will be remembered long after the revolving football coaches incident has faded, is the project that gave WSU a vastly improved football stadium and two other new and beautiful athletic facilities—a $5 million addition to the campus—at a cost of about $2.2 million.

Early in 1978, Jankovich announced a plan whereby Martin Stadium would be expanded by some 11,000 seats (to 40,000) and a new track facility built. His idea was to remove the cinder track around the football field and lower the stadium floor eighteen feet to make room for eleven rows of seats around the oval. The track would be moved to a five-acre site near the WSU Golf Course.

The intriguing part of Jankovich's plan was that he was going to accomplish most of this construction miracle with volunteer labor and equipment—with "mirrors" some detractors (and admirers) said.

OPPOSITE: *The "block" heard round the world! The Cougars Shawn Landrum crashed through and blocked this fourth quarter punt by Husky Eric Canton, and Jay Languein, 10, recovered to set up WSU's winning 32-31 score over the Huskies at Martin Stadium in 1988.* (Chris Anderson, *Spokesman Review*)

WSU's beautiful Jack Mooberry Track opened in 1981 as part of a major athletic facilities improvement project which enlarged Martin Stadium to 40,000 seats and gave WSU a new Bailey (baseball) Field. (Lewis Alumni Centre)

When Othello contractor Earl Fegert started excavation of the stadium in January of 1979 it soon became evident that the idea of moving the dirt to the golf course site and building a track there was not going to fly. Much of the dirt was frozen solid and would not thaw quickly enough to permit it to be used as a base for a running track, especially one with a composition surface.

So, in quick order, the plan was changed: move the baseball field out by the golf course and build the track down by the Field House. Bobo and Chappie gave their blessings and the deed was done. (Brayton and Chaplin directed the designing of both the baseball stadium and the track and used their great fund raising talents to secure monies for such things as scoreboards, press boxes and other amenities. Bobo also found an "angel" for lights at the new Bailey Field.)

Along about mid-winter, when the weather and the project looked mighty bleak, someone dubbed the great excavation in the bottom of Martin Stadium "Sam's Bass Hole." (It wasn't original. Some years before when the dike protecting WSU's famous Marmes archaeological dig on the Snake River started to leak, emergency funds were sought through Senator Warren Magnuson's office to preserve the site. But the leaking continued and a lake resulted. It was called "Maggie's Bass Hole.")

Sam's project went almost like clockwork. WSU did play its first two "home" football games in Spokane in the 1979 season, but then, on October 13, for Homecoming, all was in readiness and Jim Walden and the Cougars responded by dedicating the newly enlarged Martin stadium with a resounding 17-13 win over UCLA.

"Only Sam could have pulled it off!" WSU Executive Vice President Wallis Beasley said later.

Bailey Field lights dedication, May 11, 1984. (Hilltopics)

When they decided to build the track down by the Field House instead of on the golf course site, one of the contractors* approached Sam about "gettin' those goddamn scrub trees behind the North stands out of there so we can get our trucks in and out."

Before Jankovich could find his axe, architect Mason Whitney of the WSU Facilities Planning Office whipped up an Environmental Impact Statement and put a price tag on each and every one of the trees in that little grove.

That's when Sam learned that eighteen of those "goddamn scrub trees" were "golden willows," and worth $10,000 apiece.

Chappie Begins a Dynasty

When Washington State won the Pac-10 Track and Field championship in 1983, Coach John Chaplin's team accomplished what no previous WSU track team had been able to achieve.

Then, in 1984, Chaplin's Cougars repeated as Pac-10 champion, and in 1985 they made it three straight. Only USC and UCLA had done that.

"Chappie" didn't sneak up on anyone; they heard him coming, but they couldn't stop him.

The garrulous Chaplin built quickly and well after taking over the Cougar track reins from Jack Mooberry following the 1972 season. Within ten years, Chappie had a dynasty going.

A world class sprinter at WSC (he is listed in the WSU track pressbook as setting world records in the 220- and 300-yard dashes, indoors, in 1962), Chaplin came to WSU from Pasadena (California) City College.

Cougar Track Coaches John Chaplin, right, and Rick Sloan proudly display the NCAA Indoor Championship trophy their athletes won in 1977 at the meet in Detroit. (Hilltopics)

---

*Jerry Johnson and Ray Hanson, Spokane contractors, were among those heavily involved in the success of this total project, along with Earl Fegert, Othello, the excavator.

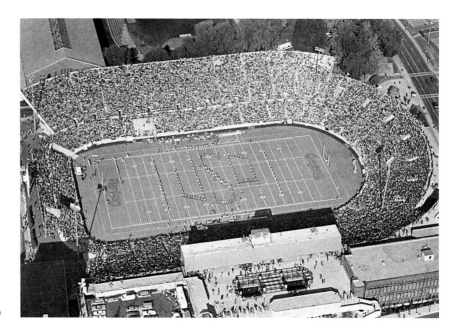

A packed house at Martin Stadium in 1984 watches the Cougar Marching Band line up for the National Anthem. (Daily Evergreen)

First in the Pac-10, first in the NCAA, WSU's Gabriel Tiacoh won a silver medal for his native Ivory Coast in the 400 meters at the 1984 Olympic Games in Los Angeles. (Hilltopics)

He was Mooberry's track Captain in 1962 and is still listed among the top ten men at 200 and 400 meters.

Chaplin coached at Wapato High School and was an assistant at Oregon State before returning to his alma mater in 1968 as Mooberry's assistant and cross-country coach. When Moob retired and Chaplin moved up to Head Coach, everyone knew his style would be different. Sportswriter Bob Payne wrote: "John Chaplin . . . is a coach considered by some the antithesis of Mooberry. . . ." But no one underestimated Chaplin's ability.

In 1971, sportswriter Tom Vogt ('70, Tacoma) noted in an article written for WSU *Hilltopics*, "By the time government grants and tuition waivers are accounted for, the Cougars can recruit five foreign athletes for every two lured over the border from Oregon and California." In the 1972 season, Mooberry had five "All-Americans" on his track team, John Van Reenen, South Africa; Peter Wright, Australia; Eilif Fredriksen, Norway; Tony Tenisci, Canada; and Chris Westman, who went to high school in Seattle but was born in France.

While not ignoring local talent, Chaplin proceeded to give the Cougar program more of an "international" look. (As of 1988, student athletes from thirty nations were represented by the banners in Chaplin's "Flag Lane" adjoining Mooberry Track at WSU.)

The results are in the track record books. Since 1974, WSU has:

* Finished in the top ten at the NCAA Championships twelve times in fifteen years and been runner-up three times.
* Won the NCAA Indoor championship (1977).
* Won the (mythical) national and dual meet title four times and finished in the top ten on seven other occasions.
* Had twenty-nine NCAA Gold Medal winners in cross-country, indoor and outdoor track; ranked in the top ten for NCAA champions.
* Had twenty-one Olympic Games entries. (Gold Medal by Julius

Korir, Kenya, steeplechase, and Silver medals by Gabriel
Tiacoh, Ivory Coast, 400 meters, 1984, and Peter Koech, steeplechase, 1988.)
* Six world record performers. (Samson Kimombwa at 10,000
meters in 1977; and Henry Rono, 3,000, 5,000, 10,000, and
3,000 steeplechase in 1978; and Peter Koech, Kenya, steeplechase, 1989.). No other U.S. university has had a student
athlete hold a world record in an Olympic distance track race.
* Won the Pac-10 Cross-Country title four times.
* Had six undefeated dual meet seasons. (Won fifty-eight straight
in 1980-1986.)

John Ngeno, of Kenya, was the first of a host of international stars at
WSU under Chaplin. Ngeno won seven NCAA gold medals (five
outdoors) at three miles, six miles, 5,000 meters, and 10,000 meters
between 1974 and 1976. He also won two NCAA Indoor three-mile
titles, and, as of 1988, was ranked among the top ten in five events in
WSU track records. His 13:08.2 indoor three-mile at Seattle in 1974 was
the second fastest ever.

WSU won its first national track team championship in 1977 at the
thirteenth annual NCAA Indoor meet in Cobo Arena, Detroit, with a
seven-man team composed of three freshmen and no seniors. This
event marked the U.S. track debut of Henry Rono, of Kenya, who the
previous fall had become the first freshman to win the NCAA cross-
country.

*Olympic Gold Medalist Julius Korir
splashes to another steeplechase win
on Mooberry track at WSU. He won
the gold for his native Kenya at the
1984 Games in Los Angeles.*
(Hilltopics)

Rono won the two-mile at the NCAA Indoor in a record 8:24.83 and
took third in the mile. Freshman Ian Campbell, of Australia, took the
triple jump at 54-3, and another frosh, Scotland's Paul Buxton, threw the
thirty-five-pound weight for only the second time and placed fourth at
65-7 3/4. Two other Kenyans, Samson Kimombwa and Joshua Kimeto,
were second in the three-mile and third in the two-mile. (On June 30,
1977, Kimombwa became Chaplin's first world record holder. He set a
new mark for 10,000 meters by running 27:31.47 in the World Games at
Helsinki, Finland.) Brian Worden, Los Angeles, tied for fourth in the
pole vault at 16-6. James Brewster, Puyallup, in the 1,000 meters, was
the seventh member of that championship team.

In an interview with *Hilltopics* Editor Pat Caraher following the team's
win at the Indoor, a disbelieving Chaplin shook his head and said, "I
honestly do not know what Rono can run between the mile and the
marathon. His best event is supposed to be the steeplechase." (Chappie
knew a great one!)

Rono had been a member of the Olympic team in Kenya in 1976, but
due to the African boycott did not compete at the games in Montreal.

In 1978, Rono had a winning string of thirty races and set four world
records in less than three months. He began with the 5,000 meters on
April 8 at Berkeley (13:08.4), and followed this with records in the 3,000-
meter steeplechase (8:05.4 at Seattle); 3,000 meters (7:32.1 at Oslo,
Norway); and wound up with the 10,000 meters (27.22.5) on June 27 at
Vienna, Austria.

Rono's romp was the greatest record onslaught in distance running
history. During his WSU career, the magnificent Kenyan ran five 10,000
races under twenty-eight minutes, a feat never before accomplished. He

Peter Koech broke Henry Rono's world record in the 3,000-meter steeplechase July 3, 1989, by running 8:05.35 at Stockholm, Sweden. The 1985 NCAA Champion, Koech won a silver medal for Kenya in the 1988 Olympics at Seoul, Korea. (Lewis Alumni Centre)

was named "Outstanding Performer in 1978" by *Track and Field News* and "Sportsman of the Year" by European sportswriters in an Associated Press poll.

"One of the greatest races I have ever seen," former Oregon Track Coach Bill Bowerman said of Rono's win over Alberto Salazar at Eugene on April 10, 1982. Rono beat Salazar, the former Oregon track star and winner of the New York City Marathon that year, by a half-stride in 27:29.90. The time was the second best by Rono and the fourth best in history for the 10,000. Salazar was clocked in 27:30.0, his best by ten full seconds. Olympic silver medalist Suleiman Nyambui, of El Paso, Texas, was third in this race.

Chaplin chalked up his first unbeaten dual meet season in 1978. The Cougars defeated Pac-10 opponents Oregon State, Arizona State, California, Oregon, and Washington in going 11-0 that year. The win over Oregon, 85-78 at Eugene, was the only sub-100-point performance by the Cougars in that dual meet season. WSU beat the Ducks in the final event, the mile relay. The Cougar mile relay team of Mike Allen, Wenatchee; Greg St. Pierre, Pullman; Darrel Seymour, New Britain, Connecticut; and Jeff Ramsey, Olympia, ran 3:16.42.

WSU captured its first ever Pac-10 (including the years in the Pacific Coast Conference, the AAWU and the Pac-8) track title in 1983, scoring 132 points to 87 for runner-up Arizona State and UCLA in the championship meet at Berkeley. Typical of the Cougar performances that weekend was that of Brent Lowery, a freshman high jumper from Bremerton. Lowery's winning jump of 7-3 was two inches higher than his previous best.

Washington State had 1-2-3 sweeps in both the 5,000 and the 3,000 steeplechase. Richard Tuwei, Peter Koech and Julius Korir took the 5,000, and Korir, Tuwei and Steve James, Tacoma, swept the steeple. Chris Whitlock, Santa Rosa, California, won the 400 meters and Tore Gustafsson, Sweden, captured the hammer throw.

At the conclusion of the 1983 season, Chaplin was named Pac-10 Coach of the Year, an honor he also was to receive following the 1984 and 1985 seasons. He enjoyed a four-year reign, 1982-1985, as NCAA District 8 Coach of the Year. During this period, WSU was ranked as the nation's number one dual meet team four times, in 1981 and 1983-1985, and placed among the top ten teams in twelve of Chaplin's first fifteen seasons as WSU Track Coach.

For the second time in less than a decade, Washington State came within a single point of the national championship at the NCAA meet in 1986 at Indianapolis. Southern Methodist University trailed WSU by nine points going into the meet's final running event, the 4 x 400-meter relay. SMU needed to win the relay to win the championship, and did it, edging the Cougars 53-52. It was the third second-place finish in the Nationals for Chaplin and the fourth by a WSU team. Twice the Cougars lost by a single point.

Chaplin had a very able assistant in these years, Rick Sloan, former UCLA great. The first Bruin high jumper to clear seven feet, and first American to exceed 8,000 points in the decathlon, Sloan came to WSU in 1973, first as Assistant Track Coach and since 1982 as Chaplin's Associate Coach.

Of the twenty-seven events in the WSU Track and Field record books, twenty-two were owned by athletes from the Chaplin era, as of 1988. The only pre-1974 records remaining were the 1:45.1 800 meters by Art Sandison, of Port Angeles, in the 1969 NCAA finals at Knoxville, Tennessee; the 3:59.2 mile by Rick Riley in the 1970 Pac-8 Championships at Los Angeles; the 2:22.00 marathon by Tom Robinson, of Spokane, at Seaside, Oregon, in 1971; and the discus throw of 208-10 by John Van Reenen, Bethlehem, South Africa, at Pullman in 1970.

School record holders at WSU in the Chaplin Era (as of 1988) were: Gary Minor, Great Falls, Montana, 100 and 200 meters (10.15 and 20.55); Gabriel Tiacoh, Ivory Coast, 400 meters (44.30); James Brewster, Puyallup, 1,000-yard run (2:08.4); Peter Koech, Kenya, 1,500 meters (3:38.12); 110 meter hurdles, Kip Ngeno, Kenya (13.49); 3,000 meter steeplechase, Henry Rono, Kenya (8:05.4); 400 meter relay, 39.54 (team of Lee Gordon, Mercer Island; Tiacoh; Dennis Livingston, Seattle; and Kris Durr, Tacoma); 1600 meter relay, 3:05.58 (team of Gordon, Livingston, Calvin Harris, Tacoma, and Tiacoh); Shot Put, Dimitrios Koutsoukis, Greece (67-6 3/4); Hammer Throw, Tore Gustafsson, Sweden (255-1); New Javelin, Jan Johansson, Sweden (257-1); Old Javelin, Laslo Babits, Canada (282-5); Long Jump, Bill Ayears, Longview (26-0 1/2); Triple Jump, Joseph Taiwo, Nigeria (56-4 3/4); High Jump, Brent Harken, Spokane (7-7); Pole Vault, Patrik Johansson, Sweden (17-5 3/4); Decathlon, Simon Shirley, Australia, (9,911).

Washington State was represented in the 1984 Olympic Games in Los Angeles by fourteen athletes who were either former or current members of the Cougar track squad. Julius Korir won the 3,000-meter steeplechase at 8:11.40 and Gabriel Tiacoh was second at 400 meters with a school record 44.54. Three others placed in the top ten in their events. Doug Nordquist, Lahabra, California, was fifth in the high jump at 7-6; Laslo Babits, Oliver, British Columbia, eighth in the javelin at 264-8; and Joseph Taiwo, of Nigeria, was ninth in the triple jump at 54-7 1/2.

In the 1988 Summer Games at Seoul, Korea, WSU's Peter Koech, '86, Kenya, ran the third fastest 3,000-meter steeplechase, 8:06.9, and won a silver medal. In 1989, Koech set a new world record in the event at 8:05.35.

The Merry-Go-Round

Jim Sweeney's departure from the Washington State football scene after the 1975 season started a merry-go-round in the Athletic Department at WSU. Before it stopped, Cougar fans were left a little dizzied by the comings and goings, and considerably distressed.

When Sweeney up and quit after the traumatic loss to the Huskies, Athletic Director Ray Nagel hired Jackie Sherrill, a top assistant at Pittsburgh, rated a bright young coach destined for big things. Then, shortly after naming Sherrill, Nagel resigned to take the AD job at the

""The greatest distance runner in track history," many have called Henry Rono, pictured here winning the steeplechase for WSU at the NCAA Championships at Champaign, Illinois, in 1977. (Lewis Alumni Centre)

Jackie Sherrill was only at WSU one year, 1976, but Cougar fans knew he was a good one. (Lewis Alumni Centre)

University of Hawaii. Assistant Athletic Director Sam Jankovich was moved up to replace Nagel.

There were rumors, even before he arrived in Pullman, that Jackie Sherrill was the heir apparent at Pitt should Head Coach Johnny Majors leave Steel City for Tennessee, his alma mater, where a coaching change was expected. Sherrill came in and did a good job in the 1976 season. His 3-8 record hardly reflects tremendous success, but Jackie beat three Pacific Northwest opponents, Idaho, Oregon, and Oregon State, and lost by a touchdown or less to Stanford and Cal. It was the USC game that thrilled Cougar fans, however, even in defeat. A strong-armed, red-shirt freshman by the name of Jack Thompson gave the Trojans a real scare on October 9 in the first college football game played in the new Kingdome in Seattle. Thompson, who Cougar fans would come to know—and cheer—as the "Throwin' Samoan," set a new WSU single game total offense mark with 356 yards, 341 of that on twenty-six pass completions in fifty attempts. USC finally prevailed, 23-14, as fullback Ricky Bell rushed fifty-one times for 346 years, but it was Thompson who caught the imagination of the fans, in what was only his second starting assignment.

At season's end, just as the rumor mill had it, Johnny Majors went home to Tennessee, Jackie Sherrill went to Pittsburgh, and Jankovich, only four months into the AD job, went looking for a new football coach for WSU.

Sam came up with Warren Powers, a former Missouri star who had played as a defensive back with the Oakland (now Los Angeles) Raiders and currently was an assistant on Tom Osborne's staff at Nebraska.

"Shrewd Sam" they called Jankovich after he turned up Powers. The Cougars had to open against Nebraska in 1977, didn't they? What could be better, said those in the know, than to bring in a guy who knew the Cornhuskers inside out. Subsequent events were to make both Jankovich and Powers look like geniuses.

"Poised, resourceful and confident, Washington State astounded the world of college football, launching the Warren Powers era with a 19-10 upset of 15th ranked Nebraska," wrote Sports Editor Harry Missildine of the *Spokesman-Review* from Lincoln on September 10, 1977.

It was one of Washington State University's greatest days in sports—at least since 1920, when another Cougar team came out of the Palouse hills and beat the widely favored Cornhuskers 21-20, also at Lincoln.

There were lots of heroes in Nebraska that day. Jack Thompson threw two touchdown passes and guided the Cougar attack flawlessly. Brian Kelly, a devilish little receiver, caught both of those scoring aerials, the second impossibly as it rolled off the shoulder pad of Nebraska defender Ted Harvey, who had covered Kelly like a blanket. Dean Pedigo, a linebacker, made seventeen tackles, and Don Schwartz, the "monster man," had eleven more. Gavin Hedrick, a punter with dynamite in his foot exploded it nine times for a 44.3-yard average. Running backs Tali Ena and Mike Washington kept the Huskers honest inside and out, hitting up the middle and catching short tosses from Thompson on flare patterns, and split end Mike Levenseller, another great receiver, complemented Kelly with four catches for forty-nine yards.

Sure-handed Brian Kelly goes airborne to haul in another pass for the Cougars. He later became the all-time Canadian Football League receiver, setting records for TDs and total yards. (Lewis Alumni Centre)

Defensive standouts also included George Yarno, who tackled Cornhusker quarterback Randy Garcia for a safety that sewed up the win, after Hayward "Spud" Harris dropped a Nebraska runner on the two the previous play. Don Hover, Terry Anderson, Ken Greene, John Troppman, and Mark Patterson also stood out on defense, and workhorses like Pat Beach, Allan Kennedy, Tom Larson, Mark Chandless, Larry Finan, and Barry Zanck up front gave the backs running room and protected Thompson nobly.

The Cougars won five more games that fall (six counting a later forfeit of the UCLA game) as the Throwin' Samoan blossomed into a full-fledged national star. Kelly and catching mates Mike Levenseller and Dan Doornink hauled in 122 of Thompson's 202 completions, and Jack wound up with more passing yards than any junior in NCAA history, 5,485.

And then, while Cougar players and fans were still celebrating their first winning season in football since 1972, they looked up and saw their leader, Warren Powers the miracle worker, disappearing into the sunrise, headed for Columbia, Missouri, to become head coach of his alma mater.

Like Sherrill the year before, Powers still had two years left on a three-year contract. There was great wailing and gnashing of teeth from the media, the alumni, and football fans in general.

Why doesn't somebody do something about these coaches who jump contracts? Why doesn't college athletics run its program like a business?

Jankovich chested the brickbats for a time, letting the critics have their say about how he should have given Powers more money, or promised him Bryan Hall—or at least signed him to an iron-clad contract, especially after watching Sherrill trot off with two years still owing.

Then, when the ruckus reached its peak, Sam dropped it on 'em. Powers owed old WSU $55,000, plus interest, for those two years on his contract, and he, Sam Jankovich, had the papers to prove it. Sam did, and Powers paid.

Jim Walden, quarterback coach under Powers, was named Head Football Coach at WSU in January of 1978. The former Wyoming QB became the fourth Cougar football coach in four years, so it was not inappropriate that the first question asked the new coach at his introductory news conference in Wilson Compton Union was: "If the Nebraska job opens up next year, would you be interested?"

Without even taking time to switch his chaw from one cheek to the other, Walden quipped: "I wouldn't take it. They had their chance and missed it." He had been an assistant coach at Nebraska when Bob Devaney was bumped up to Athletic Director and Tom Osborne got the Cornhusker job.

"I'll be at WSU long enough to see all my kids graduate from Pullman High School," Walden added. (his youngest, Murray, was ten at the time.)

"The merry-go-round is over at Washington State. I'm goin' to pull the plug on the machine."

Dan Doornink shows one of the moves that put him into the WSU Athletic Hall of Fame in 1987. Doornink, who had a fine career with the Seattle Seahawks after leaving the Cougar campus in 1977, now is pursuing a career in medicine. (Lewis Alumni Centre)

A pensive, dimpled Jim Walden observes the action in Martin Stadium while communicating with assistants in the scout box on "What next!" (Lewis Alumni Centre)

Even the scoreboard operator got into the act (Fans 2, Security 0) as delirious WSU students toppled the Husky goalpost in 1982 following the Cougars' great upset win over Washington. It was the first WSU-UW game on Rogers Field since 1954 and the Cougar win knocked the Huskies out of the Rose Bowl. (Ernie Hoover)

Walden did just that. He stayed nine seasons, the longest of any post-World War II WSU football coach, took the Cougars to a bowl game for the first time in fifty years, and beat the Huskies three times in four games, twice knocking them out of the Rose Bowl.

Jim had only three winning seasons out of nine, but, like Sweeney before him, he had a way of making people listen to his homespun Mississippi stories and expressions (with Sweeney it was Montana or the Irish) instead of looking at the scoreboard or the record book.

In spite of their overall record, the Cougars were nobody's patsies in the Walden years. Jim built a solid red-shirt program and gave WSU the closest thing to a reservoir of Pac-8 talent it had ever had. (A couple of Walden's good option quarterbacks, Steve Grant and Samoa Samoa, did not get to start until their senior seasons, 1979 and 1980, and Junior Tautalatasai, who later made the Philadelphia Eagles as a running back, found himself behind Rueben Mayes and Kerry Porter through most of 1984 and 1985.) Walden's offense, a solid mix of run and pass, was one of the most productive, year in and year out in the Pac-10, a conference famed for its offense, and earned the Cougars the respect of all their opponents.

WSU's first winning season under Walden came in 1981, when the Cougars finished their regular season 7-3-1, missing the Rose Bowl by one game, a bitter 23-10 loss to the Huskies. That was the season of the dual quarterbacks, Ricky Turner, of Compton California, and Clete Casper, of Issaquah. Walden defied coaching precedent and alternated the pair. Turner, quick and a tricky runner, was an excellent option quarterback; Casper was the better passer.

The Cougars were unbeaten through the first seven games of the 1981 season. They opened with a 33-21 win over Montana State in Spokane,

"Outta my way, Bruin!" WSU's Rueben Mayes eludes Lupe Sanchez of UCLA en route to a good gain. (Lewis Alumni Centre)

and then pulled a minor miracle to upend Colorado at Boulder. Trailing 0-10 with 2:36 remaining, WSU scored on two Buff kicking miscues and won 14-10. The winning score came when wide receiver Jeff Keller, of Baldwin Park, California, blocked a Colorado punt and safety Paul Sorensen, of Walnut Creek, California, returned it forty-three yards for a touchdown.

WSU went on to defeat Arizona State 24-21, Pacific 31-0, and Oregon State 23-0 before being tied by UCLA, 17-17. The Cougars then beat Arizona 34-19 at Tucson. The unbeaten string, the longest of the postwar years at WSU, ended with a 47-17 loss to USC in Los Angeles, but the Cougars rebounded with wins over Oregon, 39-7, and Cal, 19-0, before dropping their final game to the Huskies.

WSU's appearance in the 1981 Holiday Bowl was the first post-season game for the Cougars since they lost to Alabama in the 1931 Rose Bowl. In a wild-scoring affair in San Diego, California, on December 28, Walden's team dropped a 38-36 thriller to Brigham Young. WSU rallied from a 31-7 deficit shortly after halftime with a crunching ground attack that very nearly blew BYU away.

Stars for the Cougars in that Holiday Bowl year included Paul Sorensen, a superb defensive back, and Pat Beach, of Pullman, now a veteran tight end with the Indianapolis Colts (both Sorensen and Beach were named to All-America teams); Matt Elisara of American Samoa,

•

Sam Jankovich *resigned in mid-August of 1983 to take the Athletic Director's position at the University of Miami (Florida) and was succeeded by* Dick Young, *former Athletic Director at Oklahoma State University. Young, in turn, left in 1987 to become Athletic Director at Florida International University, in Miami.*

Jim Livengood, *who came to WSU in 1980 as an Assistant Athletic Director and subsequently moved up to AD at Southern Illinois University, Carbondale, in 1985, returned to Washington State in the fall of 1987 to replace Young. A native of Quincy, Washington, Livengood graduated from Brigham Young University in 1968 with a degree in Physical Education.*

•

tough nose guard; running back Tim Harris, of Compton, California (who set a career rushing record in 1982); Milford Hodge, of San Francisco, later with the New England Patriots, and Lee Blakeney, Concord, California, linebackers. Mike Walker, a tackle from Indianapolis, was the Bohler Award winner; Ken Collins, Cashmere, tackle, won the Laurie Niemi Award; and Jeff Keller won the Frank Butler award.

After his big season in 1981, Walden signed a four-year contract which, among other things, stipulated that all home games against the Huskies be played on campus. The outspoken coach was often critical of the lack of fan support for his teams, and he demanded the games be brought back to Pullman for the home field advantage. It paid off the very next year.

The Cougars were only 2-7-1 going into the Washington game in 1982, but rose to the occasion and defeated the Huskies 24-20 in the first game of the series played in Martin Stadium. The loss knocked Washington out of the Rose Bowl. Prior to the game in 1982 the Cougars and Huskies had played their eastside games every other year in Spokane. They had not met in Pullman since 1954, when WSC won 26-7 on then Rogers Field.

Walden had back-to-back winning seasons in 1983 and 1984, going 7-4 and 6-5 in those two years. The Cougars knocked their cross-state rivals out of the Rose Bowl again in 1983, winning 17-6 in Seattle. Only a 24-14 loss to UCLA that year kept the Cougars out of Pasadena.

Rueben Mayes of North Battleford, Saskatchewan, the greatest running back in the first century of Washington State football, put some fantastic rushing numbers in the WSU and NCAA record books in the 1984 season. In a 50-41 win at Oregon, Mayes rushed thirty-nine times for 357 yards, an NCAA record. (He gained 216 against Stanford the previous week as WSU beat the Cardinal 49-42.) Rueben had seven 100 yard-plus games in 1984, winding up with a school record 1,637 yards rushing.

Mayes continued his onslaught on the records in 1985 with 1,236 yards, the second most productive rushing season in Cougar history, and wound up with a career total 3,519, which erased the three-year-old mark of 2,830 set by Tim Harris in 1982.

Drafted by the New Orleans Saints of the NFL, Mayes became an almost unanimous choice for Rookie of the Year honors in the National Football League in 1985. Unfortunately, although practically every organization or publication picking a rookie of the year in the NFL named him, Mayes did not, officially, win the honor. The Saints had failed to nominate him!

Walden was rumored for just about every coaching position that opened up after the Cougars' Holiday Bowl season in 1981, but, true to his promise, he stayed until his son graduated from Pullman High School. At the end of the 1986 season, following two disappointing years when his Cougars finished 4-7 and 3-7-1, Walden accepted the head coaching job at Iowa State University in Ames.

Jim—and a lot of Cougar fans—shed tears over his departure. He'd not only stopped the merry-go-round of Cougar coaches, he'd stayed longer than anyone since the legendary Babe Hollingbery's seventeen seasons between 1926 and 1942, and he'd taken WSU to a bowl game, something only Hollingbery (in 1931) and Lone Star Dietz (in 1916) had done previously. He also defeated every team in the Pac-10 at least once; only Hollingbery had accomplished that, although it was the PCC in Babe's years, and did not include Arizona or Arizona State.

Typical of Walden, although his final season was a disappointment to Jim as well as to the fans, he left the Cougars with another great memory, a 34-14 win over the Southern California Trojans on October 11, Homecoming 1986. That rounded out his record of beating every team in the Pac-10 at least once while he was at WSU.

Miss Pigtails

You never had any trouble identifying Walla Walla's Jeanne Eggart— on the basketball court or throwing the javelin. Her trademark was two waist-long, auburn pigtails. Jeanne wore them to glory for four seasons between 1978-1982 at Washington State.

"Miss Pigtails" did it all at WSU, on the athletic field and in the classroom. Jeanne was an All-America choice in basketball and track and, with a 3.40 grade average, made the COSIDA (College Sports Information Directors' Association) Academic All-America. (She was on the first ever Parade All-America in 1981.)

Men's and women's athletics at WSU were merged in a new Department of Intercollegiate Athletics on July 1, 1982, with Sam Jankovich *as director.* Joanne Washburn, *who had been Director of Athletics for women, returned to her teaching position. The first integrated athletic department had* Marcia Saneholtz, Jim Livengood *and* Dick Beechner, *Associate Athletic Directors as assistants to the Athletic Director.*

"Excuse me! Pardon! Sorry, I've got to score," says WSU's Jeanne Eggart in this 1979 action in the Coliseum. (Hilltopics)

Bobby Waits set an NCAA record for stolen bases with fifty-nine during the 1971 season at WSU. It's still the Cougar record. (Lewis Alumni Centre)

The 5-8 guard was one of the most complete basketball players in WSU hoop history. She wound up as the school's all-time scoring leader, men and women, with 1,907 points in four seasons. That eclipsed 6-11, 255-pound Steve Puidokas's total of 1,894 set in the 1974-1977 seasons. In addition, Jeanne was the women's career leader in assists, steals, scoring average (18.7), field goal percentage (48.1), field goals and free throws. When she scored a school record forty points in a game against Santa Clara, she passed off for seven assists. She also was a strong rebounder and played very tough defense.

"In terms of competitiveness, on a scale of one to ten she's a twelve," said Sue Durrant, Eggart's basketball coach.

A finalist for a spot on the U.S. Olympic team in the javelin in 1980, Jeanne placed fourth. Her career best throw was 178-3.

In 1988, the first year she was eligible for the honor, Jeanne Eggart was elected to the WSU Athletic Hall of Fame.

Bobo Passes the Buck

Washington State finished first in all but three of the nineteen Northern Division baseball races between 1970 and 1988. That gives you an idea of just how Coach Chuck Brayton's Cougars dominated the Pacific Northwest collegiate baseball scene for those two decades.

In twenty-seven seasons after he took over from Buck Bailey in 1962, Bobo won or shared nineteen Division pennants.* It took him only nineteen years to pass Buck's thirty-two-year record of 603 wins. Bobo won his 604th game on March 27, 1980, with a 13-1 pasting of Eastern Washington University, and in 1988 passed the 900-win mark, beating Clemson University 6-5 in the Best in the West Classic at Fresno, California, on March 16.

Brayton would want it known that his teams have played many more games than did Buck's, but Bobo's winning percentage is over .700 and that's fantastic in the competition he keeps. Clemson, for example, was ranked in the top ten nationally when WSU beat the Tigers.

That's the good news. The bad news is that Pac-10 teams have won fourteen College World Series titles in those twenty-seven years and the league has had a team in the CWS every year. In one stretch during the 1970s, for example, when WSU had won the Northern Division five years in a row (1970-1975), the Cougars met USC each year in the play-offs and each time the Trojans won and went on to win the College World Series.

Bobo has had his share of bad bounces, too. The 1966 play-offs at USC, for example. (See Bobo Goes to Omaha.) In 1971, when the play-offs were scheduled in the north, the Cougars lost Barry Sbragia with a knee injury. The San Mateo, California, right-hander was figured to be

---

* WSU has played in the Northern Division and the Pac-8 in Brayton's years and now (as of 1989) is in a baseball loop with Oregon State, Washington, Portland, Portland State, Gonzaga and Eastern known as the Pac-10 Northern Division. It's a misnomer, since only three of its teams are in the Pac-10, but it's a good baseball league. The University of Idaho dropped its baseball program in 1980 because of budget problems, and Oregon followed in 1981. Same reason.

WSU's number one pitcher. (He came back in 1972 with a 5-2 record and a 1.40 ERA and WSU again won its Division.)

Even without Sbragia in 1971, the Cougars battled past Stanford and Oregon in the play-offs at Pullman, and beat USC 10-5 in a game which featured back-to-back home runs by 5-9, 142-pound Bobby Waits, the WSU second baseman*. Waits, from Fresno, set an NCAA base-stealing record with fifty-nine thefts and was named to the All-America first team. USC prevailed 6-3 in the final game of the 1971 play-offs and went on to Omaha and won its seventh World Series title.

In 1973, when WSU again won its Division, right-hander Joe McIntosh, of Billings, Montana, set new season records for games started (16); wins (13); and innings pitched (120-2), and career marks (modern) for complete games (24); wins (34); and strikeouts (251). McIntosh, who came to WSU from old Cougar Eddie Bayne's Billings Legion program as a shortstop, was a three-year first team Academic All-American—in a pre-med program. Joe pitched for the San Diego Padres in the National League before a shoulder injury ended his career. (He then switched career goals, attended law school and became a successful tax attorney.)

In 1976, WSU took its seventh straight Division title, with a 16-2 record, and won the Western Regional at Pullman against Pepperdine, Cal State-Fullerton and Northern Colorado for a berth in the College World Series at Omaha. Right-hander Bob Sherwood, of Pocatello, Idaho, beat defending College World Series champ Fullerton State twice in that series and won MVP honors. Sophomore first baseman Phil Westendorf, of Tacoma, had four RBI in the 7-2, title-clinching win over the Titans. Eric Wilkins, of Seattle, pitched an 8-2 win over Pepperdine in that series.

At Omaha, Spokane lefty Chris Camp beat second-ranked Oklahoma 6-1 in an opening round game played before a record crowd of 15,107, but WSU dropped its next two, losing 9-3 to Arizona State and 6-3 to Maine.

Stars of that 1976 season included outfielders Greg Herrick, Bothell, who hit a team-leading .396; Tom Jobb, Spokane, hit .315 and played great centerfield; Tim Tveit, Centralia, home run leader with nine; third baseman Marty Maxwell, Lethbridge, Alberta; first baseman Westendorf; and catcher Greg Chandler, of Everett. Camp was 6-1 on the season and Sherwood, who was 21-7 for his WSU career, was 9-4 in 1976, pitching 119 innings with an ERA of 2.20.

Doc Bohler, the grand old man of Cougar athletics, once said back in the mid-1920s that Washington State won so often in baseball that its fans expected a championship every year. It certainly has been that way in the Brayton era. After that College World Series season of 1976, Bobo won four more Pac-North titles before dropping to second in 1981. In the last seven seasons (including 1988), WSU won the Northern Pac-10 three times and tied for first on two other occasions.

Cougar pitchers Joe McIntosh, left, and Barry Sbragia congratulate each other after combining to beat Oregon 3-2 for WSU's third consecutive Northern Division pennant in 1972. Sharing their glee are shortstop Terry Heaton, right, and first baseman Frank Jackson, center. (Lewis Alumni Centre)

---

* Bobby Waits died of cancer on September 16, 1984, at age 35.

"Aw shucks, fellas. Put me down."
Freshman Scott O'Farrell gets a
victory ride from teammates Mike
Kinnunen, Tony Provenzo and
Steve Wilke after hitting a three-run
homer out of Stanford's sunken
diamond and giving WSU a 7-6 win
over UCLA in a District Eight NCAA
playoff game. O'Farrell went in as a
pinch-hitter with two out in the
ninth inning and the Cougars
trailing 4-6. (Lewis Alumni Centre)

One game that sticks out in Cougars' memories was the sudden-death meeting with UCLA at Stanford's sunken diamond following the 1978 season. WSU had dropped a pair of heartbreakers, 3-2 and 5-4, to USC in the Coast play-offs in Pullman. Two days later, the Cougars and UCLA met at Stanford for a single game to determine an at-large entry in the NCAA Rocky Mountain sectional at Tempe, Arizona.

In that sudden-death game, UCLA jumped on WSU starter Mike Kinnunen, of Seattle, and led 6-1 in the fifth when Bobo brought in Eric Snyder, of Pleasant Hill, California, the hard-luck loser to USC in the first play-off game at Pullman the previous Friday. Pitching with only two days' rest, the gutty Snyder proceeded to shut out the Bruins on two hits the rest of the way.

In the eighth, with WSU trailing 6-1, Northern Division batting champ John Seefried, of Spokane, belted a two-run homer and the Cougars picked up an unearned run to make it 6-4. Snyder, who struck out seven in his 4 2/3 innings of relief, held UCLA scoreless in the ninth.

First sacker Jim Lauer, Oroville, California, and second baseman Dan Wodrich, Kennewick, singled for the Cougars in their last at-bats, and after two were out Bobo waved freshman Scott O'Farrell, of Redmond, to the plate as a pinch-hitter. O'Farrell had been at bat only five times the entire season and had one hit, a single that beat Oregon State for the Nor-Pac title. The big freshman connected with a 1-1 pitch by Bruin reliever Tim O'Neill and drove it out of Stanford's sunken diamond at the 390-foot mark for a three-run homer and a 7-6 Cougar victory.

WSU had to enjoy that moment. The Cougars lost at Tempe the following weekend, 7-1 to Gonzaga and 14-8 to Arizona State. (Arizona State went on to the finals of the College World Series before losing—yep, to Southern Cal, 10-3.)

If you asked Cougar fans what Bobo's biggest contribution to Cougar Baseball has been to date—other than all those championships, that is—they most probably would point to the new Bailey Field. Brayton practically built the thing. He located the field, designed the stands and surrounding facilities, and had a major hand in raising the funds to finance their construction. Then he went out and got a major donor to pay for lighting the park. (On May 11, 1984, Bailey Field became the first lighted college baseball park west of Tempe, Arizona, and the Cougars "dedicated" the lights by beating the Huskies 3-2 with a three-run rally in the ninth inning.)

In 1988, Bobo found another "angel" or two and put up a first-class wooden fence inside the steel one that came with the park. Late that same year, he started work on a memorial alcove and "Wall of Fame" behind the main stands, a place where all Cougar baseball greats, past and present, could be honored with plaques, pictures and memorabilia, and fans could learn more about the sport's great tradition at Washington State.

In 1987 and 1988, however, Cougar fans had more to talk about than their beautiful stadium and Bobo's championships. They were wondering if there had ever been another player in collegiate baseball history to match their left-handed pitcher-first baseman-designated hitter, John Olerud, of Bellevue.

The eighteen-year-old son of Bobo's first All-American, John E. Olerud, the catcher and Captain of the 1965 World Series team, set the fans to talking as a freshman in 1987 when he led the Cougar pitching staff with an 8-2 record (3.00 ERA) and hit .414 at first base and as a DH. That was only the beginning. Eschewing the sophomore jinx, young Olerud won fifteen games without a loss and set WSU season records for wins, innings pitched (122-2), and strikeouts (113). He hit .464, another record,* and set new season marks for hits (108); RBI (81, tie); and home runs (23), and had a WSU record twenty-three-game hitting streak.

The young left-hander was an unprecedented first team All-America choice as a pitcher AND designated hitter, and was named *Baseball America's* NCAA Player of the Year, the first Pacific Northwest player to be so honored.

Every honor that could come to a collegiate baseball player was Olerud's at the conclusion of the 1988 season—both as a pitcher and hitter—yet, beyond belief, he was ignored by the coaching staff picking the U.S. baseball team for the 1988 Olympic Games.

As of 1988, Bobo had not been back to Omaha, but the thirty-two-team format for the College World Series he drew up and promoted while serving on the National Rules Committee gave college baseball its greatest showcase—and made more money than anyone except Brayton ever dreamed was possible for the college series.

Bobo literally gave his heart to WSU and collegiate baseball. He had bypass surgery in 1977, and again in 1987, and came back both times to win pennants with his Cougars the following season.

At the conclusion of the 1988 season, Bobo's teams had 940 wins and

"Home Run Hooper," was the title earned by 4th generation Cougar Jeff Hooper as he wound up his career with 21 round-trippers in his senior season of 1987. (Lewis Alumni Centre)

---

* Olerud's .464 average beat the .438 by Bob Garretson, of Yakima, in 1964. Ironically, Garretson's son Jeff, a WSU student, was official statistician for Cougar baseball in 1988.

Chip Hanauer flashes a victory smile from his Miller American hydroplane. (Hilltopics)

his 1988 squad set yet another Cougar record—fifty-two wins in one season.

From here on in, Cougar Baseball's Bobo Brayton is only breaking his own records.

The Rooster Tail Boys

Lee Edward Hanauer, better known to the fans of unlimited hydroplane racing around the world as "Chip," won seven straight Gold Cup races between 1981 and 1988. Heading into WSU's Centennial, the Cougar had a chance of becoming the greatest boat race driver in history.

Hanauer, of Bellevue, a 1976 WSU graduate in Education, is the most successful of three former Cougars in hydroplane racing. Col. Russell E. "Russ" Schleeh, '42, a test pilot for the Boeing airplane company, and Dallas P. Sartz, '51, of Spokane, were prominent in the sport in the 1950s and 1960s.

Hanauer won his seventh straight Gold Cup in the "Thunder on the Ohio" races June 26, 1988, at Evansville, Indiana. He was driving a backup boat built from the wrecks of his Miller High Life and a sister ship, Miss Circus Circus. Chip averaged 128.406 mph over the two-mile course. He needs only one more Gold Cup win to tie the record of eight by Seattle's Bill Muncey.

Colonel Schleeh took the Seafair race on Lake Washington in Seattle in 1956 driving Shanty I and claimed the national championship. Russ came to WSC from San Francisco and played football for Babe Hollingbery, lettering in 1939 at halfback. He was in the Air Force twenty years before joining Boeing.

Sartz broke a leg and was in a body cast for months after cracking up the "Seattle Too" in the 1962 Gold Cup on Lake Washington. A former Washington Air National Guard pilot, Sartz entered WSC in 1948 from Everett. He was a varsity boxer and competed in track and football, graduating in Physical Education in 1951.

She's a "First"

When she was inducted into the WSU Athletic Hall of Fame in 1982, the write-up that accompanied her introduction asked:

> * Who is the only professional golfer to have scored two holes in one in a regular Tour tournament?
> * Who was the first woman golfer to earn $100,000 in a single season—without winning a tournament?
> * Who is the only Washington State University student/athlete to have participated in national championships in two sports?
> * Who was the first athlete to attend WSU on a Chick Evans Scholarship?

The answer to all of the above questions is, of course, JoAnn Washam, the 1972 WSU graduate who has been one of the leading players on the Ladies' Professional Golf Association circuit better than fifteen years. JoAnn was an outstanding basketball player while attending WSU, and participated in the 1972 national tournament as a guard on the Cougar team. The previous year, as a junior, she played in the National Intercollegiate Women's Golf Championship.

JoAnn started playing golf at age eight in Auburn, Washington, and at thirteen won the Auburn Club Championship. While at WSU, she won back-to-back Pacific Northwest Golf Association titles. She since has won many titles, including the Patty Berg Classic and the Portland, Oregon, Classic in 1975. JoAnn teamed with Chi Chi Rodriguez in 1976 to win the Pepsi Cola Mixed Team title, and with Nancy Lopez captured the Portland Ping Team Championship in 1979. She is recognized as one of the longer hitters among the regulars on the tour.

In 1980, JoAnn won $107,063, finished ninth in final LPGA Tour standings, and had a 73.1 scoring average for twenty-eight tournaments.

Yes, she was the *first* woman elected to the WSU Athletic Hall of Fame.

A Great One

The headline in his hometown newspaper, the Port Townsend *Leader*, read: "Art McLarney, Still 'Going on Guts' at 72, Wins Hall of Fame Honor at WSU"

That was August 19, 1981. On December 20, 1984, Washington State's first major leaguer and one of the all-time great Cougar baseball and basketball players, was dead, a heart victim. But not before he received his WSU Athletic Hall of Fame plaque from Executive Vice President Emeritus Wallis Beasley at a special ceremony at his home in Port Townsend.

A tall—for those days—skinny kid, 6-1 and 155 pounds, McLarney won Varsity letters at WSC in both basketball and baseball in 1930-1932. He was an All-Coast guard as a sophomore in 1930 and twice was named to the All-Northern Division team. In baseball, McLarney was an outstanding shortstop, and at the conclusion of his collegiate career in 1932 was signed by the New York Giants. (Some, including Joe Caraher, who is about as good a WSC sports historian as there is, swear that Art was the college's first All-American in baseball, in that 1932 season.) But he had trouble with the curve ball, and wound up first at Williamsport, Pennsylvania, in the Eastern League and then with the Seattle Indians of the Pacific Coast League for a couple of seasons.

Art came back to WSC and worked with Coach Jack Friel while getting his teaching credentials. He started in coaching at Burlington, then moved to Cleveland High in Seattle, and later Roosevelt. His teams at Roosevelt won forty-three games and lost only four in taking city titles in 1944 and 1946, and Art's 1946 Roughriders also won the state championship. That earned him a job at the University of Washington in 1947, as assistant to Clarence "Hec" Edmundson in basketball and head baseball coach.

Art took over the Husky basketball reins when Edmundson retired. His 1948 team beat Oregon State in a playoff for the Northern Division title and went on to defeat California in a three-game series at Berkeley for the Pacific Coast Conference championship.

At the conclusion of the 1983 football season, WSU Athletic Director Dick Young announced that Washington State henceforth would play its "Home" football games at home. "Home" being Pullman. Over the years since 1896, when WAC played its first away-from-home "Home" game in Colfax (where the high school field is today), against Company C of the National Guard of Washington (from Walla Walla), Washington State has played "Home" games in Portland, Oregon (15); Tacoma (3); Seattle (3); and many times in Spokane, including the entire "Home" schedules in 1970 and 1971 after the main stands at Rogers Field burned.

*Kelvin Sampson became Men's
Head Basketball Coach in 1988.*
(Sports Information)

*Most valuable player on the court
and in the classroom. Brian
Quinnett was named the Pac-10's
Player-of-the-Week (Jan. 22-29,
1989) when he scored forty-four
points in WSU's 72-65 win over
Southern Cal. At season's end the 6-
9 forward was chosen to the
Academic All-America first team.*
(Lewis Alumni Centre)

After Sixty-two Years, Another Indian Coach

When George Raveling left WSU for the basketball job at Iowa after the 1983 season, his top assistant, Len Stevens, took over from Raveling. Stevens had been at WSU since 1981, joining Raveling after being Head Coach at St. Martin's College, Lacey.

Stevens coached the Cougars four seasons, his best year being 1986 when WSU was 15-16 overall and 8-10 in Conference. But Len slipped to 10-18 the following season and moved along to the University of Nevada-Reno.

Kelvin Sampson, Stevens's thirty-one-year-old assistant from Pembroke, North Carolina, was promoted to head coach in 1987. The North Carolinian became Washington State's first American Indian coach since A. A. Exendine, the last of four Indian football coaches here between 1898 and 1925. Sampson is a Lumbee.

Sampson came to WSU from Montana Tech, at Butte, where he had compiled a 73-45 record in three seasons. Prior to that he had spent a year as a graduate assistant at Michigan State under Jud Heathcote while working on a master's degree at East Lansing.

The young Sampson brought intensity and defense back into the WSU basketball program. His first team in 1988 earned the respect of every coach in the Pac-10. The Cougars finished 13-16 and beat all but two of the other conference schools, even though their senior star and leader, 6-9 forward Brian Quinnett, of Cheney, was sidelined the entire year with a broken foot. WSU upset UCLA 73-71 in the first round of the Pac-10 tournament at season's end, and lost to Oregon State 74-68 in overtime.

In the 1989 season, Sampson's team again was plagued by injuries, going without starting guard David Sanders, of Spokane, and their sixth man, Neil Evans, of San Jose, California. Sampson nevertheless rallied the Cougars, brought them on strong in the closing weeks of the season and opened the Pac-10 tourney with another win, this time over Oregon, 78-56. WSU then took number one-ranked Arizona down to the wire before losing 62-54.

Leading players in the Stevens-Sampson years at WSU have been Keith Morrison, twice an All-Pac-10 guard from Los Angeles, and Quinnett, who set an individual scoring mark with forty-five points against Loyola-Marymount on December 5, 1986, at the Amana Classic in Iowa City and twice was named to the All-Pac-10 Academic basketball team. In the summer of 1988, Quinnett was named to the Conference All-Star Team (coached by Sampson) which played in England, and at the conclusion of his playing career in 1989 was chosen by the American Basketball Coaches Association to participate in a series of all-star games played across the country.

The Erickson "Era"

Jim Walden should have left some oil for that "merry-go-round" when he took off for Iowa State in 1987. It started up again early in 1989.

Quarterback Timm Rosenbach signals "Touchdown!" as Steve Broussard steps into the end zone. (Daily Evergreen)

When Dennis Erickson, late of Wyoming and the University of Idaho, came aboard in January of 1987 as the people's choice to replace Walden, it was heralded as the start of the "Erickson Era" at Washington State. It turned out to be more "Er, uh." But it was fun while it lasted.

Erickson upped and opted for Miami in March of 1989, succumbing to the wiles (and wallet) of athletic director Sam Jankovich, who needed a replacement for his departing coach, Jimmy Johnson. Sam found Dennis and it was love at first sight—of a $250,000 contract (minus $150,000 to pay off WSU for unfinished business in the Palouse).

Erickson had good "Cougar" credentials, when he took the WSU job. He grew up in Everett, Washington, where his father, Robert "Pinky" Erickson, was a high school football coach. Pinky later was an assistant coach at WSU under Jim Sweeney, and Dennis served as a graduate assistant at WSU during spring practice in 1970 after playing quarterback for Sweeney's teams at Montana State.

The Cougars had a little trouble making the transition from Walden's option offense to Erickson's "Air Express" in the 1987 season. They

Keith Jackson, WSU '54, has won the National Sportscaster of the Year Award five times since his days starting out on KWSC Radio doing Cougar games. (Courtesy ABC Sports)

finished 3-7-1, staggering to a 17-17 tie with Cal in something called the "Mirage Bowl" in Tokyo, Japan, on November 28.

Although Erickson finished shakily in his first year, all was forgiven after the first two games of the 1988 season. The Cougars jumped up and intimidated Illinois 44 to 7 at Champaign and manhandled Minnesota 41-9 at Minneapolis. If any doubt remained about Washington State's scoring punch after those wins, it disappeared when the Cougars trampled Tennessee 52-24 at Knoxville on October 1.

Junior Quarterback Timm Rosenbach, of Pullman, operating behind the biggest offensive line in the school's history (it averaged somewhere around 275 pounds), directed Washington State to eight victories in eleven starts, including a nationally televised 34-30 upset of number-one-ranked UCLA in the Rose Bowl at Pasadena on October 29. That win alone was a season!

WSU had lost two games in a row, to Arizona and Arizona State, and the bloom, so to speak, had gone off the Roses. The Cougars also faced UCLA without their number one tailback, Steve Broussard, of Los Angeles, who'd rushed for over 100 yards in six straight games but injured an ankle in that traumatic 31-28 loss to ASU. (Rosenbach threw an interception when WSU appeared on its way to the winning score in the final minutes.)

Trailing the heavily favored Bruins 27-6 in the third quarter, the Cougars became aroused. Led by Rosenbach and Broussard's replacement, 5-8, 175-pound Rich Swinton, of Canoga Park, California, WSU scored twenty-one unanswered points, added a fourth quarter touchdown and then held off Bruin quarterback Troy Aikman's desperation passing assault with a brilliant goal line stand. Artie Holmes (Rialto, California), Ron Lee (Tulare, California), and Vernon Todd (San Jose, California) knocked down three straight Aikman passes to save the victory, the greatest upset in the first century of Cougar football.

Wide receiver Tim Stallworth (Pacoima, California) also was a hero in that one. He caught seven of Rosenbach's passes for 170 yards and two touchdowns, one an eighty-one-yarder, and was named WSU's "Player of the Game."*

For for the game, Rosenbach completed sixteen of twenty-five passes for 272 yards and two touchdowns (with no interceptions), and Swinton rushed twenty-seven times for 117 yards and two scores.

The Cougar defense performed more heroics the following week, preserving a 24-21 win over Stanford when Chris Moton (Inglewood, California) picked off a Cardinal pass in the end zone with 1:17 remaining.

As always, the frosting (and it was frosty!) on the season was the win over the Huskies. In Martin Stadium on November 19, in the traditional Apple Cup game, WSU came from behind in the fourth quarter, and this time won 32-31.

Again it was Swinton, subbing for the injured Broussard (a pinched nerve after sixty-six yards rushing in the first half), who sparked the

* Keith Jackson, WSU '54, did ABC-TV's play-by-play of that game.

The smile says it all: WSU 32, Huskies 31. A delirious Coach Dennis Erickson hugs quarterback Timm Rosenbach in Martin Stadium on Nov. 19, 1988. (Daily Evergreen)

Cougar ground game with 102 yards rushing, and Rosenbach, passing for 148 yards and rushing for another fifty-seven, who led the Cougar attack. But the big break came when defensive back Shawn Landrum (Long Beach, California) blocked Eric Canton's punt in the fourth quarter and Jay Languein, of Port Orchard, recovered for WSU on the Husky thirteen. Rosenbach scored the winning TD on a five-yard run.

WSU's offensive line was awesome throughout the season. Big (6-6, 290) Mike Utley, of Seattle, was a consensus All-America choice at tackle on six first teams (including the Associated Press). Utley was ably assisted up front by John Husby, 258, Bellevue; Jim Michalczik, 268, Port Angeles; Chris Dyko, 296, Spokane; Paul Wulff, 270, Davis, California; Dave Fakkema, 266, Oak Harbor; Ken Kuiper, 277, Spokane; and Doug Wellsandt, 236, Ritzville.

Defensive standouts in the 1988 season included end Ivan Cook, Roseville, California; tackle Tony Savage, San Francisco; and linebackers Dan Grayson, Woodland; Maury Metcalf, Sacramento, and Bobby O'Neal, Marysville, California.

The Cougars also had a solid kicking game in 1988, with punter Rob Myers, of LaCanada, California, and placekicker Jason Hanson, of Spokane.

Washington State met the University of Houston in the Aloha Bowl in Honolulu on Christmas Day 1988 and defeated their fellow "Cougars" 24-22 in yet another gut-wrencher for WSU fans.

After apparently blowing the game open with 24 points in the second quarter to lead 24-3 at half, the Northwest Cougars went into an early hibernation and Houston closed to within two. It was time for more defensive heroics. The WSU defense again was up to the chore.

Just when the Houston Cougars had a win dancing like Christmas sugar plums before their eyes, linebacker Tuineau Alipate (Union City,

John Traut, Laguna Hills, California, ended his football career at WSU in 1985 owning every single-season placekicking record and all but one career mark. He was the all-time scoring leader with 231 points on 43 field goals and 102 extra points.

California) relieved Houston wide receiver Jim Dixon of the pigskin with a jarring tackle and Holmes recovered at the WSU five.

Wide receiver Victor Wood, of Seattle, was voted MVP with two touchdowns and an Aloha Bowl record 218 all-purpose yards. Wood accounted for 175 yards in kickoff and punt returns. (He had a forty-yard punt return and caught four passes for 43 yards.)

No one gave it much thought when University of Miami Athletic Director Sam Jankovich showed up in Honolulu on Christmas. But on March 5, 1989, everyone knew Sam hadn't been on a Hawaiian vacation. That's when he introduced Dennis Erickson as the Hurricanes' new football coach.

On March 14, Mike Price, forty-two, Head Football Coach and Athletic Director at Weber State College in Ogden, Utah, was introduced by WSU Athletic Director Jim Livengood as Washington State's new football coach.

A native of Everett, Price played for the Cougars of Coach Bert Clark in 1966 and then came back in 1974 as an assistant coach under Jim Sweeney. He stayed four seasons, also assisting coaches Jackie Sherrill and Warren Powers, and then went back to Missouri with Powers in 1978. He'd been head coach at Weber State since 1981.

Price is listed as WSU's twenty-ninth football coach since the sport was introduced in 1894. They're still counting Robert R. Gailey in 1897, and Gailey still holds the record for short stays among all WSU football coaches. One day!

$\mathcal{T}$he Tenth Decade, 1981-1990

Kelly Smith, of Longview, leading off for WSU in the first game played on new Bailey Field, April 12, 1981, hit a home run and the Cougars went on to defeat Oregon State 8-7.

•

On May 2, 1981, the pool in the New Gym at WSU was named for long-time Cougar Swim Coach *Douglass F. Gibb* (Doug died of cancer November 3, 1983.)

•

That's how the old ball bounces! WSU was trailing 10-0 with 2:36 left in 1981 at Boulder, Colorado, when *Tim Harris*, of Compton, California, dived into the line from the Colorado two—and fumbled. The ball bounced backward and quarterback *Ricky Turner*, of Compton, scooped it up and went untouched around the left side and into the end zone. Colorado could not make a first down after the ensuing kickoff, and its punt attempt, by *Art Woods*, was blocked by *Jef Keller*, of Baldwin Park, California, and *Paul Sorensen*, of Walnut Creek, California, picked up the ball on a good bounce on the Colorado forty-three and ran it in for a touchdown. Final score: WSU 14, Colorado 10.

•

Best sports headline of the decade? From the Eugene *Register-Guard*, November 8, 1981:
The sad state of Oregon football: 102-16
WSU 39, Oregon 7 Stanford 63, OSU 9

•

Family Affair: *Jay Torchio* was the Cal quarterback when WSU defeated the Bears 19-0 in wind-blown Albi Stadium, Spokane, on November 14, 1981. Jay's Dad, *Lloyd Torchio*, a former Bear center, was an assistant coach on *Jim Sutherland's* original staff at WSC in 1956. A week later, in Husky Stadium, it worked the other way. *Steve Pelluer*, son of the late Cougar end *Arnie* Pelluer (Bremerton, 1953-1955), directed Washington to a 23-10 win over the Cougars and knocked WSU out of the Rose Bowl. (Steve's mom is the former *Jodie Gustafson*, '55, Vancouver, and his grandfather was *Carl Gustafson*, '28, great Cougar fullback and 1927 Bohler Award winner.)

•

WSU defeated Oregon State 108-1/2 to 47 1/2 and Idaho 115-41 on April 17, 1982, on Mooberry Track and the Cougars had three men over 250 feet in the javelin, *Laslo Babits*, 265; *Gerald Lyons*, Walla Walla, 256-6; and *Tom Diehl*, Bremerton, 250-4. Coach *John Chaplin* said it was a first for one school in a single meet.

•

When Washington State knocked Washington out of the Rose Bowl with a 24-20 defeat on November 20, 1982, it had been 28 football seasons since the Huskies had shown their Purple and Gold in Pullman—and they lost then, too. *Al Kircher's* WSC team of 1954, led by halfback *Jim Hagerty*, of Temple City, California, clobbered the UW 26-7 on a cold November 20. It was Hagerty's finest day as a Cougar. Jimmy scored on a forty-four-yard pass from *Frank Sarno* (Somerville, Massachusetts) on plunges of two and one yards. Kirch, by the way, split with the Huskies in four games, losing 27-33 in Spokane in 1952; winning 25-20 in Seattle in 1953, and losing 7-27 in Seattle in 1955. Only *W. H. Namack,* 1-0 (10-0 in 1901), and *William H. "Lonestar" Dietz* , 1-0 (14-0) in 1917, among all WSU coaches have better records against the UW. *Forest Evashevski* was 1-1, losing 21-52 in Spokane in 1950, and winning 27-25 in Seattle in 1951.

He won $200,000 and stayed an "amateur." Now *there* is one for Ripley—and, believe it or not, it's true. *Scott Thompsen*, of Tacoma, won the "High Rollers" tournament at Las Vegas, Nevada, in 1985 while still a student at WSU. Thomsen was voted Amateur Bowler of the Year in 1985 and 1986 while winning the Association of College Unions-International all-events title both years. He was a double gold medalist in the 1985 *Fédération internationale des quilleurs* American Zone tournament in Bogota, Colombia, and finished fourth in the AMF World Cup in 1986 in Copenhagen, Denmark, improving on his eighth-place finish the year before in Seoul, Korea.

•

Wendell Ellis, Yakima, won his second straight Pac-10 Heavyweight wrestling title in 1986 and went to the quarter-finals of the NCAA tournament. The 350-pounder was 30-6 in his senior season.

•

Dick Melhart, '67, Chehalis, former WSU Athletic Trainer, was the "hero" of an airplane hijacking in Pakistan on September 5, 1986. Overseas for a series of sports medicine clinics, Melhart was aboard a Pan American jumbo jet when it was taken over by four terrorists at the airport in Karachi. After fifteen hours, during which time his captors killed several people aboard (seventeen died eventually and 127 were injured), Melhart kicked open an emergency exit, climbed out on a wing and jumped to safety, to be followed by many of the remaining passengers.

•

Brian Quinnett, of Cheney, scored forty-five points, a new WSU single game record, against Loyola Marymount in the Amana (basketball) Classic in Iowa City in 1986—but the Cougars lost, 96-89.

•

The 1987 WSU baseball team, Pac-10 North Champions, racked up nine individual career records: *Jeff Hooper*, Bellevue, At-Bats, 644; Hits, 225; Doubles, 47; Home runs, 40; Total bases, 402; RBI, 172; and Grand slam home runs, four. *Rob Smith*, Klamath Falls, Oregon, Games, 203; Runs, 178. That '87 club also set new team records for Runs, 571; RBI, 499; Home runs, 100; At-bats, 2,180; Hits, 695; Strikeouts, 333; Double plays, 82; and Hit by pitch, 65.

•

Jim Livengood was named Athletic Director at WSU on August 11, 1987, succeeding *Dick Young*, who resigned to take the AD job at Florida International University, in Miami. Livengood had been at WSU from 1980 to 1985 before becoming athletic director at Southern Illinois University. He attended high school at Quincy, Washington.

•

Dan Doornink, '78, Wapato, was named to the WSU Athletic Hall of Fame in 1987. A seven-year veteran with the Seattle Seahawks, Doornink was third in career rushing and sixth in pass receiving at WSU in 1974-1977. He played one year with the NY Giants before joining Seattle.

•

Penny Grupp, East Wenatchee, was the National Association of Sport and Physical Education "Student of the Year" in 1987. Grupp was a member of the ski team and had a 3.60 grade average.

•

Five Cougars were picked on the 1988 Pac-10 North All-Star team: *John Olerud*, Bellevue, pitcher; *Jim Connor*, Renton, outfield; *Steve Webb*, Spokane, first base; *Greg Hunter*, Kirkland, second base; and *Pete Blanksma*, Rochester, third base. Olerud, Webb, Blanksma and Connor also were NCAA District 8 All-Star selections.

Olerud and *Brian Sojonia*, of Seattle, tied the season record for most pitching starts with sixteen in 1988, and right-hander *David Wainhouse*, Mercer Island, drafted in the first round by Montreal, set a new season record with 27 relief appearances.

Appendix

Washington State University
Athletic Hall of Fame

The Washington State University Hall of Fame was begun in 1978 by WSU President Glenn Terrell. It is comprised solely of former WSU athletes, coaches, and administrators. Nominations for membership are accepted from the general public each spring, and the WSU Atheltic Hall of Fame Council votes to determine membership.

Applequist, Hackenschmidt "Hack" *1989 Football*
Bailey, Arthur "Buck" *1978, Baseball Coach*
Bailey, Byron *1986, Football*
Bates, Stan *1980, Administrator*
Benke, Loren *1984, Track*
Berry, Bill *1989, Football and Wrestling*
Bishop, Gale *1978, Basketball*
Bohler, J. Fred "Doc" *1978, Administrator*
Bohm, Wilbur "Doc" *1978, Administrator and Trainer*
Brayton, Charles "Bobo" *1981, Baseball and Football*
Buckley, Archie *1984, Football, Basketball, and Baseball*
Campbell, Hugh *1978, Football*
Cey, Ron *1981, Baseball*
Chambers, Cliff *1984, Baseball*
Clark, Asa V. "Ace" *1978, Football*
Cogdill, Gail *1982, Football*
Conley, Everett *1984, Boxing*
Conley, Gene *1979, Basketball and Baseball*
Deeter, Ike *1978, Boxing Coach*
Dietz, William H. "Lone Star" *1983, Football Coach*
Doornink, Dan *1987, Football*
Edwards, Glen "Turk" *1978, Football*
Eggart, Jeanne *1988, Basketball*
Eischen, Clem *1983, Track*
Ellingsen, Carl *1980, Football, Basketball, Baseball, and Wrestling*
Ellingsen, Don *1984, Football and Track*
Ford, Dale *1983, Baseball*
Foster, Earl *1979, Administrator*
Foster, Wes *1981, Track*
Friel, Jack *1978, Basketball Coach*
Gambold, Bob *1988*
Gary, Robert *1989, Track*
Gayda, Ed *1983, Basketball*
Gentry, Dale *1988, Football, Basketball*
Goddard, Ed *1978, Football*
Hanley, Dick *1986, Football and Football Coach*

Hanson, Vince *1986, Basketball*
Harshman, Marv *1986, Basketball Coach*
Hein, Mel *1978, Football*
Hollingbery, Orin E. "Babe" *1978, Football Coach*
Hooper, Pete *1984, Basketball and Baseball*
Jenne, Eldon *1978, Track*
Kelly, Brian *1989 Football*
Kennedy, Bob *1988, Football*
Lincoln, Keith *1979, Football*
Lindemann, Paul *1980, Basketball*
Lindgren, Gerry *1978, Track*
Lufi, Dubi *1989, Gymnastics*
McKinnon, Ed *1978, Track*
McLarney, Art *1981, Basketball and Baseball*
McIntosh, Joe *1988, Baseball*
Marker, Chris *1986, Swimming*
Mataya, Frank *1989, Football, Basketball, Baseball, and Track*
Meeker, Herbert "Butch" *1978, Boxing*
Mooberry, Jack *1978, Track Coach*
Nelson, Jack *1979, Track*
Niemi, Lauri *1978, Football*
Nollan, William *1981,Basketball, Baseball, and Tennis*
Olerud, John *1986, Baseball*
Orr, Lee *1978, Track*
Paul, Don *1980, Football*
Petragallo, Roy *1979, Boxing*
Rademacher, Pete *1982, Boxing*
Reed, George *1982, Boxing*
Reese, W. B. "Red" *1983, Basketball Coach*
Rohwer, Ted *1989, Football, Basketball, and Baseball*
Rono, Henry *1987, Track*
Sarboe, Phil *1980, Football and Baseball*
Schwartz, Elmer *1981, Football*
Sewell, Bill *1987, Football and Baseball*
Spiegelberg, Fred *1983, Football Coach*
Steiger, Bill *1988, Football*
Sundquist, Ray *1979, Basketball*
Svare, Harland *1982, Football*
Theodoratos, George *1987, Football, Track, and Boxing*
Thompson, Jack *1987, Football*
Torgeson, Laverne *1979, Football*
Van Reenen, John *1982, Track*
Washam, JoAnn *1982, Golf and Basketball*
Williams, Clancy *1986, Football*
Williams, Jerry *1979, Football*
Zimmerman, Clarence *1978, Football*

Index

Numbers in italic make reference to photographs or to material contained in photo captions.

Numbers followed by an italicized letter *n* make reference to material contained in footnotes.

Material in the decade summaries at the end of each chapter is not indexed. In these sections, the names of prominent athletes and other sports figures have have been highlighted in italic type.